WINGATE JUNIOR COLLEGE

HISTORY OF THE
LATIN-AMERICAN NATIONS

HISTORY OF THE LATIN-AMERICAN NATIONS

BY

WILLIAM SPENCE ROBERTSON

Emeritus Professor of History in the University of Illinois

THIRD EDITION

D. APPLETON-CENTURY COMPANY

INCORPORATED

NEW YORK   LONDON

vi   PREFACE TO THE SECOND EDITION

constitutional changes, yet social, economic, and international developments have not been neglected.

Though several years there has been a steady increase in the interest
taken by citizens of the United States in the history and politics of the
other independent nations of the New World. I am often told the feeling
of those nations which separate them the colonies of Spain and

PREFACE TO THE SECOND EDITION

The purpose of this book is to outline the chief events in the history of
Latin America or, as it is sometimes called, Hispanic America. As a
preliminary I have described the physical features and the aborigines of
those portions of the New World which were colonized by Spaniards and
Portuguese—factors which have had a permanent influence upon the life
of Latin-American peoples. My account of the chief events in their early
history includes a description of the conditions in Spain and Portugal
that affected the colonial enterprises of those nations; a survey of the
romantic era of discovery and conquest; a sketch of the penetration of
Spaniards and Portuguese into the American wilderness; an account of
the administration and of social, economic, and intellectual conditions
under the old régime; and the story of the separation of the Spanish and
Portuguese colonies from their motherlands. The story of the events of
the national period includes a survey of the development of the Latin-
American nations from the achievement of independence to the present
time, with an account of their political parties, constitutional history, and
existing governments; a description of their international disputes and their
economic development; a survey of their economic, social, and intellectual
conditions on the eve of World War I; and a sketch of their progress
from the close of that titanic conflict to the present. In the present edition
I have also included an account of Haiti, where certain conditions resemble
those existing in the insular republics of Cuba and the Dominican Republic. In addition, the book contains a discussion of common problems and
ideals of the Latin-American nations, as well as a description of the relations of those nations with Great Britain, with other European powers,
and with the United States.

When I undertook to write the story of Latin America, I decided to
survey the history of the Latin-American peoples from the age of the
Incas to the present day from a viewpoint that would consider each of
those peoples since the winning of independence as a distinct political
entity constituting a nation. Certain resemblances naturally exist among
the Latin-American nations, yet there are many differences—differences
which are influential in determining their destinies. In composing this
book, I have aimed to present such facts and tendencies as might enable
the reader to understand the present conditions and problems of Latin-
American nations. Emphasis has necessarily been laid upon political and

constitutional changes, yet social, economic, and international developments have not been neglected.

During recent years there has been a steady increase in the interest taken by citizens of the United States in the history and politics of the other independent nations of the New World. A portion of the reading public has evinced a keen interest in the present condition and the future prospects of those nations which sprang from the colonies of Spain and Portugal. Courses in the history of Latin America are now being given in numerous colleges and universities from New York to California. It is out of my investigations as a student and my experience as a teacher that this volume has taken its present form. I have aimed to write a book that would be instructive to the general reader who desired a survey of Latin-American history and that might also be used as a text for college and university classes in the history of Latin America. As an indication of the interest of Europeans in Latin America, it is perhaps worthy of mention that a translation of this *History* into Spanish has been undertaken by Juan M. Aguilar, Professor of Spanish History in the University of Seville, and José de la Peña, Professor of the History of Spanish Law in the same institution.

In the planning of this book I have been confronted with certain problems which other writers would perhaps have solved in a manner different from that in which I have solved them. Instead of appending a formal bibliography, I decided to furnish for each chapter a list of the best references for further reading which might serve as a guide to other works —particularly in English—containing material upon important topics discussed in the chapter. Those references, like the references to bibliographical aids, have been prepared in the hope that they may prove of special service to teachers. To aid students and teachers in the comprehension of significant tendencies or of disputes concerning territory, I have prepared from the best available data a number of maps to elucidate the text. In addition, I have given references to other maps which, when available, will illustrate the history of the Latin-American nations. Although I have striven to write a fair and accurate history, yet I do not expect to have avoided all the pitfalls of error which beset a writer who ventures into paths that are more or less untrodden. In the composition of this work I have utilized materials accumulated as the result of my travels in Spain, Mexico, and South America. The *History* has also profited, I believe, by the study that I have for years been making of the relations between European powers and Latin America.

I am grateful to various persons for aid in the collection of material for this book. I am thankful to those teachers who have made suggestions for the improvement of the text. To Latin-American friends I am indebted for information about special phases of history and for pamphlets concerning particular events. To the Division of Economics and History of the Carnegie Endowment for International Peace I wish to acknowledge my indebtedness; that Endowment courteously allowed me to use a graph and some statistical tables which were published in my book entitled *Hispanic-American Relations with the United States*. To my publisher I am indebted for authorizing me to quote some verses from Miss Blackwell's book entitled *Some Spanish-American Poets,* as well as for allowing me to engage in the venture of enlarging this volume. I am under obligations to members of the staff of the University of Illinois Library because of their constant courtesy and helpfulness to me in the use of the valuable collection of Latin-American books in that library. My wife has read the entire manuscript carefully and has aided me in reading the proof.

NOTE FOR THE THIRD EDITION

The revisions made in this book have been designed to give it greater accuracy and up-to-dateness. In the second edition new chapters were added on social, economic, and intellectual conditions. The present revision includes a selected list of works in English for each chapter in the text and brings the story down to the present. Among numerous books and articles used in bringing the narrative up to date, the author has found very useful the coöperative *Historia de América* (14 volumes, Buenos Aires, 1940-1941) edited by the eminent Argentine historian, Señor Ricardo Levene. That history contains selected bibliographies for every country of the New World. A list of works in English was furnished in the booklet entitled *Latin America* (Oxford, 1941) compiled by the English scholar, Dr. Robin A. Humphreys, under the auspices of the Royal Institute of International Affairs. The maps drawn for this history were carefully prepared after the designs of the author by Professor Leo S. Baldwin of the Milwaukee Branch of the University of Wisconsin.

W. S. R.

CONTENTS

CHAPTER I

THE LAND

CHAPTER II

THE PEOPLE

CHAPTER III

THE EUROPEAN BACKGROUND

CHAPTER IV

DISCOVERY AND CONQUEST

CHAPTER IX

THE CULTURE OF COLONIAL SPANISH AMERICA

CHAPTER X

REVOLUTIONARY MOVEMENTS IN THE EARLY NINETEENTH CENTURY

CHAPTER XI

THE WINNING OF INDEPENDENCE

CHAPTER XII

IMPERIAL AND REPUBLICAN RULE IN BRAZIL

CHAPTER XIII

THE GROWTH OF THE ARGENTINE NATION

CHAPTER XIV

URUGUAY

CHAPTER XV

PARAGUAY

CHAPTER XVI

CHILE

CHAPTER XVII

BOLIVIA

CHAPTER XVIII

PERU

CHAPTER XIX

NEW GRANADA OR COLOMBIA

CHAPTER XX

ECUADOR

CHAPTER XXI

VENEZUELA

CHAPTER XXII

THE INSULAR REPUBLICS

CHAPTER XXIII

THE CENTRAL AMERICAN REPUBLICS

CHAPTER XXIV

IMPERIAL AND REPUBLICAN RULE IN MEXICO

CHAPTER XXV

SOCIAL PROBLEMS AND POLITICAL IDEALS OF THE
LATIN-AMERICAN NATIONS

CHAPTER XXVI

RELATIONS OF LATIN-AMERICAN NATIONS WITH OTHER STATES

ILLUSTRATIONS

HISTORY OF THE
LATIN-AMERICAN NATIONS

CHAPTER I

THE LAND

The term "Latin America" signifies those regions of the New World that were colonized by emigrants from the Latin nations of Europe. In a sense it might be taken to mean the countries which were settled by people from France, Portugal, and Spain. It might include New France as well as Haiti, Brazil, and Spanish America. In a narrower sense, however, Latin America signifies simply those sections of the Americas that were colonized by wayward children of the Iberian Peninsula. When we speak of the Latin-American nations or of the Hispanic-American nations— as some scholars prefer to designate them—we ordinarily mean those independent nations of the New World which developed from settlements that were planted by Spaniards and Portuguese.

"Latin America" Defined

The history of Latin America constitutes a part of the long epic of human life. A story of the introduction of European man into the Americas, in part it deals with his adaptation to an environment different from that which existed in the Old World. This environment was composed of two factors, the land and its inhabitants.

America is more approachable from Asia than from Europe. The north Atlantic, across which some early voyagers made their way, is the stormiest ocean in the world. Its currents and winds are often contrary to vessels sailing westward from European ports. Once the Americas are reached, however, they are more accessible from the eastern than from the western side.

As regards form and climate South America is one of the southern group of continents. It belongs with Africa and Australia, which have their widest parts near the equator. Yet the South American continent bears some resemblance to North America. Both North and South America are triangular in form. In the northeast both continents have an area of ancient rocks. North America has Labrador, while South America has the plateau of Guiana. To the east there are plateaus of old rocks in both continents: the northern continent has the Appalachian Mountains; and the southern continent has the mountainous plateau of Brazil. Along the western side of each continent are found a series of complex, rugged mountain chains, which are skirted by a coastal plain that in South

North and South America

1

America is extremely narrow. Between the mountainous masses of the east and those of the west are vast plains that stretch from north to south. Through those plains flow several great rivers which are bordered by alluvial lowlands.

Though there is a similarity between the physiography of North and South America, they are not equally suited for the abode of civilized man. This is partly due to differences in the ocean currents that affect large sections of the two continents. In latitudes corresponding to those where North America is laved by warm seas from the equator and the Mexican Gulf, South America is bathed by icy streams from the Antarctic region. Northeastern South America is washed by equatorial currents, while that part of North America is lapped by icy seas from the northern oceans. Great rivers in South America mostly flow through regions that are fundamentally different from those through which flow the corresponding rivers of North America. The western mountain range of South America is much more rugged; its chief peaks are considerably higher than those of the sister continent.

The chief physiographic provinces of South America may be listed as follows: (1) the Atlantic Coastal Plain; (2) the Brazilian highlands; (3) the highlands of Guiana; (4) the basin of the Orinoco River; (5) the basin of the Magdalena; (6) the Amazonian basin; (7) the basin of La Plata River; (8) the Patagonian plains; (9) the Cordilleras; (10) the great plateaus; and (11) the Pacific Coastal Plain.

Chief Physiographic Provinces of South America

The Atlantic Coastal Plain of South America is not large. A very narrow plain borders the Caribbean Sea and, in disconnected strips, extends south from the mouth of the Amazon. The extreme eastern portion of that plain is subject to terrible droughts. At the beautiful Bay of Rio de Janeiro a rocky mountain range almost reaches the ocean. Near La Plata River the coastal plain merges into the pampas; then, after encircling a spacious harbor at Bahía Blanca, it skirts the Patagonian plains.

Large stretches of the eastern coast have a heavy rainfall that sometimes exceeds forty inches a year. Mostly covered with luxuriant vegetation, a considerable portion of the interior of Brazil is a table-land which is occasionally separated from the sea by a mountain fringe. To the north and the south the plateaus sink into great river valleys. These highlands, with lofty peaks that reach some ten thousand feet above sea level, stretch from the interior of the present state of Uruguay almost to the Amazon River. They contain the mineral deposits of Uruguay and Brazil.

Between the basins of the Amazon and the Orinoco rivers lie the highlands of Guiana. A few of their highest peaks rise to about eleven thousand feet above sea level. The northern slopes of this plateau have a heavy rainfall from the northeast trade winds, while its southern slopes are almost arid. Here and there throughout this varied region gold is found in paying quantities.

The northern slopes of the Guianan highlands gradually merge into the llanos. These are plains where trees, swamps, and lagoons are often found along the watercourses, and where tropical grasses are flooded in rainy seasons and parched in dry seasons. The llanos sink into the alluvial plains of the Orinoco basin which are nowhere much more than eight hundred feet above sea level. In the islands of the Orinoco delta the vegetation is most luxuriant. Dense forests, tufted grasses, and shifting sand dunes vary the physiography of this basin. Its most important mineral deposit is asphalt. With the aid of the trade winds, vessels can sail far up the sweltering Orinoco River. As its branches join the tributaries of the Amazon, it furnishes a convenient entrance into the vast interior of South America.

A less important river than the Orinoco is the Magdalena. Still it is navigable with steamboats at a distance of some five hundred miles from the sandbars at its mouth. Its valley and the valleys of its tributaries form a tropical physiographic province. The Magdalena River drains the beautiful Cauca Valley and, by a winding channel that often overflows its banks, furnishes an approach to the plateau of Bogotá. Islands, lagoons, and swamps make its lower course resemble portions of the Amazon Valley.

The Amazon is the largest stream in the world. The basin of that vast river system includes about two-fifths of the South American continent. With many side channels that cut the lowlands into islands, that river flows through dense forests and luxuriant savannas—large portions of which are often submerged. After receiving the waters of more than a dozen great tributaries, it empties into the Atlantic at the equator. Ocean tides sweep up its main channel for several hundred miles. Its branches, particularly on the north, form a veritable network that is linked to the adjacent river systems, especially in flood time. Still, a hot, humid, and enervating climate has prevented the Amazon Valley from becoming the chief gateway into the continent.

La Plata River is a very spacious but shallow estuary which is formed by the junction of the Uruguay and the Paraná rivers. The Paraná River, with tributaries that are navigable for hundreds of miles, reaches to the Brazilian highlands and also to the foothills of the Andes. A most important tributary is the sluggish Paraguay River, which joins the Paraná after receiving the waters of the Pilcomayo and the Bermejo. The other branch of La Plata, the Uruguay River, flows for a large distance through low-lying plains. Along the lower banks of the tributaries of La Plata River are found treeless plains or pampas which, before the advent of Europeans, were covered with tussocks of grass. These pampas are comparable to North American prairies.

To the far south the pampas merge into the plains of Patagonia. These vary from prairielike districts in the north to bleak steppes in the south. Petroleum seepages have been discovered there.

The dominant physiographic feature of South America is the great cordillera which stretches from the Isthmus of Panama to Cape Horn. At its southern extremity the cordillera is composed of one mountain chain. About 25° south of the equator, however, that chain divides into two ranges which gradually diverge as they proceed northward. Embracing at first only a narrow table-land, those mountains later enclose a large plateau that contains lakes and valleys. Through this plateau rivers occasionally break their way and proceed to the sea. On the east various streams descend sharply to the lowlands and join the great river systems. The Andes Mountains, as the lofty cordillera is ordinarily called, reach their culmination in the icy peak of Mount Aconcagua, which has an elevation of 22,860 feet. Volcanoes are still active, especially near the equator. In the rocks of the high cordillera there are found rich and varied mineral deposits.

The territory between the lofty Andean chain and the coastal cordillera is a plateau that rises thousands of feet above sea level. Probably it is more accurate to say that this region is composed of a series of plateaus, which are more or less broken by hills and mountain peaks, lakes and river valleys. Because of the great altitude, which often ranges from ten to twelve thousand feet, the climate of those plateaus is temperate. Fish are found in their lakes and streams. Timber for building purposes is furnished by their forests. Their mountains contain stone. Among their flora and fauna are some of the most useful gifts of the American continent, namely, quinine, the potato, and the llama. In fine, the plateaus of Titicaca, Quito, and Bogotá furnish natural conditions favorable to the development of civilization.

A plain, which is about eighty miles wide at its maximum under the equator and becomes little more than a fringe of islands in the south, stretches along the western coast. A southern portion of the Pacific Coastal Plain has sufficient rainfall for profitable agriculture. The western coast of South America has few rivers of any kind. Emptying at the equator is the short, sluggish Guayas River which drains unhealthful plains. Farther south are a few short rivers that wind their way from the cordillera to the Pacific. The central portion of the Pacific Coastal Plain is deprived of rain throughout the year because the moisture-laden winds are intercepted by lofty mountains. South of the Camarones River it is extremely arid. The most uninviting portion of the barren plain is the desert of Atacama, which covers some twenty degrees of latitude. Yet nitrate deposits in certain arid regions, guano upon adjacent islands, and copper in the Andean foothills, furnish the bases for important industries. Indeed the gifted Peruvian poet, Chocano, has epigrammatically said of Latin America's mineral wealth:

> Bright in America's deep chests there lies
> Wealth to outshine the sun in heaven's height,
> Peru's rich gold roused longing's fiercest might
> In ancient nations; silver's precious prize
> Mexico yields in streams no summer dries;
> Chile her coppers, burning ruddy bright;
> Pearls, Panama, like fine teeth, dainty white;
> Diamonds, Brazil, that flash like sparkling eyes.

Physiographic and climatic resemblances that exist between Central America and present Mexico, at least as far north as the Tropic of Cancer, have caused those regions to be designated "Middle America." Its chief physiographic provinces may be considered as follows: (1) the cordillera; (2) the highlands; (3) the Atlantic and the Pacific coastal plains; and (4) the peninsula of Yucatan.

"Middle America"

In Central America the cordillera dominates the landscape. As a geographer has aptly said, it seems as though in that section the eastern plateaus and plains had been swept away by the ocean, leaving only the elevated western regions. At the Isthmus of Panama indeed the cordillera becomes a low, narrow range; but to the north it rises and is surmounted by lofty peaks. North of the Isthmus of Tehuantepec the continent widens again. As it expands the cordillera expands also. Near its highest point the mountain chain divides into an eastern and a western range which enclose extensive highlands.

Elevated portions of Central America have been styled miniature pictures of the Andean plateau. In present Mexico the highland is broken by peaks that glisten with eternal snow. To the north the highland sinks into a dusty desert. Though the greater portion of this plateau lies between the tropics, yet, because of an altitude which varies from six to eight thousand feet, the climate is so temperate that it has been called eternal spring. Rich in minerals, and containing lakes and fruitful valleys, this highland, which was called Anáhuac by the aborigines, was naturally suited to become the site of a high culture.

In Central America there are low coastal plains of varying width. Toward the north a narrow plain is left on each side between the expanding cordillera and an ocean. Even there the land generally slopes more abruptly to the Pacific than to the Atlantic. Along the coastal plains the climate is humid and tropical or semitropical. Other depressions besides those of the coastal plains are the marshy sections and the Isthmus of Tehuantepec.

Between the bays of Campeche and Honduras lies the peninsula of Yucatan. With a comparatively slight elevation above sea level, its climate is tempered by the adjacent waters. It is a hilly, fertile region. In pre-Columbian days it evidently possessed some of the attractive features of the neighboring highlands.

"Middle America" possesses few rivers. Exclusive of the Río Grande —whose northern banks are now held by the United States—this region contains no important river systems. The Usumacinta River, flowing in large part through present Mexico, empties into the Gulf of Campeche. On the east coast there are scarcely any good harbors: Vera Cruz is only an indentation in the coast line. But on the west are the Gulf of California, the harbor of Acapulco, and the Bay of Panama.

In contrast with North America, the widest part of the South American triangle lies near the equator. Another condition makes Latin America less adapted to settlement by white men, namely, the presence of a vast forest. From the southern portion of present Mexico, with only one large break, a tropical forest extends along the eastern coast of Central and South America to 30° south of the equator. Giant hardwood trees amidst an exuberant jungle have presented an almost impenetrable front to civilization.

Portions of Latin America are marked by sharp climatic differences. In proceeding from the coast to the interior in Mexico, Central America, and South America abrupt changes are often experienced. During a single day's journey a traveler may pass from a coastal jungle through a tropical forest; and, rising through scrub timber, he may reach a delightful plateau covered with luxuriant grass and adorned with deciduous trees. If he proceeds still higher he may reach a lofty, barren plateau or *páramo* which is surmounted by icy peaks. It was upon the favored uplands that some of the best aboriginal cultures developed.

Latin America had a varied offering of flora which were useful for food. Foremost perhaps among such plants that were indigenous to America was maize. Ears of Indian corn have been found in pre-Columbian graves in various parts of South America. The aborigines of Mexico sculptured ears of corn in stone and modeled them in clay. Aborigines of the Andean plateaus cultivated the *quinoa* plant, which produced a grain that was used for food. Various species of beans have been found in prehistoric graves of Aztecs and Quechuans. Certain beans were evidently used by Indians for medicinal purposes. Pre-

Columbian funeral urns were frequently encrusted with decorations of peanuts. Among the gourds of aboriginal South America were found various kinds of squashes. The Indians of Peru seem to have eaten cakes made out of the ground seeds of pumpkins. Inca vases were frequently decorated with conventionalized designs of red peppers. Potatoes, both white and yellow, grew wild in the Andes from present Colombia to Chile. A related tuber called manioc was in certain parts of northern South America perhaps even more useful than the potato. Yams were also found there. In the Inca Empire nuts that resembled almonds were highly esteemed by the aborigines. Among fruits that now flourish in Europe, the delicious pineapple was a native of the New World. Many other fruits, seeds, and nuts that were strange to Europeans were indigenous to tropical America.

Flora and Fauna

From the cinchona tree that flourished upon Andean slopes was derived the so-called "Peruvian bark," the invaluable quinine. The leaves of the coca plant—which the Peruvian Indian still chews mixed with lime or ashes—furnished cocaine. Aborigines of Mexico evidently made a beverage from cacao seeds. Vanilla was indigenous there. In central South America there flourished *yerba mate,* the "Paraguayan tea." Tobacco was widely cultivated in America before the discovery; Columbus beheld the Indians smoking rude cigarettes made of tobacco wrapped in corn husks! Prehistoric man in America used several sorts of fiber. In Peruvian graves there has been found cotton of different colors: white, tawny, and maroon. From the century plant of Mexico and Peru the aborigines made a fiber resembling the henequen of Yucatan. After the advent of Europeans, the viscous sap of certain trees and shrubs in Mexico and South America became the rubber of commerce.

America was also well endowed with fauna. It was particularly rich in birds and insects. The turkey was indigenous. Of domesticated animals the aborigines of the New World had few. The American bison was undomesticable. Aborigines of North and Middle America had, in general, only one domesticated animal, the dog. In tropical sections of Latin America there were venomous reptiles.

South America had, however, a useful quadruped that was strange to Europeans. Aborigines in the western and southern portions of the continent made use of certain indigenous animals which were related to the camel. These New World camels were the guanaco, the vicuña, the llama, and the alpaca. Upon the Patagonian plains the Indians hunted the guanaco. Inhabitants of the elevated plateaus used the wool of the vicuña to weave fine cloth. They employed llamas and alpacas for domestic purposes: the llama was the common beast of burden;

the fleeces of the llamas and alpacas were used in weaving cloth, while their flesh served as meat.

With many river valleys and low plains, South America possessed a relatively large area that was adapted to agriculture. Nevertheless, narrow plains with a regular coast line were often bordered by steep highlands that hindered communication with the interior. Certain great river valleys were covered with dense forests which could scarcely be traversed except by river courses and which at times were plagued with disease. Passes in high mountain ranges were often very difficult to scale. Here and there swiftly flowing rivers afforded abundant water power; but generally the plains, the hills, and the mountains lacked coal. Of the great river systems upon the east, two were poor door-ways for Europeans because they were in the equatorial region. Not a few of the best harbors of Latin America were "mountain-locked." Thus in many sections of the western hemisphere imposing physical obstacles confronted European man.

SUGGESTIONS FOR FURTHER READING

BOWMAN, I., *South America, A Geography Reader,* 1915.

CARLSON, F. A., *Geography of Latin America,* 1936.

CHURCH, G. E., "South America, An Outline of Its Physical Geography," *Geographical Journal,* Vol. XVII, pp. 333-409.

CLEVEN, N. A. N., *Readings in Hispanic American History,* 1927.

GLADWIN, H. S., "Aboriginal Man in Arizona and His Fore-Runners," *Grand Canyon Nature Notes,* Vol. VII, No. 10, 1933.

HUNTINGTON, E., *The Red Man's Continent,* 1919.

JAMES, P., *Latin America,* 1942.

KEANE, A. H., *Central and South America,* Vol. II, 1911.

MILLER, B. L., and SINGEWALD, J. T., *The Mineral Deposits of South America,* 1919.

SHANAHAN, E. W., *South America, An Economic and Regional Geography with an Historical Chapter,* 1929.

TRUEBLOOD, H. J., "Raw Material Resources of Latin America," *Foreign Policy Reports,* Vol. XV, No. 10, 1939.

VERRILL, A. H., *Foods America Gave the World,* 1937.

WHITBECK, R. H., and Others, *Economic Geography of South America,* 1940.

CHAPTER II

THE PEOPLE

The problem of the origin of man in the New World is related to the question of prehistoric man. In the absence of convincing evidence about the origin of the American race many theories have been formulated. One of the most careful students of American aborigines took the view that their ancestors came from western Europe by a land bridge across the Atlantic Ocean.

Origin of
American
Man

Notable remains of early man have been discovered in South America. Kitchen middens have been found in various parts of Brazil. In Argentina innumerable vestiges of prehistoric human activity have been unearthed. Remains of monkeys have been exhumed in Patagonia. Human bones have been found in Brazil and in the Paraná delta.

Basing his views upon the study of such remains, an Argentine geologist, paleontologist, and ethnologist named Florentino Ameghino formulated a theory that startled some men of science Ameghino asserted that in present Argentina, which had emerged from the waters even before European men chipped rude implements out of stone, sub-man originated from monkeys. He maintained that "man-monkey" (*tetraprohomo Argentinus*) developed there and became differentiated into a number of species. From the pampas man migrated by a convenient land bridge to Africa and Oceanica; he spread over South America, and eventually migrated to North America by way of the Isthmus of Panama, accompanied by colossal animals. In time man proceeded from North America to Asia, where he became the ancestor of the Mongolian peoples, and to Europe, where he became the progenitor of the Caucasian race. According to Ameghino's hypothesis, the cradle of the human race was neither in Asia nor in Europe, but in Argentina.

Other students of prehistoric man, notably certain members of "the North American school," challenged that hypothesis. To test the soundness of Ameghino's theory in 1910 Aleš Hrdlička, a prominent ethnologist of the United States, made a short visit to Argentina for an independent study of the supposed remains of early men. A capable geologist who accompanied him reached the conclusion that probably most of the pampean alluvium in which those remains were found had been deposited in comparatively recent times. Hrdlička reached the conclusion that the evidence at hand did not substantiate the claim that "geologically ancient man" or "any precursors of the human race" had ever lived on the pampas.

In an article which he published later that scholar made an interpretative summary of the views commonly accepted in the United States about the origin of man. Hrdlička declared that there was no probability that mankind originated in the New World. He reasoned not only that man did not reach there until after reaching a development higher than that of the glacial period but also that the main physical features of the American race had not been obliterated. He described the characteristic features of the American aborigines, excluding the Eskimos, in brief, as follows: brown skin; hair of head black, medium, coarse, and straight; beard scanty; eyes generally of a deep brown color with eyeslits often having a "slight upward slant"; rather large ears; upper incisor teeth shovel-shaped; and projecting jaws.

Basing his hypothesis upon the substantial identity of physical characteristics and elaborating a theory previously propounded by Shaler, Hrdlička expressed the view that the American Indians belonged to a single stem of people. He argued that immigration had taken place gradually, and that the ancestors of the aborigines who peopled the Three Americas came from Asia to North America after man had attained a relatively advanced stage of development. Those migratory waves were followed by the multiplication, diffusion, and differentiation of man in America. Hrdlička admitted that, in addition to these Asiatic immigrants, small bands of Polynesians or even of Europeans might have settled in certain parts of America within the last two thousand years. This theory of the Asiatic derivation of the American aborigines has even been accepted by some of the leading ethnologists of Latin America.

Ethnologists who accept this theory generally incline to the opinion that the pre-Columbian inhabitants of America belonged to one race, with the possible exception of the Eskimos. Still, by 1492 the aborigines of America had so far differentiated that many different languages and dialects had developed. Even in this diversity, however, a certain unity has been found; there were related languages, each of which was ordinarily used by affiliated Indian tribes. Each group of Indians using a closely related speech has been termed a stock.

The process of classifying aboriginal stocks has not progressed so far with regard to Latin America as it has with regard to the United States and Canada. Recent classifications include twenty-nine linguistic stocks in Mexico and Central America and more than eighty in South America. To those lists additions or subtractions may subsequently be made, as

MAP SHOWING THE DISTRIBUTION OF INDIANS IN LATIN AMERICA
ABOUT 1500

(Adapted from maps by J. W. Powell, C. Thomas, J. R. Swanton, and A. E.
Chamberlain)

investigations proceed. Such classifications are significant to historical students because they afford clews that help to determine, with more or less definiteness, the extent of the respective regions that were influenced by one or another of the Indian cultures.

The American aborigines were in different stages of development, which depended largely upon their environment. Some Indians in North America, Central America, and South America had not emerged from the Stone Age. Certain tribes of Mexico, Central America, and South America had reached a higher stage of culture, for they made articles out of bronze. Among those tribes were the Aztecs, Mayas, Chibchans, and Incas. At the time of the discovery none of the Indians smelted iron. Various theories have been formed to explain why they had not advanced farther along the pathway of civilization. Among these hypotheses are the following: the scarcity of domesticated animals; the lack of adaptability in the American race; and the absence of contact with the culture which was developing in the Old World. It seems safe to assert that at the time when Columbus made his landfall, the most advanced American aborigines were in some respects hundreds of years behind their European contemporaries.

During the pre-Columbian epoch a more or less constant mingling of the aborigines evidently took place. At the opening of the sixteenth century in various sections of South America there lived Chief Cultural Regions, of South America aborigines belonging to different stocks. Yet, using as criteria the prevalence of certain traits besides language, our present knowledge indicates that the South American Indians may be viewed as congeries of tribes living within regions that were the sites of somewhat different types of culture. They may be conveniently grouped in three culture regions which had some relation to the great physiographic provinces of the continent: (1) The region which stretched in a southwesterly direction from the Brazilian highlands to the Strait of Magellan. In that culture area the aborigines still lived mainly by hunting, fishing, and gathering nuts. It was made up of the Brazilian highlands, a part of the Atlantic Coastal Plain, the lower basin of La Plata River, the southern portion of the cordillera, and the Patagonian plains. (2) A triangular-shaped region located in the middle of the continent which had its base upon the northern coast. In this culture area the aborigines lived partly by agriculture; and they had made some progress in the industrial arts. It was composed of the basin of the Orinoco River and the basin of the Amazon with adjacent tracts, and also of some portions of the Atlantic Coastal Plain. (3) The region that comprised most of the western part of the continent. There those aborigines lived who made implements from copper and bronze. It included the major portion of the cordillera with the great plateaus and also large portions of the Pacific Coastal Plain.

The Tapuyan Indians were probably the most northern members of the lowest culture group in 1492. At that juncture they were hemmed in by tribes of a higher culture, the Caribans and the Tupians. The Tapuyans were often called by their neighbors "the Ancients." They were nomads who lived by hunting. The Portuguese called them "Botocudos" (lip-pegs) because of a custom which the men had adopted of ornamenting their lips with a peg for each enemy killed in battle. Southwest of the Tapuyans were the Guaycuruan Indians who inhabited the region later designated as the Chaco.

The Charrúas or the Charruan Indians, as they are sometimes designated, occupied the lower banks of the Uruguay River. They were a taciturn, brave, and warlike people. In time of war they were led by a cacique. They made a livelihood by war, by hunting, and by fishing. Apparently they were polygamous. Their women often accompanied them on their forays. As implements of warfare they used clubs, bows and arrows, and *bolas*, which were stones fastened to thongs. Only in cold weather did they cover their bodies with long, sleeveless shirts made from the skins of wild beasts. They were very fond of an intoxicating beverage called *chicha* that was made from cane juice. Their religion was a species of fetish worship.

To the south and west of La Plata River were located the Puelchean, the Tsonekan, and the Chonoan Indians. These warlike aborigines had not emerged from the Stone Age. Their chieftains were hereditary. As described to us by travelers, their manners and customs much resembled those of the neighboring Araucanians.

Living mainly between the Andes and the Pacific Ocean, and between the parallels of 27° and 40° south latitude, was a group of related aborigines who became known as the Araucanians. Perhaps that word was derived from the Indian word *auco*, meaning the free. Scantily dressed in the skins of foxes and lions, they gained their livelihood by farming, fishing, and hunting. From juicy fruits they made intoxicating liquors of which they were very fond. Cruel to their enemies, they were superstitious in their religious beliefs. Athletic, brave, and patriotic, they were keen lovers of liberty. In some respects they resembled the Iroquois of North America.

A group of Araucanian families constituted what was designated a tribe. They recognized no chief except when they were waging war. During times of peace they most respected the oldest head of a family or the bravest warrior. When war seemed imminent they chose a chief designated the *toqui* to manage military operations. At such times the Araucanians held military assemblies; they sent an arrow dipped in blood from group to group as a signal that war had been agreed upon. They used as implements of warfare lances, wooden clubs, lassos weighted by stones, and the bow and arrow. They were implacable warriors who savagely tormented their captives. Intellectually they had not progressed far: they do not seem to have been able to count above ten; and they measured time by the movements of the sun and moon. It can scarcely be said that they possessed a literature. As workmen they were not artistic; their music was a melancholy and monotonous chant. Yet, because of their energetic and warlike patriotism, Alonzo de Ercilla, a noble Spaniard who fought against the Araucanians, immortalized them in an epic which he styled *La Araucana*.

In 1492 the Arawakans were scattered from the headwaters of the Amazon to its mouth; they also occupied isles of the Caribbean Sea. They lived by farming and fishing: maize, manioc, and fish were staples in their diet. They displayed much skill in molding earthen vessels. They made stone hatchets and sabers of hard wood to use in war. Eventually the Arawakans became involved in a struggle with the Cariban Indians.

The Caribans made a livelihood by farming, hunting, and fighting. It was their custom to eat adult males whom they captured. So addicted were they to this abominable practice that the Spaniards called them "Caribs," which meant cannibals. Just before the Spanish conquest began, the fierce Caribs were rapidly spreading over the Antilles; and they also dominated parts of the northeastern coast of South America.

The mode in which the Tupian Indians were scattered about South America furnished a basis for the view that their primitive home was near the northern tributaries of La Plata River. They seem to have made their way down the tributaries of that river to the Atlantic and then to have proceeded northward to the Amazon's mouth. At the opening of the fifteenth century they were found some distance up the Amazon River. They made a livelihood mainly by hunting and fishing. Those members of the Tupian stock who were located in the south near the junction of the Pilcomayo and Paraná rivers were noted for their bravery: they called themselves Guaraníes, which, being interpreted, meant warriors. They also were cannibals.

Neighbors of one group of the Tupians were the Calchaquian Indians who are sometimes called the Diaguites. The Calchaquians were located in the mountains of the eastern Andes. They had reached a higher stage of culture than Indians to the east. Ordinarily they clad themselves in a tunic made out of the wool of the llama. They wore their hair long, tied it in a knot, encircled it with a band, and decorated it with colored plumes. Their villages were generally composed of stone houses grouped together—somewhat after the fashion of the Pueblo Indians—upon a cliff or the side of a ravine. The Calchaquians were farmers whose chief crop was maize. They had domesticated the llama, the turkey, and certain kinds of ducks. They had a peculiar custom of burying dead children in funeral urns. Besides urns and vases, they manufactured basins, pipes, stone hatchets, spoons of wood, and implements of copper. A rude fresco ascribed to these aborigines depicts them as engaged in a fierce struggle with the Aymaran Indians. Originally they had a language of their own which was eventually displaced, however, by the language of the conquering Incas.

Inca civilization arose upon the ruins of earlier civilizations. During the pre-Inca age several indigenous cultures flourished in western South America. Among them were the Nazca, the Chimú or Yunca, and the culture that was focused, in a religious aspect at least, at Tiahuanaco. Nazca society developed **Pre-Inca Civilizations** in the valleys of Chincha, Ica, and Nazca; the Yunca civilization centered around Trujillo. Farmers and fishermen, who had attained distinction in the making of pottery, spread the arts and crafts of the Yuncas and the Nazcas. Both those peoples were addicted to human sacrifices.

The chief pre-Inca civilization, however, developed upon the elevated plateau of Tiahuanaco, near the southeastern shores of Lake Titicaca. There ruins are still found of what were perhaps the most imposing architectural structures of pre-Columbian America. Among these are fragments of a temple erected to a god called Viracocha. Near the temple have been found enormous stones decorated with symbolic figures and colossal monolithic statues. This city was perhaps the religious center of an empire which had a political capital elsewhere.

With regard to the aborigines that built this metropolis there has been a difference of opinion among scholars. Careful students of Peruvian antiquities, basing their views upon the belief that the people of Tiahuanaco had developed a distinct type of architecture, have ascribed it to a people called the Aymarans, a large-chested people who deformed their children's heads by compressing them between boards. A prominent Peruvian scholar has ascribed it to the Quechuan Indians. Other students have attributed it to a mysterious people distinct from either the Aymarans or the Quechuans. In any case, during an age which perhaps antedated the arrival of Pizarro by one thousand years, the rulers of Tiahuanaco had spread their civilization over a large section of the Andean highlands. During that era there also flourished along the coast some less important aboriginal cultures, notably that which centered around the sacred city of Pachacamac.

The Tiahuanaco civilization was overthrown—possibly by savages—and a period of anarchy succeeded. During that period in various districts aggressive peoples emerged into prominence and extended their influence over neighboring territory. Among them were the warlike Quechuans inhabiting the valleys near Cuzco. The name Inca seems originally to have been applied to their chieftain and also to members of the ruling family. It eventually became the designation of the expanding Quechuan tribe.

According to legend, the founder of the Inca dynasty was Manco Capac, who led his people from Tampu-Tocco, which may have been at a place called Machu Picchu, to the fertile, protected valley of Cuzco. It is conjectured that in the mists of the twelfth century those people began to extend their influence from that center into the neighboring valleys. Chieftains, who became less and less legendary, undertook to subjugate the neighboring aborigines In the fourteenth century the Incas apparently undertook to unify their conquests.

At its greatest extent the Empire of the Incas stretched from present Ecuador to the Maule River; on the west to the Pacific Ocean, and on the east to the Amazonian jungles. By its inhabitants **The Inca Empire** the vast Empire was designated Tahuantisuyo. It was divided into four administrative districts. (1) Chinchasuyo, which extended north from Cuzco. (2) Ccollasuyo, which included the basin of Lake Titicaca and stretched south to the river Loa. (3) Antisuyo, which lay to the east of Cuzco and included certain Andean slopes. (4) Contisuyo, which extended from Cuzco westward to the Pacific Ocean. In certain regions beyond these districts the influence of the Incas had been felt, especially to the east. To the north their sway had not spread much farther than the highlands where llamas and alpacas were employed as domestic animals.

The exact population of Tahuantisuyo about 1492 is not known. No census of the Empire was ever taken. Ruins of towns and fortresses indicate that its population was most dense in fruitful oases near the coast and in fertile Andean valleys. A conservative Peruvian scholar has estimated that its population numbered some ten million. The city of Cuzco, the capital and metropolis, possibly contained some fifty thousand souls. There were a score or more of smaller cities. Various tongues were used: besides the Quechuan speech, which remained the language of the Incas and also became the official language of the Empire, the people of certain districts used special dialects. Many subjects of the Incas continued to use the speech of the conquered Aymarans.

Quechuans were organized into clans or *ayllus* that occupied villages. The council of the Quechuan tribe was composed of delegates chosen by the clans. A clan acknowledged a common ancestry through the female line. Originally each clan seems to have had its own religious cult with distinct ceremonies and social obligations. Even after the conquests had been consolidated, members of the same clan continued to furnish each other mutual aid in the tillage of the soil and the construction of houses. Apparently the right of private property existed to some extent; members of the upper classes, at least, could bequeath their patrimonies. A father might leave his movable property to his sons. If he had no descendants, his property went to the State. Incas of royal blood—called *orejones* by the Spaniards—and certain privileged classes formed a sort of nobility. Inca society was stratified.

The various tribes which composed the Inca Empire were also made up of clans. Each tribe occupied a more or less definite territory within which it had special rights. Sometimes the vanquished peoples were confederated under the leadership of the Incas. Upon the conquest of a certain tribe, its lands were ordinarily divided into three parts. One part was assigned to the inhabitants for their livelihood: every individual thus had the use of a portion of land. Each father of a family had the right to a strip of land, the size of which depended upon the number of his children. He was allowed to keep the produce that was necessary for the subsistence of his family. A second part of the conquered territory belonged to the cult of the Sun. The third part was the property of the Incas. Produce derived from the second and third parts was used for the support of civil and religious officials. The Incas and the Sun, with a few members of the nobility, owned most of the herds and flocks. Alpaca wool and cotton were distributed among certain artisans either for the manufacture of their clothing or for the fabrication of textiles for the use of the government.

The religion of the Incas was founded mainly upon the reverence of natural phenomena, which were sometimes personified, and the worship of the dead. Natural objects of adoration varied according to the region inhabited. The coastmen·adored the sea, the mountaineers reverenced lions and bears, while the plateau people worshiped the lightning and the rainbow. With the conquests of the Incas the number of their gods increased: the personified forces of nature, which were adored by subjugated tribes, were added to the gods in the Inca pantheon. Each family reverenced its ancestors, whose bones were preserved in special sepulchers. Every clan worshiped its dead caciques and heroes. Inca rulers were the objects of special reverence: during life they were adored, and religious exercises were addressed to their mummies. Certain cults survived the Inca conquest, notably the mysterious religion of Pachacamac. Above all, the Inca tribe was devoted to the worship of the Sun, which naturally became the religion of the State. All the gods of the Empire were declared to be children of the Sun. It is believed by some students of the ancient Peruvians that at Cuzco and Pachacamac human beings were occasionally immolated.

The military organization of the Incas was of paramount importance, for the army and war were the bases of their power. A fighting and farming people, no sooner had they conquered a region Military than they undertook to cultivate the land. At the apex of Organization Inca organization was a species of military nobility that defied death. Common soldiers were recruited from the agricultural classes. It seems to have been the custom of the Incas to keep groups of those soldiers under arms for a short time and then to replace them by others. The families of men engaged in military service were supported and their fields were cultivated. War was waged in a barbarous fashion. After a victory the soldiers often became inebriated. Denizens of a conquered territory were compelled to furnish provisions for Inca soldiers and to construct forts. Eventually the Empire was held together by a series of military fortresses which were ordinarily located at strategic points. Sometimes these fortifications were constructed with salients and angles so as to permit of lateral fire upon attacking forces. In the construction of their fortresses the Incas occasionally used stones that weighed several tons.

The Incas planted what may be termed military colonies within territories which they overran. Such colonies were styled *mitimaes*. Inca military colonists were Quechuan Indians who were ordered to learn the language of a vanquished people without forgetting their own tongue. They acted not only as police but also as spies. They wore a distinctive dress and might neither return to their native districts nor change their residences without permission. The purpose of the Incas in establishing these colonies was to decrease or to destroy opposition to their rule in outlying districts.

Another mode by which the Incas consolidated their conquests was by the construction of highways. The inhabitants of conquered regions were compelled to build roads and to maintain them. From Cuzco roads extended in various directions. One highway proceeded by a serpentine route northward from Cuzco to Quito and also southward towards the region inhabited by the Araucanian Indians. Another road ran in a southerly direction from the Gulf of Guayaquil to the desert of Atacama. Those main highways were connected by secondary roads that descended from the mountains to the coast. In connection with their roads the Incas also built bridges. Inca highways scaled lofty crags by stairways, and at certain points were provided with storehouses for provisions and munitions. Still they were sometimes mere footpaths for Indian couriers.

In architecture the Incas had reached a high stage of development.

They used stone in the construction of their fortresses. They carefully fitted or keyed stones together by means of irregularities on their inner surfaces. Lime or cement they used seldom, if indeed at all. Few circular or semicircular edifices of the Incas have been found; their structures were generally rectangular in shape. The walls, doors, and windows of their buildings ordinarily converged towards the top. In their stone houses the Incas had a number **The Arts** of clever devices. They employed lock holes to fasten the bars of doors. They used stone cylinders for hooks and supports, as well as for ventilation and drainage. Occasionally Inca workmen showed engineering skill. They straightened watercourses and dug irrigating ditches along mountain sides. At Sacsahuaman, which is upon a crag overlooking Cuzco, at Ollantaytambo, in a valley near that city, and at Machu Picchu, an almost inaccessible stronghold northeast of that capital, have been found massive and intriguing remains of Inca architecture.

The Incas modeled animal forms in clay. Their decorative art reached its highest development in pottery. So graceful are the lines of Inca vessels found at Machu Picchu that they have been compared to Grecian vases. Inca workmen made many articles out of bronze: hatchets, knives, bells, mirrors, tweezers, needles, spoons, rings, spangles, and bracelets. Surgical tools they manufactured from bronze or obsidian. Occasionally the Incas used those instruments to trepan skulls or for dental surgery. Their women wove colored ponchos that were adorned with unique designs.

Aboriginal customs and traditions were preserved by the Incas in dancing and music. Dances took place at private and public entertainments and at religious festivals, as the feast of the Sun. Occasionally dances were used to incite warriors to combat; at other times they were employed to soothe the emotions of excited chieftains. They were also used to portray scenes in national life. The music of the Incas was ordinarily composed of a few notes in a minor key, which were repeated over and over again. In connection with dances and music, their minstrels chanted songs of love and conquest. A historical canto in praise of an Inca has been translated from the Quechuan language into Spanish.

In one most important respect the Incas had lagged behind the Aztecs. Despite rumors of an Inca system of writing, careful scholars have reached the conclusion that the Incas did not develop an alphabet or even a system of hieroglyphics. At the time of the Spanish conquest the chief device which they used for the preservation and transmission of their thoughts was the so-called *quipu*. This was made up of colored and knotted strings of different lengths which were pendant from a cord and variously arranged. Somewhat after the fashion of an English tally, those strings were used to keep records which had to be deciphered. Unfortunately the conquistadors wantonly destroyed the collections of quipus at the Inca capital.

Neighbors of the Quechuans on the north were the Cañarian and other Indian stocks that had been influenced, if not indeed conquered, by the Incas. According to aboriginal traditions, the equatorial plateau was originally inhabited by the Quitus Indians; hence the adjacent region was often designated the "Kingdom of Quito." In the equatorial region of the west coast various cultures intermingled. Certain Indians living there had been affected by the culture of aborigines whom the Spanish conquerors called the Muiscas.

Those Indians, who became known in history as the Chibchans, occupied the most northerly area of high culture in South America.

The Chibchan Indians They lived east of the Magdalena River upon a plateau that was traversed by rivers and dotted by lakes. The main habitat of the Chibchan tribe was upon the fertile plateau around the towns of Bacatá and Tunja with the contiguous valleys. In their early history these Indians were apparently divided into many small communities ruled by caciques. Ultimately the number of caciques was reduced to five, who began a fight for supremacy. Just before the advent of the Spaniards a cacique named Zipa, who was located at Bacatá, became involved in a desperate struggle with the cacique called Zaque, whose capital was at Tunja. Declining centers of Chibchan culture were at Sogamoso, Tundama, and Guatabita.

Though some of the Chibchans lived in a comparatively cold region, they had developed a high culture. Their chief occupation was agriculture; their crops were mainly cotton, corn, fruits, and potatoes. They manufactured coarse cloth and mined salt, copper, and emeralds. By commerce with neighboring aborigines they secured other products. They made various articles out of beaten gold. In the early sixteenth century Bacatá had possibly twenty thousand inhabitants.

Chibchan houses were ordinarily round in shape with pyramidal or conical roofs. Their walls were made out of tree trunks set in the earth which were plastered with a mixture of mud and straw. The size and character of the houses varied according to the social standing of their occupants. Doors and windows were small and few in number. Protected by a wall and by rude fortifications, Bacatá contained the home or "palace" of the ruler, which was reputed to have a dozen doors.

Very few ruins of stone structures constructed by the Chibchans have been found. They made various kinds of pottery, which were often decorated in dark colors. In alloys of variable proportions of gold, silver, and copper, they cast statuettes which they chiseled by means of copper tools. A gold urn found by the conquistadors in Tunja weighed about thirty pounds. Strangely enough, though many Chibchans lived in a region which possessed a wonderfully diversified flora, no representations of trees, leaves, or flowers have been found on their pottery. There is no evidence to prove that they had developed the art of transmitting their ideas beyond the drawing of rude pictographs.

Their priests apparently composed a caste. Tradition ascribed to a creative god called Bochica the origin of their civilization. The Chibchan religion was a species of nature worship. Every home had its fetish: every house possessed its idol of clay, wood, wax, copper, silver, or gold. Mountains, rocks, trees, shrubs, and especially streams and lakes, were supposed to be inhabited by divine beings. Such natural objects were accordingly venerated. Lake Guatabita was the scene of peculiar religious rites. The ceremonious sacrifices that were offered there to the gods upon the selection of a new ruler furnished a basis for the alluring myth of El Dorado.

According to a story handed down by Spanish chroniclers, upon coronation day the young chief was taken to the shores of Lake Guatabita. There he embarked on a boat which was laden with gold and emeralds. After being clad in gay robes by the priests, the prince was smeared with sticky earth and covered with gold dust. In the middle of Lake Guatabita—so ran the legend—the monarch offered his precious treasure to the gods by emptying it into the lake amid the rejoicings of his people. From this story arose the legend of the gilded man, which lured adventurers to make expeditions in search of a country where gold was plentiful.

Far from attractive was the Chibchan practice of human sacrifices. Those sometimes took place at sunrise. Occasionally a victim was bound to poles and shot to death by arrows. At times captive children seem to have been sacrificed. When a cacique died, slaves and women were often interred alive beside his body, which was adorned with jewels and anointed with a preservative balsam.

The Chibchans also occupied parts of the Isthmus of Panama and Central America. To the north of them was an area where different cultures mingled and affected Indians that were in a primitive stage of development. Possibly the most noteworthy of the aborigines that were located in this intermediate area were the Cunan and the Ulvan Indians, both probably related to the Chibchans, and the Mosquitoan Indians. Three Indian stocks of "Middle America" developed or assimilated a high civilization. Those were the Maya, the Zapotecan, and the Nahuatlan or Nahua Indians who lived mainly upon the highlands or upon a favored peninsula. On the northern outskirts of the Nahuas were some related peoples possessing a low culture. Among these were Indians designated by the Spanish conquerors as "Chichimecs" whom ethnologists have classified linguistically with the Nahuas. Farther to the north were other Indians: as the Yaqui and the Piman who have been grouped by ethnologists with the Nahua stock; and the Yuman whose culture resembled that of Indians inhabiting the southwestern part of the present United States. Hovering upon the northern borders of present Mexico were the Athabascans that included the vengeful Apaches.

The Empire of the early Mayas included almost all of Central America. Their history has been divided into two periods: the "Old Empire," including the period from the beginning of the **The Mayas** Christian era to 600 A.D.; and the "New Empire," including the period from 600 to the Spanish conquest. The oldest Maya culture had its site in the northern part of Central America. This civilization was based upon farming; the chief crop was corn. Probably because of unfavorable agricultural conditions that had developed in their original habitat, in the fifth century the Mayas began to emigrate to northern Yucatan, where they established a new empire.

Ruined cities found in Yucatan and Central America indicate the character of the Maya Indians. Important seats of their civilization were Tikal, Copán, Palenque, Quirigua, Chichen Itza, and Uxmal. Upon those sites were found the ruins of stone buildings that had apparently been used for religious purposes. Located at strategic points, certain cities were protected by walls and fortresses. Palaces and temples constructed of cut stone were often built upon pyramids. It is believed that centuries ago each of these acropolises was the center of a large and flourishing community which contained many inhabitants.

Scant evidence has been found regarding the social and political organization of the Mayas. It appears, however, that they were arranged in exogamous clans in which descent was traced in the male line. The clans were located in villages; every clan was headed by a chief. Land was the collective property of each family: apparently the labor of tilling the soil was performed in common. Every village had a hereditary military leader. Justice was administered by local officials.

Though their homes were ordinarily only adobe or wooden huts covered with thatched straw or palm leaves, the Mayas were fine artisans. Among them the manufacture of pottery was highly advanced. Especially did they excel in the decorative art; their vases were occasionally adorned with human masks. Frequently their flasks were decorated with profiles and with hieroglyphics in relief. The discovery of Maya vases bearing animal or human representations has led to the conclusion that those vessels were probably used in religious rites. In Maya temples many walls were covered with designs in stucco or in relief on stone. Huge statues of men, richly carved wooden panels, and poorly executed paintings of animals have been found in Maya ruins. The serpent motive was much used. Interior decorations of their temples sometimes depicted priests and divinities.

The Arts of the Mayas

The government of the Mayas was theocratic. In their life, religion played an important part. They had several divinities. Their chief god was Itzamma, "the Roman-nosed god," who was regarded as the creator of all, the founder of their civilization, and the source of light and life. He was ordinarily depicted as an old man with an aquiline nose and a distorted and almost toothless mouth. Almost equally important was a god whose face was a "humanized serpent." This divinity was Kukulcan, a feathered snake, who was the Maya representative of the Aztec god Quetzalcoatl. The face of this "long-nosed god" was often worn by priests and rulers as a mask or headdress. In Maya codices, Kukulcan is represented as a deity of diverse powers, but it seems probable that his chief function was that of a rain god. The chief god of evil was Ahpuch, the god of death, who was sometimes represented as a skeleton. A youth adorned with a lofty headdress was the maize god. Though ordinarily the offerings to Maya gods consisted of fruits of the land, after the Toltec conquest slaves or children were occasionally sacrificed. A striking pictorial representation of the Mayas represents a man being sacrificed to Kukulcan.

Their religious rites were based upon astronomical observations. Their priests studied the heavens carefully. So accurate were their calculations that they co-ordinated the lunar month with the solar calendar. Recent investigations show that the Mayas had for centuries used a more accurate calendar than that employed by the conquering Spaniards. In the decoration of Maya temples much use was made of the cross as a symbol of the four quarters of the heavens. Certain achievements of the Mayas were the outcome of their interest in religion.

The Mayas had learned how to preserve and transmit their thoughts by writing. As yet, their hieroglyphics are not fully intelligible, but these have been serviceable in setting limits to their civilization. In the Maya system of writing, phonetic symbols were evidently displacing ideographic symbols. The arithmetic of the Mayas has been reconstructed with so much success that it has helped to determine the age in which their culture flourished. They used the principle of indicating number values by the relative position of digits with respect to a character used to represent zero. Their system was vigesimal. Stone

monoliths of the Mayas bearing carved hieroglyphics have been designated five-year "almanacs in stone."

Long before the Spaniards saw the Yucatanese coast, the Maya
civilization, which marked the highest point of development reached
by aboriginal Americans, had fallen into decay A confederacy of their
city-states, Chichen Itza, Uxmal, and Mayapán, which had for some
time dominated the peninsula, was disrupted by an internecine quarrel.
During the twelfth century important Maya cities in Yucatan were
subjugated by aborigines from Mexico.

North of the Mayas were located other tribes that had attained a comparatively high development. Probably the most important of the Indian
stocks occupying the territory between the Mayas and the Aztecs was
the Zapotecan. The center of Zapotec culture was the city of Mitla;
its architecture still demonstrates the skill of its workmen. With stone
tools those aborigines hewed massive blocks out of quarries and constructed great buildings which vie with those of the Incas. At Monte
Alban, their religious center, exquisite gold jewelry has been found.

For many years the originators of Mexican and Central American
culture were supposed to have been the Toltecs. Critical students of
Indian civilizations, however, have discarded that tradition. It is now
believed that about the year 800 A.D. there existed upon the plateau
of Anáhuac a tribe known as the Toltecs whose capital was at Teoti-
huacán. The original state of the Toltecs was a small kingdom that
flourished from 1000 to 1200. In the twelfth century their successors,
who have been called "dynastic Toltecs," started to expand and ultimately subjugated all the non-Mayan peoples of Central America and
of central and southern Mexico. In an epic attributed to the Aztecs,
the achievements of the fair god, Quetzalcoatl, who was reputed to
have given culture to the Toltec people, were thus described:

> Houses had he wrought of emeralds;
> Dwellings made of gold and silver;
> Edifices worked from coral;
> Had his palace built of sea shells
> And his wondrous habitations
> Fashioned in artistic woodwork
> And adorned with precious feathers.
> Wealth untold there was in Tula;
> Emeralds in gold uncounted;
> Treasures unsurpassed they guarded.
> Wondrous rich were all the Toltecs;
> Masters they of wealth uncounted.

The Nahuas were related tribes, whose members upon the eve of
the Spanish conquest held sway from the Isthmus of Tehuantepec to

the Panuco River. Their legends affirm that their early home was on a great water in the far north. Through the Toltecs the Nahuas secured a knowledge of writing, architecture, and calendars, besides certain religious ideas, as the cult of Quetzal- coatl, the feathered snake.

Nahuas

The last of the Nahuas to reach the pleasant central valley in the plateau of Anáhuac were the Mexicans or, as they were commonly called, the Aztecs. It was perhaps about 1325 when they settled upon two small islands in Lake Texcoco under a chief named Tenoch. As the Aztecs eventually triumphed in the struggle for subsistence, the city of Tenochtitlán became the center of their power. Gradually they extended their influence and authority over adjacent peoples. With the people of two other tribes, the Texcocans and the Tlacopans, they organized a confederacy which subjugated peoples who were far distant from Anáhuac. At its largest extent, including some tribes that had been enveloped but not subdued by the Aztecs, their Empire stretched from Yucatan almost to the river Panuco and from the Gulf of Mexico to the Pacific Ocean. On the north and west the Aztec Empire was bounded by the Tarascan and Otomian Indians and by the Chichimecs. On the south its sway extended to the Isthmus of Tehuantepec.

Much dispute has been waged about the exact stage of civilization reached by the Aztecs. Basing their views upon the imaginative accounts of Spanish chroniclers, early historians of the conquest entertained an exalted notion of Aztec culture. As a reaction some writers have aimed to reduce them to the level of other North American Indians. In recent years, however, the general tendency among students of the aborigines has been to consider the Aztec civilization as a highly developed form of an indigenous culture.

A prime object of the Aztec confederacy was to wage war. Each of the confederated tribes possessed an independent organization and had a right to certain land. Upon this territory the town from which the respective tribe took its name was located. Each tribe might not only wage war on its own account

The Aztec Confederacy

but also levy tribute upon the people whom it conquered. Taught how to fight at an early age, the men of all the tribes were warriors. Military officers were elected by the tribe or by the clans. The clan was the military unit.

The spoils of a war waged by the three confederates were divided among them. In time of joint action the Aztec war chief was the commander of the combined forces; but when the war had terminated the tribes resumed their independent military organizations. A council advised the war chief, who almost possessed the powers of an Emperor. Conquered tribes had to furnish tribute to the confederates. Apparently the Aztec conquests extended from about 20° north latitude to the borders of Central America.

The Aztec tribe was composed of twenty clans. Each clan occupied a number of adjacent, communal houses. A clan was governed by a council composed of elected chiefs. Ordinarily each clan had a political as well as a military chief. Certain lands were reserved for the use of markets, temples, and other public buildings. A section of tribal territory was assigned to each clan. The land of a clan was divided into portions which were allotted to the married men for agricultural purposes. Originally the title to the land, however, remained in the tribe; the tiller of the soil could neither sell his allotment nor transfer it. Tribal officials, who could not till their own allotments, were given the products of lands which were cultivated for them by a dependent class. Public lands were set apart for clan councils and for officials of temples and other public buildings.

The central government of the Aztec tribe was vested in a council composed of members representing the different clans. It settled disputes and initiated men into office. The Aztecs had two chiefs selected by the council: the civil chief called the "snakewoman;" and the war chief, known as the "chief of men." Just before the Spanish conquest the Aztec war chief exercised some important religious functions and was consequently viewed with great veneration.

Tenochtitlan or, as it was later styled, the City of Mexico, was the stronghold of the Aztecs and the center of their culture. The marshy islands upon which it had been built were linked to the mainland by three long causeways with gates that regulated the flow and the depth of the water. From a neighboring hill potable water was conveyed to the city by an aqueduct. Mexico City was arranged around a great square that was surrounded by a stone wall which had gates leading to the three causeways. Trade was carried on where trees shaded the narrow streets and also in the great square where public gatherings were held. In and around that square were large communal structures, official buildings called *tecpans,* armories or "houses of javelins," and pyramidal temples, which included educational buildings and the residences of priests. Communal buildings were one or two stories high with low parapets. The main tecpan was capped by observation towers. Temples were mounted by steps; they were crowned by wooden oratories and also by sacrificial stones. Inhabitants of the capital city appear to have had a different status from those of the adjacent towns. Estimates of the population of Mexico City at the time of the conquest differ greatly. Recent estimates vary from fifty thousand souls to three hundred thousand.

As the culture of the Aztecs was essentially urban, so was Mexico

City their religious center. Their religion was a species of idolatry: they worshiped gods of wood and stone. The largest temple in the great square was dedicated to the cult of Huitzilopochtli, the god of war and of the sun. Some three hundred feet long at the base, it was about one hundred and fifty feet high.

Aztec Society

A Spanish chronicler described it as the altar upon which human sacrifices were offered by priests who stank of blood and sulphur. Tezcatlipoca was the god of the sky, whose cult was practiced in the same temple as that of the god of war. Tlaloc was the Aztec god of rain and fertility. Quetzalcoatl was the feathered god of learning and of priesthood—the fair god of romance.

A most abominable feature of the Aztec religion was the terrible custom of offering human sacrifices to Huitzilopochtli. Upon the summit of the chief temple captives and children were at special times stretched upon sacrificial stones, their breasts were opened at one fell blow, and their bleeding hearts were thrust into a receptacle as a sacrifice to the awful deity! Terror caused by the cult of human sacrifice strengthened the prestige of the Aztecs among the neighboring peoples. Occasionally a warrior destined for the sacrifice was fastened to the altar and then allowed to fight with Mexican warriors until he succumbed. After the Roman analogy, the Spaniards designated such a combat the gladiatorial sacrifice.

Among the Aztecs there were various ranks. Antisocial acts might cause individuals to lose their civil rights. Even when such persons could not be called slaves, they formed a dependent class. Merchants belonged to a special group: they made distant expeditions not only for trading purposes but also to gather information about neighboring territories—in fact, they acted as spies. Mechanics did not belong to a closed caste; for a son was not compelled to learn his father's craft. Still, certain artisans, as goldsmiths and silversmiths, were held in special esteem. Soldiers who had distinguished themselves in war could join an order like the Knights of the Eagle. Although such titled leaders could scarcely be considered a noble class, yet from them the Aztecs often selected their chiefs.

The chief occupation was agriculture. Some manufacturing was carried on; certain towns produced special products. The Aztecs were skilful artisans. They manufactured textiles out of a great variety of materials which they dyed in rich tints. They colored feather plumes beautifully. From stone, particularly obsidian, they made armatures, mirrors, and the tips of lances. Excellent examples of their pottery have been found: among them were many fine bowls, and also amorphous, cylindrical, and globular vases. Sometimes they decorated their vases with symbolic designs or adorned them in relief. They sculptured in stone and carved bas-reliefs on their temples and statues; they had attained a high degree of skill in cutting precious stones, and even manufactured mosaics from jade and turquoise. Of the metals they used copper, tin, silver, and gold. As the gold jewelry was melted by avaricious Spaniards, very few golden ornaments fashioned by, the Aztecs have been preserved.

Their civilization reached its culminating point in the so-called "picture writing." Upon the skins of animals or upon paper made from the fiber of an agave, the Aztecs drew paintings which conveyed ideas. To draw the design they used a pointed instrument —possibly the thorn of an agave—and the design was tinted with vegetable or mineral colors. Though many of the picture writings were wantonly destroyed, some precious codices dating from the pre-Columbian epoch have been preserved. Their character varies according to the epoch to which they belong. Among them are drawings which depict the migrations of the Aztecs in northern Mexico, their religious rites and domestic scenes, the payment of tribute by subject tribes, and the advent of the white strangers. Aztec hieroglyphs were often composed of descriptive figures—like illustrations in books—and of signs, which apparently had the values of actual writing. Comparable to charts or plans accompanied by written explanations, they were composed of two elements: the figurative and the ideographic. The system has been likened to writing in rebus form. The Aztecs had apparently taken a timid step toward a phonetic system of writing.

Picture Writing

The best aboriginal cultures in Latin America were seated upon the fertile plateaus in or near the tropics where the climate was spring-like. There the Indians had developed the highest form of political organization known to pre-Columbian America—a type of primitive confederation. But partly because of natural obstacles, and partly because of lack of transportation facilities, the Aztecs and the Incas were isolated. Little or no communication took place between them: the Aztecs knew nothing about the potato or the llama, while the Incas had not developed the art of picture writing. Because of physiographic or climatic conditions, the aboriginal tribes were thus not so easily conquered in Latin America as in the English colonies of North America. Early colonies of the Spanish and the Portuguese in America were much influenced by the physical environment and by the customs of the aborigines. In the lands of the Aztecs, the Chibchans, and the Incas, the conquistadors planted settlements upon or near the sites of Indian towns and villages. Aboriginal trails were slowly transformed into the highways of a hybrid civilization. At the present day, in the lands once dominated by the Aztecs, the Mayas, the Chibchans, the Incas, the

Guaraníes, and the Araucanians, Indian blood courses through the veins of a not inconsiderable part of the population.

SUGGESTIONS FOR FURTHER READING

ALEXANDER, H. B., *Mythology of All Races; Latin America,* 1920.

THE ANONYMOUS CONQUEROR, *Narrative of Some Things of New Spain,* 1917.

BINGHAM, H. C., *Machu Picchu: A Citadel of the Incas,* 1930.

CASTETTER, E. F., and BELL, W. H., *Pima and Papayo Indian Agriculture,* 1942.

CHAMBERLAIN, A. F., "Linguistic Stocks of South American Indians, with Distribution Map," *American Anthropologist,* New Series, Vol. XV, pp. 236-247.

CHURCH, G. E., *Aborigines of South America,* 1912.

GARCILASO DE LA VEGA, *The First Part of the Royal Commentaries of the Yncas,* Vol. I, 1871.

HRDLIČKA, A., "The Peopling of America," *Journal of Heredity,* Vol. VI, pp. 79-91.

JOYCE, T. A., *Maya & Mexican Art,* 1927.

————, *Mexican Archaeology,* 1914.

————, *South American Archaeology,* 1912.

LEHMAN, W. and DOERING, H., *The Art of Old Peru,* 1924.

MEANS, P. A., *Ancient Civilizations of the Andes,* 1931.

MORLEY, S. G., *An Introduction to the Study of the Maya Hieroglyphs,* 1915.

————, "Yucatan, Home of the Gifted Maya," *National Geographic Magazine,* Vol. LXX, pp. 591-644.

RADIN, P., *Indians of South America,* 1942.

SPINDEN, H. J., *Ancient Civilizations of Mexico and Central America,* 1928.

————, "The Population of Ancient America," *Geographical Review,* Vol. XVIII, pp. 641-660.

VAILLANT, G. C., *Aztecs of Mexico,* 1941.

WISSLER, C., *The American Indian,* 1938.

CHAPTER III

THE EUROPEAN BACKGROUND

Jutting far into the Atlantic, the Iberian Peninsula is the natural home of a people that seeks its fortune upon the sea. There is no physiographic basis for the existing political division of the peninsula. During the Middle Ages, however, because of historic reasons, it became the abode of two distinct nationalities. Yet as they were subject to similar geographic influences, and as they sprang from almost identical stocks, the Spanish and the Portuguese peoples had some common characteristics.

The Iberian Peninsula is geographically *multum in parvo*. Its physiography is determined by mountains, plateaus, and river systems. High mountain ranges divide the peninsula roughly into four physiographic provinces which are subdivided into smaller provinces by minor ranges and by the Ebro, the Guadalquivir, the Guadiana, the Tagus, and the Duoro rivers. With mountains and plateaus that slope more or less gradually to the sea, the Iberian Peninsula has marked contrasts in climate. Those contrasts accentuate the differences of physical geography.

The isolation of certain physiographic provinces of Spain was partly responsible for the absence of a fixed national type. As a leading Spanish historian has emphatically declared, there is in the true sense no "Spanish race." In the veins of the modern Spaniard there mingle the blood of several different peoples or races. Iberians, Celts, Phœnicians, Greeks, Carthaginians, Romans, Visigoths, and Vandals had invaded and occupied portions of the Iberian Peninsula. At an early period the Jews became a noticeable factor in the population. In the eighth century a large part of the Peninsula was conquered by the Moslems. This added another element to its population and left an enduring impress upon its civilization. Though the dialect spoken in that portion of northern Spain named Castile had by the opening of the fifteenth century become predominant at court and in literary circles, in certain regions there still existed linguistic peculiarities—some of which persist to the present day.

In the early fifteenth century the Iberian Peninsula was not a coherent political entity. Over the embattled city of Granada there still waved the Moslem Crescent. The little Kingdom of Navarre was independent. The kingdoms of Castile and León had indeed become united under one crown, but their sovereign ruled over some provinces that had once been Christian or Mohammedan principalities. Portugal had been hewn out of the side of the Castilian state. Incorporated with the Kingdom of Aragon was not only the region called Catalonia but also the former Moslem principality of Valencia. In Aragon, and possibly to a less extent also in Castile, former kingdoms retained their own customs, laws, and administrative systems. The marriage in 1469 of Princess Isabella, the leading claimant to the Castilian throne, to Prince Ferdinand, the heir to the throne of Aragon,—an event that was followed some years later by the recognition of Isabella's title as Queen of Castile, and by the accession of Ferdinand to the kingship of Aragon,— united those kingdoms into a dyarchy.

Spain in the Fifteenth Century

The unification of Spain was promoted by the masterful and gracious personalities of Ferdinand and Isabella, "the Catholic Monarchs." The introduction or adaptation of certain institutions of government also stimulated unification. Spain's territorial unity was ensured by the capitulation of Granada in 1492, by the annexation of the border counties of Cerdagne and Roussillon, and by the conquest of Navarre. The subjugation of the Moslems encouraged a spirit of religious unity.

During the reign of Ferdinand and Isabella, 1479-1516, there took place a great increase of royal power. Their hands, which sternly repressed rebellious nobles, checked the activity of legislative assemblies in Aragon and Castile. The Castilian Cortes, composed of representatives of clergy, nobles, and deputies of towns and cities, which had been developing into a bicameral legislature that suggested laws to the sovereign or endorsed his fiscal proposals, was gradually allowed to fall into disuse.

The royal government exercised an increasing authority through the development of the institution called the Council of Castile. The factious barons, who had secured predominance in this council, were so reduced in number that control was virtually vested in officials and lawyers of the crown. This council advised the monarch about grants and appointments. Acting as the supreme court of justice in Castile, it promoted centralization.

The Catholic Monarchs displayed a tendency to assign the judicial functions of the Council of Castile to a tribunal designated an *audiencia*, which had served as a high court of the nation. In 1480 the monarchs definitely established the seat of that tribunal at Valladolid and provided that it should have both civil and criminal jurisdiction. Another audiencia, which was founded at Ciudad Real in 1494 and transferred to Granada in 1505,

Special Institutions

had jurisdiction over that part of Spain lying south of the Tagus River. Subsequently a third audiencia was established in Galicia; and audiencias were later created in other sections of Spain. Yet the audiencia of Valladolid was considered the most important tribunal: it continued to enjoy the highest prestige. Its judges held their offices by royal appointment for one year. In 1499 an elaborate ordinance made stipulations concerning the jurisdiction of Castilian audiencias and described the cases which they should consider.

Another important institution, which developed largely under Aragonese auspices, was the viceroy. As early as 1323 the King of Aragon had appointed a viceroy to represent him in Sardinia. Though that official's term was strictly limited to three years, he was an almost absolute ruler under the crown, except in fiscal affairs. In Sicily the Aragonese viceroy also played an important rôle, especially in judicial matters, and a practice developed of sending appeals from his decisions to Spain. Created early in the sixteenth century, the viceroy of Naples was aided in his administration by a special council that was dominated by Spaniards. In Castile the title of viceroy was sometimes given with that of governor to the rulers of outlying territories.

Two other institutions of Castile deserve notice, the captain general and the *adelantado*. During the later Middle Ages, captains general or governors, as they were sometimes called, who were appointed directly by the King, controlled extensive territories in Castile. They exercised military, as well as civil, functions. In the thirteenth century the King suppressed the captains general and replaced them by agents called adelantados, who were entrusted with more civil than military authority. It was the duty of the adelantado of the Canary Islands to distribute land among his followers.

The institution or process styled the *residencia* developed in Spain during the fifteenth century. Apparently this process was first applied to a royal official designated the *corregidor*. It became customary to require him to remain at his post for fifty days after his appointment had expired in order that complaints might be brought against him and justice dispensed. During the reign of the Catholic Monarchs the period of the residencia was decreased to thirty days, and checks were provided to prevent evasion. A special judge was charged to make known the procedure to the inhabitants of the particular district. He was to search for the truth and to make a written report to the Council of Castile. Early in the reign of Charles I, 1516-1556, the residencia was applied to other royal officials, such as governors. This inquest was obviously intended to ensure the efficiency and honesty of crown officials. In time it became another instrument of royal power.

Municipal government in Castile reached its highest development during the fourteenth century. That régime centered about the municipal assembly or *concejo* which made regulations for the management of the city. A council was usually composed of property owners or the heads of families living within the city limits. It annually invested the magistrates of the city **Castilian Cities** or town who sometimes held office by virtue of special privilege. The *alcalde* served as a judge in civil and criminal cases. *Regidores* acted as municipal overseers. An *alguacil* performed the functions of a police officer. The *alguacil mayor* led the city's soldiers to war, while the *alférez* carried the municipal standard. In conjunction with various other officers, who performed minor duties, those magistrates were styled the *ayuntamiento* or the *cabildo*.

Queen Isabella acquired control over the appointment of members of the ayuntamiento by placing their offices on sale. She increased the authority of the corregidores who after 1480 were sent out annually to inspect the cities. When the corregidor became rooted in a certain district the Catholic Monarchs adopted the practice of sending a *visitador* or inspector to examine into the administration of justice and finance.

Ferdinand and Isabella also promoted legal reforms. In the thirteenth century Alphonso X of Castile had codified the most important laws of his kingdom in the *Fuero Real* or Royal Charter and had supervised the preparation of the *Siete Partidas*, **Legal Codes** which was a compilation of Roman, canon, and Spanish law. To standardize the Spanish laws the Catholic Monarchs entrusted the task of collecting the ordinances and decrees that had been issued since the age of King Alfonso to a jurist named Díaz de Montalvo. He accordingly prepared a collection of those decrees that was known as the *Ordenanzas Reales* (Royal Ordinances). These ordinances, however, did not reconcile conflicts between the decrees and the codes. In response to protests at the ambiguity and confusion prevailing in the existing legislation of Spain, in 1505 the Cortes of Toro issued eighty-three interpretative laws which were ordinarily styled the *Leyes de Toro* (Laws of Toro). A thorough codification of Spanish law was not completed, however, until the reign of Philip II, 1556-1598, when the code known as the *Nueva Recopilación* was promulgated.

In Castile the *fueros* were constituent elements of law. A fuero was often a grant by a king to the inhabitants of a certain city or town. Though such grants were at times made to rural districts within the realm, they were frequently conceded to promote the settlement of devastated regions which had been torn from the Moslems. As those regions were located within a debatable land that was subject to hostile irruptions, special privileges were offered in the fueros to prospective settlers. Towns planted on the frontiers of Castile were generally invested by their charters with some autonomy. The fuero of a Castilian city in the borderlands was often a species of charter which granted certain political privileges to its inhabitants.

Most influential in its effects upon national unity was the crusade against the Moslems. From their impregnable stronghold in the Asturias, and from Catalonia, the Spaniards during long centuries had driven the Moslems farther and farther south. In the spring of 1490 soldiers of Ferdinand and Isabella encamped upon the plain near the last Moslem stronghold, the city of Granada. After some chivalric encounters between Christians and Moslems, negotiations for the surrender of Granada were begun in October, 1491. As a result of conferences between their commissioners, on November 25, 1491, the terms of the surrender of Granada were framed.

The Siege of Granada

The capitulation of Granada contained generous pledges to the vanquished. The Christians promised that the Moslems should be allowed to retain their religion, their mosques, their law, their property, and their distinctive dress. For the time being, they were to be ruled by their own magistrates or by Jews who had held public office. The tribute that might be levied upon the vanquished people was restricted to certain specified taxes. Those Mohammedans who desired to leave Spain were to be provided with free transportation to northern Africa. They should be allowed to pass freely through Spanish territory without being molested in person or property. In no case should they be forced to become Christians. On January 2, 1492, the Alhambra was occupied by the jubilant soldiers of the Cross.

The conquest of Granada was supplemented by the acquisition of Cerdagne and Roussillon. Upon the accession of Ferdinand and Isabella those borderlands were in the possession of the French King who had held them some thirty years. By the Treaty of Barcelona in 1493, on certain conditions, Charles VIII of France restored Cerdagne and Roussillon to Ferdinand and Isabella.

Lying like a saddlebag upon the Pyrenees, the little Kingdom of Navarre had long been coveted by both France and Spain. By treaties which were negotiated between 1476 and 1500 the Catholic Monarchs brought the rulers of that mountain kingdom under their tutelage. Using as a pretext a claim of his second wife to the throne of Navarre, in July, 1512, Ferdinand sent an army into that kingdom. The King fled and the Duke of Alva captured Pamplona. In a Cortes at Burgos in 1515 Ferdinand solemnly declared that Navarre was incorporated with Castile. Before Ferdinand's death the entire peninsula, with the exception of Portugal, was thus united under one crown.

The establishment of the territorial unity of Spain was bound to have great effects. A crusade of centuries against the Moslems had deeply influenced the life and habits of the Spanish people. It had stimulated their military spirit at the frequent expense of the arts of peace. Near the border- lands Castilian cavaliers had ofttimes lodged under the same roof with their armed steeds, in order that they might sally forth promptly at the battle cry of *Sant Iago*. Though, as the Castilian arms spread southward, the arts of civilization revived within the regions that seemed secure from Moslem attack, the crusading spirit was kept alive. Spaniards of the upper class, especially the nobles, came to view menial occupations as low and despicable: they deemed that agriculture and manufactures should be left to captives, to serfs, and to the lower classes. The conquest of Granada intensified the fervent religious spirit of Aragonese and Castilians. Trained to fight the battles of the Cross against the Crescent, they developed a proselyting ardor that was destined to endure long after the fall of Granada.

Effects of Unification

The intense religious spirit engendered by the Moslem crusade stimulated the activity of the Inquisition. That institution had been established in Aragon and Navarre as early as 1238. There it was used against heretics and Moslems who had ostensibly accepted the Catholic faith. Soon after their accession Ferdinand and Isabella decided to introduce the Inquisition into Castile. A bull of November, 1478, authorized them to appoint inquisitors who were given jurisdic- tion over heretics. Two years later a court of this so-called "New In- quisition" was installed at Seville. Inquisitorial courts were subse- quently founded in other Castilian cities, while tribunals of the "Old Inquisition" in various parts of Spain were revived or reënforced. Mean- time the Pope authorized the creation of a Council of the Inquisition, which was given jurisdiction over all matters concerning the faith, and which ultimately established its virtual independence of the Papacy.

Under the zealous direction of Tomás de Torquemada, the Spanish Inquisition soon became an instrument of religious repression and persecution. In theory the only persons exempted from its jurisdiction were the bishops. Through its mediæval procedure, its unfair rules of evidence, its ubiquitous familiars and other agents, and its edict of faith, which made every person a spy upon his neighbor, it tried to extirpate heresy from the soil of Spain. It was used particularly against those Jews and Moors who professed Christianity. Besides its attempts to eradicate unorthodox belief, the Inquisition exercised a censorship over books and manuscripts which had a stifling effect upon freedom of thought.

In general the Spanish Church had discarded the rites used by its communicants in the Gothic age and had adopted the ritual approved by Rome. Spanish priests possessed the *fuero* or right of immunity known as "benefit of clergy," which entitled them to exemption from the jurisdiction of civil courts, at least in religious cases. From time to time the clergy held councils.

Religious Life

Various religious orders played influential rôles in Spanish life. At the accession of Ferdinand and Isabella two orders were especially important, the Franciscans and the Dominicans. The Franciscans were accustomed to make pilgrimages while begging alms and preaching repentance. The Dominicans were especially interested in the extirpation of unorthodox belief. In the latter part of the thirteenth century there were in Spain some two thousand Dominican and Franciscan monasteries. The Company or Society of Jesus, possibly the most important order of all, was founded after the death of King Ferdinand. Eventually the militant Jesuits developed many functions: they supported the papal prerogative, planted missions, and founded academies and seminaries.

The regular and secular clergy were not only exempt from the jurisdiction of the State in some matters, but on the accession of Ferdinand and Isabella, they were also exempt from the payment of certain taxes. Against this practice of immunity, which often became a glaring abuse, the Catholic Monarchs set their faces. They prohibited archbishops and bishops from engrossing national revenues. They tried to prevent certain religious orders from obtaining bequests of property from wealthy laymen. For by such methods the clergy of Spain had acquired control of immense, remunerative properties.

Church and State

Ultra-Catholic though the Spanish monarchs were, they exalted their authority at the expense of the Papacy. At the time of their accession the Pope exercised the right to appoint ecclesiastics to vacant sees in Spain. During a dispute over an appointment to a vacancy in the bishopric of Cuenca, however, the Catholic Monarchs asserted the prerogative of the crown to make such appointments. In consequence, they secured from Pope Sixtus IV an acknowledgment of their right to make nominations to important ecclesiastical sees that might fall vacant. As a matter of course, the Pope appointed such nominees. By engrossing the rents of nominees who were displeasing to them and in other ways, Ferdinand and Isabella succeeded in obtaining control over the appointment of candidates to minor benefices. As a reward for their services in the crusade against the Moslems, the Pope conceded to those monarchs the right of patronage over all the churches of the former Kingdom of Granada. It was a logical result of the policy pursued by Ferdinand

and Isabella that under monarchs of the House of Austria, who came into power in 1516, the Pope was compelled to agree that no bulls should be published by his nuncio in Spain without the consent of the King.

Exact figures regarding the population of Spain upon the accession of Ferdinand and Isabella are not available. The Spanish economist Colmeiro estimated the population of Spain under the Catholic Monarchs at 10,000,000, which seems excessively high. In 1482 a Spanish official reported to the Catholic Monarchs that there were, exclusive of Granada, 1,500,000 resident property holders in Castile. With an estimate that the relative proportion of resident property holders to inhabitants was one to four, the total population of Castile would be 6,000,000. Estimating the population of Granada and Aragon at 1,500,000 or 2,000,000, a total for Spain is reached of 7,500,000 or 8,000,-000, which is presumably rather high. The eminent Spanish historian Altamira calculated that in 1594 the inhabitants of Spain, which by that date had annexed Portugal as well as Navarre, numbered some 8,000,000 souls.

The chief social strata in Spain were the upper, middle, and lower classes. The upper class was composed of nobles and higher clergy. Despite the weakening of its power and prestige by the monarchs, the upper class continued to enjoy many advantages. Its members possessed extensive estates, upon which there were numerous peasants in a servile condition. Many nobles and ecclesiastics lived in castles with stables filled with fine steeds and with hoards of gold and silver plate and jewels. The most frequent noble titles were count, duke, and marquis. Among the lower nobility the most common title was *hijo-dalgo* or simply *caballero*. All of those nobles enjoyed numerous privileges, such as exemption from certain taxes.

Under the Catholic Monarchs the position of the middle class was improved in various ways. The increasing attention paid to commerce and industry encouraged some members of the lower nobility to enter the ranks of the mercantile class; while, on the other hand, the movement of emancipated peasants from the lower into the middle class, which was under way before the accession of Isabella, went on at a rapid pace. A royal ordinance of 1480 confirmed to Castilian peasants the right to leave the estates of nobles and to take with them their own properties and products.

In Aragon, especially in Catalonia, where feudal or quasi-feudal customs had secured a firmer root than elsewhere in Spain, the serfs encountered special difficulty in securing their emancipation. By virtue of a decision rendered by King Ferdinand in 1486, however, the manual labor due from Aragonese peasants to their lords was replaced by money payments, and emancipated serfs were placed under the King's jurisdiction. A firm basis was thus laid for a class of free peasants.

In general, the nobles held offices or dwelt upon their hereditary estates. Ordinarily they viewed all manual labor with contempt. The lower classes were mainly engaged in agriculture, manu-

Social and Economic Conditions

factures, commerce, and sheep raising. Over these occupations the Spanish sovereigns exercised a supervision that was paternalistic. In 1500 they made the senior member of the Council of Castile the president of the *Mesta* or guild of sheep owners. His duty was to manage the affairs of that guild and to act as a link between it and the crown. The extension of the privileges enjoyed by the Mesta in the beginning of the sixteenth century indicated that agriculture was on the decline. At times there was apparently a lack of agricultural produce in Castile as many fields lay untilled. To an extent agriculture was also injured by the interest which developed in manufactures.

The cities of Granada, Seville, Córdova, Toledo, Segovia, and León became flourishing centers of industry. Seville and Córdova became noted for the manufacture of arms, especially swords. To promote the manufacture of woolen cloth the Catholic Monarchs decreed that not over two-thirds of the wool produced in Spain should be exported, while woolen cloth should not be imported. They also tried to influence commercial development. In 1500 the exportation of merchandise in foreign vessels from a Spanish port was forbidden, if there were Castilian vessels in the same harbor. In important cities the merchants selected officials called consuls who undertook to settle disputes about commercial matters. As a result the crown undertook to establish *consulados* or commercial tribunals. These were local councils composed of merchants who were empowered to make regulations to promote commerce and even to try cases relating to trade. A model grant of this sort was made by Ferdinand and Isabella in 1494 to the merchants of Burgos. The grant of privileges to a consulado in northern Spain became widely known as the Ordinances of Bilbao, and served as a pattern.

In certain parts of Spain conditions prevailed which partook of a feudal character. This was especially true of Catalonia,

Quasi-feudal Customs

where estates were held of the Aragonese King by a quasi-feudal tenure. Ordinarily, however, in mediæval Spain lands were not held upon condition of military or other honorable service: the functions of government were not partitioned out as in a feudal state; and great landowners were not organized in hierarchical tiers. The relations existing between a lord and his vassal were often personal rather than feudal or semi-feudal. Yet at this epoch there existed in Spain large estates which were regularly tilled by a vassal peasantry or by peasants who had scarcely emerged from serfdom. Even in Castile, free peasants and small proprietors sometimes commended themselves to the protection of a neighboring noble by a practice that was designated the *encomienda:* the peasants furnished service to the noble in return for protection.

Another practice, which developed hand in hand with the reconquest of Spain, is worthy of special notice. This was the custom of dividing lands among the followers of the conquering kings. Strips of land which James I of Aragon allotted to his followers in regions taken from the infidels were termed *repartimientos.* In their conquest of the principalities of Murcia and Seville a similar policy was adopted by Castilian monarchs. The lands of the conquered regions, as well as the estates and houses vacated by the Moslems, were distributed among Christian cavaliers. Presumably captive Moslems and their serfs were at times transferred with portions of land.

For many years before the accession of Ferdinand and Isabella the Jews had played an important rôle in the social and intellectual life of Spain. Racial and religious antagonism toward them increased rapidly during the fifteenth century. Frequent **The Jews** attempts were made to convert them to Christianity; Jews who were converted by force were often contemptuously designated *Marranos.* In 1479 and 1480 the Cortes renewed certain obsolete laws concerning the Jews: they were prohibited from wearing silk dresses and jewels; they were ordered to live in separate quarters in the towns and cities, and their relations with the Christians were restricted in various ways.

Apparently the expulsion of the Jews from Andalusia was seriously considered by Queen Isabella as early as 1480. Not until the fall of Granada, however, did Ferdinand and Isabella make their momentous decision. In March, 1492, a decree was promulgated which provided for the expulsion of professed Jews from the kingdoms of Castile and Aragon within three months. This decree provided that the Jews might sell or dispose of their movable property freely; they were declared to be under the royal protection, but prohibited from taking gold or silver with them. Soon there fled to Africa, Italy, and Portugal a multitude of Jews who, according to a conservative estimate, numbered about 165,000. About 20,000 died because of mistreatment. In all, Spain lost some 185,000 inhabitants: physicians, scholars, farmers, skilful artisans—the best types that she could possess.

The solution of another racial and religious problem again carries the story into the age of the Austrian monarchs. Despite provisions concerning the Moslems in the capitulation of Granada, the Spaniards soon made attempts to convert them by force. Some additions were thus made to the converted Mohammedans, the so-called Moriscoes. A commission appointed by Charles I decided that Moslems who had been baptized should be considered as Christians. In April, 1525, King Charles issued a decree approving this decision and declaring that any mosque in which mass had once been celebrated became thereby a Christian church. Meanwhile the Papacy stimulated antagonism to the unconverted Moslems, who were designated *Mudéjares*. In November, 1525, the King issued a decree announcing that within a short time all the Mohammedans who would not accept the Catholic faith should be expelled from Spain unless they wished to become slaves. As a result many Mudéjares were converted, some arose in revolts that were rudely suppressed, while others fled to Africa. Mosques were shut; Korans were burned. Mudéjares in the legal sense disappeared, and only Moriscoes remained in the Spanish dominions.

Moslems and Moriscoes

The suspicious Spaniards soon enforced against the Moriscoes, however, many restrictive laws that had been enacted under the Catholic Monarchs. Moriscoes were enjoined not to enter the former Kingdom of Granada. A law of 1572 provided for the preparation in each community of a register of free and slave Moriscoes who should not be allowed to leave their homes without a royal permit. Yet even this rigorous law did not prove effective, while Spanish dread of a rebellion by Moriscoes, who might be aided by Mohammedans from northern Africa, did not decrease.

After the age of Philip II many schemes were formed for the disposal of the Moriscoes. Although violently opposed by nobles who employed the industrious Moriscoes on their estates, a radical solution steadily gained favor. At last, in 1609 an edict was issued providing for the expulsion of the Moriscoes from Valencia and portions of Castile. This edict, which resembled the decree for the expulsion of the Jews, was later applied to other sections of Spain. Because of this barbarous measure some five hundred thousand Moriscoes disposed of their properties and sailed from Spanish ports.

In an age when population was declining, and when interest in the industrial arts was decaying, Spain thus deprived herself of a class similar to the Jews whom she had banished in 1492. Not only did she drive those industrious classes from her shores, but she also persistently strove to exclude them from her vast, unpopulated dominions overseas.

At many points the history of Portugal resembles that of Spain. Portucalia, the nucleus of mediæval Portugal, developed from a grant of land made by the King of León about 1095 to a Burgundian adventurer. More than two hundred years of crusade against the Moslems, which was complicated by struggles against the suzerainty of Castile, resulted in the formation of a new nationality. In the thirteenth century Portuguese crusaders completed the conquest of a region called the Algarve. In April, 1385, after the death of King Ferdinand of Portugal, a Cortes which had been convoked to settle the succession to the throne elected a brave crusader named John, who was a natural brother of the deceased ruler, as King of Portugal. On August 14 of the same year at the battle of Aljubarrota the Portuguese, who were aided by English archers, decisively defeated an invading Castilian army. Thus Portugal's independence from Spain was sealed.

Portugal Achieves Independence

The reign of John I was an introduction to the Golden Age of Portugal. During his rule the Portuguese language was introduced into the courts of law. The calendar was changed from the Augustan era to the Christian. Lisbon became the metropolis of the Portuguese Empire.

Kingship in mediæval Portugal was at the same time hereditary and elective. The daughters, as well as the sons, of the King, were eligible to the throne. The Cortes was convoked by the King to furnish advice when circumstances demanded. In its sessions the clergy, the nobility, and the representatives of towns and cities deliberated together. Unanimity was necessary for an agreement. Upon the accession of John I, a long and strenuous conflict between Church and State had terminated; for in 1361 an agreement had been reached between the contending interests by which ecclesiastics were confirmed in the enjoyment of all privileges that were not contrary to the royal prerogative.

The clergy played a most important part in Portuguese politics. The nobles, originally composed of persons styled *ricoshomens* and *infançoes,* were very numerous. During the crusade against the Moslems the Portuguese kings had made to the nobles numerous grants of land which carried with them political and judicial privileges of a semi-feudal nature. As in Castile, charters granted by the kings to towns and cities constituted their organic laws. But Portugal's municipalities did not enjoy so much autonomy as those of Castile; they were carefully watched by royal officers and powerful prelates.

Portuguese law found its origins in the Roman law, the Visigothic code, the Church decretals, and the regulations of the King and the Cortes. The chancellor of John I started the work of codification which was continued by João Mendes. The *Livro das leis e posturas* of Mendes, which was published near the opening of the fifteenth century, constituted an important source of later codes. The Ordinances of Duarte, which were completed in 1436, constituted another source. During the reign of

Portuguese Law and Custom

Alphonso V those two compilations, supplemented by customary law, municipal charters, concordats with the Papacy, judicial decisions, and royal ordinances, formed the basis of a famous code that was called the *Ordenações Affonsinas* (Ordinances of Alfonso). Early in the sixteenth century King Manuel appointed jurists to prepare a new code which was based upon the Ordinances of Alfonso and supplemented by subsequent laws. That revised code, which was published in 1514, was designated the Manuelian Ordinances. After the conquest of Portugal by Philip II in 1580, he directed that the legal codes should be revised by certain jurists. This compilation, which was based upon the Ordinances of Alfonso and the Manuelian Ordinances, with the addition of laws subsequently issued, was promulgated in January, 1603. It was designated the *Ordenações Philippinas*.

In Portugal, as in Spain, the kings had followed the custom of distributing among their followers the territory which was wrested from the Moslems. During the age of John I, many portions of land were held by ecclesiastics or nobles to whom they had been given by royal favor. Other portions had been granted by charters to communes or municipalities, while the rest of the land remained under the direct control of the King. Residents upon the royal estates were either nobles or tenants. The King was the direct proprietor of the mines and the seaports. He paid the expenses of his government with the income from his estates and the revenues accruing from navigation duties.

A large part of Portuguese soil was held by members of the upper nobility to whom it had been granted by the kings either in return for services or to secure their support. Occasionally those lands had been granted within Portucalia; but more often they had been carved out of regions that had been torn from the Moslems. Ecclesiastics or nobles who were thus favored were often called donatories. Although in theory the Portuguese King might revoke the land grants at pleasure, in practice he had little control over them, and their limits were frequently extended by aggressive nobles. Even in the reign of John I, who strove to strengthen the royal authority over those semi-feudal estates, noble landowners were ordinarily exempt from the payment of certain taxes; they exercised a large amount of judicial authority, and acted as the military chieftains of their tenants.

Despite the limitations placed upon the power of the clergy by the agreement of 1361, ecclesiastics still exercised a large amount of authority. They frequently belonged to the King's council and played an important rôle in the Cortes. Early in the sixteenth century the King's chaplain became the head of the Portuguese Church. He was at a later date recognized as the patriarch of Lisbon.

Portuguese municipalities did not possess as much autonomy as the cities of Castile. For the kings of Portugal, as well as the nobles and the clergy, had infringed upon municipal rights. The *foraes* or charters that had been given to municipalities in return for services against the Moslems ordinarily granted them certain administrative and judicial privileges. Among those was the right to send delegates to the Cortes. During the fifteenth century royal judges called *juizes da fóra* displaced judges who had been elected by the inhabitants of the chartered district; while other royal officials who were designated corregedores undertook to interfere in local affairs. The inhabitants of a municipality ordinarily belonged to three strata: the serfs, the middle classes, and the members of the lower nobility.

A Portuguese historian has estimated that, on the eve of the great discoveries, the total population of his country was about one million souls. The main occupation was agriculture; but some attention was paid to commerce and mining. As in Spain, the long and bitter struggle against the Moslems had engendered, especially among the upper classes, a dislike for menial occupations and a love for warlike adventure.   The Population of Portugal

The Mohammedans and the Jews of Portugal were not treated exactly like their Spanish brethren. Conquered Moslems apparently did not constitute so distinct an element in Portugal as in Spain. Presumably more traces of Mohammedan blood were found to the south than to the north of the Tagus River in Portugal. The Jews, however, belonged to a class that was separate and distinct. Active and enterprising, they were viewed with disdain and envy by the proud Portuguese; they were often forced to live in special quarters in the towns and cities. They did not always enjoy the same rights before the law as did their Christian neighbors. Hence John I secured a bull from the Pope which aimed to protect Portuguese Jews from persecution. During his reign they could only be held responsible by Jewish magistrates for offenses against the civil and the criminal law. By virtue of this guardianship and of their own ability, Jews at times held important positions in the government of Portugal. A large part of her foreign commerce fell into their hands.

It was reserved for King Emmanuel "the Fortunate," who desired to unite the kingdoms of the Iberian Peninsula under one scepter, to decide the fate of unbaptized Jews and Moslems. About 1496—to please the Catholic Monarchs—King Emmanuel issued orders for the expulsion of the Jews. Members of that unfortunate race either had to become Christians or to depart from Portuguese soil within six months. With numerous Jews that were expelled there went also some unbaptized Moslems, who had fled into Portugal from Spain. To persecute those Jews who had professed Christianity in order that they might remain in Portugal, in 1536 a tribunal of the Holy Office was erected at Lisbon. To a less extent perhaps than in Spain did the Inquisition in Portugal exert a blighting influence upon the life and development of the people. Four years after the establishment of the Inquisition at Lisbon, the Jesuit order was introduced into Portugal where it soon acquired the control of educational institutions.

The two nations that inhabited the Iberian Peninsula in the later Middle Ages had many resemblances. Though there were some local variations, similar strains of blood mingled in the veins of Spanish and Portuguese. Political tendencies in both Spain and Portugal had encouraged the growth of royal power. Both Spanish and Portuguese governmental systems mirrored the King's prerogative. Institutions like the ayuntamiento, the audiencia, and the viceroy furnished the Spaniards, at least, with materials for the fabric of a colonial system. In both Spain and Portugal there prevailed a system of landholding which was based upon the existence of large estates tilled by a servile peasantry. The policy pursued toward the Jews and the Moslems had an injurious effect upon industry and commerce, especially in Spain, while the ubiquitous activities of the Inquisition checked freedom of thought and intellectual progress. Because of the geographical location of Spain and Portugal, because of the rooted dislike of Spaniards and Portuguese for menial occupations, and because of the termination of the arduous crusade against the Moslems, in the end of the fifteenth century the upper classes in the Iberian Peninsula were seeking for new domains to conquer. At a juncture when conditions for colonization in the Iberian kingdoms were far from being so auspicious as they were in contemporary England, it was the audacious enterprise of Columbus, Cabral, and their followers that gave adventurous cavaliers a chance to enter upon a new crusade. More or less unwittingly they thus undertook to transplant Iberian customs and institutions to strange lands far beyond the Pillars of Hercules.

SUGGESTIONS FOR FURTHER READING

ALTAMIRA, R., *A History of Spanish Civilization*, 1930.

ARMSTRONG, E., *The Emperor Charles V*, Vol. II, 1902.

BELL, A. F. G., *Portugal of the Portuguese*, 1915.

CHAPMAN, C. E., *A History of Spain*, 1918.

DIEULAFOY, M., *Art in Spain and Portugal*, 1913.

HAMILTON, E. J., *American Treasure and the Price Revolution in Spain, 1501-1650*, 1934.

HERCULANO, A., *History of the Origin and Establishment of the Inquisition in Portugal*, 1926.

HUME, M. A. S., *Philip II of Spain*, 1897.

KLEIN, J., *The Mesta; A Study in Spanish Economic History*, 1920.

LEA, H. C., *A History of the Inquisition of Spain,* Vol. III, 1907.
————, *Chapters from the Religious History of Spain,* 1890.
MERRIMAN, R. B., *The Rise of the Spanish Empire in the Old World and in the New,* Vol. II, 1918.
NEUMAN, A. A., *The Jews in Spain,* Vol. II, 1942.
PALMER, T. W., *Guide to the Law and Literature of Spain,* 1915.
PRESCOTT, W. H., *History of the Reign of Ferdinand and Isabella,* 1838.
SEDGWICK, H. D., *Spain, A Short History,* 1925.
STEPHENS, H. M., *The Story of Portugal,* 1903.
VANCE, J. T., *The Background of Hispanic-American Law,* 1937.
VAN DYKE, P., *Ignatius Loyola,* 1926.
WATTS, H. E., *The Christian Recovery of Spain,* 1907.
WILLIAMS, L., *Arts and Crafts of Older Spain,* Vol. I, 1907.

CHAPTER IV

DISCOVERY AND CONQUEST

The discovery of the New World by Columbus was foreshadowed by the maritime achievements of the Portuguese. Among the princes and scholars who prepared the way for the great Genoese the name of Prince Henry is preëminent. In the prime of life, Henry, the son of King John I of Portugal, relinquished the prospect of military fame and devoted himself to the advancement of geographical knowledge, the planting of colonies, and the expansion of commerce. Under his guidance sailors and navigators were trained for exploration. An increasing interest in Africa directed his attention to that continent.

"Prince Henry the Navigator"

A beginning was made by the rediscovery of islands along the African coast that had been known to the ancient world. Near the end of the second decade of the fifteenth century mariners from Portugal reached the islands of Porto Santo and Madeira. About 1432 they discovered the island of Santa Maria in the Azores. About 1434 Gil Eannes sailed past Cape Bojador. Prince Henry had planted a colony in the distant Azores by 1443; and about that time Portuguese sailors passed Cape Verde. In 1486 Bartholomew Dias rounded the southern extremity of Africa which he named Stormy Cape. Upon his return to Portugal, however, because of the promise that this discovery seemed to hold, King John II designated it the Cape of Good Hope.

In 1496 King Manuel decided to give the chief command of an exploring expedition to Vasco da Gama. Four vessels were carefully prepared for a voyage to the Indies. On July 8, 1497, bearing the pilot who had accompanied Dias, the fleet sailed from Portugal. About four months later Gama passed the farthest point that Dias had reached. On Christmas Day he caught sight of land which he called Natal. Early in March, 1498, he anchored off the island of Mozambique. About May 17 he sighted the highlands of India, and a few days later he anchored before Calicut. Gama had thus reached India by sailing around Africa. A Portuguese geographer attributed this significant achievement to the divine inspiration of "Prince Henry the Navigator."

Within a year after Gama's return, King Manuel entrusted a noble named Pedro Alvares Cabral with an expedition to Calicut in order

46

to establish commercial relations with India. Accompanied by the most skilful seamen, with a fleet of thirteen ships that were armed with artillery and laden with presents, Cabral set sail in March, 1500. His fleet took the beaten route down the   Cabral African coast until the Cape Verde Islands had been   Discovers Brazil passed. Then, influenced presumably by reports of inconspicuous Portuguese voyagers concerning land in the west, he deliberately proceeded in a southwesterly direction. On April 22, 1500, he caught sight of a mountain peak in South America. Supposing that the land which he had discovered was an island, he named it Vera Cruz. This name was later changed because a dye wood found there resembled the Brazil wood brought to Europe from Asia. Cabral formally took possession of the new land in the name of Portugal; and, on May 1, he set up a wooden cross as a sign of ownership.

Largely because of the teachings and the inspiration of Prince Henry, the African coasts had thus been explored, the Cape of Good Hope had been rounded, the sea route to India and the Far East disclosed, and Brazil discovered. The Portuguese claim to that country rested partly upon Cabral's discovery. There is no doubt that from the explorations of the Portuguese, Christopher Columbus received a definite stimulus. His son Ferdinand declared that it was in Portugal that Columbus began to surmise that, if her navigators could sail so far south, he might also sail west and discover land in that direction.

Few characters in history have been the subject of so much controversy as the Great Admiral. More than a dozen towns have claimed to be the place of his birth. It is now generally agreed, however, that Christopher Columbus, the son of a woolweaver, was born in Genoa. A critical scholar named Henry Vignaud presented evidence to show that the great Genoese was born in 1451. As a lad Columbus learned the weaver's trade. There is evidence which indicates that he went to sea when about twenty years of age.

However that may be, Columbus was affected by the spirit of his time. He eventually learned about the scientific equipment of a navigator: the astrolabe, the compass, sea charts, and tables of declination. He not only read the travels of Marco   Influences Polo but may also have been influenced by the writings   Affecting Columbus of Pierre d'Ailly, who in a volume entitled *Imago Mundi* had collected the sayings of the ancients concerning the size and sphericity of the earth. A belief was current for many years that Columbus received a decisive impulse from the celebrated Florentine scientist Paolo dal Pozzo Toscanelli, who was supposed to have composed letters and a map that served him as sailing directions. Vignaud maintained, however, that those letters were forged by Bartholomew Columbus to destroy the tale that his brother Christopher was inspired to make the voyage because of a tale told him by an obscure mariner regarding new lands to the west. Though some historical scholars nevertheless believe that Columbus was influenced by those letters, it is a mistake to maintain that the discoverer would not have sailed without that stimulus.

About 1477 Columbus took up his residence in Portugal. He soon married the daughter of a Portuguese who had been governor of the island of Porto Santo. In 1484 he presented a petition to King John II of Portugal. It appears that Columbus proposed to lead an expedition in a westerly direction in order to discover populous islands and main-lands that were rich in gold, silver, and precious stones. He petitioned the Portuguese monarch to equip a fleet of three vessels with supplies for one year. He solicited the title of grand admiral, the viceregal power, and the perpetual governmental control over all lands that might be discovered. Among other conditions he asked to be assigned one-tenth of the revenues and precious metals derived from such lands. Whatever may have been the exact terms of this proposal, King John submitted the project to a group of scholars who rejected it. In 1485 Columbus left Portugal to seek his fortune elsewhere.

Soon after landing in Spain, he visited the Franciscan monastery of La Rábida. He then proceeded to Seville where the Duke of Medina Sidonia and the Count of Medina Celi became interested in his plan. Apparently Columbus held his first interview with Ferdinand and Isabella at Córdova in 1486. Four years later a commission formally disapproved the proposals of the Genoese, evidently expressing the opinion that they were illusory and impracticable. As the monarchs seemed to be engrossed in the crusade against the Moslems, he reluctantly decided to appeal to France. Yet the intervention of faithful friends, including a navigator named Martín Alonzo Pinzón, induced Queen Isabella to grant Columbus another hearing. At Santa Fé a new commission considered his proposals. Again the decision was against the Genoese, who sadly took leave of the Catholic Monarchs. However, the treasurer of Aragon, Luis de Santangel, persuaded the Queen to support the enterprise. Hence, on April 17, 1492, Columbus and the Catholic Monarchs signed a contract.

The so-called capitulations of Santa Fé provided that Columbus and his heirs were to have the hereditary office of admiral in all islands and lands that might be discovered or acquired by him or through his industry. Columbus was also to be the viceroy and governor-general over such lands; he was conceded the right to nominate candidates for the chief magistracies of the islands and provinces so discovered. He was to have one-tenth of the pearls, precious stones, and spices

Columbus in Spain

that might be found, bought, bartered, or gained within the newly discovered lands. He or his lieutenant should have the sole power to judge all disputes about commercial relations between those regions and Spain. The admiral should be allowed to contribute one-eighth of the expense of any subsequent expedition and should get one-eighth of the accruing profit. To judge by this agreement, the object of Columbus was to discover and to take possession of certain islands and lands in the Atlantic Ocean concerning which he had evidently secured information. A passport furnished the voyager by the sovereigns, however, stated that he was to sail toward India.

Of the total cost of the expedition, which Vignaud estimated at two million maravedís, the Spanish monarchs furnished about one-half. A fraction of the cost, possibly not more than one-eighth, was advanced by Columbus probably from loans, while the remainder seems to have been supplied by his friends. **The First Voyage of Columbus** It is accordingly clear that though patronized and supported by the State, the expedition of Columbus was not a purely governmental enterprise. Through orders of the Catholic Monarchs urging compliance with the capitulations, and by the aid of Pinzón, Columbus ultimately succeeded in equipping three caravels, the "Niña," the "Pinta," and the "Santa María." With this small fleet and accompanied by about one hundred and twenty men, he left the harbor of Palos on August 3, bound for the Canaries. Thence the expedition sailed westward across the Atlantic, and after many bickerings, doubts, and discouragements, on the evening of October 11, the sailors were inspirited by detecting a faint light.

The dawn of the following day revealed the outlines of an island that was called by the aborigines Guanahani. This island, which the best scholars have identified with what is now called Watling's Island, Columbus named San Salvador. Whatever ideas the Genoese may originally have entertained about his object, he now evidently thought that he had reached the Indies. He called the inhabitants Indians and entertained notions that he would soon behold the Great Khan. After he reached Cuba, he sent two of his followers to seek for that Oriental potentate. Then he sailed to an island which, because of a fancied resemblance to Spain, he named Española—an isle later designated Santo Domingo. The "Santa María" was wrecked upon the coast of that island. After laying the foundations of a fort, and leaving some forty men there, early in January, 1493, Columbus sailed for the Iberian Peninsula. He took with him a few Indians and some ornaments of gold.

In March he arrived at Lisbon where a report that he had reached the Indies caused great excitement. It soon became apparent that his discovery had provoked the jealousy of the Portuguese. John II took the view that the newly-discovered lands were within the territory of Guinea which had been assigned to him by the Pope. On March 15 Columbus reached Palos. From Seville he proceeded to Barcelona where he was benignantly received by the Catholic Monarchs who asked him to sit beside them upon an improvised throne. He was given a coat of arms upon which the sovereigns graciously allowed him to place a gold castle on a green field and a purple lion rampant on a white field. Upon these arms the legend was later inscribed, "For Castile and for León Columbus found a New World."

Meanwhile Pope Alexander VI had been asked to define the rights of Spain. On May 3, 1493, he issued a bull which granted to Ferdinand and Isabella all lands which they might discover that did not belong to any Christian prince. Another bull dated May 4 was issued which drew an imaginary line from north to south, one hundred leagues west of the Azores and Cape Verde Islands. Any discoveries of land lying west of this line, not already possessed by a Christian prince, were to belong to Spain. Portugal was thus restricted to territories east of this line. On September 26 still another bull provided that Ferdinand and Isabella should have the title to lands which they might discover in India.

The
Demarcation
Line

King John was not satisfied with that adjustment. Commissioners appointed by the contending nations signed a convention at Tordesillas on June 7, 1494. The Treaty of Tordesillas provided that the demarcation line should be drawn three hundred and seventy leagues west of the Cape Verde Islands: lands found to the east of that meridian should belong to Portugal, while lands to the west should be the property of Spain. This meridian crossed the continent of South America near the mouth of the Amazon. In conjunction with Cabral's discovery, this demarcation assigned to Portugal the title to Brazil, while it restricted the Spanish claim in America to the region that lay west of that imaginary line.

The three remaining voyages of Columbus will be briefly described. During his second voyage, which was made from 1493 to 1496, he explored Cuba and discovered Jamaica. On his third voyage in 1498, he caught sight of the island of Trinidad, coasted along what proved to be the adjacent mainland of South America, and passed the mouth of the Orinoco River. Meanwhile complaints against the colonizing policy of Columbus induced the Spanish monarchs to appoint Francisco de Bobadilla as judge and governor of the newly-discovered islands and mainland. When that official reached Santo Domingo he cast the discoverer into chains. Upon his arrival in Spain the monarchs released him and declared that Bobadilla had exceeded his instructions. Upon his last voyage in 1502, Columbus sailed along the shores of Central America from Honduras to Panama.

Other explorers had meantime been busy. Alonso de Ojeda, a companion of Columbus, led an expedition in 1499 which reached the northwestern coast of South America. An Indian village built upon piles in the Gulf of Maracaibo reminded him of Venice, so that he called the region Venezuela (little Venice). In 1508 he was made the governor of a region which was called Castilla del Oro. He soon undertook to plant a settlement upon the mainland.

Interested in the colonizing activities of Ojeda was a lawyer named Enciso. In 1510 he led from Santo Domingo a band of settlers bound for a colony which Ojeda had planted in South America. Upon a ship belonging to the expedition there was concealed a bankrupt Spaniard named Vasco Núñez de Balboa, who narrowly escaped being marooned on a desert isle. When Ojeda's settlement was found to be deserted, the stowaway suggested that the expedition should sail to a region where food was plentiful and where the Indians did not use poisoned arrows. On the southeastern margin of the Isthmus of Panama, the colonists founded a town called Darien. Two alcaldes were chosen, one of whom was Balboa. That adventurer soon refused to obey Enciso, shipped him to Spain, and stigmatized him as a devil. He also expelled the titular governor of the district and became the dominant personality of the settlement.

Balboa sent out expeditions from Darien to explore the surrounding territory. He heard reports of a favored region where the natives ate and drank out of golden dishes and where Indians in vessels propelled by oars and sails navigated a Great Water. On January 20, 1513, he addressed a letter to the King to explain his actions. In this letter Balboa said that there was gold in the land which he had discovered. He mentioned a rumor to the effect that at three days' journey beyond the mountains of the isthmus there was another sea.

News that Enciso had denounced him to King Ferdinand made Balboa realize that he must justify himself at once. Instead of waiting for the aid which he had solicited from Spain, he immediately prepared an expedition. Accompanied by some two hundred Spaniards and a large number of Indians, on September 1, 1513, he sailed from the harbor of Darien. Five days later, he marched from Caledonia Bay in a southerly direction. On the forenoon of September 25 his guides assured him that the Great Water could be seen from the top of a mountain. Before reaching its summit, Balboa halted his men; then, alone on a peak in Darien, he beheld a new sea that faded away in the distance. According to a Spanish chronicler, he gave thanks to God who had permitted

Balboa Discovers the Pacific Ocean

a lowly person like himself to discover the great, main sea. He named the newly discovered gulf San Miguel. A few days later, with a naked sword and the royal standard in his hands, he waded into its billows and by a pompous proclamation took possession of the salt sea and all its adjacent lands for the crown of Spain! The discoverers christened this ocean the *Mar del Sur,* the South Sea. Six years later, upon the shores of that ocean, a Spaniard named Pedrarias Dávila founded the city of Panama.

Ferdinand Magellan, a brave and honorable Portuguese who had visited the Molucca Islands, laid before his King a proposal to reach those islands by sailing west. As the Portuguese monarch did not accept his plan, Magellan, who seems to have believed that the Moluccas lay upon the Spanish side of the demarcation line, proceeded to Spain. On March 22, 1518, a contract was arranged between Magellan and King Charles I. By that contract the King agreed to furnish five vessels for the expedition, to equip them with arms and men, and with provisions for two years. On his part Magellan agreed to discover in the ocean, within the Spanish half of the world, islands, mainlands, and "rich spiceries." As he evidently believed that there was a channel connecting the Atlantic Ocean with the South Sea, Magellan agreed to seek for a strait. The agreement also contained a stipulation about the division of any profits that might accrue from the lands discovered.

With five ships, bearing some two hundred and seventy men, Magellan sailed from Sanlúcar on September 20, 1519. After coasting slowly along the shores of Brazil, the party wintered at 49° south of the equator. In spite of storms and privations, they discovered the much sought strait. The first passage of Magellan's Strait took thirty-eight days. His men named the new sea the Pacific Ocean. After three months' sailing across that ocean they reached a group of islands which, because of the thievish propensities of their inhabitants, they designated the Ladrones. In the middle of March, 1521, Magellan caught sight of an archipelago which was subsequently called the Philippines. The bold navigator was killed in a skirmish with the natives upon one of those islands, but his remaining followers continued the adventurous voyage. Only one vessel of the expedition, the "Victoria," reached Spain in September, 1522, laden with spices.

The First Circumnavigation of the Globe

The exploration of the interior of America by the Spaniards was begun by leaders dispatched from the West Indies. From Santo Domingo, Governor Diego Columbus, the son of the Great Admiral, sent a prosperous planter named Diego Velásquez to conquer Cuba. Among his followers there was an adaptable, brave, and persuasive young

Spaniard named Hernando Cortés who had sought his fortune in the New World.

After alluring reports reached Cuba of a strange land to the west that had been seen by Juan de Grijalva, Cortés was selected by Governor Velásquez to lead an exploring party. To prepare for this trip Cortés used all his available resources. How much money Velásquez contributed is not clear. The expedition was composed of some five hundred and fifty Spanish soldiers, one hundred and ten marines, and two hundred Indians. Cortés was given ten brass cannon and four small falconets. Besides swords and spears, his followers were equipped with crossbows, firelocks, and much powder and ball. Most important of all were sixteen horses, clad in mail.

The Expedition of Hernando Cortés

On February 18, 1519, in "eleven ships, both great and small," the Spaniards left Cuba despite the attempt of the governor to recall their leader. Instructions prepared for Cortés by Velásquez directed him first of all to find Grijalva. He was then to liberate certain Christians who were supposed to be in captivity in Yucatan. He was to explore the harbors, bays, and inlets, "to look carefully into everything," and to inquire after pearls, spices, and gold. Any treasure that he might obtain was to be placed in a box having three keys. He was to treat the Indians kindly, and to instruct them in the Catholic faith. The main purpose of the expedition was to gather information.

Greatly outnumbered though he was, the Spanish leader soon decided to invade the Aztec Empire. In the conflict that ensued certain circumstances favored his enterprise. Cortés was the resourceful leader of mailclad men with firearms and horses, while Montezuma, the Aztec war chief, was the hated and vacillating leader of a barbarous and disintegrating confederacy. Further, Lady Marina, the clever daughter of an Indian chief, faithfully served the Spaniards as guide and interpreter. A widespread tradition that the feathered god of the Mexicans would some day return from the east also favored the daring Spaniards. Rumors that penetrated the Aztec Empire about the white strangers seemed to herald the approach of the god Quetzalcoatl.

After landing at Vera Cruz, despite Montezuma's warning that he should leave Mexico, Cortés decided to scuttle his fleet. On August 16, 1519, he started for Tenochtitlan. Through the strange neglect of the Aztec warlord, he was allowed to pass the stone wall that served as the Empire's outer defense. After defeating the Tlascalan Indians in battle, he negotiated an alliance with them against the Aztecs. By fire and blood Cortés steadily marched toward the capital city. He traversed the plateau of Anáhuac until his men caught sight of the beautiful valley

Cortés Invades the Aztec Empire

of Mexico. Pressing farther, and escorted by agents of Montezuma who made a virtue of necessity, on November 8 Cortés reached the southern causeway of Tenochtitlan where he was met by the Aztec monarch and his chieftains.

The Spanish chroniclers penned extravagant accounts of the vast extent of the capital city, its gardens, temples, and other public buildings. Lodged in a tecpan near the great temple, Cortés was soon warned by his allies that the Aztecs contemplated an act of treachery. He accordingly decided upon a sudden coup. Accompanied by a few mailclad knights, he boldly seized Montezuma and escorted him to a building which was occupied by the Spaniards. There the captive monarch was induced to issue an official declaration recognizing the supremacy of the Spanish King. Meanwhile reports of the unauthorized steps taken by his agent had reached Velásquez, who consequently equipped another expedition under Pánfilo de Narváez to capture the recalcitrant leader. To face that menace Cortés divided his forces: he left a cruel and dashing leader named Pedro de Alvarado in charge of Montezuma, and led a detachment to meet Narváez. As negotiations for a pacific settlement were futile, Cortés swooped down upon Narváez's men and decisively defeated them. Thus he acquired fresh prestige, munitions, followers, and a new fleet.

While Cortés was engaged in this exploit, the Aztecs, who had become enraged because of the slaughter by the Spaniards of some Indians who were engaged in a festival, turned upon Alvarado's followers and besieged them. Informed by messengers of this untoward event, Cortés hastily rejoined his men in the capital city, accompanied by Indian allies and some followers of Narváez. Stricken in the forehead by a missile while haranguing his people, Montezuma soon died; Indian chroniclers ascribed his death to the Spaniards. After the Spanish forces had decided to retire from the city, the Aztecs fell upon them with the utmost violence, and during the "sorrowful night" of July 5, 1520, numerous Spaniards were slaughtered. The tree under which the survivors reposed is still shown to tourists.

Taking refuge in the territory of friendly Indians, Cortés gathered strength for a fresh attack upon the stronghold of Aztec power. From the West Indies, Spanish adventurers came to join his forces. In May, 1521, he laid siege to Tenochtitlan. After a siege of three months, the city was taken by the jubilant Spaniards. Cuauhtemoc, the doughty successor of Montezuma, was tortured over a slow fire that he might disclose the hiding place of Aztec treasure. By a series of regulations for the conquered metropolis Cortés proved himself to be a wise administrator. Under his guidance the Spaniards soon began to subjugate Indians who had been under the rule of the Aztecs.

The region called Central America was occupied by the Spaniards from 1522 to 1524 through expeditions that were sent out, on the one side by Hernando Cortés, and on the other side by Pedrarias Dávila, who had been made governor of Darien and the adjacent territory. In January, 1522, Gil González Dávila started from the Gulf of San Miguel along the Central American coast in a westerly direction. Soon compelled to beach his poor vessels, he continued his expedition by land; and, after many hardships, he heard rumors of a wise Indian chief in the interior, who was named Nicaragua. González and his followers visited this cacique in his capital which was located upon the shores of a lake only a few leagues from the Pacific Ocean. After baptizing and catechizing many Indians, González returned to Panama with news of his discovery. While he was striving to secure a royal grant of the region that became known as Nicaragua, Governor Pedrarias sent Francisco Hernández to occupy it. After founding settlements there Hernández came to blows with González, who was finally seized by one of the conquerors.

Stories of wonderful lands to the south incited Cortés to select Pedro de Alvarado to lead an expedition to a region that was called Guatemala. In December, 1523, Alvarado left Mexico City with a large force of Spaniards and Indians bound for the south. After a series of bloody conflicts, he captured the important towns of Guatemala and even penetrated into a district that was designated Salvador. On July 25, 1524, he founded a city named Santiago de Guatemala. Cortés also sent a veteran fighter named Cristóbal de Olid to Honduras with a force of Spaniards and Indians to seek a strait and to make a settlement. As Olid proved to be intractable, Cortés sent another conquistador to subjugate him, and later, in spite of many hardships, made a march to Honduras himself. In 1540 King Charles I gave a grant of land in a district denominated Costa Rica to Diego Gutiérrez who undertook to conquer it. Meanwhile Francisco de Montejo and his son had overrun the peninsula of Yucatan.

Thus did the Spaniards undertake the conquest of Central America, or, as they designated it, Guatemala. This task did not monopolize the attention of an outstanding figure like Cortés. Neither did it attract a person like Francisco Pizarro, the conqueror of Peru.

Francisco Pizarro spent some of his youthful days as a swineherd upon the hills of Estremadura. To his ears there came alluring tales of the New World; hence he left his herd and embarked for the West Indies. In 1510 he turned up in Santo Domingo. He was a companion of Balboa on the expedition that resulted in the discovery of the Pacific Ocean. Upon the shores

Exploration and Conquest of Central America

Francisco Pizarro

of the new sea Pizarro heard tales of a land in the south where the natives used domesticated animals as beasts of burden. He was given an additional stimulus in 1522 when a sick cavalier called Pascual de Andagoya returned from an expedition beyond the Gulf of San Miguel with glowing reports of a mysterious region that was denominated Birú.

Pizarro was bold, resourceful, and persevering, but illiterate and poor. He was accordingly compelled to seek aid for his project of conquering Peru. He secured as partners a soldier of fortune named Diego de Almagro and Fernando de Luque, who was a vicar at Panama. Apparently the arrangement was that Luque should furnish the necessary funds, that Almagro should equip the expedition, and that Pizarro should assume the command. As Governor Pedrarias gave his consent, he was assured a part of the accruing profits. In November, 1524, with possibly two hundred men in one small vessel, Pizarro sailed from Panama in a southerly direction. Despite great hardships, he proceeded a short distance along the inhospitable coast of South America. Almagro brought back to Panama from his trip, which was distinct from that of Pizarro, rumors of a rich Indian Empire far to the south. The voyagers had gathered some gold.

As Pedrarias now withdrew from the enterprise for a monetary consideration, on March 10, 1526, the three remaining parties framed a contract. According to this agreement Almagro and Pizarro undertook to devote themselves exclusively to the discovery and subjugation of Peru until that Empire was conquered. As Luque had furnished funds for the promotion of the expedition, he was promised one-third of the lands, aborigines, incomes, treasures, and spoils that might be secured. Almagro and Pizarro gathered reënforcements at Panama; and with some two hundred soldiers, munitions, and a few horses, the two captains resumed the enterprise. On his second expedition, after waiting for fresh reënforcements on the island of Gallo, Pizarro and thirteen men reached Tumbes near the mouth of the Guayas River. There some Spaniards were sent ashore who were hailed by the aborigines as children of the sun. Those messengers brought back to Pizarro reports of a fortress, a temple, and vases of gold. In 1528 he returned to Panama with llamas and golden ornaments. Yet, as the governor did not look with favor upon another expedition to a region clearly beyond his jurisdiction, the three partners were compelled to turn for aid and sanction to the Spanish crown. Pizarro accordingly left Panama for Spain early in 1528, apparently agreeing to secure his partners' rights, as well as his own.

At Toledo the adventurer told his wonderful story to Charles I. The result of the interview was a contract between Pizarro and the

Spanish Queen dated July 26, 1529. This agreement gave Pizarro the right of discovery and conquest in Peru for two hundred leagues south of the island of Puná, a region that was designated New Castile. The Queen promised him the titles of governor, captain general, and adelantado of that region, with an annual salary. He was not only accorded the right to build forts but also to assign lands and Indians to colonists. Pizarro was thus practically made the viceroy of the prospective conquest, while Almagro was merely declared to be commander of the fortress of Tumbes, and Luque was made the bishop of that place. On his part Pizarro agreed to equip a force of two hundred and fifty men for a Peruvian expedition within six months after his return to Panama. The contract contained a stipulation that some priests should be taken along to convert the Indians. Special privileges were granted to emigrants; among these concessions was the exemption from certain taxes. The Spanish government agreed to facilitate the purchase of vessels for the expedition. It was promised a share of any precious metals that might be found.

After Francisco Pizarro had secured some recruits in Spain, including his brothers Gonzalo and Hernando, he returned to America to organize another expedition. A rupture between Pizarro and Almagro because of the contract with the Queen was narrowly averted. Eventually a detachment of the third expedition for Peru sailed from Panama. It was composed of three vessels bearing about one hundred and eighty men, some thirty horses, and the Pizarro brothers. The arrangement was that Almagro should follow this detachment with reënforcements. Aided by Hernando de Soto with adventurers from Nicaragua, Francisco Pizarro again landed at Tumbes. As he encountered only slight opposition from the aborigines, in May, 1532, he marched into the Inca's dominions. Soon afterward he founded a town called San Miguel, where he left some of his discontented followers. The Inca Atahualpa, who had succeeded to power after a sanguinary civil war, sent a courier who brought the Spaniards greetings, presents, and an invitation to visit his master, who was encamped on the other side of the mountains.

Pizarro Invades the Inca Empire

After scaling the snow-capped cordillera, Pizarro and his followers presented themselves before the Inca's pavilion. Assigned quarters in a public building of Cajamarca, some of the adventurers, who at night beheld the Peruvian watch-fires twinkling around them as numerous as the stars of heaven, began to despair of their enterprise. Not so Pizarro, who, influenced perhaps by the example of Cortés, had conceived the desperate plan of ambuscading the Inca in the presence of his army. When on November 16, 1532, Atahualpa unsuspectingly visited the Spanish camp, thousands of his companions were wantonly slain and he was captured.

In Peru, as in Mexico, the capture of their leader stupefied the Indians. It was as though "the keystone had fallen from an arch." Atahualpa vainly endeavored to satisfy the cupidity of the Spaniards by undertaking to fill a large room with gold or golden vessels. After dividing the treasure which was brought to the Inca's feet by his submissive subjects, the conquerors strangled the unfortunate monarch. Pizarro, who meantime had been joined by Almagro, made his triumphal entry into Cuzco on November 15, 1533. In January, 1535, upon the banks of the Rimac River, the conqueror of Peru founded the city that soon became known as Lima. He dispatched an expedition to subjugate the Charcas Indians upon the elevated plateau beyond Lake Titicaca. Far to the south of that lake, in 1538 or 1539, one of his followers founded the city of Chuquisaca.

After the seizure of Atahualpa, one of his commanders called Rumiñahui left Cajamarca, led some Indians to the city of Quito, and mastered the adjacent region. Upon learning that the Kingdom of Quito had not been subdued by Pizarro, Pedro de Alvarado led a band of gallant adventurers from Central America to conquer it. In March, 1534, he disembarked on the equatorial coast of South America and prepared to march to the city of Quito. Rumors of Alvarado's expedition reached Peru in time to hasten the departure for Quito of Sebastián Moyano, a bold follower of Pizarro who had been made governor of San Miguel.

Sebastián Moyano was born of humble parents in the Spanish village of Belalcázar. As Sebastián de Belalcázar or Benalcázar he became known to contemporaries and to historians. Orphaned at an early age, the adventurous youth was attracted by the golden romance of America. Apparently he proceeded to the New World in the third expedition of Columbus.

Conquest of Quito by Benalcázar

After participating in various exploits of the Spaniards in Central America, he accompanied Francisco Pizarro to Peru. In the northern part of the former Inca Empire Benalcázar gained the support of the Cañarian Indians who had been disaffected toward Atahualpa, routed the partisans of Rumiñahui, and in December, 1533, entered the city of Quito. Meantime, Francisco Pizarro had sent Almagro to aid Benalcázar against Alvarado, and the latter was induced in return for a large sum of gold to relinquish his project of conquering the kingdom. Benalcázar soon undertook to reconstruct Quito. He took formal possession of that city for the King of Spain in December, 1534. After he extended his authority over the coastal region under the equator, he turned his eyes toward the land of the Chibchans.

Allured by the legend of the gilded man, in 1535 he sent two of his followers into the region north of his capital. Those explorers penetrated as far as the Cauca Valley. Benalcázar continued the exploration of that attractive valley; and on July 25, 1536, he planted a settlement there that was named Cali. In the following December he founded the city of Popayán. After gathering reënforcements, in 1538 he scaled the lofty cordillera that separated the sources of the rivers Cauca and Magdalena. A number of years earlier settlements had been made by Spaniards at Santa Marta and Cartagena on the coast of the Caribbean Sea. Thus it was that, after descending the Magdalena River for some distance, Benalcázar heard rumors of white men who had traversed the highlands to the east.

These were Spaniards who had been sent on an exploring expedition by Fernández de Lugo, who in 1535 had entered into an agreement with the Spanish crown to conquer and colonize a region called Santa Marta which lay east of the Magdalena River. As commander of the expedition Lugo had selected Gonzalo Jiménez de Quesada, a resolute lawyer who was a native of the kingdom of Granada. Leaving Santa Marta in April, 1536, and dispatching a flotilla to ascend the Magdalena River, Jiménez de Quesada started on the long and hazardous trip overland to the upper Magdalena. Though tormented by insects, hunger, and disease, he proceeded up the inundated valley of that tropical river, repelled the attacks of Indians who used poisoned arrows, scaled the mountains, and at last caught sight of verdant plains which reminded him of his native province. After defeating the discordant Chibchans, Quesada occupied the valley of Bacatá without opposition. He captured Tunja and Sogamoso, where he secured quantities of gold, textiles, and emeralds. In this valley on August 6, 1538, he founded the city of Santa Fé—that later came to be known as Santa Fé de Bogotá. The conqueror called the land which he had subdued the New Kingdom of Granada.

Jiménez de Quesada Conquers the Chibchans

Shortly afterward he heard of the approach of a party under Nicolás Federmann that had proceeded from Venezuela through the Amazonian wilderness. About the same time he learned of Benalcázar's expedition. In February, 1539, Benalcázar, Federmann, and Quesada made a triumphal entry into Santa Fé. Soon afterward the three conquistadors became involved in an acrimonious controversy concerning the territories to which they were respectively entitled. Finally in 1546 the Spanish King granted Quesada a coat of arms bearing a symbolic representation of emeralds to commemorate the fact that he had discovered valuable mines in New Granada.

Meantime, the conquest of the region south of Peru had been undertaken by Almagro. To him the Spanish crown had conceded the territory designated New Toledo which extended for two hundred leagues beyond the grant made to Francisco Pizarro. In July, 1535, accompanied by a large number of Indians, and some five hundred Spaniards who were lured by false stories of gold in the south, Almagro started on a long journey. He marched slowly over the elevated plateau, struggled across the *puna* or bleak plain of Atacama, and finally caught sight of the green valleys of Chile. From the valley of Coquimbo he marched to the valley of Aconcagua, whence he sent out exploring parties. Disappointed in their search for gold, Almagro's followers soon clamored to return to Peru. In the end of 1536, they rendezvoused in Copiapó, and then marched across the desert of Atacama toward Cuzco. There Almagro engaged in a bitter struggle with Pizarro for supremacy; on July 8, 1538, he was captured and condemned to death.

Although the conquest of Chile was next confided by the Spanish crown to an obscure adventurer, yet Francisco Pizarro commissioned one of his followers named Pedro de Valdivia to perform that difficult task. Valdivia was a persevering native of Estremadura, who had served his King in Venezuela. In Peru he had commanded Pizarro's forces against Almagro upon the latter's return from the south. With some two hundred men, besides Indians, he left Cuzco early in 1540: his object was to plant a permanent settlement in Chile. On February 12, 1541, he founded a city called Santiago de Nueva Estremadura—later called Santiago de Chile—that was defended by a fort placed upon a hill. Rebuilding the city after it had been destroyed by the Araucanians, Valdivia then proceeded to found settlements on the Pacific coast. In 1553, however, the aborigines, led by a valiant youth called Lautaro, defeated the Spaniards and captured their leader, who was slain by a vengeful Araucanian.

Conquest of Chile by Valdivia

The story of the exploration and conquest of the Atlantic coast of South America is linked to the history of the Pacific Ocean. When news of Balboa's discovery reached Spain, it stimulated interest in the search for a strait. Juan Díaz de Solís, who had made a voyage to America in 1508, and had become chief pilot of Spain, was commissioned to explore the coast of South America to a distance of seventeen hundred leagues or more beyond the Isthmus of Panama, if that was possible without crossing the demarcation line into the Portuguese half of the world. On October 8, 1515, with three small vessels bearing seventy men and provisions for two years and a half, Solís sailed from Sanlúcar. He proceeded along the coast of America south of the region discovered by Cabral; in February, 1516, he reached a vast expanse of fresh water—later found to be the estuary of the Río de la Plata—

which he called the *Mar Dulce* (Fresh Sea). After discovering the island of Martín García in that estuary, Solís disembarked with some of his companions. The explorers were unexpectedly attacked by the Charruan Indians, however, and Solís and many of his companions were slaughtered. The remaining Spaniards fled from those ill-omened coasts, loaded their vessels with Brazil wood, and returned to Spain. The task which Solís had essayed was soon taken up by other hands.

The conquest of southern South America was undertaken by a Spanish knight named Pedro de Mendoza who had gained distinction in the Italian wars. In 1534 he entered into a contract with the King of Spain which provided that he should equip an expedition for the banks of the Río de la Plata, build three stone fortresses there, and seek a route across the continent to the South Sea. Granted the title of adelantado, he was allowed a salary payable from revenues accruing from a region that stretched for two hundred leagues south of the grant made to Almagro. A share of the gold, silver, pearls, and precious stones possessed by any people that might be conquered should belong to the King. In August, 1535, with a company containing some distinguished members of the Spanish nobility, as well as a few Germans, Mendoza sailed from Seville for the New World. Upon his arrival in La Plata River, Mendoza founded the city of Buenos Aires which was soon violently attacked by the Indians. He sent one of his followers named Juan de Ayolas to explore the upper stretches of the rivers Paraná and Paraguay and to seek a route to Peru. Some time afterward the disillusioned adelantado left America for Spain.

Mendoza's Expedition to La Plata

Ayolas ascended the Paraná River. After a skirmish with the Guaraní Indians, on August 15, 1537, near the junction of the Pilcomayo and the Paraguay rivers, he built a fort called Asunción. Then the intrepid leader ascended the Paraguay River farther, and proceeded overland to Peru. Upon his return trip he was killed by Indians. Meanwhile an officer of Mendoza's expedition named Dominguez Martínez de Irala had assumed the leadership. Buenos Aires was forsaken, the remaining colonists ascended the river in 1537, and settled at Asunción.

The story of Venezuelan colonization begins with pearl fishers and slave hunters. In 1528 certain Germans, who had been granted by Spain the right to discover, conquer, and colonize the northern coast of South America between Cape Vela and Maracapana, transferred their right to the Welsers, a banking firm of Augsburg. The assignment stipulated that within two years this firm should plant two settlements, build three forts, and secure fifty German miners for Spanish America. Among other privileges it was granted exemption from certain taxes and was conceded the right to exploit twelve square leagues of land upon its own account. Early in 1529 the Welsers began a career of conquest and exploitation in Venezuela, which lasted until their privileges were revoked in 1556.

After the middle of the sixteenth century the Spaniards devoted special attention to the conquest of certain fertile valleys in Venezuela that were inhabited by warlike Indians. In 1560 Francisco Fajardo planted a settlement called San Francisco in the Guaire Valley. Under the rule of Governoi Ponce de León the subjugation of the Indians was entrusted to a noble Spaniard called Diego de Losada, who had won renown as a conqueror. After defeating the Indians, who lived in the valley of Caracas, on or about July 25, 1567, Losada laid out in that valley, a city which he christened Santiago de León de Caracas. It was not until the Caracas Indians, who conspired to annihilate the colonists, had been overwhelmingly defeated by Losada that the existence of this city was assured.

Diego de Losada Founds Caracas

While Spaniards were exploring and conquering the western and southern parts of South America, navigators under the Spanish or the Portuguese flag were coasting along the shores of the land that had been discovered by Cabral. Vicente Yáñez Pinzón, a companion of Columbus, led an expedition in 1499 from Palos to South America. In January, 1500, he caught sight of that continent south of the equator. While proceeding in a northerly direction, he discovered the mouth of a great river which he named the Marañón—later called the Amazon—where he filled his casks with sweet water. He then sailed past the delta of the Orinoco River and proceeded as far as the Gulf of Paria. Taking on a cargo of Brazil wood, he left for Palos. It appears that in 1501-1502 Amerigo Vespucci, a Florentine who had been in the Spanish service, made a voyage under the Portuguese flag to the New World and coasted along the shores of Brazil in a southerly direction. For more than a decade after the discovery of Cabral, however, the Portuguese government, engrossed by its East Indian enterprises, paid little attention to the colonization of Brazil. Still, by private enterprise a few small settlements were scattered here and there along the extensive coast.

After the accession of King John III, who ruled from 1521 to 1557, the Portuguese began seriously to consider colonization in America. In 1525 John III sent a small fleet to the Brazilian coast to protect it against the attacks of the French. Five years later that King appointed Martin Affonso de Souza, a member of his council, as commander of an expedition and governor of the lands which he might discover in Brazil. Affonso de Souza coasted along the shores of Brazil, started a

John III Carves Brazil into Captaincies

colony at São Vicente, and made a short trip into the interior. Meantime the Portuguese King formulated a plan for colonization in America. This was an adaptation of a scheme which had been followed in India: the establishment of settlements that would be entrusted to illustrious Portuguese, who were to be designated captains-donatory. With the avowed purpose to extend the Catholic faith, in September, 1532, the King decided to divide Brazil into districts, each of which stretched some fifty leagues along the coast. In theory those districts extended inland to the vague Tordesillas line. To each donatory should be assigned a grant of land.

A donatory was made the almost absolute lord of his particular district. He was the lawful and hereditary owner of the land; he was given the right to judge civil, criminal, and religious disputes. He was to plant settlements and to assign lands within his jurisdiction. To the Portuguese crown there was merely reserved a shadowy, feudal right of sovereignty. The twelve districts thus carved out of Brazil were designated captaincies. These were named Santo Amaro, São Vicente, Parahyba do Sul, Espirito Santo, Porto Seguro, Ilhéos, Bahia, Pernambuco, Itamaracá, Ceará, Rio Grande, and Maranhão.

As the Brazilian coasts were ravaged by pirates, the Portuguese King soon decided to abolish the captaincies and to establish one common government. In December, 1548, he framed instructions for the guidance of the first governor-general. That official was to seek a spot in the captaincy of Bahia which would serve as a site for his capital. The governor-general and also the captains-donatory should strive to convert the natives to the Catholic faith. The enslavement of the aborigines was prohibited. No colonist should sell them firearms. All the Brazil wood that might be found should belong to the King. This governor was directed to promote the exploration of the Brazilian wilderness. He should visit the various captaincies and arrange for the erection and the repair of forts. The foundations were thus laid for the colonization of Portuguese America that took place in the second half of the sixteenth century.

The New World, as Columbus ultimately called the land which he had discovered—whether or not in recognition of the greatness of his discovery may never be known—was eventually named after Amerigo Vespucci. There is no need here to enter *Amerigo Vespucci* into the dispute raised by Vespucci's statement that he reached the mainland of South America as early as 1497. In 1504 he wrote a letter to a friend describing four voyages which he claimed to have made. A Latin copy of this letter fell into the hands of a teacher of geography named Martin Waldseemüller.

From a printing press at St. Dié in Lorraine in 1507 Waldseemüller published a volume entitled *Cosmographiae Introductio* (*Introduction to Cosmography*), which contained a Latin version of Vespucci's letter describing his alleged voyages. The geographer suggested that the new continent should be christened "Amerigo" or "America," after Amerigo Vespucci, its discoverer. From time to time other names were suggested as designations for the newly-discovered continents. In 1506 Bartholomew Columbus printed the name "Mondo Novo" on the new southern continent. Las Casas suggested that the New World should be called "Columba." The official name which prevailed in Spain, however, was "The Indies." The name given by Cabral, "Vera Cruz," was sometimes applied; and a Latin version of it, "Terra Sanctæ Crucis," was also used. During the sixteenth century perhaps the most common name was "Mundus Novus." In 1512 the Lenox globe used the name "Terra de Brazil." Eight years later a German cartographer named Schöner proposed that the New World should be designated "America," "Brazil," or "Peacock's Land." In 1541 the name "America" was applied to the two continents by Mercator, the famous Flemish geographer. In 1550 Münster printed upon the northern part of the New World the phrase *Insula Atlantica quam vocant Brasili et Americam*. Though Spanish cartographers did not use the name America upon their maps until 1758, yet by the early seventeenth century most geographers had adopted as names for the new continents the terms North America and South America.

Whether Columbus made his discovery because of his own convictions, or because of reports of Portuguese voyages to strange lands, or because of the influence of an age when geographical traditions were being shattered, certain it is that he unfolded to the amazed eyes of Europeans a new book. By a strange chance, those venturesome conquistadors who followed in his wake struck the Americas where the aboriginal culture had reached its highest development, the plateaus occupied by the Aztecs, the Chibchans, and the Incas. Spanish activity in the New World thus at first ordinarily assumed the aspect of an enterprise of conquest. Settlements which daring leaders planted in southern South America, where conditions naturally favored the development of what may be designated agricultural colonies, progressed very slowly. This was largely because of the desire to find gold which constantly lured men into the wilderness. By the middle of the sixteenth century certain patterns that Spanish and Portuguese colonial enterprises were destined to follow had been sketched. Portuguese settlements, which originally showed more traces of feudal customs than did the Spanish, were located along the eastern coast. Within the area delimited by the demarcation line of 1494 the Portuguese came into contact with the

Tupian and the Tapuyan Indians. Because of the establishment of captaincies, the Portuguese system of colonization made a more lasting impress upon Brazil than early royal grants left in Spanish America. But, in both Spanish and Portuguese America, wherever the steel-clad knight and the sandaled monk penetrated, there soon began a curious mingling of European civilization and aboriginal culture.

SUGGESTIONS FOR FURTHER READING

ALVARADO, P. DE, *An Account of the Conquest of Guatemala*, 1924.

ARCINIEGAS, G., *The Knight of El Dorado*, 1942.

BIRNEY, H., *Brothers of Doom; The Story of the Pizarros of Peru*, 1942.

BOURNE, E. G., *Spain in America, 1450-1580*, 1904.

DÍAZ DEL CASTILLO, B., *The True History of the Conquest of Mexico*, 1927.

GRAHAM, R. B. CUNNINGHAME, *The Conquest of New Granada*, 1922.

———, *The Conquest of the River Plate*, 1924.

———, *Pedro de Valdivia, Conqueror of Chile*, 1926.

GREENLEE, W. B. (trans.), *The Voyage of Pedro Alvares Cabral to Brazil and India*, 1938.

JAYNE, K. G., *Vasco da Gama*, 1910.

KIRKPATRICK, F. A., *The Spanish Conquistadores*, 1934.

MACNUTT, F. A., *Fernando Cortés and the Conquest of Mexico*, 1909.

MADARIAGA, S. DE, *Hernán Cortéz, Conqueror of Mexico*, 1941.

OLIVEIRA MARTENS, J. P., *The Golden Age of Prince Henry the Navigator*, 1914.

MORISON, S. E., *Admiral of the Ocean Sea*, Vol. I, 1942.

———, *Portuguese Voyages to America in the Fifteenth Century*, 1940.

PIZARRO, P., *Relation of the Discovery and Conquest of the Kingdoms of Peru*, Vol. I, 1921.

PRESCOTT, W. H., *History of the Conquest of Mexico*, 1843.

———, *History of the Conquest of Peru*, 1847.

PRESTAGE, E., *The Portuguese Pioneers*, 1933.

PRIESTLEY, H. I., *The Coming of the White Man*, 1929.

RICHMAN, I. B., *The Spanish Conquerors*, 1919.

SANCHO, P., *An Account of the Conquest of Peru*, 1917.

THACHER, J. B., *Christopher Columbus*, Vol. II, 1904.

VIGNAUD, H., *Toscanelli and Columbus*, 1902.

CHAPTER V

THE LATIN-AMERICAN COLONIES IN THE SIXTEENTH CENTURY

The Spanish conquerors paid little attention to agriculture. For many decades the regions that were best adapted for farming colonies were neglected by the gold-hunting Spaniards. In both Spanish and Portuguese America avaricious adventurers captured the aborigines and sold them into slavery. Influenced by the eloquent pleas of priests, the governments of Spain and Portugal intervened between the conquerors and the Indians. Yet the Spanish crown did not succeed in establishing its authority without a struggle. With regard to its intention to protect the aborigines, it can scarcely be said to have succeeded at all.

Nature of the Latin Colonies in America

Upon conquering a certain region the Spaniards ordinarily attempted to persuade the Indians to adopt settled life. Sometimes the natives nominally accepted the Christian religion and undertook to live in villages. To this process of transformation the term *reducción* was ordinarily applied. As the Spanish conquerors arrived in small numbers and generally disliked to work in the fields and mines, they soon undertook to use the aborigines as laborers. In order to manage the Indians more readily, the conquerors adopted the practice of dividing them into groups or squads and assigning a squad or more to each of the leading colonists. Those squads were designated *repartimientos*.

The term *encomienda* was soon applied to the right conceded by the Spanish crown to a colonist to receive tribute from a group of Indians. The grantee was styled an *encomendero*. From time to time the Spanish monarchs urged encomenderos to instruct in the Catholic faith the Indians who had been entrusted to their care, to teach them to live orderly lives, and to protect them. Laws were soon issued to the effect that an encomendero who failed to protect his wards and to promote their political and religious welfare should lose his encomienda. At first encomiendas were given for a limited time. As the years passed the custom developed of allowing them to pass to the heir of the grantee. The number of Indians included in such grants varied greatly; it depended upon the influence and merit of the persons to whom they were granted.

Sometimes a modified form of the repartimiento was used. Where

66

squads of natives were employed in mines or on plantations, the term *mita* was applied to a group of Indians who were compelled to labor under the Spanish overseers. In certain sections Indians with their families were required to dwell all their lives on the estate of the individual or corporation to whom they belonged. Upon the Peruvian highlands such an Indian, who was transferred with the land, was designated a *yanacona*. Eventually, the tendency was to use the term encomienda as the equivalent for repartimiento. The custom of employing aborigines in mines or on plantations of Spanish America became a system of Indian slavery that left an enduring impression. In a futile effort to protect the Indians against mistreatment, in 1542 the Spanish government promulgated the so-called "new laws."

During the early conquest many Spaniards proceeded to the New World from the Castilian portion of the Peninsula. A number of the prominent leaders in the Spanish Indies were natives of Estremadura. Some of these were adventurers who, because of personal reasons, or because of the fall of Granada, felt that the pent-up Spanish Peninsula confined their powers. Animated by intense religious emotion, other colonists saw in the unfolding of the New World a rare opportunity to extend the gospel of Christ to a benighted people. Although early in the sixteenth century the Spanish government tried to promote the settlement of artisans and farmers in the West Indies by special concessions, such as the grant of extensive estates to persons taking groups of colonists to Santo Domingo, yet the governors found it difficult to restrain settlers from proceeding to the adjacent continents to hunt for treasure.

Sustained efforts were made by the Spaniards to transmit European culture to the New World. Besides some prospective settlers, on his second voyage Columbus brought to the West Indies mares, sheep, heifers, calves, goats, ewes, pigs, and chickens. Wheat, barley, and other cereals, the grapevine, and also the seeds of oranges and melons were presented by the Old World to the New. These and other European fauna and flora were distributed through America by the conquistadors. European stocks were grafted on to native grapevines. Cortés ordered that for every one hundred aborigines held in repartimiento, a Spaniard should for a term of years plant annually one thousand shoots of vines or other useful plants. A Spanish writer declared that when Gonzalo Pizarro started to take charge of the district of Quito he had a herd of no less than five thousand swine. When Valdivia left Cuzco to undertake the conquest of Chile, he took with him not only war horses but also domestic animals. Wheat was introduced into Peru by a Spanish lady who made its usefulness widely known among the colonists.

As has been indicated, the Spanish colonial Empire was largely founded through the initiative, the funds, and the enterprise of indi-

Conquista-
dors Are
Displaced
by Royal
Agents

viduals who undertook the conquest of certain regions in the New World by virtue of agreements with the Spanish monarchs. This was true of Columbus, Cortés, Pizarro, Mendoza, and other adventurous Spaniards. Partly because of complaints about the shameful treatment of the aborigines, the Spanish crown subsequently attempted to establish its *authority upon the rude foundations which had been laid by the conquistadors. Early in the sixteenth century the privileges conferred upon Columbus were totally abrogated. Cortés was soon deprived of his position as governor, captain general, and chief justice. In 1526 a portion of his authority was transferred to a commissioner who was sent to act as his judge in residencia. That judge was soon succeeded by a governor; and in 1528 an audiencia was established in Mexico City.

As administration by means of that tribunal did not produce satisfactory results, the Spanish government decided to transplant another institution to America. In October, 1535, Antonio de Mendoza arrived in Mexico to act as viceroy. In Peru the authority of the Pizarro family, which well-nigh became a dynasty, was not easily superseded. Upon learning of the quarrels of the Peruvian conquistadors, in 1540 Charles I appointed Cristóbal Vaca de Castro his special agent in Peru. After Vaca de Castro defeated the followers of Gonzalo Pizarro, who had inherited the authority of his brother Francisco, an audiencia was established in Lima; and in 1543 Blasco Núñez Vela was appointed viceroy of Peru. Six years later an audiencia was created for the city of Santa Fé de Bogotá which was granted jurisdiction over the territory that had been conquered by Benalcázar, Federmann, and Quesada.

An officer of prime importance in the exploration and settlement of the Spanish Indies was the adelantado. Though that title was often associated with other titles in early Spanish-American history, it indubitably signified an officer with distinct powers and duties. The first adelantado in the New World was Bartholomew Columbus, who was granted that post by his brother. As an American office under royal control, it began through the appointment in 1514 of Vasco Núñez de Balboa as adelantado of the coast of the South Sea. In agreements made by the Spanish King with enterprising subjects in the sixteenth century some thirty persons were promised the title and privileges of adelantado. Among those were many prominent explorers and colonizers of Spanish America.

The contract of an adelantado with the crown contained specifications about the territory which he was to explore, to conquer, or to colonize. It was his duty to equip the expedition that should include some priests or friars. In every case he agreed to promote the conversion of the Indians to Christianity. He was conceded special privileges, such as the right to grant encomiendas of Indians; and he was granted some exemptions, as from the payment of certain duties. He was ordinarily pledged to build forts for the protection of his settlement. Every adelantado was made governor and captain general of the province which he planned to settle. He promised the Spanish crown one-fifth of the gold and other precious metals that he might discover. Powers and privileges might be granted to an adelantado for one generation or for a longer period.

By the extension of royal power over regions subjugated by the conquerors, and by the enactment of laws which aimed to protect the Indians against enslavement by encomenderos, the tendency, in some parts of the Indies, was to decrease the importance of the encomienda. In time the missionary became an important factor in Spanish colonization. Missionaries in Spanish America generally belonged to the regular clergy. Among the religious orders that came to the Indies in the sixteenth century were Augustinians, Capuchins, Franciscans, and Jesuits. To members of those orders, groups or tribes of aborigines were assigned for conversion to the Catholic faith. Friars not only founded missions among Indians who had been subjugated by the conquistadors but to a varying extent they also played the rôles of encomenderos.

Ordinarily missionaries were independent of the civil officials in a particular region. They could partition the land and its inhabitants, and could organize villages or pueblos of Indians that were managed by friars. Favorite sites for their pueblos were often far distant from the settlements of Spaniards: in a pleasant valley, upon a protected plain, or on the banks of a navigable stream. Missionaries of the Catholic faith in Spanish America were frequently pioneers of civilization. Agents of the State as well as of the Church, they were preachers, teachers, chroniclers, explorers, and colonists.

At the forefront of Spanish colonial administration was the King. Largely because of the increase of royal power that had taken place in the motherland, the title to her colonies was not vested in the Spanish people, but in the Spanish monarch. Spain and her colonies were united in a personal union: His Catholic Majesty was the connecting link. It became clear that the crown intended to govern the Indies through a distinct set of institutions.

Spanish Colonial Administration

From a rudimentary organization in which one magistrate acted as a minister for the colonies, the Spanish colonial administrative system developed into complex institutions in the Peninsula and in America. The earliest institution that appeared was the *Casa de Con-*

tratación or House of Trade which was founded at Seville about 1503. Originally that board was composed of a treasurer, a comptroller, and a business manager. A chief pilot was added in 1508; in 1514 a post-master-general was created. The House of Trade had commercial, judicial, and scientific functions. It regulated commerce and immigration between Spain and her colonies. It soon exercised jurisdiction over disputes relating to mercantile affairs. It directed the training of pilots who wished to navigate in America, and undertook the preparation of charts and maps of the new discoveries. Though in time the House of Trade became subject to the Council of the Indies, it was not extinguished until 1790.

The administration of the Spanish colonies under the King was soon vested in the Council of the Indies. At least as early as the second decade of the sixteenth century that council appeared in a rudimentary form; but it was not definitely organized until 1524. Members of the Council of the Indies were appointed by the King from officials who had served in America. A fundamental law respecting the personnel of the council provided that among its members should be a president, a chancellor, eight councilors, an attorney, and two secretaries who should be prudent persons of orthodox ancestry.

That council was expected to hold its meetings at court, for the King was always supposed to be present. It had administrative, legislative, and judicial authority. The King listened to its advice about such important matters as appointments. It made laws for Spanish America by a two-thirds majority. Cases were appealed to it from colonial audiencias. Reports about the Indies were laid before it, whether concerning a residencia or other matters. It gathered information respecting the colonies. The Laws of the Indies declared that to promote good government and the administration of justice the Council of the Indies could in consultation with the King enact general and special laws, ordinances, and provisions, which should be obeyed throughout the colonies. Yet its very omnipotence constituted a grave defect; for it was considered the fountain of law and patronage. The Spanish monarch saw his extensive domain in America only through the eyes of his council.

As the territories in the New World were brought under the direct control of the Spanish crown, various administrative districts were carved out of them. Attempts were soon made to organize those districts politically. The most important executive officers who came into existence during the early period of Spanish colonization were the viceroys, governors, and captains general.

The Chief Royal Agents in America

The first viceroy who regularly represented the Spanish King in his

American dominions was Antonio de Mendoza. His jurisdiction originally extended over all the Spanish dominions in Central and North America. In other words, he was the chief colonial official in the vast district which stretched from the Isthmus of Panama as far north as the Spanish authority extended. The capital of the viceroyalty of New Spain was at Mexico City. The earliest law concerning the viceregal institution declared that the kingdoms of New Spain and Peru were to be governed by viceroys who should represent the Spanish monarch. These officials were to exercise the superior governmental authority; they should administer justice equally to all Spanish subjects and vassals. They should study everything that might promote the pacification, tranquillity, and welfare of their provinces just as the King would do if he were present in person.

Viceroy Blasco Núñez Vela established his capital at Lima. Originally the jurisdiction of the Peruvian viceroy extended over all the Spanish possessions in South America. Shortly after the establishment of the viceroyalty of Peru, the Spanish government issued a fundamental statute concerning viceregal authority. This statute declared that in all matters arising within his jurisdiction a viceroy could take such measures as seemed to him wise: unless there existed some special prohibition, he could act with the same power and prerogatives as the King himself. It commanded the audiencias, governors, judges, subjects, vassals, ecclesiastics, and laymen of whatsoever class or condition, to obey the viceroys as personages who represented the Spanish King.

An American viceroy normally held his office for three years. That term might be lengthened or shortened at the King's pleasure. In the seventeenth century the salary of the viceroy of New Spain was twenty thousand ducats, while the stipend of the Peruvian viceroy was thirty thousand ducats. Ordinarily a viceroy considerably increased his salary through perquisites. Instructions were often sent by the Council of the Indies to the viceroys to direct their actions in certain matters or upon special occasions. Upon leaving office a viceroy was expected to hand to his successor a detailed report regarding the condition of his viceroyalty.

During the early period of Spanish rule in America a viceroy was in general charge of the financial administration of his district. From the very beginning a Spanish viceroy in America occupied a threefold position: he was captain general, president, and viceroy. As captains general, the viceroys of New Spain and Peru were in charge of the military and naval forces of their respective viceroyalties. In their rôles as presidents they often acted as chairmen of the audiencias which were established at their respective capitals. While in their positions as viceroys—in the narrow sense—they were the chief civil rulers of the provinces within their respective jurisdictions. Special directions with regard to the manifold duties of a viceroy were given in more than seventy laws. The viceroy of a particular region was expected to be the patron of monasteries and hospitals, the protector of the poor, and the defender of the oppressed. He was the King's *alter ego*.

In time the Spanish crown became convinced that an American viceroy exercised jurisdiction over too extensive a territory. The result was the appointment of an official specifically designated as captain general, who was given control of a district that was carved out of a viceroyalty. The King placed a captain general in charge of the administration of the provinces of Central America. For decades that captain general was subordinate in certain matters, especially in military affairs, to the viceroy of New Spain; but in other respects his authority within his own district was that of a viceroy in miniature.

In Spanish America the need was early felt of judges who might check the judicial authority of petty officials. During the first decade of the sixteenth century colonists in the West Indies invoked such protection against the son of Columbus. Hence in 1511 a tribunal of royal judges was established in Santo Domingo to hear cases by appeal from local magistrates. This court was the precursor of the royal audiencias that were soon established in certain cities of the New World. Those audiencias developed into institutions that were scarcely inferior in importance to the viceroys. Indeed they were often viewed as the primary units in the administration of the Spanish Indies.

The rudimentary audiencia which had been functioning in the West Indies was definitely established at the city of Santo Domingo by a royal order of September 14, 1526. It was composed of a president, four judges, an attorney, and some minor officers. Originally its jurisdiction included the islands of Santo Domingo, Cuba, Puerto Rico, and also the continental provinces of Venezuela and Guiana. At a subsequent date its authority was extended over Louisiana and Florida. In 1528 ordinances were formulated for its administration and management, ordinances that were based upon the procedure of the tribunals of Valladolid and Granada. The audiencia of Santo Domingo was granted jurisdiction over both civil and criminal matters. It was to consider cases in the name of the King. Its magistrates could not engage in mercantile transactions. In certain cases appeals might be made from their judgments to the Council of the Indies. Any one disregarding the decisions of this tribunal should be punished by a fine of fifty thousand maravedís.

Problems that were not settled by these ordinances were to be determined by the laws of Spain.

Another audiencia was established in Mexico City by a decree issued in 1527. It provided that the viceroy should act as the presiding officer of the tribunal. Besides the president, this court should be composed of eight civil judges, four criminal judges, two attorneys, and other minor officials. The audiencia of Mexico was to have jurisdiction over the territory between Florida and Honduras, and was to include the peninsula of Yucatan. On account of the disturbed condition of affairs in Mexico, this tribunal was instructed to perform various political duties: it was to take the residencia of Cortés, to delimit certain provinces, to make fiscal reforms, and to protect the Indians. Ordinances formulated for its direction in 1528 much resembled those pertaining to the audiencia of Santo Domingo. The officials and colonists living within its jurisdiction were ordered to obey its mandates just as though the King had issued them.

In February, 1535, an audiencia was set up at the city of Panama, with a president, four judges, and an attorney. The earliest ordinance concerning the jurisdiction of that tribunal assigned it control over Spanish America from the Strait of Magellan to Nicaragua. In 1563 its jurisdiction was restricted to the district between the Darien River and the Bay of Fonseca. Meanwhile, by a decree of 1542, another audiencia had been established at Lima. This tribunal was originally composed of a president and four judges—a personnel that was later increased. Its jurisdiction was to extend over Peru.

Several other audiencias were established in Spanish America during the sixteenth century. A court was created in 1543 which was to be located in the city of Santiago de Guatemala. A fundamental ordinance provided that it should have five judges and one attorney. In 1548 provision was made for the establishment of an audiencia in the city of Guadalajara, Mexico, which was to have jurisdiction over the northern part of the viceroyalty of New Spain. That tribunal followed the traditions and customs of the tribunal in Mexico City to which it was subordinated. On July 17, 1549, the Spanish King authorized the establishment of an audiencia at Santa Fé de Bogotá. Under its jurisdiction were placed the provinces of New Granada, Santa Marta, Cartagena, Popayán, and Guiana. Ten years later the King provided for another audiencia in the viceroyalty of Peru, which was to be located at the city of Chuquisaca in the province of Charcas. For a considerable period, this court, which was ordinarily called the audiencia of Charcas, had jurisdiction over the territory that stretched from Arica to Montevideo. On November 29, 1563, the King issued an ordinance creating an audiencia for the city of Quito. The president and judges at Santa Fé de Bogotá were ordered not to exercise any jurisdiction within the boundaries of that new tribunal. The audiencia of Quito was given control of territory lying on both sides of the equator and stretching from the Pacific Coast far beyond the Andes. In 1565 an audiencia was established at the city of Concepción in Chile.

In the process of making territorial adjustments the Spanish government frequently employed as a convenient unit the jurisdictional area controlled by an audiencia. An audiencia in the Spanish Indies at first signified not only a tribunal of justice but also a territorial division. The courts that were thus established throughout the Spanish Indies were composed of a varying number of members who were appointed by the King. In order that they might preserve their impartiality, the judges of those tribunals were required to live secluded from the world. They were not to own real estate, to keep more than four slaves, to accept gifts, or to become familiar either with ecclesiastics or laymen. If an emergency arose, they might correspond directly with Madrid. Upon more than one occasion the Spanish monarch declared that a colonial audiencia should be considered as a representative of his royal person.

The original function of an audiencia in the Indies was judicial. It was the supreme court of a certain district with original and appellate jurisdiction. In cases of minor importance its decisions were final; in important cases appeals might be carried to the Council of the Indies. Members of a particular tribunal were expected to make periodical visits to towns and cities within its jurisdiction. In general, the magistrate who presided over the meetings of the audiencia in a certain town or city, whether he was designated as viceroy, captain general, or president, was the chief executive of the surrounding region. In Spanish America the audiencia developed important administrative functions. When the viceroy was absent or disabled, the senior judge, or, in special cases, the entire court, assumed the executive authority. Gradually the Spanish-American audiencias became advisory councils to the chief executives. They shared with the viceroys or captains general of their respective districts the responsibility for the management of military affairs. They also exercised authority in ecclesiastical affairs, especially in matters of patronage and finance. As they heard complaints from persons who considered themselves injured by the acts of viceroys or governors, they checked the powers of such magistrates.

To the magistrate who presided over the meetings of an audiencia which was not located at the seat of a viceroy or a captain general, the term president was applied. In consequence the territory over which he exercised jurisdiction was often designated a presidency. The regions controlled by the respective courts located at Guadalajara,

Quito, and Chuquisaca were presidencies. As neither a viceroy nor a captain general resided at those cities, their tribunals exercised some political authority. The audiencia located at Guadalajara, however, being not far distant from Mexico City, was kept subordinate to the adjacent viceroy. But the isolated audiencias of Quita and Chuquisaca were in a sense governments within governments. The circumjacent areas were under the control of those courts, and especially of the jurists who presided over their meetings.

Minor Officials

Under the audiencias, viceroys, and captains general in Spanish America were governors, alcaldes, and corregidores. Governors were in charge of those divisions of a viceroyalty, captaincy general, or presidency that were designated *gobiernos*. A gobierno varied in size: sometimes it included the entire jurisdictional area of an audiencia; more commonly it was a subdivision of such an area. Ordinarily a gobierno included several regions that were denominated provinces. A province was frequently composed of a group of cities and towns that had been settled by Spaniards; it might also include the adjacent villages of subject Indians. Otherwise it might designate a region inhabited by savage tribes that had not been induced to adopt village life. A governor exercised political, judicial, and military authority.

Over a Spanish town or city and the adjacent villages of dependent Indians, an alcalde or a corregidor ordinarily ruled. In general that official was selected either by the chief executive of a particular district or by the Spanish King. An alcalde or corregidor resided at the most important town of his province. By the aid of minor officials, who were often natives, he exercised functions of a varied character: judicial, fiscal, and military. A corregidor was given jurisdiction over civil and criminal disputes arising among Spaniards and aborigines. Among his fiscal duties was the collection of tribute from Indians and taxes from encomenderos. In some parts of Spanish America he also exercised military authority within his district.

According to an official report dated 1574, there were some two hundred towns or cities in the Spanish Indies. One-half of them were in South America. The limits of municipalities were more or less carefully defined according to the density of the population. Where the territory was thickly settled, a town was described as extending to the boundaries of the neighboring towns or cities. In thinly settled portions of Spanish America, the city included a considerable extent of adjacent territory. Politically the Spanish-American city was modeled after the Castilian municipality. A royal order of 1563 provided that every adelantado should found at least three cities. Ordinarily the founder of a city was allowed to appoint alcaldes and regidores for the ayuntamiento or, as it was sometimes called, the cabildo. He was to assign to each settler a lot in the city and a tract of land for cultivation beyond its gates. He also had the power to allot encomiendas to settlers. Where there was no adelantado or other authorized leader, ten married men might join to establish a settlement and to organize a town government.

Spanish laws made careful specifications about the plan of a town. Its center was the *plaza mayor* or great square. Around that square were built the town hall, the prison, and the church. Streets intersecting at right angles enclosed the blocks in which the colonists built their town houses. After a town or city was founded, the authority to grant lands passed from the adelantado to the cabildo. This "chessboard plan" of municipalities was often followed in Spanish America.

An important check upon the actions of crown officials in the Spanish Indies was furnished by the residencia, which was modeled after the Spanish practice. This inquest was an examination into the career of an official, an audit of his accounts, and a formal trial. Aggrieved persons were invited to enter complaints against him within sixty days. Then the commissioner or judge of the residencia opened a court in the town where this official had resided. A law of 1582 provided that the formal trial might last sixty days in case of presidents, judges, alcaldes, attorneys, governors, and corregidores. In important cases appeal might be taken to the respective audiencia and thence to the Council of the Indies. Apparently minor officials were subjected to this ordeal whenever their superiors were investigated. Though the residencia seemed like an admirable check, yet a Peruvian viceroy compared it to a whirlwind that raised dust and chaff.

Special officers were appointed to look after fiscal affairs. In the course of time instructions were framed for the guidance of a treasurer, a comptroller, and a factor or business manager, who, during a considerable period, were the principal fiscal officers of the Spanish crown in various administrative areas in the Indies. Such officials were strictly prohibited from engaging in mercantile transactions and were required to keep their accounts in a specified manner. In 1605 tribunals of the treasury were established at Mexico City, Lima, and Santa Fé de Bogotá with the power to audit the accounts of fiscal officials within the extensive territory subordinate to the magistrates in each of these cities.

As a mode of holding colonial officials to strict account, the Spanish government, in addition to the residencia, dispatched inspectors to America. Visitadors might be sent at any time to make investigation of the conduct of a particular official or of a group of officials. It was the custom to require a visitador to send the evidence which he had gathered, together with a summary defense of the accused officials, to the Council of the Indies, which gave a final judgment upon the matter. For example, in 1543 a member of the Council of the Indies was appointed to inspect the conduct of the viceroy, the audiencia, and royal fiscal officials in New Spain. A law of 1588 provided that inspectors should go to the capital or chief city of the particular district in order to examine into the execution of justice, the conduct of ecclesiastical officials, and the administration of the royal finances.

Taxation in Spanish America originated in the age of the conquistadors. Founders of colonies were sometimes authorized to levy a capitation tax upon the aborigines and to collect the tithes designed for the support of the Church. At an early date the cabildos of Spanish-American towns and cities proceeded to levy taxes upon commercial, industrial, or professional enterprises, which were used for the support of the local administration. Early in the sixteenth century the Spanish government decreed that the crown should be paid a royalty of one-fifth of all the gold, silver, and quicksilver which might be mined in the Indies. The fifth of the precious metals and precious stones became the chief source of revenue to the Spanish monarch from his American dominions.

As the Spanish conquerors brought little money with them to the Indies, and as the aborigines ordinarily managed their commercial transactions by a species of barter, the earliest colonists had to resort to various devices to carry on trade. Grains of cacao were used for exchange in certain sections. In agricultural and pastoral districts, such as the basin of La Plata River, the colonists used yerba mate, tobacco, goats, sheep, wool, tallow, and horseshoes as money. Where gold was plentiful, that metal in powder or in bars was sometimes used as a medium of exchange. The conquerors of the Chibchans circulated aboriginal tokens of gold. In regions where the white metal was plentiful, silver tokens were manufactured. Crude mints were soon established at Cuzco and Lima. About 1540 a silver token called the peso was minted in Peru that was probably the first peso coined in the New World. In 1572 a mint was opened at Potosí, which coined a variety of silver coins that were widely circulated in southern and western South America.

Intellectual life in the Spanish colonies centered around the universities. As early as 1551 King Charles I had issued a decree providing for the establishment of universities at Lima and Mexico City that were to enjoy the same privileges as the University of Salamanca. The Royal and Pontifical University of Mexico, which was founded two years later, became famous in the Indies and well known in Spain. The University of San Marcos at Lima developed from an institution which was founded by a Dominican friar in 1553. Royal orders were issued that chairs of Indian languages should be founded in both of these institutions.

By virtue of successive papal grants, the Spanish monarchs had secured extensive rights over the Catholic Church in the Indies. A bull of Alexander VI of May 4, 1493, had entrusted to the

Church and State

Catholic Monarchs the task of converting the aborigines. Another bull dated November 16, 1501, granted to them the tithes collected in the churches of the Indies. At the instance of King Ferdinand, on July 28, 1508, Pope Julius II issued a bull by which he conferred upon the Spanish sovereigns extensive jurisdiction over the Church in the Indies as follows:

After mature deliberation with our brothers, the cardinals of the holy Roman Church, and by their advice, by these presents we concede with apostolic authority, other constitutions, ordinances, and laws to the contrary notwithstanding, to the said King Ferdinand and Queen Isabella and to the future monarchs of Castile and León, that nobody without their consent can construct or build large churches in the above-mentioned islands which are now conquered or which may be conquered, and we concede to those monarchs the right of patronage and of presenting suitable persons for vacancies in cathedral churches, monasteries, dignities, colleges and other ecclesiastical benefices and pious places. . . .

Whether it granted to Spanish rulers for the first time the general authority of making ecclesiastical appointments in the Indies, or whether it merely recognized a privilege that had been earlier conceded by the Pope, the bull of 1508 formed the basis of the right of the Spanish crown to exercise jurisdiction over the Catholic Church in the Indies. In explicit terms the Pope thus conceded to the monarchs of Spain the patronage in Spanish America.

By virtue of this bull, the Spanish crown appointed the first prelates, sketched the limits of bishoprics, and decided questions concerning benefices in the New World. The decisions of the King on ecclesiastical matters became crystallized in the Laws of the Indies. In a law of June 1, 1574, Philip II avowed that the right of patronage throughout Spanish America was a perpetual prerogative of the Spanish government. By subsequent laws this claim was enlarged to include the appointment of church dignitaries, the erection of churches and monasteries, the supervision of all ecclesiastical establishments, and the right to prevent any bull, brief, or dispensation of the Pope from being promulgated in the colonies without the consent of the Council of the Indies.

In the early history of the Spanish colonies some inquisitorial functions were exercised by bishops. Later the Church was reënforced by the Inquisition. That powerful institution was extended to the New World ostensibly to promote the extension of the Catholic faith and to eradicate heresy. A royal decree of January, 1569, announced the decision to establish inquisitorial tribunals in Spanish America. A year later two inquisitors, appointed by the King, were sent to Lima. Originally the jurisdiction of the Peruvian tribunal extended over all of Spanish South America. In 1571 two inquisitors were installed in Mexico City. Their court had control over the region extending from the Isthmus of Panama to the unknown regions of the north. In 1610 an inquisitorial tribunal, which was given jurisdiction over the Caribbean region with the exception of Central America, was established at Cartagena.

While this development of Spain's administrative machinery was taking place, cavaliers and monks were busily engaged in exploring the hinterland in North and South America, and bold navigators were reconnoitering the coast.

Even before the deposition of Cortés, expeditions had been sent in a northerly direction along the coast of Mexico. In 1533 Jiménez discovered the peninsula of Lower California. Viceroy Mendoza sent out an expedition under López de Villalobos which in November, 1542, reached the Philippine Islands. During the same year another expedition led by Juan Rodríguez Cabrillo, an experienced Portuguese mariner **Exploration of the Pacific Coast and the Interior** who was accompanied by a daring pilot named Ferrelo, sailed from Navidad along the coast of California. Upon the death of Cabrillo, Ferrelo led the expedition as far north as the coast of present Oregon. In 1595 a prosperous merchant named Sebastián Vizcaíno was commissioned by the viceroy to colonize Lower California. Two years later he planted a colony there, which, however, was soon destroyed by Indians. In 1602 Vizcaíno entered a bay which was later called San Diego; on December 16 of that year, he discovered the Bay of Monterey, and then proceeded north to Cape Mendocino.

In 1513 Ponce de León explored the coast of Florida, where in 1521 he was mortally wounded by Indians. Five years later Lucas Vásquez de Ayllón attempted to plant a settlement farther north on the Florida coast. In 1527 Narváez, the hapless antagonist of Cortés, led an expedition from Spain to the coast of Florida and proceeded from Tampa Bay to Galveston Bay. At that point Narváez's boat was unexpectedly driven out to sea and lost.

Influenced by the imaginative tales of a Franciscan friar about wonderful cities in the distant wilderness, in 1542 Francisco Vásques de Coronado led an expedition from Compostela up the valley of the Zuñi River. There the magical cities proved to be merely Indian pueblos. Coronado then divided his expedition into detachments: one squad discovered the Grand Cañon of the Colorado; while a band led by Coronado himself pursued another will-o'-the-wisp across dusty plains into present Kansas. At the very juncture when the dispirited Coronado was retracing his steps toward Mexico, a daring cavalier named Hernando de Soto, who had led an expedition from Cuba to Florida, was turning back from a trip into the interior of North America during which he had discovered the Mississippi River.

In 1582 Antonio de Espejo, a Mexican merchant, led a party up the valley of the Río Grande in order to rescue some hapless friars. During his trip Espejo explored present Arizona and New Mexico and discovered some veins of silver. In 1595 Juan de Oñate agreed to conquer and colonize New Mexico. Three years later he left Santa Bárbara with a magnificent company of well-dressed cavaliers and seven thousand head of cattle. In April, 1598, he pompously declared that he took possession "of all the kingdoms and provinces of New Mexico" for the King of Spain.

During the sixteenth century corsairs and buccaneers harassed the West Indies and the coast of Central America. Bartolomé de las Casas, "the Apostle of the Indians," tried to protect them from enslavement. Dominicans and Franciscans, who were slowly penetrating into Chiapas and Guatemala, at times had bitter quarrels about the possession of sites for their respective monasteries. Meanwhile the conquest and conversion of the aborigines proceeded at a slow pace. At the end of the sixteenth century, León, the chief city of Nicaragua, was falling into decay, while Granada had only about two hundred inhabitants.

Expansion in Central and South America

In 1540 a companion of Jiménez de Quesada named Jorge Robledo founded Cartago in the Cauca Valley. He then conquered a region on the banks of the Cauca River and started a settlement at Antioquia. Shortly after an audiencia had been established in New Granada, Ibagué and other towns were founded in the Magdalena Valley either for defense against Indian attacks or for commercial purposes. Before the close of the sixteenth century settlements had also been made at Buga, Honda, and Ocaña. Meanwhile far to the east Dominican and Franciscan friars were making explorations and establishing missions in the region that was designated Guiana. Years before Caracas was settled, Diego de Ordaz had explored the Orinoco Valley beyond the mouth of the Caroní River. About 1531 upon the banks of the Orinoco River, a town named Santo Tomé was founded—a town that subsequently became known as Angostura. In spite of the bitter hostility of the aborigines, during the latter half of the sixteenth century settlements were made at a number of harbors on the coast of the Caribbean Sea.

To commemorate the defeat of Gonzalo Pizarro, in October, 1548, the Spaniards founded the city of La Paz near Lake Titicaca. In 1540 a companion of that conquistador named Orellana embarked with a small party on one of the upper tributaries of the Amazon. After reaching that river he followed it through the continent to the sea. The advance of Spanish power in western South America was promoted by viceroys of Peru who sanctioned expeditions for the exploration of the Andean highlands and the Amazon basin. In 1567 in the name of the Spanish King, Juan Alvares Maldonado was conceded the government of the territory stretching from Lake Opotari, which was a short distance northeast of Cuzco, to the mouth of the Amazon. Maldonado even led an expedition from Cuzco to take possession of his extensive grant. After founding a town and struggling against a rival explorer, he penetrated the Amazonian wilderness near the source of the river Madre de Dios.

The settlement of the Peruvian highlands was stimulated by the discovery of mineral deposits. About 1545 rich silver mines were found at Potosí. The exploitation of quicksilver mines at Huancavelica and the use of that metal in the separation of ores much stimulated the mining industry. Viceroy Toledo framed wise ordinances to regulate the exploitation of mines. From time to time daring Spaniards were entrusted with the task of planting outposts for defense against Indian attacks. A settlement was made at Tarija on the banks of the Nuevo Guadalquivir River in 1570. During the same year in a pleasant valley upon the eastern plateau Gerónimo de Osorio founded an outpost that became known as Cochabamba.

After the untimely death of Valdivia, the conquest and settlement of Chile was taken up by García Hurtado de Mendoza, a son of the Peruvian viceroy. In 1557 he led a formidable expedition into the interior and routed the Araucanian Indians. He repopulated devastated cities, founded new towns, and proceeded as far south as the Chiloé Archipelago. Meantime a Genoese mariner who had been employed by Valdivia had explored the Chilean coast from Valparaiso to Llanquihue In 1557 a daring navigator named Ladrillero proceeded from Valdivia to the Strait of Magellan, and sailed through its main channel to the Atlantic Ocean. There he took possession of the strait and the adjacent territory for the Spanish King. A stream of settlers crossed the cordillera from Chile into a region called Cuyo. Before the end of the sixteenth century, Chileans had founded the city of Mendoza near the foothills of the Andes.

In 1541 Cabeza de Vaca, who had gained fame in North America, led a party of Spanish colonists from Santa Catharina by land to Asunción. Gonzalo Pizarro dispatched expeditions from Peru to explore the unknown interior. At his instance an adventurous Spaniard named Prado founded a town in the lofty region inhabited by the Calchaquian Indians. Colonists from the Peruvian viceroyalty made settlements near the western fringes of the pampean plains. With a company of settlers from Asunción in 1561 Nunflo de Chaves founded a city named Santa Cruz de la Sierra upon the plateau at a considerable distance east of Cochabamba. Several years later another party proceeded down the Paraguay River from Asunción and made a settlement at Corrientes on the left bank of the Paraná. Lower down that river, in 1573 Juan de Garay, an enterprising Spaniard who came to America in the train of a Peruvian viceroy, founded Santa Fé. On June 11, 1580, with colonists from Asunción, he made a permanent settlement at Buenos Aires.

In January, 1549, King John III selected Thomé de Souza as captain general of Brazil and also appointed him as ruler of the captaincy of

The Portuguese Settlements Bahia. At the same time the King decided that the seat of government in Portuguese America should be in that captaincy. Thomé de Souza reached Brazil on March 29, 1549, accompanied by some governmental officials, several hundred soldiers and convicts, and a few Jesuits. In the same year Souza founded the city of Bahia which remained the capital of Portuguese America for two hundred years. During the next half century a number of other settlements were made along the Brazilian coast.

The early colonists of Brazil were not all of the best character. Some of them were convicts who had been banished from the motherland. Others were adventurous persons belonging to the middle class, *fidalgos* who fled from the persecutions of the Inquisition or who sought their fortunes beyond the seas. As most of the Portuguese colonists disdained menial labor, they soon had recourse to the natives to supply servants for their homes. Aborigines were soon induced by the settlers to labor upon their plantations. But Indian servants were not entirely satisfactory, and as the spread of sugar cane culture stimulated the demand for labor, the Portuguese eventually looked to Africa for aid. In the second quarter of the sixteenth century Negroes were brought to Brazil. In the captaincy of Bahia, Negro slavery became the economic basis of society.

During the sixteenth century Portugal did not develop much special machinery for the administration of her colonies. Governors, princes, and kings exercised authority which was not clearly differentiated. In many particulars the administration of Portuguese America was not distinct from that of the motherland. The only special official of importance that appeared in Portugal was the inspector of finance, who managed the finances of the kingdom. He also oversaw the *Casa da*

India that was entrusted with the freighting of vessels for the Indies. That rudimentary colonial minister was restricted, however, by an ecclesiastical council designated the *Mesa da Consciencia e Ordens* which was created in 1532. In the Portuguese colonies the most important local officer was the corregedor who exercised judicial and military authority. As in Spanish America, so also in Portuguese America, the government of towns and cities was modeled after that of the mother country.

To Brazil the Portuguese brought elements of Old World culture. The most important of these perhaps was sugar cane which, planted in 1532 in the captaincy of São Vicente—later known as Bahia—spread thence to other captaincies, and in time to Spanish America. Horses, cattle, sheep, and goats that were imported by the early colonists multiplied in numbers. Wheat, barley, and other European cereals were brought to Brazil and also the grapevine. A species of pepper from Africa was introduced.

Transfer of Old World Culture

At the instance of John III, who was the patron of the Society of Jesus, six members of that society went to Brazil in 1549 led by Manoel de Nobrega. The Jesuits began their labors in and about the city of Bahia. They not only tried to keep the Portuguese colonists from forsaking the Catholic faith but also preached fervently against their vice and immorality. On the other side they strove to convert the aborigines, and urged them to give up cannibalism. They built churches, translated the church litany into Indian languages, and founded schools. Shortly after the arrival of another company of Jesuits in 1553, who were led by José de Anchieta, Nobrega established upon an elevated plain an academy which he designated the College of São Paulo. These friars founded academies or seminaries in other parts of Brazil, made settlements along the frontier, and undertook the conversion of the natives.

The first bishopric of Brazil was established at Bahia in 1551. Originally this bishop was a suffragan of the bishop of Lisbon. For more than a century the bishop of Bahia exercised jurisdiction over all of Brazil. For that reason, and because of the multitude and splendor of its temples, that city was long considered the center of Brazilian religious life.

The fundamental provision about the relations between Church and State in Brazil was the bull issued by Pope Julius III to King John III in 1551. That bull conceded to the King and his successors in perpetuity, as Grand Masters of the Orders of Aviz, Christ, and Santiago, complete ecclesiastical and spiritual jurisdiction over their conquests. It conceded to him the right

Church and State

to appoint bishops, to collect tithes, to dispense revenues for churches, alms, and religious feasts, and to hear cases by appeal from ecclesiastical courts. In consequence the royal treasury was to bear the expense of the religious establishment. The King was thus made the patron of the Church in Portuguese America.

About the middle of the sixteenth century Brazilian magistrates began to sanction the founding of houses of mercy which were often managed by religious orders. Those houses served as lodgings for pilgrims, asylums for orphans, hospitals for the sick, and almshouses for the poor. It became the custom to establish in each important town or city an institution consecrated to such purposes, which was frequently designated the *Sancta Casa de Misericordia*. In 1582 a house of mercy was founded at Rio de Janeiro. This became the most opulent and famous charitable institution in Latin America.

About the middle of the sixteenth century the French, whose mariners had occasionally visited the American coast, became deeply interested in South America. Admiral Coligny formed a plan to establish there a refuge for persecuted Calvinists. Henry II of France encouraged the project; and in 1555, under the command of an adventurer called Nicolas Villegagnon, a company of Huguenots sailed for Brazil. Upon a rocky islet in the Bay of Rio de Janeiro they built a fort named Coligny. There they suffered from the scarcity of food and water. Further, they soon suspected that their leader was not a true Protestant. Religious dissensions broke out among them; and Villegagnon severely punished those colonists who conspired against his arbitrary rule. Though other Huguenots soon arrived at Fort Coligny, the vanguard of what promised to be a great migration, they did not find there the much desired toleration.

Meanwhile Governor-General Mem de Sá undertook to expel the French from the Bay of Rio de Janeiro. By the aid of reënforcements from Portugal, he blockaded the entrance to that bay, defeated the French garrison, and demolished Fort Coligny. As a check against the return of Frenchmen who had fled into the interior, in 1567 Mem de Sá founded the city of Rio de Janeiro. Later the designs of the French upon other portions of the Brazilian coast were thwarted, and though they eventually planted settlements upon the coast of Guiana, which have lasted until our own time, their dream of "Antarctic France" was forever shattered.

Significant events in Portugal profoundly affected Brazil. In 1578 the imprudent young King Sebastian was defeated and killed at the battle of Alcacer Quibir, while aiding the Sultan of Morocco against a pretender. A senile, childless cardinal, Henry of Aviz, succeeded to the Portuguese throne. Intrigue was rife about the succession, even before King Henry died in January, 1580. Prominent among candidates for the crown were Antonio, prior of Crato, the Duchess Catherine of Braganza, and Philip II of Spain. Scarcely had Portuguese patriots proclaimed Antonio as their King, when Philip II sent an army under the Duke of Alva into Portugal to support his claim. The patriots were soon dispersed, their fortresses were given up to the Spaniards, and a price was placed upon the head of the fugitive Antonio. A Cortes which assembled at Thomar in April, 1581, proclaimed Philip II of Spain as the lawful king. As King Philip I of Portugal he was accordingly recognized not only in Lisbon but also in Rio de Janeiro.

Philip II of Spain Becomes King of Portugal

The early Spanish colonies in America were ordinarily colonies of conquest. To settlements in the New World the flora and fauna of the Old World were transported. Reciprocally flora of the Americas were taken to the Old World. In Brazil, as well as in Spanish America, the Jesuits and other religious orders started a zealous crusade to convert the aborigines—a crusade in which they often served as pathbreakers of civilization. Certain Iberian institutions were transplanted to America, where in a fresh soil some of them were much altered in form and spirit.

Of all the institutions adapted in Spanish America probably the most primary was the audiencia that frequently furnished the framework to which other institutions were fitted. It was during the sixteenth century that Spain laid the foundations of her system of colonial administration. She undertook to do this by taking the place in colonial life of the conquistadors or of their successors. As has aptly been said of Spain by an eminent American historian, she often tried to reap where she had not sown. In contrast with the main course of English expansion in North America, the advance of Spanish power in South America was marked by the founding of towns and cities at strategic points. Vast intermediate areas were left unsettled. Portugal was slower in developing a colonial system than Spain, if indeed she may be said to have developed a distinctive system at all. Partly because of the economic system prevailing in their motherlands, both the Spanish and the Portuguese were constrained to use the aborigines as laborers. The Spaniards soon used the Indians in the exploitation of gold and silver mines, while the Portuguese employed them in the tillage of their sugar plantations. They thus erected a social structure that long endured in Latin America.

SUGGESTIONS FOR FURTHER READING

AITON, A. S., *Antonio de Mendoza, First Viceroy of New Spain*, 1927.
BOLTON, H. E., *The Spanish Borderlands*, 1921.
GRAHAM, R. B. CUNNINGHAME, *A Vanished Arcadia*, 1901.
HANKE, L., *The First Social Experiments in America*, 1935.
HARING, C. H., *Trade and Navigation Between Spain and the Indies in the Time of the Hapsburgs*, 1918.
HELPS, A., *Spanish Conquest in America*, Vol. IV, 1900.
MAGALHÃES, P. DE, *The Histories of Brazil*, Vol. II, 1922.
MARCHANT, A., *From Barter to Slavery*, 1942.
MEANS, P. A., *Fall of the Inca Empire*, 1932.
MECHAM, J. L., *Francisco de Ibarra and Nueva Vizcaya*, 1927.
MOSES, B., *The Spanish Dependencies in South America*, Vol. I, 1914.
NASH, R., *The Conquest of Brazil*, 1926.
SIMPSON, L. B., *The Encomienda in New Spain*, 1929.
SMITH, D. E., *The Viceroy of New Spain*, 1913.

CHAPTER VI

THE OLD RÉGIME IN BRAZIL

Events during the sixty years' captivity, 1580-1640, when Spain ruled over Portugal and her colonies, form an interlude in the history of Brazil. Yet this era was not without influence upon the administration of Portuguese America. Governmental policy toward Brazil tended to approximate the practices followed with respect to the Spanish Indies. Further, the Portuguese colonies became involved in the struggle between the Spaniards and the renaissant Dutch.

The desire of the Dutch to free themselves from Spain inspired them to attack her colonies. In the last part of the sixteenth century the "Beggars of the Sea" began to prey upon the Brazilian settlements. They founded the Dutch West India Company to promote colonization. Soon after the termination of the twelve-years' truce between Spain and Holland in 1621, the Dutch equipped a fleet to attack Portuguese America. **The Dutch Conquer Northern Brazil** In 1624 an expedition under Admiral Willekens captured Bahia; but that port soon surrendered to a Spanish fleet. Still, the Dutch did not relinquish their colonial designs. In February, 1630, with a fleet of fifty vessels they besieged Pernambuco. They soon captured that city; and, after several years of struggle, they conquered the northern part of Brazil. In 1637 the Dutch West India Company entrusted the conquered territory to a prince of the House of Orange, Count Maurice of Nassau-Siegen, who proved to be a wise, enterprising, and magnanimous ruler. During his administration, which lasted until 1644, the somber Portuguese and the gay Fleming lived together in peace.

During Spanish rule some progress was made in the exploration and settlement of certain portions of Brazil. Attempts to plant colonies were made in the captaincies of Sergipe, Parahyba, Rio Grande do Norte, and Ceará. As reports of the navigability of the Amazon River frequently reached settlements upon the coast, the Spanish government decided to equip an exploring party. On October 28, 1637, an expedition led by Pedro Teixeira, which was composed of about seventy soldiers and a thousand natives, left Pará at the mouth of the Amazon and started up that river. After reaching the highest navigable point, Teixeira proceeded overland to Quito, where bull fights were held in honor of his achievement. At the request of the Peruvian viceroy, the daring explorer returned by the same route in order to perfect his survey. He reëmbarked upon a tributary of the Napo River and descended the Amazon to Pará, where he landed on December 12, 1639. While upon that marvelous trip Teixeira heard rumors about a race of woman warriors without husbands who were called "Amazons." This name was later applied to the Great River.

The administration of Portuguese America was modified by its Spanish rulers. Philip II soon suppressed the inspectors of finance and replaced them by a Council of Finance, which exercised jurisdiction over Brazil. Under his successor Portuguese administration was further assimilated to Spanish administration; for, though the Council of Finance was left in control of the commerce and revenues of Brazil, in 1604 it was supplemented by a Council of the Indies which was granted jurisdiction over the civil and religious affairs of the former Portuguese colonies. After December, 1640, when Portuguese patriots took possession of Lisbon, and the Duke of Braganza became King of Portugal with the title of John IV, the subordination to Madrid ended. Yet the administration of Brazil did not return to its former condition. To the Council of the Indies and the Council of Finance there was added a Council of State and also a Privy Council. The Council of State made civil appointments for the Portuguese colonies, while the Privy Council nominated candidates for judicial offices. The legal code of Brazil remained the *Ordenaçoes Philippinas,* which in 1643 were confirmed by King John IV.

Soon afterward an uprising against the Dutch broke out in Pernambuco. This movement spread throughout northern Brazil. By a treaty signed at The Hague in 1661 Holland formally relinquished her Brazilian possessions. A noted Portuguese historian has not inappropriately styled the reconquest of Pernambuco by his compatriots the "Brazilian Iliad." Nevertheless the Dutch succeeded in retaining their settlements upon the coast of Guiana.

A significant movement of expansion started under the Spanish monarchs. This was the spread of Portuguese influence through expeditions from São Paulo. At first those expeditions, which began about 1603 and often proceeded up the Tieté River, were largely designed for the purpose of capturing Indians and of selling them as slaves in the markets of São Paulo and Rio de Janeiro. "Paulistas," as the half-breed adventurers from São Paulo were called, gradually penetrated farther and farther into the interior. In 1618, after gold was discovered in a region that had been explored by Paulistas, Philip II framed ordinances for the regulation of the

Brazilian mines. Before the end of the seventeenth century gold was also found in a section that was designated Minas Geraes; early in the following century diamonds were discovered there. From Minas Geraes pioneers ventured next into a district that was called Goyaz. In the second quarter of the eighteenth century a Paulista named Cabral discovered gold mines at Cuyabá within a region that was eventually called Matto Grosso. In 1742 by way of the Guaporé, Madeira, and Amazon rivers, Manuel Felix de Lima made a voyage from Matto Grosso to Pará. Bold adventurers even menaced the Jesuit missions in Paraguay. To the south Paulistas were making explorations as far as Rio Grande do Sul. In 1680 the Portuguese founded a town at Colonia on the banks of the Río de la Plata. At many other points daring pioneers planted settlements far beyond the imaginary demarcation line that had been sketched by the Treaty of Tordesillas.

In this task they were aided by the friars. In 1653 there arrived in northern Brazil a remarkable Jesuit named Antonio Vieira. At once he began to preach fervently against the enslavement of the Indians. Thwarted in his designs by the opposition of planters and slave hunters, he went to Lisbon, where in 1655 he secured a royal decree that placed the aborigines under the guardianship of his order. While Vieira was striving with more or less success to protect them, some of his coadjutors were planting missions in the interior of Brazil. Long after his death, the Jesuits founded missions and built chapels along the Great River and its chief tributaries. By the middle of the eighteenth century, they had constructed a chain of missions across the continent. Portuguese Jesuits from Pará had met Spanish Jesuits from Quito near the headwaters of the Amazon River. Spanish missionaries near the Orinoco River were in communication with Portuguese missionaries on the river Negro, while far to the south Jesuits from Brazil, as well as from Paraguay, were catechizing the Indians of La Plata basin.

As a result of the expansion of the Portuguese settlements, some changes were made in the administrative divisions. In 1621 a so-called "State of Maranhão," including a portion of Brazil southeast of the mouth of the Amazon, was organized and made directly subordinate to the government in the Peninsula. During the following century this state split into the captaincies of Pará, Maranhão, Piaúhy, and Ceará. Meanwhile new districts designated as Parahyba do Norte and Rio Grande do Norte were being organized farther south. The captaincy of Bahia was absorbing the two adjacent captaincies of Ilhéos and Porto Seguro, while a region called Sergipe was gaining some autonomy. Springing from the old district of São Vicente and including a

portion of the captaincy of Santo Amaro, the new division of São
Paulo was definitely recognized in 1709. Eleven years later Minas
Geraes was made a separate captaincy. In the hinterland there were
also organized during the first half of the eighteenth century the new
captaincies of Goyaz and Matto Grosso. The captaincy of Rio de
Janeiro included the original district of Parahyba do Sul. Colonists
who had spread into the southern portions of Brazil in the second
quarter of the eighteenth century were laying the foundations of a
new captaincy in the region designated Santa Catharina. In the debatable land still farther south settlements were being made in Rio
Grande do Sul, which was organized as a new division early in the
nineteenth century.

In theory, until the middle of the eighteenth century, the limits
between Spanish and Portuguese America were indicated by the
demarcation line drawn by the Treaty of Tordesillas.

The
Boundary
Treaty of
1750

That boundary was never surveyed. It was probably
because of the cordial relations existing between the
crowns of Spain and Portugal that on January 13, 1750,
a treaty was signed at Madrid by commissioners of those
nations which sketched a new demarcation line between the Spanish
and the Portuguese territories in the Indies. By the Treaty of Madrid
the Portuguese government recognized the Spanish title to the Philippine Archipelago. On the other hand, this treaty transferred seven
flourishing Jesuit missions on the left bank of the Uruguay River to
Portugal in return for Colonia which was ceded to Spain. It acknowledged the Portuguese claim by settlement to large portions of the
Amazon and Paraná basins. It further stipulated that the contracting
parties should select commissioners to survey the boundary line.

Some time afterward the two governments appointed such commissioners who encountered many difficulties when they attempted to
determine the boundary. Furthermore the mission Indians upon the
Uruguay River fought for three years to prevent the transfer of the
Jesuit reductions to Portugal.

Under both Spanish kings and Portuguese monarchs the power of
the captains-donatory steadily decreased. By the middle of the eighteenth century royal agents had displaced the donatories as the chief
executives throughout Portuguese America. At the end of that century
there were seventeen captaincies in Brazil. The governor who administered a captaincy was frequently designated as captain general.
Ten of those executives, who controlled important captaincies, could
correspond directly with the Portuguese government, while the others
were subordinated to the captains general of the first class. For a
time the governors of Espirito Santo, Santa Catharina, and Rio

Grande do Sul were subordinated to the captain general of Rio de Janeiro.

Each captain general oversaw all branches of public administration within his district. He was the commander of the military forces; he directed the civil administration, founded cities, and supervised the finances. He presided over a tribunal of accounts, and was further assisted in the fiscal administration by such officials as customhouse officers and superintendents of the mint. Judicial power in each captaincy was in the hands of superior and inferior judges. The highest judicial authority in Brazil was vested in two supreme courts: one established in 1609 at Bahia; and the other set up in 1751 at Rio de Janeiro. In certain cases appeals might be taken from those courts to a tribunal in Lisbon.

The Civil Administration of Brazil

The captain general residing at the capital city was early designated the governor-general. After 1640 he was sometimes styled viceroy. Until 1763 he was obliged to live at Bahia. The viceroy's term of office was ordinarily three years. At the end of his term he was expected to return to Portugal at once "in the same ship that had brought his successor." His conduct while in office was subjected to an inquest similar to the residencia used in the Spanish colonies. Both viceroys and governors general were early placed under certain prohibitions. They were not to interfere in financial or judicial affairs except as specified by law. They were not to meddle in the administration of those captaincies that were directly subject to the crown except in times of war or of public calamity. Yet they could reach a common agreement with the captains general of such districts in case emergencies arose which involved matters of common interest.

At the end of his term of office a governor general was expected to inform his successor regarding the conditions that prevailed in the colony. He was also to submit to the King a comprehensive report concerning the "most important matters that had been decided, as well as those that were still unsettled, without which he should not be paid his salary for his last year of service." As time passed, despite the legal restrictions imposed by the mother country, the governor general became so powerful that one Jesuit father stigmatized his authority as "monstrous."

In 1763 the viceregal seat was transferred from Bahia to Rio de Janeiro. The extent of the powers finally granted by the Portuguese crown to the Brazilian viceroy may be shown by quoting from the instructions given in 1763 to the Conde da Cunha, who is reckoned by Brazilian historians as being the first viceroy in the distinctive sense of that term. The King conceded to him the "entire authority over all generals, colonels, commanders of fortresses, persons who may be in these fortresses and in fleets or expeditions that may proceed to Brazil, and also over all noblemen and other subjects of whatever quality, state, or condition. He shall have complete jurisdiction over all cases, whether civil or criminal, even including cases of deaths from natural causes, and shall also have authority to carry out his orders without the parties having any further appeal, and without the exception of any person whomsoever." These instructions also expressly granted to this viceroy authority to supervise the royal finances in the following passage: "He may direct the officials of my treasury and the commissioners and clerks of my customhouses that in all matters in which I have given directions with regard to my treasury or its expenditures, and in all other affairs relating to it they shall fully execute his commands."

It is clear that the administration of Portuguese America ultimately became very centralized; the most important check was exercised through the town councils.

In some respects Brazilian municipalities played a rôle resembling that of the cities of Spanish America. A town in Brazil frequently included the surrounding area. Ordinarily its administration was vested in a council designated a *senado da camera*. The powers of that council were frequently determined by a royal grant which was often modeled upon the charter of a Portuguese city. In theory the officials of a Brazilian city were elective: in practice they were frequently designated by the royal agent who presided over the meetings of its council. Brazilian town councils made regulations concerning local affairs; the council of an important city might even temporarily fill a vacancy in the position of captain general. Upon exceptional occasions these town councils might even act as deliberative assemblies. Indeed at certain times their functions were almost unlimited.

In many parts of Brazil the most important occupation was agriculture. The cultivation of sugar cane soon spread extensively in several captaincies. Cotton was indigenous; it flourished **Industry** best perhaps in the captaincy of Maranhão. The culture of wheat and rice spread widely in southern Brazil. From the captaincy of Bahia, the raising of tobacco extended into other parts of the colony that were adapted to it. In that captaincy cacao also throve well. In 1728 the first coffee beans were brought from Cayenne and planted in the captaincy of Pará. About thirty years later the cultivation of coffee was begun in the captaincy of Rio de Janeiro, whence it spread to the rich lands of São Paulo, where it flourished remarkably. Eventually the coffee tree was also introduced into the provinces of Espirito Santo and Minas Geraes. The progress of agricultural industry, however, was delayed by the scarcity of labor, which was only partly remedied by the importation of Negro slaves, who, in 1800, comprised about one-half of the population.

The process of refining sugar was at first very primitive. The introduction into Brazil of the *engenho*, or sugar mill operated by horse power, which seems to have been brought there from Peru by a Spanish priest, transformed the industry. The juice from the mill was poured into huge kettles, where it was boiled down; then the saccharine mass was dumped into refining vats. By the opening of the eighteenth century there had been erected in the captaincy of Bahia 146 sugar mills; in Pernambuco, 346; and in Rio de Janeiro, 136. By that time the total production of sugar in Brazil amounted to 19,000 tons per annum.

Besides the sugar mills, the only factories of consequence in Brazil were those engaged in the manufacture of coarse cotton or linen cloth. The government of Portugal displayed a paternalistic attitude toward certain industries. A decree providing that no manufacturer of sugar in Brazil should be detained for debt indicated its policy toward a colonial industry that did not compete with home manufacturers. After the ambitious statesman, the Marquis of Pombal, became the chief minister for King Joseph I, he exempted colonial indigo and rice from imposts for a term of years. During his ministry Brazilian sugar had to be transported across the Atlantic in a crude form in order that it might be refined in Portugal. A share of Brazilian tobacco was by law reserved for factories in the motherland. In the end of the sixteenth century the cultivation of the grapevine was prohibited in the captaincy of São Paulo. The exportation of wheat from the colony of Rio Grande do Sul was prohibited in 1785. In the same year a royal decree was issued which declared that all Brazilian factories where articles were manufactured out of gold, silver, silk, flax, and cotton should cease to operate. At the opening of the nineteenth century certain weavers were condemned to deportation from Portuguese America.

A mining ordinance which was promulgated by the Portuguese government about 1750 stipulated that, with the exception of a plot reserved for the discoverer of the mine, the ore lands of Brazil should not be sold but should be distributed by lot for usufructuary purposes upon the payment of specified fees. After the rush to the gold fields began, it was found increasingly difficult to collect the fifth of the precious metal which was due to the King. To ensure the collection of the fifths, at one time the government rigorously prohibited the exportation of gold from the mining district. At other times it required the payment of annual fees which were proportioned according to the number of slaves that were employed in the respective mines. The gold rush had evil effects upon agriculture, for slaves were bought up by miners and cultivators deserted the plantations.

For several years the diamond mines which were discovered in the second quarter of the eighteenth century along certain tributaries of the São Francisco River were exploited by private enterprise. At first the government merely imposed a tax which varied according to the value of the diamonds found. Later it resorted to a capitation fee which resembled the charge that was laid on the production of gold. The government was next compelled to encircle the diamond region with a cordon of customhouses. It gradually increased the capitation tax; and at last it nominally transformed the exploitation of the diamond district into a government monopoly.

As the ports of Brazil were closed to the vessels of foreign nations, for a considerable period the commercial intercourse with the mother country was carried on by fleets of vessels convoyed by Portuguese warships. Brazilian products were transported to the markets of Lisbon, Oporto, and other Portuguese cities, while the merchandise from Portugal was sent to various colonial ports, whence it was distributed throughout the country. During the sixteenth century Brazilian sugar and tobacco became known in many marts of trade.

Commerce and Revenue

Soon after the accession of John IV the Portuguese government relinquished its policy of carrying on trade with Brazil by convoyed fleets. It sanctioned the formation of a commercial company that was conceded a monopoly of commerce and transportation between Portugal and Brazil. Merchant ships sailed in fleets escorted by ships of war; one fleet per year left Portugal for Brazil. In 1765 another commercial company was organized for the development of the captaincies of Pará and Maranhão. This company was assigned the task of promoting agriculture and increasing the population in that region. The government not only gave it the use of two warships, but also the land on which to construct warehouses, and the monopoly of taking slaves to Brazil. It exercised a favorable influence upon the development of the Amazon Valley. The company of Pernambuco and Parahyba, which was founded for similar purposes in 1769, was not so successful. After the downfall of Pombal in 1777, the commercial companies were forthwith abolished. Yet the vessels of foreigners were strictly prohibited from entering Brazilian ports.

Sources of revenue for the Portuguese government were furnished by monopolies of important colonial industries. Prominent among these were salt, Brazil wood, the whale fisheries, the gold mines, and the diamond mines. Certain Portuguese taxes closely resembled those imposed by the Spaniards; most important among these perhaps were the taxes levied at the customhouses. The domestic commerce of Brazil was often carried on by means of barter. In mining districts quills filled with gold dust or rude bars of gold were used as media of exchange. In farming regions cattle or cotton or slaves were employed as money. The first coins minted in Portuguese America were struck off during hostilities with the Dutch in order to pay the soldiers engaged in that war.

During the seventeenth and eighteenth centuries the organization of the Brazilian Church became complex. In 1676 Pope Innocent XI issued a bull that made the bishop of Bahia the archbishop of Brazil. By other bulls of the same date the Pope created two new dioceses in Brazil: one was located at Rio de Janeiro and the other at Pernambuco. Soon afterward he installed a bishop at Maranhão who was, however, made a suffragan of the archbishop of Lisbon. At those cities canons and other ecclesiastical dignitaries were installed. Before the end of the eighteenth century bishops were also established in five other cities. Two of the Brazilian bishops, those located at Pará and Maranhão, still remained subject to the archbishop of Lisbon. In sharp contrast with the Spanish Indies, tribunals of the Inquisition were not established in Portuguese America.

Nevertheless, troublesome problems arose in the relations between Church and State. In accordance with the bull of 1551, the Portuguese monarchs undertook to compensate the Brazilian clergy for the transfer of their tithes to the crown by conferring upon them certain offices, honors, and emoluments. **Church and State** As many abuses became apparent in the administration of ecclesiastical courts, the government provided for appeals from their judgments. In this manner the decisions of church courts were in some cases modified and in other cases completely nullified. The crown also tried to shield its subjects from exploitation by grasping ecclesiastics.

At times aggressive clerics even tried to interfere with the civil administration. A bishop of Maranhão attempted to check a war that was being waged against the aborigines. Another ecclesiastic dispatched expeditions into the interior in order to kidnap Indians to be used as domestic slaves; a bishop of Pará placed a magistrate under the ban of excommunication. Monastic establishments refused at times to pay tithes for the lands that they held. The clergy of the city of Rio de Janeiro even launched an anathema against the city council because of certain privileges that it had accorded to the poor.

Against these attempts, which seemed to threaten temporal power by the skillful use of spiritual weapons of the Church, the government took a firm stand. Orders were dispatched from Lisbon to the effect that an excommunication laid against either an individual or a corporation should be lifted whenever it was not justified. The founding of new monasteries within the limits of Portuguese America was prohibited. Ecclesiastics were to be kept within the bounds of their authority as prescribed by episcopal provisions and the dispositions of the Council of Trent.

The religious orders in Brazil played an influential rôle in education. Immediately upon their arrival there the members of the Company of Jesus proceeded to found educational institutions. When **Education** the Jesuits erected a monastic house, or established a mission, or built a church, they also founded elementary schools. In connection with their establishments in the various captaincies they proceeded to open primary schools that were adapted to local needs. When northern Brazil was being settled, and when aggressive Paulistas were penetrating into the hinterland, Jesuit fathers accompanied the pioneers. Other religious orders that later arrived in Brazil followed the example of the Jesuits in educational work. Schools were opened in monasteries and missions where boys could be catechized in the Catholic faith and instructed in the rudiments of knowledge.

At the end of the seventeenth century, however, higher education in Brazil was limited to a few seminaries and academies. In 1699 an academy of artillery and military architecture was created at Bahia; and in 1738 a similar academy was established at Rio de Janeiro. Two years earlier there had been established in that capital the seminaries of São José and São Pedro. The seminary of São Pedro had professorships of rhetoric, Christian doctrine, Latin, and music, while the seminary of São José had chairs of Latin, philosophy, theology, and liturgy. About 1776 certain Franciscans attempted to set up in Rio de Janeiro a university modeled upon the statutes which Pombal had granted to the University of Coimbra. Though a few academies and seminaries were thus erected in the latter part of the colonial régime, the children of Brazilian aristocrats were sometimes sent to Portugal to study in Coimbra's classic halls.

Not until after the expulsion of the Jesuits did the home government display an interest in elementary instruction. In 1772 it issued a decree providing that the revenues accruing from certain taxes should be placed in a special fund which was to be used for the promotion of public education. During the following year it directed that the number of schools for children in Brazil should be increased.

The Portuguese government did not follow a liberal policy with respect to the press either at home or in the colonies. During the seventeenth century it maintained an inquisitorial inspection of manuscripts intended for circulation in Portugal or Brazil. When in the beginning of the eighteenth century an enterprising colonist established a printing press at Recife in order to print bills of exchange and prayer books, the governor of the province was directed by royal order to sequestrate the press and to notify the proprietor that he should publish no more books. About the middle of that century a printing press was set up in the city of Rio de Janeiro by Antonio Isidro, who printed some booklets concerning a Brazilian bishop. Isidro's activities as a publisher, however, were short-lived; for a royal decree was soon issued that closed his office "in order that ideas which were contrary to the true interests of the state should not be disseminated." No periodicals were published in Brazil; indeed almost the only journal that circulated in the Portuguese dominions was the *Gazette of Lisbon* which printed very little news.

Poets of colonial Brazil were influenced by two great factors: the poetry of Camoes and the scenery of their native land. In a sense early Brazilian poets were sectional. They often sang about the natural beauty of Pernambuco, Bahia, or Rio de Janeiro. Bento Teixeira composed a póem entitled *Prosopopéa* in which he chanted about the port of Recife.

Literature, Science, and Art

At Bahia in the seventeenth century certain poets imitated the rhythm of anonymous verses entitled *Dialogos das grandezas do Brazil*. A lyric note was struck by Gonzaga, when in 1792 there appeared from the Lisbon press the first edition of his *Lyras de Dirceu*, which described the tragedy of an unfortunate Brazilian lover who had been compromised in a mining conspiracy and banished to Africa. Among prose writings the works of eloquence held a high place: ·those began in sermons of the Jesuits. Certain literary productions of the friars partook of the nature of history. In 1587 Gabriel Soares, a Portuguese sugar planter who had resided in Bahia, wrote a notable geographical tract concerning the Brazilian coast, which was not published for many years. Possibly the most important historical production of the colonial period in Brazil was Rocha Pitta's *History of Portuguese America*. During the Old Régime there appeared the faint beginnings of the picaresque novel: the most striking example of this was the *Peregrino da America* of Nuno Margues Pereira. The origins of Brazilian histrionic art may be clearly found in rude dramas depicting the lives of saints and in comedies or comic tragedies.

The beginnings of investigation into the natural history of Brazil were made under the direction of the Prince of Nassau. At his instance the first purely scientific expedition from Europe to the New World was organized. A Dutchman named Wilhelm Pies was appointed the leader of the party, while among others a German scientist, Georg Marcgraf, was selected to accompany him. During his sojourn in

Brazil the leader made many observations concerning diseases and medicinal plants, which he published in 1648 in the first part of his *Historia Naturalis Brasiliensi*. Meantime Marcgraf was serving as the astronomer and geographer of the party. In the course of a number of exploring expeditions into the wilderness he made a large number of geographical observations which he published at Amsterdam in 1647. He also carefully collected data concerning the solar eclipse of November 13, 1640. In a tower at Mauritzstadt this scientist carried on the first astronomical observations made by a European in South America.

Aside from certain scientific observations which were the by-products of attempts to delimit the Spanish-Portuguese boundary, the most significant contribution to scientific knowledge of Brazil that was made in the eighteenth century was the result of the mission of Alexandre Rodrigues Pereira, a native of Bahia who had studied and taught at the University of Coimbra. At the instance of the Portuguese government, from 1783 to 1792 he traversed the valley of the Amazon and its tributaries and collected data concerning the Brazilian animal, vegetable, and mineral kingdoms. So important were his services to natural science that he has been styled by admiring countrymen as "the Humboldt of Brazil."

Portuguese America had no such artistic heritage as Spanish America. The Portuguese had no such masters of the brush as Velásquez from whom to draw inspiration; they had no such cathedrals as Burgos to serve as models for their religious architecture. Their prevailing architectural style was a species of ornate Gothic designated as Manuelian. The Prince of Nassau brought some Dutch painters to northern Brazil, but they made no enduring artistic impression. Though an occasional priest painted pictures or offered lessons in art, and a painter named Tauny brought a fleeting luster to the French name, the colonial milieu did not encourage the establishment of a school of art. In fact, the government of Portugal took steps that effectively discouraged the development of certain arts and crafts which were intimately related to architecture. A royal order of 1621 directed that no Negro or mulatto or Indian should be permitted to ply the trade of a goldsmith or a silversmith. In 1698 the governor-general decreed that "the flourishing workshops of silversmiths, goldsmiths, and sculptors should be closed"—a prohibition that remained in force until 1808. Not until the second half of the eighteenth century did some precursors of Brazilian painting open their rude ateliers in Bahia and Rio de Janeiro. The scene was indeed not properly set for the formation of a distinctive school of art until the arrival in the capital of a coterie of French painters in 1816.

During the early colonization of Portuguese America criminals were transported there in considerable numbers. Heretics were even allowed to settle there. Until the reign of Philip II the colonies of Portugal were not shut to Jews; during that reign, as well as at a later epoch, many of them emigrated to Brazil to escape the persecution of the Inquisition.

Immigration and Population

Immigration policy with respect to aliens was not consistent: the early policy of Portugal was to admit anyone professing the Catholic faith, but foreigners were strictly prohibited from trading with the Indians, and they were compelled to pay special taxes. In 1591, however, a royal decree provided that aliens of whatever faith were to be excluded from the Portuguese colonies.

A notable attempt to encourage Portuguese emigration to America was made in 1744, when King John V directed that four thousand families should be transported at public expense from Madeira and the Azores to southern Brazil. Besides granting them bounties, the government agreed to furnish such colonists with supplies for the first year. Each family was to be conceded a quarter of a square league of land; the men were to be exempt from military service. But this wise colonial policy was not continued.

Negroes from Guinea gradually displaced the Indians as laborers upon plantations. African slaves thus became an important element in Brazil's population. Even in the sixteenth century there was considerable mingling of the whites, the Negroes, and the Indians in Brazil. In time freedmen, Negroes who had been emancipated, formed a considerable element in Brazilian society. As the policy of Pombal was to encourage the amalgamation of whites and Indians, during the eighteenth century Brazil became a huge melting-pot. At least in certain parts of that colony, the tendency was toward the formation of new types of mankind.

A Portuguese agent sent to demarcate the boundary sketched by the treaty of 1750 was a brother of Pombal. Soon after visiting the missions in the Amazon Valley, he accused the Jesuits of keeping the aborigines in ignorance and serfdom. The Portuguese government consequently deprived the Jesuits in Brazil of their temporal authority. In 1759, after the discovery of a conspiracy against the life of King Joseph, a royal edict was issued that the Jesuits, who were suspected of being involved in the conspiracy, should be expelled from the Portuguese dominions. Their properties were confiscated, their reductions were neglected, and their neophytes vanished into the wilderness.

Partly because of the serious difficulties encountered in the survey of the boundary line sketched in 1750, on February 12, 1761, a convention was signed between Spain and Portugal that completely annulled the Treaty of Madrid. In theory, for the time being, the line of Tordesillas again marked the limits between Brazil and Spanish America. But on October 1, 1777, a new treaty was signed at San Ildefonso between Spain and Portugal which sketched the boundary between their American possessions. It provided for the choice of commissioners who should not only determine the boundary line exactly but should also prepare a map of the Spanish-Portuguese frontiers in America. At many points that line followed the demarcation of 1750. In the south, however, the Treaty of San Ildefonso recognized the Spanish claim to Colonia and to the seven missions on the left bank of the Uruguay River. On the other hand, that treaty acknowledged Portugal's claim to the island of Santa Catharina, to the adjacent mainland, and to extensive interior districts that had been explored and sparsely settled by Jesuits and Paulistas.

Boundaries between Spanish and Portuguese America

It is scarcely an exaggeration to say that by this treaty Portugal obtained a clear title to territory in South America which was more than twice as large as the domain conceded to her by the Treaty of Tordesillas. Yet, because of various difficulties, the boundary drawn by the Treaty of San Ildefonso was never completely surveyed. In a report which he made to his King more than ten years after that treaty was signed, a Spaniard, who had been acting as a commissioner to determine this boundary, complained that the Portuguese were planting new settlements beyond the demarcation line of 1777. He recommended that a definitive treaty should be framed which would end controversies over the limits.

Signs of discontent with the existing régime appeared in Brazil at various times. Still, few movements took place there that could be designated rebellions. In 1787, when Thomas Jefferson was in France, a Brazilian student named Maia informed him that certain of his fellow countrymen desired to emulate the United States by establishing a republic in Brazil. That student later became a leader of those colonists who aspired for independence in the captaincy of Minas Geraes. There in 1789 an ensign in the Brazilian cavalry, who was nicknamed "Tiradentes," headed a band of conspirators who wished to separate from Portugal and to establish their independence. They designed a national flag, drafted some laws, and formulated certain reforms. But their plot was betrayed to the viceroy, they were imprisoned, and in 1792 Tiradentes was executed. Discontent with the rule of the motherland was much less pronounced in Brazil than in Spanish America.

Revolutionary Tendencies

The more or less futile attempts that were made accurately to define

MAP SHOWING THE SPANISH-PORTUGUESE BOUNDARY AND THE
AUDIENCIAS IN SOUTH AMERICA NEAR THE END OF THE
EIGHTEENTH CENTURY

the boundaries between Spanish and Portuguese America derive much of their importance from the fact that they indicate the extent to which Portuguese pioneers had penetrated the Amazonian wilderness. While the Spaniards had been dominating Portugal and profoundly influencing her system of colonial administration, and also after the Portuguese King was restored to his throne, Brazilian pioneers had been exploring the hinterland, making settlements along the waterways, and thus gaining for Portugal a claim to the territory which her clever diplomats secured by the Treaty of San Ildefonso. In Brazil the old divisions into captaincies still to an extent persisted and furnished a model for other divisions that were eventually organized under a viceroy located at Rio de Janeiro. Brazilian social and intellectual life radiated from the cities. The only Portuguese colonial institution that resembled Anglo-American self-governing institutions was the *senado da camera*. Yet that council furnished no such political training as was afforded by the local institutions of the Thirteen Colonies.

SUGGESTIONS FOR FURTHER READING

BRAGANÇA CUNHA, V. DE, *Eight Centuries of Portuguese Monarchy*, 1911.

CALLCOTT, M. D. G., *Journal of a Voyage to Brazil and Residence Therein*, 1824.

CARDOZO, M. S., "The Collection of the Fifths in Brazil," *Hispanic American Historical Review*, Vol. XX, pp. 359-379.

EDMUNDO, L., *Rio in the Time of the Viceroys*, 1936.

DAWSON, T. C., *The South American Republics*, Vol. I, 1903.

DENIS, P., *Brazil*, 1911.

GALVÃO BUENO, A. DE, "The Bandeirantes: Their Deeds and Their Descendants," *Bulletin*, Pan American Union, Vol. LIV, pp. 456-480.

KOEBEL, W. H., *South America, An Industrial and Commercial Field*, 1923.

MAWE, J., *Travels in the Interior of Brazil*, 1812.

MEDINA, J. T. (ed.), *The Discovery of the Amazon*, 1934.

OAKENFULL, J. C., "*Brazil*," *Past, Present, and Future*, 1919.

OLIVEIRA LIMA, M. DE, *The Evolution of Brazil Compared with That of Spanish and Anglo-Saxon America*, 1914.

SOUTHEY, R., *History of Brazil*, Vol. III, 1822.

WATSON, R. G., *Spanish and Portuguese South America*, Vol. II, 1884.

CHAPTER VII

THE EXPANSION AND ADMINISTRATION OF THE SPANISH COLONIES

During the seventeenth and eighteenth centuries the Spaniards made many advances in the New World. Not the least notable of those movements was the extension of Spanish influence from the ancient center of Aztec power. Itinerant padres strove to convert the aborigines and to teach them the rudiments of civilization. Persevering missionaries pushed into the region occupied by the Yaqui Indians. By the middle of the seventeenth century Jesuit missions had been planted in the upper Sonora Valley. In 1687 a scholarly Jesuit named Eusebio Kino founded the mission of Nuestra Señora de Dolores on the banks of San Miguel River. From that mother mission he made many exploring expeditions and eventually proceeded beyond the northern frontiers of present Mexico. This indefatigable pioneer undertook in 1695 to promote the establishment of missions in Lower California, a project in which he was only temporarily successful. Meanwhile missionaries and miners were advancing northward over the central Mexican plateau.

In the province which Oñate had explored and where missions were being founded by Franciscans, in 1609 Governor Peralta founded the town of Santa Fé. A fierce insurrection of the Pueblo Indians against their Catholic overlords that began in 1680 was not subjugated until the end of the century. Meantime the Spaniards were pushing their settlements beyond the frontiers of the province of Nuevo León. In 1687 a new province called Coahuila was organized. Incited by reports of French designs upon Texas, in 1686 Alonzo de León led an exploring party into that region. An enterprising Franciscan named Hidalgo, who proceeded from the College of Santa Cruz at Querétaro, planted a permanent settlement in 1718 at San Antonio, which became the center of Spanish operations in Texas. The activities of English smugglers upon the borders of Louisiana, which Spain had acquired from France at the end of the Seven Years' War, incited the Spaniards to employ French officers and fur traders to fasten their hold upon that vast province.

The settlement of Upper California, a land fabled to be rich in gold, pearls, and diamonds, was repeatedly undertaken by Spaniards from Mexico. At last, as the result of expeditions by land and sea directed by the enterprising governor of Lower California, Gaspar de Portolá, who was aided by a Franciscan padre named Junípero Serra, in 1769 a mission was founded at San Diego and the beautiful Bay of San Francisco was discovered. In the following year Portolá succeeded in planting a mission at Monterey. In 1771 and 1772, three other Franciscan missions were established in Upper California. In 1776 a toilsome migration of settlers overland from Sonora led by a venturesome frontiersman named Juan Bautista de Anza resulted in the founding of a colony at San Francisco. Subsequently the indefatigable Padre Serra, the leading Spanish pioneer of California, planted nine other missions on the Pacific coast. By the opening of the nineteenth century Franciscan friars were directing a chain of missions along the coast of Upper California. Those missions were guarded by forts that were called *presidios*.

The colonization of Central America proceeded slowly. Here, too, the exploration of the interior and the planting of settlements was largely carried on by members of religious orders. Jesuits were active in Nicaragua, Franciscans in Honduras, and Recollets in Guatemala. By the middle of the seventeenth century the city of Santiago contained monasteries belonging to six different religious orders.

Meanwhile many towns and cities were founded in northern South America. Near a sand bar at the mouth of the Magdalena River there **Progress in Central and South America** was founded in 1629 a town called Barranquilla that became a terminus of navigation and a commercial emporium. Shortly afterward, as a result of the activities of Jesuit padres who had been converting the aborigines, a town named Quibdó was established upon the left bank of the Atrato River. In the vicinity of Antioquia mining towns were built, and in time some attention was paid to agriculture. Rude roads were constructed, which linked Antioquia to adjacent towns and to the Magdalena River. Near the heart of this busy region a thriving village developed which became known as Medellín. A few years later the town of Socorro, which had been erected upon the ruins of an Indian pueblo, was transferred to another site upon the banks of an eastern tributary of the Magdalena. Among other towns and cities that were founded during the eighteenth century were Bucaramanga, Cúcuta, and Rionegro.

In 1637, after the aborigines had been subjugated by Juan de Urpin, the city of Barcelona was founded on the Caribbean coast. During the seventeenth and eighteenth centuries members of the Capuchin and Franciscan orders were busily engaged in the conversion of Indians in northeastern Venezuela. Meantime Spanish colonists in Guiana were not only compelled to struggle against the aborigines but also to resist the intrusion of Dutch, English, and French pioneers who proceeded from the European settlements north of the Amazon.

In the vast viceroyalty of Peru the process of settlement often went hand in hand with the exploitation of mines. In 1604, at the base of a group of hills a mining town was erected which was called Oruro. About 1630 silver mines were discovered in a lofty mountain range at Cerro de Pasco. Those mines were subsequently exploited by Indian laborers under the direction of Spanish overseers. Friars of the Franciscan order penetrated the wilderness as far as the Ucayli River. Jesuit fathers built rude missions along the upper tributaries of the Amazon. Both Jesuits and Franciscans explored portions of its upper basin. Throughout that remote region and also in parts of the Peruvian highlands those missionaries gathered the Indians into villages which were called reductions.

In Chile the colonists had to carry on an intermittent warfare with the Araucanian Indians. The Spanish government vainly endeavored to subdue those Indians by the use of Jesuit and Franciscan missionaries. To fortify this attempt the governor of Chile made settlements along the exposed frontier. North of Santiago the towns of San Felipe and Copiapó were founded; and to the south Rancagua, San Fernando, and Los Angeles. Subsequently other settlements were planted near Concepción and upon the island of Juan Fernández.

Explorations were also being carried on east of the Andes. In 1683 colonists from Tucumán founded the city of Catamarca. From time to time daring explorers and Jesuit missionaries ventured into the savage wilderness called the Chaco. In 1779 when Colonel Cornejo was about to relinquish his plan to descend the Bermejo River from Peru, a Franciscan monk continued the trip to Corrientes. Meantime, Jesuit fathers had made explorations along the Atlantic coast south of La Plata River. Early in 1779 an expedition commanded by Juan de la Piedra, which was directed by a pilot named Villarino, discovered the mouth of the Río Negro. Soon afterward Villarino ascended that river some distance and returned to the city of Buenos Aires. Acting under instructions to check the southward advance of the Portuguese, in December, 1726, Governor Zabala of the province of Buenos Aires authorized the founding of a town called Montevideo on the northern banks of La Plata River. Twenty-three years later the Spanish King created the post of governor of that city.

Partly because of the expansion that was taking place, the administration of the Spanish colonies in America was made more complex by changes in the system of audiencias. In 1609 the seat of the Chilean audiencia, which had been at Concepción, was transferred to Santiago de Chile. It was subordinated to the Peruvian viceroy and was given jurisdiction over the territory stretching from the Strait of Magellan northward to the limits of the province of Cuyo. In 1661 King Philip IV decided to establish an audiencia at Buenos Aires with jurisdiction over the provinces of Río de la Plata, Paraguay, and Tucumán. That court was abolished in 1671 but reëstablished in 1783. Three years later the Spanish King resolved to withdraw the islands of Trinidad and Margarita with the continental provinces of Maracaibo, Cumaná, and Guiana from the jurisdiction of the audiencia of Santo Domingo so that he might erect a new tribunal at Caracas. In 1787 he ordered that an audiencia was to be established at Cuzco which should have jurisdiction over that bishopric and possibly over other districts. Meanwhile the Spanish government had created officials named regents who were to preside over colonial audiencias.

The margin note: The Creation of New Administrative Districts

Until the beginning of the eighteenth century the audiencias of Panama, Quito, and Santa Fé de Bogotá were subordinated to the viceroyalty of Peru. In 1717, however, King Philip V provided for the installation of a viceroy at Santa Fé de Bogotá. Six years later that vice-regal office was abolished. Yet in 1739 the King reëstablished the viceroyalty of New Granada. The new viceroy was to have jurisdiction over South America from the northern limits of the audiencia of Panama to the southern boundary of the region controlled by the tribunal at Quito.

Three years later, because of the great distance between Santa Fé de Bogotá and Caracas, Philip V ordered that the governor and captain general of Venezuela should be entirely independent of the viceroy of New Granada. In 1777 Charles III directed that the provinces of Cumaná, Guiana, and Maracaibo, with the islands of Margarita and Trinidad, should be placed under the military and political control of the Venezuelan captain general. The captaincy general of Venezuela was thus definitively established. In the same year the King provided for the creation of the captaincy general of Cuba. The chief executive of Chile, who as governor and president of the royal audiencia had been subordinate to the Peruvian viceroy, was designated a captain general in 1778. Twenty years later by a royal decree this captain general was declared completely independent of the Peruvian viceroy. By that date the captain general of Central America had become practically independent of the viceroy of New Spain.

In 1776 the viceroyalty of the Río de la Plata was created. It included the provinces of Buenos Aires, Paraguay, Tucumán, Potosí, Charcas, Cuyo, and Santa Cruz de la Sierra. A large portion of this territory had been originally assigned to the viceroy of Peru, and a small part had been placed under the captain general of Chile. The capital of the viceroyalty of La Plata was the city of Buenos Aires. On the west it reached the boundary of the captaincy general of Chile, while on the northwest it extended to the limits of the audiencia of Charcas. It stretched from the mouth of the Río de la Plata to the Pacific Ocean, and from the Strait of Magellan to the southern sources of the Amazon.

During the reign of Charles III important reforms were made in the administration of Spain and her colonies. The custom of dispatching to the Indies a special representative of the King was revived. The duty of a visitor general had merely been to place on trial such officials as had been accused of malfeasance in office. Copies of the evidence that was collected with the opinion of the royal agent were sent to the Council of the Indies which was to pass a final judgment on the accused. The most noteworthy of these visitations was that of Gálvez.

José de Gálvez was sent to Mexico in 1765. He was instructed by the King and the Council of the Indies to visit the courts in all the towns and cities of the viceroyalty. He was to inspect the offices and bureaus of the royal treasury with a view to the improvement of their administration. In particular this visitor general was to report upon the feasibility of introducing into Mexico the system of intendancies of the army and the treasury which had been set up in Spain. As a result of his visitation, which lasted until 1771, Gálvez recommended administrative changes that were both special and general in character. Besides a number of minor reforms in the judicial and fiscal régime of Mexico, he urged that a new administrative area, designated a commandancy general, should be carved out of the northern part of the Mexican viceroyalty, that the monopolistic commercial system of the motherland should be abolished, and that intendants of the army and treasury should be established throughout Spanish America. Upon his return home, Gálvez became the minister of the Indies, and thus was able to promote these major reforms.

The Visit of José de Gálvez

Significant administrative reforms accordingly took place in the Spanish Indies. A new subdivision, which was designated the interior provinces of New Spain, was outlined by a decree of August 22, 1776. This decree provided that northern New Spain should be placed under the military and political control of a commandant general who was conceded independence of the Mexican viceroy. On paper this was little less than the establishment of another viceroyalty in North America. In 1804 provision was made that the interior provinces should be divided into two districts: the interior provinces of the east, and the interior provinces of the west. Obviously the intention was to place each of those regions under the control of a separate commander. This reorganization has been interpreted as an attempt by Spain to prevent the disintegration of her vast domain in America.

An official who proved a galling restraint upon viceroys, captains general, and presidents was the intendant. That institu-

The Introduction of Intendants   tion had been tentatively introduced into the Spanish West Indies before the visitation of José de Gálvez to Mexico. On October 31, 1764, a royal decree had provided for the establishment at Habana of an intendant of the army and the treasury. This decree transferred the management of civil, ecclesiastical, and military revenues from the captain general of Cuba to the new official. He was also given charge of such matters as fortifications, royal lands, and contraband trade. Equal in rank to the captain general, the intendant received his instructions from the King with whom he might correspond directly. He presided over the tribunal of accounts at Habana, which in 1775 supervised the finances of Louisiana, Cuba, and other islands.

On September 8, 1777, the King appointed an intendant of the army and the treasury for Venezuela who was to reside at Caracas. This intendant framed the fiscal regulations for the captaincy general, audited its accounts, and appointed treasury officials. He regulated agriculture, trade, and navigation, and for a time acted as a judge in cases relating to commerce. He used the governors of the provinces as his agents in financial affairs. Nominally, at least, he was entirely independent of the other officials of the captaincy general and might correspond directly with the King.

In 1782 an ordinance was issued by the Spanish government which provided for the establishment of intendancies in the viceroyalty of La Plata. As modified in 1783, that ordinance divided the viceroyalty into eight intendancies and some subordinate districts. A chief intendant with supervisory authority was to reside at Buenos Aires, while seven subordinate intendants were to be located at the cities of Asunción, Cochabamba, Chuquisaca, La Paz, Potosí, Salta, and Córdoba, Each intendant was given charge of affairs relating to justice, police, finance, and war in his respective district. The intendant general at Buenos Aires was in reality made an administrative head of the viceroyalty, who for a brief period vied in authority with the viceroy.

In 1784 Viceroy Teodoro de Croix framed regulations for the introduction of intendants into Peru; the viceroyalty was soon divided into seven intendancies. A little later an intendant with direct control over northern Chile was placed at Santiago, while a subordinate intendant was placed in Concepción with jurisdiction over the terri-

THE VICEROYALTY OF LA PLATA SHOWING THE INTENDANCIES
(Adapted from Biedma and Beyer, *Atlas histórico de la república argentina*.)

tory stretching from the river Maule to the Araucanian frontier.

On December 4, 1786, an ordinance of intendants for New Spain was promulgated. This ordinance divided that viceroyalty, including Yucatan and the interior provinces, into three provinces and twelve intendancies. Again, the magistrate located at the capital city was made the chief intendant. Subordinate intendants were located at the cities of Vera Cruz, Mérida, Oaxaca, Puebla, Valladolid, Guanajuato, San Luis Potosí, Guadalajara, Zacatecas, Durango, and Arispe. Intendants were given control over matters relating to justice, police, finance, and war in their respective districts. Each intendant was to see that, justice was administered in his district with rectitude, celerity, and economy. He was to superintend agriculture and industry within his intendancy; he was to oversee markets, inns, bridges, public granaries, the currency, and also the police of towns and cities. He was to supervise public finance within his district: he was given charge of confiscations, prizes, and royal properties; and he was entrusted with the collection of the revenues from tithes, tributes, monopolies, and taxes. He had charge of arsenals and hospitals, and of the inspection, provisioning, and transfer of troops within his jurisdiction. Intendants in other sections of Spanish America were instructed to follow the ordinance of intendants for New Spain as far as conditions would allow.

The Ordinance of Intendants of 1786

About 1790 the system of intendants was extended to Central America. The provinces of the captaincy general were arranged in four intendancies: Chiapas, Honduras, Nicaragua, and Salvador. As the intendancies sometimes coincided in area with existing provinces, in certain parts of Spanish America the new system of fiscal administration encouraged a spirit of particularism within the grand administrative areas.

By the end of the eighteenth century twelve audiencias had been established in America. The most important of these were located at the capitals of viceroyalties or captaincies general but scarcely of minor importance were the tribunals of Quito and Charcas. In the areas subject to those tribunals and, partly because of historic reasons, also in the district under the control of the audiencia of Cuzco, there had gradually developed an autonomous spirit. There were four captaincies general—in the special sense of that term—in the Spanish Indies: Chile, Cuba, Venezuela, and Guatemala or Central America. By 1800 the captains general of Chile, Central America, and Venezuela had become practically independent of the neighboring viceroys. At that date there were four viceroyalties in the Indies: New Spain or Mexico, New Granada, Peru, and La Plata or Buenos Aires.

Political Jurisdictions in Spanish America

Early in the nineteenth century the jurisdiction of the viceroyalty of Peru was extended. A royal decree of July 15, 1802, ordered the transfer from the president of Quito to the Peruvian viceroy of a region designated the commandancy of Mainas, a frontier district where Franciscan missionaries were converting the aborigines. According to the decree, this commandancy included land that was drained by the upper tributaries of the Amazon. It stretched from the Yavarí River to the river Caquetá, and extended on the east to the Portuguese frontiers. On July 7, 1803, a similar royal order was issued which provided for the transfer of the province of Guayaquil from the viceroy of New Granada to the viceroy of Peru. After the colonies had separated from Spain, these administrative decrees caused serious disputes between Peru and Ecuador concerning their boundaries.

An important institution of local government was the cabildo. Colonial cabildos were ordinarily composed of alcaldes or judges, and regidores, who may be compared to aldermen. Ordinarily there were two alcaldes in each cabildo, while the number of regidores depended upon the size of the town. About 1800 the cabildo of Caracas was composed of the captain general ex-officio, two alcaldes, twelve regidores whose offices might be bought or sold, four regidores nominated by the King from Spanish residents of the city, and four other officials whose offices were purchasable. In Spanish-American cities it was the custom to convoke upon extraordinary occasions an open meeting of the cabildo (*cabildo abierto*), which was composed of the town council reënforced by other citizens whom the town officials had invited to attend. A cabildo abierto, which was the assemblage most closely resembling a New England town meeting, might, however, only be held with the consent of the chief executive of the city. The open meetings of town councils became in troublous times the organs through which the views of the colonists might be expressed and training in self-government obtained.

Town and City Government

In time steps were taken to regulate the administration of towns and villages inhabited by Indians who had been civilized by the Spaniards. Attempts were made to preserve the rights and privileges of the caciques. The Indians of a reduction or a village were allowed to select alcaldes and regidores, who had duties similar to those of corresponding officials in Spanish cities. In some parts of the Indies the Spanish government appointed corregidores to reside in Indian towns and villages in order to represent the government and to protect the Indians against oppression.

Almost from the beginning emigration from Spain to Spanish America was under the control of the House of Trade. According to the laws of the Indies, a Spaniard might only embark for America when granted a license and after he had proved that he was an orthodox Catholic.

Emigration to Spanish America

Partly because of the harassing restrictions concerning emigration the number of Spaniards who proceeded to the Indies was very small. In the early nineteenth century a well-informed Frenchman residing at Caracas estimated that not more than one hundred Spaniards annually emigrated to the captaincy general of Venezuela.

Despite prohibitory laws, some foreigners occasionally ventured into Spain's colonies. Hence the Laws of the Indies contained various provisions concerning aliens. In the eighteenth century such persons were permitted to reside in the Spanish Indies upon the payment of a license tax, but they did not enjoy all the privileges of Spanish citizens. Some persons who had been born outside of Spain took advantage of her naturalization laws; for a citizen by naturalization was ordinarily allowed in the Indies the rights of a natural-born citizen. Spain aimed to prevent foreigners from engaging in commerce with her colonists. In 1776 a royal order directed that no foreigners should be permitted to reside in Spanish America or to trade with its inhabitants without a license. Unlicensed foreigners were to be deported immediately.

In accordance with the doctrine that the supreme authority resided in the King, the legislation for Spanish America was promulgated and executed in his name. The laws which early applied in the colonies were those Spanish codes that existed at the epoch of the conquest, supplemented by special laws formulated for the regulation of American affairs. The Spanish codes that lay at the basis of the legal system of the Indies accordingly were the *Siete Partidas,* the *Leyes de Toro,* and the *Nueva Recopilación.*

Spanish Law in America

Other legislation was soon found to be necessary. Special laws formulated by the Council of the Indies regulated various branches of administration. The number and peculiar character of those laws soon created a crying demand for their codification. Philip II accordingly ordered that a code of the laws of the Indies should be prepared, which was to omit what was unnecessary, to make additions where necessary, and to reconcile discords. Various jurists labored upon the compilation which was finally promulgated in 1680. This was styled the *Recopilación de leyes de los reinos de las Indias,* a code which was concerned with both civil and ecclesiastical affairs.

Almost every page of this comprehensive code reveals the humane intentions of the Spanish monarchs. It was composed of nine books which were subdivided into titles. Twenty-four titles dealt with universities, learning, ecclesiastical imposts, the Church, and the Inquisition.

Thirty-four titles dealt with certain administrative matters, such as the audiencias and the Council of the Indies. Sixteen titles were concerned with viceroys, military affairs, corsairs and pirates, and the mail service. Twenty-six titles of a miscellaneous character were concerned with discoveries, colonization, cabildos, repartimientos, public works, mines, banks, and pearl fisheries. Fifteen titles related to such matters as governors, corregidores, alcaldes, trials, appeals, and the residencia. Nineteen titles were devoted to the aborigines: tribal properties, pueblos, tributes, caciques, and personal services. Eight titles dealt with divers matters which were mainly judicial, such as judges, punishments, prisons, mulattoes, Negroes, and vagabonds. Thirty titles, which were mainly fiscal in character, dealt with such things as monopolies, taxes, the mines, the royal fifths, the tribute from Indians, and the sale of offices. Forty-six titles, which were largely commercial, concerned such topics as ports, navigation, the House of Trade, and the freighting of vessels.

When the Laws of the Indies were promulgated Charles III ordered that there should still remain in force all the decrees and ordinances that were not contrary to those laws, and that wherever deficient they should be supplemented by the laws of Castile. With respect to the subsoil resources of the Spanish dominions, in 1783 Charles II promulgated the Ordinances of Aranjuez. Those ordinances provided that the ownership of all mines was inalienably vested in the Spanish King, that they might be exploited by his subjects, and that his rights included not only metals but also fossils, "bitumens, or juices of the earth." In the age of Charles IV the Spanish laws were newly codified in the *Novíssima Recopilación,* which was promulgated in 1805.

The conditions attending the Spanish invasion of the Indies, as well as the crusading zeal of the conquerors, ensured that eventually there would be a species of military organization in America. The epoch at which a system of defense developed in a   Military Defense particular colony depended largely upon local circumstances. With the passing years volunteer soldiers were needed for the defense of encomiendas against slave-hunters, for protection of the frontiers against Indian attacks, or for the garrisoning of ports against the aggressions of pirates. Eventually there were found in each of the important administrative divisions of Spanish America defensive forces composed of regular soldiers and militia. Ordinarily composed of cavalry and infantry, the militia were not placed under arms except for reviews or in time of need. The common soldiers in these forces were largely composed of aborigines or of persons of mixed descent who were trained in the art of war by creoles and peninsular Spaniards. A position as officer in the militia was an honor often purchased by a landed proprietor. It was not until the latter part of the eighteenth century that regulations were framed for the organization of the volunteers in the captaincy general of Venezuela. Speaking of the Venezuelan militia, a keen observer said:

This organization, so nearly approaching that of regular troops, has flattered the ambition of all the distinguished creoles to such a degree, that there is none of them who does not feel honored by being incorporated in it, with the title of officer. An epaulette, on whichever shoulder it may be placed, is coveted by all persons of rank. The Spanish sub-lieutenant wears the epaulette on his left shoulder, the lieutenant on the right, and the captain on both.

Near the end of the colonial régime the number of regular soldiers in the captaincy general of Venezuela was 10,000. The Mexican publicist, Lucas Alamán, declared that at this time the number of regular soldiers in the viceroyalty of Mexico, including the garrisons at important ports, did not exceed 6,000, while, including those soldiers who were employed in guarding the Californias and the Mexican Gulf, the militia numbered 28,000. A Peruvian historian estimated that after the creation of the viceroyalty of La Plata, the veteran forces maintained in Peru did not exceed 6,000, while the militia aggregated 50,000. The English attack on La Plata gave the military spirit there such a stimulus that a citizen soldiery was organized in the city of Buenos Aires, which, in October, 1806, included 6,000 men.

Important harbors such as Vera Cruz, Callao, Buenos Aires, and Cartagena were protected by forts. Small vessels guarded sections of the coast where illicit trade was common or where danger of attack was imminent. During the eighteenth century a few Spanish warships proceeded to the Pacific shores of South America in order to check the contraband traffic. It is surprising that, despite the great distance of the Indies from the motherland, despite the persistence there of thousands of barbarous Indians, and despite the prevalence of graft and corruption, the colonies were kept so long under Spanish suzerainty with so small a defensive force.

During the seventeenth and eighteenth centuries new audiencias were created in Spanish America. The separation of the captaincies general of Chile, of Caracas or Venezuela, and of Guatemala or Central America, from the adjacent viceroyalties was recognized. Certain administrative areas that were thus delimited on paper came to be viewed by the Spanish colonists as definite political entities that possessed a distinctive character. The limitary lines that were vaguely sketched by Spain for her chief colonial administrators in America, which at a later date were ordinarily designated the *uti possidetis* of 1810, suggested the metes and bounds of nations that were yet to be. Regions within the boundaries of viceroyalties, captaincies general, and presidencies later became the habitats of independent nations.

But the only Latin-American colonial institutions which remotely resembled Anglo-Saxon self-governing institutions were the town councils, and especially the cabildos abiertos. Yet even the open town councils furnished no such opportunity for political training as the town meetings of New England. Further, there were in the Latin-American colonies no deliberative assemblies like the colonial legislatures in English America to fulminate complaints against the mother country. Neither were there ever held in either Spanish America or Portuguese America any intercolonial congresses resembling the Albany Congress or the Stamp Act Congress. Faint suggestions that the Spanish colonists should depute agents to represent them in Spain had fallen on deaf ears. The almost complete absence of the machinery of self-government is perhaps the most severe arraignment that can be brought against the colonial régime of the Iberian nations.

SUGGESTIONS FOR FURTHER READING

CHAPMAN, C. E., *Colonial Spanish America,* 1933.
———, *The Founding of Spanish California,* 1916.
CUNNINGHAM, C. H., *The Audiencia in the Spanish Colonies,* 1919.
ENGLEHARDT, Z., *Missions and Missionaries of California,* Vol. I, 1908.
FISHER, L. E., *The Intendant System in Spanish America,* 1929.
———, *Viceregal Administration in the Spanish-American Colonies,* 1926.
HUSSEY, R. D., *The Caracas Company, 1728-1784,* 1934.
LEA, H. C., *The Inquisition in the Spanish Dependencies,* 1908.
MACNUTT, F. A., *Bartholomew de las Casas,* 1909.
MOSES, B., *The Establishment of Spanish Rule in America,* 1898.
PRIESTLEY, H. I., *José de Gálvez,* 1916.
RICHMAN, I. B., *California under Spain and Mexico,* 1911.
THOMAS, A. B., *After Coronado; Spanish Exploration Northeast of New Mexico, 1696-1797,* 1935.
WHITAKER, A. P., *The Huancavelica Mercury Mine,* 1941.
WILGUS, A. C. (ed.), *Hispanic American Essays, A Memorial to James Alexander Robertson,* Chaps. VIII, IX, 1942.
ZIMMERMAN, A. F., *Francisco de Toledo,* 1938.

CHAPTER VIII

SOCIAL AND ECONOMIC CONDITIONS
IN THE SPANISH INDIES

Industry in the Spanish colonies was based largely upon the use of mining, pastoral, and farming lands. Just as the distribution of such lands varied in different sections of Spanish America, so did the occupations vary, and also the kind of life. Subsoil resources in portions of the viceroyalties of Mexico, Peru, and New Granada ensured the development of the mining industry. In other sections, notably in the viceroyalty of La Plata, fertile, grassy plains encouraged the formation of an agricultural and pastoral colony. Occasionally the presence of different kinds of land in the same region made possible the evolution of a varied society. Wherever mining was a chief industry, the advance of the frontier signified not progress along a more or less definite line, as in English America, but the successive establishment of mining camps at sites where the lodes of gold or silver made possible a rapid or ephemeral growth.

The exploitation of mining lands in the Spanish Indies was based upon the concept that the mines were the property of the government, which, without subtracting them from its patrimony, could grant to certain of its subjects a usufructuary right on condition that the outcropping ores or the subsoil should be worked and that a specified share of the product should be contributed to the royal treasury. Mining was thus not a free industry but a fiscal interest of the crown. In the sixteenth century the introduction of the amalgam process, which made use of quicksilver to extract metals from the ore, induced the Spanish government to establish a monopoly of the extraction and sale of that metal. The mining ordinances of Peru, which were codified in the end of the sixteenth century, stipulated that labor in a mine could not be suspended for more than twenty days during the calendar year without the loss of the usufructuary right.

The mode of extracting the ore from gold and silver mines was essentially the same from the Río Grande to the Strait of Magellan. Shafts were first sunk into the earth; then horizontal or oblique galleries were tunneled until pay ore was struck. The metalliferous ore was thrown into bags made out of hides, which Indian laborers carried to the surface on their backs. The ore was then transported to the reduction plant where the metal was separated from the dross. After this was done, the molding of the metal into bars or coins was ordinarily performed in establishments under the direct control of the royal treasury.

In conjunction with a system of royal monopoly the forced labor of the aborigines made possible the extraction of enormous quantities of gold and silver. Aside from the precious metals that remained in the Indies in such forms as money, jewels, silverware, and gold ornaments, there passed to Spain up to 1803, according to the calculations of Humboldt, gold and silver amounting to 4,851,000,000 pesos.

Conditions attendant upon mining operations in Spanish America kept the control of the industry in the hands of a small, prosperous upper class. Entrepreneurs of the silver industry became wealthy, especially in Mexico. A classic example of this tendency was the Conde de Regla, who paved the pathway for his daughter's wedding procession with tiles made of silver. At the bottom of the social pyramid were the poor Indian laborers who, after toiling up crude ladders with heavy bags of ore on their backs, returned at the end of their shift to huts of clay and straw to live in misery and squalor.

Miners had to be supported by the produce raised by agriculturists. In both Mexico and Peru farming towns were eventually interspersed among mining camps. These towns were often founded by the initiative of enterprising individuals. Around such towns there generally settled groups of farmers known as *hacendados* or ranchers. In Mexico many settlers were assigned grants of a square league of land. On such *haciendas* were built large man- **Agriculture and Cattle Raising** sions with barns, stables, and huts for the laborers. The methods of farming employed were very primitive: a bent stick was sometimes used as a plow; and brush from a tree served as a harrow. Before the end of the eighteenth century most of the arable land in Mexico had been taken up. There, as well as in Chile and La Plata, the drift was toward the formation of large estates. Throughout Peru a diversified form of agriculture developed and much attention was devoted to the pastoral industry.

The invasion of America by the Spaniards involved a most significant change in the ownership of real property. A system of communal landholding was gradually displaced by a species of private ownership, which was often affected by the Spanish practice of entail, and which in the case of subsoil resources was subject to the right of the crown.

Agriculture developed slowly in the viceroyalty of La Plata. In 1788 royal orders were issued conceding to its inhabitants the right to export wheat to Spain. But the financial embarrassment of one of the concessionaires interrupted this trade. Hence, in 1793 certain farmhands petitioned the King of Spain, in these words, not to restrict the exportation of their products:

Who doubts Sire, that agricultural land is the source of wealth? The conditions prevailing in this country ensure this: its location in a temperate clime; the good quality of its lands which raise good crops without the use of fertilizers; the boundless territory that it has for cultivation; the disposition of the country people to cultivate wheat and legumes, even without more prospect than is afforded by the consumption of the city of Buenos Aires. Although they live in the midst of such opportunities as we have indicated, yet the laborers of these extensive plains are in a condition of the greatest poverty and depression because they have no market for their products on account of the lack of commerce and exportation.

The most important occupation in La Plata was stock-raising. Cattle left on the pampas by early Spanish explorers and settlers multiplied rapidly. At first only the hides of these animals were utilized commercially. But after Spain modified her commercial policy by the use of registered vessels, the exportation of hides increased so much that it seemed as though the cattle-raising industry would be brought to an untimely end through the extermination of the herds. Up to 1778 the number of hides annually exported from La Plata came to about one hundred and fifty thousand; after that date the number mounted so rapidly that by 1783 it had increased almost tenfold.

The industry of salting meat became important in the last quarter of the eighteenth century. After a beeve was slaughtered, it was hung up and divided into convenient pieces, which were placed in brine. At the end of a month this beef was packed and covered with salt in barrels holding about two hundred pounds apiece. The preserved meat was exported chiefly to Cuba and Spain. In a memorial that the landowners of La Plata presented to the Spanish government in 1794 the estimate was made that 380 vessels of some 350 tons apiece could be laden annually with the meat, tallow, hair, and bones resulting from the slaughter of 450,000 head of cattle, without making any allowance for the hides, and that ample meat products would be left for domestic consumption.

In certain parts of Spanish America the culture of the grape had so far developed that sufficient wine was produced for domestic use. Despite restrictions laid by the home government, vineyards flourished in various sections of Mexico, Peru, and La Plata. During the eighteenth century the viniculturists of the province of San Juan sold wine in the city of Buenos Aires at 58 pesos per barrel. A reform law greatly injured the colonial producers of wine by bringing it into direct competition with Spanish wines, for the high cost of overland freight placed it under a serious handicap.

Coarse cotton and woolen cloth was manufactured in considerable quantities in various sections. In the Platean province of Tucumán huge wooden carts were manufactured. In Paraguay vessels were constructed out of fine native timber. A **Manufactures** tannery was established in the city of Buenos Aires. The ceramic art was practiced in Chile and La Plata. A large silver production and the strength of the religious sentiment caused the art of the silversmith to flourish in many towns of the Spanish Indies. On the northern coast of South America, the inhabitants engaged in pearl-fishing. In the viceroyalty of New Granada the Spaniards took up the search for emeralds. Jewelry of unique design was made out of native materials by craftsmen in various towns and cities. Franciscans in Californian missions taught the Indians to make chairs and tables of a distinctive style. Fine wood-carving was done in the Jesuit missions in Paraguay. Manufactures indeed merged into the handicrafts that border on the fine arts.

As the Spaniards had an inherent dislike for manual tasks, most of the labor in mines or on farms was performed by aborigines or Negro slaves. The trades were ordinarily monopolized by whites and mestizos. In the large cities such artisans as carpenters, hatters, candlemakers, silk manufacturers, saddlemakers, masons, shoemakers, weavers, and silversmiths organized themselves into groups modeled after the trade guilds of Spain. Ordinarily a species of apprenticeship had to be served before a workman could become a recognized artisan. Near the end of the colonial régime there were in Mexico City about one hundred trade guilds.

Among the industries, perhaps mining was the most highly organized. The miners of Mexico were slow to form a protective organization. Not until 1777 did they establish a mine operators' guild that was provided with a court. Two years later ordinances for the mining industry of Mexico were compiled. These regulations recognized that the ownership of bituminous substances was vested in the Spanish crown. Royal decrees issued in 1792 and 1793, however, declared that the proprietors of land where coal was found might freely export it to Spain and also to her colonies.

Partly because of the monopolistic Spanish commercial policy, there was a good deal of coastwise trade between the colonies. Commerce with southern South America could for many **Intercolonial** decades be carried on legally only through Porto Bello. **and Illicit Trade** For two centuries Peruvian merchants forwarded European goods to Chile, while in return that colony sent products of its farms and mines. The government of Peru did not allow articles from either New Granada or La Plata to pass through its territory. During the last quarter of the eighteenth century, however, Spain framed liberal regulations concerning intercolonial commerce. In 1774 Charles III authorized Peru, New Granada, Central America, and Mexico to exchange their own products. Two years later this permission was extended to La Plata. After war broke out with England in 1796, Spain not only allowed freedom of commerce with friendly or neutral nations, but also freedom of intercolonial trade.

Illicit trade with the Spanish Indies was often coupled with the depredations of corsairs who sacked both ships and ports belonging to the Spaniards. About the middle of the sixteenth century bands of French pirates sacked Cartagena, Habana, and Santiago de Cuba. During the seventeenth century English buccaneers had a rendezvous in Jamaica, whence they sallied forth to pillage Spanish towns on the Caribbean Sea and the Gulf of Mexico. In January, 1571, freebooters under the notorious Henry Morgan plundered the city of Panama. The wars of the Spaniards with the Dutch encouraged a series of attacks upon Spanish settlements on the Pacific coast of South America. In 1624 Dutch pirates besieged Callao and looted Guayaquil. When rich prizes became scarce, English buccaneers secured a foothold on the coast of Central America where they engaged in cutting logwood and gradually established a claim to territory.

Foreign commerce with the Indies sprang from clandestine trade. Even in the sixteenth century foreigners covertly transferred goods to Spanish vessels destined for America. When the fleet returned to Spain, these interlopers, as they were called, secured a share of the colonial products in a similar fashion. A conservative estimate made in the end of the seventeenth century was that French trade with the Spanish Indies carried on through Cadiz amounted to 10,000,000 francs per annum. Among the chief articles thus sent to Spanish America were cotton and linen cloth, hats, laces, silks, haberdashery, codfish, saffron, and drugs. In 1698 a trading company, designated the Royal Company of the Pacific, was granted by the French government for fifteen years a monopoly of commerce with the region between Cape Horn and the Río de la Plata and also with the coasts and islands of the South Sea not already occupied by Europeans. This was contrary to the Spanish view that the Pacific Ocean was a closed sea.

In 1701 certain Frenchmen entered into a contract with the King of Spain to furnish all the Negro slaves that might be necessary in the Spanish Indies. As a consequence, the French Asiento Company was formed, which undertook to carry on the slave trade with the Indies under the convoy of French ships. By virtue of this grant, and through licenses granted by the Spanish King, a part of the commerce of the Indies fell into foreign

French
Commerce

hands. A considerable amount of illicit trade was carried on between French merchants and Spanish colonists. French goods were taken to Habana, Panama, Cartagena, Caracas, and Buenos Aires. Armed expeditions were even sent from France to southern South America. In 1703 Philip V of Spain agreed to allow some French vessels to proceed from Spanish ports to the South Sea in order to trade there. By virtue of this permission, the commerce of France with South America greatly increased. Colonial officials in the viceroyalty of Peru became much alarmed over the situation, as will be illustrated by the following passage from one of their protests:

The number of French ships, both great and small, engaged in commerce in this region is so extraordinary that there scarcely passes a day when one of them does not appear on the coast of the South Sea, and when one of them does not enter a harbor on these coasts. It is almost impossible to prevent them from entering because they often unite their forces, and because, as the ports which they approach are unprotected, they intimidate those persons who wish to prevent the disembarkation of their cargoes. They send their armed crews on shore, and thus ensure themselves freedom of commerce by force and violence in such a manner that it is very difficult to prevent fraud, unless indeed his Catholic Majesty should give most stringent orders concerning this contraband trade or should send troops to these coasts in order to pursue those traffickers and to prohibit their enterprise.

The commerce of Europeans with Spanish America had meantime become an issue in the War of the Spanish Succession. In the apprehension that open negotiations for peace might cause Spain to prohibit French voyages to the Indies, the government of France granted permits to vessels bound to South America on pretended voyages of discovery. During the negotiations that closed the war, one of the English diplomats proposed that his country should be granted for thirty years the asiento contract which France had enjoyed since 1701. On her part, France agreed that she would not secure for her subjects in Spain or in the Indies any change in the commercial conditions that had existed in the Spanish dominions during the reign of Charles II. Commerce with the Spanish colonies was technically to be reserved to the mother country.

The Treaty of Utrecht transferred certain privileges that had been enjoyed by France in Spanish America to England. It granted to the English a monopoly of the importation of slaves into the Spanish Indies. It also conceded to the English the **The Treaty of Utrecht** privilege of sending there annually one vessel of 500 tons laden with their goods. Further, it authorized them to establish warehouses at Panama, Cartagena, and Buenos Aires. In accordance with that treaty, agents of the South Sea Company, which came into the possession of this monopoly, were permitted to penetrate Spanish America in order to sell their "black ivory."

This asiento clause furnished the English an entering wedge for trade with the Spanish Indies. It came to be the custom to reload the 500-ton vessel as soon as its cargo was discharged and to unload the fresh cargoes also in colonial ports. English colonies in the West Indies became the entrepôts of smugglers who traded with the adjacent Spanish colonies.

Traders from North America took part in illicit commerce with the Spanish Main. Before Thomas Jefferson penned the Declaration of Independence, whaling vessels manned by hardy New Englanders had pursued their gigantic game in southern waters and had visited ports in various sections of Latin America. As early as 1790 trade was being carried on between the United States and Spanish-American countries. Molasses, coffee, brown sugar, salt, and indigo were being brought into that country, while flour, lumber, and products of the fisheries were being carried to the Spanish Indies. Early in the nineteenth century American vessels were transporting manufactured articles to ports in Venezuela, La Plata, and Chile, and returning to the United States with cargoes of agricultural and pastoral produce.

Modes of transportation in the Spanish Indies varied greatly. As the Spaniards penetrated into the interior of the country, primitive roads were laid out, which frequently followed aboriginal Transportation trails. Along these roads travelers were ordinarily conveyed, after the Spanish fashion, in coaches drawn by horses or mules. In mountainous regions litters were employed for the convenience of passengers. Freight was carried for short distances or over mountain passes on the backs of Indians. In one region or another donkeys, mules, llamas, and oxen were used as pack animals. Huge, lumbering oxcarts were often employed for the transportation of individuals belonging to the lower classes and also for the transport of freight across the plains or the pampas. Trains of pack mules bearing valuable consignments of wines or other produce were occasionally convoyed on long trips to market. Barges, which sometimes were merely rude adaptations of Indian boats, were much used for transportation of freight and passengers by water. The rivers Magdalena, Guayas, Orinoco, and La Plata, with their tributaries, long remained the chief arteries of communication between the seacoast and their respective basins. Oceanic ports were indifferently served by Spanish or colonial ships, and more rarely by vessels of England or France that were surreptitiously trading with the colonists.

In early colonial times communication between the widely separated colonies was extremely difficult, partly because of the enormous distances and the rugged terrain that separated them. Aside from the occasional arrival of a trading ship at a river or ocean port, almost the only mode of communication was by itinerant merchants or Indian couriers. During the seventeenth century, however, a rudimentary postal system for the Indies was organized under the direction of the House of Trade. It was first established in the viceroyalties of Mexico and Peru. It was next introduced into the viceroyalty of New Granada. By 1760 the postal service of that viceroyalty had been extended, on the one hand, as far as Caracas, and, on the other hand, as far as Guayaquil. Bogotá was thus placed into communication with Spain through Caracas and Cartagena. The mail with the motherland was much improved after 1765, when Spain took over the administration of the transatlantic service. Charles III provided in 1764 that one mail packet per month was to leave Coruña for South America. A few years later this service was extended to the city of Buenos Aires.

Commerce with the Indies was for a long period managed by the House of Trade. As that institution was first located at Seville and later at Cadiz, trade with the Spanish colonies was for many decades restricted to merchants of those cities. **Commerce** Until the middle of the eighteenth century the commerce **between** between Spain and Spanish America was regularly car- **Spain** ried on by fleets of merchant vessels which were con- **and Her Colonies** voyed across the Atlantic Ocean to Mexico or to the Isthmus of Panama. At that time direct trade might legally be carried on only between a few ports in Spanish America and certain ports in the Spanish Peninsula.

By a series of measures, however, Spain gradually abandoned certain features of her commercial system. Partly due to the influence of liberal political economists, she abolished the practice of carrying on commerce with the Indies by fleets. These were replaced by registered vessels which were conceded permits to sail from Spain to particular ports of Spanish America. In the third decade of the eighteenth century permission was granted to certain Spanish merchants to carry on direct trade from Spain with Buenos Aires. By a royal decree of October 16, 1765, Spaniards were conceded the right freely to carry on commerce between nine specified Spanish ports and certain ports in the islands of Cuba, Santo Domingo, Puerto Rico, Margarita, and Trinidad. A few years later this freedom of intercourse was extended to Yucatan, Campeche, and Louisiana. About the same time the King swept away some of the restrictions that had long hindered the direct interchange of products between certain regions in the Spanish Indies.

On October 12, 1778, a law was promulgated that marked a significant change in Spanish colonial policy. In addition to the ports specified in the decree of 1765, this law named thirteen other places in the Balearic and Canary Islands and in Spain that might carry on commerce directly with Spanish-American ports. It opened to that trade twenty-four additional harbors in Spanish America, including Buenos Aires, Montevideo, Valparaiso, Arica, Callao, Guayaquil, Cartagena, and Santa Marta. With regard to the payment of duties, those Spanish-American towns and cities were grouped into major and minor ports: the minor ports should collect duties of 1½ per cent upon the value of Spanish products that might be imported, and duties of 4 per cent upon the products of foreign countries; while the major ports should collect duties of 3 per cent upon Spanish and of 7 per cent upon foreign products. Article XXII of this law provided that all goods manufactured in Spain from wool, cotton, and flax should be exempt from duties at Spanish-American harbors for ten years.

In order to promote the development of the national merchant marine, the law further provided that Spanish vessels which were exclusively burdened with national products should enjoy a reduction of one-third of the regular duties, while those Spanish vessels which had cargoes composed of two-thirds national products should enjoy a reduction of one-fifth. This reform law gave the commerce between Spain and her American colonies a great stimulus. It has been calculated that from 1772 to 1776 there entered Buenos Aires only thirty-five vessels, while during each year from 1792 to 1796, there entered that port more than fifty ships. Another liberal measure was adopted because of a war between Spain and England. In 1797 a royal decree was issued providing that, subject to certain restrictions, neutral vessels might engage in the carrying trade with the Spanish Indies.

Spain's policy toward her colonies was not only animated by a spirit of monopoly but also by a spirit of paternalism. At various times

Spain's Policy toward Industry

viceroys were instructed to encourage the cultivation by the Indians of flax and hemp. In the end of the sixteenth century the Spanish government prohibited the extension of grape culture in the Indies. Soon afterward Peruvian viniculturists were further harassed by a prohibition upon the export of their wines. The government thus aimed to prevent Peruvian wines from competing with Spanish wines in colonial markets. Another illustration of Spain's restrictive policy may be found in a decree of 1614 which provided that tobacco might be freely planted in Spanish America only upon condition that that portion of the product which was not consumed in the colonies should be transported directly to Seville. Early in the nineteenth century, wool produced in the Indies was allowed to enter Spain free of duty, but a heavy tax was laid upon its exportation from the colonies to foreign countries.

PORTS OF SPANISH AMERICA AUTHORIZED TO RECEIVE SPANISH SHIPS
IN 1778

Duties upon goods entering the ports of the Indies were levied so as to favor the home producer at the expense of the colonist. Certain colonial products were subjected to duties when exported from the colonies. Here an illustration may be taken from Venezuela. At the end of the eighteenth century products raised or manufactured in Spain which were imported into that colony were so lightly taxed that they were termed free articles. Articles produced abroad but finished in Spain paid imposts aggregating about 12½ per cent before they were landed at Venezuelan wharves. All goods of foreign manufacture paid duties upon entering Spain that amounted to 15 per cent, upon departing for America 7 per cent, and upon arriving there 7 per cent, besides various port dues which further increased the price of all foreign products imported from the mother country. Raw materials that went to supply foreign industries paid heavy duties upon exportation from Spain. These discriminatory taxes gave Spanish manufacturers an advantage.

The consulado was transplanted from Spain to Spanish America. During the sixteenth century consulados were established at Mexico City and Lima, which were patterned after the tribunals at Burgos and Seville respectively. Before the end of the eighteenth century such tribunals had also been established at Vera Cruz and Guadalajara. King Charles IV issued a decree in 1793 establishing a commercial tribunal at Caracas and providing that it should be administered according to the Ordinances of Bilbao. Early in 1794 that King issued a decree creating a consulado at Buenos Aires which was modeled after that of Seville. Among the officials of the tribunal of Buenos Aires were two consuls, nine councilors, a secretary, an accountant, and a treasurer. It acted not only as a court of justice in mercantile disputes but also as a council to promote the advancement of agriculture and commerce. A later order provided that its members should be composed in equal part of merchants and ranchers. Within this consulado some important problems were debated, such as the commercial relations of the viceroyalty of La Plata with foreign nations.

As the aborigines had no metallic tokens, and as the conquerors brought little money with them, the early colonists had to resort to barter in commercial transactions. In certain regions, **Media of Exchange** especially before mints were established, various substitutes were used for money. Silversmiths were soon employed in Mexico to make crude pesos of gold. In 1535 a mint was established at Mexico City which was used for the coinage of silver. Gold dust and bars of gold were used in New Granada as media of exchange. In Peru discs of gold were early coined that were supposed to be of a certain weight and fineness. In that viceroyalty the term peso was also applied to rough discs of silver of a certain size made in its primitive mints and stamped on both sides with a cross.

In the viceroyalty of La Plata, goats, sheep, wool, tallow, and horse-shoes were used instead of money. In Paraguay twenty-five pounds of yerba mate were reckoned as being worth two pesos; while a bundle of leaf tobacco was worth twice as much as twenty-five pounds of Paraguayan tea. Coins or metallic tokens were sometimes made by private citizens. In October, 1618, Philip II ordained that in the pay-ment of duties and imposts the various media of exchange in the Spanish Indies would be considered as specie, but that a colonial unit of value reckoned as one peso of eight reals should be worth only six reals. Thus there was brought into existence the peso *hueco,* which was worth only three-fourths as much as the peso *fuerte,* the current unit of monetary value in the mother country.

Pesos fuertes were first coined in the Spanish Indies during the sixteenth century in the mints of Mexico and Peru. In 1572 a mint was established at Potosí which regularly made cut silver pesos of eight reals that were designated *macuquina* money. At this mint other coins were made of an alloy of silver and copper; such coins were termed *plata sencilla.* As a good deal of counterfeit money was in circulation, during the seventeenth century the Spanish government ordered that a new peso should be coined which should be stamped with the name of the place where it was minted. The new pesos were to bear on one side the arms of Castile and León; and on the other side they were to bear the columns of Hercules with the legend "Plus Ultra" in the middle. These pesos were consequently known as columnar money. In 1622 a mint was set up at Santa Fé de Bogotá, where the money used in northern South America was coined; and in 1750 another mint was established at Santiago de Chile.

The coins which circulated in the Indies in the eighteenth century were the same as those of Spain. Gold coins were the doubloon of eight, which was worth sixteen pesos fuertes; the doubloon of four worth four pesos; and the escudo worth two pesos. Silver coins were the peso, the half-peso, and the real. A silver peso was nominally worth eight reals, while a real was of the value of thirty-four maravedís. At one time or another copper coins were introduced into the Spanish Indies, which were not always received with favor by the lower classes. In addition, other subsidiary coins composed of an alloy of copper and silver were widely used. Partly because of diverse practices pre-vailing at various mints, the coins that circulated in different parts of Spanish America were frequently not of the same standard of weight and fineness.

During the reign of Charles III attempts were made to improve the colonial monetary system. In 1775 an ordinance was issued directing that all cut coins should be collected, taken to the mints, and there transformed into monies of standard weight and fineness. So great was the scarcity of money in certain regions, however, that much macuquina money was still used. Finally by a secret royal order of 1786 the mints of the Indies were directed to coin only gold money of the required legal quality, namely .875 fine, while all silver money that was minted should be .903 fine. Employees in the Peruvian mints— for by this time there was also a mint at Cuzco that made gold coins— were required secretly to swear that they would carry out this regulation. Nevertheless cut silver coins remained in circulation.

Throughout Spanish America means were lacking for the easy transmission of funds from one city to another. As the use of drafts was not common, the payment of balances between colonial merchants living in different sections was generally accomplished by the actual transfer of money. Payments to the crown or to Spanish merchants, however, were made in *plata doble,* which signified money of the legal weight and fineness. As such currency was drained away to Spain, in certain parts of the Indies the standard money of gold and silver appreciated in value. In La Plata at the end of the eighteenth century silver money of the legal standard was at a premium of 3 per cent, while standard gold money was enjoying a premium of 8 per cent.

The revenues collected by royal agents at the opening of the seventeenth century were of a diverse character. Most of the regular income of the royal treasury can be conveniently grouped under four overlapping heads. (1) The payments due to the King as the lord of the land. These included the royal tribute which was paid by the Indians, the King's profits of the coinage carried on at the various mints, and his share of the precious metals and precious stones found or mined in the Spanish Indies. (2) The payments due to the King in his capacity as the patron of the colonial church. These included the first fruits of ecclesiastical benefices, the revenues arising from the sale of indulgences, and the King's share— ordinarily one-ninth—of the tithes that were nominally collected for the support of the ecclesiastical establishment. (3) The payments due to the King from various royal monopolies. Among these were the sale of municipal offices, the sale of land, and the monopolies of tobacco and quicksilver. (4) The payments due to the King from various taxes on trade or on commercial transactions which included the tax on stamped paper; the tax on certain articles of consumption such as spirituous liquors; the *almojarifazgo,* a duty levied on imports into or exports from the country; and the *alcabala,* a percentage tax on the barter, transfer, or sale of a large number of articles.

The Royal Revenues

By the end of the eighteenth century the jurisdiction over disputes concerning the royal revenues had been vested in the intendants. There existed, however, in Buenos Aires, a junta of the treasury composed of fiscal officers of the crown, which was clothed with supervisory authority over the administration of justice not only in matters respecting the royal treasury but also with regard to the financing of the military establishment.

The population in Spanish America was composed of three basic elements, the whites, the aborigines, and the Negroes. These elements were present in varying proportions in different sections. **Population** Whites were found chiefly along the coast and in the capital cities. In general the aborigines were gradually pressed back into the interior; seldom were they exterminated as in the English settlements in North America. Negroes were found mainly in the low, hot, coastal regions.

From the intermixture of white, black, and red races there resulted a large number of ethnic types. Mestizos were the children of Indians and whites, while the offspring of Indians and Negroes were called zambos. Mulattoes were the descendants of Negroes and whites. The children of whites and mulattoes were designated *pardos*. From the crossing of those types there resulted an almost infinite number of blends. White inhabitants were divided into two great castes: the natives of Spain, and the so-called creoles, who were persons of Spanish blood that had been born in the Indies. Peninsular Spaniards took precedence of all other classes. By the favor of the Spanish government, they monopolized most of the important offices in Church and State. Creoles played a peculiar rôle in society. Proud of their American birth, they often viewed the European Spaniards with intense jealousy: sometimes they courted the favor of the office-holding class; and at other times they displayed signs of resentment toward their rulers. With a fondness for intrigue, the creole caste constituted the volatile, uncertain element in the colonial population—the class most receptive to new ideas.

Numerous festivals furnished the inhabitants of colonial towns and cities opportunities to display their sentiments. Shortly after the conquest of the Aztec Empire was assured, the Spaniards **Festivals** began to celebrate their triumph by a stately procession —the *paseo del pendon*—through the streets of Mexico City, a procession in which the royal standard was displayed and which was later imitated in other Spanish-American capitals. During Holy Week, upon the arrival of an archbishop or a viceroy, or when the oath of allegiance was taken to a new monarch, other festivals were held. A Bohemian naturalist named Thaddeus Haenke, who was in Lima in 1793, thus described the procession of Corpus Christi, which he beheld passing through its streets:

The procession was composed of the religious orders of St. John, the Mercedarians, the Augustinians, and the Franciscans. After them came the archbishop and the ecclesiastical cabildo; the pallium was carried by the guard of halberdiers of the viceroy. The procession was closed by a regiment of dragoons and another regiment of infantry. . . . The festival of Corpus Christi was the only occasion upon which there was conveyed out of the cathedral the magnificent tabernacle which in this city is of great richness. Some of the Negroes who assisted in this ceremony had decorated their heads with the feathers of cocks; others, who bore shields ón their arms and cudgels in their hands, pretended to be engaged in a species of combat. To the rhythm of the music certain Negroes would strike the shields of other Negroes, who would respond in a similar fashion. Nor did these poor people lack the cleverness to act like clowns. Thus they forgot their serfdom and displayed various customs of their native land.

Masquerade festivals were favorite diversions in Mexico. In the seventeenth century the Jesuits arranged a masquerade procession for the students at their college, which meandered through the streets of the capital city for two hours. Some of the students arrayed themselves in facetious and ridiculous fashion as Negroes, Negresses, mulattoes, cowboys, and monkeys. Others masqueraded as Montezuma, Cortés, or grandees of the Spanish court. A triumphal car adorned with representations of castles and lions bore maskers representing the King and the Queen of Spain and the heir presumptive to the throne. On the occasion of the marriage of the Spanish King in 1691, the students of the University of Mexico arranged a masked festival. "Many persons who participated in it were on horseback; some persons appeared in the guise of such animals as eagles or lions; while others were attired in the costumes of different nations as Turks, Indians, and Spaniards." In another masquerade that occurred on November 6, 1800, the men were dressed as women, while the women were attired as men. Upon the processional car, which was adorned with a portrait of St. John, a richly attired stripling recited some chosen words of praise.

In connection with such celebrations cockfights were often held, especially in Mexico and Peru. Another favorite pastime of the lower classes was pelota, which was a species of handball.
Amusements   With the passing years, however, in many places the Spanish sport of bullfighting came to be the most popular public amusement. Sometimes these performances were arranged by an empresario by virtue of a contract with the cabildo of the particular town or city. At other times a town council arranged directly for the construction of an amphitheater to serve as the scene of the sport. Ordinarily places were reserved in these arenas for public officials, while the rest of the space was left for the people. After the officials had

taken their places, the bullfighters, who might be either amateurs or professionals, entered, and the sport of teasing and tiring and killing the bulls was on. A band of musicians or buglers ordinarily announced the changes of the scene by a blast on the bugles or by a strain of music. In certain cities of Spanish America the populace was profoundly dissatisfied whenever *corridas de toros,* as bullfights were designated, were not provided at more or less regular intervals. After fulfilling other requirements, candidates for the doctor's degree at the University of San Marcos were required to arrange for bullfights at their own expense for the entertainment of their preceptors. Spacious arenas were erected in the large cities for the accommodation of the lovers of this sport. In the last decade of the eighteenth century Manuel Tolsa, a noted architect and sculptor who had recently arrived from Spain, designed a bull ring for the capital of Mexico that was modeled after the great amphitheater at Madrid.

In the upper circles of colonial society there was no small amount of luxury. Accounts are still extant of the expensive, ceremonious journey of a viceroy from Cartagena to Bogotá in 1797, which, including charges for beer and snuff as well as port wine, Luxury cost over $35,000. In a description of the reception hall in the remote, viceregal palace at Santa Fé de Bogotá were mentioned the following furnishings: "a tapestry of damask with curtains of the same material at the doors and windows, a dais covered with damask and adorned with gold braid," a chair lined with velvet and adorned with silver trimmings, a table trimmed with silver and covered with a damask cloth, two full-length gilded mirrors, two gilded tables, a gilded clock, and two portraits of the King and Queen of Spain in frames of crystal. In the antechamber were several portraits of other members of the royal family; while in the hall where the audiencia assembled there were two pictures of scenes in the life of the Virgin Mary, one of the Assumption, and another of the mystery of the Immaculate Conception.

An inventory of the property of a minor royal official of the viceroyalty of Buenos Aires mentioned more than a dozen Negro slaves; two finger rings worth 100 pesos apiece; a gold chain with a rosary worth 150 pesos; two mate bowls with drinking tubes and two trays, "all made of silver with gold adornments," which cost 700 pesos; "a silver table with feet shaped like those of a goat"; a set of diamonds, which were valued at 700 pesos; and "a coach made in Holland, with its glass windows, linings, pear-shaped ornaments, iron axles . . . two pair of mules, and gilded harnesses," which had cost more than 1,400 pesos.

So far as economic matters were concerned, until near the end of the eighteenth century Spain followed a policy of monopoly and paternalism. Like other colonizing nations of Europe, she viewed her colonies as estates that were to be exploited for the benefit of the mother country. As will be later indicated, her oppressive fiscal régime provoked much discontent, especially among the lower classes. With regard to social life, the Spaniards naturally undertook to transplant Iberian customs to America. This process was hindered, however, because of the vast extent of the terrain that had to be settled by a limited number of immigrants, and also because of the presence of an aboriginal race which had to be exterminated or civilized or driven into the wilderness. Nevertheless, society in towns and cities was essentially Spanish, with adaptations to suit the particular environment, and modifications because of the presence or the assimilation of an aboriginal element. Here and there, in torrid regions along the coast, Spanish-American colonial civilization was affected by the presence of Negro slaves. And in both northern and southern South America the allegiance of the colonists to Spain was being slowly undermined by the insidious neglect of law not only by their own administrators but also by contraband traders of foreign nations.

SUGGESTIONS FOR FURTHER READING

EXQUEMELIN, A. O., *The Buccaneers of America*, 1924.

HARING, C. H., *The Buccaneers in the West Indies in the XVII Century*, 1910.

HUMBOLDT, F. W. H. A. VON, *Political Essay on the Kingdom of New Spain*, 1811.

————, *Personal Narrative of Travels to the Equinoctial Regions of America during the Years 1799-1804*, Vol. III, 1908.

KOEBEL, W. H., *The Romance of the River Plate*, Vol. I, 1914.

MARKHAM, C. R., *History of Peru*, 1892.

MOSES, B., *South America on the Eve of Emancipation*, 1908.

————, *Spain's Declining Power in South America*, 1919.

PONS, F. R. J. DE, *Travels in South America*, Vol. I, 1807.

SCHURZ, W. L., *The Manila Galleon*, 1939.

SIMPSON, L. B., . . . *The Repartimiento System of Native Labor in New Spain and Guatemala*, 1938.

ULLOA, G. J. and A. DE, *A Voyage to South America*, Vol. I, 1806.

WHITAKER, A. P., *The Huancavelica Mercury Mine*, 1941.

WILGUS, A. C. (ed.), *Colonial Hispanic America*, 1936.

CHAPTER IX

THE CULTURE OF COLONIAL SPANISH AMERICA

The varied culture that developed in the Spanish Indies depended upon such factors as the section of Spain from which the settlers came, the policy adopted toward the aborigines, the prevailing economic order in a particular colony, and the relative influence of the impact from foreign lands. Something, too, depended here, as in the case of other colonial societies, upon the policy pursued by the metropolis. In innumerable particulars conditions in the Spanish colonies were curiously mediæval; or to be more exact a series of attempts was made to graft an Iberian civilization upon an Indian stem. Here little else can be done than to describe the more or less prevailing pattern of colonial Spanish-American civilization.

Special attention must be paid to the imposing machinery of the church establishment. In the Spanish Indies the Roman Catholic Church was a colonizing factor and a civilizing influence of the greatest importance. By means of the right of patronage, the Spanish crown exercised an ascendancy over the Church in the American colonies. Indeed it is almost correct to say that the King of Spain was, in most ecclesiastical matters, the Pope of the Spanish-American Church.

The Spanish monarchs clung tenaciously to the right to make ecclesiastical appointments in the New World. A concordat between the Papacy and Spain in 1783 avowed that there never had been any controversy concerning the appointments which had been made by her kings to vacant archbishoprics, bishoprics, and benefices in America. Yet the right of patronage was jealously watched by the Spanish government through its agents in the Indies. This policy may be illustrated by a passage from the instructions of King Charles III to the Marquis of Loreto who, in 1783, was made viceroy of La Plata:

Church and State

I also charge you to take special care with respect to the conservation of the right of royal patronage. You should guard the patronage yourself and make certain that neither regular nor secular prelates infringe upon that right, except in the manner that has been made known to the kings of Spain by the Holy Apostolic See and as has been specified in the regulations issued concerning it. You should not allow the prelates to intermeddle—as some of them have attempted—in matters that do not pertain to them. You should be careful to inform me of the prebends and benefices which have been vacated and to which appointments must be made. I shall see that they are promptly filled, while you should make certain that the churches are furnished with the necessary service.

Ecclesiastical divisions in Spanish America did not always coincide with the administrative areas. After the captaincy general of Chile was carved out of the viceroyalty of Peru, the bishop of Santiago remained for some time a suffragan of the archbishop of Lima. By the authority of the Spanish King or of a colonial magistrate provincial councils were occasionally held in dioceses of Spanish America. After being endorsed by the respective bishop, the resolutions of such councils had to be approved by the chief executive or by the audiencia of the particular district before they were put into force. If the local authorities disapproved them, they had to be sent to the Council of the Indies to be sanctioned or disallowed. Though no bishops or archbishops from America were present at the Council of Trent, the Pope held that the Indies were under its jurisdiction. A royal order, however, and not a papal brief, made known that the dispositions of the Council of Trent should be applicable throughout the American dominions of Spain.

With the progress of the Catholic faith in America, the Church gradually developed its own organization. By the end of the eighteenth century there were six archbishoprics in Spanish America: Santo Domingo, Mexico, Guatemala or Central America, Lima, Charcas, and Santa Fé de Bogotá.

Ecclesiastical Organization

At that time, the archbishopric of Santo Domingo was composed of five bishoprics: Caracas, Cuba, Cuayaba, Louisiana, and Puerto Rico. In the archbishopric of Mexico there were eight dioceses: Puebla, Valladolid, Oaxaca, Guadalajara, Mérida, Durango, Linares, and Sonora. There were three suffragan bishops in the archbishopric of Guatemala. The archbishopric of Santa Fé de Bogotá was composed of four bishoprics. Among the nine episcopates in the archbishopric of Lima were Arequipa, Quito, Cuzco, Panama, and Santiago de Chile. In 1802 another bishopric was created in the missions of Mainas. The archbishopric of Charcas was composed of five dioceses, namely, La Paz, Tucumán, Santa Cruz de la Sierra, Asunción, and Buenos Aires. After the creation of the viceroyalty of Buenos Aires, the diocese of Tucumán was divided into the bishopric of Salta and the bishopric of Tucumán. The latter episcopate was enlarged by the addition of the province of Cuyo which was separated from Chile. In 1803 an archbishopric was established at Caracas that included the provinces within the captaincy general of Venezuela.

In each cathedral church there was a chapter composed of a variable number of canons, prebendaries, and other dignitaries who formed the bishop's council. When an archbishop died, the respective chapter governed the archbishopric through a vicar. The spiritual jurisdiction in certain cities was controlled by a cabildo of ecclesiastics. In towns and cities where there was no chapter or ecclesiastical council the spiritual authority was ordinarily exercised by vicars who had delegated powers. In accordance with Spanish custom, ecclesiastics in the Indies enjoyed a number of special privileges. Perhaps the most important of these was the privilege of being tried before an ecclesiastical court instead of before a civil court.

The activities of the secular clergy were supplemented at many points by the work of the regular orders. Augustinians, Dominicans, Franciscans, and Jesuits proceeded to the Spanish Indies in large numbers. Many of them took up their residence in towns and cities where they founded religious houses and came into possession of large properties. In Lima, at the end of the eighteenth century, there were three Augustinian monasteries, four Dominican monasteries, three Franciscan monasteries, and three houses of Mercedarians, besides four convents and other establishments that were held by pious women. Members of the regular orders were either dependent upon certain ecclesiastical provinces of Spain or else they were organized into provinces distinct from those of the mother country. According to canon law, monks were not permitted to become parish priests, but necessity compelled several popes to allow them to become curates. In the middle of the eighteenth century this practice was modified so that only two parishes in an ecclesiastical province could be filled by friars.

The Regular Clergy

Many members of the Dominican and Franciscan orders were engaged in converting and civilizing the aborigines. Little Brothers of St. Francis planted missions in Mexico, Venezuela, and New Granada. Members of the Company of Jesus founded missions and schools from Mexico to Chile. The most distinctive work of the Jesuits was done in the interior of South America.

After penetrating La Plata as far as Córdoba, they reached the wilderness inhabited by the Guaraní Indians. Authorized by a royal order, in the seventeenth century they proceeded to the basin of La Plata River. The center of their system in Spanish South America was at Candelaria. By the middle of the eighteenth century they had established more than thirty reductions near the rivers Uruguay, Paraná, and Paraguay. The mission buildings were erected after the same pattern: a square plaza was surrounded by houses upon three sides; on the remaining side was built a church, with the homes of the Jesuit fathers and other structures. Lands were cultivated after a communistic method. In and about the missions were gathered thousands of Indians who were trained by the Jesuits in manual arts and catechized in the Catholic faith.

Under the paternalistic rule of Jesuit fathers, however, the Indian neophytes were deprived of initiative, if indeed they were not actually kept in a servile condition. The administration of the missions was completely controlled by the friars. As the mild-mannered Indians of the reductions were captured by marauding Portuguese half-breeds and by Spanish slave-hunters, the crown conceded the Jesuits the right to arm their neophytes. The region of the *misiones,* as it was called, accordingly became little else than a Jesuit empire, which served as a bulwark for the Spanish colonists against the expanding Portuguese.

As Charles III suspected the Jesuits of engaging in intrigue against his rule, in 1767 he ordered that they should be expelled from his dominions. The missions consequently fell into decay, the Indians relapsed into barbarism; and the Jesuit seminaries were transferred to other orders. At this policy some Spanish Americans felt much aggrieved.

Meantime, the inquisitorial tribunals located at Cartagena, Lima, and Mexico City had not been idle. They regularly published the edict of faith and staged *autos-de-fé* in those cities. In less important cities the Holy Office was represented by resident commissioners. Besides, it had inspectors who scrutinized books, images, and manuscripts. The inquisitors persistently strove to prevent infringements upon ecclesiastical or inquisitorial privileges, and to extirpate bigamy, sorcery, and heresy. The sessions of the tribunals of the Holy Office were secret: its punishments were chiefly fines, confiscations, exile, and death. After a sentence of death had been rendered, the hapless victim was handed over to the secular arm for punishment.

The inquisitorial court located in New Granada wasted much time in vain quarrels with secular officials. During the period extending to 1761 the tribunal at Lima judged some 370 persons, 40 of whom were burned at the stake. A prominent Mexican historian has estimated that, exclusive of a score of persons who were tried by various agents of the Inquisition before a court was established at the city of Mexico, during the period from 1570 to 1803, that tribunal placed on trial 932 persons. Nevertheless, it seems that the effect of Spanish-American inquisitorial tribunals upon the purity of the Catholic faith was slight, while the stifling influence which they exerted upon intellectual life was not inconsiderable.

Edicts of the Council of the Inquisition prohibiting the circulation of certain books were regularly published in the Spanish Indies. The officials of inquisitorial tribunals soon undertook to examine book-shops and to inspect the literature introduced into their respective juris-dictions. In the viceroyalty of Mexico almanacs and catechisms were printed by permission, but all other writings had to be submitted to examination by the civil and ecclesiastical authorities before they could be published. The University of San Marcos was not even allowed to print, without a license, the addresses delivered on the arrival of a new viceroy. All booksellers were required to furnish inquisitorial officials with lists of the volumes offered for sale and to keep on hand a catalogue of prohibited books. A censorship was enforced at seaports so that the importation of prohibited books might be prevented. At Buenos Aires a commissioner of the Inquisition was much disturbed over certain wall papers that were decorated with figures of Cupid, Venus, and Hercules.

Early in the nineteenth century the Council of the Inquisition issued a formal decree ordering the suppression of an Italian satirical poem directed against "the vices and follies of kings and courts." All Jewish, Mohammedan, and Protestant religious books were strictly prohibited, and also the writings of such authors as Addison, Defoe, Montesquieu, Rousseau, Voltaire, and Tom Paine. A French agent who resided in Venezuela declared that "every work written by a heretic, or which treats in common language of matters in controversy between the Catholics and modern heretics is entirely prohibited. . . . Every work that treats only of love, of magic, of witchcraft, or of superstition, is deservedly condemned." Nevertheless, prohibited books were treasured by leading colonists. In 1809 the mattress of a Peruvian monk was found to be stuffed with seditious literature.

Elementary education was largely in the hands of religious orders. Wherever a monastery was built, a school for boys was founded. Children of the upper classes were there taught to recite the catechism, to read Latin, and to write in Spanish chirography. In some places poorly educated servants were entrusted with the task of teaching the children of the vicinity. The education given to girls was ordinarily inferior to that of the boys; for they were not supposed to need other instruction than that which concerned household duties. By the close of the eighteenth century, in the city of Buenos Aires some primary schools were supported by the municipality. With regard to primary instruction in that viceroyalty a contemporary expressed the following low opinion:

Elementary and Secondary Education

In the schools there was no system of education. The teachers of elementary subjects were for the most part ignorant and vicious; their entire teaching was what might have been expected of them. Each child read the book that he could bring from home: profane histories, the narratives of which neither they nor their masters understood, books of chivalry, or similar productions. The most pious fathers gave their sons ascetic works to read which were products of an ill-digested piety or lives of the saints which had been written by authors without judgment and which were consequently laden with apocryphal passages and pretended miracles.

Secondary education eventually developed in academies located in the capital cities. In their halls attention was paid to what may be styled general culture, as well as to theology. Some of these institutions ultimately blossomed into universities.

During the early seventeenth century a Franciscan friar in La Plata endowed the University of Córdoba. The faculty of that university was eventually grouped in two colleges: the college of arts, which furnished instruction in such subjects as logic, physics, and metaphysics; and the college of theology, which gave instruction in scholastic and moral theology. On the other side of the Andes, the University of San Felipe at Santiago de Chile, which was founded in accordance with a royal decree of 1738, had an irregular and languid existence until 1759, when Valeriano Ahumada became its rector. Patterned after the University of San Marcos, it furnished a great stimulus to intellectual life in the captaincy general of Chile. By a royal decree of 1721 the College of Santa Rosa at Caracas was transformed into a university. In the eighteenth century that university had nine chairs: Latin, philosophy, theology, music, ethics, medicine, canon law, civil law, and the Scriptures. One of the most notable educational institutions in the Spanish Indies was located at Chuquisaca on the remote Andean plateau. The University of San Francisco Javier, which was founded there upon a preëxisting college in 1624, became a great center of legal study. The official language in all of these universities was ordinarily Latin. The mode of instruction was by texts and lectures, which were occasionally varied by disputations. In conjunction with the universities that had been founded in the sixteenth century, these institutions served the colonists as nurseries of learning.

Early in the eighteenth century the University of San Marcos at Lima had almost two thousand students. A French engineer who visited it declared that its training was good in scholasticism but weak in science. A Spanish scholar reported that "the university makes a stately appearance without, and its inside is decorated with suitable monuments." The main subjects of study were medicine, philosophy, theology, Spanish grammar, civil and canon law, and certain Indian languages. According to viceregal orders, "zambos, mulattoes, and other low castes" were excluded from its cloisters. Some of its teachers were paid out of the income from an endowment that had been set apart for the university by Viceroy Toledo, while those friars who served as professors were paid from funds of their respective religious orders. Professorial chairs were filled as the result of competitive contests between learned candidates, which sometimes provoked bitter litigation. A Peruvian historian states that near the end of the eighteenth century the University of San Marcos had given the degree of master of arts to six candidates, while it had conferred the degree in medicine on twelve persons, the degree of doctor of theology on 134, and the degree of doctor in civil and canon law on 164.

At the Royal and Pontifical University of Mexico, in addition to theology, civil and canon law, and science, some attention was paid to aboriginal Mexican dialects. Its chief administrative official was a rector who was elected annually by the secret vote of a board of councilors. The constitution of the University of Mexico—first printed in 1668 and reprinted in 1775—contained instructive provisions concerning both students and teachers. It stipulated that the teachers should hold their classes a full hour by the university clock or hourglass: one half of the period should be spent by the teacher in dictating and writing; and the other half in explaining in Latin what had been dictated. If the subject was very difficult, the explanation should be in the Spanish language. Severe penalties were to be imposed on teachers who were frequently absent from their classes. This constitution also contained instructive regulations concerning the life of the students. They were to dress in simple costume; they were "not to wear colored stockings, nor gold lace, nor embroidery, nor long hair, nor toupees"; and the students who wore gowns or cassocks were not to be admitted into classes unless they wore caps. Students attending the various colleges were expected to wear distinctive academic costumes.

The degree of bachelor of arts was granted after a successful three years' course of study. Every candidate had also to defend a thesis and to pass an oral examination. A bachelor might secure the degree of licentiate in law after four years of additional study. In theology or medicine a similar degree was to require additional study extending over three years. The doctor's degree in theology or law or medicine might be secured only on petition by a candidate already holding the degree of licentiate in the respective subject. In the preamble of the constitution of the University of Mexico the statement was made that by 1775 the degree of bachelor had been granted to no less than 29,883 persons, and the degree of doctor had been conferred upon 1,172. Among these were mentioned alumni who had risen to places of distinction in the Old World as well as in the New: archbishops, bishops, judges, governors, lawyers, physicians, teachers, inquisitors, corregidores, missionaries, and royal councilors.

At an early date in the history of the Spanish Indies viceroys and captains general were prohibited from allowing books to be printed within their respective jurisdictions unless they had been censored. A Catholic catechism for the Indians, the first book printed in the viceroyalty of Peru, was published in Lima by permission of the audiencia in 1584. The earliest printing in certain parts of Spanish America was done under the direction of the Jesuits. In 1738 a religious tract was issued from the printing press of the Society of Jesus at Santa Fé de Bogotá. It seems that the Jesuits set up a printing press at Córdoba in 1765 and printed the first book upon that press in the following year. Upon granting the Jesuits permission to use this press the Peruvian viceroy stipulated that they should not print any book about the Indies without a special license from the King, nor should they print any book concerning the law or the Indian languages unless it had been examined and censored. The printing press earliest used in the city of Buenos Aires was brought there about 1780 from the former Jesuit college at Córdoba.

Printing and Journalism

During the eighteenth century certain gazettes were printed intermittently in Mexico. The first number of the *Periodical Journal of Santa Fé de Bogotá* was published in 1791. In the following year a journal with a similar name was issued from the press of the Jesuits at Ambato in the presidency of Quito. As early as 1790 there began to appear the *Erudite, Commercial, and Economic Diary of Lima*. A year later the initial number of the epoch-marking *Peruvian Mercury* was printed in the same city. In 1801 the first number of the *Mercantile Telegraph* was issued at Buenos Aires. Because of the English occupation of Montevideo, in 1807 a journal styled the *Star of the South* was published there in English and Spanish. The *Gazette of Caracas* issued from the press in 1808. In general such periodicals contained only a small amount of news besides brief notices concerning the activities of public officials.

Literature in Spanish America during the seventeenth and eighteenth centuries was of a varied character. In his old age Francisco Núñez de Pineda wrote an instructive account of his experiences while held a captive by the Araucanian Indians. By a defense of Gongorism, a literary style of affected elegance which was flourishing in Spain, in a book published in 1694, Juan de Espinosa Medrano, a professor at the University of Cuzco, made himself widely known in South America. Another Peruvian named Pedro de Peralta Barnuevo Rocha y Benavides was an erudite poet, dramatist, and essayist. In addition to scientific studies, a Mexican professor, Carlos de Sigüenza by name, wrote a poem that

Literature of Spanish America

narrated the story of the miraculous appearance to an Indian of the Virgin of Guadelupe. A Mexican beauty who assumed the veil under the name of Sor Juana Inés de la Cruz produced three volumes that included plays and poems.

Though some poems were written in Santa Fé de Bogotá, the special claim which the viceroyalty of New Granada had to literary distinction during this period was because of its historical productions. Of those only two may here be mentioned: *Historical News,* which was written by a Franciscan named Pedro Simón; and the *General History of the New Kingdom of Granada,* which was penned by Lucas Fernández de Piedrahita. The first poet born upon the soil of Argentina was Luis de Tejada, who composed an autobiographical poem entitled *El peregrino en Babilonia* and also some mystical poems which have only recently been edited. Manuel José de Labarden was the author of a poem entitled *Oda al Paraná,* which suggestively described the course of that great river as it meandered through the pampas.

The Spaniards brought to America virulent epidemic diseases. Consequently the Indians were scourged with smallpox, measles, and tuberculosis. Though members of religious orders frequently acted as physicians, the science of medicine was not well served. Though a hospital was built in the Mexican mining town of Zacatecas in the sixteenth century, two centuries later there were no physicians in that place. A physician who practiced medicine in two other places besides the capital of Mexico composed a curious treatise about the physical marvels and medical problems of that country. In Peru the art of medicine was in so backward a state that a century after Harvey had made known the circulation of the blood the professors of medicine at the University of San Marcos were still ignorant of that discovery. Chile was perhaps better served by the medical profession than Peru, for a number of doctors who practiced there were graduates of French or Spanish medical schools. In 1756 a Frenchman was installed in the chair of medicine of the University of San Felipe. Veterinarians, who were supposed to be able to make "divers cures of diseases and of old sores of horses," were allowed to practice medicine in the capital of the viceroyalty of La Plata. In 1805 the first vaccinations against smallpox were performed in that city; the vaccine was soon used to render the Indians immune.

Scientifically, the Spanish Indies furnished a vast field of observation for scholars of Europe. During the reign of Charles III an Aragonese officer named Azara, who had been engaged in the delimitation of the possessions of Spain and Portugal near La Plata, made a careful study of the fauna of that region. His *Description and History of Paraguay and the Río de la Plata* contained such valuable zoölogical observations that he has been styled the Buffon of Spain. Antonio de Ulloa, a Spanish scholar who accompanied a French expedition that undertook to measure the length of a degree on the equator, recorded scientific facts as well as his observations concerning the oppressed aborigines. In 1760 there arrived in Santa Fé de Bogotá a learned Spanish monk named José C. Mutis, who soon undertook to make a botanical survey of New Granada. With the aid of artists, draughtsmen, and collectors he labored for many years on a scholarly study of the flora of that viceroyalty.

Francisco Caldas, a gifted creole pupil of Mutis, also achieved distinction. Caldas gathered astronomical, geographical, and meteorological data concerning New Granada. He composed a notable work about the influence of the climate upon vegetation. He made a valuable study of Peruvian bark. José A. Alzate, a Mexican priest, was an astronomer and mathematician of note who observed the transit of Venus across the sun and published scientific articles in his gazettes of literature. In the Peruvian viceroyalty, Hipólito Unanue recorded some *Observations on the Climate of Lima*. The German savant, Alexander von Humboldt, declared that Alzate and Mutis were the two greatest scholars of America, and that Mexico had taken up the study of exact science with an ardor that he had not witnessed "in the great university centers of the Old World."

On December 20, 1619, an eclipse of the moon was observed at Huehuetoca, which lay on the same meridian as Mexico City, by an engineer named Enrico Martínez. Data obtained from observations of the same eclipse in Europe were carefully studied by Fray Diego Rodríguez of the University of Mexico, who reached the conclusion that the Mexican capital was 101° 27′ 30″ west of Paris, a calculation which excelled in accuracy the result reached by Humboldt about a century and a half later. During the eighteenth century the results of the astronomical observations of Antonio León Gama, a learned scholar of Mexico, were published in a Parisian scientific journal.

The study of comets was begun in Mexico in the seventeenth century. In 1681 Carlos de Sigüenza y Góngora, who was professor of cosmography and mathematics at the University of Mexico, published a tract assuring his countrymen that comets were not a manifestation of divine wrath. A Flemish nobleman named Martin de la Torre, took issue with Sigüenza, whereupon the latter responded with a pamphlet entitled *Mathematical Bellerophontes against Astrological Chimeras*. When the erudite Father Kino took part in the debate against Sigüenza, the latter retorted with a declaration of faith in his *Philosophical and Astronomical Book* by which he challenged the accuracy of Kino's data. This debate, which was precipitated by the tracts of a Mexican professor, was probably the earliest instance in America "of a clash of intellects in public print on a scientific question."

Progress in the mining industry was much facilitated by the enterprise of Bartolomé Medina, a miner domiciled at Pachuca, Mexico, who in 1557 introduced, if indeed he did not discover, the use of an amalgam of salt and quicksilver for the reduction of ores. The use of mercury quickly spread beyond the frontiers of New Spain; about 1590 it was being employed in the extraction of silver from the ore of the famous silver hill at Potosí. Nevertheless, the study of natural science in the Spanish Indies was much hampered by the trammels imposed by religion and scholastic theology. In the eighteenth century the Peruvian, José Eusebio Llano Zapata, undertook to investigate nature for himself in the great book that lay before his eyes. The result of his researches was a learned work entitled *Historic-Physical and Critical-Apologetic Memoirs of South America.* He published only one tome of this treatise, which was an intensive study of the natural history of Peru and in particular of its mineral kingdom.

In the captaincy general of Chile, scientific investigation often took a practical trend. Much time was spent in the study of the processes employed in the extraction of metals from ores. In 1787 Joaquín Granados introduced into the Chilean mining industry a machine for pumping water out of flooded mines. In 1803 Dr. Juan Egaña prepared an encyclopædic report concerning Chile that contained an illuminating survey of its mineral wealth. Egaña was discerning enough even to record the existence of deposits of coal there. Near the end of the eighteenth century Thaddeus Haenke introduced a chemical process by which nitrate of soda could be readily separated from the deposits found in the coastal region of Tarapacá.

Private houses in the Indies ranged from rude, fortified huts of timber or adobe to beautiful homes on the prevailing Spanish model. Elaborate residences often showed the influence of the prevailing styles of public buildings. Public architecture was **Architecture** a curious and fascinating mixture of styles, which varied according to the purpose of the particular structure, the epoch when it was erected, and the accomplishments of the architect and his workmen. In early colonial times attempts were made to construct chapels in the degenerate Gothic or early Renaissance style of contemporary Spain. The Plateresque style, a decorative type of architecture that developed in Spain, was widely employed. Moorish influence may also be traced, as in the use of glowing colors, iridescent and bright-colored tiles, and richly ornamented ceilings.

During the seventeenth century, when Baroque architecture spread from Italy into the Iberian Peninsula, that florid style had a great vogue in the Spanish Indies. The façades and interiors of many churches and chapels, especially in Mexico, show the dominant influence of that style. Baroque was also widely used in the construction of residences in Mexico and in western and southern South America. During the eighteenth century the exceedingly decorative form of Baroque designated Chirrigueresque spread from Spain to Spanish America. In later colonial days chapels and churches and missions in the colonies were often constructed by Indian laborers with or without the aid of Spanish masters. These buildings were ornamented in varying styles and frequently bore traces of the handiwork of aboriginal craftsmen. In regions where Indian decorative art had flourished, motifs were occasionally borrowed from Aztecan or Incan art. In the Platean city of Córdoba a fusion took place between the Andalusian Baroque and elements of the architectural technique of the Calchaquian Indians.

Cathedrals or churches that were under construction during a long term of years often showed the influence of different styles of architecture. The largest church edifice in the New World, the cathedral at Mexico City, which was erected from designs drawn by the court architect of Philip III in the form of a rectangle some four hundred feet in length, is in general a massive example of Baroque architecture. It also shows the influence of other styles. Another example of Spanish Baroque is the stately cathedral at Puebla, Mexico, which was constructed after a plan drawn by the architect of the Escorial.

The walls of Spanish-American churches and cathedrals were sometimes adorned with canvases attributed to Spanish painters. A European artist occasionally took up his residence in a colonial city. For the most part, however, the products of the brush in the Spanish Indies were by local talent. Colonial painting was ordinarily little else than the imitation or the adaptation of Spanish religious painting. In the capital of Peru the portraits drawn of prominent personages by native artists were ordinarily harsh and lacking in grace. A notable school of painting, however, developed in Quito. The most talented painter of that city was a mestizo, Miguel de Santiago by name, who had visited Spain and been influenced by Velásquez, Zurbarán, and El Greco. Among Santiago's best works were a painting depicting the birth of St. Augustine that adorned the cloister of the Augustinians in Quito, and two portraits of friars that hung on the walls of the Franciscan monastery there. His nephew, Gorivar González, who followed in his footsteps, painted, among other pictures, "The Prophets" on pillars of the Jesuit church in the same city. Thus a Quitian school of painting came into existence.

In Mexico City a coterie of men cultivated the fine arts. Their most distinguished representative was Sebastián de Arteaga, whose finest painting perhaps was "The Betrothal of the Virgin." On December 25, 1783, acting on the recommendation of a group of Mexican patrons of art, Charles III issued an order approving the establishment of the Academy of San Carlos of New Spain, which was to be devoted to the study of painting, sculpture, and architecture. The King endowed this academy and pre- Painting, Sculpture, and Music sented to it a valuable collection of plaster casts.

Sculpture in the Spanish colonies was also a derivative art which was stimulated by religious sentiment. Cathedrals and churches were sometimes adorned with carved chair stalls or with fine wooden carvings of saints. Splendid examples are the wonderful carvings in the choir of the church of San Francisco at Cuzco and in the cathedrals at Lima and Mexico City. In the city of Quito there were artists in carving who excelled in making polychrome wood sculptures. During the seventeenth century an Indian known as Caspicara (Manuel Chili) gained fame as the sculptor of such wood carvings as "The Assumption of the Virgin" and "The Impression of the Wounds of Saint Francis." A distinguished sculptor in wood was Baltazar Gavilán of Lima, who was the son of a Spaniard by an Indian woman. Among other figures, he carved the gruesome wooden skeleton representing death which Augustinian friars carried through the streets of Lima on Holy Thursday. In Peru polychrome wood statuettes of Christ and the Virgin were made by the thousands.

In both Peru and Mexico statues were occasionally cast in bronze. The most artistic bronze statue fabricated in colonial times was the equestrian statue of Charles IV that was cast in Mexico City in 1802. The molten metal was poured into a mold that had been fashioned by Manuel Tolsa. This colossal statue, which now stands at the head of a beautiful boulevard in the Mexican capital, bears an inscription stating that it had been erected as "a monument of art."

Indigenous music was naturally influenced by the music introduced by the conquerors, and, in certain sections, it was also affected by that of Negro slaves. In the viceroyalty of Peru the Incan musical scale of five tones was eventually modified by the addition of *mi* and *si*, so that the scale became a septachord. Aboriginal music was also improved by the use or adaptation of such European instruments as oboes, trumpets, and violins. Indians soon undertook to imitate Spanish musical compositions. Echoes of the Aragonese *jota* or of popular Andalusian dances found their way into the folksongs of the Peruvians. At times there was mingled with these elements an African strain; thus eventually a hybrid form, which was often styled "creole music," was brought into existence. During the eighteenth century Italian music had considerable influence upon the musical compositions that were

enjoyed by the upper classes in certain colonies. As in the case of
Baroque architecture, so also in regard to theatrical performances,
which were originally more or less religious in character, the activities
of Jesuit priests served to multiply such spectacles. Dramatic compositions in Peru took their themes and motifs largely from the contemporary Spanish drama. A remarkable drama called *Ollanta* appeared
there, written in the Quechuan idiom, which faithfully depicted some
features of Inca life. Critical scholars, however, have demonstrated that
though this drama was presumably based upon a rudimentary, pre-
Columbian dramatic work, it had been much influenced by the productions of Spanish dramatists.

During the last decades of the eighteenth century discontent with
Spanish rule was manifested in various sections of the Indies. In 1780

**Early
Uprisings
in Spanish
America**

two Frenchmen who were living in Chile, Antoine Berney
and Antoine Gramuset, with the aid of a Chilean named
José Antonio Rojas, formed a conspiracy to promote the
independence of that captaincy general from Spain. The
Frenchmen sketched a program for a revolution and
framed a constitution for a republic, but the plotters were denounced
to the audiencia of Santiago. The "three Antonios" were arrested,
secretly tried, and condemned to deportation. In November, 1780, an
insurrection was started in Peru by Tupac Amaru, a descendant of
the Incas. He denounced the Spanish government because of its heavy
taxes and other oppressive measures. As a large horde of Indians joined
him, some Spanish officials were terrified. But the Peruvian viceroy
gathered a large army, marched against the Indian rebels, and put
them to rout. Tupac Amaru, who seems to have planned the creation
of an independent state, was captured, and in May, 1781, he was bru-
tally executed in the plaza of Cuzco.

During the same year, provoked by oppressive monopolies and taxes,
the inhabitants of certain towns in the viceroyalty of New Granada
rose in revolt. The *comuneros,* as they were known, were so successful
that they proposed terms of settlement to the viceregal government—
terms which urged the abolition or modification of the multiform
taxes. Colonial officials agreed to those terms, the tumult was stilled,
but the Spanish government did not fulfill the pledges that had been
given to the rebels. In 1795 and 1797 uprisings occurred in the neighboring captaincy general of Venezuela which were partly caused by
foreign influence. The chief conspirators were thrust into dungeons,
while others escaped to the West Indies. The captain general stated that
these conspirators aimed to subvert Spanish rule and to establish an
independent republic.

In certain parts of Spanish America a keen interest was shown in literature and science. Two great centers of the intellectual awakening were Peru and New Granada. At their capitals literary societies were formed which were largely composed of creoles. In both of these viceroyalties literary journals were founded which disseminated new ideas and aspirations among the people. Even more important than such tendencies were influences that emanated from foreign lands. The doctrines of the Spanish physiocrat Jovellanos became known in certain parts of South America. The botanical research of Mutis spread an intellectual leaven among the inhabitants of New Granada.

The Intellectual Awakening

A special stimulus was given to some Spanish colonists by doctrines that emanated from France. Noteworthy among the French works that influenced intellectual leaders in various sections of the Spanish Indies were the following: Montesquieu's *Spirit of the Laws,* which praised the division—as he understood it—of executive, legislative, and judicial authority in the English Constitution; Voltaire's essays, histories, and poems which criticized the Church and other institutions in witty phrases; Raynal's *Philosophical and Political History of the Indies,* an informing volume about colonization that denounced priests and princes; and Diderot's *Encyclopedia* which epitomized the results of free inquiry. Rousseau's *Social Contract,* published in 1762, which discussed the evils of monarchical rule and formulated the doctrine that governments were properly based upon compacts, also conveyed the leaven of revolt to certain Latin Americans. To dissatisfied colonists in Spanish and Portuguese America the French Revolution served as a great example. Some Spanish-American leaders were profoundly influenced by its philosophy. Through a Spanish translation published at Santa Fé de Bogotá in 1794 by an enterprising creole named Antonio Nariño certain colonists in northern South America became familiar with the classic theories of liberty which the French National Assembly had embodied in its "Declaration of the Rights of Man and of the Citizen."

Nor was England without an influence in certain quarters of South America. Prominent creoles of Buenos Aires read Adam Smith's *Wealth of Nations.* An unauthorized expedition led by Commodore Popham and General Beresford against the viceroyalty of La Plata in 1806, which resulted in the temporary conquest and occupation of Montevideo and Buenos Aires by English redcoats, weakened the prestige of Spain. This invasion afforded some of her colonists training in the art of war. Further, as the invaders lowered the duties on certain kinds of merchandise imported into the viceroyalty of La Plata, they encouraged there a spirit of opposition to the Spanish commercial system.

To certain South Americans the United States served as a grand exemplar. A Chilean journalist named Camilo Henríquez aptly said that the revolution of the thirteen colonies against England had lighted the sacred fire of liberty upon the American continent. North American revolutionary philosophy had a widespread influence in South America. Early in the nineteenth century a Spanish translation of the Declaration of Independence of July 4, 1776, was circulated in the viceroyalty of New Granada and the captaincy general of Venezuela. The Articles of Confederation were translated into Spanish and circulated in that captaincy general and also in the viceroyalty of La Plata. Spanish versions of the Constitution of the United States were circulated in La Plata, Venezuela, and New Granada.

The last decades of the Old Régime in Latin America were marked by violent expressions of discontent with economic conditions, especially among the lower classes. In both Spanish and Portuguese America revolutionary doctrines emanating from France and the United States were being secretly introduced. Yet it would be a grave mistake to believe that this philosophic leaven was affecting the majority of the population in any section of Latin America. These doctrines scarcely seem to have spread beyond the circles of well-educated and ambitious creoles in important towns and cities. A spark was needed from without to ignite the powder magazine in the Spanish colonies.

SUGGESTIONS FOR FURTHER READING

BAXTER, S., *Spanish-Colonial Architecture in Mexico*, Vol. I, 1901.
COESTER, A., *The Literary History of Spanish America*, 1916.
KILHAM, W. H., *Mexican Architecture of the Vice-regal Period*, 1927.
LANNING, J. T., *Academic Culture in the Spanish Colonies*, 1940.
MOSES, B., *The Intellectual Background of the Revolution in South America*, 1926.
———, *Spanish Colonial Literature in South America*, 1922.
———, *Spain Overseas*, 1929.
NAVARRO, J. G., "Art in Ecuador," *Bulletin, Pan American Union*, Vol. LIX, pp 800-817.
PRIESTLEY, H. R., *The Mexican Nation*, 1923.
Twenty Centuries of Mexican Art, 1940.
WHITAKER, A. P. (ed.), *Latin America and the Enlightenment*, 1942.
WILLIAMS, M. W., *The People and the Politics of Latin America*, 1942.

CHAPTER X

REVOLUTIONARY MOVEMENTS IN THE EARLY NINETEENTH CENTURY

The immediate cause for the separation of the Latin-American colonies from their motherlands was Napoleon's policy toward the Iberian Peninsula. Animated by a notion that the best mode of securing a permanent peace was to isolate England from the continent of Europe and to close all European ports to her commerce, early in the nineteenth century the French Emperor adopted a policy of intervention toward Spain and Portugal. For several years Napoleon duped Spain and secured her support in his schemes against her neighbor. In 1801 he obtained from Charles IV and from his all-powerful minister, Godoy, Prince of the Peace, the promise of coöperation in his designs. A secret clause in the Treaty of Fontainebleau, which was signed by France and Spain in October, 1807, provided that French soldiers should be permitted to march through Spain to the Portuguese frontiers. This treaty also provided for the dismemberment of Portugal.

At that juncture the monarch of that country was the demented Queen Maria I. Her son, Prince John, whose wife was a daughter of Charles IV named Carlota Joaquina, was acting as regent. In July, 1807, Napoleon had informed the Portuguese ambassador at Paris that his country must close her ports to English commerce. At the court of Lisbon the French envoy made three specific demands: all Portuguese ports should be closed to English commerce; all Englishmen residing in Portugal should be detained; and all British property there should be seized. Those demands frightened the Regent. He yielded to the first demand; but, fearing the wrath of England, he hesitated to grant the other demands. Napoleon therefore seized Portuguese vessels in French ports. On October 22, 1807, a secret treaty was signed between the English secretary for foreign affairs, George Canning, and the Portuguese minister in London, which provided that, if the Regent should decide to leave Lisbon to escape French soldiers, England was to furnish a squadron to escort the fugitive prince to his American dominions.

Upon receiving news of the approach of French invaders, the members of the dynasty of Braganza prepared to flee. On November 29,

1807, a Portuguese fleet bearing the royal family sailed from the Tagus. Escorted by a British squadron under Admiral Sir Sidney Smith, the Portuguese vessels crossed the Atlantic Ocean, and ,in January, 1808, they reached Bahia. Regent John signalized his arrival by promulgating a decree which opened Brazilian ports to foreign vessels. The fugitive dynasty arrived in Rio de Janeiro in March, 1808. The seat of the Portuguese government was thus transferred from Lisbon to a colonial capital.

Flight of the Braganza Dynasty

The administration of Brazil was soon reorganized. The viceroy was displaced by Regent John. He selected secretaries and councils to aid him in the government. In other captaincies than Rio de Janeiro he permitted the captains general to continue in the exercise of large powers. In April, 1808, the Regent promulgated a decree which removed the prohibition upon the free exercise of industries. Six months later he issued another decree that established the bank of Brazil. Such measures constituted an important step toward independence.

About the time that Junot's soldiers swarmed into Portugal, Napoleon intervened in Spanish affairs. Intrigues of the heir apparent, Ferdinand, Prince of the Asturias, against his father, furnished the French Emperor with a clew to the situation. Early in 1808 French troops seized fortresses in northern Spain. On March 19, alleging that his health would no longer permit him to act as sovereign, Charles IV abdicated his throne in favor of the heir and declared that Prince Ferdinand should be recognized as king in all the Spanish dominions.

Napoleon Intervenes in Spain

That prince at once informed Murat, the lieutenant of Napoleon, that he had received from his father the domains of Spain and the Indies. Ferdinand expressed his earnest desire to strengthen the ties which united Spain with France. Nevertheless, Murat, who soon entered Madrid with a French army, carefully refrained from recognizing Ferdinand as King. Although the former King soon regretted his abdication and declared that this act was null, yet on April 10, at the request of the idolized prince, the Council of the Indies addressed to important royal officials in America a note announcing that the Spanish crown had been transferred to Ferdinand VII.

The French Emperor thwarted this policy by his machinations at Bayonne. After an uprising took place in Madrid against Murat's soldiers, Napoleon induced the ex-King to renounce by treaty his sovereign rights. The treaty stipulated that the integrity of the Spanish monarchy should be preserved, that the prince whom Napoleon would enthrone at Madrid should be independent, and that the boundaries of Spain should not be altered. This act of renunciation was embodied in a decree of May 8, 1808, by which Charles announced that he had given to Napoleon the sovereignty over Spain and the Indies, and by which he ordered magistrates throughout the Spanish dominions to obey the French. On May 10 Ferdinand agreed to a treaty with Napoleon in which he declared that he endorsed his father's abdication, and stated that, as Prince of Asturias, he relinquished his right to the throne of Spain. Ten days later the Council of the Indies addressed to the chief officials in Spanish America documents conveying the news that both Charles IV and Ferdinand VII had renounced the Spanish crown.

Napoleon had meanwhile formulated plans for the government of the Spanish dominions. Shortly after the deposition of Ferdinand VII, Murat issued an ordinance which invited Spanish notables to assemble in Bayonne. At that city on June 6 Napoleon issued a decree announcing that his brother Joseph, who had been ruling over the Kingdom of Naples, was King of Spain and the Indies. A few days later, when the notables met, they recognized Joseph as their King. On July 7 this Assembly adopted, with slight modifications, as the Constitution for Spain a Napoleonic statute which declared that the Spanish crown should be the patrimony of the male descendants of Joseph Bonaparte. This charter stipulated that the Spanish-American colonies were to enjoy the same rights as the Peninsular provinces. In the presence of the Spanish dignitaries, on July 8 King Joseph swore to observe the Constitution and to preserve the integrity and independence of Spain. The new ruler used the title "King of Spain and the Indies."

Joseph Bonaparte Proclaimed King

Reports of the startling events in Spain were transmitted to the Indies in various ways. Soon after the deposition of Ferdinand, Murat sent the news of the fall of the Spanish dynasty to South America. Napoleon dispatched vessels from French ports which carried letters, proclamations, and instructions to Spanish officials in the colonies. By these measures and by means of emissaries, accounts of the change of dynasties in Spain were sent to Mexico, New Granada, Venezuela, Chile, and La Plata.

Meantime, however, significant changes took place in Spain. Reports of the abdication of Charles IV, of the enforced renunciation of the Spanish crown by the beloved Ferdinand VII, and of the installation of Joseph, *el rey intruso,* provoked a national uprising—the beginning of the war of the peoples. As if by magic, from Oviedo to Granada, juntas, or local councils, sprang up which assumed the functions of government, and declared that they ruled on behalf of Ferdinand VII. The junta of Seville dispatched commissioners to announce to Mexicans and South Americans the steps which had been taken against Napoleon and to solicit contributions for the support of the Spanish cause.

The changes in Spain provoked significant reactions in the New World. Reports about the abdication of Charles IV evoked many expressions of loyalty to Ferdinand VII. He was formally proclaimed King in Mexico City, Caracas, Bogotá, Chuquisaca, and Buenos Aires. In some cities contributions were made by the colonists for the support of the war against Napoleon. News of the formation of juntas in the motherland created among the creoles a desire to imitate that example. In July, 1808, the cabildo of Caracas presented a memorial to the captain general proposing that a governmental junta should be established in that capital. During the next month, the viceroy of New Spain issued a proclamation to the inhabitants which announced that a junta in the capital city had pledged itself to obey no orders of the French Emperor. A junta which was convoked by the viceroy of Buenos Aires decided that the seditious papers brought by an emissary of Napoleon should be cast into the flames. Nevertheless, not all of the colonial leaders were at heart loyal to Spain. Occasionally an original thinker argued that the deposition of Ferdinand VII had broken the link which joined Spain to the Indies.

Effects of These Changes

A Central Junta that had been established at Seville issued a decree on January 30, 1809, which announced that the American colonies were an integral part of the Spanish monarchy. It further declared that the colonists were entitled to representation in the government. Each viceroyalty and captaincy general was invited to sent delegates to the Cortes. In certain cities of Spanish America those proceedings merely added fresh fuel to insurrectionary flames.

At Chuquisaca, on May 25, 1809, President Pizarro was deposed; and the audiencia assumed the supreme military and political authority. In July citizens of La Paz in the same presidency deposed the intendant, organized a junta, and drew up a declaration that they would defend to the utmost the independence of their native land. Led by Pedro Murillo, those insurrectionists, who nevertheless protested their loyalty to the captive prince, waged a brief and unsuccessful war against Spanish soldiers. On August 10 a band of colonists deposed Ruiz de Castilla, president of the audiencia of Quito, incarcerated him, and created a junta of government which proclaimed its allegiance to Ferdinand. During the following month a junta at Santa Fé de Bogotá selected Camilo Torres to frame a memorial of grievances for presentation to the Central Junta. It appears that several conspirators schemed to start a revolution at Caracas in December, 1809. In the same month a conspiracy was unearthed in Valladolid, Mexico, which evidently had as its object the formation of a junta that should rule the viceroyalty on behalf of Ferdinand VII.

LATIN AMERICA ON THE EVE OF THE REVOLUTION

(From Robertson's *Rise of the Spanish-American Republics*)

The patriot government of distracted Spain soon took an important step. In January, 1810, the Central Junta created a Regency to which it transferred the supreme authority. In the following month the Regency addressed a proclamation to the inhabitants of Spanish America which invited them to choose delegates to a national Cortes. It announced that Spanish Americans were now elevated to the dignity of freemen; that they would no longer be viewed with indifference, vexed by cupidity, and destroyed by ignorance; and that their destinies did not depend upon ministers, governors, or viceroys, but upon themselves. Such statements stimulated the liberal spirit that was spreading among the creoles in Spanish America.

On April 19, 1810, after commissioners had arrived from Spain with orders that the Regency should be recognized, an extraordinary cabildo in Caracas deposed Captain General Emparán and created a governmental junta which professed to act for King Ferdinand. The junta soon deported Emparán and other Spanish officials, established certain administrative bureaus, and undertook some political reforms. It not only issued a manifesto disavowing the authority of the Spanish Regency but also addressed a proclamation to Spanish Americans asserting that Venezuela had taken a place in the ranks of free nations. It also issued an address to cabildos at Spanish-American capitals which asked them to join the insurrectionary movement.

After the viceroy at Buenos Aires had incautiously published a manifesto announcing the victories of French arms in Spain, in May, 1810, a cabildo abierto in that city replaced him by a provisional junta which was ostensibly formed to preserve the authority of Ferdinand VII. On July 20, 1810, an extraordinary cabildo at Santa Fé de Bogotá established a junta which declared that it would not abdicate the sovereign rights of the people to any other person than the unfortunate Ferdinand. In the following month a junta was formed at Quito. Rumors of those events, as well as the unpopularity of Acting Captain General García Carrasco, promoted dissatisfaction in Santiago de Chile. On September 18, 1810, García Carrasco was displaced by a governmental junta which proclaimed its fidelity to the captive King. The sequel will indicate that, despite the protests of fidelity to Ferdinand VII, in certain parts of the Indies venturesome leaders of these movements had visions of independence from Spain.

A sketch of the Great Revolution in Spanish America may rightly begin with the movement initiated in Mexico by Miguel Hidalgo, the curate of Dolores. Around his insurrectionary banner, which depicted the Virgin of Guadelupe, the patron saint of the Indians, there gathered a large number of dissatisfied Mexicans who were mainly aborigines or mestizos. His followers were

Hidalgo in Mexico

successful against royalist soldiers in various encounters: after a stubborn defense, they sacked the prosperous mining town of Guanajuato; they captured Valladolid, the capital of the province of Michoacán; and on October 30, 1810, they almost destroyed a small force of royalist soldiers in a bloody conflict on the Monte de las Cruces near Mexico City. If the curate had next led his forces against the castle of Chapultepec, he might have captured the capital and ended the revolution in triumph.

Hidalgo failed to do so, however, and his revolt soon encountered an increasing opposition. Unfortunately for his cause, he never promulgated a definite scheme for the government of emancipated Mexico. He merely made an announcement that he intended to convoke a Congress which should enact wise laws. Furthermore, his revolt encountered the stubborn resistance of the Church and of many persons belonging to the wealthy and influential classes. The Inquisition stigmatized the curate of Dolores as a libertine, a heretic, and a rebel. It declared that every person who supported him, who failed to denounce him, or who spread revolutionary doctrines, would be fined and excommunicated.

Viceroy Francisco Venegas took energetic steps to suppress the insurrection. He ordered the experienced and skillful military commander, Félix María Calleja, to defeat the rebels. Though the Indian hordes who followed the banner of Guadelupe greatly outnumbered the royalists, they were no match for the trained royalist soldiers. On November 6, 1810, General Calleja checked Hidalgo at Aculco. At a bridge across the river Calderón, near Guadalajara, on January 17, 1811, Spanish soldiers decisively defeated the revolutionary army. Shortly afterward while traveling through the desert plains near Monclova, Hidalgo and other leaders were captured by a discontented compatriot who had deserted the patriot banner. After being incarcerated and summarily tried, early on the morning of July 30, Hidalgo was shot by the royalists.

José María Morelos, a capable priest, now assumed the leadership of the revolution. In October, 1810, Hidalgo had appointed him commander of the insurrectionary forces in the territory south of Mexico City. Morelos dispersed the royalists in a brief campaign and revolutionized a region which extended to the mountain ridge that surrounded the capital. Meantime another leader named Ignacio Rayón had convened a meeting of revolutionists at Zitácuaro. There, on August 19, 1811, they drew up an act which announced the establishment of a supreme national junta composed of three men. Its members undertook to support the rights of the Church and of Ferdinand VII. They issued a circular asking revolutionary chieftains to take an oath of allegiance to the "Supreme Governmental Junta of America." Though appointed a member of this junta, Morelos held aloof from it, apparently because he disliked its declarations of fidelity to the Spanish King.

On March 18, 1812, a Cortes which the Regency had convoked at Cadiz promulgated a Constitution for Spain. This fundamental law declared that sovereignty was vested in the Spanish nation which included all Spaniards in both hemispheres. Roman Catholicism should be the national religion. The government was to be a hereditary monarchy. Executive authority was vested in a King, while legislative power belonged to the King and the Cortes. A unicameral legislature was to include deputies chosen by Spanish citizens in Spain and the Indies. Each province in the Spanish dominions was to be administered by a political chief selected by the King. An important article provided that all Spaniards should have the right to express their political ideas. The Regency declared that every Spanish subject should consider the Constitution of 1812 as the fundamental law of the monarchy. In May, 1812, the Cortes decreed that an oath of allegiance should be taken to this Constitution throughout Spain's dominions in the Old World and the New. On October 30 of that year the chief magistrates of the viceregal government of Mexico solemnly swore to observe it. Prisoners entitled to amnesty were set free.

Political Changes in Spain and Mexico

Meanwhile, Morelos had invited Mexican revolutionists to meet at Chilpancingo. At his instance the provinces which had been liberated from Spanish rule elected representatives to an assembly, while he chose deputies to represent districts that were still under Spanish rule. To that Congress on September 14, 1813, Morelos made an address expounding his political ideas. He suggested that Mexico should be declared free and independent of Spain and of all other nations, that Roman Catholicism should be the state religion, and that a government should be created based upon the sovereignty of the people. Under his inspiration, on November 6, 1813, Congress framed a Declaration of Independence from Spain. This declaration announced that because of the circumstances existing in Spain, the Mexicans had recovered the exercise of their usurped sovereignty and that the bonds uniting them to the Spanish throne were forever dissolved. It stated that Congress had power to enact laws, to negotiate treaties with foreign nations, and to make concordats with the Papacy. Only the Roman Catholic religion should be tolerated. All opponents of independence were to be considered as guilty of treason.

Though Ferdinand VII was released from captivity early in 1814, his restoration to the throne of Spain did not recall Spanish-American revolutionists to their allegiance. At Apatzingan, on October 22, 1814, the Mexican Congress adopted a provisional Constitution which set up a rudimentary government, yet, so far as a large part of Mexico was concerned, that organic law remained a paper Constitution.

About a year after it was promulgated, while guarding the flight of Congress, Morelos was captured by royalists. Jubilant soldiers took him to Mexico City, where they cast him into a dungeon. After the most expeditious trial in the annals of the Inquisition, he was unfrocked, condemned to death, and shot in the back. Subsequently a brave Navarrese named Mina strove to promote the emancipation of Mexico with a band of followers mainly recruited in the United States. He failed, however, to enlist the sincere coöperation of Mexican guerrillas. After some initial successes, he was captured, and sentenced to the same ignominious fate as Morelos. In Mexico the star of the Revolution seemed to have set.

The precursor of the South American Revolution was Francisco de Miranda. An energetic native of Caracas, who became a Don Quixote of liberty, Miranda spent a large part of his mature life in attempts to interest certain nations in the cause of Spanish-American independence. He had just persuaded the English government to equip an expedition to revolutionize South America, when the Spanish uprising against Napoleon began. That movement and an alliance which England soon formed with the Spanish patriots against the French Emperor caused Miranda to relinquish the hope of English aid in the emancipation of Spanish America. In December, 1810, he returned to his native land.

On July 5, 1811, largely as a result of his influence, the Congress to which he had been elected a delegate formally announced that Venezuela was independent. In their Declaration of Independence the Venezuelans denounced the policy which the government of the Spanish patriots had adopted toward their country. They said that the policy of Spain had forced them out of a position of political ambiguity. They spoke of the imprescriptible right of a people to destroy any political agreement that did not fulfill the great purpose for which governments were established. The "representatives of the United Provinces of Venezuela"—as they styled themselves—solemnly declared that those provinces were independent states. Venezuela was the first of the revolted Spanish colonies formally to declare through delegates assembled in a Congress that she was independent of the motherland.

Venezuela Declares Independence

The next step of the Venezuelans was to frame a Constitution for the new state. After considerable discussion concerning the type of government to be established, on December 21, 1811, Congress adopted a federal plan. Some of its clauses had been patterned after the United States Constitution, while others showed the influence of the French

Declaration of the Rights of Man. Yet the first Constitution of Venezuela was scarcely put into operation. In July, 1812, largely as the result of a terrible earthquake, which ruined cities, dispirited the patriots, and encouraged the royalists, the patriot commander, General Miranda, who had been made dictator of Venezuela, capitulated to the Spanish commander, General Domingo Monteverde. This commander treated the inhabitants of the former captaincy general as the denizens of a conquered province. Miranda was betrayed to the Spaniards by embittered compatriots.

A greater captain than Miranda was Simón Bolívar. The scion of a distinguished family of Caracas, who had been educated in Europe, he was living on a plantation in the beautiful valley of Aragua when the sudden death of his young bride induced him to forsake agriculture for politics. In 1810 he became an outspoken champion of independence. After Miranda's betrayal he succeeded in escaping from the toils of Monteverde and fled to the West Indies. He soon decided to join the revolutionists in the viceroyalty of New Granada.

In the city of Cartagena, on November 11, 1811, a revolutionary junta adopted a Declaration of Independence from Spain. Those revolutionists declared that the cession of the crown to Napoleon had severed the bonds that joined the Spanish King to his people. They stigmatized as imprudent and provocative the measures which the patriot government of Spain had adopted toward New Granada. They declared that, using the imprescriptible rights which they had acquired as a result of Napoleon's usurpations, they erected the province of Cartagena into a free and independent state. On July 16, 1813, a Congress of delegates from Cundinamarca, the central province of New Granada, which assembled at Santa Fé de Bogotá also adopted a Declaration of Independence. Even before that declaration was framed, a Congress of delegates from other provinces had formed a confederate Constitution for the United Provinces of New Granada.

Early in 1813 Bolívar entered the military service of the junta seated at Cartagena. He soon drove the Spanish soldiers from the lower Magdalena Valley. He then marched against the royalists in Venezuela. At Trujillo on June 15, 1813, he issued a proclamation of war to the death against the Spaniards; in August he triumphantly entered his native city. About two months later an extraordinary cabildo of that city proclaimed him Liberator. Forced to leave Venezuela because of the fierce campaigns of the royalist commander, Boves, the Liberator was next sent against the province of Cundinamarca which was maintaining an organization distinct from that of the other provinces of New Granada. Bolívar soon forced the dictator of Santa Fé de Bogotá to capitulate. Early in 1815 the seat of the government of New Granada was fixed at that city. After a strong expeditionary force dispatched by Ferdinand VII had landed in Venezuela, Bolívar embarked at Cartagena for the West Indies. Under the command of General Morillo, a veteran of the Peninsular War, by the middle of 1816, the royalists had completed the reconquest of New Granada and Venezuela.

The "provisional junta of the provinces of La Plata River," which was established at Buenos Aires in May, 1810, selected Colonel Saavedra as its president. It entrusted the administration of the government to two departments which were placed in charge of secretaries.

Revolutionary Tendencies in La Plata

Juan J. Paso was made secretary of finance, while Mariano Moreno, "the soul of the revolution of 1810," was made secretary of military and political affairs. In the columns of the *Gazette of Buenos Aires* which he edited, Moreno argued in favor of the establishment of independent and democratic governments in South America. Under his influence, the junta of Buenos Aires rejected the authority of the patriot government in Spain; it also tried to extend its jurisdiction over important provinces of the former viceroyalty of La Plata. To the intendancy of Paraguay and to the *Banda Oriental del Uruguay*—a region lying between the Uruguay River and the Atlantic Ocean—it sent letters and messengers inviting the people to join the insurrectionary movement. It equipped an expedition against Paraguay under Manuel Belgrano which served to disseminate there the news of the kaleidoscopic changes that had taken place upon the banks of La Plata River. Yet its attempts to extend authority over all the provinces of the former viceroyalty proved unsuccessful.

In July, 1811, a provisional junta at Asunción decided against the recognition of the Spanish patriot government. Paraguayan leaders were not only incited by reports of the changes that had taken place in Spain, but they were also provoked by rumors concerning Portuguese designs against their province. On October 12, 1813, a Congress of delegates at Asunción adopted a fantastic plan of government which provided that the supreme power should be conferred upon two citizens who were to be designated "Consuls of the Republic of Paraguay."

About a year afterward a subservient Congress made the first consul, José de Francia, dictator of the Paraguayan state. Francia was a capable and astute lawyer who had gained the reputation of being an honest man. A Congress which assembled on June 1, 1816, declared that he should be "perpetual dictator" of the republic.

The hero of the movement for independence on the eastern bank of the Uruguay River was José Artigas, a picturesque and forceful leader who was influenced by federal ideas. To delegates whom he sent to a Constituent Assembly at Buenos Aires to urge the adoption of a declaration of independence, Artigas gave instructions that have become famous in South American history. The Instructions of the Year Thirteen—as they have been designated—proposed that a confederation should be formed by the provinces of the former viceroyalty of La Plata. Each of the provinces should be allowed to organize its own government, the central government should direct only the general business of the state, and other affairs should be managed by the provinces. Every province should have the right to sanction the constitution that was approved by the Constituent Assembly. Other provisions regarding relations among the united provinces were obviously modelled upon the Articles of Confederation and the Constitution of the United States.

The Constituent Assembly at Buenos Aires, however, declined to admit the delegates from the Banda Oriental. In 1814 Artigas left the soldiers of Buenos Aires who were besieging Montevideo. At that date the people upon the eastern bank of the Uruguay River began a movement for independence under his leadership. They struggled against the King of Spain, the Regent of Brazil, and the Director of the revolutionary government at Buenos Aires. By 1815 Artigas dominated Montevideo, several provinces of La Plata, and the missions on the banks of the Uruguay River.

Meanwhile the government at Buenos Aires had undergone radical changes. In December, 1810, deputies from the provinces had been incorporated in the provisional junta. Mariano Moreno had died while on a mission to England. On April 5 and 6, 1811, after a tumult of the populace, the junta was reorganized. In September of that year the executive authority was lodged in a triumvirate, while the junta acted as a legislative chamber. In October, 1812, that triumvirate was overthrown, and a quadrumvirate was formed. This body convoked an Assembly which vested the executive authority in a director and enacted laws that promoted the movement for independence.

On March 9, 1812, José de San Martín landed at Buenos Aires. The fourth son of a captain who had served Spain in the viceroyalty of
San Martín La Plata, at an early age the boy was taken to the Iberian Peninsula where he soon enlisted under the Spanish banner. For several years he fought for his King in Africa, Portugal, and Spain. In 1808 he was presented with a medal for his valiant service and promoted to the rank of colonel. Upon hearing of the revolt in South America, he relinquished his colonelcy in order that he might promote the liberty of his native land.

A few days after his arrival, the government at Buenos Aires entrusted San Martín with the organization of a regiment of mounted grenadiers. He soon established a military training school and stimu-

lated the morale of the citizen soldiery of Buenos Aires in various
ways. On February 3, 1813, at the head of a regiment of his grenadiers,
he defeated a band of marauding Spanish soldiers at San Lorenzo on
the banks of the Paraná River.

Meanwhile General Belgrano was battling with the royalists in the
interior. At Tucumán on September 24, 1812, he checked Spanish
soldiers who were invading the viceroyalty. On February 20, 1813, his
soldiers forced the royalists to capitulate at Salta. Upon entering the
presidency of Charcas, however, his army was routed in a bloody battle
at Vilcapugio on October 1; and on November 26, it was again defeated upon the plains of Ayohuma.

Because of these reverses, in December, 1813, Colonel San Martín
was given command of an expedition which was sent to reënforce
Belgrano. On January 18, 1814, that colonel was appointed commander
in chief of the soldiers of Buenos Aires who were stationed near the
city of Tucumán. After reaching the defeated army, he took steps to
train its officers. While reorganizing and inspiriting the army, his study
of the military situation convinced him that the project of the government at Buenos Aires to defeat the royalists by driving them out of
the presidency of Charcas was unwise. In April, 1814, he accordingly
gave up his post as commander of the army of Upper Peru. In August
the Director appointed him governor-intendant of the province of
Cuyo, which lay south of Tucumán and included some eastern slopes
of the Andes.

That appointment was doubtless in accord with the wishes of the
patriot commander. As early as April, 1814, he had written to a compatriot and declared that in Upper Peru he could wage only a defensive
war. In confidence he imparted the project that he had conceived for
the prosecution of the war for independence:

A small well-disciplined army in Mendoza to cross the Andes in order to exterminate the royalists in Chile and to aid a government of trusty friends to put
an end to the anarchy which reigns there. Then, allying our forces, we shall go
by sea to capture Lima. This is the road and not the other. You may be sure
that the war will not be finished until we capture Lima.

In February, 1816, San Martín sent from Mendoza to Buenos Aires
a plan of his campaign for the liberation of Chile.

The Assembly and the Director at Buenos Aires had meanwhile been
carving the former viceroyalty into provinces. On March 24, 1816,
delegates from that region assembled at Tucumán. In that Congress
there were no representatives from Paraguay or the Banda Oriental,
and, as the presidency of Charcas was occupied by royalists, there
were only a few delegates from that section. The Congress of Tucumán

appointed Juan Martín de Pueyrredón the "Supreme Director" of the nascent state. San Martín wrote to the delegate who represented the province of Cuyo to urge that it should adopt a declaration of absolute independence from Spain. While Belgrano lent his voice to those delegates who favored the establishment of a monarchical government. After an animated discussion, on July 9 they adopted a Declaration of Independence from Spain, as representatives of the "United Provinces of South America." A few days later Congress made a minor addition to the declaration to the effect that the new nation should be considered as independent not only of Ferdinand VII but also of any other foreign power. The political entity which was thus formed was ordinarily styled the United Provinces of La Plata.

The scene now shifts to Chile. The provisional junta that had displaced the captain general soon convoked a Congress at Santiago for the purpose of forming a government. When the delegates met in July, 1811, they took an oath of fidelity to Ferdinand VII, and also swore to support the constitution and laws which Congress might establish. From that ambiguous position José M. Carrera, an ambitious military officer who had served in Spain, undertook to lead those Chileans who favored independence from the motherland. In September, 1811, he overthrew the existing government. During the following year he sanctioned a republican Constitution, which, however, recognized the sovereignty of Ferdinand VII. This Constitution vested the supreme authority in a junta of three members which was controlled by Carrera.

Revolts in Chile and Peru

As the leader of a faction that opposed the domination of Carrera and his brothers there stepped forward Bernardo O'Higgins, the impetuous, natural son of an Irishman who had a notable career in the Spanish colonial service. Followers of Carrera and O'Higgins were defeated in October, 1814, at the battle of Rancagua by a royalist army which was partly composed of soldiers who had been sent to Chile by the Peruvian viceroy. After this disastrous defeat O'Higgins and José Carrera led bands of Chilean émigrés beyond the snow-capped Andes where they sought a refuge with the followers of San Martín at Mendoza.

Peru was perhaps the most important stronghold of Spanish power in South America. In 1810 reports of conditions existing in Spain, and rumors of movements in certain parts of Spanish America encouraged plots against the existing régime. Discontented Peruvians held meetings to discuss reforms. A prominent leader of those coteries was José de la Riva Agüero, an aristocratic, clever, and well-educated creole who had traveled in Europe. Under his inspiration secret clubs were formed which stimulated the smoldering disaffection. The fomenters of discontent, however, were denounced, and Riva Agüero was banished to an interior province.

The most formidable indication of discontent with the existing régime was a revolt led by a brigadier of aboriginal descent called Pumacahua. Followed by a large number of creoles and Indians who resented the heavy taxes and were incited by reports of the revolution in the provinces of La Plata, in August, 1814, he deposed the Spanish officials in Cuzco and created a loyalist junta there. From that city he sent out military expeditions in various directions. But on March 11, 1815, his followers were defeated by soldiers of the Peruvian viceroy.

Early in 1816 a contemporary might have prophesied that the insurrection against Spanish power in America had been fought in vain. Restored to the throne of Spain, the idolized Ferdinand VII was determined to establish his absolute authority in the Indies. Calleja, the indomitable military commander who had become the viceroy of New Spain, had apparently almost stamped out the insurrection there. The persevering royalist commander Morillo had reconquered a large part of northern South America. Dissatisfied Peruvians had been expatriated, pacified, or subjugated. Leaders of the Chilean revolution had taken refuge in the camp of San Martín at Mendoza.

SUGGESTIONS FOR FURTHER READING

FISHER, L. E., *The Background of the Revolution for Mexican Independence,* 1934.

GARCÍA CALDERON, F., *Latin America; Its Rise and Progress,* 1918.

GRIFFIN, C. C., *The United States and the Disruption of the Spanish Empire, 1810-1822,* 1937.

LATIMER, E. W., *Spain in the Nineteenth Century,* 1907.

MANNING, W. R. (ed.), *Diplomatic Correspondence Concerning the Independence of the Latin-American Nations,* Vol. I, 1925.

MARCHANT, A., "Tiradentes in the Conspiracy of Minas," *Hispanic American Historical Review,* Vol. XXI, pp. 239-257.

MITRE, B., *The Emancipation of South America* (trans. by W. Pilling), 1893.

NOLL, A. H. and MCMAHON, A. P., *The Life and Times of Miguel Hidalgo y Costilla,* 1910.

PETRE, F. L., *Simón Bolívar,* 1910.

ROBERTSON, W. S., "The Juntas of 1808 and the Spanish Colonies," *English Historical Review,* Vol. XXXI, pp. 573-585.

——, *The Life of Miranda,* Vol. II, 1929.

——, *Rise of the Spanish-American Republics,* 1918.

RYDJORD, J., *Foreign Interest in the Independence of New Spain,* 1935.

SENCOURT, R., *The Spanish Crown, 1808-1931,* 1932.

SHEPHERD, W. R., *The Hispanic Nations of the New World,* 1919.

YBARRA, T. R., *Bolívar,* 1929.

CHAPTER XI

THE WINNING OF INDEPENDENCE

From 1817 to 1820 the revolutionary cause in Mexico declined.
Many of its leaders sought pardon of Ferdinand VII. In 1820, however, events occurred in Spain which profoundly affected
conditions in the colonies. On January 1, Rafael Riego,
the commander of an Asturian regiment, announced his
adherence to the Constitution of 1812. As a result of the
revolution which ensued, Ferdinand VII was soon compelled to relinquish his absolute power and to declare his intention to support
that Constitution.

The Spanish
Revolution
of 1820

Reports of the Spanish revolution reached Vera Cruz in April, 1820.
Government officials in Mexico City soon took an oath to support
the Constitution of 1812. Its promulgation encouraged liberal ideas;
the freedom of the press was again proclaimed in Mexico. In September deputies were chosen to represent that viceroyalty in the Spanish
Cortes. Before they sailed for Spain, however, that legislature indiscreetly passed decrees which suppressed certain religious orders
throughout the Spanish dominions. Such measures much disturbed
leaders of the Mexican Church. Even conservative Mexicans began
to hearken to revolutionary whispers.

In the end of 1820 the Mexican insurgents who still fought for
independence were waging a guerrilla warfare against the royalists
in the mountainous region south of the capital city. After the execution of Morelos, Vicente Guerrero had become the indomitable leader
of the revolutionists. The commander of the royalist army operating
against Guerrero was Colonel Armijo. The viceroy hoped that Armijo
would soon complete the pacification.

When, after failing to subdue the revolutionists, Armijo relinquished
his post, Viceroy Apodaca selected as his successor the
enigmatical Colonel Agustín de Iturbide, a creole who in
April, 1816, had been recalled from his post because of
alleged misconduct. On November 9, 1820, Colonel
Iturbide accepted the appointment; about a week later, he left Mexico
City to take charge of the royalist forces. After a few encounters
with insurgent guerrillas, however, he undertook to negotiate with
Guerrero, without informing the viceroy of this step. Those negotia-

Iturbide and
the Plan
of Iguala

tions culminated in an agreement between Guerrero and Iturbide to unite their forces and to pacify Mexico.

Their agreement was embodied in a plan for the independence of Mexico that Iturbide first made known on February 24, 1821, in the obscure town of Iguala. That plan was a pronunciamiento which not only contained a Declaration of Independence from Spain but also a sketch of a provisional government for Mexico. The preamble of the Plan of Iguala reasoned that the independence of Mexico was destined to be established in the natural course of events. It alleged that the evils which existed in Mexico because of the remoteness of Madrid could be cured by the absolute independence of that viceroyalty. It declared that only a union of Europeans, Indians, and creoles would furnish an enduring basis for the happiness of the Mexican people. Roman Catholicism was to be the only religion tolerated in the new state, while both regular and secular clergy were to be protected in all their rights and properties.

A monarchy was to be established in Mexico that should be regulated by a constitution. The ruler should be Ferdinand VII, a member of his family, or a scion of some other European dynasty. Until an emperor was selected, the governmental authority should be exercised by a junta which was to frame regulations for the election of delegates to a Mexican Congress. The new government was to be supported by the army of independence which should be designated "the army of the three guarantees." That army should sacrifice itself, if necessary, for the preservation of the Roman Catholic religion, the establishment of independence, and the union of Mexicans and Spaniards.

This sagacious plan, which virtually provided that the titular sovereignty over Mexico might be held by a Spanish prince soon won support. Among the factors which prompted the acceptance of the plan was Iturbide's wide acquaintance with military commanders, his wise direction of the campaign, and his conciliatory and humane policy toward his antagonists. The viceroy was soon deposed by a mutiny of his own troops. When his successor, Juan O'Donojú, arrived at Vera Cruz with a small escort, he found that the plan of Iturbide had won general acceptance throughout Mexico. Hence at Córdoba, on August 24, 1821, O'Donojú signed a treaty with that leader. The Treaty of Córdoba embodied the main provisions of the Plan of Iguala, but it also provided that if a Spanish prince did not accept the crown, the Cortes of Mexico should elect a monarch.

On September 27, 1821, the army of the three guarantees marched into the City of Mexico. At once the victorious commander selected the members of a governmental junta which on September 28 signed an act that proclaimed the independence of the Mexican Empire. The junta soon appointed a regency which was to act as an executive body until an emperor was elected. Iturbide was made president of the Regency. After news reached Mexico that the Spanish Cortes had disavowed the Treaty of Córdoba, on May 18, 1822, a military officer proclaimed him as Emperor Agustín I. Upon the following day Congress passed an act which stated that it had selected him as the constitutional Emperor of Mexico, according to the Plan of Iguala. On July 21 in the spacious cathedral of the capital city, Iturbide was crowned Emperor.

Meanwhile the Mexican revolution had affected the neighboring regions. Early in September, 1821, a junta in the province of Chiapas declared its intention to seek independence from Spain and to support the Plan of Iguala. A little later, a junta that had been convoked by the captain general in Guatemala City declared in favor of independence. Other provinces of the captaincy general expressed their desire to become independent of the motherland. Near the end of 1821 Iturbide dispatched a military expedition into Central America. In September, 1822, his government issued orders that he should be proclaimed Emperor in the principal Central American towns and cities. Agustín I thus became the ruler of an Empire that stretched from the forty-second parallel of north latitude to the Isthmus of Panama.

Simón Bolívar had meanwhile not been idle. In December, 1816, he sailed from the West Indies and disembarked in the island of Margarita. With a small band of guerrillas, he persistently led the struggle against the royalists. He drove them out of a region in the lower valley of the Orinoco River and established the provisional capital of Venezuela at Angostura. Early in October, 1818, he decided to assemble a congress there. On February 15, 1819, he delivered an eloquent address to the Congress of Angostura in which he expounded his ideas about political systems. He not only criticized the federal system of government but also reasoned that the powers of the Venezuelan executive should be analogous to the prerogatives of the English King. He was induced to accept the presidency of the republic. Some of his political ideas were embodied in a provisional Constitution which was adopted by that Congress on August 15, 1819.

Bolívar had meanwhile led his army into New Granada by a daring march over the ice-capped Andean range. After crossing the desolate plateau of Pisba—thirteen thousand feet above the level of the sea—Bolívar's soldiers intercepted the Spanish forces under General Barreiro at a bridge across the river Boyacá. There on August 7, 1819, the royalists were decisively defeated. Two days later the last viceroy of New Granada fled precipitately from the capital. The battle of Boyacá freed from Spanish rule the viceroyalty of New Granada, with the exception of the presidency of Quito. Under the influence of this victory, on December 17, 1819, the Congress of Angostura, which had been afforced by some delegates from New Granada, enacted a law proclaiming the union of the former viceroyalty of New Granada and the captaincy general of Venezuela into a state that was styled the Republic of Colombia. The republic was divided into three departments: Venezuela, Cundinamarca (New Granada), and Quito. The capital of Cundinamarca was henceforth to be styled Bogotá. Bolívar was made president of the new nation which—to distinguish it from a state that emerged later—has sometimes been designated "Great Colombia."

Battles of
Boyacá,
Carabobo,
and
Pichincha

The patriot commander next prepared for an expedition against the royalists who were entrenched in Venezuela. In April, 1821, he decided to assemble the soldiers of Venezuela and New Granada at a central point and there to give battle to the enemy. While certain patriot divisions attacked the royalists at Caracas, San Felipe, and Valencia, other soldiers marched toward the chosen rendezvous. At Tinaquillo the Liberator reviewed the united army which was about six thousand five hundred strong. He then led it against the royalists under General La Torre who had succeeded Morillo. On June 24, upon the plains of Carabobo, revolutionary soldiers routed the royalist army.

Though some royalists still clung tenaciously to fortified posts along the seacoast, the battle of Carabobo ensured the independence from Spain of northern South America. As a result of this victory, on August 30, 1821, the Congress which had met at Cúcuta adopted a Constitution for the dual state of Colombia. Soon afterward it elected Bolívar president.

The Liberator had decided that he would next turn his conquering arms against the royalists in the presidency of Quito, where a revolutionary junta had been established in October, 1820. In January, 1821, Bolívar ordered his ablest lieutenant, General Antonio de Sucre, to lead an expedition by sea to Guayaquil. On May 24, 1822, General Sucre defeated General Aymerich, the President of Quito, upon the slopes of Mount Pichincha which overlooked the capital city. The resulting capitulation provided that the presidency should be relinquished by the Spaniards. Sucre's victory aided Bolívar who on his southward march had fought a fierce battle against royalists at Bomboná. Soon after entering the city of Quito, Bolivar announced that the liberated presidency had been incorporated with Colombia.

The revolutionary fires in La Plata had meanwhile spread westward and northward. They were destined soon to merge with the flames that had swept down the Pacific coast from Colombia. At Mendoza, from August, 1814, to February, 1817, San Martín had been organizing an army for the invasion of Chile. Early in 1817 this army made an heroic march into that country through lofty mountain passes. The Uspallata Pass by which part of the Army of the Andes surmounted the cordillera was some twelve thousand feet above the level of the sea.

On the morning of February 12, 1817, San Martín's soldiers issued from mountain paths and attacked the royalist soldiers, who, under the command of Colonel Maroto, had gathered to dispute their advance. After an obstinate defense, the royalists were dislodged from a hill near the village of Chacabuco. The captain general fled from Santiago, and San Martín soon entered the capital. A cabildo abierto in that city selected him to be the governor of Chile but he declined the office in order that he might carry out his designs against Peru. Prominent citizens of Santiago then elected O'Higgins supreme director of the new state.

Battles of Chacabuco and Maipú

Early in January, 1818, O'Higgins and his secretaries wrote the Declaration of Independence. This document declared that Chile constituted a free and sovereign state which would forever remain separate from the Spanish monarchy. On February 7 the new government issued a proclamation stating that upon February 12 the independence of Chile from Spain would be formally announced. Upon that day in the great plaza of Santiago, San Martín and other leading officials took oath to sustain the absolute independence of the Chilean nation. It was not until April 5, 1818, however, when San Martín routed the royalists upon the plains of Maipú, that her independence was ensured.

Soon afterward, with the aid of O'Higgins and Pueyrredón, San Martín took energetic steps to organize an expedition against Lima. In April, 1819, he was appointed brigadier general of Chile's army. Lord Cochrane, an English naval officer, joined the Chilean patriots and helped to organize the expedition which was destined for the liberation of Peru. In August, 1820, vessels bearing revolutionary soldiers from Chile and La Plata sailed out of Valparaiso harbor. After landing upon the coast south of Lima, San Martín started a propaganda to promote Peruvian independence. Upon the evacuation of Lima by Viceroy La Serna, the revolutionary general entered that city. In its great plaza, on July 28, 1821, he formally proclaimed the independence of Peru from Spain.

On August 3 San Martín issued a proclamation announcing that the supreme military and civil authority of Peru was vested in himself with the title of protector. He expressed the opinion that to convoke a congress while there still were royalists in a country was dangerous. On October 8 he issued a provisional decree concerning the government. This decree provided that the laws of Spain which harmonized with the new régime should remain in force. It defined the Protector's powers and provided for a council of state which was to advise him in governmental affairs. By subsequent decrees San Martín made further arrangements for the reorganization of Peru.

Yet the war for the liberation of South America had not terminated. For the royalists still controlled the Peruvian highlands and also the presidency of Charcas. San Martín felt that the junction of the Colombian forces with his soldiers would perhaps ensure the subjugation of the Spaniards. In July, 1822, he accordingly sailed for Colombia to discuss the destiny of South America with Bolívar. The result of a mysterious interview at Guayaquil was, in brief, that the high-minded San Martín withdrew from the South American war for independence and allowed Bolívar to assume the undisputed leadership of the patriot cause.

San Martín as Protector of Peru

Bolívar soon sent General Sucre to Peru. There Sucre established intimate relations with certain Peruvians. Soon their aspiring leader, Riva Agüero, declined in authority and decided to leave his native land. After the arrival of the Liberator at Lima in September, 1823, the two Venezuelan generals prepared for a campaign against the royalists under General Canterac. During the following months Sucre organized and equipped the united army of liberation which was mainly composed of soldiers from La Plata, Chile, Peru, and Great Colombia.

In the middle of June, 1824, those soldiers broke camp and marched in separate detachments toward an appointed rendezvous. On August 6 the patriot forces defeated royalists under Canterac upon the elevated plain of Junín. Shortly afterward Bolívar left Sucre in charge of the army and proceeded to the seacoast. After some complicated maneuvers, Sucre, who had been directed by Bolívar to avoid a battle, was conceded permission to fight the royalists. On December 9, 1824, he overwhelmingly defeated them upon an old Incan battlefield at Ayacucho. This battle sealed the fate of Spain's Empire in the Three Americas: on the one hand, it supplemented the labors of San Martín; while, on the other hand, it virtually completed the work of Bolívar.

Battles of Junín and Ayacucho

Sucre proceeded from Ayacucho into the presidency of Charcas where the remaining royalists soon laid down their arms. He issued a proclamation to the people on February 9, 1825, which announced that the presidency would remain under the control of his army until delegates from its provinces could assemble. He further proposed that those representatives should decide the political fate of Upper Peru. Bolívar reluctantly sanctioned that measure. On August 6, 1825, delegates who assembled at Chuquisaca formally declared the independence of the presidency of Charcas. They justified this step because of the

misgovernment and oppression of Spain. They expressed their intention to establish a sovereign state that would be independent of all
nations. Five days later this Congress decreed that the new state
should be designated the Republic of Bolívar or, as it came to be known
—Bolivia. Its capital, Chuquisaca, was to be rechristened Sucre.

The Brazilian movement for independence from the motherland
dates from the arrival of the Braganza family in America. On Decem-

Origins of
Brazilian
Independ-
ence

ber 16, 1815, Regent John proclaimed that the colony
of Brazil was a kingdom, which placed it upon the same
constitutional basis as Portugal. Citizens of Brazil were
thus accorded the same rights as Portuguese citizens.
Further, after Queen Maria I died on March 20, 1816, her son John
was formally proclaimed King of Portugal and Brazil with the title
of John VI. Yet some Brazilians were not satisfied. In 1817 a revolt
broke out in the province of Pernambuco where conspirators attempted
to establish a republican government but without success.

The position of King John VI was unique. He remained the titular
monarch of Portugal where a Regency had been ruling under English
protection. In 1820 revolutionists overthrew that régime, established a
new Regency, and convoked a Constituent Cortes. Some Brazilians
championed the cause of the Portuguese revolutionists, while others
advocated the formation of a separate constitution for their country.
By a decree of February 24, 1821, John VI prematurely approved the
national Constitution which was being framed by the Portuguese
Cortes; two days later his eldest son Pedro solemnly swore to support
it. Propaganda spread in Rio de Janeiro, however, in favor of the
Spanish Constitution of 1812. King John accordingly issued another
decree on April 21, 1821, by which he proclaimed that fundamental
law to be in force until the Portuguese Constitution should be definitively formed. But the King soon changed his mind; for, on the next
day, he issued a decree revoking the Spanish Constitution of 1812 and
again proclaiming the organic law which was being elaborated in
Lisbon. It has accordingly been said of Brazil that in 1821 it had
"two constitutions in two months."

On April 22, 1821, John VI issued a decree which granted to his son
Pedro the authority of regent in Brazil. Accompanied by members of
his family, King John embarked on board a warship on the evening
of April 24. Two days later he sailed for Portugal. Just before his
departure the King addressed a letter to his son expressing apprehensions about the future of Portuguese America and advising Pedro to
place the Brazilian crown upon his own head rather than to allow an
adventurer to seize it.

On taking the reins of power, Regent Pedro swore to defend the

Portuguese Constitution that had been framed by the Cortes. At this juncture, however, that legislature passed certain decrees which affected Brazilians unfavorably. It established juntas of government in the provinces. It reduced the supreme court in Rio de Janeiro to a provincial court. It stipulated that local Brazilian magistrates should correspond directly with Portuguese authorities. It ordered the young prince to return to Portugal "in order to complete his political education." Many Brazilians consequently thought that the Portuguese Cortes intended to reduce their country to the status of a colony. A Brazilian scholar who played a prominent part in the ensuing reaction was José Bonifacio de Andrada e Silva. An address to the Regent from a patriotic junta of the province of São Paulo, which was composed by Bonifacio, contained this appeal:

How dare these Portuguese deputies, without waiting for the Brazilian deputies, promulgate laws which affect the dearest interests of this realm? How dare they dismember Brazil into isolated parts possessing no common center of strength and union? How dare they deprive your Royal Highness of the Regency with which your Royal Father, our monarch, had invested you?

In 1822 Bonifacio became Pedro's chief minister. In that capacity, on June 3, 1822, he signed a decree convoking at Rio de Janeiro a Constituent Assembly of delegates from the Brazilian provinces.

On August 14 following he addressed a circular to the diplomatic corps at Rio de Janeiro which announced that Brazil considered itself as independent as Portugal, that the colony had been freed from the yoke with which the mother Kingdom had   Grito de Ypiranga aimed to enslave it, and that it was almost ready to proclaim its independence. Almost resolved to declare that Brazil was independent of Portugal, on the same day Regent Pedro left the capital city on a trip to the south. After he had perused letters from Rio de Janeiro which voiced the sentiments of many inhabitants of that city in favor of a complete separation of Brazil from Portugal, and after he became aware of further measures of the Portuguese Cortes directed against Brazil's autonomy, Pedro decided upon a momentous step. On September 7, 1822, on the banks of the Ypiranga, a small stream near the city of São Paulo, he proclaimed the independence of Brazil from Portugal. This informal proclamation, which Brazilian writers have styled the *Grito de Ypiranga,* constituted the Brazilian Declaration of Independence.

On September 21 the municipal council of Rio de Janeiro announced its intention to make Pedro the constitutional emperor of Brazil. Pedro accepted the proffered dignity on October 12 and promised to put into operation the constitution that should be framed by the

Constituent Assembly. On December 1, 1822, the Regent was solemnly crowned as Constitutional Emperor of Brazil. Meantime the separatist spirit was spreading through the interior Brazilian provinces. Aided by Lord Cochrane, who now organized Brazil's navy, the patriots soon subdued the Portuguese party that opposed separation from the motherland. The Portuguese fleet which had besieged Bahia was dispersed. By November, 1823, Brazil was practically freed from the Portuguese.

The first Constituent Assembly of Brazil met on April 17, 1823, in Rio de Janeiro. This Assembly entrusted the task of framing a Constitution to a committee composed of José Bonifacio and other leaders. Various members of the committee drafted constitutional projects. At last the task was entrusted to Antonio Carlos, who, after determining certain fundamental principles, selected features from various constitutions, and in about two weeks prepared a fundamental law. This project, which was considered favorably by the Assembly, provided that the government of Brazil should be an hereditary monarchy vested in the dynasty of the Emperor Pedro I. It declared that the Emperor and a bicameral Assembly were the representatives of the nation. It further declared that the powers of the executive, legislative, and judicial departments were all delegated by the sovereign people.

Evidently this liberal project, which limited the Emperor's power, displeased him grievously. On November 12, 1823, an imperial military officer arbitrarily dissolved the Constituent Assembly. The Emperor soon selected a commission to frame a constitution for Brazil. In one month this commission, which was mainly composed of Pedro's councilors, drafted a new project that was partly based upon the project of Antonio Carlos.

The Constitution of 1824 declared that Brazil was an independent nation. The government was to be monarchical and hereditary, constitutional and representative. Pedro, the head of the ruling dynasty, was styled Emperor and Perpetual Defender of Brazil. Roman Catholicism was to be the religion of the State; but the exercise of other religions was to be permitted in special edifices that should not have the external forms of temples. This Constitution provided that the patronage, which had been conceded by the Holy See to the Portuguese King in 1551, should be exercised by the Emperor. Pedro was given the authority "to appoint bishops and to fill ecclesiastical benefices." He was also given the right to pass upon the admission into Brazil of "the decrees of councils, apostolic letters, and other ecclesiastical provisions that were not repugnant to the Constitution."

The chief executive authority was granted to the Emperor, who was

Brazilian Constitution of 1824

to be aided by secretaries of state and by a Council of State. He was to appoint the chief civil and military, as well as ecclesiastical, officers. He could negotiate treaties with foreign nations. He could issue ordinances to promote the proper execution of the laws. Among the so-called moderative powers conferred upon him was the right of suspensive veto upon bills passed by Congress, and the authority to approve or temporarily to suspend the acts of provincial councils.

The Congress or General Assembly, as it was designated, was composed of a Chamber of Deputies and a Senate. Acting jointly the houses were to pass, revoke, or suspend laws, to lay taxes, to authorize loans, to administer national property, to regulate the coinage, to administer oaths to the rulers, to fix the powers of the guardian of a young Emperor, to determine the succession when it was doubtful, and to select a new dynasty, if the ruling dynasty became extinct.

The judicial department was declared to be independent of the other departments. A superior court was to exist in every province. In the capital city there was to be a supreme court which, among other powers, should decide conflicts between the superior courts of the provinces about their respective jurisdictions.

The existing captaincies were now styled provinces. The chief executive of a province, who was called president, was to be appointed by the Emperor. Each city, town, or village in the Brazilian Empire should have an elective council to manage its municipal affairs.

During the early stages of the Spanish-American Revolution the government of the United States remained neutral but showed a keen interest in the struggle. After the Treaty of 1819 concerning the Floridas had been ratified by the Spanish King, and after Iturbide, Bolívar, and San Martín had triumphed over the royalists, President Monroe felt that the time was ripe for the acknowledgment of Spanish-American independence. On January 30, 1822, the House of Representatives asked the President to lay before it documents and information about the governments of Spanish America. In response he sent a special message on March 8, 1822. His recommendation was that the new nations of Spanish America which had established their independence should be recognized. Despite the protests of Spain, both houses of Congress approved this view, and on May 4, 1822, Monroe signed an act that appropriated money for diplomatic missions to independent nations on the American continent.

On June 19, 1822, Secretary of State John Quincy Adams presented the Colombian chargé d'affaires, Manuel Torres, to President Monroe. By that act the United States acknowledged Colombia as an independent nation. On December 12 following Adams presented José

Manuel Zozaya, minister plenipotentiary from the Mexican Empire, to the President. Recognition by the United States of other Spanish-American nations which were included within the purview of the law of May 4, 1822, was consummated by the appointment of diplomatic agents to those states. Caesar A. Rodney was appointed the American minister to the United Provinces of La Plata on January 27, 1823. On the same day Heman Allen was appointed minister to Chile. Peru and certain Spanish-American nations that did not appear distinctly upon the map of South America in 1823 were recognized subsequently. Paraguay was not recognized by the United States until 1852.

On January 21, 1824, the minister of foreign affairs of Emperor Pedro I appointed José Rebello chargé d'affaires to Washington. Rebello's instructions declared that the United States ought to recognize the Brazilian Empire. Upon his arrival in Washington, Monroe's cabinet carefully considered whether or not the independence of that Empire should be acknowledged at once. After the Brazilian agent had submitted to Adams a memoir about the separation of his country from the motherland, on May 26, 1824, President Monroe received Rebello as Brazilian chargé. This act constituted the recognition of that Empire by the United States.

The acknowledgment of the independence of Latin-American nations by the United States was not without influence upon certain nations of Europe. Further, the news of the Doctrine promulgated by President Monroe in his message to Congress of December 2, 1823, stimulated those Englishmen who, largely because of commercial motives, advocated the immediate recognition of the revolted Spanish colonies. In January, 1825, the English minister, George Canning, announced to the diplomatic corps in London his intention to recognize the Spanish-American states. On February 2, 1825, a commercial treaty was accordingly signed at Buenos Aires by diplomats representing England and the United Provinces of La Plata. The negotiation of this treaty was an acknowledgment of Argentine independence by the court of London. At Bogotá on April 18 following a similar treaty was signed by diplomats of England and Colombia. A treaty between England and Mexico was signed at London on December 26, 1826.

England's Policy toward Latin America

In the recognition of the Brazilian Empire by European nations, England played an important rôle. In November, 1823, the minister of foreign affairs of Brazil sent two agents to London who were empowered to negotiate for the recognition of Brazilian independence. They soon held a series of conferences with the Portuguese minister at London. Between the conflicting views of those negotiators Canning strove to find a compromise ground. On May 13, 1825, John VI signed a certificate to the effect that he recognized Brazil as an independent Empire, with an administration distinct from that of Portugal. On August 29 of that year through the good offices of the able English diplomat, Sir Charles Stuart, a treaty was signed at Rio de Janeiro between the two countries. By that treaty Portugal acknowledged Brazil as an independent Empire. In 1827 a treaty of amity and commerce between England and Brazil was ratified by the contracting parties. In that manner England formally recognized Brazilian independence.

France did not early recognize the new Latin nations. During the revolutionary struggles her government more than once contemplated the founding of Bourbon monarchies in the revolted Spanish colonies. At various times French agents were **French Policy** dispatched to Mexico and South America who were charged to investigate conditions and to report. Foreign Minister Chateaubriand urged Ferdinand VII to allow foreign nations freely to trade with the Indies. For several years, however, the Bourbon Family Compact of 1761 and also the presence of French troops in Spain, effectually restrained France from following the example of England with regard to the Spanish nations of the New World.

No such considerations restrained France with respect to Portuguese America. Incited by the policy of England, on April 18, 1825, the French minister, Baron Damas, instructed Count Gestas, the French consul at Rio de Janeiro, to negotiate a commercial treaty with the government of Brazil. On January 8, 1826, Gestas signed with two Brazilian diplomats a treaty of amity, navigation, and commerce, which expressly recognized the independence of the Empire of Brazil and the imperial dignity of Pedro I.

After the July Revolution, when Louis Philippe d'Orléans ascended the throne of France, Count Molé, the minister of foreign affairs, recommended to the King that political recognition should be accorded to several Spanish-American states in principle and that this policy should be put in force by the negotiation of treaties with those states. In August, 1830, this recommendation was approved by Louis Philippe. Certain Spanish-American governments were soon notified of the new policy that had been adopted by France. On November 14, 1832, a treaty of amity, commerce, and navigation was signed between France and Venezuela. Commercial treaties were subsequently arranged between France and other Spanish-American nations.

Not until the death of King Ferdinand VII, when a number of Liberal statesmen returned to power, did the Spanish government decide to end the protracted family quarrel. Influenced by commercial motives, by the fact that other important states had recognized the independence of the Spanish nations of the New World, and by the conviction that they should cultivate friendly relations with those

Spain and Spanish America nations, Spanish Liberals reluctantly decided to relinquish the claim to their continental heritage in the New World. On December 4, 1836, the Cortes adopted a decree which authorized the government to conclude treaties of peace and amity with the nations of Spanish America upon the basis of the acknowledgment of their independence.

In accordance with that decree, on December 28, 1836, a treaty was signed between Mexico and Spain by which Isabella II recognized that republic as "a free, sovereign, and independent nation, composed of the states and countries specified in her constitutional law." Article V provided that the citizens of her Catholic Majesty and citizens of the Mexican republic should be considered reciprocally as citizens of the most favored nation, except in cases where mutual concessions were agreed upon. Mexico was thus the first nation carved from Spain's colonial Empire to be recognized by the motherland.

Other Spanish-American nations soon indicated their desire to foster commercial relations with Spain. In a series of fifteen treaties, Spain acknowledged the independence of her former colonies upon the American continent. By the exchange of treaty ratifications with Honduras in 1895, the Spanish government concluded the negotiations which had been authorized by the Cortes in 1836. This tardy recognition marked the dawn of Pan-Hispanism.

Soon after the struggle for the independence of Spanish America began, revolutionary leaders took the view that the control of relations

The Papacy and the Latin-American Nations with the Papacy, including the right of patronage, had passed directly from the Spanish King to the patriot governments. In general, the papal policy toward those governments was opportunistic. Desirous to avoid giving offense to Ferdinand VII, for a time the Pope refrained from sanctioning ecclesiastical appointments made by revolutionary authorities. When the Liberals came into power in the motherland, however, Pius VII made known his intention to receive those Spanish-American agents who might wish to consult him concerning spiritual matters. The dispatch from Rome in the spring of 1823 of a vicar apostolic to Buenos Aires and Santiago de Chile signalized the informal beginning of diplomatic relations between the Holy See and the Spanish-American nations. But after the restoration of Ferdinand VII to absolute power, Leo XII exhorted the bishops of Spanish America to support that King. On January 28, 1826, shortly after John VI had recognized his son Pedro as the Emperor of Brazil, the Pope publicly acknowledged the independence of the Brazilian Empire. By a bull issued in August, 1831, Pope Gregory XVI announced his intention to enter into relations with *de facto* governments of Spanish America. On November 26, 1835, the Papacy formally recognized the independence of New Granada. Unlike the papal policy toward Brazil, the recognition of Spanish-American independence which was thus initiated by the Vatican left the thorny problem of the patronage unsettled.

As the result of a train of events precipitated by the designs of Napoleon upon Spain and Portugal, new nations thus appeared in America. The colony of Brazil became an independent nation through a series of steps which began with the flight of the dynasty of Braganza from Lisbon and ended by the promulgation of a monarchical Constitution in 1824. So quietly was the transformation from a colony to an independent Empire accomplished in Portuguese America that the separation of Brazil from the motherland might almost be styled bloodless. In sharp contrast with this development was the separatist movement in the Spanish Indies. The Spanish-American Revolution, which in reality terminated with the victory of Sucre upon the plains of Ayacucho in December, 1824, was for the most part a bloody, protracted, internecine struggle which devastated large areas, destroyed capital, property, and many lives, and encouraged revolutionary habits. Yet, with the exception of the stormy meetings of extraordinary cabildos and the agitated deliberations of revolutionary juntas or occasional congresses, few opportunities had been furnished Spanish Americans for training in the art of politics.

Though the War for Independence had terminated in triumph on the American continent, the struggle for true democratic government had scarcely begun. While the Brazilians had founded an Empire, in the Spanish Indies only the Mexicans began their national career by establishing an imperial régime. Most of the other nations that were clearly outlined upon the map of Latin America in the second decade of the nineteenth century had created systems of government that were republics in form. During early years of that decade Central America was attached to the Mexican Empire. In northern South America there had been founded by Bolívar the republic designated "Great Colombia," which was composed of the regions formerly styled the viceroyalty of New Granada, the captaincy general of Venezuela, and the presidency of Quito. The independent republic denominated Peru claimed jurisdiction over a large portion of the ancient viceroyalty of that name. In 1822 the people living in the territory which had been controlled by the captain general of Chile constituted an independent nation under Director O'Higgins. A loosely organized political entity called the United Provinces of La Plata was attempting to exercise jurisdiction over the major portion of the former viceroyalty of La Plata. A small part of that viceroyalty upon the east bank of the Uruguay River—the region later styled Uruguay—had not achieved its independence in 1824. Dictator Francia dominated another fragment of the former viceroyalty of La Plata which was styled "the Republic of Paraguay." In 1825 through the influence of Sucre the presidency of Charcas had become the republic of Bolivia. Leaders of the Spanish-American nations ordinarily maintained that their limits were determined by the *uti possidetis* of 1810. To the east of the Spanish-American peoples the statesmen of Brazil maintained that her limits extended to the bounds sketched by the Treaty of San Ildefonso.

SUGGESTIONS FOR FURTHER READING

ANGELL, H., *Simón Bolívar*, 1930.

ARMITAGE, J., *The History of Brazil*, Vol. I, 1836.

BELAUNDE, V. A., *Bolivar and the Political Thought of the Spanish-American Revolution*, 1938.

BOLÍVAR, S., *An Address of Bolívar at the Congress of Angostura*, 1919.

CHISHOLM, A. S., *The Independence of Chile*, 1911.

COCHRANE, T., *Narrative of Services in the Liberation of Chile, Peru, and Brazil from Spanish and Portuguese Domination*, Vol. II, 1859.

HALL, B., *Extracts from a Journal, written on the Coasts of Chile, Peru, and Mexico*, Vol. II, 1824.

HASBROUCK, A., *Foreign Legionaries in the Liberation of Spanish South America*, 1928.

HUMPHREYS, R. A. (ed.), *British Consular Reports on the Trade and Politics of Latin America, 1824-1826*, 1940.

LOCKEY, J. B., *Pan Americanism; Its Beginnings*, 1920.

MEHEGAN, J. J., *O'Higgins of Chile*, 1913.

ROBERTSON, W. S., *France and Latin-American Independence*, 1939.

———, "Metternich's Attitude Toward Revolutions in Latin America," *Hispanic American Historical Review*, Vol. XXI, pp. 538-598.

———, "The United States and Spain in 1822," *American Historical Review*, Vol. XX, pp. 781-800.

SCHOELLKOPF, A., *Don José de San Martín*, 1924.

SHERWELL, G. A., *Antonio José de Sucre*, 1924.

SPRAGUE, W. F., *Vicente Guerrero*, 1939.

TEMPERLEY, H., *The Foreign Policy of Canning*, 1925.

WEBSTER, C. K., *Britain and the Independence of Latin America*, Vol. I, 1938.

WHITAKER, A. P., *The United States and the Independence of Latin America, 1800-1830*, 1941.

CHAPTER XII

IMPERIAL AND REPUBLICAN RULE
IN BRAZIL

On March 25, 1824, the first Emperor of Brazil solemnly swore to observe the new Constitution. This step completed the process by which the Portuguese colony was transformed into an independent empire. The agitated years from 1824 to 1831 have aptly been designated the second period of the reign of Pedro I. He played a strange rôle in Brazilian history: he championed a movement that culminated in the separation of the colony from the motherland but was finally induced to return to Portugal, for he was unable to check a propaganda directed against himself. Pedro I was a mixture of good and bad qualities. His morals were not always above reproach. Ambitious, impulsive, and ingenuous, although deficient in education and political experience, yet he had some imagination. The brilliant Brazilian littérateur, Euclydes da Cunha, characterized Pedro as part soldier, part king, and part *condottiere*. Seated on a throne in the hall of the Senate, wearing an imperial mantle, with a crown adorning his brows, and grasping a scepter, on May 6, 1826, the only Emperor then ruling in America opened the first session of the Brazilian Congress.

Emperor Pedro I was confronted by difficult problems. One task was to put the new Constitution into operation. Even before he swore to observe the fundamental law, the Emperor had suspended that article which guaranteed personal liberty. In certain sections of Brazil opposition to the new Constitution did not die out for several years. When Pedro sent imperial soldiers to crush a revolt that aimed to establish a union of the northern provinces in the so-called "Confederation of the Equator," his policy was **Problems of Pedro I** opposed by some Brazilians. His appointment of certain persons to act as the presidents of recalcitrant provinces did not restore them to tranquillity.

Constitutional problems also arose regarding the Emperor's relations with Congress. The two houses, which first assembled in 1826, found it difficult to agree upon certain matters of legislative procedure. When Congress became aware that in the treaty by which Portugal acknowledged the independence of Brazil the Emperor had promised to pay a large indemnity to the motherland, his policy was bitterly criticized.

Further, prominent congressmen wished that the Emperor's ministers should have seats in the national legislature. A ministry of that type was eventually formed on November 20, 1827, headed by Araujo Lima, a member of the House of Deputies. When John VI died in July, 1825, the crown of Portugal reverted to the Emperor of Brazil, who reluctantly conceded it to his little daughter Maria. Some Brazilians suspected that Pedro preferred the Portuguese crown to that of Brazil.

A serious problem for Pedro I was the condition of the Banda Oriental del Uruguay. After Artigas renounced the government at Buenos Aires, his native land became the dark and bloody ground of South America. On the one side, it was claimed by the United Provinces of La Plata: on the other side, it was claimed by Portugal; for that nation maintained that her jurisdiction extended south to La Plata River. After the downfall of Artigas in 1820, Portuguese soldiers under General Lecor took possession of Montevideo; an assembly in that city declared that the Banda Oriental was incorporated with the Kingdom of Portugal and Brazil under the title of the cisplatine province. When Brazil separated from Portugal, some of the soldiers who occupied the debatable land declared in favor of John VI, while others acclaimed Pedro I.

In 1825 some thirty-three natives of Uruguay, led by Juan Antonio Lavalleja, invaded that country and at Florida on August 25 they framed a Declaration of Independence. Yet that declaration was linked to a pledge of their adherence to the United Provinces of La Plata. The Congress at Buenos Aires accepted the pledge and informed Pedro I of its action. He accordingly declared war against the United Provinces on December 1, 1825. After the Brazilians had been checked in conflicts by land and sea, on February 20, 1827, they were decisively defeated by soldiers of Argentina and Uruguay at Ituzaingó. In the following May a preliminary convention of peace was signed between Argentina and Brazil which contained a provision that Uruguay should be free and independent. Not only did the Emperor thus fail to retain control of a valuable province; but the defeats of the Brazilian army had injured his prestige, and the expense of an inglorious war had drained his treasury. A buffer-state had appeared on the map of South America.

Partly because of his fondness for absolute rule, Emperor Pedro I became unpopular with his subjects. Though the Constitution guaranteed the liberty of the press, leading journals were censored or suppressed. The Emperor frequently interfered with the work of his ministers; his ministry occasionally assumed legislative authority. Cliques or party groups began to form whose alignments were determined by their attitude toward the imperial administration. A conservative party appeared that was mainly composed of absolutists and constitutionalists. Absolutists were largely wealthy Portuguese or officeholders who supported the unconstitutional measures of the Emperor. Constitutionalists disliked Pedro's arbitrary measures but favored the existing Constitution. **Growth of the Liberals** On the other side, the Liberals were opposed to the Emperor's method of government: certain of them, influenced by the example of the United States, dreamed of founding a republic in Brazil; while others desired to establish a system of responsible government, such as had developed in England. As the opposition to Pedro's dictatorial rule increased, Liberal journals were founded. Among them was the *Aurora Fluminense*, edited by Evaristo da Veiga, which criticized the government and exposed the Emperor's extravagance. Another journal called the *Republic*, spoke ironically of Pedro as the "very dear Emperor"! In 1829 he had a serious quarrel with the House of Deputies, which in consequence he arbitrarily dissolved.

When news arrived in Brazil of the revolution of July, 1830, in Paris, which placed Louis Philippe on the throne of France, the discontented Liberals received a fresh stimulus. Pedro I now decided to visit the province of Minas Geraes, which seemed the focus of agitation against him. In some parts of that province he was very coldly received. The festivities that celebrated his return to Rio de Janeiro ended in disputes between the Portuguese and the Brazilians. On March 13, 1831, the Conservatives in the capital engaged in conflicts with the Liberals, among whom were officers of the army. Those quarrels increased the hatred of natural-born Brazilians for the Portuguese and diminished the popularity of the Emperor, who was a native of Portugal.

Twenty-three deputies and one senator took counsel together about the critical condition of public affairs. They selected Evaristo da Veiga to frame an address to the Emperor. In this address those Congressmen alleged that the imperial government had neglected to check the attacks of Portuguese Conservatives upon the Liberals; they declared that the Brazilians were justly indignant, and demanded punishment for the offenders. They boldly spoke of the traitors who surrounded the throne: in menacing language they declared that, unless the Brazilians were granted redress, the public peace, the stability of the State, and the very existence of the throne would be endangered. Upon responding for the Emperor, the minister of justice, Viscount Alcantara, declared that his government had taken the steps necessary to preserve public tranquillity.

A series of significant events soon occurred which showed that the monarch's prestige was rapidly waning. On March 20, 1831, Pedro I dismissed the majority of his ministers and replaced them by native Brazilians who did not suit the Liberals. When on March 25 he appeared at a solemn *Te Deum* that was attended by many Liberals in the church of São Francisco de Paula, he was joyfully acclaimed by many people. Some worshipers, however, limited their good wishes for Pedro I to the period when he would remain a Constitutional Emperor. To those persons he replied that he was and always had been a constitutional ruler. There is a tradition that to other persons who acclaimed Pedro II, the Emperor responded that his heir was still a child. Early in the following month Pedro I abruptly dismissed his ministers and replaced them by a group of unpopular aristocrats. Meantime seditious meetings were being held; and the spirit of discontent was spreading rapidly, especially among the imperial soldiers.

Increasing Unpopularity of Pedro's Rule

Some inhabitants of the capital city demanded that the Emperor should dismiss his aristocratic cabinet and reinstate the ministry of Brazilians that had preceded it—a demand to which he would not accede. Pedro I then issued a justificatory proclamation: he declared that he would always support the existing Constitution; he asserted that his cabinet was animated by constitutional principles, and implored the Brazilians to preserve tranquillity. To agents of discontented citizens who asked him for the restoration of the previous ministry, he responded epigrammatically that he would do everything for the people but nothing by the people. Upon learning of that response the populace of Rio de Janeiro rose in a revolt which was vigorously supported by imperial soldiers. It appears that some Liberals were uncertain whether they wished to retain the monarchy or to found a republic.

Deserted by his soldiers and unable to get the support of Brazilian leaders, early on the morning of April 7, 1831, in his spacious palace at Boa Vista, the Emperor wrote an act of abdication. That brief state paper was a curious document. Pedro I declared that, availing himself of his constitutional right, he voluntarily abdicated in favor of his very beloved and esteemed son, Dom Pedro de Alcantara. So perturbed was the monarch that he omitted to state that he was abdicating the Brazilian crown. The people of Rio de Janeiro joyfully acclaimed the new Emperor, who was only five years of age.

At the request of his ministers, the ex-Emperor soon dismissed them, with the exception of the Marquis de Inhambupe, who was to transfer the government to the new authorities. Early on the following morning, accompanied by his wife, his daughter, and a few servants, Pedro embarked on the English vessel "Warspite." On board that warship, under date of April 8, Pedro addressed a letter to Brazilian deputies

THE LATIN-AMERICAN NATIONS IN 1831

(From Robertson's *Rise of the Spanish-American Republics*)

and senators which stated that in the exercise of his constitutional right he had appointed José Bonifacio as the tutor of his children.

The Regency After the abdication of Pedro I was announced, a special session of the Brazilian Congress assembled which appointed a Provisional Regency. Soon afterward the regents issued a proclamation which announced that Pedro de Alcantara was the Constitutional Emperor, which expressed confidence that this prince would learn to love Brazil in his childhood, and which declared that the Regency would remain in power only until a regular session of Congress should assemble. With sanguine words the Provisional Regency thus ushered in a most distracted period of Brazilian history.

When the two houses assembled in regular session, as provided by the Constitution, they appointed a Regency composed of three persons, namely, General Francisco de Lima e Silva, José da Costa Carvalho, and João Braulio Muniz. This Regency ruled from 1831 to 1835. The insubordination of the soldiers and the growth of a sectional spirit in various provinces made that period very tumultuous. The revolution of April had evidently spread the taint of disaffection in the army. In the capital city soldiers started a mutiny. In the province of Para they deposed their commanders and assassinated the civil magistrates, thus starting a rebellion that lasted about four years. In the province of Pernambuco the citizens had to arm themselves for defense against the rebellious soldiery. In the province of Maranhão revolutionists deposed the chief civil and military commanders. In the province of Ceará a certain Pinto Madeira plotted to restore the province to Pedro I. In the interior province of Matto Grosso anarchic disturbances took place.

But the great littoral provinces of São Paulo and Rio de Janeiro, with the extensive interior province of Minas Geraes, served as the ballast of the Empire. Further, a Moderate party supported the Regency. The commanding figure that emerged during this period was the minister of justice, Father Feijó, who created a national guard and quelled uprisings in and about the capital city. A Brazilian littérateur likened him to Carlyle's providential heroes.

The spirit of reform was manifested by attempts to amend the fundamental law. On May 6, 1831, Miranda Ribeiro **Proposed Amendments to the Constitution** introduced a motion into the House of Deputies which proposed the revision of certain articles of the Constitution. A special committee was consequently appointed composed of three deputies. It soon reported to Congress in favor of certain constitutional amendments. Among its recommendations was an amendment abolishing the life tenure of senators. Another amendment proposed that the government of Brazil should be a federal monarchy. A compromise between the two houses was the law dated October 12, 1832, which authorized the electors of deputies to the next Congress to confer upon their representatives the power to amend specified articles of the Constitution.

Accordingly the Congress of 1834-1837 seriously considered the revision of the Constitution. By a vote of seventy against sixteen the lower house of Congress resolved to revise the Constitution without the sanction of the Senate. With the approval of the Regency the House of Deputies embodied certain proposed amendments in the Additional Act, which was adopted on August 12, 1834. This act abolished the Council of State. It provided that, in the absence of an adult heir to the throne, electoral colleges in the provinces should select a Regent who was to serve for four years. It also provided that instead of councils with very restricted functions, the provinces should have autonomous legislative assemblies. The exiled ex-Emperor died in Portugal in the same year as that in which the Brazilian Constitution was thus amended by concessions to the spirit of sectionalism.

On October 12, 1835, Congress installed Father Feijó as sole Regent. This step marked a temporary loss of power by the Liberals. Feijó pursued an independent policy and did not select his ministers from Congress. He was compelled not only to   **Regent Feijó** establish the supremacy of the civil government against revolutionists but also to carry on a struggle with Congress that was determined to assert its authority. In September, 1835, a federalist revolt gained startling headway in the southern province of Rio Grande do Sul. Though the leader of the republican partisans in that region was captured, Feijó was unable to suppress the revolutionary movement. A decree restricting the liberty of the press added to his unpopularity. Parliamentary opposition, which was based upon the union with moderate Liberals of those reactionaries who wished a restoration of previous conditions, hastened Feijó's downfall. Prominent in the formation of the new party group were Bernardo de Vasconcellos and Pedro de Araujo Lima, who later became the Marquis of Olinda. The new party won the elections of 1836; Regent Feijó gave up his position in September, 1837. In that month Araujo Lima assumed the functions of the Regent, who acted in the name of Emperor Pedro II.

The accession of Araujo Lima to the Regency signalized the triumph of those politicians who wished a species of responsible government adopted. The new Regent chose a ministry from members of Congress. A law was soon passed that restricted the provincial autonomy which had been conceded by the Additional Act. Civil wars did not entirely subside during the Regency.

There was a significant agitation concerned with the youthful

Emperor. In April, 1840, an association was founded to promote the accession of Pedro II to the throne. On July 23, 1840, the Liberals succeeded in passing through both houses of Congress a declaration that Prince Pedro had attained his majority. A project of a proclamation was framed announcing that decision; and a committee was appointed to inform the prince of the step which Congress had taken. The spokesman of this committee informed Pedro de Alcantara that Congress, the sole repository of the sentiments of the Brazilian nation, had become convinced that the best remedy for the existing evils was the immediate acclamation of his majority and his consequent elevation to the Brazilian throne. Pedro was invited to take the oath of office as Emperor. This step was evidently in accord with his wishes. Upon the afternoon of July 23, accompanied by a splendid retinue, the youthful prince proceeded to the hall of the Senate. There he took an oath to maintain the Catholic religion and the integrity of the Empire, to execute the imperial laws and Constitution, and to promote the general welfare of Brazil. The coronation ceremony took place on July 18, 1841, amid great festivities.

The American prince became Emperor Pedro II of Brazil in his fifteenth year in spite of a constitutional provision that the heir to the throne should be considered a minor until he had completed his eighteenth year. It is scarcely an exaggeration to say that Pedro II asumed imperial power by virtue of a parliamentary revolution. Shortly afterward the youthful Emperor married a daughter of the King of the Two Sicilies. For many years deprived of his mother's care, trained by his tutors to sit at the imperial council table, and withal something of a bookworm, Pedro II had an attractive personality. His dignified demeanor and unostentatious manners won for him a high measure of popularity. Though a model of domestic virtue, he was accused of resorting to personal influence in politics. Unfortunately for the continuance of imperial rule, he lacked initiative; he was not a champion of political progress; and he neglected to cultivate the army. With some of the characteristics of a benevolent despot, Pedro the Magnanimous served long as the chief magistrate of "a republican Empire."

Emperor Pedro II

The youthful Emperor began his long rule by selecting a ministry of Liberals. His mode of government may be termed parliamentary. The political complexion of his ministries varied with that of the House of Deputies: from 1840 to 1889 his ministers were alternately Liberals and Conservatives. Certain constitutional and legal reforms soon strengthened his hands. After the Council of State was reëstablished by a law of November 23, 1841, it exercised a steadying influence upon public policies. On December 3 of that year a code of

procedure was promulgated which standardized legal processes. By
the end of 1845 civil wars which had raged in the provinces of São
Paulo, Minas Geraes, and Rio Grande do Sul had been suppressed by
imperial soldiers. A revolt in the province of Pernambuco, which was
precipitated by persons who wished that commerce should be monopolized by native Brazilians, was suppressed in 1848. Pedro II thus
gave the land a good peace. On the other hand, dissatisfied with
Argentina's foreign policy, in 1851 Brazil became involved in the war
which Platean Liberals undertook to wage against Rosas, the dictator
of Argentina. Complications with Uruguay followed which culminated
in a war against Paraguay that will be described in a subsequent
chapter.

The long reign of Pedro II was an epoch of great progress. In 1850
the first regular line of packets was established between Brazil and
Europe. Four years later the first railway line in Brazil
was opened to traffic. More than five thousand miles of   Social and
railway had been laid by 1889. By that date some eleven   Economic
thousand miles of telegraph lines were in use, besides   Progress
submarine cables. Between 1831 and 1889 the revenues of the Empire
increased about fourteenfold. From 1840 to 1889 the value of its
products increased about tenfold. Immigration from Europe was
encouraged: in 1888 about one hundred and thirty thousand immigrants landed in Brazilian ports.

As Brazil possessed extensive lands bordering upon the Amazon
River, her policy toward the navigation of that river was of interest
not only to South American nations but also to leading commercial
nations of the world. Through diplomatic negotiations with republics
owning territories along the Amazon River the Empire tried so to
influence the policies of those states as to exclude from the navigation
of that river nations which did not possess land upon its banks. After
Uruguay, Argentina, Paraguay, and Bolivia had conceded the freedom
of navigation of their international rivers, however, an increasing
propaganda in Brazil in favor of similar action induced the imperial
government to alter its policy. On December 7, 1866, the minister of
foreign affairs published a decree which announced that, after the
lapse of nine months, the navigation of the Amazon River and its
tributaries should be free to the merchant vessels of all nations up
to the Brazilian frontiers. By a supplementary decree of July 31,
1867, the Brazilian government made known that the main channel of
the Amazon would be open as far as Tabatinga.

More than one student of Brazilian politics has said that the "personal" influence which the Emperor exercised by virtue of the so-called
moderative power was largely responsible for the progress made dur-

ing the years from 1840 to 1889. This influence was not without an effect upon politics. Apparently he aimed thus to hold the balance between

Political Problems

Conservatives and Liberals. During his reign certain ministries were dissolved because they did not have the sanction of public opinion. Discerning Brazilians have asserted that Pedro II used such occasions to enhance his own political prestige as the permanent factor in national politics. Though he permitted a large measure of freedom to public opinion and the press, a certain senator once stigmatized his rule as a "veiled despotism."

A most significant development of his long reign was the appearance of a new political party. On December 3, 1870, the first number was published of a journal named the *Republic,* which became the organ of the Republican party. The founding of that journal, said the Brazilian statesman, Joaquim Nabuco, "was an event, which, if there had been prescience in politics, would have eclipsed all other events." A manifesto which that issue contained, signed by fifty-seven leaders of the new movement, declared that an organization of Republicans was legitimate and necessary. They proposed that a constituent assembly should be convoked with power to consider social and political reforms and to inaugurate a new régime. Their program was favorably received in certain provinces, especially in São Paulo and Minas Geraes, where Republican clubs were formed.

A grave politico-religious problem arose to disturb party alignments. The tranquil relations that had existed between Church and State in Brazil were seriously disturbed in 1872 because of a dispute precipitated by the Bishop of Olinda who ordered Catholic societies to expel such members as belonged to Masonic lodges. In the opinion of the Brazilian government that action was unauthorized. It accordingly directed the bishop to withdraw the interdict which he had laid upon the brotherhoods where his order had not been obeyed. As the offending bishop refused to obey the commands of the government, it dispatched an ambassador to the Holy See who was told that the conduct of the bishop had been censured by Pope Pius IX. The government then prosecuted two bishops who were sentenced to imprisonment with hard labor. This verdict antagonized the Brazilian clergy, who consequently harbored resentment against the imperial régime.

Other disturbing incidents were caused by the ambition of certain military officers, who were not excluded by law from a political career, to exert an influence in politics. The issue was raised in 1883 when a Brazilian colonel contributed articles to a periodical of Rio de Janeiro criticizing a reform bill which had been introduced into the Senate. The government assumed the position that military officers should obtain the consent of the minister of war before they presumed to make contributions to the newspapers. As the government declined to abide by the decision of certain military officers to the effect that soldiers had the constitutional right to express their views in newspapers, an influential general named Manoel Deodoro da Fonseca, who had been vice-president of the province of Rio Grande do Sul, espoused the soldiers' cause. In February, 1887, he sent an open letter to the Emperor accusing the government of injustice to the soldiers. When, in consequence, the government relinquished its views upon the moot point, its prestige was sadly injured, and the militaristic influence in politics was strengthened.

While the balance of political power was thus slowly shifting from the government to the army, another cloud loomed ominously on the horizon. That was the problem of the emancipation of the slaves. In time, besides the Conservatives, the Liberals, and the Republicans, the abolitionists and the slavocrats formed factions which, however, scarcely crystallized into definite parties.

The Slavery Issue

Slavery had struck its roots deeply into Brazilian soil. Yet, partly because of the anti-slavery policy pursued by England, on November 7, 1831, a law had been enacted which aimed to abolish the African slave trade: it provided that, with certain exceptions, all Negroes brought into Brazil should be free. On September 4, 1850, a law was sanctioned which contained effective provisions for the abolition of the domestic trade in slaves. In the course of the war with Paraguay the Emperor and his advisers were forced to realize that Brazil was despised by her neighbors because she had about one and one-half million bondsmen. During that war Pedro II decided in favor of the gradual emancipation of the Negroes. In April, 1868, a commission of the Council of State headed by Joaquim Nabuco was selected to frame a project of a law concerning Negro slavery. With a few modifications, his project became the basis of the law of September 28, 1871, which was vigorously championed in Congress by the distinguished statesman and diplomat, Viscount Rio Branco.

The law of September 28, 1871, often designated as the "Rio Branco Law," provided that the children of slaves born after that date should be free. Such children should remain under the guardianship of their mothers' masters until they had attained the age of eight years, when those masters might either accept an indemnity from the State or avail themselves of the services of the freed minors until they became twenty-one years old. The names of all slaves should be inscribed in official records by their owners, while children freed by law should be recorded in distinct registers. Slaves who had been abandoned by their masters were declared to be free. This law, which provided for the gradual abolition of slavery, made possible a steady decrease in the number of slaves, but it did not please either the radical Liberals or the extreme abolitionists. Nine years later prominent publicists founded an anti-slavery society. In various quarters of Brazil progressive planters liberated their slaves. On September 28, 1885, a law was sanctioned which provided that all slaves who had reached the age of sixty years should be free. It stipulated, however, that such freedmen should serve their former masters for three years.

This law did not satisfy the radicals. Some of them favored the emancipation of all Negro slaves without compensation to their owners.

Abolition of Slavery In 1887 when the Emperor decided to make a trip to Europe, leaving his daughter, Princess Isabella, who had married Comte d'Eu, to serve as Regent, conditions were ripe for a further change. Italian immigrants in the province of São Paulo, believing that slave labor was inimical to their interests, encouraged slaves to flee from the plantations of their masters. Regent Isabella profited by that incident to advocate immediate emancipation. At her instance, on May 8, 1888, the minister of agriculture introduced a bill into the Chamber of Deputies which provided that slavery should at once be declared extinct. After some debate the bill passed both houses; on May 13 it was sanctioned by Regent Isabella.

This law, which liberated some six hundred thousand Negro slaves without compensation to their owners, may be likened to a two-edged sword. It cut down an institution that had influenced the social and economic life of Brazil for more than two hundred years. It signalized the triumph of the extreme abolitionists and caused Brazilian laborers to rejoice. On the other side, it naturally provoked great discontent among the landowners and furnished a pretext for political disaffection. Rich planters, who had been the mainstay of the monarchy, became affiliated with discontented ecclesiastics, Republicans, and military officers. On June 11, 1889, in the House of Deputies a member exclaimed: "Down with the monarchy! Long live the Republic!"

In November, 1889, at the instigation of Professor Benjamin Constant, who had become a champion of positivist principles, discontented civil and military leaders formed a conspiracy to over-

Deposition of the Emperor throw the monarchy. Early on the morning of November 15 a brigade of Brazilian soldiers commanded by General Deodoro da Fonseca marched from a barracks in the suburbs into the capital city and took possession of the government buildings almost without opposition. The cabinet promptly resigned. Although the aged Emperor, who had just returned from

Europe, still hoped to form a new cabinet, yet his palace was surrounded by soldiers and he was placed under arrest. Revolutionary leaders headed by Deodoro da Fonseca issued a decree which proclaimed that Brazil had been transformed into a federal republic. They declared that the Brazilian provinces joined by a bond of federation now constituted the United States of Brazil. Further, they stated that, pending the election of a Constituent Congress, the nation would be ruled by a provisional government.

On November 17 the imperial family sailed for Portugal. On the next day the provisional government announced that it would recognize and respect all obligations, contracts, treaties, and debts which had been legally contracted by previous governments of Brazil. Certain nations of South America and also the United States soon recognized the new government. Accordingly, by a bloodless revolution, the political system of a vast domain that had harbored a European dynasty was transformed from an empire into a republic. Though monarchical rule in America was thus terminated, many Brazilians long cherished fond recollections of their last Emperor.

The proclamation of the Brazilian republic was followed by a brief interregnum. By a series of decrees the provisional government initiated various reforms. By a decree of December 3, 1889, it appointed a commission to frame a constitution. On January 7, 1890, it issued a decree that provided for freedom of religious worship. On June 22 following it issued a decree convoking a Constituent Assembly which was to meet on November 15. A draft of a constitution for Brazil, which had been framed by Ruy Barbosa and other Republican leaders and had been approved by Deodoro da Fonseca, was soon laid before the Constituent Assembly. That Assembly referred the project to a committee of twenty-one members who represented the states and the district that included the capital city. After a few modifications were made in the plan, it was adopted by the Constituent Assembly. The republican Constitution of Brazil was promulgated on February 24, 1891. This fundamental law announced that the nation was composed of the former provinces united in an indissoluble union which was designated the United States of Brazil.

This Constitution provided for executive, legislative, and judicial departments of government. The President and Vice-President were to be elected by direct popular vote for four years. A cabinet, composed of men who should not sit in Congress, was to be appointed by the President. With the **Constitution of 1891** approval of the Senate, the President might appoint other important federal officers. He was the commander in chief of the army and navy: in case of a foreign invasion, he might declare war at once. He had the right to sanction laws, or to veto them; but Congress might override his veto by a two-thirds vote. He might issue decrees to promote the faithful execution of the laws and might pardon criminals or commute punishments. The Senate was to be made up of three members from each state and from the federal district who should be elected by direct popular vote. The Chamber of Deputies was to be composed of members elected by each state in proportion to its population. Congress, which should hold annual sessions, was given extensive legislative powers. Only registered citizens who were over twenty-one years of age might vote. The judiciary of the Brazilian Union was to be composed of a federal supreme court located at the capital and of inferior courts in the states.

In harmony with a decree of the provisional government, this Constitution provided for the complete separation of Church and State. It prohibited both federal and state governments from establishing, subsidizing, or embarrassing the exercise of religious worship. No church or religious cult was to be supported by the national government or the state governments. Only civil marriage was to be recognized by law. Cemeteries were to be under the control of the civil authorities. No citizen was to be deprived of civil or political rights because of his religious belief. The instruction given in public educational institutions was to be laical. But the right of patronage was relinquished by the Brazilian national government and naturally reverted to the Holy See.

The federal government was prohibited from interfering in the affairs of the states except in specified cases. That government was also prohibited from making discriminations for or against the ports of any state. The states of Brazil were, however, conceded the right to levy export duties. A clause in the Constitution provided that each state must be organized according to the republican form. Shortly after the federal Constitution had been adopted, the Brazilian states also promulgated constitutions. The Brazilian fathers had modeled their republican system after that of the United States.

In accordance with a constitutional provision, Congress in joint session proceeded to elect the chief magistrate. General Deodoro da Fonseca was elected president and another military man,

Deodoro da Fonseca Becomes President

Marshal Floriano Peixoto, was elected vice-president. Deodoro da Fonseca's rule closely resembled his dictatorship during the interregnum. He interfered in the affairs of the state of São Paulo upon the pretext that its president was acting in an irregular fashion. On March 18, 1891, a group of prominent Brazilians accordingly issued a protest against this unconstitutional rule. So strong did the opposition to the President become in Congress that it even refused to vote the appropriations which were necessary to carry on the government.

On November 3, 1891, the President issued a decree by which he dissolved Congress and invited the nation to select representatives to an assembly that should revise the Constitution. To justify his measures he asserted that monarchical conspirators were intriguing against the republic. His dictatorial policy provoked opposition, especially in the states of Pará, São Paulo, and Rio Grande do Sul. The navy stationed at Rio de Janeiro displayed disaffection. On the morning of November 23, 1891, Admiral Custodio José de Mello, who was disgusted with arbitrary rule, assumed charge of the navy and thus assured the overthrow of the dictator. Upon the same day Deodoro da Fonseca resigned the presidency and made way for his constitutional successor, Marshal Peixoto, who at once convoked an extraordinary session of Congress.

Still, the presidency of Peixoto, 1891-1894, was in the main a continuation of arbitrary rule. Brazil had merely passed from the hands of one military dictator to those of another. Some Brazilians suspected that the President desired to perpetuate his power; for he vetoed a bill providing that a vice-president who became president should not be eligible for the presidency during the ensuing term. By a decree of April 10, 1892, Peixoto announced that the federal district should be considered as under martial law. Against this measure, Ruy Barbosa protested and insisted that accused persons were entitled to the privileges of the writ of habeas corpus. Successful in his contention, in May, 1893, Ruy Barbosa took charge of the *Journal of Brazil* which became a champion of constitutional government. So active a campaign did the new editor wage against "praetorian centralization" that the President evidently contemplated casting him into prison. Hence in September, 1893, Ruy Barbosa fled to Buenos Aires.

On September 6 the marines in the harbor of Rio de Janeiro rose against the government. Admiral Mello issued a manifesto declaring that Marshal Peixoto had corrupted the people, emptied the national treasury, and abused the Constitution. As many insurrectionary sympathizers resided in the capital, Mello could only threaten to bombard it. He accordingly left the harbor of Rio de Janeiro in one vessel and established a capital in the city of Santa Catharina, where he hoped to obtain the support of Gumercindo Saraiva who had placed himself at the head of a revolt in the state of Rio Grande do Sul. Saraiva's invasion of that state however, ended in failure. Admiral Mello sailed for Buenos Aires, and his revolt also collapsed. Marshal Peixoto had triumphed. As he did not covet another term in the presidency, the successful candidate in the campaign of March, 1894, was Prudente de Moraes Barros, who had presided over the Constituent Assembly of 1889-1890.

Moraes Barros, who was chief magistrate from 1894 to 1898, has aptly been styled the first civilian president of Brazil. A lawyer by training and a Republican, he transformed the administration of his country. During his presidency the smoldering embers of civil war were extinguished. Early in 1895 an amnesty was conceded to all enlisted men who had participated in revolts. Praetorian methods were gradually discarded; life and property were again respected. Upon his return from exile, Ruy Barbosa was joyfully acclaimed by the people. In 1896 Antonio Maciel, who was called "Conselheiro," a missionary among the half-breeds and Indians of the hinterland of the state of Bahia, became involved in a quarrel with the secular authorities which developed into an insurrection. In October, 1897, when the misguided fanatic's stronghold at Canudos fell into the hands of the republic's soldiers, the revolt, which was attributed in part to the influence of monarchists, collapsed. Henceforth monarchical traditions were decidedly on the wane. The republican government had found itself.

During the administration of Moraes Barros the finances of Brazil were seriously embarrassed. This was partly due to the fact that at times the government had been corrupt and extravagant. In part it was due to attempts to relieve the treasury by issues of paper money. Further, the wars with Argentina and Paraguay had caused large deficits, and the revolts that had ensued after the downfall of the Empire had compelled extraordinary expenditures. The expenses of the army alone amounted to some five million pounds sterling per annum. Under this President, deficit followed deficit: two war vessels had to be sold to alleviate the financial stringency. In 1897 a large amount of inconvertible paper money was in circulation; the rate of exchange descended to its lowest point. A Brazilian economist has calculated that, as the interest on the heavy loans which Brazil had contracted since 1824 was payable in Europe, the low rate of exchange absorbed about one-quarter of the national revenue. The government feared that it would be unable to pay the interest due on its foreign debts in June, 1898, while it could scarcely hope under the existing circumstances to negotiate another foreign loan. Nor could it anticipate much aid by an increase of the tariff duties from which most of its revenues were derived. It faced bankruptcy.

A prominent candidate in the presidential campaign of 1898 was Manoel Ferrez de Campos Salles, who had declared himself against the adoption of a parliamentary régime, and had instead championed the division of the government into executive, legislative, and judicial departments. Campos Salles had also pronounced himself against the intervention of the national government in the affairs of the states. He favored a federal republic instead of a unitary or a centralized republic. The campaign of 1898 resulted in his election to the presidency.

The president-elect had also meditated about his country's financial ills. Before his inauguration Campos Salles took a trip to Europe to seek a remedy for them. During that journey he consulted prominent bankers in England and France. The Rothschild banking firm proposed that certain foreign loans should be consolidated; it advised him that this was the only feasible solution of the fiscal stringency. As the basis for a loan of ten million pounds sterling, that firm asked for certain pledges and guaranties. To some of its proposals Campos Salles could not agree. The basis for an agreement was, however, reached before the president-elect left for his native land. A contract framed in July, 1898, provided that the Rothschilds would fund not over ten million pounds of the Brazilian debt at 5 per cent interest per annum. It made provision for a sinking fund. It provided that, as a guaranty for the payment of the obligations that were being incurred, the nation should hypothecate her customs revenues, especially those of the capital city. Until July, 1901, no other debt should be incurred by Brazil, except by the consent of the Rothschilds. Paper money equivalent to the amount of the loan should be retired from circulation. Upon returning to Brazil the president-elect submitted this contract to Congress which ratified it with scarcely a dissenting vote.

The Campaign of 1898

During the presidency of Campos Salles a dispute respecting the bounds between Brazil and France in South America became acute. The contending parties gave different interpretations to Article VIII of the Treaty of Utrecht by which France in 1713 had acknowledged the claims of Portugal to the territory between the Amazon River and the river Japoc (Vicente Pinzón). In the latter half of the eighteenth century pioneers from French Guiana had penetrated into territory which was claimed by Brazil; while France maintained that the river Japoc was not identical with the Oyapoc River, as maintained by Brazil, but that it was a different river. At last, despairing of a settlement by diplomatic negotiations, Brazil and France agreed to submit the question in dispute to the arbitration of the President of Switzerland. As her representative Brazil selected Baron Rio Branco. The decision, which was announced on December 1, 1900, was mainly in favor of the Brazilian contention. The arbiter took the view that the Oyapoc River, emptying in latitude 4° 10′ north of the equator, was the river

Boundary Disputes

Japoc or Vicente Pinzón. France obtained little more than one thousand square miles of the disputed territory.

In 1902 Rodrigues Alves was elected president. During his administration two other boundary controversies were peacefully adjusted. One of those concerned the boundary between Brazil and British Guiana that had been in dispute for some time. Both Brazil and England had caused surveys of the disputed territory to be made by boundary commissions, but the two nations were unable to reach a settlement by negotiation. Hence they agreed to submit their claims to the arbitration of the King of Italy. To plead her cause Brazil selected the distinguished publicist, Joaquim Nabuco, who was aided in the preparation of his case by Rio Branco. The arbitral award of Victor Emmanuel III, which was announced on June 6, 1904, divided the disputed territory between the parties. The Brazilian government soon took steps to adjust another boundary dispute. By an agreement with Holland in 1906 a boundary line was sketched between Brazil and Dutch Guiana.

The internal administration of President Alves was distinguished by the improvement of the metropolis. In 1902 Rio de Janeiro, located upon one of the finest sites in the world, was still in many respects a colonial city. A guiding force in the movement for civic improvement was the prefect of Rio de Janeiro, Pereira Passos. His elaborate plan, approved in September, 1903, was executed with remarkable celerity. On March 8, 1904, a new street named the Central Avenue was begun; there splendid municipal and national buildings were soon constructed. A long, stone quay was built. Several delightful public gardens and parks were plotted. Notable among the streets that were laid out was the Avenida Beira Mar, a charming boulevard that soon stretched for miles along the ocean front. Not of least importance, under the direction of the eminent physician, Oswaldo Cruz, so stubborn a fight was waged against the mosquito that eventually the terrible scourge of yellow fever was thoroughly eradicated from the renaissant capital city.

President Alves had been succeeded in 1906 by Affonso Penna. During his presidential campaign Penna had expressed his wish to provide a stable currency. In arguing for the creation of a bank for the redemption of paper money, he was presumably desirous to imitate the example of Argentina. After his election President Penna continued to champion fiscal reform, and, on December 6, 1906, he signed a law providing for the establishment of an institution for the redemption of paper which was to be styled the Bank of Redemption. This law provided for the issue upon gold deposited in the bank of new paper notes which might be convertible into gold by the bank at the rate of fifteen pence for a milreis. By the end of December, 1907, that bank had on hand gold amounting to some six million two hundred thousand pounds sterling, while it had placed in circulation about the same amount of redeemable paper currency.

Upon the death of President Penna in 1909 he was succeeded by Vice-President Nilo Peçanha. The leading candidates in the presidential campaign of 1910 were the Liberal Republican, Ruy Barbosa, and Marshal Hermes da Fonseca, a Conserva- **Political Dissensions** tive Republican. The views formulated by Ruy Barbosa in the campaign of 1910 bear a close resemblance to the platform of a political party. Among other principles this Liberal leader declared against any interference by the government in judicial tribunals or in their decisions. The federal government should not refuse to execute a law because of its alleged unconstitutionality. That government should not interfere in federal, state, or local elections. Except in grave emergencies, it should not declare martial law.

In spite of the eloquent appeals of Ruy Barbosa, which evoked enthusiastic popular support in certain quarters, when Congress assembled to count the votes, it declared that the military candidate was elected president for the term 1910-1914. Partisans of Ruy Barbosa styled the ensuing rule of Hermes da Fonseca a dictatorship. A revolt that soon broke out in the navy was sternly repressed: the offending sailors were embarked on board a vessel and shot upon the high sea. Bahia, the natal city of Ruy Barbosa and of other prominent Brazilian publicists, was bombarded.

In 1912 in the lower house of Congress a coterie of deputies formed a society which was opposed to the rule of Hermes da Fonseca. The convention of the party which opposed his administration met at Rio de Janeiro in July, 1913, and nominated as its vice-presidential candidate, Alfredo Ellis, and as its presidential, anti-militaristic candidate, Ruy Barbosa. Because of a grave financial crisis that confronted the nation, however, the candidates of the Liberal Republican party withdrew from the contest. They expressed the view that the voters ought to elect to the presidency a publicist who should represent not a faction or certain factions but all people. On March 1, 1914, Wenceslao Braz was chosen president.

During the quarter-century that had elapsed between the deposition of Pedro II and the election of 1914 many monarchists had passed from the political stage. Still Brazil had scarcely emerged from the period of personal politics. Frequently the attitude of a voter toward a presidential candidate had been determined by his opinion of the personality of a candidate rather than by the candidate's political views. Occasionally—as in 1897 and 1910—a candidate stated his views trenchantly on moot problems.

Attention will next be directed to social, economic, and intellectual life before the first World War disturbed the structure of society.

A law of 1907 provided that every citizen between the ages of twenty-one and forty-four capable of bearing arms should be responsi-

Conditions on the Eve of the First World War

ble for military service. Every citizen was liable for two years of active service and seven years in the reserve. There were perhaps not more than eighteen thousand regular soldiers. In addition, however, there were many military associations and shooting clubs, especially in southern Brazil; and important municipalities had their own military guards or military police. About 1914 Brazil had three battleships, fourteen destroyers, five torpedo cruisers, and five submarines.

Immigration to Brazil from other European nations than Portugal had begun during the reign of John VI. As early as 1818 some Swiss immigrants had settled at Novo Friburgo, near Rio de Janeiro. With the current of settlers from Switzerland, there soon mingled an increasing stream of settlers from the German Confederation. During the reign of Pedro II a large number of Germans became segregated in southern Brazil where they preserved to a remarkable extent their own language, customs, and ideals. Under that Emperor immigrants from the United States also arrived in Brazil. During the last decade of the nineteenth century certain Brazilian states passed laws to encourage immigration. In 1907 the federal government issued a decree declaring that the peopling of Brazil would be encouraged by the national administration in agreement with state governments, with railway companies, and with private individuals, provided that certain regulations were observed. This decree contained provisions about the rights and privileges of immigrants and the aid to be furnished them by the national and the state governments. A conservative scholar estimated the number of immigrants that landed in Brazil from 1820 to 1912 at 3,200,000. Italians led the list with 1,300,000, followed by Portuguese with 900,000, and by Germans with 116,000.

The population was composed of three racial elements: white, black, and red, besides the resulting mixed classes. Though the white

The Population

element was the least numerous, it was politically predominant. Its members, belonging chiefly to the Latin peoples, possibly amounted to one-third of the total population. The Negroes were composed mainly of former slaves and their descendants. Indians inhabited the interior of Brazil; frequently they were fierce warriors, and occasionally they were cannibals. A low estimate placed their number at half a million. From the blending of those elements a mixed class had emerged that possibly comprised a larger portion of the population than the white element.

The most densely populated states were Bahia, São Paulo, and Minas Geraes. The increase of population had been very marked in the progressive state of São Paulo. As Brazil comprised some 3,200,000 square miles of territory, the average population per square mile was less than eight persons. In the main, the habitat of the people was a narrow strip of land that stretched south on the Atlantic coast from Pará to Uruguay and narrow fringes that extended along the Amazon River and its chief tributaries. In southwestern Brazil settlements had been made at some distance in the interior of the plateau and along the rivers. An official survey made in 1920 indicated that the population of Brazil exceeded thirty millions.

The official language of Brazil was Portuguese. In certain regions that language had been modified because of the environment and because of immigration. In the north it was influenced by the language of the Tupian Indians. In the south it was affected by the language of Spanish and German immigrants. Near the bounds between Brazil and her southern neighbors a Spanish-Portuguese mixed dialect was often used. There were many local differences in idioms, vocabularies, and even the meaning of words.

The Empire was Roman Catholic in its religion. After the provisional government decreed the separation of Church and State, the Catholic Church retained its communicants, buildings, lands, and incomes. By 1914 the Brazilian Catholic Church was organized into seven archbishoprics. The archbishop of Rio de Janeiro became the first cardinal created in South America. Nevertheless, the Protestant faith had made some progress in that republic. Throughout southern Brazil the Lutheran church had many adherents; while in important towns and cities Presbyterians from the United States had established missions, churches, and schools.

Social and Economic Conditions

Transportation between Brazil and foreign countries was mainly by steamships touching at ports along the coast and on the Amazon River. The federal government controlled the Lloyd Brasileiro line plying between Brazil and the United States. Communication between the Brazilian states in the north and those in the south was mainly by ocean or river steamers; for there was no through railroad communication between those sections. Brazil's railroads had mainly been laid where the population was most dense, along the coast and in the immediate hinterland. Most of the railroads were located in the productive agricultural and mining lands of the south.

The chief occupations in Brazil were agriculture, mining, manufacturing, and commerce. The gathering of crude rubber and of Paraguayan tea were important industries. In 1914, with thirty million head of cattle, many inhabitants were engaged in pastoral occupations. At that date Brazil had an extensive dried beef industry, but the meat packing industry had hardly begun. Brazilian authors had printed long lists of their country's minerals: veritable mountains of iron were known to exist; diamond mines and gold washings were still being exploited. Within the last half century some cotton mills have been established. In the large cities a considerable number of inhabitants, especially those of Portuguese extraction, have always been employed in mercantile pursuits.

After the abolition of slavery, the cultivation of sugar cane greatly declined. But the attention paid to coffee culture steadily increased, especially in the state of São Paulo. During the present century the coffee interests acquired an almost dominant interest in Brazilian economic life. By 1914 Brazil was producing about three-fourths of the world's supply of coffee. Over-production, however, had caused a decline in prices: in 1908 the government of São Paulo prohibited an increase in the acreage devoted to coffee plants. That state also decided upon a system of valorization which provided for the purchase by the state of the surplus coffee when the price was low and the storage of that surplus until prices rose. The states of Minas Geraes and Rio de Janeiro also adopted this plan which involved economic coöperation on their part. The national government soon proceeded to make large loans to the coffee states to enable them to carry on this scheme. It even undertook to purchase coffee when the price was low. This interlocking policy on the part of state and national governments not only protected certain planters, but also tended to create a bloc of states that exercised an increasing influence in the national councils.

A concrete notion of the chief economic interests of Brazil will be furnished by statistics of her foreign commerce. In 1914 she exported over eleven and one-quarter million sacks of coffee (of one hundred and thirty-two pounds apiece) which brought some £27,000,-000 sterling. In round numbers other important exports were as follows: crude rubber, £7,000,000; cacao, £1,000,000; cotton, £1,864,-000; leather, £2,956,000; Paraguayan tea, £1,856,000; tobacco, £1,162,-000; and hides, £741,000. These amount are given in English pounds because fluctuations in the value of Brazil's money in international exchange often compelled her merchants to reckon their exports in foreign gold. When Ruy Barbosa withdrew from the presidential race, his country was on the verge of bankruptcy. At the end of 1913 there was a deficit in Brazil's treasury of about £1,715,000 sterling. In addition to a large domestic debt, there was in circulation a considerable amount of inconvertible paper money. The total foreign debt aggregated £100,000,000 and it was plain that Brazil could not even pay the interest on it. The government of Wenceslao Braz was thus forced to initiate negotiations for a foreign loan in order to tide the ship of state over the rocks. Not without considerable difficulty was another funding loan negotiated with the Rothschilds in October, 1914, which amounted to £15,000,000, was to bear interest at 5 per cent, and was to fall due during the period, 1914-1977.

Elementary instruction, which was in charge of the secretaries of interior of the various states, was backward, particularly in the interior and in the north. In primary schools education was free but not compulsory. A large number of private **Education** schools and of schools established by Protestant missionaries throughout Brazil were also devoted to elementary instruction. Secondary education was provided by the federal government, by state governments, and by various private institutions. Normal schools were found in important towns and cities. Under the control of the federal government at the capitals of various states there had been established institutions for the study of engineering, medicine, pharmacy, dentistry, and law. At São Paulo was located Mackenzie College, an institution founded by Presbyterian missionaries, which offered courses in commerce, engineering, and the humanities. At the capital of the republic were located academies of fine arts. Near that capital was located a zoölogical laboratory—the best in Latin America—that had been named after its distinguished founder, Oswaldo Cruz.

A long list of authors entitles Brazil to a place in the front rank of American literary nations. Among her essayists and novelists may be mentioned the following: J. Manoel de Macedo, author of *A Moreninha*, whose novels showed the influence of **Literature** the romantic movement; José de Alencar, the brilliant **and Art** author of many realistic novels about Brazilian life, such as *Guarany, Cinco Minutos,* and *Sonhos de ouro;* Tavares Bastos, whose essays stimulated Brazilian publicists to open the Amazon to the world's commerce; Machado de Assis, the distinguished novelist and essayist, who wrote *Braz Cubas* and *Varias Historias;* Raul Pompéa, a psychological novelist, author of *Atheneu,* and other stories; Escragnolle Taunay, who produced novels and historical essays; Euclydes da Cunha, who composed *Os Sertoes;* and Baron Rio Branco, author of political essays and geographical studies.

Prominent among historical writers are Joaquim Nabuco, who wrote *A Statesman of the Empire;* Pereira da Silva, author, among other works, of the *History of the Founding of the Brazilian Empire;*

Francisco A. Varnhagen, who wrote a *General History of Brazil;*
João Lisboa, who gathered *Data for the History of Maranhão;* Manoel
de Oliveira Lima, the diplomat and littérateur, author of *King John VI
of Brazil;* and Helio Lobo, who among illuminating diplomatic studies
has written *From Monroe to Rio Branco.* Besides writing literary
histories of Brazil, both Sylvio Roméro and José Verissimo edited or
produced works of poetic merit.

Independent Brazil produced many poets. Domingos José Gonçalves
de Magalhães showed the religious phase of Brazilian romanticism in
his volumes *Suspiros Poeticos e Saudades* and his *Mysterios e Cantos
Funebres.* Manoel de Araujo Porto Alegre in his *Brasilianas* and other
poems chanted about the rural scenes of his native land. A great lyric
poet, Antonio Gonçalves Dias, in whose veins flowed Indian, Negro,
and Portuguese blood, has been characterized as the best poetic exponent not only of the aborigines but also of the citizens of Brazil.
Manoel Antonio Alvares de Azevedo, author of the *Lyra dos vinte
annos,* showed the influence of various intellectual currents of his
age. Castro Alves, a poet of Bahia, sang passionately about the evils
of slave society in *O poema dos escravos.* In spontaneous verse Olavo
Bilac chanted historic incidents, as in *Delenda Carthago,* or sang of
love, as in *Via-lactea.* A pure Negro named Cruz e Sousa was characterized by Sylvio Roméro as being in many respects the best poet that
Brazil had produced.

Music was a favorite art. A national school of music was founded
in 1847. It was reorganized in 1890 under the auspices of Leopoldo
Miguez, the composer of various symphonies. Carlos Gomes won a
lasting place in the hearts of Brazilians by his opera, *Guarany.* The
academy of fine arts, which was founded by John VI, has trained some
notable painters and sculptors. From the atelier of Rodolfo Bernadelli,
who studied in Rome, have come some notable sculptures, as "Christ
and the Adulteress." Under the stimulus of Italian and French painters
a native school of painting developed. Notable among Brazilian artists
was Pedro Americo who portrayed that spirited scene at Ypiranga in
1822 which he styled the "Proclamation of Independence."

After several different projects of a civil code had been framed by
prominent jurists, in January, 1899, the minister of justice authorized
Professor Clovis Bevilaqua to frame a code. His draft
was revised by Ruy Barbosa, and after being modified
by the Brazilian Congress, was sanctioned by President
Wenceslao Braz, with the stipulation that it should go
into force on January 1, 1917. The material for the code was mainly
drawn from Portuguese ordinances, Brazilian laws, and Brazilian
juristic writings. An introduction composed of one hundred and twenty-

**The
Brazilian
Civil Code**

one articles, was followed by a general division composed of three books dealing with persons, property, and juridical acts; and by a special division made up of four books concerning family law, the law of property, the law of obligations (including contracts), and the law of succession. A provision about what may be termed "homestead rights" shows that in a few minor clauses the framers of the code were influenced by precedents that had developed in foreign lands. The civil code of the United States of Brazil was virtually a general federal statute which not only superseded the national laws and regulations in regard to such matters as land-holding, contracts and judicial proceedings but also superseded the respective laws of twenty-one states.

The struggle between Germany and Austria, on the one side, and England, France, and Russia, on the other side, which began in August, 1914, had a profound influence upon South America. At an early stage in the first World War the publicists of Brazil realized that Germany's submarine policy was a danger to their nation. The situation became critical, when, in January, 1917, the German imperial government announced a ruthless submarine campaign. In his reply to this announcement the Brazilian secretary of state not only protested against the submarine blockade but also informed Germany that the responsibility for any acts contrary to international law which might affect Brazilian citizens, merchandise, or ships would devolve upon her. As in duty bound, Brazil issued a proclamation of neutrality in the war between the United States and Germany. *Policy toward the First World War*

After a report reached Rio de Janeiro that a Brazilian vessel had been torpedoed by a German submarine without warning, on April 11, 1917, Brazil announced that diplomatic relations with Germany had been severed. When news reached the capital that another Brazilian ship had been torpedoed, President Wenceslao Braz urged Congress to take steps for national defense and recommended that the German merchant vessels which were interned in Brazil's ports should be seized. Congress acted favorably on the message, and, on June 2, 1917, the President issued a decree providing that Brazil should use the interned German ships. This decisive act was soon followed by a law which revoked Brazil's neutrality. On October 25 President Wenceslao Braz notified Congress that another Brazilian vessel had just been torpedoed and that the captain of that vessel had been cast into prison. Further, he declared that Brazil could not avoid the war which Germany had imposed upon her.

On October 26, 1917, the President signed a law which announced that a state of war existed between Brazil and Germany. The government soon took steps to raise and equip soldiers to aid the Allies on the battlefields of Europe. Warships of Brazil were dispatched to join the navies of England and the United States in the North Sea.

This war affected conditions in Brazil in various ways. Restrictions that were placed by certain belligerent nations upon their exports, lack of vessels for the carrying trade, and high prices checked the importa-tion of manufactured articles. The decrease in imports reduced the government's revenues. In December, 1914, the President was authorized to suspend the redemption of paper money in gold. During the war the level of international exchange for Brazil was lowered. It became difficult for Brazilians to procure rolling stock for their railroads. After the United States, as well as the Allies, had restricted the trade in coffee and rubber, Brazil's exports of those staples necessarily decreased greatly. A trend accordingly became manifest toward a more diversified system of agriculture. New foodstuffs, especially rice, meat, corn, beans, and cassava meal, entered in considerable quantities into Brazil's exports. Many small factories of different sorts were erected throughout the country. Of those the most important were tanneries, paper mills, cotton factories, and meat-packing establishments. The war seriously impeded certain projected public improvements, for it hindered the flow of foreign capital into Brazil.

Influence of that War upon Brazil

On March 1, 1918, Rodrigues Alves was again elected president. •As he soon became seriously ill, Vice-President Delfim Moreira tem-porarily administered the government. In a special elec-tion held on April 13, 1919, Dr. Epitacio Pessoa, who was acting as head of the Brazilian delegation at the Versailles Conference, was chosen president. After his inauguration, which took place on July 28, 1919, President Pessoa filled his cabinet positions with men from civil life. In May, 1922, his secretary of the treasury floated a large loan in London and New York. A grand exposition, which was opened in the capital on Septem-ber 7, 1922, to celebrate the progress made in Brazil during the century that had elapsed since independence from Portugal was for-mally proclaimed, was honored by a visit from United States Secretary of State Hughes. On November 6, 1922, the Brazilian Ambassador at Washington and the American Secretary of State signed a contract by which the United States agreed to send a number of naval officers under a rear-admiral to Rio de Janeiro to assist Brazil to reform her obsolete navy.

President Epitacio Pessoa

In the election of 1922 the administration candidate, Arturo da Silva Bernardes, President of the state of Minas Geraes, was opposed by the military element led by Hermes da Fonseca that favored the

candidacy of ex-President Pecanha. After Bernardes had been declared elected, Captain Fonseca, the son of Hermes da Fonseca, started
an uprising in a fortress that dominated the capital city, but this
insurrection was soon quelled. Bernardes was inaugurated on November 15, 1922. His program of fiscal reform was initiated by a law of
January 8, 1923, which vested the right to issue paper money in the
Bank of Brazil. Nine months later, by an exchange of notes the United
States and Brazil accorded each other the most-favored-nation treatment in matters relating to the customs.

But the President's plans for retrenchment, which were based upon
the advice of British experts, were badly obstructed by the military
faction which incited a revolt that broke out in July,
1924, in the state of São Paulo. Although the rebels   Political
                                                        Discontent
captured the capital of that state, federal troops soon
forced them to evacuate the city. Because of distracted conditions,
President Bernardes was thenceforth compelled to maintain a species
of martial law in various parts of the republic.

In the election of 1926 Washington Luis, a prominent publicist of
the state of São Paulo, was chosen president. In many respects his
policies were simply a continuation of those of his predecessor. He
suppressed uprisings in various sections of the republic. With the
intention of improving economic conditions, heavier import duties
were laid upon various articles in order to secure funds with which to
ensure the construction of roads in states along the Atlantic seaboard.
Nevertheless, a spirit of social and political discontent prevailed in
certain quarters.

In the election of 1930 the President favored the conservative
candidate, Julio Prestes, president of the state of São Paulo. After
his election Prestes made a trip to the United States and Europe. His
relations with foreign bankers, especially in England, caused much
dissatisfaction in Brazil, where he was accused of being willing to
make great concessions to foreigners in order to obtain a public loan.
A frightful wave of economic depression struck South America; the
value of the milreis, as measured by international exchange, fluctuated
alarmingly; while, despite the attempts of the government to stabilize
the market by valorization, the price of coffee sank very low. Dissatisfied politicians bitterly criticized the Paulista President as well
as the Paulista president-elect.

President Washington Luis was accused of striving to perpetuate
the dominant influence of the state of São Paulo in national politics.
He was accused of trying to promote a transient prosperity by a
governmental building program during the elections. He was accused
of failing to bring to the bar of justice the assassins of the governor

of the state of Parahyba, who had been the candidate of the Liberals for the vice-presidency. The Liberals avowed that the election of Prestes, whom they declared to be a tool of the President, was due to election frauds promoted by officials of the national government.

Unsatisfactory conditions in business as well as in politics thus furnished the occasion for the development of a belligerent spirit of sectionalism. The southern states, which have a temperate clime and are inhabited largely by people of **The Revolution of 1930** European stock, harbored resentment at the haughty domination of the Paulistas in national politics. On October 3, 1930, Getulio Vargas, a lawyer who was president of the cattle-raising state of Rio Grande do Sul and the defeated Liberal candidate for the presidency, raised the standard of revolt. Planters of the state of Paraná, whose fortunes had been much injured by the collapse of coffee prices, followed his example. To the north of the capital city the great state of Minas Geraes, which had ordinarily stood with the Federal District and the influential middle states of São Paulo and Rio de Janeiro, now became gravely disaffected. The ensuing strife was rendered more formidable by the fact that the rebellious states controlled their own militia systems, while in their important cities the police forces could readily be transformed into rebel squadrons.

A grave economic crisis, occurring in juxtaposition with resentment at Paulista domination of the national government, precipitated a civil war. A revolution that had been transforming many forms of industry and unsettling old manners of life had become vocal through the army. Liberalism had become the watchword of dissatisfied sectional leaders who wished to share in the spoils of national office. Bitter discontent with the existing régime had penetrated even into the ranks of federal officials. After three weeks of civil war, President Washington Luis was deposed by prominent army and naval officers of the federal government. On October 24, 1930, his administration was supplanted by a military junta.

The entry of Getulio Vargas into Rio de Janeiro on November 3, 1930, marked the opening of a new era in the political life of the Brazilian people. The Constitution of 1891 was soon discarded: on November 11 a provisional organic law was put into force. During the interregnum measures were taken to reduce the production of sugar and to stabilize the price of coffee. Opposition to dictatorial rule culminated in July, 1932, in a rebellion in the state of São Paulo which lasted three months. Vargas then decided to hold elections for a constitutional convention which met in October, 1933. On July 16 of the next year, the President promulgated a new Constitution.

Though the federal union formed in 1891 was left intact, some changes were made in the relations among the states and in the rôle of the national legislature. The Chamber of Deputies, reënforced by representatives of labor and of professional organizations, was given additional powers. Although restrictions were placed upon the authority of the federal government with respect to the proclamation of a state of siege and with respect to intervention in provincial affairs, yet in some particulars the power of that government was increased. Certain clauses restricted immigration, while others recognized a public interest in commerce, industry, and labor. The President was made ineligible for immediate reëlection.

Vargas was elected president for a term of four years. Disturbances soon took place. In 1935 a military revolt was suppressed. Plinio Salgado headed the Integralists, a Brazilian species of Fascists clad in green shirts, who were rooted in German and Italian elements of the population. Persons suspected of communism were sentenced to imprisonment. Though **Vargas and Totalitarianism** presidential elections had been set for January, 1938, as authorized by Congress, in October, 1937, the President proclaimed a state of war throughout the country. Alleging that the army was in favor of a change, that civil war was imminent, and that communist doctrines were spreading, on November 10, 1937, he not only dissolved Congress but also announced that the Constitution was superseded by a new fundamental law.

The Constitution of 1937 declared that Brazil was composed of states, territories, and the federal district bound together in an "indissoluble union." All internal customs barriers were swept away. The President's term of office was extended to six years and his powers were much increased. Among his new prerogatives was the right to issue "decree-laws" as well as to prorogue the Chamber of Deputies. The "Supreme Authority of the State," as the President was styled, was authorized to interfere in the government of a state by appointing an "interventor" who was to replace the chief magistrate. If the choice of a new national executive by an electoral college composed of specified members did not please the President, he could select another candidate and present both names to the voters in a national election. Article CLXXX declared that, until Congress assembled, the President should have the power to issue decree-laws in all matters within the scope of legislative authority. A careful, American student of the Vargas régime has declared that this article is "a legal tail which wags the constitutional dog."

In a book entitled *The National State* Francisco Campos, the ideologist of the Vargas dictatorship, who was reputed to be the author of the new Constitution, explained that the "Brazilian State, while democratic, is at the same time totalitarian, supreme authority being vested in the President of the republic who exercises it in the name of the people in the interest of their welfare."

As yet, this Constitution has not been submitted to the required referendum. Though it provides for a "National Parliament" composed of a Chamber of Deputies and a Federal Council, both of these are still non-existent. Neither has the Council of National Economy provided by the fundamental law been set up. Again, in December, 1937, political parties were declared to be dissolved. Not only have interventors been introduced into several states, but in each state an "administrative department" has been established, namely a legislative council composed of from four to ten members which passes upon all proposed laws and decrees of the respective state. Steps have also been taken to revise the legal codes. In September, 1940, the states were deprived of the right to tax their mineral resources of which they had been given control by the Constitution of 1891.

The totalitarian traits of the Brazilian republic encouraged some persons to feel that Vargas and his advisers had fallen under Nazi influence. Yet in Rio de Janeiro on May 11, 1938, he ruthlessly suppressed a Nazi-Integralist *putsch* against his government. Plinio Salgado and other agitators fled from Brazil. On January 28, 1942, the government announced that it had severed relations with the Axis powers. A few months later, a spy hunt unearthed hundreds of Nazi agents and caches of radios, dynamite, and military supplies. Many persons suspected of disloyalty were imprisoned. After vessels of Brazil's merchant marine were sunk by Axis submarines along her eastern coast, Vargas decreed that thirty per cent of the assets of Axis citizens was confiscated.

In August, 1942, after five Brazilian ships had been torpedoed in three days with the loss of hundreds of women, children, and soldiers, the government denounced these sinkings as an "ignominious outrage" and announced that "such crimes against the lives and goods of the Brazilians" would not go unpunished. Indignant citizens burned the Nazi flag on the steps of the municipal theater of the capital city. On August 22, 1942, after nineteen of her ships had been thus blown up, Brazil dispatched notes to Germany and Italy which stated that they had committed acts of war against her, thus "creating a belligerent situation," which she was "forced to recognize" in defense of the dignity, sovereignty, and safety not only of herself but of all America. Two days after Brazil thus recognized the existence of a state of war, Vargas issued a decree which closed one Italian and two German banks. Further, he confiscated seventeen Axis vessels interned

MAP ILLUSTRATING TERRITORIAL GAINS MADE BY BRAZIL FROM HER
SPANISH-AMERICAN NEIGHBORS

(After maps by M. Mercado M., and E. S. Zeballos)

in Brazilian ports. On September 16 orders were issued for the complete mobilization of the army.

The only independent nation that long endured under a monarchical form of government in the Americas, under the direction of able leaders, in 1889 Brazil made a sudden change to republicanism. The sharpness of that transition helps to explain why monarchical traditions continued to have an influence in her constitutional and political life. Its sharpness helps to explain the emergence of military governments at certain epochs and also the influence of militaristic parties in the country. With the passing years, however, the people, as well as the publicists, of the Brazilian republic became adapted to the new order. In Brazil, the great melting-pot of America, a distinct national type is being formed. There Portuguese manners and customs still largely persist among the people. Facing the Atlantic, with a domain larger than that of the United States exclusive of Alaska, possessed of enormous natural resources, if she can satisfactorily adjust her financial burdens and secure the needful capital and labor for the development of her potential wealth, the Brazilian republic may look forward hopefully to a vigorous and influential national life. The people of Brazil have passed through a cycle: from imperial government to an imperialistic republican régime, and from that status to what may be termed a dictatorial democracy. In the face of circumstances similar to those that took place during the first World War but more insulting to her honor, Brazil pursued a logical course which again culminated in her entry into a war against Germany.

A salient feature of the development of Brazil has scarcely been touched in the present chapter, namely her extraordinary success in disputes with neighbors about her boundaries. As will be shown in the chapters that concern the Spanish-American nations of South America, Brazil has not only held possession of the territory so generously assigned her by the Spanish-Portuguese Treaty of 1777, but has also gained a clear title to lands far beyond the limits which it sketched. Forts and missions planted by venturesome pioneers furnished the bases for claims successfully urged by her farsighted and scholarly diplomats to extensive territories in the fertile basins of great rivers.

SUGGESTIONS FOR FURTHER READING

AGASSIZ, L., *A Journey in Brazil*, 1869.
BATES, H. W., *The Naturalist on the River Amazon*, 1910.
CALOGERAS, J. P., *A History of Brazil*, 1939.
GOLDBERG, I., *Brazilian Literature*, 1922.
———, *Brazilian Tales Translated from the Portuguese*, 1921.

GRAHAM, M., *Journal of a Voyage to Brazil*, 1824.

GRUBB, K. G., *The Lowland Indians of Amazonia*, 1927.

GUENTHER, K., *A Naturalist in Brazil*, 1931.

HAMBLOCH, E., *His Majesty the President of Brazil*, 1933.

HARING, C. H., *South American Progress*, 1934.

HERRING, H., *Good Neighbors*, 1941.

JAMES, H. J., *The Constitutional System of Brazil*, 1923.

——, *Brazil After a Century of Independence*, 1925.

JOBIM, J., *Brazil, 1939-40, An Economic, Social, and Geographic Survey*, 1940.

KELSEY, V., *Maria Rosa: Everyday Fun and Frolic with Children in Brazil*, 1942.

KIDDER, D. P., and FLETCHER, J. C., *Brazil and the Brazilians*, 1857.

KIPLING, R., *Brazilian Sketches*, 1940.

LOWENSTEIN, K., *Brazil under Vargas*, 1942.

MAACK, R., "The Germans of South Brazil—A German View," *Quarterly Journal of Inter-American Relations*, Vol. I, pp. 5-23.

McCREERY, W. G., and BYNUM, M. L., *The Coffee Industry in Brazil*, 1930.

MANCHESTER, A. K., *British Preëminence in Brazil*, 1933.

NORMANO, J. F., *Brazil, a Study of Economic Types*, 1935.

ROOSEVELT, T., *Through the Brazilian Wilderness*, 1914.

SIMONSEN, R. C., *Brazil's Industrial Evolution*, 1939.

"South America VI: Brazil," *Fortune*, Vol. XIX, No. 6, pp. 43 ff.

TORRES-RÍOSECO, A., *The Epic of Latin American Literature*, 1942.

WADDELL, A. S., "The Revolution in Brazil," *Foreign Policy Reports*, Vol. VI, No. 26, 1931.

WILLIAMS, M. W., *Dom Pedro the Magnanimous*, 1937.

CHAPTER XIII

THE GROWTH OF THE ARGENTINE NATION

Argentina sprang from the heart of the viceroyalty of La Plata. The action of the junta of Buenos Aires, which was crowned by the measures of the Congress of Tucumán in 1816, had brought into existence the nebulous political entity known as the United Provinces of La Plata. In 1819 a Congress at Buenos Aires framed a "unitary" or centralistic Constitution which was opposed by certain of these provinces. During the stormy years which followed that step the advocates of a centralized political system were opposed to those who favored a federal system, namely, a national government that would be based upon provincial autonomy. The years from 1816 to 1829 have indeed been designated the "Period of Anarchy."

Origin of Argentina

A publicist who rose above provincialism was Martín Rodríguez, who in September, 1820, became governor of the province of Buenos Aires. Rodríguez chose as one of his secretaries Bernardino Rivadavia, who wished to promote social and political reforms. At his instance amnesty was granted to expatriated citizens. The cabildo of Buenos Aires, which had occasionally served as a center of dissension, was abolished. Three million pesos were borrowed in Europe for internal improvements. A bank of discount was established that was later designated the national bank. Tithes and ecclesiastical immunities were swept away. In 1821 an institution designated the University of Buenos Aires was founded which took charge of primary, secondary, and higher education. The notion of federalism was kept alive by means of reciprocal agreements regarding amity, commerce, and navigation among the governors of certain provinces. Steps were taken in various sections to authorize the convocation of a constitutional convention that might organize a general government. Some provincial leaders, however, did not favor this plan.

This project was realized during the administration of Juan de las Heras, governor of the province of Buenos Aires. In December, 1824, the delegates of certain provinces of the former viceroyalty assembled at the capital city. On January 23, 1825, this Constituent Assembly promulgated a fundamental law, which provided that the provinces should be administered by their own institutions until a national constitution was adopted. Meanwhile the central executive power was to be vested in Governor Las Heras, who was thus made the chief magistrate of all the provinces represented in the Assembly. As the war with Brazil concerning the status of Uruguay broke out soon afterward, he relinquished his office and recommended that Congress should create a national executive.

By a law of February 6, 1826, Congress established the executive power of the United Provinces. By an almost unanimous vote it elected Bernardino Rivadavia to fill that position. It then proceeded to frame a new constitution. Despite the arguments of certain delegates who championed a federal régime, on July 19, 1826, Congress adopted a centralistic Constitution. This organic law provided that executive authority should be vested in a President. Legislative authority was granted to a Senate and a House of Representatives. A supreme court was given jurisdiction over all disputes to which a province might be a party. By a law of Congress the city of Buenos Aires was made the capital of "the Argentine Republic." Several provinces having declared their opposition to a centralized system, the Constitution was bitterly criticized in certain sections. The governor of the province of Córdoba, General Busto, rejected it and started a rebellion. This example was followed by another local political chieftain, Juan Facundo Quiroga, "the tiger of the pampas." In July, 1827, appealing to his countrymen to suppress their local interests, their partisan differences, and their personal passions, Rivadavia resigned the presidency.

Vicente López, who became president *ad interim*, dissolved Congress, and convoked the legislature of the province of Buenos Aires. On August 12, 1828, this legislature selected Colonel Dorrego as governor. Dorrego had fought in the South American war for independence. While an exile in the United States, he had become an ardent admirer of the federal system, which, upon returning to his native land, he championed in the Constituent Assembly of 1826. Upon becoming governor, he aptly declared that the era was terrible and that his path was "strewn with thorns." While he was governor a treaty with Brazil was signed on August 27, 1828, that guaranteed the independence of Uruguay and terminated the war with the Brazilian Empire. When they returned to the city of Buenos Aires, however, some soldiers who had been engaged in that war revolted under the leadership of a dissatisfied general named Juan Lavalle. Dorrego consequently left that city to secure the aid of Colonel Juan Manuel de Rosas.

The fickle populace of the capital city soon acclaimed Lavalle. That general pursued Governor Dorrego and defeated him at Navarro. When Dorrego was betrayed by one of his own officers, Lavalle arbitrarily ordered him to be executed within two hours. On December 13 he was shot without a trial, and without legal cause: impartial history has judged that this arbitrary act was, in reality, an assassination! Dorrego's execution provoked many protests from the provinces. Quiroga denounced it as an outrage. A convention which met at Santa Fé stigmatized it as high treason and summoned the interior provinces to furnish soldiers to make war on the province of Buenos Aires under the leadership of Estanislao López, governor of the province of Santa Fé. In April, 1829, soldiers commanded by López and Rosas defeated Lavalle. Arrangements were soon made for the cessation of hostilities, for the appointment of a provisional governor of the province of Buenos Aires, and for the withdrawal of Lavalle who took refuge in Uruguay.

Execution of Dorrego

Out of the somber shadow of Dorrego there emerged Juan Manuel de Rosas. He possessed "a coat of arms, blue eyes, and the spirit of a ruler." Rosas was descended from a well-known colonial family. He spent part of his boyhood on his father's ranch, attended school in the capital city, and, when a mere lad, took part in the expulsion of the invading redcoats. Soon afterward he left the paternal roof and engaged in the curing of fish. He then bought land, became a model rancher, an expert horseman, and a prime favorite of the hybrid inhabitants of the pampas who were called gauchos. A leader of the country gentry, he exerted his influence in favor of peace and order whether checking vagabondage and robbery or leading militiamen against Indians.

Shortly after the deposition of Lavalle, the provisional governor of the province of Buenos Aires convoked a legislature which on December 8, 1829, appointed Rosas governor and captain general for three years. If we may trust the memoirs of an Argentine contemporary, when Rosas thus came into power he secretly cherished a scheme to use the customs and the external forms of a federation to mask his centralistic and selfish ambitions. The years from 1829 to 1852 have been appropriately designated the "Age of Rosas."

Shortly after his accession to power, an army under General La Paz defeated federalist soldiers led by Quiroga. Several provinces then proclaimed the victor as supreme military chief. Yet he was soon imprisoned, Quiroga routed his soldiers, and the centralistic cause seemed lost. Meanwhile the legislature of Buenos Aires had conferred extraordinary powers upon Rosas. When peace was restored, that dictator insisted upon relinquishing his authority. General Balcarce, who was appointed by the legislature to succeed him, assumed power on December 17, 1832. Rosas then added to his prestige by leading an expedition against troublesome Indians on the frontiers.

On March 7, 1835, the legislature of the province of Buenos Aires again appointed Rosas governor. It granted to him the sum total of public authority. Rosas accepted the office, but upon the express condition that the voters of the province should approve this appointment. By a referendum which was taken in the end of March, with only a few dissenting votes, the people sanctioned the grant of all public authority to Rosas. To aid him in the administration, he selected secretaries of foreign relations, of the treasury, and of war and the navy. Some early measures of the dictator were as follows: the abrogation of laws that confiscated the property of political offenders; the negotiation of a treaty with England which abolished the slave trade; the founding of a provincial bank upon the ruins of the national bank; the emission of large quantities of paper money; and the reëstablishment of the Jesuit order. Twelve provinces now delegated to him the attributes of national executive: thus there was created the political system that was sometimes styled the Argentine Confederation.

Rosas Becomes Supreme Ruler

So happy were the people of the metropolis at the restoration of peace and tranquillity, that they idolized their ruler. A commission appointed by the legislature to recognize his services decided to present a sword of gold to the dictator, who was styled the "Illustrious Restorer of the Laws." During a festival held in the capital city prominent citizens dragged through the streets a triumphal cart which bore the portrait of Rosas—a cart to which the populace made humble obeisance. Chiefs of friendly Indian tribes adjured their followers to be faithful to Juan Manuel. His pictures were even placed on the altars of churches; from their pulpits the priests exhorted the people to obey him. A secret organization called the *Mazorca* or Ear of Corn, because of the cohesion of its members who were followers of Rosas, harried his enemies and committed all sorts of outrages. An Argentine enemy of the tyrant estimated that during his rule over twenty thousand persons were poisoned, beheaded, shot, or killed in other ways.

Contemporaries described this extraordinary man as endowed with both craft and force. Though his physiognomy was ordinarily tranquil and even mild, yet, upon occasion, the contraction of his lips, said a French diplomat named Brossard, gave him "a singular expression of deliberate severity." Rosas was an accomplished poseur: "when encountered face to face, he could intimidate, or deceive, or seduce." Brossard likened him to those men portrayed by Tacitus, "who placed liberty to the fore so as thereby to overthrow the existing order." This shrewd observer suggestively interpreted the rôle of Rosas in La Plata as being that of a man from the country, who had become "the leader of the reaction of the men of the campo against the predominant influence of the capital city."

The reign of terror fostered by Dictator Rosas was not accepted blindly by every one. His dictatorship had scarcely begun when certain young scholars, including Juan Bautista Alberdi, Esteban Echeverría, and Juan María Gutiérrez founded a club ostensibly for the discussion of literary questions. After the dictator had closed the doors of this club, its members created an organization designated the Association of May, which has been not inappropriately compared to the *Carbonaro*.

Reactions against Rosas

In 1839 Berón de Astrada, governor of the province of Corrientes, who was leading a revolt, was defeated by a partisan of Rosas, captured, and executed. Shortly afterward, upon being informed of a conspiracy led by Colonel Maza, the dictator imprisoned that officer who was soon condemned to death upon the charge that he had plotted to assassinate Rosas. On November 7, 1839, insurrectionists who had arisen against dictatorial rule in southern Argentina, were defeated at Chascomús. With the aid of exiled Argentine citizens, Lavalle organized an expedition in Montevideo, invaded Argentina, and formed a coalition with the governor of Tucumán; but his army was defeated by General Oribe who was allied with Rosas, and Lavalle was shot by a follower of that dictator. The reaction against Rosas was next led by Generals Paz and Rivera, who after some successes were forced to retire to Uruguay. In conjunction with the governor of Corrientes, General Paz organized a revolt in that province, which was subdued by Urquiza in 1847.

During the Age of Rosas a peculiar controversy arose about the Falkland Islands. As those islands were by Spanish officials included within the viceroyalty of Buenos Aires, they were claimed as national territory by the magistrates of the United Provinces of La Plata. In 1831 two sealing vessels from the United States were seized by the governor of the islands for violation of the fishing laws. This seizure provoked an animated diplomatic correspondence between Argentina and the United States. Meanwhile Captain Duncan of the United States corvette "Lexington" arbitrarily dispersed the Argentine settlers in the Falkland Islands. Against that action Argentina protested. The American chargé d'affaires at Buenos Aires responded that the Argentine government had no right to prevent citizens of his country from fishing near the Falkland Archipelago.

Foreign Complications

In January, 1833, the captain of an English warship took possession of the islands in the name of his King and hauled down the Argentine flag. Against that step the government at Buenos Aires protested in 1841 through its minister in London; but the English secretary of state for foreign affairs, Lord Palmerston, asserted England's prior claim to the archipelago against Spain. Palmerston based that claim upon discovery and previous occupation, which had not been invalidated by the withdrawal of the English in 1774.

In 1839 José M. Alvear, the Argentine minister in Washington, presented to the secretary of state of the United States a claim for damages caused by the acts of Captain Duncan. In reply Secretary Webster stated that as Argentina's claim to the islands was disputed by England because of rights acquired at a period long before 1833, he took the view that the United States should not give a definitive answer to Alvear's communication until the dispute between England and Argentina was adjusted.

The expanding ambition of Dictator Rosas gradually involved him in difficulties with other nations. He took the side of General Oribe in the latter's struggle with Rivera for the domination of Uruguay. Provoked by the mysterious death of a French lithographer, who had been suspected of a design to transfer military plans of the Argentine Confederation to Bolivia, France protested against the policy of Rosas who compelled her citizens to serve in his army. In March, 1838, having failed to obtain satisfaction from the dictator's secretary of foreign relations, the French consul announced that the coast of Argentina was blockaded. In conjunction with Rivera and Argentine exiles, a French admiral took possession of the island of Martín García. Early in 1843, with the help of Rosas, Oribe invested Montevideo, which provoked a protest from the governments of France and England. As Dictator Carlos López of Paraguay had made an alliance with the governor of the Argentine province of Corrientes against Rosas, in retaliation the latter laid an embargo upon all commerce with that province or with Paraguay. In April, 1845, English and French fleets blockaded the Río de la Plata; Anglo-French forces were stationed at Montevideo and other points in Uruguay. After various negotiations for an adjustment had failed, in 1850 conventions were signed between Rosas, on the one hand, and France and England, on the other hand, by which the European powers agreed to withdraw their warships from the blockade of La Plata River, and Rosas promised to recall his legions from the siege of Montevideo.

Among lieutenants of the dictator who at length became weary of a régime that was complicated by strife with foreign powers was General Urquiza. Governor of the Province of Entre Ríos, he had long chafed at the barbed bit that had been fastened in his mouth. On April 22, 1851, Urquiza addressed a letter to Colonel Costa, who was serving under Oribe, **Program of General Urquiza** which denounced Rosas as a tyrant and invited that colonel to make war upon him. Urquiza said that his program was to restore order and liberty to the Argentine republic and to allow Uruguay to govern herself. In a letter transmitting this communication to Oribe, Costa characterized its author as a savage, a traitor, and a madman.

On May 1, 1851, General Urquiza issued a pronunciamiento. He announced that the province of Entre Ríos had reassumed the powers which it had delegated to the tyrant. He said that that province desired to see delegates of the Argentine provinces gather in a constituent assembly to establish a republic. On May 25, in a gazette entitled the *Regeneration,* that general published a proclamation addressed to Argentine civilians and soldiers. He declared that for them the hour of republican organization had struck in the great clock of destiny. Four days later, representatives of Entre Ríos, Uruguay, and Brazil signed an offensive and defensive treaty which was aimed against Rosas. In a daring campaign Urquiza led his army from Entre Ríos across the Uruguay River and forced Oribe to capitulate, thus relieving Montevideo. After recrossing that river and fording the Paraná, the victorious general led soldiers of the allied peoples against the dictator's army.

At Caseros, on February 3, 1852, Urquiza routed the demoralized army of Rosas. That enigmatical man at once resigned his dictatorship.

Battle of Caseros He asserted that to the extent of his ability he had supported Argentina's independence, integrity, and honor. The fallen dictator escaped from Buenos Aires in disguise on an English steamboat and lived in poverty at Southampton until his death. The Age of Rosas was a period of transition between anarchy and constitutional reorganization. Despite the existence of evil tendencies, despite the fact that he could not always keep peace, his long and arbitrary rule had improved the efficiency and honesty of public administration in Argentina and had restricted or destroyed the power of *caudillos* or local tyrants whose faces were set against nationalism. A unique product of social conditions, Rosas used against the local chieftains in extreme fashion the same methods of terrorism that had been employed by previous rulers of La Plata.

After the governors of four provinces had agreed that the management of foreign affairs should be entrusted to him, Urquiza issued a decree of amnesty to all exiled Argentine citizens. On May 31, 1852, the governors of eleven provinces, including the province of Buenos Aires, framed an agreement at San Nicolás which was composed of nineteen articles. Some of its provisions were as follows: that a convention composed of two delegates from each province should be convoked, that in case disturbances broke out Urquiza should be authorized to use all prudent means to restore tranquillity, and that he should also be entrusted with the command of the military forces.

He was given the title of "Provisional Director of the Argentine Confederation." In the belief that the governors of the provinces had conferred excessive powers upon the Director, the province of Buenos Aires disavowed this agreement; but the thirteen remaining provinces approved it and proceeded to elect delegates to a Constituent Assembly which in November, 1852, met in the city of Santa Fé.

To that Assembly an envoy of Urquiza read his address. The Provisional Director declared that the Argentine flag had space for more than fourteen stars but that it was impossible to erase any one of those. Interior provinces of Argentina sent as their delegates intellectual leaders who were acquainted with the constitutions of 1819 and 1826. Into their hands *Constituent Assembly at Santa Fé* had come by a strange chance a copy of *The Federalist*. There was also circulated among the delegates a copy of a notable treatise by Alberdi entitled *Bases and Suggestions for the Political Organization of the Argentine Republic* which was accompanied by a draft of a constitution. That great South American political philosopher reasoned that the new Argentine constitution should reflect the condition of the country; that it should be neither absolutely centralistic nor absolutely federalistic; that it should be a compromise which would recognize the political existence of both the nation and the provinces, but more centralistic than the United States Constitution. His views on the framing of South American constitutions are worth quoting:

What is important for us in South America is to have a free movement of population, immigration, free commerce, and a general guarantee of progressive reform. Political constitutions of to-day have the task of organizing practical means to lead emancipated Spanish America out of the obscure and inferior condition in which it finds itself. So, as at an earlier date we placed in our constitutions, independence, liberty, and religion, to-day we must provide in them for free immigration, liberty of commerce, railways, and free industry; not in the place of these grand principles but as essential means to cause them to cease to be words and to become realities. To-day we must promote population and railways, the navigability of our rivers and the wealth of our states. We must elevate our people to the habit of a free government which necessity has imposed upon us.

By the perusal of Alberdi's *Bases* and *The Federalist* and by a direct study of the Constitution of the United States the fathers at Santa Fé became acquainted with North American political principles. On May 1, 1853, the Assembly sanctioned a new Constitution for Argentina. In reality this Constitution was an attempt to harmonize two political tendencies which had long struggled for domination—the federalistic and the centralistic. It recognized that some autonomy was possessed *The Argentine Constitution of 1853* by the provinces, while it gave large and significant powers to the national government.

This Constitution declared that aliens should have the same rights as citizens. It vested executive power in a President and a Vice-President to be chosen by electoral colleges in the provinces for a term of six years. The President should be the commander in chief of the army and navy; he was given charge of civil and ecclesiastical patronage. With the advice of the supreme court, he might refuse to allow the promulgation of papal bulls. He might summon or prorogue Congress and could veto its legislative acts. He could grant pardons and commutations of punishment, except in cases of impeachment. He was to be aided by five secretaries who might participate in congressional debates, but who should not have the right to vote. The Argentine fathers evidently did not favor a parliamentary government.

Legislative authority was vested in a Senate and House of Deputies. The two houses were given the authority to levy direct taxes which did not necessarily have to be proportioned to the population. A significant power was the right to grant subsidies to the provinces when their own revenues might prove insufficient to meet provincial expenses. Judicial power was vested in a supreme court and such inferior courts as Congress might establish.

The Constitution declared that the provinces should retain all powers which were not delegated to the national government. No province was to declare war upon another province. Provincial governors should be the agents of the nation in the enforcement of her laws. The central government was given the right to intervene in the provinces to suppress domestic violence, to repel foreign invasion, or to preserve the safety of the nation.

In respect to relations with the Papacy, the Constitution of 1853 followed precedents that had been set during the revolutionary epoch. A certain article gave to the President the right to make appointments of bishops to vacant sees upon the nomination of the Senate. Another article gave him the power, with the advice of the supreme court, to exclude from the republic the decrees of church councils and also papal bulls, briefs, and rescripts. It further specified that whenever such a communication contained provisions of a general and permanent character which were agreeable to the government a national law would have to be enacted to put them into force.

This fundamental law was patterned after the Constitution of the United States. Nevertheless, as the distinguished Argentine historian, Ricardo Levene, rightly says, Argentine federalism could not be of the same character as North American federalism, "where the states that formed the Union had independent, autonomous traditions."

In November, 1853, the first elections were held under this Constitution. Urquiza was chosen president of the "Argentine Confederation." He decided to fix the seat of government in the city of Paraná, the capital of the province of Entre Ríos. President Urquiza Inaugurated on March 5, 1854, he at once appointed secretaries of the interior, foreign relations, justice and public instruction, war, and the treasury. The relations of Argentina with foreign powers were soon placed on a firm basis. Conventions were signed with the United States, France, and England stipulating that the Paraná and Uruguay rivers might be freely navigated by the merchant vessels of all nations. Treaties of navigation and friendship were negotiated with other European powers and with certain nations of South America. The University of Córdoba was made a national institution; the federal government made appropriations to the provinces for the promotion of primary instruction. Urquiza not only took steps to encourage the settlement of the national domain but also to promote the construction of railways.

Thirteen provinces soon framed constitutions which were approved by the national government. Grave complications, however, developed between statesmen at Buenos Aires and magistrates at Opposition of Buenos Aires Paraná. A clash of arms between national and provincial forces resulted in a victory for President Urquiza. The government of the province of Buenos Aires accordingly signed a peace with the Confederation. In September, 1860, amendments to the national Constitution which were proposed by a provincial convention at Buenos Aires were incorporated in the fundamental law by a National Convention. Among those amendments was an article providing that the enacting clause of all laws should use the term "The Argentine Nation." At this critical time Santiago Derqui became president of the Confederation; while General Bartolomé Mitre, an energetic, resourceful, and versatile native of the metropolis, became governor of the province of Buenos Aires. The attempt at reconciliation failed when deputies from the province of Buenos Aires to the national Congress at Paraná were refused seats because they had not been elected according to the provisions of the new Constitution.

On September 17, 1861, the national army under Urquiza and soldiers led by Mitre struggled for the mastery upon the plains of Pavón. Both generals claimed to be the victor, but Urquiza, who was not supported by Derqui, retired from the field of battle. The prestige of victory thus lay with the soldiers of the dissentient province.

Soon afterward certain Argentine provinces issued laws which granted General Mitre provisional authority until a new administration might be organized. On April 22, 1862, Mitre announced that he assumed control of the national government with the title of the governor of Buenos Aires who was entrusted with the national executive

Mitre as Supreme Ruler

power. He called for the election of a Congress, which assembled on May 25. In accordance with a constitutional amendment, Congress adjusted the delicate issue concerning the location of the capital by a compromise which provided that the seat of the national government should be in the city of Buenos Aires for five years. In October, 1862, Mitre was elected president of the republic.

President Mitre was the first chief magistrate of the Argentine republic who ruled over all of her territory. Though his ascendancy marked the triumph of metropolitan influence, he promoted national unity in many ways. He signed a law which provided for the assumption of the debt that had been incurred by Urquiza. Insurrections which broke out in several provinces Mitre subdued. His secretary of the interior improved relations among the provinces by promoting the postal and telegraphic service. His minister of instruction founded national academies. His secretary of the treasury reformed the customs service. With the aid of Argentine citizens, General Flores, an exiled leader of the *Colorado* party of Uruguay who had fought under Mitre at Pavón, prepared an expedition against the *Blanco* party that was in control of the government at Montevideo. The war waged against Paraguay during Mitre's administration will be described in connection with the history of that country.

In November, 1867, the President wrote a significant letter to a friend named José M. Gutiérrez. Mitre declared that his task had been to prepare the way for the free election of a president. He expressed the opinion that the chief magistrate of the Argentine republic should not use his official influence in favor of any presidential candidate. In other words, he announced that he did not intend to be used as an electoral instrument. This letter has been styled Mitre's "political testament." Many years passed, however, before his counsel was taken to heart by Argentine presidents.

In pursuance of precedents established during the colonial and revolutionary periods Argentina's Constitution provided that the national government should enact civil, commercial, and

The Civil Code of Argentina

other codes. A commercial code adopted in 1862 was based largely upon foreign codes of commerce. When Mitre became president he selected Vélez Sársfield, a prominent jurist, to frame a civil code. That jurist's draft was submitted to Congress which adopted it in September, 1869. The civil code of Argentina was an amalgam composed of some four thousand articles which were largely taken from Brazilian, French, Spanish, and Chilean

ARGENTINA

SCALE OF MILES

0   100   200   300   400   500

Territories are underlined.

sources. Those articles were arranged in four books: Book I dealt with persons; Book II with personal rights; Book III with property rights; and Book IV with various provisions about real and personal rights, especially succession and inheritance.

Domingo F. Sarmiento, who was unexpectedly elected president of Argentina in 1868, was a distinguished educator and pugnacious publicist. While an exile from his native land during the tyranny of Rosas, he had taught school in Chile and had made an extensive tour to study European and American educational systems. When elected to the presidency he was serving as the Argentine minister to the United States.

President Sarmiento promoted public education in various ways. He signed a law which provided for the establishment of national normal schools. He issued a decree which reorganized the curricula of secondary schools. He promoted the introduc- **Sarmiento as President** tion of the methods and teachers of the United States into his country. When López Jordán, the avowed assassin of Urquiza, became governor of the province of Entre Ríos, Sarmiento sent a military expedition to that province to restore order. Provincial authorities viewed that step as an attack upon their autonomy. The civil strife which ensued between national and provincial soldiers did not terminate until López Jordán was routed. This was the first time that the national government had recourse to the dangerous expedient of intervening by force in a province.

During Sarmiento's administration railroads were built from Córdoba to Tucumán, and from Concordia to Mercedes. Telegraph lines were extended. Immigration from Spain, France, and Italy was encouraged. Commerce with England, France, Spain, and the United States increased and with it the public revenues.

In 1874 Nicolás Avellaneda, who had been secretary of justice and public instruction under Sarmiento, was elected president. A journalist and statesman who used both the spoken and the written word to great effect, he was admirably fitted for the **Political and Economic Progress** presidency. To him fell the task of suppressing a revolt led by ex-President Mitre, who protested against the use of official influence in elections. President Avellaneda continued the educational reforms which had been initiated by Sarmiento; he founded numerous primary and secondary schools throughout the republic. Foreign commerce increased greatly. In 1879 Argentina exported some forty-seven million pesos' worth of products and imported forty-four million pesos' worth of merchandise.

A step which marked the decline of animosity between the national government and the province of Buenos Aires was a law of September

20, 1880, by which the city of Buenos Aires was declared to be the nation's capital. When it approved this measure, the legislature of the province of Buenos Aires provided for the establishment of its new capital at a place called La Plata. The region which had been under the control of the municipality of Buenos Aires thus became the Argentine federal district. In 1879 General Julio A. Roca had led an expedition against the troublesome Patagonian Indians and advanced the southern frontier of the republic to the Río Negro. Upon his return the conqueror of the wilderness was proclaimed a candidate for the presidency.

No uprisings against the government occurred during the presidency of General Roca, 1880-1886. In 1884 Argentina instructed her minister at Washington to urge upon the United States the claim concerning the Falkland Islands which had been presented by Alvear. Estimating the value of the colony which Captain Duncan had destroyed at over two hundred thousand pesos, the Argentine government declared that it was willing to submit the dispute to arbitration. But in a message to Congress in December, 1885, President Cleveland described the Argentine settlement in the Falkland Archipelago as "a piratical colony," and stated that his government considered Argentina's claim to the islands as "wholly groundless." Her minister to the United States, Vicente G. Quesada, soon tried to correct those statements. He argued that the action of the United States in virtually supporting the seizure of the Falkland Islands by England was "in flagrant opposition" to the Monroe Doctrine. Yet Quesada's protest was in vain and the issue remained open.

Reopening of the Falkland Controversy

President Roca authorized several military expeditions against the Indians in northern and southern Argentina, thus opening up more territory to settlement. His administration was distinguished by great material progress. During the years from 1880 to 1886 the national revenues increased almost one hundred per cent, while the number of immigrants and the railway mileage almost doubled. But no such advance was made in politics. Long before the expiration of his term, Roca began to lay plans for the presidential succession: his candidate was a relative named Celman, who had been governor of the province of Córdoba. In spite of the activity of the opposition party, the candidate who was supported by the President was successful in the election. In October, 1886, Celman was inaugurated president, while Carlos Pellegrini became vice-president.

Celman reaped the whirlwind in politics as well as in finance. Excessive speculation and large issues of inconvertible paper money during the early years of his administration prepared the way for a crisis. As the President renounced his own political party, the opposition to his administration increased. A tumult in the city of Buenos Aires on April 13, 1890, signalized the birth of a new political party, the Civic Union or the Radical party, whose members engaged in armed struggles against the government in the streets of the capital. After the rebels were compelled to desist because of lack of munitions, some sixty congressmen asked the President to resign. In consequence Vice-President Pellegrini assumed the presidency in August, 1890. As the national bank and the bank of the province of Buenos Aires closed their doors in March, 1891, in the following December the government opened a new banking institution at Buenos Aires known as the Bank of the Argentine Nation. With the right to establish branches in the provinces, this bank soon became a powerful force in Argentine finance.

Rise of the Radical Party

In 1892 Luis Sáenz Peña became president. The agitation of the Radical party stimulated an insurrectionary spirit in various provinces. That party even proclaimed one of its leaders the provisional president of the republic; but Sáenz Peña proclaimed martial law, and soldiers under General Roca subdued the insurrectionists. After several cabinet crises, in January, 1895, the President gave way to the Vice-President, José E. Uriburu. During his administration a serious controversy between Brazil and Argentina about their boundary line was adjusted. This question originated mainly from the fact that the limits between Spanish and Portuguese America, as sketched in the Treaty of San Ildefonso, had never been thoroughly surveyed. The debatable region included a part of the territory where Jesuit fathers had planted missions. After a long dispute as to which of two river systems in reality marked the limits, the contending nations decided to submit the question to the arbitration of the President of the United States. The functions of arbiter devolved upon President Cleveland. After carefully considering the arguments and the documents presented by the distinguished representatives of Argentina and Brazil, on February 5, 1895, the arbiter announced his decision, namely, that the boundary line between the two republics should follow the westerly of the two river systems, which was the Brazilian contention.

Soon afterward General Roca again became president. Important measures of his second administration were concerned with the currency and international relations. On November 3, 1899, he signed a law which provided that the nation should redeem her paper pesos of one hundred centavos apiece for forty-four centavos in gold. The redemption was to be made through a financial institution called the Bank of Redemption. In international relations a significant move was made by Argentina in connection with the attempt of three European nations in 1903 forcibly to collect from Vene-

New Issues

zuela debts which she owed their citizens. Luis M. Drago, the secretary of foreign relations, protested to the government of the United States and formulated a doctrine denying the right of a European government forcibly to collect debts owed by a Latin-American nation. This protest became known as "the Drago Doctrine."

Upon the conclusion of the second presidency of Roca in 1904, Dr. Manuel Quintana was elected the chief magistrate. A few months after his inauguration a revolt broke out which was ascribed to members of the Radical party who, alleging that liberty of suffrage was not permitted, had refrained from voting in the presidential election.

In 1910 Roque Sáenz Peña, the candidate of the so-called Nationalist party, was elected president. He came to the Pink House with a determination to abstain from official interference in national elections. In his first message to Congress the President proposed a reform in the election laws. In February, 1912, he signed a law which aimed to compel every properly qualified voter to cast his ballot at national elections. It provided that in a room without windows the ballot of each voter was to be enclosed in an envelope which should then be deposited in a ballot box. A voter who, without good cause, failed to exercise the electoral franchise was to be prosecuted; if convicted, he should be punished by a fine. Other provisions aimed to protect the voter from intimidation. When Sáenz Peña was compelled to retire because of ill health, and Vice-President Victorino de la Plaza became president, he notified provincial and municipal magistrates that the national executive would endeavor to prevent any official interference in the approaching presidential campaign. By the measures of this administration, the basis was accordingly laid for a radical political change.

Article XXI of the Constitution declared that every natural-born Argentine citizen should be subject to military service as provided by law. In 1901 a law was enacted which made military
Conditions about 1914 — service compulsory upon natural-born citizens between the ages of twenty and forty-five for a nominal period of twenty-five years. In 1913 the standing army comprised some twenty thousand men. The provisions for service in the navy resembled those for the army. Some seven thousand men were enrolled in the active naval service; the fleet included three armored cruisers, four protected cruisers, five iron-clads, five torpedo boats, and two torpedo-boat destroyers, besides small craft, river gunboats, and auxiliary vessels.

Argentine statesmen have been much influenced by Alberdi's famous dictum that rightly to govern a country is to populate it. Article XXV of the Constitution declared that the federal government was to encourage European immigration. In 1876 a law was enacted which provided that the national government should assist immigrants in various ways. An Argentine statistician has calculated that from 1857 to 1909 some three and one-half million immigrants landed at Buenos Aires. European countries had contributed contingents in the following order: Italians, Spaniards, French, Russians, Syrians, Austrians, English, Germans, and Swiss. Early in the present century the government undertook to restrict immigration by the passage of laws for social defense. Of a total population of 7,905,502 in 1914, 2,378,217 were foreigners. The most densely populated regions were the federal district, the province of Buenos Aires, and the provinces bordering on the river Paraná, while the most sparsely populated region was southern Patagonia.

Social and Economic Conditions

The official language of the Argentine Nation was Spanish. In popular usage, at least, that language had been modified because of the presence in the republic of a large foreign element. The citizens of Argentina also inherited the Roman Catholic faith, which was a privileged religion. As prescribed in the Constitution, the State supported that religion; the Argentine President must be a Catholic. Still, the organic law provided that other religions should be tolerated.

The city of Buenos Aires was the hub of the Argentine transportation system. Steamships from Uruguay, Chile, the United States, and various European countries regularly touched at that port. Side-wheel steamers plied regularly from Buenos Aires up the Paraná and Paraguay rivers as far as Asunción. The railways of Argentina had been promoted by North American enterprise, by English capital, and by national subsidies. By 1914 some twenty thousand miles of railway radiated from the metropolis.

In 1914 Argentina was primarily an agricultural and pastoral country. Enormous numbers of cattle, sheep, horses, goats, and swine roamed over her pampas, plains, and steppes. Large packing houses furnished occupation for many people. Argentine agriculture was diversified: corn and wheat were the most important cereals; in certain zones viniculture was an important industry; and, especially in the province of Tucumán, much attention was paid to the cultivation of sugar cane. Gold, silver, and copper were mined in the Andean zone. Along the Atlantic coast the fisheries were a minor industry. Flour and sugar mills, creameries, cheese factories, tanneries, cigar and cigarette factories had been established, besides a few factories of shoes, clothing, and furniture. With the development of Argentina's foreign commerce, an increasing number of persons had found employment in mercantile transactions, especially in the city of Buenos Aires.

An index of economic development is found in Argentine commerce. Statistics of her foreign trade in 1914 indicate the lines of greatest development. In that year the exports of her agricultural products, including wheat, flax, corn, oats, flour, and bran, amounted to 184,367,-331 pesos of gold. The exports of her pastoral products, including livestock, preserved meat, extract of beef, wool, butter, tallow, blood, and bones, totaled 151,746,228 gold pesos. The total value of her exports was 349,254,141 pesos of gold. In the same year her imports, which consisted mainly of manufactured articles, came to 271,811,900 gold pesos.

According to the Constitution, the management of primary education was entrusted to the provincial governments. Because of the alarming
Education increase of illiteracy, however, a law was enacted in 1905 which authorized the national government to establish primary schools in the provinces. Both national and provincial governments thus participated in the support of primary schools; and in a few provinces the municipalities also supported such schools.

Secondary education was mainly given in academies designated as *colegios* which were supported by the national government. Almost all of the important institutions of commercial or technical education were national. Though partly supported by the national government, the universities of Santa Fé and Tucumán were under the direction of their respective provinces. The great national universities of Argentina were the University of Córdoba, the University of La Plata, and the University of Buenos Aires. The metropolitan university was composed of six colleges: economic science; law and social sciences; philosophy and letters; medicine; exact, physical, and natural sciences; and agronomy and veterinary science. The three national universities, which were supported by fees and by appropriations from the general government, had in 1914 an aggregate attendance of some eight thousand students.

Since May 11, 1813, when Vicente López y Planes read the national hymn to a Constituent Assembly at Buenos Aires, the Argentine people have produced a varied literature. Juan C. Varela was a
Literature lyrical poet on the classic model, who also wrote tragedies and whose last poem, *Al 25 de Mayo de 1838*, was directed from exile against Dictator Rosas. Even before those verses were written, Esteban Echeverría had published a poem called *Elvira* which signalized the introduction of romanticism into Argentina. A thinker as well as a poet, he was the author of *Dogma Socialista*. Another versatile spirit, who was an historian, was Juan María Gutiérrez. While an exile in Montevideo, Gutiérrez won a prize for his *Canto á Mayo*. A frequent contributor to the *Revista de Buenos Aires* and to the *Revista del Río de la Plata*, he was perhaps the most distinguished man of letters that Argentina had produced. One of the most sympathetic of Argentine poets was Carlos Guido y Spano. The alliance of Argentina with Brazil and Uruguay against Paraguay provoked him to write

Nenia, a lyric poem in which a Guaraní maiden mourns the loss of her nearest and dearest relatives in the Paraguayan War. A most patriotic poet was Olegario V. Andrade, whose verses on national themes quickened the pulses of Argentinians.

A literary man who detested Rosas was the publicist Bartolomé Mitre. One of his anti-Rosista poems entitled *Invalido* became a popular song; in his poems of the pampas he sang of the Argentine gaucho. His *History of San Martín* established his reputation as one of the foremost Latin-American historians. Mitre would have won undying fame had he done nothing more than found *La Nación* of Buenos Aires, which, under his liberal editorship, became one of the leading newspapers of Latin America.

Another voluminous prose author was Domingo F. Sarmiento, whose articles, books, and reports fill some fifty volumes. His most famous book is *Facundo, or Civilization and Barbarism;* it is a picturesque account of life on the Argentine plains and of struggles between the Federalists and the "Unitarians." Juan Bautista Alberdi, a thinker who lived many years in exile because he dissented from "those twin colossi, Mitre and Sarmiento," wrote voluminously about social and economic conditions in South America. Among a host of historical critics, only one may be mentioned, Pablo Groussac, who served many years as the director of the national library. The Argentine capital has become the home of a coterie of younger scholars who are putting all students of Latin America deeply in their debt by their learned and illuminating contributions to the history of their native continent.

The earliest painters and sculptors of note were Frenchmen, Spaniards, and Italians, who in some cases served as teachers of art. Della Valle, an artist of Italian descent, painted a vivid picture **Fine Arts** of Indians returning home with captives who had been seized in a raid upon the white settlements. Pridiliano Pueyrredón made a portrait of Manuelita Rosas, the daughter of the dictator. The most charming picture of Eduardo Sivori was perhaps that entitled "The Pampa at Olavarría," which subtly conveyed the atmosphere of the Argentine prairies. Other phases of Argentine life were portrayed by Agosto Ballerini, who for many years served as illustrator for *La Nación.* Among other paintings he produced "The Apotheosis of Mariano Moreno" and "The Sister of Charity." In "The Song by the Fire" Carlos P. Ripamonte depicted a party of gauchos under an ombú tree, who were listening to a companion chanting a lay to the accompaniment of a guitar. Still another phase of society was portrayed by Ernesto de la Cárcova in a picture that was entitled "Without Bread and Without Employment." More than one artist has used camera or pencil or brush to depict scenes on the busy waterfront of the capital city.

Among Argentine sculptors may be mentioned Francisco Cafferta, who chiseled statues of Manuel Belgrano, Mariano Moreno, and Bernardino Rivadavia. Another prominent sculptor was Mateo Alons, from whose atelier came such sculptural representations as "The Carousal," "Amen," and "The Dying Indian." During the presidency of Quintana a school of painting at Buenos Aires was by law transformed into the National Academy of Fine Arts. Partly as the result of private generosity, within the walls of that academy there had been gathered many products of the Argentine brush or chisel.

Perhaps the most significant political development in Argentina since the battle of Pavón has been a steady growth in power of the national government. Its powers have been interpreted liberally. To a considerable extent this has meant the **Political Tendencies** political predominance of the city of Buenos Aires. Argentine nationalism has been stimulated by a practice adopted by the federal government of making grants of money to the provinces to promote internal development. The provinces have been further subordinated to that government because of its armed intervention in their affairs.

Political groups or parties had altered. The Socialists had become an extreme party largely made up of laborers who advocated such reforms as the single tax and proportional representation. The main political principle held by the Radical party prior to 1916 was that a complete change should be made in the existing political situation. Though they wished to turn the conservative politicians out of office, they were not economic radicals. Against those groups which wished to change the established order, the National party and other conservative parties drew closer together but did not unite.

The electoral reform of 1912 gave the Radical party its opportunity. A political revolution resulted from the campaign of 1916. Hipólito Irigoyen, the candidate of the Radical party, was elected president. Of Basque descent, he had been a prominent leader of the Radical party for many years: he had not, however, held any important political office. Neither he nor his party had made any definite statement of political principles.

Argentina early felt the disturbing effects of the World War. European capital was withdrawn from the country, projected material improvements were retarded or laid aside, and attempts were made to replace by domestic manufactures articles **Influence of the First World War on Argentina** that had formerly been imported. Alcohol, blankets, dyestuffs, furniture, saddles, and shoes were manufactured for home consumption and occasionally for export. The currents of Argentine foreign commerce shifted toward the Allies and the United States.

Here again, a menacing problem was raised by Germany's submarine policy. The Argentine government expressed regret at Germany's note announcing the renewal of an unrestricted submarine campaign. On April 10, 1917, Argentina notified the United States government that she recognized the justice of its decision to make war upon the imperial German government. Shortly afterward two Argentine merchant vessels were sunk by German torpedoes. After a fruitless exchange of notes, on August 5, 1917, the Argentine government sent to Berlin a categorical demand for an indemnity because of ships that had been sunk by submarines. To the surprise of some publicists, on August 28 Germany agreed to its demand for an indemnity; and also gave a guaranty that there would be no further destruction of Argentine ships by German submarines. Two days later Argentina accepted that adjustment. After the United States government published some intercepted correspondence, which demonstrated that the German envoy at Buenos Aires had secretly advised his government either to spare two Argentine ships that were soon to enter the submarine zone or else to sink them without leaving any trace (*spurlos versenkt*), in September, 1917, both houses of Congress by large majorities adopted resolutions declaring that diplomatic relations with Germany should be severed. The President handed the imperial envoy his passports. Nevertheless, apparently influenced by persons who believed that Argentina should formulate a policy of her own, Irigoyen took no further measures against the imperial German government. A fellow-countryman said of the radical leader: "He did not wish to be either pro-Ally or pro-German: he was simply Argentinian."

In protest at this attitude the Argentine ambassador at Washington resigned his post. Early in 1918 a serious railroad strike—ascribed to pro-German agitation—occurred, which evidently aimed to prevent the shipment of grain abroad. New export duties were levied to check the outward flow of foodstuffs. **Aftermath of that War** In accordance with a law which placed the control of articles of necessity in his hands, in August, 1918, the President prohibited the exportation of certain products. A proposed loan of some two hundred million pesos to the Allies to be used in the purchase of foodstuffs from Argentina was blocked in her Senate. In October, 1919, Germany tried in vain to get a smaller loan for a similar purpose. Plans were nevertheless formed for a renewal of German immigration to Argentina. Indicative of social and economic unrest, several strikes occurred in 1919. The fears entertained in 1916 that President Irigoyen would become a dictator were not entirely dissipated.

In the campaign of 1922 Marcelo de Alvear, the scion of a distinguished Argentine family, who was serving his country as minister to

France, was nominated for the presidency by the Radical party. Despite much dissatisfaction with the radical régime, on April 2 Alvear was elected president. On his return from France the president-elect visited Italy, England, Spain, Brazil, and Uruguay; he was inaugurated on October 12, 1922. Shortly afterward news of a naval mission sent by the United States to Brazil provoked sharp criticism of that policy by newspapers of Buenos Aires and incited Argentine statesmen to form plans to modernize their navy and to improve the equipment of their army. On August 28, 1923, the President signed an anti-trust bill which was designed to prevent monopolistic combinations or manipulations in commerce or industry. To secure gold to be used in the redemption of paper currency in the following month the Argentine government floated a loan of $55,000,000 in the United States.

Gradually a split appeared in the ranks of the Radical party; a majority of its members (Irigoyenistas) continued to recognize Irigoyen as their champion, but a faction repudiated his leadership and became known as the Anti-Personalista Radicals, or simply the Anti-Personalistas. This faction nominated Senator Leopoldo Melo for the presidency. In the election of 1928 that Senator received half a million popular votes, while the ex-President polled twice as many. In the electoral college this decision was ratified by an overwhelming majority.

During his second administration Irigoyen lost popular support. In December, 1929, he directed the Bank of Redemption to cease paying gold for Argentine paper. This imprudent step was followed by a bad slump of the peso in international exchange. The domestic prices of wheat and meat declined. A wave of economic depression swept the country; the blame for strikes and unemployment was cast on the administration. The anti-personalista wing of the Radical party bitterly criticized the President's policies. It declared that he had violated the Constitution and hindered the normal development of the country. Other opposition parties denounced Irigoyen's despotic rule, his irregular and demoralizing financial measures, and his practice of intervening by force in the provinces.

On September 5, 1930, the President was induced to transfer his functions to Vice-President Martínez, who declared martial law in the capital. But, on the next day, revolting troops, led by José F. Uriburu, a general who had been slighted by the septuagenarian President, took possession of Buenos Aires. At the city of La Plata, on September 7, Irigoyen resigned his magistracy. The former President was subsequently escorted to the island of Martín García, where he was kept under surveillance. Meanwhile Uriburu had compelled Martínez to relinquish his post. In this manner the administration of the Argentine

Irigoyen Overthrown by the Revolution of 1930

Nation passed into the hands of the aristocratic, conservative party which had dominated her politics prior to the political revolution of 1912.

On September 8, 1931, a *de facto* government headed by General Uriburu assumed control. It censored the press and declared a state of siege. Many offenders were cast into prison. At elections held in the province of Buenos Aires in April, however, the Conservatives were outvoted by the Radicals. As a result, elections in other provinces were postponed and an announcement was made that general elections would be held on November 8. The anti-personalista faction of the Radical party soon rallied around ex-President Alvear, who opportunely returned from Paris. Apprehensions were not allayed, however, when it became known that a number of Radical leaders had been deported.

As the *de facto* government had issued a decree which prohibited the Irigoyenistas from supporting their candidates at the polls because they had not repudiated the radical régime, the members of that party did not vote in the presidential election of 1931. During the campaign General Agustín P. Justo, the candidate of the Anti-Personalistas, declared himself in favor of a return to constitutional normalcy and pleaded for peace and harmony in politics. On February 20, 1932, Justo became president. His first step was to end the state of siege. Among the reforms which he soon instituted were the following: economy in the financial administration, measures to promote discipline in the military and naval forces, and the formulation of an organic law for all the universities of the country. Congress enacted laws providing for the improvement of roads, for the establishment of a bureau to manage the oil industry, and for the creation of a national commission of culture. A most important law founded the Central Bank of the Republic. The discovery of a Radical plot to overthrow the existing régime led the President temporarily to reimpose a state of siege.

Among important international events was an anti-war pact signed with Brazil in October, 1933, by which the two nations bound themselves not to recognize the legality of a title to territory which had been acquired by a nation through force. In October, 1934, the Thirty-third Eucharistic Congress of the Catholic world gathered in Buenos Aires. At the instance of President Franklin D. Roosevelt, there assembled in that city in December, 1936, an Inter-American Conference for the promotion of peace which was attended by delegates from all the independent nations of America.

By 1937 the supporters of President Justo had joined a new political group designated the *Concordancia* which was composed of Conservatives and Anti-Personalistas. This coalition party selected as its candidate for the presidency and vice-presidency respectively Dr. Roberto M.

Attitude toward the Second World War Ortiz, a well-known lawyer and a one-time Radical; and Ramón Castillo, a former Conservative who was nicknamed "The Fox." The election held on September 5 was won by the Concordancia.

On February 20, 1938, Ortiz became president. During his administration various cultural institutions were founded throughout the country. Steps were taken to improve primary education. Domestic issues, however, soon paled before the Nazi menace. In March, 1939, evidence was discovered to show that Germans were conspiring to get control of Patagonia. On May 10 the President issued a decree announcing that all foreign political organizations were outlawed and that no foreign insignia were to be displayed nor any foreign songs sung in Argentina. In July another decree provided that an investigation should be made of Nazi and Fascist underground activities. Congress approved a budget which included large appropriations for military purposes. After German legions had subjugated France, the government secured large loans from the United States which were destined for the purchase of industrial equipment in that country.

Because of ill health, early in July, 1940, Ortiz delegated his authority to the Vice-President. A new cabinet was then organized. When the Uruguayan government proposed that the Latin-American nations should grant non-belligerent rights to American states at war with non-American powers, Castillo's cabinet opposed this policy. It reasoned that such a step would not be in harmony with the decisions reached by the American republics in inter-American conferences. On June 20, 1941, however, the Chamber of Deputies, in which the Radicals had a majority, selected a committee to investigate the activities of Nazis, Fascists, and other alien groups in South America. Leading newspapers of the capital city criticized the administration policy of prudent neutrality in the second World War. Signs that Castillo was ready to improve his country's relations with other American states were not altogether absent. On October 14, 1941, Argentina and the United States signed a commercial treaty based upon the principle of reciprocity. Shortly after the Japanese attack on Pearl Harbor, Argentina granted non-belligerent rights to the United States.

In June, 1942, Ortiz resigned his position. He died on July 15. This untoward event strengthened the hands of Castillo in the crisis. In April, 1942, the Argentine tanker *Victoria* had been torpedoed, an act for which Berlin apologized. In June the freighter *Río Tercero* was sunk in the Atlantic by a German submarine. Soon afterward Argentine merchant ships were ordered to evade the Nazi blockade by docking at American ports in the Gulf of Mexico. But the Chamber of Deputies unanimously approved a motion to the effect that relations with Germany, Italy, and Japan should be severed. The Castillo administration, however, was content to dispatch a vigorous protest to Berlin. In July, 1942, the lower house of Congress chided the minister of foreign affairs for accepting Germany's explanation that the sinking of the *Río Tercero* was a mistake. By way of explanation the minister revealed that he had undertaken to furnish the German government with data on Argentine shipping routes and sailing dates: "Germany leaves the seas open and safe for Argentine shipping." In August, 1942, however, when Brazil declared the existence of a state of war with the European members of the Axis, the President promptly issued a decree conceding to her the status of non-belligerency. Early in October, the Chamber of Deputies voted, 67 to 64, in favor of the immediate rupture of relations with the Axis; but, declaring that he would take note of this action, Castillo advised that foreign affairs were in his hands.

After the American ambassador had made complaints about subversive Nazi activities in South America which had their mainspring in Buenos Aires, the Argentine government started a spy hunt. Espionage operations were traced to the German legation in that capital. The government then set up a strict control over cable, telephone, and wireless communications with foreign lands. A little later, however, it temporarily suspended the publication of a leading, liberal newspaper which had criticized the sympathetic attitude of the secretary of foreign affairs, Enrique Ruiz Guiñazú, toward the Axis powers. As an Argentine official bulletin had suggested that England approved Castillo's policy of cautious neutrality, Downing Street retorted that it had been at pains to inform that government that it deplored Argentina's continued relations with "the enemies of humanity." At this critical juncture Berlin refused to accede to a request of the Argentine Supreme Court that an air and naval attaché of the German legation should be instructed to waive his privilege of diplomatic immunity in order to face charges of espionage. Hence late in January, 1943, the Argentine government asked that the intriguing attaché should be recalled from his post. Nevertheless Castillo maintained that the international position of Argentina would not be altered.

Argentina has progressed farther than her great neighbor on the north. Out of an age marked by social chaos and political anarchy, with bounds vaguely defined and imperfectly understood, and with smaller nationalities tugging at her apron strings, Argentina has developed into a strong nation with definite boundaries and a cosmopolitan population. Spanish though her civilization is in many of its admirable traits, yet her people, especially in Buenos Aires, are drawn from the four quarters of the earth. Indeed, if it were not for the intense spirit of nationalism that pervades the intelligent, native citizenry of Buenos Aires, one might be tempted to designate the capital city as a battlefield where foreign, or at least non-Argentine, influences are struggling for the mastery. With a physical environment similar to that of the United States, the Argentine republic seems destined to remain for a considerable period an agricultural and pastoral country that will furnish tribute to a metropolis which in some particulars vies with Paris and New York. With the ambition to make their country an arbiter of international politics, some Argentine statesmen have been attempting to shape their national policies by the scale of a hemisphere. A most hopeful sign in Argentine political life has been the emergence of a genuine desire for democratic government. The advent to power of a progressive party, which was rooted in the Argentine provinces, and which was in the main opposed to aristocratic privilege and to prerogatives of class and caste, seemed to signalize the dawning of a new era in Argentine politics. But the intense dissatisfaction that developed with Irigoyen's personal rule and increasing ineptitude incited military leaders to head a revolution that drove the Radicals from office. This revolution seemed to herald the return to influence of the conservative elements of the nation. Yet Castillo's attitude toward the second World War resembles the policy pursued by Irigoyen toward World War I.

SUGGESTIONS FOR FURTHER READING

ALBERDI, J. B., *The Crime of War*, 1913.
BIERSTADT, E. E. (ed.), *Three Plays from the Argentine*, 1920.
BLACKWELL, A. S., *Some Spanish-American Poets*, 1937.
CADY, J. F., *Foreign Intervention in the Río de la Plata*, 1929.
CHAPMAN, C. E., *Republican Hispanic America*, 1937.
FRANK, W. D., *Tales from the Argentine*, 1930.
HOLDICH, T. H., *The Countries of the King's Award*, 1904.
HUDSON, W. H., *Tales of the Pampas*, 1939.
JEFFERSON, M. S. W., *Peopling the Argentine Pampas*, 1926.
KING, J. A., *Twenty-four Years in the Argentine Republic*, 1846.
KIRKPATRICK, F. A., *A History of the Argentine Republic*, 1931.
KOEBEL, W. H., *Argentina, Past and Present*, 1911.
LEVENE, R., *A History of Argentina*, 1937.
MACDONALD, A. F., *Government of the Argentine Republic*, 1942.
MARTINEZ, A. B., and LEWANDOWSKI, M., *The Argentine in the Twentieth Century*, 1915.
NICOLS, M. W., *Sarmiento, a Chronicle of Inter-American Friendship*, 1940.
———, *The Gaucho*, 1942
OCHS, R. D., *A History of Argentine Immigration, 1858-1924*, 1939.

PARKER, W. B. (ed.), *Argentines of Today*, 1920.

PHELPS, V. L., *The International Economic Position of Argentine*, 1938.

ROBERTSON, W. S., "Argentina's Attitude to the War," *The Nation*, Vol. CIV, pp. 234-235.

———, "Foreign Estimates of the Argentine Dictator, Juan Manuel de Rosas," *Hispanic American Historical Review*, Vol. X, pp. 125-137.

ROWE, L. S., *The Federal System of the Argentine Republic*, 1921.

SEOANE, M., "Castillo is not Argentina," *The Nation*, Vol. CLVI, pp. 12-13.

"South America IV: Argentina," *Fortune*, Vol. XVIII, No. 1, pp. 27 ff.

TORNQUIST, E. A., *The Economic Development of the Argentine Republic in the Last Fifty Years*, 1919.

UGARTE, M., *The Destiny of a Continent*, 1925.

WEDDELL, A. W., *Introduction to Argentina*, 1939.

WHITE, J. W., *Argentina. The Life Story of a Nation*, 1942.

WILLIAMS, J. H., *Argentine International Trade under Inconvertible Paper Money, 1880-1900*, 1920.

CHAPTER XIV

URUGUAY

Uruguay sprang from a part of the viceroyalty of La Plata which had been a debatable land between Spain and Portugal. On the eve of the revolution against Spanish rule, the Banda Ori-
The Creation of Uruguay ental del Uruguay included that portion of the intendancy of Buenos Aires which stretched from the river La Plata to the junction of the Uruguay and the Peperí-Guazú rivers. In spite of the efforts of Artigas, when General Sucre won the battle of Ayacucho in December, 1824, the soil of Uruguay was still occupied by Brazilian soldiers. But the battle of Ituzaingó was followed by the Argentine-Brazilian Treaty of 1828 which guaranteed the independence of the region on the east bank of the Uruguay River. A clause of this treaty provided that the proposed constitution of Uruguay was to be approved by representatives of both Argentina and Brazil before it should be put into operation. It seems curious that this significant treaty contained no stipulations concerning the boundaries of the new state.

In November, 1828, a Constituent Assembly met at San José. It appointed a provisional governor, who, on December 13, 1828, issued a decree announcing that all foreign officials should cease to exercise authority within Uruguayan territory. Soon afterward the soldiers of Argentina and Brazil evacuated the region east of the lower course of the Uruguay River. Meanwhile the Constituent Assembly had appointed a committee to frame a constitution. After some debate the Assembly decided to designate the new state *La República Oriental del Uruguay*. On September 10, 1829, it approved a Constitution for this state. About nine months later Uruguayan envoys returned from Brazil and Argentina with the welcome news that those governments had approved the Constitution. On July 18, 1830, the civil and military officials of Uruguay swore to support and defend it.

The Uruguayan Constitution of 1830 provided for a
Constitution of 1830 centralized form of government. The President was to be elected by Congress for four years. He was the commander in chief of the army and navy; he was granted the right to appoint the chief civil officers; he could introduce bills into Congress

and was given the power of veto; he could suspend the operation of federal laws, and could commute sentences. His cabinet was to be composed of as many executive officers as might be necessary. They were to report to Congress on their respective departments.

The President was given the function of passing upon the admission into Uruguay of papal bulls, briefs, and rescripts. He was to exercise the right of patronage. Roman Catholicism was declared to be the state religion.

A permanent committee of seven congressmen was empowered, during the recess of Congress, to watch over the execution of the Constitution and the laws. Congress was composed of a Senate and a House of Representatives. Judicial authority was vested in a high court of justice, a court or courts of appeals, and courts of the first instance. The judges of the high court of justice were to be appointed by the President.

The unit of local government was the department. In the chief town of each department a political chief appointed by the President should act as the executive magistrate. In minor towns subordinate officials were to be placed who should be responsible to the political chief.

To a Congress elected under the Constitution of 1830 two names were presented in candidacy for the presidency: Juan A. Lavalleja, and Fructuoso Rivera. Lavalleja had been the leader **Rival Chieftains** of "the thirty-three immortals" of 1825, while Rivera had been one of his trusted lieutenants in the struggle for independence. A spirit of rivalry had unfortunately sprung up between them even before the Constitution was framed. Congress elected General Rivera as president; he was installed in office upon returning from his military post. In July, 1832, General Lavalleja started a revolt against Rivera; but two months later the President routed the insurrectionists at Tupambay. His rival was consequently forced to seek a refuge in Brazil. Two years later he started another revolt which was also thwarted.

Upon the expiration of his term, Rivera quietly gave up his office. Congress elected as his successor Manuel Oribe, another general who had won distinction during the war for independence. During the first year of his presidency, it seemed as though the republic was entering upon an era of tranquillity and prosperity. A little later, however, President Oribe permitted the Lavallejistas to return from exile. After he had removed Rivera from the command of the army, that general was aroused to action, especially as suspicion was rife that Oribe was acting under the influence of the Argentine dictator. Rosas sent soldiers under Lavalleja to aid Oribe in his struggle against Rivera.

On September 19, 1836, Oribe defeated Rivera at the battle of
Carpintería. This battle, where Oribe's soldiers carried white pennants,
while Rivera's soldiers bore red pennants, signalized the
first appearance in the internecine struggles of Uruguay
of the Blancos and the Colorados, factions or parties
which for many decades divided the sympathies of the Uruguayan
people.

Blancos and
Colorados

In 1838 Rivera routed the forces of Oribe, who resigned the presidency and fled to the Argentine capital. After a brief interregnum,
when the presiding officer of the Senate acted as chief magistrate of
the republic, General Rivera was reëlected president. On March 10,
1839, the President, who was assured of support from the French and
from Argentine émigrés, issued a proclamation which announced that
he was declaring war against the Argentine tyrant. A treaty between
Rosas and the French agent Mackau dated October 29, 1840, contained an ambiguous clause which stated that the Argentine government would consider Uruguay as an independent nation so long as
this might be demanded by the justice, the honor, and the security of
the Argentine Confederation.

After defeating Rivera by the aid of Argentine soldiers, in 1843
Oribe invested Montevideo, where the Colorados were entrenched.
The period from 1843 to 1851 in which Montevideo was besieged is
known in Uruguayan history as the "great war." Upon the eve of the
downfall of Rosas, on October 8, 1851, in accordance with an agreement between himself and the government at Montevideo, General
Urquiza made a treaty with Oribe which provided for the cessation of
the war and left the Colorados in power. Article V of that treaty
declared that among the warring factions of Uruguay there were left
neither victors nor vanquished.

Shortly after the close of this struggle, Brazilian diplomacy scored
a triumph by the negotiation of a group of treaties with the Uruguayan minister in Rio de Janeiro. By the second article
of the treaty of limits signed on October 12, 1851, an
agreement was reached that the boundaries between
Uruguay and Brazil were defined in the act by which
a Congress at Montevideo had declared in 1821 that the Banda Oriental del Uruguay belonged to Portuguese America. That act defined
the limits of this territory on the west and the north to be the Uruguay River. On the north and the east the boundary line was declared
to be the river Cuarerim, the ridge of Santa Anna, the Yaguarón
River, and Lake Merim by way of San Miguel to the Atlantic Ocean.
The adjustment of 1851 accordingly sanctioned the retention by
Brazil of portions of the rich, mission territory which she had oc-

Foreign and
Domestic
Complica-
tions

cupied after the Treaty of 1777 had acknowledged them to belong to
Spanish America. It also conceded to her the exclusive right to navigate the Yaguarón River and Lake Merim.

During the presidency of a Blanco named Bernardo Berro, Uruguay
returned to Argentina the island of Martín García, which had been
seized by Uruguayans in 1845. General Venancio Flores, a Colorado
who became president in 1854, asked Brazil to intervene in Uruguayan
politics; hence for three years imperial soldiers were stationed upon
the soil of the distracted republic. In 1857 a politician named Gómez
formed a chimerical plan for the annexation of his country to the
province of Buenos Aires and the creation of a republic to be called
the "United States of La Plata." A band of Uruguayans that aimed
to carry out this plan was defeated, and its leaders were ruthlessly
shot. During the presidency of Pereira some administrative reforms
were made and the Jesuits were expelled from the country. Berro, who
became president for the second time in 1860, essayed certain reforms,
but during his administration civil war flared up again.

In May, 1864, the government of Brazil dispatched an envoy named
Saraiva to Montevideo to make a final plea for the settlement of claims
for damages to life and property that had been suffered by citizens
of the Empire residing in the republic. Uruguay met this demand by
the presentation of counter claims. When Saraiva's attempt at a reconciliation failed, on August 4, 1864, he presented an ultimatum demanding the immediate fulfillment of the Brazilian claims and threatening reprisals if satisfaction was not granted. After Uruguay had
rejected these terms, Brazil issued orders to Admiral Tamandaré and
General Menno Barreto to occupy certain Uruguayan cities. In October Admiral Tamandaré reached an agreement for concert of action
with General Flores, who was leading an insurrection against President Aguirre's government. As Dictator López of Paraguay apparently
had an understanding with the Blancos of Uruguay that he should
support Aguirre, he protested at the proceedings of Brazil. Yet forces
of Tamandaré and Flores blockaded Salto and Paysandú. Salto soon
capitulated, and Paysandú fell in January, 1865, after an heroic defense. Government officials at Montevideo publicly burned the originals
of the treaties existing between Uruguay and Brazil.

Meanwhile the imperial government had dispatched Silva Paranhos
—who later became Viscount Rio Branco—on a special mission. In
the end of January, 1865, this diplomat made an agreement with
Flores, "general in chief of the army of liberation," by which that
general promised to satisfy Brazil's claims against Uruguay and to
observe existing treaties, while Silva Paranhos gave a pledge that
his government would protect Uruguayan citizens within the Empire

and would satisfy their legitimate claims. On Feburary 22 General Flores led his victorious army into Montevideo and assumed the title of Provisional Governor. Brazilian diplomacy had scored a triumph: it had secured a satisfactory peace with Uruguay and had gained the Empire an ally in the impending war with Paraguay.

In 1870 under the leadership of Colonel Aparicio the Blancos defeated the Colorados and even laid siege to Montevideo. After the revolutionists were vanquished in the battles of Sauce **The Insurrection of Aparicio** and Manantiales by soldiers of the government, on April 6, 1872, through the mediation of the Argentine consul, a significant peace was signed which reconciled the warring factions. It provided that rewards were to be distributed among the soldiers of Aparicio, that his officers were to retain the military grades which they had enjoyed before the uprising, and that certain of his leaders were to be made the administrative heads of departments. The people joyfully hailed this adjustment of the contending factions, which was designed to satisfy the Blancos by conceding them a share in the functions and emoluments of government. Such an open admission that the prime motive for a revolt was a desire by rebellious leaders for participation in the spoils of office goes far to explain why alterations in the form of government have often been accomplished in Latin America by the sword rather than by the ballot.

The improvement in social conditions which resulted from this pact of reconciliation, however, was only temporary. A collapse of public credit because the debts of the government were paid in depreciated paper instead of in gold caused 1875 to be designated the "Terrible Year." At this time gold reached a premium of over 800 per cent. In the face of bitter and increasing opposition to his domination, on March 13, 1880, President Latorre resigned his magistracy and issued a proclamation declaring that Uruguay was "ungovernable." During the presidency of General Máximo Santos abuses in the management of the finances were responsible, in part, for an increase in the national debt. President Julio Herrera y Obes, who was a well-known lawyer, strove to avert a panic and to prevent uprisings. His very arbitrariness helps to explain why he enjoys the distinction of being the first President of Uruguay who saw his constitutional term of office end without being compelled to fight against rebels.

Juan Borda, who became president in March, 1894, was not so fortunate. Three years later, the so-called "Nationalistic **Nationalistic Revolts** Revolution," which was supported by Blanco leaders, broke out. After several sanguinary conflicts had taken place between government soldiers and insurrectionary forces, on August 25, 1897, while reviewing his troops in the capital city, Borda was shot in the heart. He was succeeded by Juan L. Cuestas as provisional president. On September 18, 1897, a pact of reconciliation was signed at Montevideo by commissioners of the government and agents of the malcontents. By that compact the members of the National party agreed to lay down their arms. As Congress opposed the candidacy of Cuestas for the presidency, he arbitrarily dissolved it and continued to hold supreme power for one year longer. On March 1, 1898, a new Congress elected him constitutional president. In religious matters Cuestas was intolerant. Although the Constitution declared that the state religion was Roman Catholicism, he placed restrictions upon its exercise and even tried to prevent the ingress of priests and friars. His religious policy has been ascribed to Masonic influence.

José Batlle y Ordóñez, the son of a former president of the republic, now came to the front of the political stage. In 1885 this new leader founded *El Día,* a newspaper that became his mouthpiece. A fearless journalist, he criticized the corrupt rule of civilian presidents and revivified the Colorado party. He felt that this party should adapt itself to new conditions by becoming democratic, and that it should promote social and political reforms. In 1898 he was elected Senator to Congress from Montevideo. Five years later, when he became a candidate for the presidency, he issued a manifesto declaring that, if elected, he intended to keep in mind the material and moral interests of the nation and to regulate his actions by constitutional precedents.

Soon after his inauguration the Nationalists rose against the government. Armed strife was temporarily averted by mediation, however, and an agreement was reached resembling the settlement with Aparicio in 1872. This adjustment was little more than a truce between contending factions: in 1904 a revolt occurred that lasted almost nine months. After a battle which resulted in the death of the rebel chieftain, Aparicio Saravia, on September 24, 1904, a peace was signed. That agreement provided for a general amnesty; for the supervision of elections by party committees; and for the recognition of the existing government by the rebels. Further, they were to lay down their arms and to give up their fortified towns; while a mixed commission was to distribute one hundred thousand pesos among the civil and military leaders of the insurrection. It seemed as though the sanguinary political feuds which had been provoked during the revolutionary epoch had thus been extinguished.

The administration of Claudio Williman, a leader of the Colorado party who was inaugurated on March 1, 1907, was signalized by important reforms. He soon issued a decree reorganizing the cabinet. Intendants and subintendants were introduced to aid in the administration of the departments. Capital punishment was abolished; a statute was enacted which permitted absolute divorce. An organic law for the University of Montevideo was sanctioned. Another law established a national institute for the deaf and dumb. The moles in the harbor of Montevideo were completed. So carefully did President Williman husband the nation's revenues that he left in the treasury an unprecedented surplus of nine million pesos.

Political and
Social
Reforms

On March 1, 1911, Batlle y Ordóñez became president for the second time. Notable among his plans for public improvements was a project for a splendid capitol which should be in the midst of new streets and plazas. Political persecutions ceased, freedom of the press was observed, and significant reforms were contemplated. The government began a serious study of the social welfare of its citizens. Experts from foreign lands were employed to investigate Uruguay's problems. The secretary of finance directed that statistics should be collected about wages, the cost of living, and the demand and supply of labor. Seeds and agricultural implements were exempted from import duties. A tax was levied upon useless expenditures for jewelry. In July, 1914, Congress discussed a bill granting full political rights to women. After his inauguration in 1915, President Viera announced his intention to follow the policies of his predecessor. He sanctioned various bills that aimed to promote the social welfare of Uruguayans. Among those measures were the following: a law introducing an eight-hour day, a law aiming to prevent accidents to workingmen, a law providing for industrial education in primary and secondary schools, a law concerning old-age pensions, a law levying a national inheritance tax, and a law establishing government control of telegraph and telephone lines.

The stream of immigration to Montevideo resembled that to Buenos Aires. In 1875 Uruguay had a population of less than half a million: in 1914 the population had trebled. A Uruguayan writer calculated that in a total population of about one million in 1908, the foreigners numbered about 180,000: of these Italians composed about 35 per cent; and Spaniards, 30 per cent. As the aboriginal race in Uruguay was largely exterminated, and as Negroes were found mainly along the Brazilian frontiers, the basic element in her population was Spanish. Immigrants were assimilated in the Uruguayan population with comparative ease. Children born of foreign parents in Montevideo often took pride in their Uruguayan citizenship.

Conditions
about 1914

The two chief occcupations of the people were agriculture and stock-raising. Their rich soil sustained a varied agriculture. In the north the main crops were tobacco, peanuts, and grapes, while in the south, wheat, corn, oats, flax, and barley were the most important products. According to the census of 1908, there roamed over the plains of Uruguay some 3,600,000 cattle, almost 2,000,000 sheep, and more than 500,000 horses. Uruguayan factories were mainly dependent upon agriculture and cattle-raising. The chief manufactures were butter, leather, flour, macaroni, and preserved meat. Many Uruguayans were engaged in mercantile affairs, especially in Montevideo. Uruguay had one of the most stable currencies in South America.

In comparison with some other Latin-American countries the republic of Uruguay was well supplied with transportation facilities. At Montevideo most of the steamship lines plying to Buenos Aires touched with considerable regularity. As it was only a one-night trip by water from Montevideo to the Argentine capital, Uruguayans could make good connections with sidewheel steamers plying up the Paraná and its tributaries. From 1869—when the first railway, which ran between Montevideo and Piedras, was opened to traffic—to 1914, over 1,500 miles of railway were constructed in Uruguay. The chief cities of the republic were thus linked with the metropolis.

In 1914 the commander in chief of the army was the secretary of war and the navy. The soldiery was mainly composed of a standing army and of reserves that constituted a national guard. The total strength of the standing army amounted to some ten thousand men. Uruguay's navy was composed of a few cruisers for coast defense and some smaller vessels.

The foundations of the existing educational system of Uruguay were laid by Dictator Latorre. In 1877 he issued a decree that placed education in charge of a board of public instruction. All public education, which was to be compulsory and sup- **Education, Literature, and Art** ported by the State, was placed under the control of the central government. Latorre's decree was supplemented by laws which marked Uruguay as one of the most progressive of the Latin-American states in educational legislation. Special attention was paid to the establishment of schools in rural districts. In or about Montevideo were located normal schools, a commercial school, a school of agriculture, a school of arts and trades, and a national university.

The literature of Uruguay resembled that of Argentina. Her poets and novelists wrote of the relations between the Indians and Spaniards, of the adventurous life and daring deeds of the gaucho, as well as of the evils of high society. *Ismael*, a romance by Acevedo Díaz, suggested the rôle of the half-breed in the formation of Uruguayan society. Zorilla de San Martín's poem, *Tabaré*, described the love of a half-breed Charruan Indian for a Spanish maiden. Among other productions

Alejandro Magarinos Cervantes wrote a poetic novel entitled *Celiar*, which depicted life during the colonial régime. Perhaps the most important historical writers were Francisco Bauzá, author of the *History of Spanish Domination in Uruguay*, and Luis Acevedo, who wrote an erudite commentary upon documents concerning the national hero, Artigas. One name only may be mentioned from the list of critical writers: José Rodó, the author of that intellectual breviary of South American youth entitled *Ariel*.

First in the list of Uruguayan artists is the name of Juan Blanes. He drew a vivid picture of an incident in the visitation of Buenos Aires by yellow fever in 1871. Uruguayan heroes he depicted in "Artigas in 1810" and in "The Oath of the Thirty-three." His son, Nicanor Blanes, modeled two remarkable statues of aborigines of the pampas, which were exhibited in the National Museum of Fine Arts.

After the outbreak of the first World War, the Congress of Uruguay established a food control board which was authorized to fix prices upon articles of prime necessity. Though less threatened **Uruguay and the First World War** than her great southern neighbor by the depredations of Germany upon the high sea, Uruguay took a positive attitude. In reply to the announcement of the United States that war existed between it and the imperial German government, Baltasar Brum, the Uruguayan secretary of foreign relations, declared that his government protested against Germany's submarine policy, that, while determined to maintain her neutrality, yet his nation expressed her "sympathy and moral solidarity" with the United States cause. After news reached Montevideo that the Uruguayan ship "Rosario" had been sunk by a German torpedo, President Viera published a remarkable decree announcing the decision of his cabinet that no American nation which was forced into a war "with nations of other continents" in defense of her own rights would be considered by Uruguay as a belligerent. On October 7, 1917, in secret session both houses of the Uruguayan Congress voted by overwhelming majorities that diplomatic relations with Germany should be severed. Upon the same day the President accordingly issued a decree which declared that his government had broken off both diplomatic and commercial intercourse with that country. Soon afterward, the government revoked the decrees that had proclaimed with regard to England and her Allies the observance by Uruguay of a state of neutrality in the first World War.

Dissatisfied with conditions, upon the expiration of his first term as president, Batlle had paid a visit to Europe where he sought a remedy for evils of the Uruguayan political régime. He believed that the existing presidential system should be altered. He decided that a plural executive similar to that of Switzerland might banish rebellions and civil wars from his country.

In May, 1913, a follower of Batlle named Arena ably explained the motives which inspired that President. His explanation is worth quoting not only because it presents the view-point of Batlle but also because it is an exposé of the evils of presidential government in Latin America: **Batlle Advocates Political Reforms**

> Batlle firmly believes that this long *via crucis* which the republic of Uruguay has traversed—longer and more sorrowful than Christ's—is largely the work of the President. He believes that the blood which has been shed in torrents, has almost always been shed either because of the presidents or because of presidential ambition. He is permanently obsessed by the thought that the country juggles with its fate in every presidential election. . . . Batlle has noticed that scarcely has the president-elect occupied his post, than there arise in his vicinity candidates for the future presidency; he has observed how these candidates, how the friends of these candidates, and how the friends of the friends of these candidates, do not take a single step, do not make a single gesture that is not affected by the mirage of the future presidency. Finally, he has beheld in this perennial spectacle of the struggle for the presidency a constant and profound disturbance of the politico-administrative mechanism and of the entire national life.

Batlle's proposal for a plural or collegiate executive, which came to a head after he had been succeeded by Viera in 1915, found some of his countrymen apathetic. Certain progressive leaders favored it, but the opposition was so strong that a party was formed which opposed the introduction of a collegiate executive. A law was enacted, however, providing for the use of the secret ballot. This system was first used in the election of delegates to a Constitutional Convention, which resulted in the defeat of the *Colorados Batllistas*. The result was that the new fundamental law adopted on October 15, 1917, did not embody the ideas of Batlle; it was rather in the nature of a compromise between his political ideals and the views of the triumphant Blancos. This Constitution went into operation on March 1, 1919, the very day on which Baltasar Brum was inaugurated president.

Uruguay's second Constitution preserved the main features of the centralized form of government established in 1830. Among its innovations was a provision that the President should be chosen by direct popular vote. It not only abolished the perma-nent committee of Congress but also provided for a **Changes in the Constitution** council of administration composed of nine members chosen by the people to serve for six years. This council was to prepare the budget, as well as to supervise elections. It might require the opinion of the President about legislative proposals concerning fiscal and currency matters and international commerce. It could authorize its members to participate in the deliberations of Congress without the right to vote. The same privilege was conceded to "ministers of state," who were to be appointed by the national council; but whose duties were not clearly differentiated from the functions of members of the President's cabinet. Local government was vested in representative assemblies and in autonomous administrative councils that were to be elected in the departments by popular vote.

Article V separated Church and State. It declared that all religious faiths were free, that the State would not support any religion, and not only that buildings actually used for religious purposes should remain in the possession of the Catholic Church but also that they were to be exempt from taxation.

The Uruguayan Constitution of 1917 deprived the President of considerable power and prestige. Whatever authority he had left was concerned chiefly with political functions. The control of all administrative matters not expressly reserved to him was transferred to the Council of Administration. It was vested with almost complete control over the ministries of public instruction, public works, and commerce and industry.

Under this Constitution the Colorados began a series of significant social reforms. Among these were a new election law, an eight-hour law, old-age pensions, indemnities for accidents, and government inspection of factories. It appeared that henceforth the policies of the Colorado party were to be determined largely by party conventions. After the campaign of November, 1930, however, serious charges of fraud and irregularities were brought against the officials who supervised the elections in Montevideo. Linked with these charges was the complaint of the Riverista faction of the Colorado party that other factions of that party had violated an ante-election agreement and thus excluded its candidate from the presidency.

Shortly afterward the announcement was made that Gabriel Terra, an experienced administrator and diplomat, who was the candidate of the Batllista faction of the Colorado party for the presidency, had won the elections. On March 1, 1931, Terra was quietly inaugurated. A brief experience with the Constitution of 1917 convinced the President that it had failed to improve political conditions. In particular he objected to the control of appointments by the Council of Administration. On March 31, 1933, he dismissed that council, dissolved Congress, and assumed dictatorial authority. In June delegates were elected to a Constitutional Assembly.

In some particulars the new fundamental law harked back to the Constitution of 1830. The two-headed executive was abolished, the Council of Administration was replaced by a president, a vice-president, and a cabinet. An attempt was made to hold cabinet ministers responsible for their acts by clauses which made possible their censure by Congress. The cabinet of nine members was to include three members from the second strongest political party. Provision was also made for minority representation in the lower house of the legislature. Women were admitted to suffrage. Dual nationality was permitted to naturalized citizens. Clauses concerning social legislation even dealt with the socialized practice of medicine. Departmental juntas were accorded legislative authority.

Terra was reëlected president. Revolts of Blancos and Colorados against his rule were suppressed. On March 27, 1938, General Alfredo Baldomir, an architect by profession, was elected president. The most significant events of his administration were connected with the second World War. In June, 1940, intense excitement was provoked by the discovery of a Nazi underground plot which had extensive ramifications. It appears that Germans in Argentina and Brazil had conspired to co-operate with their compatriots in Uruguay to establish in the basin of La Plata an agricultural colony of the Third Reich which was to form the nucleus of an extensive Nazi dependency. Soon after this plot became known, two United States cruisers opportunely cast anchor in the harbor of Montevideo. On September 25, 1940, the Uruguayan government issued a decree directing all good citizens to search for individuals and organizations suspected of connections with the Nazi régime.

Uruguay and the Second World War

Early in 1941, Argentina, Bolivia, Brazil, Paraguay and Uruguay took part in a regional conference at Montevideo which framed treaties embodying measures designed to check the economic ravages caused in the Platean basin by the second World War. On June 14, 1941, after the President had dissolved Congress and set up a council of state, he issued an announcement that Uruguay's ports and air bases could be used by any American country "in defense of the interests of democracy." The Brazilian government approved this declaration but the Argentine government frowned upon it and championed the doctrine of "strict neutrality." Nevertheless, in January, 1942, Uruguay severed relations with the powers of the Axis. Soon after Vargas issued a declaration of war, on August 26, 1942, Baldomir announced that his country viewed her northern neighbor as a non-belligerent: Brazil was conceded the use of Uruguayan territory for her air, military, and naval forces so as to ensure "a more efficient common defense against possible aggression."

On November 29, 1942, Juan J. Amézaga, the candidate of the liberal Colorados, was elected president for the next term. Constitutional reforms were adopted which not only provided for a system of proportional representation in the election of members of Congress but also restored to the President the right to select his cabinet. In a radio address Amézaga declared that he would carry on his predecessor's policy of continental solidarity.

One of the small states of South America, certain pages in the history of Uruguay reflect the story of her origin—she was a buffer state between Argentina and Brazil. Essentially a pampean land, her industrial life seemed destined to develop for a time mainly in channels similar to those of central Argentina. Uruguay's political waters have been more troubled than those of her great Latin-American neighbors. The party that was unsuccessful at the Uruguayan ballot box frequently appealed to the sword to secure a share of the spoils of office. Occasionally a dissentient party secured a portion of the spoils by an arrangement with the rival faction which was curiously like a treaty between belligerent nations. At present, however, the citizens of Uruguay seem to have settled down to a life that is industrious, meticulously regulated, and vehemently patriotic. Uruguayans are endowed with the aspiring Latin-American spirit that plans magnificent structures without always reckoning about the means with which to complete them. Though in large part drawn from other nations than Spain, her citizens have erected their civilization upon a basis that is mainly Spanish. They are very receptive, alert to utilize progressive ideas, and much inclined to adopt new vogues. Uruguay has become a vast laboratory of social, economic, and political experimentation. With regard to both the great world wars of the present age, she soon made public her intention to favor any American country that was fighting against nations of other continents to sustain democracy.

SUGGESTIONS FOR FURTHER READING

AKERS, C. E., *A History of South America*, 1904.
BROWNING, W. E., *The River Plate Republics*, 1928.
CLARK, S. A., *The East Coast of South America*, 1940.
CLEMENCEAU, G. E. B., *South America Today*, 1917.
GOLDBERG, I., *Studies in Spanish-American Literature*, 1920.
HANSON, S. G., *Utopia in Uruguay*, 1938.
HUDSON, W. H., *The Purple Land*, 1927.
KOEBEL, W. H., *Uruguay*, 1911.
PARKER, W. B. (ed), *Uruguayans of Today*, 1921.
RODÓ, J. E., *Ariel*, 1922.
ROSS, G., *Argentina and Uruguay*, 1916.
WILGUS, A. C. (ed.), *South American Dictators*, 1937.

CHAPTER XV

PARAGUAY

The state of Paraguay was formed in a region which in the seventeenth century had been styled the province of Guairá or Paraguay. A portion of that vast province was later made an intendancy of the viceroyalty of La Plata. When leaders in Asunción decided to separate from Spain they signed a convention with agents of the junta of Buenos Aires which not only regulated commercial relations between that city and Asunción but also provided that their province would be considered as independent. This convention further declared that, until the limits of Paraguay should be definitely demarcated, it was to include the department of Candelaria on the left bank of the Paraná River. For some years, however, the new state remained in a nebulous form.

Origin of Paraguay

After 1816, when José Rodríguez de Francia was made perpetual dictator of Paraguay, he became increasingly despotic. Evidently he was convinced that the Paraguayans were not ready for self-government. European visitors who ventured into his dominions described him as endowed with remarkable ability but vain, ambitious, and cruel. As the dictator became obsessed with the notion that his subjects were constantly conspiring against him, his capital became a veritable whispering gallery. Paraguayans who were suspected of disaffection toward the supreme ruler were arbitrarily imprisoned, manacled, and tortured. Occasionally they were exiled from their homes or executed in a shocking manner under the windows of Francia's palace. In a mood of fearful adoration the people called him *El Supremo*.

Though ordinarily aided by a secretary who acted as a minister, for the most part Francia's mode of government was personal. Chief executive, sole legislator, and supreme judge of the nation, Francia also made himself the head of the Paraguayan Church. In 1830 he abolished the tithes. A lover of South American independence, he levied forced contributions upon the Spaniards in Paraguay, and generously gave an asylum to Artigas. He soon adopted a policy by which his country was secluded from the world, both commercially and politically. A special license was even required to emigrate from Paraguay. The roving French botanist, Aimé Bonpland, was virtually kept a prisoner there for many years. As very

El Supremo

few articles might legally be imported into Paraguay, her people were forced to manufacture furniture, leather goods, and coarse cotton cloth. Upon receipt of a note from Simón Bolívar asking him to abandon his policy of isolation, Francia haughtily replied that Paraguay would not abandon that policy so long as he remained at the head of her government. On September 20, 1840, just after a terrible storm had burst over Asunción, the dictator died.

As Francia had made no disposition about a successor to his power, the government of Paraguay soon passed into the hands of a military junta. On March 12, 1841, a Congress decided to vest **The Two Consuls** executive authority in the hands of two consuls who should serve for three years. Of those rulers the rising man was Carlos A. López, a clever lawyer, who had been living in seclusion. The consuls soon initiated important reforms. Among other measures, they encouraged commercial relations with neighboring countries, founded a literary academy at Asunción, reorganized the judicial system, and provided for the gradual extinction of Negro slavery.

At the instance of the consuls, in 1842, an extraordinary Congress of four hundred deputies met at Asunción. On November 25 they signed a formal act stating that Paraguayan independence had been a solemn and incontestable fact for more than thirty years. Categorically they declared that Paraguay was by fact and right a nation free and independent of all foreign powers, that she would never become the patrimony of any person or of any family, and that all civil, ecclesiastical, and military officials should before assuming office, take an oath to defend the independence and integrity of the republic. This declaration was to be made known throughout Paraguay and to the neighboring countries. On the same day Congress enacted a law sanctioning the use of the flag and the seal that had been employed by Francia, which bore the inscription "Republic of Paraguay."

In 1844 the Congress assembled again. The consuls made a report to it concerning their activities. They also submitted the project of a law which reorganized the administration. On March 13, **Carlos López Becomes President** 1844, Congress approved the project which made provision for three departments of government and which vested large powers in a president, who should hold office for ten years. On the following day the legislators acclaimed López as president.

During the next decade certain nations of America acknowledged Paraguay's independence. In 1852 the United States recognized Paraguay as an independent nation. Argentina, whose publicists had entertained hopes of incorporating Paraguay within their domain, acknowledged her independence after the battle of Caseros. But negotiations to determine the boundaries of independent Paraguay were only partly successful. A treaty was signed between diplomats of Argentina and Paraguay on July 15, 1852, which stipulated that the boundary line between the two nations should be the rivers Paraná and Bermejo, and that a narrow strip along the right bank of the Paraguay River between the mouth of the Bermejo River and the river Atajo should be neutral territory. Yet, as this convention was not ratified by the legislature of the Argentine Confederation, Paraguay continued to exercise jurisdiction over a portion of the mission territory which stretched along the left bank of the Paraná from the Iguassú River to Candelaria. Attempts by Paraguay to determine by treaty her boundaries with Brazil to the east of the Paraguay River failed, and the expanding Empire continued to claim territory south of the Río Blanco. To the west of the river Paraguay, however, Brazil recognized that the northern boundary of the republic was the river Negro.

In 1854 Congress reëlected López, but, at his request, it limited his term of office to three years. After that term had expired, the President changed his mind and was again reëlected. Between 1857 and 1862 various disputes arose between Paraguay and foreign powers. With the United States a controversy took place chiefly because of the colonizing and mercantile activities of a bustling agent named Hopkins who had been driven out of Paraguay by López. This was complicated by a dispute concerning the "Water Witch," a United States vessel engaged in making a scientific exploration of South American rivers which was fired upon by Paraguayan gunners when entering the Upper Paraná River. With France difficulties arose because of the treatment accorded to Frenchmen who had been induced to emigrate to Paraguay as the result of a mission to Europe of the President's eldest son, Francisco S. López. With England a dispute took place because of the imprisonment by Paraguayan authorities of an English citizen named James Canstatt, who was accused of being implicated in a conspiracy directed against the life of the President. Though upon more than one occasion those acrimonious disputes brought Paraguay to the verge of war, yet after intermittent negotiations, they were all settled peacefully.

The elder López died on September 10, 1862. About a month later Congress elected his son, Francisco Solano López, as president for ten years. Shortly after the accession of the younger López, the Brazilian minister to Paraguay stated that espionage prevailed there to so great an extent that even the servants of foreign diplomats were compelled clandestinely to divulge to the police whatever took place within the respective legations. He asserted that any person who made the least

Accession of the Younger López

criticism of the government was doomed to end his life in a dungeon. Either because of a passion for military prestige, or because of suspicions about the designs of one or more of the neighboring nations, President López soon undertook to improve Paraguay's military establishment. Forts were built at strategic points along the limitary rivers, rude barracks were constructed, and thousands of quasi-civilized Guaraníes were placed under arms. In September, 1864, the Brazilian minister at Asunción informed his government that some Paraguayans considered a foreign war as the only event that would relieve their country from the "tyrannical régime" of López.

Edward Thornton, the British minister at Buenos Aires, who paid a visit to Asunción at this juncture, took a similar view. In a dispatch to Lord Russell, he thus explained the attitude of the Paraguayans toward the dictatorship: "The great majority of the people are ignorant enough to believe that there is no country as powerful or so happy as Paraguay, and that they are blessed with a President who is worthy of all adoration. The rule of the Jesuits, of the Dictator Francia," and of the López dynasty had imbued those people "with the deepest veneration for the authorities." Thornton further declared that among the three or four thousand Paraguayans who knew better there was such a lack of confidence that no combination against the tyrant seemed possible.

The Paraguayan War, as it is designated, was the outcome of a complex and strained international situation. Paraguay's boundaries with

Origins of the Paraguayan War

Argentina and Brazil were unsettled. Dictator López was suspected of harboring the ambition to become the Napoleon of South America. For some time the Blancos of Uruguay had been soliciting his intervention. Even before an opportunity for action presented itself, he had decided to play a part in the troubled politics of neighboring states.

Resentment over an old quarrel with Rosas and his refusal to recognize their independence had not died out among Paraguayans. Economic differences between Asunción and Buenos Aires helped to fan the spirit of animosity. The discord in Argentina between Federals and Liberals encouraged López's hope that he would succeed in a war against that country. A general mobilization that the dictator ordered in Paraguay in 1864 was originally directed against Argentina on behalf of the Blancos, but when Brazilian activities in Uruguay became threatening López altered his immediate objective.

On the other side Pedro II may have invited a foreign war in order to draw attention from troublesome domestic problems. In any case, it is clear that complications with the Brazilian Empire, with which Paraguay had been on strained relations for some time, furnished an occasion for war. In 1865, though her neighbors knew it not, Paraguay was a formidable military power.

As indicated in the preceding chapter, to atone for injuries which Brazilian subjects had suffered in the civil wars of Uruguay, the imperial government announced that it would make military reprisals on the Uruguayan frontiers. On August 30, 1864, the Paraguayan government, which favored the Blanco régime in Uruguay, protested vehemently against this announcement and declared that it "would consider any occupation of Uruguayan territory by imperial troops... an attack upon the balance of power of the states of La Plata, a balance which interests the republic of Paraguay as the guarantee of her security, peace, and prosperity. That government protests in the most solemn manner against such an act, and at once disclaims all responsibility for the ultimate consequences of the present declaration." Thus boldly did the hermit republic formulate to a giant neighbor her doctrine concerning the political equilibrium of the nations that occupied the spacious La Plata basin.

In consequence of the movement of Brazilian troops against the Uruguayan frontier, on November 12, López notified the imperial government that diplomatic relations between Paraguay and Brazil were severed. Further, he prohibited Brazilian vessels from navigating Paraguayan rivers. Evidently convinced that, as war with Brazil was inevitable, it had best be precipitated at once, he ordered a Paraguayan gunboat to capture a Brazilian packet which had passed Asunción on its way to Matto Grosso. In December, 1864, he dispatched a military expedition against that province. The dictator then asked President Mitre for permission to march his soldiers across the Argentine province of Corrientes in order to attack the Brazilian province of Rio Grande do Sul. Mitre declined to grant that request. In response to a message from López, the Paraguayan Congress passed a law on March 18, 1865, which approved his warlike measures against Brazil. That Congress also imprudently voted to declare war upon Argentina.

A note communicating this decision was apparently not received by the Argentine secretary of foreign relations until May 3. Meantime, in the port of Corrientes on April 13 Paraguayan gunboats seized two Argentine vessels. This high-handed outrage caused an outburst of popular indignation throughout Argentina and made feasible a rapprochement with her great rival, Brazil. Urquiza wrote a characteristic note to Mitre in which he aptly declared that words must give way to deeds: "Now it falls to our lot to fight once more under the flag which at Caseros united all the Argentinians!" To intensify the crisis, Paraguayan soldiers invaded Rio Grande do Sul. The domineering ambition of Paraguay's chief magistrate had far outleaped the bounds of sane policy. Instead of formulating a doctrine of the balance of power in South America acceptable to the Platean nations, he had provoked the formation of a coalition directed against himself.

Upon the other side, the policy of Pedro II had won favor. When Mitre began to negotiate with Flores for joint action against Paraguay, the Uruguayan dictator declared that he could not join such an alliance unless Brazil became a party. The result was that on May 1, 1865, Argentina, Uruguay, and Brazil signed a secret treaty which arranged a defensive and offensive alliance against Paraguay. The allies agreed that the chief command of their military forces should be given to General Mitre, while their naval operations should be directed by the Brazilian, Admiral Tamandaré. They pledged themselves not to lay down their arms except by common agreement after the existing Paraguayan régime had been overthrown. They expressly declared that the war was not undertaken against the Paraguayan people but against their government. They agreed to guarantee the independence, sovereignty, and territorial integrity of Paraguay. After the completion of the war her people should be permitted to establish their own governmental institutions. The free navigation of the Paraná and Paraguay rivers should be assured. But the offending republic was not only to bear the cost of the war but also the ensuing indemnities.

Article XVI of the Tripartite Treaty sketched the boundaries of Paraguay so as to suit Argentina and Brazil. The boundary between Brazil and Paraguay should be the Paraná River to a stream on the right bank that was called the Igurey; from its sources the boundary should follow the peaks of the cordillera of Maracayú to the sources of the river Apa, and then follow that stream to the Paraguay River. The limits between Paraguay and Argentina on the east should be the river Paraná to the Brazilian frontier; that is, to the mouth of the Iguassú River upon the right bank of the Paraná.

The exacting terms of this secret treaty serve to indicate the apprehensions that the younger López had provoked in the minds of statesmen of neighboring countries. The two great allies had conceded to each other their utmost territorial claims against their mutual antagonist. This treaty proposed to deprive Paraguay of about one-half of the territory over which she had claimed jurisdiction; it forecasted a dismemberment that might not inappropriately be likened unto a partition of Poland. After the Tripartite Treaty had been unexpectedly published by the English government, its territorial clauses evoked protests from certain South American nations which felt that their interests were threatened.

Both Emperor Pedro and President Mitre expected that hostilities would be of short duration. To a vociferous populace that gathered in front of the President's palace, Mitre gave a slogan which implied that in three months he would be in Asunción.   **Course of**
the War
Despite the great numerical inequality of the opposing powers, the war lasted about five years. Soon after the Tripartite Treaty was signed, Brazil sent warships up the Paraná River. On June 11, 1865, her fleet dispersed an enemy squadron near Corrientes. The Argentine-Uruguayan army defeated Paraguayan soldiers on the banks of the Yatay River; that army then besieged Uruguayana and compelled the Paraguayan commander to capitulate. After those defeats López skilfully withdrew his soldiers within the boundaries of his country and confined himself to defensive warfare. In April, 1866, allied soldiers forded the Paraná River. On May 24 they defeated the enemy in a bloody battle at Tuyutí; but on September 22 the Paraguayans checked the allies at Curupaití. It was the beginning of 1867 before the fleet of the allies succeeded in passing a strategic fort which guarded the Paraguayan frontiers at Huamitá. The allies then besieged that fort, which fell on August 15, 1868. After other sanguinary conflicts with the brave soldiers of Paraguay, early in January, 1869, the invaders occupied Asunción. Driven from one refuge to another, deserted by most of his remaining followers, but refusing to surrender, López was finally overtaken by Brazilian soldiers and shot near the banks of the Aquidaban River on March 1, 1870. Apparently the dictator died in the conviction that Paraguayan nationality perished with him.

The American minister to Uruguay, who visited Asunción shortly afterward, indeed doubted whether Paraguayan nationality would survive. In a letter to his government he thus transmitted his impressions of the vanquished country:

No candid person on near view of the facts can fail to perceive that there has been enacted in Paraguay a terrible tragedy of blood and crime. It is truthful and just to say that the chief actors in this sanguinary and criminal destruction were López and Brazil. . . . While the present condition of the people who made such a wonderful defense of its nationality for five years is very sad to observe, it is safe to say that the newspaper and other accounts of the numerical loss of life and existing hopelessness of the country are an exaggeration. There is left alive of the original population a larger proportion than has been represented. The financial status is far from hopeless. As the López government paid the soldiers comparatively nothing, the close of the war left but a small debt to be provided for by the new government.

This war was significant to all participants. It destroyed a large portion of the male population of Paraguay, caused the death of many soldiers of the allied nations, and brought some Brazilians into contact with the citizens of republics. It drained the treasuries of the belligerents. In accordance with the Tripartite Treaty, Argentina and Brazil attempted to saddle the vanquished people with a huge war debt. The "Paraguayan War" ended the rule of the López dynasty and prepared the way for constitutional government in the hermit state. Six years passed after the death of López, however, before the last detachment of Argentine and Brazilian soldiers left the soil of Paraguay.

Meantime a provisional government, which had been formed from nationals living in the conquered territory and from a Paraguayan legion that had fought with the invaders, had established a governmental junta. In October, 1869, at the instance of the Brazilian military commander, the junta issued a decree which announced that all slaves upon Paraguayan soil were free. On June 2, 1870, the allies signed a treaty of peace with this provisional government. Soon afterward the junta convoked a Constituent Assembly which met in August, 1870, in the hall of the cabildo at Asunción. A committee of five men, headed by Juan Silvano Godoi, a Paraguayan publicist who had been educated at a college at Santa Fé in Argentina, was selected to frame a constitution. On November 25, 1870, the Assembly promulgated a Constitution for Paraguay which declared a dictatorship to be unlawful.

The Paraguayan fathers stipulated that their country should be free and that her government should be republican. The executive authority was vested in a President, a Vice-President, a cabinet, and a permanent committee. After the first election—when the chief executive magistrates were to be selected by the Constitutional Assembly—the President and Vice-President should be chosen by electors. The President should be the commander in chief of the army and navy as well as the chief administrator of the State. He might veto acts of Congress. With the consent of Congress, he might negotiate treaties, declare war, or make peace. Five secretaries, appointed by the President, should form his cabinet. They might attend Congress, and take part in its debates; but they could not vote. The Chamber of Deputies was to be made up of members chosen by direct vote from election districts. The Senate was to be composed of members elected by direct vote at the ratio of one member for every twelve thousand inhabitants. Besides the power to levy direct taxes and to establish a national bank, Congress was given the right to accept or reject the resignation of the President and the Vice-President as well as the authority to permit foreign soldiers to enter the territory of the republic. The judiciary was to be composed

Constitution
of 1870

of a supreme court and of as many inferior courts as might be established by law.

Article III declared that the Roman Catholic Apostolic faith was the religion of state. Nevertheless, the government was not to prohibit the free exercise of any other religious faith. The President was to exercise the right of patronage; with the consent of Congress, he might refuse to admit papal rescripts. The Constitution contained no provisions about local government. At a later time the territory was divided into districts which resembled Uruguayan departments.

Cirilio Rivarola was elected president. A difficult problem which confronted the new government was the adjustment of frontiers. Just before the end of the war the provisional government had made a treaty with Brazil and Argentina stating **Bounds of the New Paraguay** that Paraguay should be free to urge the bounds which she thought consistent with her rights. Shortly after the war terminated, while insisting upon her claims as a conqueror, Brazil agreed to support Paraguay in her opposition to the contention of Argentina. On January 9, 1872, diplomats of Paraguay and Brazil signed a convention by which the Empire was conceded a clear title to the territory north of the Río Apa that she had been promised by the Treaty of 1865.

Encouraged by Brazil's sympathetic attitude, Paraguay persisted in her opposition to Argentina's demands. During the administration of President Gill, on February 3, 1876, the government signed a treaty which provided for an adjustment of the disputed boundary. This treaty stipulated that Argentina should have a clear title to the mission region on the left bank of the Paraguay between the Bermejo River and the Pilcomayo River, that she should relinquish her claim to territory between Bahía Negra and the Río Verde, and that the title to the region between the rivers Verde and Pilcomayo, including Villa Occidental, should be submitted to the arbitration of the President of the United States. On November 12, 1878, President Hayes decided that Paraguay was justly entitled to the territory between the Pilcomayo and the Verde Rivers. Nevertheless, as a result of the war, Paraguay was compelled to relinquish her claim to about fifty-five thousand square miles of territory.

The political history of Paraguay after her war with the allies was profoundly affected by its results. Her first President soon resigned because of differences with Congress and was **Politics and Diplomacy after the War** succeeded by the Vice-President—this was a prelude to Paraguay's subsequent history. Presidents or vice-presidents, who succeeded presidents after their resignation or deposition, followed each other in rapid succession. Parties, which originated from the cliques that sided for or against López in the war, rent the country by their dissensions. The policy which the nation should follow toward one or another of her antagonists in that struggle was often a crucial problem in her politics and diplomacy. During most of the period that elapsed between 1870 and the opening of the twentieth century, the Colorado or Radical party controlled the national government. It does not appear that this party had any well-defined principles except to remain in power. Some presidents did not serve out their terms of office: they were induced to resign, they were deposed, or they were assassinated. The military element played an important rôle in Paraguayan life. At times presidents were removed from power by bloodless revolts; at other times the uprisings were barrack insurrections. Occasionally Paraguayan revolutions partook of the burlesque. The period between 1902 and 1910 was checkered by such events as the proclamation of martial law, the bombardment of public buildings by rebels, a compromise between opposing factions, and mediation by the diplomatic corps.

Meanwhile a dispute had been brewing over the northern portion of the Chaco, a semi-tropical plain composed of moist lowlands drained by the rivers Bermejo and Pilcomayo. Maintaining that the audiencia of Charcas had exercised jurisdiction over the right bank of the Paraguay River, publicists of Bolivia had laid claim to the very region which Brazilian diplomacy had aided Paraguay to keep from Argentina. In 1879 Bolivia dispatched Antonio Quijarro to Asunción where on October 15, 1879, he signed a treaty with José S. Decoud, the Paraguayan secretary of foreign relations. By the Quijarro-Decoud Treaty a boundary line was sketched between the two parties which extended directly west from the mouth of the river Apa to the river Pilcomayo.

A Bolivian agent named Tamayo found, however, that Paraguay did not favor the ratification of that treaty. Instead a Paraguayan diplomat named Aceval proposed that a boundary line should be drawn in a westerly direction from Fort Olimpo. Tamayo finally agreed that the title to a zone of territory which the Quijarro-Decoud Treaty had acknowledged as belonging to Bolivia should be submitted to arbitration. Accordingly the Tamayo-Aceval Treaty of 1887 stipulated that that title should be passed upon by the King of Belgium. But this treaty also failed of ratification by both parties.

In 1894 another attempt was made to reach an adjustment. Bolivia sent Telma Ichaso to Asunción with instructions stating that his country was ready to arbitrate. Ichazo entered into negotiations with Gregorio Benites. On November 23, 1894, they signed the Ichazo-Benites Treaty which undertook to divide the Chaco between the two

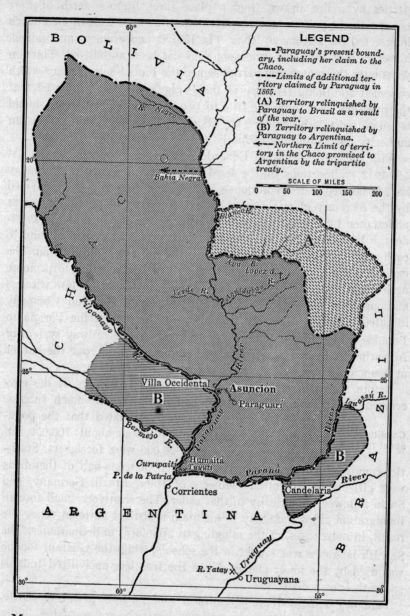

LEGEND

— Paraguay's present boundary, including her claim to the Chaco.

---- Limits of additional territory claimed by Paraguay in 1865.

(A) Territory relinquished by Paraguay to Brazil as a result of the war.

(B) Territory relinquished by Paraguay to Argentina.

←— Northern Limit of territory in the Chaco promised to Argentina by the tripartite treaty.

SCALE OF MILES

0   50   100   150   200

MAP SHOWING TERRITORIES RELINQUISHED BY PARAGUAY TO ARGENTINA AND BRAZIL AFTER THE WAR OF 1864-1870

parties by a line drawn from a place three leagues north of Fort
Olimpo to the point where the meridian of 61° 26′ west of Greenwich
intersected the Pilcomayo River. The Bolivian government maintained,
however, that this new concession had not been authorized. Thirteen
years later the contending parties signed the Pinilla-Soler Treaty which
conceded additional territory to the Paraguayans and stipulated that
the question concerning the title to two vaguely defined zones should
be submitted to arbitration. "The claims of Paraguay," said a Bolivian
authority, "increased mysteriously and by every treaty."

With the inauguration of Eduardo Schaerer as president, on August
15, 1912, "alterations of the legal order"—as a writer of Paraguay
has designated her revolutions—became less frequent. A revolt led
by the secretary of war soon collapsed. A survey of public lands was
undertaken by the national government. At the instance of the President, a homestead law was enacted which promised a strip of land to
each applicant who would agree to till the soil and build a home. The
capital of the Agricultural Bank, which had been created to promote
agriculture and industry, was considerably increased. A few wireless
stations were erected. The Central Paraguayan Railroad Company
initiated a ferryboat service from Encarnación across the Paraná to
Posadas, which linked Paraguayan railroads to the railway system of
Argentina. A United States firm was employed to improve the harbor
at Asunción. Steps were taken to encourage immigration.

Before the outbreak of the first World War, attempts of the government to encourage immigration had not met with much success.
A careful Paraguayan scholar estimated that the popu-
Conditions about 1914 lation of his country in 1905 was about 700,000. Of
these inhabitants perhaps 20,000 were foreigners. Statis-
tics computed a few years earlier indicated that one-half of the aliens
were citizens of Argentina: subjects of Italy, Brazil, Germany, and
Spain followed numerically in that order. The relatively small foreign
immigration aided Paraguay to maintain a distinct national type—the
result, in most cases, of the mingling of Spaniards and Guaraníes. The
Spanish language was taught in the schools, while the Guaraní tongue
was used by the lower classes. Upon the frontiers uncivilized Indians
spoke their own dialects.

Paraguay remained an agricultural and pastoral country. Cattle,
sheep, horses, and goats browsed upon her rich, grassy plains; hides
were an important export. Crude rubber, tobacco, cotton, oranges,
Paraguayan tea, and timber were her main agricultural products.
Cigars, cigarettes, tannin, sole leather, and nandutí lace were her chief
manufactures. Her development had been retarded because of her distance from the seaboard. Until recently the only mode of communica-

tion between this country and the outside world was the Paraguay River which was navigable by vessels of light draught as far as Asunción. The first railroad in Paraguay, opened between Asunción and Paraguarí in 1861, was later extended to Encarnación.

The Tripartite Treaty stipulated that Paraguay should pay the expense of her own subjugation. Aside from indebtedness due to the war, which was not pressed by the victors, the Paraguayan government floated loans in London and Buenos Aires. It was frequently much embarrassed because of its inconvertible paper currency. Indeed commercial transactions between Paraguayan merchants and foreigners were not infrequently reckoned in terms of the gold peso of Argentina.

Article VII of the Paraguayan Constitution provided that primary instruction should be compulsory. Yet the percentage of illiteracy in Paraguay was high. Academies where students prepared for higher education had been founded at the capital city and elsewhere. A law of 1889 provided for a university which opened its doors in Asunción in the following year. The National University of Paraguay was composed of a college of law and social sciences, a college of medicine, and a college of mathematics. Besides this university, there were normal schools, a military academy, and an ecclesiastical seminary.

Paraguay soon felt some effects of the first World War. In August, 1914, a moratorium was declared by Congress. During the administration of Manuel Franco, a Liberal-Radical who was inaugurated in August, 1916, the moratorium was extended. Imports decreased and with them the customs revenues. Disturbed economic conditions, which were partly the result of the war, induced the government to establish a bureau that was to arrange for the redemption of paper money and to regulate the currency. A treaty was negotiated with Argentina providing that, with few exceptions, the products of each country were to be admitted into the other country free of duty for five years. Compulsory military service was established by law. With regard to the declared policy of the United States toward the German submarine campaign, the Paraguayan government expressed its sympathy for her advocacy of neutral rights. In 1918 in a message to Congress the President stated that Paraguay accepted the principles of American solidarity as voiced by President Wilson.

Paraguay after the Outbreak of the First World War

Despite attempts to frame a treaty of limits the controversy between Paraguay and Bolivia concerning the title to territory on the right bank of the Paraguay River above Villa Occidental remained unsettled. The essence of Paraguay's contention was that as this hinterland had been first explored and colonized by her pioneers, she had earned the title to it. Acrimonious discussion took place between the parties about the maintenance of the *status quo*. In December, 1928,

The Chaco War

a clash between Paraguayan soldiers and a Bolivian garrison took place at Fort Vanguardia. A peace was patched up by an agreement to submit the differences to a mixed commission. After fresh endeavors to settle the controversy by negotiations had failed, and after other conflicts had occurred on the frontiers, the Chaco War took place.

On September 9, 1932, Paraguayans commanded by Colonel José F. Estigarribia routed a Bolivian force that had seized Fort Boquerón. Under the command of a German officer named Kundt the Bolivians waged an aggressive campaign. In December, 1933, however, their forces were decisively defeated. Among the Bolivians who eluded the victors was the brave General Enrique Peñaranda. At the head of a new Bolivian army, he soon resumed the sanguinary conflict in the swamps and tangled thickets of the Chaco. The Paraguayan warriors continued to push forward, however, and on January 15, 1935, Estegarribia pitched his camp on the banks of the Parapití, a river which marked the farthest limit of his country's claim. On June 12, 1935, while the warring nations were still fighting, a peace protocol was signed.

This protocol, framed at Buenos Aires by a conference which met at the instance of neutral American states, provided for the suspension of hostilities, the immobilization of the contending armies, and the delimitation of a Bolivian-Paraguayan boundary. On October 10, 1938, a treaty which sketched that boundary was signed at Buenos Aires by the two parties. This treaty drew a jagged line from a place at 20° 9′ 58″ south latitude on the western bank of the Paraguay River to a point at 62° 37′ 19″ west longitude on the eastern bank of the river Pilcomayo. By this agreement Paraguay secured territory into which she had fought her way beyond the limits drawn in 1907 by the Pinilla-Soler Treaty. On the other hand, Bolivia was not only left in control of the Andean slopes, but was also conceded a clear title to a bit of territory northeast of the land assigned to the victor which assured her an outlet on the Paraguay River.

Shortly after Estigarribia became president in August, 1939, he dissolved Congress. He appointed a commission to frame a new fundamental law, which he approved on July 10. This Constitution provided that the President should hold his office for five years. He was granted very extensive powers, such as the control of patronage, the declaration of a state of siege, and the right to initiate laws and to negotiate treaties. Legislative authority was given to a unicameral legislature. Judicial authority was vested in a supreme court and in-

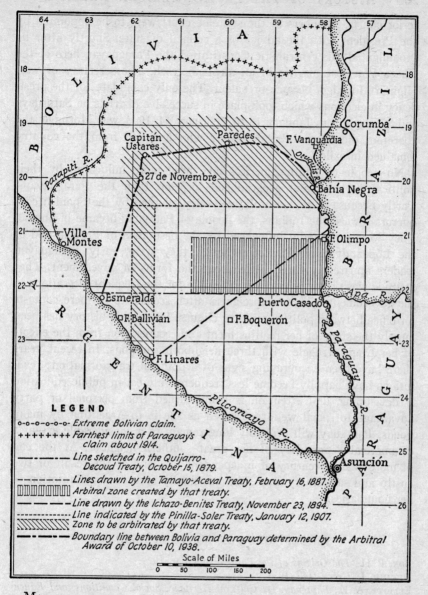

LEGEND

o-o-o-o-o-o- Extreme Bolivian claim.
+++++++++ Farthest limits of Paraguay's
claim about 1914.
—·—·— Line sketched in the Quijarro-
Decoud Treaty, October 15, 1879.
——————— Lines drawn by the Tamayo-Aceval Treaty, February 16, 1887.
▨▨▨▨ Arbitral zone created by that treaty.
— —— —— Line drawn by the Ichazo-Benites Treaty, November 23, 1894.
············· Line indicated by the Pinilla-Soler Treaty, January 12, 1907.
▨▨▨ Zone to be arbitrated by that treaty.
━━━━━ Boundary line between Bolivia and Paraguay determined by the Arbitral
Award of October 10, 1938.

Scale of Miles
0   50   100   150   200

MAP ILLUSTRATING THE BOUNDARY DISPUTE BETWEEN PARAGUAY
AND BOLIVIA

ferior courts. Members of the supreme court were to be appointed by the President with the advice of a council of state. Shortly after he promulgated this centralistic Constitution the Paraguayan hero of the Chaco War lost his life in an airplane crash. The secretary of war, Higinio Morinigo, became president. The only candidate for the presidency in elections which took place in successive districts on Saturdays and Sundays from January 16 to February 14, 1943, was Morinigo, the "barefoot dictator." Liberal leaders who had fled from the country remained in exile.

No people of South America have been more influenced by their political heritage and geographical location than the Paraguayans. Partly because of the assimilative policy adopted by the Spanish conquerors toward the Indians, the people of Paraguay became bi-lingual. They were profoundly influenced by the despotism of Francia and of the López dynasty. Patriotic though they were, early Paraguayan leaders apparently cared little about the forms of government. That attitude was probably partly responsible for the frequent alterations in the government, which to foreigners often seemed to be mere contests for office between politico-military cliques. Paraguay's history has been largely the story of her readjustment and recuperation from the effects of her tragic struggle with three neighboring nations. In recent years there have been encouraging signs of a political transformation: revolutions have happily become less frequent, interest in public education is developing, and attention is being turned from personal or party advantage to social welfare. Linked as she is to Argentina by many bonds, Paraguay will probably long remain to a considerable extent a commercial dependency of her great southern neighbor. At the end of more than a century of independent life, and as the result of two costly and sanguinary wars, she has finally secured a delimitation of her boundaries.

SUGGESTIONS FOR FURTHER READING

Box, P. H., *The Origins of the Paraguayan War*, 1929.

Duguid, J., *Green Hell*, 1931.

Elliott, A. E., *Paraguay, Its Cultural Heritage, Social Conditions, and Educational Problems*, 1931.

Graham, R. B. Cunninghame, *Portrait of a Dictator*, 1933.

Grubb, W. B., *An Unknown People in an Unknown Land*, 1925.

———, *A Church in the Wilds*, 1914.

Hunt, R. J., *The Livingstone of South America: The Life and Adventures of W. Barbrooke Grubb*, 1933.

Hutchinson, T. J., *The Paraná, with Incidents of the Paraguayan War*, 1868.

Koebel, W. H., *Paraguay*, 1917.

Masterman, G. F., *Seven Eventful Years in Paraguay*, 1869.

PAGE, T. J., *La Plata, the Argentine Confederation, and Paraguay*, 1859.
PARKER, W. B. (ed), *Paraguayans of Today*, 1920.
ROBERTSON, J. P. and W. P., *Letters on Paraguay*, Vol. II, 1838.
———, *Francia's Reign of Terror*, Vol. II, 1839.
THOMPSON, G. C. E., *The War in Paraguay*, 1869.
WASHBURN, C. A., *The History of Paraguay*, Vol. II, 1871.
WILDE, J. C. DE, "South American Conflicts: the Chaco and Leticia," *Foreign Policy Reports*, Vol. IX, No. 6, 1933.

CHAPTER XVI

CHILE

Chile arose from the captaincy general of that name. After that region had been freed from Spanish rule, Director O'Higgins proceeded to organize a new government. He appointed a secretary **The Reign of O'Higgins** of state and a secretary of war. Shortly afterward he placed Hipólito Villegas in charge of the finances. Meanwhile the Director had issued some reformatory decrees. All Chileans were to take an oath of fidelity to the new régime; property belonging to royalists was to be confiscated; and a Chilean army was to be organized.

In May, 1818, the "Supreme Director of the State"—as O'Higgins was styled—appointed a commission of seven men to frame a provisional constitution for Chile. A draft of a fundamental law was submitted to the Director who promulgated it in October, 1818. This Constitution placed the supreme executive authority of the nation in the hands of O'Higgins, who was to be aided by three secretaries; it gave him authority to appoint all important magistrates, as well as the right to veto legislation. It granted legislative authority to a Senate composed of five members. It vested judicial authority in a supreme court composed of five members who, like the senators, should be chosen by the Director. The territory of Chile was divided into three provinces which should be managed by officials called governors-intendant. The Constitution of 1818 contained a pledge that a Congress would be convoked when the country was freed from royalist soldiers.

Director O'Higgins remained the dictator of the new state for several years. He appointed five prominent Chileans members of the Senate; but their decisions, on the whole, merely embodied his wishes. In his foreign policy O'Higgins was comparatively successful. Despite differences between San Martín and the United Provinces of La Plata, the dictator maintained amicable relations with that state. He negotiated treaties of alliance with the governments of Peru and Colombia. His government was recognized by the Mexican Empire. In 1822 his agent in London, Antonio de Irisarri, succeeded in negotiating a loan of one million pounds with English bankers.

Dictator O'Higgins rightly felt that conditions in Chile were ripe for certain social reforms. He reopened the National Institute, an educational establishment which had been closed for several years, and improved elementary schools in various ways. He promoted the organization of a police system in the cities as well as in rural districts. He attempted to suppress brigandage by establishing special tribunals which dispensed summary justice. He decreed that all titles of nobility granted by the Spanish King to Chileans, as well as the coats of arms attesting those titles, should be swept away. Further, he aimed to abolish *mayorazgos* or entailed estates. Those reforms antagonized many members of the influential and wealthy classes, while other Chileans opposed O'Higgins because they had been partisans of the Carreras.

On May 7, 1822, the Director issued a decree which ordered that elections should be held for a "preparatory convention." Elections which took place in the municipalities resulted in the choice of delegates who had been designated by the dictator. To the Convention which was installed at Santiago on July 23 O'Higgins submitted a message resigning his position; but its members insisted that he should remain in command, and he yielded. On September 28, 1822, he sent another message to the Convention proposing that it should frame a new fundamental law for Chile. A project of a constitution was promptly formed, briefly discussed, and sanctioned by the Convention on October 23, 1822. A few days later the Director swore to observe it. Though this Constitution declared that the sovereign authority emanated from the people, and though it vested political authority in three distinct departments, yet it virtually provided that O'Higgins might wield dictatorial powers for ten years longer. But some Chilean leaders did not approve of this curious fundamental law.

Two months after the Constitution of 1822 was promulgated, a revolt led by a general named Freire occurred at Concepción. The insurrection spread throughout other districts in southern Chile, and an open meeting of the town council soon assembled in Santiago to request the Director to give up his office. On January 28, 1823, a committee from this council asked O'Higgins to resign. At first he demurred and declared that there was no competent authority to which he might transfer his functions. The insistence of the revolutionists, however, convinced him that he must yield, and he reluctantly gave up his power to a junta upon the condition that a national Congress should be convoked. After the acts of his administration had been adjudged, the ex-Director sailed for Peru.

The provisional government that succeeded O'Higgins selected General Freire to serve as director until a Constituent Congress should assemble. Freire aimed to continue the policy of reform which had been initiated by O'Higgins; and he succeeded in abolishing Negro slavery. When the Constituent Congress assembled, it promptly confirmed the choice of Freire as director. It entrusted the task of framing a constitution to a prominent jurist named Juan Egaña. After some discussion of his project, the Constituent Congress finally adopted a fundamental law which was promulgated on December 29, 1823.

Freire
Becomes
Supreme
Director

That Constitution provided for a complicated form of government. Executive authority should be vested in a Supreme Director whose term of office should ordinarily be four years. His cabinet was to be composed of three secretaries. He was to be advised by a council made up of dignitaries and magistrates. Legislative authority was granted to a bicameral Congress composed of a Senate and a "National Chamber." Judicial authority was vested in a supreme court, an appellate court, and inferior judges. The republic was to be divided into various administrative districts. Artificial though this peculiar, fundamental law was, yet, as suggested in a commemorative decree, it became a political legacy to posterity.

Evidently some of its provisions were never put into force. By a coup d'état Freire soon established himself as dictator. He led two campaigns against Spanish royalists in the Chiloé Islands and thus brought the archipelago under the rule of Chile. After he had banished the royalist bishop of Santiago, Chilean relations with Rome became strained. An agent of the Pope named Juan Muzi demanded his passports, and the Papacy would not acknowledge the right of the Chilean government to make eccclesiastical appointments. Perhaps the most awkward problem which confronted Freire was concerned with the finances; for he soon found it difficult to pay the interest upon a debt that had been incurred in England.

A significant development in Chilean politics was the appearance of a party that advocated the adoption of a federal system of government. Among its leaders were Camilo Henríquez and a publicist named José M. Infante. In a Congress which Freire had convoked the Federal party triumphed; on August 28, 1826, that Congress sanctioned a Constitution which introduced a federalistic régime. This fundamental law divided Chile

Federalism
Becomes
an Issue

into eight provinces. Each province should be administered by a governor and an assembly as provided by its respective constitution. Two years later, however, a Constituent Assembly decided that the government should be popular, representative, and republican. That Assembly promulgated the "Political Constitution of 1828." This Constitution stipulated that Roman Catholicism should be the religion of the State to the exclusion of every other faith. Executive authority was given to a President who should be selected by electors chosen by popular vote. Legislative authority was granted to a Congress composed of a Senate and a House of Representatives. Provincial assemblies, which were to be composed of members chosen by direct popular vote, were not only given the power to elect Senators but also the right to nominate intendants for the provinces.

The lack of success of the Constitution of 1826 had checked the growth of the Federal party, while discussions about constitutional changes had encouraged the formation of new political organizations. Young Chileans of the lower classes, who were styled *Pipiolos* (novices) in derision, had supported the liberal movement for a new constitution. Opponents of the Liberals were generally the aristocrats of Chile, namely the clergy and men of property. Members of other parties called those conservatives *Pelucones,* because of the large wigs which colonial aristocrats had customarily worn. The Pelucones were opposed to extreme measures or radical changes. To an extent they became a clerical party that stood for the Catholic Church and its influence. After the liberal leader Francisco Pinto became president under the Constitution of 1828, the Conservatives criticized his policies severely, and he soon relinquished his office. President succeeded president in rapid succession until 1830, when the Conservatives came into office. A civil war which broke out between them and the Liberals culminated in the battle of Lircai on April 17, 1830, where the Conservatives were victorious. Prominent among those Conservatives who were convinced that a new constitution was necessary was Diego Portales who had long felt that Chile's institutions were not adapted to her condition.

A born agitator and a merchant, he believed that Chile needed peace and a stable administration. As secretary of important departments for Vice-President Ovalle, after the battle of Lircai, Portales promoted alterations in the political order. At **Diego Portales** his instance, on October 1, 1831, Congress passed a law convoking a convention to revise the Constitution of 1828. As early as 1822, this reformer had expressed the opinion that a democratic form of government was an absurdity in "countries like the Spanish-American that are full of vices and where the citizens lack all the virtues that are necessary for the establishment of a true republic." His conception of the proper political organization for the Chileans was "a strong, centralistic government, whose leaders are true models of virtue and patriotism, and who can thus direct their fellow-citizens into the path of order and virtue."

To the Constitutional Convention, which assembled on October 20, 1831, a committee of its members headed by Mariano Egaña, a conservative lawyer, submitted the project of a constitution. After much debate, on May 25, 1833, a new Constitution was promulgated. It was based largely upon the project of the committee, which had been modified at some points as a result of the suggestions of Egaña; at other points it had apparently been molded in accordance with the advice of Portales.

The Constitution of 1833 declared that Chile embraced the territory stretching from the desert of Atacama to Cape Horn and from the cordillera of the Andes to the Pacific Ocean, as well as the Chiloé Archipelago, other adjacent islands, and the Juan Fernández Islands. Executive authority was vested in a President chosen by indirect election who was to serve for five years. In case of disability he was to be replaced by one of his secretaries. He was to be commander in chief of the army and navy and the chief administrator of the state. He could make important appointments; and he could veto laws of Congress. He was to be advised by a Council of State. A distinctive feature of this Constitution was the provision that members of the President's cabinet might at the same time hold seats in Congress.

Congress was to be composed of a Senate and a Chamber of Deputies. Senators, who must have an income, were to be chosen by indirect election from districts in the provinces for six years. Deputies should be elected for three years by direct vote from smaller districts. A permanent committee, which was to be composed of seven members of Congress chosen by that body, was to act as its representative while it was not in session. An unusual power granted to Congress was the authority to pass upon the inability of the President to perform his functions. Other clauses of the Constitution made provisions respecting a hierarchy of local officials. The republic was divided into provinces which were to be governed by intendants appointed by the President.

This Constitution contained provisions concerning the relations between Church and State that were in harmony with the precedents which had developed during the revolutionary era. It declared that the religion of Chile should be Roman Catholicism, and that no other faith should be publicly worshiped. With the advice of the Council of State, or whenever authorized by law, the President could exclude from the republic papal bulls, briefs, and rescripts. He was given power, with the consent of the Senate, to make appointments to bishoprics and archbishoprics from a list of names prepared by the Council of State. This article formulated the constitutional principle that the right of patronage was vested in the national government.

The adoption of this Constitution was a significant step in national progress. Chilean leaders had framed a Constitution that was suited to the particular stage of political development which they had reached. It preserved the system of landed estates that had descended from colonial days. It granted the President such a large measure of authority that he dominated both the executive and the legislative departments. The Chilean fathers probably did not realize that the Constitution of 1833 made possible the growth of a species of parliamentary government.

A temporary clause of the Constitution stipulated that the existing Congress should remain in session until 1834. In that year the first elections under the new Constitution took place. General Joaquín Prieto, who had become the chief magistrate in September, 1831, was elected president; he opened the sessions of the first Congress under the new régime in June, 1834. At once he was confronted with fiscal difficulties because of the embarrassed condition of the finances. In a short time he had to contend with a serious insurrection. The Liberal leader, ex-President Freire, secured two warships in Peru, and in July, 1836, sailed to the Chiloé Islands where he planned to organize a revolution that would overthrow the government. But he was captured, tried by court martial, and condemned to exile. Not only did this incident injure the prestige of the Liberal party, but it created a strong prejudice against Peru. In 1841 General Búlnes became president.

Though Búlnes was a Conservative, he attempted to govern by a cabinet composed of members of different parties. During his administration marked advances were made in various lines. A normal school was founded at Santiago. A law of November 19, 1842, provided for the founding of the University of Chile. It was opened on September 17, 1843, in the same structure as that which had been occupied by the University of San Felipe. A scholar named Andrés Bello, who was a native of Venezuela, was made rector of the new university.

Varied Progress

The military academy, which had been created by O'Higgins, was reëstablished. A debt that Chile had incurred in England, upon which considerable interest had been unpaid, was consolidated. The secretary of finance formulated regulations for the administration of customhouses. In 1843 the schooner "Ancud" sailed from the Chiloé Islands on a voyage to the Strait of Magellan, where upon the peninsula of Brunswick its company planted a settlement. Some years later Chile's claim to that strait was strengthened by the founding of a town at Punta Arenas. Meantime immigrants from Germany began to settle in the province of Valdivia where they long retained many of their customs. During the second administration of Búlnes, who was reëlected in 1846, reform tendencies alarmed the Conservatives, who selected

Manuel Montt, secretary of justice and public instruction, as their candidate for the presidency.

Manuel Montt, who served as President from 1851 to 1861, in many respects continued the policies of Búlnes. Opposition to Montt's rule resulted in an insurrection in which the Liberals were defeated on December 8, 1851, at the battle of Loncomilla. Yet the tithe was replaced by a tax. Treaties of commerce were negotiated with various nations of Europe. To promote public improvements a new loan was negotiated in England. *Mayorazgos* were abolished. The Chilean civil code, which had been framed by Andrés Bello after a careful study of Roman law, Spanish law, and the Code Napoleon, went into force on January 1, 1857. In this code Bello gave unity and cohesion to the mass of Spanish legislation which was still in force in his country and incorporated many provisions from foreign law, especially from French legislation. The civil code of Chile was composed of more than twenty-five hundred articles that were arranged in four books: Book I was concerned with persons; Book II with property; Book III with succession; and Book IV with obligations. An original feature was the clause providing that foreigners should be on a plane of civil equality with Chileans. This code had much influence upon the framers of other Spanish-American civil codes.

After Manuel Montt was reëlected, a fresh alignment of parties took place. The Montt-Varista party, so designated because its leader was Antonio Varas, one of Montt's secretaries, had strong aristocratic leanings. While the Liberal-Conservative party composed of former Liberals and Conservatives opposed the aristocratic régime which had been fostered by Montt. In 1859 the bitter strife between the contending parties culminated in civil war. A law was consequently enacted to the effect that citizens who took part in riots and revolts should be responsible with their persons and property for the resulting damage.

The Montt-Varista party nominated for the presidency José J. Pérez, a publicist of wide experience, who triumphed in 1861 by a large majority of electoral votes. During his adminis-

Foreign and Domestic Issues

tration a war broke out between Spain and Peru which ultimately involved Chile. For her the most significant event of the war was the ruthless bombardment of Valparaiso by a Spanish fleet on March 31, 1866—an event which incited the Chileans to fortify their ports and to build a navy. At the instigation of a troublesome Frenchman who assumed the trappings of royalty, the Araucanian Indians arose against the Chilean pioneers who were gradually encroaching upon their territory. But the pseudo-king, Aurelie Antonine I, was captured by Chileans and deported.

In 1865 an animated discussion about the religious provisions of the Constitution resulted in a law which provided that Protestants might practice their faith inside their own buildings. This law further provided that dissidents might establish private schools where the doctrines of their religion could be taught. Under Federico Errázuriz, a Conservative who became president in 1871, religious reform was carried farther by a decree which provided that Protestants might be buried in unconsecrated portions of Catholic cemeteries, and that cemeteries provided by the government should in the future be exempt from ecclesiastical control. Largely because of those reforms, the Catholic clergy assumed an attitude of protest toward the President. In 1873 Errázuriz decreed that the children of dissidents need not study the Catholic religion in the public schools, if their parents wished them to be exempt. Two years later benefit of clergy was greatly curtailed by a law which provided that ordinarily civil courts should have jurisdiction over all temporal matters, whatever might be the condition of the parties involved. As the result of a dispute over the choice of an archbishop of Santiago, the government secured complete control of ecclesiastical appointments. On January 16, 1884, under President Santa María, a law of civil marriage was promulgated which made possible the celebration in Chile of a legal marriage without the participation of Catholic priests. Other laws of the same year provided for the legal recognition of non-Catholic cemeteries which might be used for the interment of members of any religious sect.

Meantime, the so-called "War of the Pacific" had occurred between Chile, on the one side, and Bolivia and Peru, on the other side. The causes and significance of that war will be considered in detail in following chapters. Let it suffice to note here that, as a result of Chile's triumph in that conflict, she was permitted to retain possession of the Bolivian department of Atacama, she was conceded the province of Tarapacá by Peru, and was allowed to retain control of the provinces of Tacna and Arica, pending a referendum of their inhabitants that should decide whether those provinces should belong to her or to Peru.

A significant development took place in internal politics during the age of José Manuel Balmaceda, who had served as secretary of the interior under Santa María. A facile speaker, a journalist and a politician of no small ability, he had be- **Presidential Government** come a leader of the anti-clericals and Liberals who were sometimes styled the Reformers. His presidency, which began in 1886, was marked by progress in education and in public improvements. In politics Balmaceda attempted to unite the discordant groups of Liberals into one strong party. His cabinets, which contained politicians from different cliques, were unstable. On August 9, 1888, he sanctioned a law regarding suffrage which provided that all male citizens twenty-one years of age who could read and write and were listed in departmental registers should have the right to vote. He was accused, however, of manipulating congressional elections. Suspicions that he was preparing the way for a successor, who was not favored by the congressional majority, precipitated a conflict between him and Congress before the new electoral law was put into operation. So strong did congressional opposition to Balmaceda's administration become, that eventually only a faction of the Liberals supported him.

A crisis was precipitated when Balmaceda insisted that he was not bound to select a cabinet which was in harmony with the majority in Congress. In January, 1890, he formed a new cabinet, composed of his own adherents who belonged to a faction that was in a minority in Congress. This step not only ran counter to the fundamental principle of the parliamentary system which had been slowly developing, but was also an attempt to reassert the primacy of the executive over the legislative department. As a result of congressional opposition, the President yielded and replaced that cabinet by one satisfactory to Congress. In August, 1890, it therefore passed a law making appropriations for the expenses of government. After a crisis in the responsible cabinet, its members resigned, and Balmaceda again selected advisers composed of his own followers. At a meeting in Santiago on October 15, the day upon which Balmaceda dissolved Congress, members of the opposition adopted a resolution stating that the President had shown bad faith by the selection of a cabinet which was not supported by the congressional majority. The permanent committee protested against various acts of Balmaceda and notified him that after December 31 of the ensuing year he would have no authority to maintain the army or the navy unless Congress made appropriations.

On January 1, 1891, President Balmaceda issued a proclamation declaring that the parliamentary régime which the congressional coalition advocated was "incompatible with republican government." A few days later he issued an extraordinary decree announcing that, until Congress passed an appropiration for 1891, the budget which it had approved for 1889 should be in force. This act was not only contrary to precedent but it was extralegal—not to say dictatorial. An issue was thus clearly raised, namely, that between presidential government and congressional government. Early on the morning of January 7 vessels of the Chilean navy at Valparaiso sailed out of the harbor bearing prominent members of the Anti-Balmacedist party. The navy was in open revolt. Upon the same day a pronunciamiento, signed by a majority

The Congressional Revolt

of the congressmen, was published which declared that Balmaceda had been deposed because he had violated the Constitution.

In the civil war which ensued the congressional party controlled the navy, while the Balmacedistas dominated the army. As the struggle progressed, the fortune of arms inclined to the side of the Congressionalists who established a junta at Iquique. After some bloody conflicts by land and sea, on August 28, 1894, the soldiers of Balmaceda were badly routed near Valparaiso. On the following day the President abdicated and appointed General Baquedano, who had been neutral in the struggle, as the head of a provisional government. Balmaceda now sought a refuge in the Argentine legation, while confusion and anarchy reigned in Santiago. A little later the revolutionary junta reached Valparaiso, and it was soon installed in the capital. To avert the shame of being prosecuted by his political enemies, on the morning of September 19 Balmaceda committed suicide. Among his last letters was one known as his political testament that deserves notice:

As long as there exists in Chile a system of parliamentary government in the form in which it has been operated and that which is supported by the triumphant revolution, there will be neither electoral liberty nor a serious and constant organization of parties. Neither will there **Balmaceda's** be peace among the cliques of Congress. The triumph of the **Political Testament** revolution and the submission of the defeated party will produce a momentary calm but before long the old divisions, the bitterness, and the moral transgressions toward the head of the state will reappear.

The revolution of 1891 was sustained by public opinion which was tired of the system of governmental interference in elections. It was stimulated by the opposition of politicians to presidential omnipotence. This internecine conflict had a demoraliz- **of the Anti-** ing effect upon the finances of Chile. Her currency was **Balmaceda** swollen and her debt was greatly increased. The political **Revolution** result was the triumph of the principle that no President should govern without a cabinet supported by a congressional majority. This did not mean that presidential authority should be subjected to the public will through Congress; for the practice of dissolving the legislature after a vote of lack of confidence had not prevailed in Chile. Balmaceda had failed in his attempt to make the government of Chile "presidential" instead of "parliamentary." No amendment was made to the Constitution to register this alteration in the balance of power. Nevertheless, it is scarcely an exaggeration to say that presidential domination was replaced by congressional dictatorship. In some respects the Chilean political régime came to resemble the French system of parliamentary government.

As incidents connected with the anti-Balmaceda revolution had evidently convinced some Chileans that the United States was opposed to this movement, a dispute with that government took on a serious aspect. On October 16, 1891, a brawl occurred between Chileans and sailors of the United States vessel "Baltimore" who were on shore at Valparaiso. One United States officer was killed and several sailors were wounded. President Harrison in a message to Congress took a jingoistic attitude. As a retort, the secretary of foreign relations of Chile sent a discourteous cablegram to her minister at Washington which was communicated to the United States government and also published in Santiago. In January, 1892, the United States therefore delivered an ultimatum to Chile demanding an indemnity. That policy exasperated many Chileans, but rather than precipitate a war with the United States their government agreed to pay an indemnity of seventy-five thousand dollars for the families of the injured sailors.

Even before the suicide of Balmaceda, the victors in the civil strife had made Jorge Montt, who had become vice-admiral, the head of a junta of government. In November, 1891, a new Congress selected Montt to be president. Toward the vanquished party his policy was generous. He immediately granted an amnesty to officials of the Balmaceda régime, with certain exceptions. In fiscal and political affairs he adopted a policy of reform. On December 22, 1891, he sanctioned a law which provided for the establishment of municipalities administered by elective officers. Another reform measure was concerned with inconvertible paper currency. Despite violent opposition by the debtor classes, on February 11, 1895, he signed a bill which provided for the redemption of paper money in gold and which established the gold standard. The gold peso was made the monetary unit.

In 1896 Federico Errázuriz, a son of the former president, was elected chief magistrate by the support of the Conservatives and members of other party groups. During his administration various problems of foreign relations pressed for **Domestic and International Issues** solution: the controversy with Peru about the referendum in Tacna and Arica; the policy to be adopted in regard to Bolivia's demand for a seaport upon the Pacific; and the boundary dispute with Argentina. This dispute was an inheritance from other days. It had arisen in a serious form in 1881 when, by the mediation of the United States, a treaty had been signed by the contending parties which drew a boundary line in Tierra del Fuego and provided that the bounds in the cordillera should be a line drawn between the highest peaks that were supposed to indicate the continental watershed. As an investigation showed that the line sketched by the treaty of 1881 and this watershed did not everywhere coincide, a renewal of the old controversy took place. It seemed that Peru and Bolivia hoped to profit by Chile's foreign difficulties. Eventually, however, Chile and Argentina agreed to submit the dispute about their limits in the cordillera to the arbitration of the English King.

The passing of Balmaceda did not end his influence in Chilean political life. A tendency was indeed displayed among the lower classes to view him as the martyred champion of the cause of the people against the aristocratic classes who were entrenched in Congress. In time his disciples formed a party group that was designated the Balmacedistas. They founded their principles upon the political testament of their leader: their political program was to vindicate the President, and to protect that magistrate against alleged encroachments by Congress. Though the Liberal party had been greatly injured by Balmaceda's failure, it recovered strength in the election of 1901 when its candidate, Germán Riesco, was elected by a large majority over the coalition candidate, Pedro Montt. The Conservative party declined in influence; it became a clerical party whose chief political ambition was to establish the dominance of the Church. President Riesco's administration was notorious for political instability. There were frequent changes in his cabinet: ministerial crises caused him frequently to seek support in groupings and regroupings of cliques or parties. Perhaps that is one reason why he was unable to resist the clamor for the emission of inconvertible paper money.

Still, during his administration significant moves were made in international relations. The long-standing dispute beween Chile and Argentina about their limits was adjusted by the decision of the English King who made his definitive award in November, 1902. About the same juncture those two nations signed significant treaties stipulating that in the future their disputes should be settled by arbitration, that their military armaments should be limited, and that for five years neither party should, without previous notification, make an increase in her navy.

In 1906—the year in which a terrible earthquake visited Valparaiso —the National party sprang from the personal following of Manuel Montt. With the aid of the Radical party, which championed the application of democratic principles to politics, and of some Liberals and Conservatives, it elected to the presidency Pedro Montt, a son of the former President. In that campaign the Radical party adopted a platform advocating the election of the president by popular vote, the payment of salaries to congressmen, the modification of the Senate so as to make it a different body from the lower house, the complete separation of Church and State, and a decrease in the number of feast days. The Democratic party, which was organized to represent the interests of the laboring classes, did not frame a precise statement of political principles.

President Pedro Montt was troubled by an opposition which desired to issue more inconvertible paper currency. Still, he promoted important public works and the construction of railroads. During his administration the Chilean people celebrated the completion of the tunnel through the frozen ridge of the Andes. This formed the last link of the railroad between Santiago and Mendoza, thus affording quick communication with Argentina. Under Ramón Barros Luco, an octogenarian who served as President from 1911 to 1916 material progress continued. The railroad which Chile had agreed to construct from Arica to La Paz was completed. Along the seacoast a longitudinal railroad was extended from Iquique to Puerto Montt. The government also promoted the construction of quays, reservoirs, dams, and aqueducts. United States corporations acquired valuable mines of copper and tin where they constructed huge mining plants.

A stream of Germans that emigrated to southern Chile settled in a region that became known as "Little Germany." In 1907 some eight thousand immigrants landed in Chile. The influx was checked by regulations providing that only immigrants under contract with private individuals would be admitted. Of one thousand foreigners who arrived in Chile in 1913 about eight hundred were Spaniards; over one hundred came from Italy, and about the same number from France. In truth an important element in Chilean immigration has been the Spanish. A distinct national type consequently developed: the typical Chilean is a descendant of a Spaniard with an occasional dash of Araucanian blood.

Conditions about 1914

According to Chile's Constitution, all citizens who could bear arms were liable for military service. The organizer of the Chilean army was a German officer named Körner. On September 5, 1900, a law was enacted which provided that all citizens between eighteen and forty-five years of age were to inscribe their names in military registers. Citizens of twenty or twenty-one years of age should belong to the active contingent for at least nine months. About 1914 the Chilean army numbered some seventeen thousand men; it was almost equally divided between conscripts and soldiers of the regular army. The navy of Chile was composed of one battleship, six cruisers, four torpedo gunboats, seven destroyers, and five torpedo boats. In her naval service there were about seven thousand men.

The chief occupations were farming, mining, and manufacturing. In the southern part of the country large estates held by descendants of colonial aristocrats were tilled by laborers who were sometimes in a condition of economic serfdom. The main crops were wheat, corn, barley, and beans. Grapes were raised in various sections. Large numbers of cattle and sheep grazed upon the plains. Some bituminous coal was mined in southern Chile. In 1914 about a million tons of copper were extracted from her enormous ore deposits.

The greatest mineral wealth was saltpeter, which was found in enormous quantities mixed with other salts in the northern desert between the Andes and the ocean from latitude 19° 13′ almost to 27°. The two chief nitrate-producing regions were the provinces of Antofagasta and Tarapacá. As Chile was the only country where nitrate of soda was found in workable quantities, the deposits of *caliche*—as it is called in the crude form—constituted her most valuable asset; for nitrate was widely used as plant food and in the manufacture of explosives. This extractive industry was controlled by the national government, which from time to time sold strips of desert land to companies for exploitation. After the caliche had been mined, the saltpeter was separated from other materials in refining plants scattered throughout the desert. Unique industrial communities were thus created in two northern provinces. A heavy tax was levied on the exportation of nitrate. The income from the nitrate industry ordinarily furnished about one-third of the revenue required for the support of the national government.

Social and Economic Conditions

An important by-product of the nitrate industry was iodine. The manufactures of Chile were mainly various foodstuffs, alcoholic beverages, clothing, leather, woodwork, and pottery. Statistics of the exports in 1914, besides miscellaneous items, were as follows: beverages and liquors, 175,245 pesos of gold; agricultural products, 16,665,222; pastoral products, 21,824,705; and mineral products, 253,365,503 gold pesos.

In transportation Chile was both aided and hindered by her physiography. Along the narrow strip of land bordering the ocean there were many ports visited by vessels engaged in the coastwise trade. The South American Steamship Company, which was backed by Chilean capital, was one of the best companies that furnished service between important Chilean ports and those of Peru and Panama. Small ports were served by sailing vessels. In part railways were owned by private companies and in part by the government. By the construction of various short railways which had been linked together, a longitudinal railway had been constructed that stretched south from Pisagra in the province of Tarapacá to Puerto Montt in the province of Llanquihue. Branch railroads or transverse lines extended from the seaboard toward the foothills of the Andes. Three railroads crossed the Andes from Chile: a railroad from Lai-Lai (near Santiago) to Mendoza; a railroad from Arica to La Paz, Bolivia; and another from Antofagasta to Oruro, La Paz, and other Bolivian cities.

Upon the eve of the first World War, the general direction of education in Chile was in charge of the secretary of public instruction. Elementary education was mainly supported by the local districts. Free, and entrusted to laymen, it was not, however, compulsory. Secondary education was chiefly carried on in lyceums where courses lasting from three to six years prepared students for a university career or for technical schools.

Education

At the capital city there was a school of pedagogy affiliated with the national university. The University of Chile, which was reorganized by a law of 1879, was managed by a board of public instruction. It was composed of the following colleges: theology; law and social sciences; medicine and pharmacy; physical science and mathematics; philosophy, letters, and fine arts. Besides furnishing instruction in the social sciences, the college of law and social sciences supervised legal education throughout the republic. At the capital, besides the national university, a Catholic University had been established.

Andrés Bello is the first distinctive name in Chilean literature. Editor of a government journal called the *Araucano*, a poet of no small merit, author of a Castilian grammar, and of a standard work on international law, Bello stimulated intellectual life in Chile in various ways. His pupil Salvador Sanfuentes composed poems that dealt with dramatic incidents in the relations between Spaniards and Araucanians. Guillermo Blest Gana wrote verses about Chilean home life. Upon the occasion of the war with Spain in inspired verses Guillermo Matta summoned Spanish-Americans to rise against her attack. A poem of Eusebio Lillo was adopted as the national hymn of Chile. While upon diplomatic service for his country in Bogotá, José Antonio Soffia wrote a notable poem about Bolívar and San Martín. Among prize poems of Eduardo de la Barro was one entitled *A la independencia de América*. Alberto Blest Gana, who had resided in Paris, produced among other novels, *Martín Rivas*, a tale of Chilean society. A stimulating prose writer was José V. Lastarria, whose stories were collected and published in a volume entitled *Antaño y Hogaño*. His *Recuerdos Literarios* described the dispute in Chilean literary circles about romanticism; among his historical studies was a treatise about the Chilean Constitution.

Literature and Art

A group of great historical writers made the University of Chile famous. Miguel L. Amunátegui wrote learned monographs about the revolution against Spanish rule. Besides numerous studies and special volumes, Diego Barros Arana composed a monumental *General History of Chile*. Benjamin Vicuña Mackenna was a voluminous historical writer. The dean of American bibliographers, José T. Medina, composed or edited some two hundred brochures or volumes.

Considerable attention has been paid in Chile to the fine arts. Aspiring painters and sculptors have been much influenced by the artists of France and Spain. About the middle of the nineteenth century a French painter named Monvoisin established a school of fine arts in Santiago, and subsequently his pupils founded an academy of painting there. Among prominent painters may be mentioned Antonio Smith, the pioneer in Chilean landscape painting. The great painter of historical scenes was Pedro Subercaseaux, who depicted the embrace of O'Higgins and San Martín after the victory at Maipú. Another well-known painter was Pedro Lira, who founded the annual Beaux Arts contest.

In sculpture the Chileans won distinction. A school of sculpture was founded in Santiago in 1854 under the direction of a French artist, Auguste François. His most gifted disciple was Nicanor Plaza, who became the director of this school in 1873. Plaza was widely known as the designer of the statue that immortalized Caupolicán on the historic hill of Santa Lucia. A pupil of Plaza named Virginio Arias early displayed signs of wonderful talent. In 1882 he exhibited in Paris a bronze statue known as "El Roto Chileno," or, as the French named it, "The Defender of the Nation." This statue portrays a sturdy Chilean farmhand, who, at the summons of his country, drops a sheaf of wheat and grasps a rifle. Five years later Arias achieved a great triumph, for his sculptured representation of "The Descent from the Cross" was awarded the Grand Prize at the Paris Salon—the first laurels in art won in Europe by a South American.

On August 3, 1914, the Chilean secretary of foreign relations informed the German minister at Santiago that his government would maintain "the strictest neutrality" in the war which had begun in Europe. Chile soon began to feel the economic effects of that struggle: she lost Teutonic markets for guano and nitrate. In 1915 the attack of an English squadron upon the German warship "Dresden," which was supposed to be interned, provoked Chile to demand an apology, the acceptance of which angered Germany. Though exposed to commerce raiders, yet, because of her position upon the Pacific, she was not so menaced by Germany's submarine campaign as Argentina and Brazil. In response to the announcement of a new ruthless submarine campaign, on February 8, 1917, the Chilean secretary of foreign affairs under President Sanfuentes, who took office in December, 1916, sent a note to the German envoy at Santiago to state that Germany's blockade involved a restriction of the rights of neutrals which Chile would not endure

Attitude toward the First World War

because it was contrary to principles that had long been observed. Further, the Chilean secretary stated that his government could not approve the policy announced by the German imperial government because that would be a departure from strict neutrality.

The directive force in the recent politics of Chile has often been in the hands of a coalition. Occasionally a President has actually attempted to govern by a cabinet composed of a member **New Party Groupings** from each important political party. After the age of Balmaceda the political pendulum in Chile swung toward congressional, which ordinarily meant aristocratic, control of the administration. Parliamentary government became a régime distinguished by instability. It has been estimated that at the opening of the present century the average life of a Chilean cabinet was about three months. At that time two influential party groups were the National Union and the Liberal Alliance. The Union was mainly composed of Conservatives and Liberals of former days, while the Alliance was made up of Democrats, Socialists, and other persons with radical views. In the main the Union was representative of the landed aristocracy which has exercised a profound influence in Chilean politics, while the Alliance may not inappropriately be designated the progressive and popular element that derived its strength from the growing middle class.

In the campaign of 1920 the candidate of the National Union was Barros Borgoño, a member of an aristocratic family who had served as secretary of foreign relations. The candidate of the Liberal Alliance was an eloquent lawyer of Italian descent named Arturo Alessandri. So close was the presidential election which took place on June 25 that both parties ultimately agreed that instead of allowing Congress to scrutinize the election returns—as provided by the Constitution—they would form a special tribunal of seven members designated the Court of Honor to serve as an electoral board. By a vote of five to two that board decided that Barros Borgoño had received one hundred and seventy-six votes, while Alessandri had received one hundred and seventy-seven. Alessandri, who was inaugurated in December, 1920, selected the members of his cabinet from the different political groups that composed his party coalition.

In a message to Congress on June 1, 1921, President Alessandri outlined his program. Among social and economic reforms **President Alessandri's Program** he advocated an improvement in the legal status of women, the adoption of laws that would promote the welfare of laborers, and the stabilization of the monetary system. Pending the formulation of specific amendments to the Constitution, he suggested that the fundamental law should be modified so as to separate Church and State completely. He proposed that the administrative régime should be decentralized by transferring to provincial officials a large measure of authority which the national government had exercised in local affairs. The existing parliamentary system, said Alessandri, should be altered so as to prevent destructive collisions between the executive and the legislative departments. He asked that the permanent committee and the Council of State should be abolished. The President should be elected by direct popular vote. In place of the existing system of presidential succession, Alessandri proposed that a Vice-President should be substituted who was also to be chosen by popular vote.

With respect to foreign policy Alessandri stood forth as a vigorous advocate of disarmament in South America. Courageously did he maintain that even the crucial controversy with Peru concerning Tacna and Arica should be submitted to arbitration. In the realm of internal politics a propaganda for the concession of political rights to women assumed significant proportions; in 1923 the Progressive Feminist party framed a platform advocating political and social reforms. The presence of a hostile majority in the Senate hindered the adoption of Alessandri's constitutional reforms; his administration was checkered by some of the most acute crises known to Chilean parliamentary history. Bitter political controversies between the President and Congress apparently ended early in 1924 by a series of compromises. Congress yielded to his demand that the parliamentary system should be modified so that he should be freed from certain legislative trammels. Votes of confidence in the cabinet were henceforth to be confined to the lower house, while the President was prohibited from dissolving that house more than once during his term of office. The existing cabinet resigned and a new cabinet was chosen which gave certain electoral guarantees.

In September, 1924, a series of advanced social laws were enacted which had been vigorously opposed by the Conservatives. These laws were concerned with such matters as labor contracts, accidents to workmen, and the judicial rights of coöperative societies. The most important of these laws created an insurance institute to direct a system of compulsory insurance for laborers. But these politico-constitutional changes did not quiet Chilean politics. In September, 1925, Alessandri resigned and went into exile. Military and naval officials joined hands against a system of government that was dominated by an irresponsible Congress. Their object was to end the régime of congressional government which had been given full sway by the revolution of 1891.

On January 23, 1925, a junta was brought into existence which invited the exiled leader to return. Alessandri accepted the presidency anew, but upon the express condition that a Constituent Assembly should be convoked to make essential alterations in the fundamental law. Upon his return from Italy, however, he found that this program was opposed by the Liberal Alliance and the National Union, both of which wished that Congress should again exercise its usual functions. Hence, the President convoked an extralegal assembly composed of representative politicians and enlightened citizens to whom he entrusted the task of altering the Constitution of 1833. This assembly designated a committee headed by Alessandri, which framed a new constitution. With some modifications, the assembly approved the draft, which was completed on August 3, 1925. Instead of presenting this project to a Constituent Assembly, Alessandri decided to submit it to the voters. On August 30, 1925, by a large majority they approved the new Constitution without any changes.

The Constitution of 1925 retained many provisions of the Constitution of 1833. Some articles of the earlier organic law were omitted and other articles were modified. According to the new Con-

The Constitution of 1925

stitution, local assemblies were to meet regularly at the capitals of the provinces. A stipulation was made that proportional representation should be used in the election of deputies and senators. An electoral tribunal was established to pass upon the elections of deputies, senators, and presidents.

The provisions in the Constitution of 1833 that set up a Council of State were omitted. Clauses which provided for a permanent committee were swept away. Article LXXXI, which allowed members of the cabinet to hold seats in Congress, was stricken out. The President of the republic was to be elected by direct vote. He was no longer required to take an oath to profess and protect the Roman Catholic religion. Among his new attributes was the authority to confer judicial personality upon corporations. His authority to suspend constitutional guarantees was enlarged. Presidential authority was thus restored, increased, and fortified.

Among the constitutional guarantees was an assurance of "liberty of conscience, and the free exercise of all religions that may not be contrary to morality, good usage, and public order." Article IV of the Constitution of 1933, which declared Roman Catholicism to be the religion of the State, was omitted. The clauses which vested the appointment of archbishops, bishops, and other ecclesiastical dignitaries in the government, were also suppressed,—thus the President was no longer to exercise the right of patronage. By means of a friendly agreement between the parties, provision was made that a subsidy of 2,500,-000 pesos per annum was to be paid by the government to the Catholic

Church of Chile for five years. This aid was to promote the transformation of that church into an independent entity.

The new Constitution accordingly marked a significant change in Chilean politics. It embodied most of the reforms demanded by those persons who were dissatisfied with the excesses of congressional government: the legislative department of government was again subordinated to the executive. The fundamental law also contained provisions that aimed to encourage a democratic régime. By virtue of the reforms of 1925, Church and State were completely separated.

At the time when these constitutional reforms were being elaborated, a commission of experts from the United States, headed by Professor Kemmerer of Princeton University, was studying the financial condition of the country. It submitted a series of projects for the reform of the banking system and also the system of taxation. On August 23, 1925, the President issued a decree providing for the founding of a national bank of redemption which was to have the exclusive right to issue paper money. Other fiscal reforms recommended by the Kemmerer Commission were subsequently carried out. The levy of an income tax partly relieved Chile of undue dependence upon export taxes. The government took steps to promote irrigation and to conserve natural resources.

A new leader had meanwhile emerged. Colonel Ibañez, a masterful descendant of a Briton who settled in central Chile, had opposed congressional domination in 1924 and had served as a member of the cabinet as well as Vice-President. In May, 1927, he was elected president by an overwhelming majority. Just before his inauguration, a son of Balmaceda **The Rise and Fall of Ibañez** presented the president-elect with the presidential insignia that his father had worn and greeted Ibañez as a vindicator of Balmaceda's designs. In response Ibañez praised the President who had given his life rather than betray his political principles. Ibañez characterized the victim of the revolution of 1891 as a statesman who had foreseen his country's true political course and who had anticipated the painful results to Chilean democracy of the excesses of congressional government.

At the instance of the President, in February, 1931, Congress passed a law that granted him dictatorial powers in certain matters when it was not in session. Leading opponents of the dictator were expelled, the press was suborned, and a hateful system of espionage was introduced. In 1928 an extensive system of public improvements was begun which added enormously to the public debt. Ibañez aimed to save the day by forming a consolidated organization called the *Cosach* which was to control the production and sale of nitrate. But he could not long withstand the economic crisis which was affecting the entire world. Discontent with a military dictatorship came to a head on July 22, 1931, when students seized a university building. Though the revolutionists were ultimately ejected by the dictator's soldiers, they were given so much support by anti-administration factions, that on July 26 Ibañez transferred his authority to the president of the Senate. When that official relinquished this onerous post, the chief minister, Juan E. Montero, became acting president. He soon appointed a commission to investigate the administration of Ibañez who had meanwhile gone into exile. In the election that took place early in October the Acting President and former President Alessandri were the candidates for the chief magistracy. Montero won the election by a large majority.

His administration was a period of turmoil and after a revolution started on June 4, 1932, Montero quietly gave up his office. A junta was formed which apparently aimed to establish a social-istic republic. Constitutional guarantees were suspended.

Later Tendencies At the polls on October 30, 1932, Alessandri was again elected president. He invited both Conservatives and Radicals to join his cabinet. He was supported by Congress in his determination to suppress revolutionary agitation. Prominent opponents of the administration were driven into exile or thrust into prison. Alessandri's first official act was to dissolve the *Cosach*. This organization was replaced by the Chilean Nitrate and Iodine Corporation, which was given the exclusive right for thirty-five years to purchase those products from the factories and to sell them in the world's markets. The producers were to be relieved of certain taxes while the government was to receive one-fourth of the profits. An increase in the exportation of nitrate later enabled the government to resume payments on its foreign debt. Attempts to reform the old system of landholding known as *lati-fundismo* by distributing small strips of land among the peasants were only to a small degree successful. Alleging that the Chilean Electric Company, a foreign corporation which controlled the light and power in a large part of the country, had violated a law concerning international exchange, in March, 1936, the government expropriated it.

In 1938 two political groups solicited the votes of the electorate: the Right which was supported by the aristocratic oligarchy; and the Left or "Popular Front" which was composed mainly of Communists, Radicals, and Socialists. The Popular Front nominated a Radical named Pedro Aguirre Cerda for the presidency, while the Right nominated Gustavo Ross Santa María, who had served as minister of the treasury. In the presidential election the Popular Front was victorious; Aguirre Cerda was inaugurated on December 24, 1938. His administration was checkered by changes in the cabinet and in the alignment of political parties. He vetoed a bill that aimed to outlaw the so-called Communist party. A rupture of relations with Spain was not healed until that government had accorded safe conduct to Spanish nationalist refugees who had been given shelter in the Chilean legation in Madrid.

Because of ill health the President retired from active service on November 10, 1941. He was succeeded by Jeronimo Méndez, a leader of the Radicals. The death of Aguirre Cerda on November 25 made necessary a new election. On April 2, 1942, the victorious Radical, Juan Antonio Ríos, was inaugurated as president. As the unprecedented demand for nitrate due to the second World War could not be supplied by costly synthetic nitrate plants, and as there was also an enormous demand for copper, Chilean economy enjoyed a boom. President Ríos declared that his country would sever relations with the Axis only when such a policy was demanded by the national will. With a merchant marine immune from submarine attacks by the Nazis, the early attitude of Chile toward the war resembled that of Argentina, for her cabinet took the view that a policy of strict neutrality should be rigidly pursued. Some prominent leaders of the Popular Front, however, were in favor of a declaration that their nation was non-belligerent, while others wished to see her relations with the Axis powers severed. In August, 1942, the government protested to Germany against the sinking of Brazilian merchantmen by submarines.

As the head of a Popular Front government, President Ríos evidently considered as a hindrance to action against the Axis the opposition of conservative classes, the presence in southern Chile of thousands of persons of German lineage, and the vulnerability of the narrow Chilean terrain stretching from Peru to Cape Horn. The proud Chileans were stirred, however, by a speech in which the American Under-Secretary of State, Sumner Welles, publicly rebuked Argentina and Chile for harboring agents of the Axis who were secretly intriguing against the United Nations. On October 20 the entire cabinet resigned, which left the President a free hand. Although Chilean vessels had been immune from attacks by Axis submarines, early in December the new secretary of foreign relations, Joaquín Fernández, began to urge that the government should sever relations with Germany, Italy, and Japan. On January 19, 1943, shortly after the secretary of the interior returned from a visit to the United States, by a vote of 30 to 10 the Senate approved the decision of the President to rupture diplomatic relations with the Axis powers. In a broadcast from the Moneda

Palace on the next day Ríos declared that he was carrying out the mandate of Chilean public opinion, that Chile had "an essential interest in this fight," that the severance of relations with the Axis was for the good of his country, and that this action was an important step towards continental solidarity: "We are fighting so that all men and all nations may live in peace."

The history of Chile is a story of development. Since the establishment of independence, by war, by diplomacy, or by occupation, the boundaries of her territory have been delimited to the south and to the east, and pushed much farther to the north. Chile's industrial development has been vigorous. Though she possesses the physical basis for a diversified agriculture in the south, her economic prosperity became too largely dependent upon the sale of copper and nitrate. From a military and naval point of view, the position of Chile is much stronger than that of some other Latin-American states. Of those states Chile is the one in which for a time constitutional development most resembled that of England. Recent constitutional changes at Santiago not only contained the pledge of greater provincial autonomy but also of less friction between the executive and legislative departments. The Senate, which has been the citadel of the privileged classes, seems to be waning in power. Whatever the future may hold in store for the Chileans, of them it may more truthfully be said than of almost any other Latin-American people that they constitute a homogeneous nation. Chile is virile, progressive, and tenacious of her rights. In contrast with her neutral policy during the first World War, early in 1943 Chile severed diplomatic relations with Japan, Italy, and Germany.

SUGGESTIONS FOR FURTHER READING

BÚLNES, G., *Chile and Peru, the Causes of the War of 1879*, 1920.
DENNIS, W. J., *Documentary History of the Tacna-Arica Dispute*, 1927.
EDWARDS, A., *The Dawn*, 1931.
ELLIOTT, L. E., *Chile Today and Tomorrow*, 1922.
EVANS, H. C., *Chile and Its Relations with the United States*, 1927.
FETTER, F. W., *Monetary Inflation in Chile*, 1931.
Foreign Policy Association, *The Revolution in Chile*, 1934.
GALDAMES, L., *A History of Chile*, 1941.
HANCOCK, A. U., *History of Chile*, 1893.
HENDRICKS, F. K., "The First Apostolic Mission to Chile," *Hispanic American Historical Review*, Vol. XXII, pp. 644-669.
HERVEY, M. H., *Dark Days in Chile*, 1891-92.
JEFFERSON, M. S. W., *Recent Colonization in Chile*, 1921.
KOEBEL, W. H., *Modern Chile*, 1913.
McBRIDE, G. M., *Chile: Land and Society*, 1936.
PARKER, W. B. (ed.), *Chileans of Today*, 1920.

REINSCH, P. S., "Parliamentary Government in Chile," *American Political Science Review*, Vol. III, pp. 507-538.

ROBERTSON, W. S., "Chile and the World War," *The Nation*, Vol. CIV, pp. 305-307.

SHAW, P. V., *The Early Constitutions of Chile*, 1930.

"South America III: Chile," *Fortune*, Vol. XVII, No. 5, pp. 74 ff.

STEVENSON, J. R., *The Chilean Popular Front*, 1942.

SUBERCASEAU, G., *Monetary and Banking Policy of Chile*, 1922.

WILGUS, A. C. (ed), *Argentina, Brazil, and Chile since Independence*, 1935.

CHAPTER XVII

BOLIVIA

Bolivia originally claimed the territory of Upper Peru which had been subject to the audiencia of Charcas. In August, 1825, the Congress at Sucre adopted a flag for the new state; it made
The Creation of Bolivia
provision for the national coinage, and declared that the nation should have a representative and republican government. Shortly afterward it asked that two thousand Colombian soldiers should be allowed to remain in the country. On October 3, 1825, it enacted a law which provided that General Sucre should be the supreme ruler whenever the Liberator was not in Bolivia.

On November 1 Bolívar reached the Bolivian capital. For a short period he acted as the chief executive of the state. After making certain administrative and political reforms, on December 29 he issued a decree which announced that a Constituent Congress would assemble at the capital on May 25, 1826. At the same time he transferred his authority to General Sucre. During the months which elapsed before the Constituent Congress met, Sucre initiated important policies. In January, 1826, he issued a decree providing that Bolivia's territory should be carved into five departments which were to be divided into provinces. He soon exercised authority over the desert of Atacama, which had been under the jurisdiction of the audiencia of Charcas. In vain he aimed to secure from the Peruvian government a strip of territory that would include the port of Arica and thus furnish Bolivia a convenient outlet to the sea. By a decree of May 18, 1826, Peru recognized Bolivian independence.

On May 25, 1826, Sucre resigned his authority to the Constituent Congress. It at once elected him provisional president. This position he accepted with reluctance. Meanwhile, at the request of the Bolivians, Bolívar had framed a project of a Constitution for the new republic. In June, 1826, Sucre presented this project to the Constituent Congress. It gave executive authority to a President who should serve for life. His powers resembled those granted to the United States President; his cabinet was to be composed of three secretaries. The legislature was to be made up of three houses: a House of Tribunes, a House of Senators, and a House of Censors. Tribunes were granted special power over fiscal, military, and foreign affairs. Senators were given control of judicial, ecclesiastical, and constitutional matters. Censors were charged to observe that the Constitution, laws, and treaties of the nation were obeyed.

Judicial power was vested in a supreme court, district courts, and justices of the peace. The supreme court was granted jurisdiction over cases concerning ambassadors, consuls, and the patronage; it was to scrutinize papal bulls and rescripts. Torture in judicial proceedings was prohibited. The Constitution provided that Bolivia should be composed of departments which were to be divided into provinces. At the head of each department there should be a prefect. Bolívar held that the Constitution should contain no stipulation concerning religious faith. Yet after several months of debate it was adopted with an amendment providing that Roman Catholicism should be the state religion.

Sucre was promptly elected president. On December 9, 1826, he made an address to Congress announcing his intention to retire from office on August 2, 1828. President Sucre laid the administrative foundations for the Bolivian state. In July, 1827, the judges whom he had appointed members of the supreme court were installed at the capital. He warned **The Presidency of Sucre** Brazil to evacuate Bolivian territory upon which she was encroaching. He negotiated a treaty of limits with Peru which stipulated that Bolivia should have possession of the Pacific coast from Cape Sama to the river Loa; but unfortunately for Bolivia the Peruvian executive, General Santa Cruz, declined to sanction the arrangement.

Hence, on the Pacific coast Bolivia merely held title to a narrow strip of territory between the Loa River and the river Paposo. Despite the politic measures of Sucre, the presence of Columbian soldiers in Bolivia created much dissatisfaction. There were suspicions that Peru viewed Bolivia as an outpost of Colombia. Conspiracies which were formed against the President have been ascribed to the nefarious influence of Peruvians.

On April 18, 1828, disaffected soldiers in the garrison of the capital city rebelled against Sucre, whom they wounded severely in the right arm. This mutiny was followed by an invasion by Peruvian soldiers under General Gamarra. So far did the invaders penetrate into Bolivia that on July 6, 1828, her invalid President was constrained to agree to a capitulation which provided that he should resign the presidency, that Colombian soldiers should soon depart from the soil of Bolivia, and that a Constituent Assembly should be convoked to revise the Constitution. On August 2, 1828, in his message to Congress resigning the presidency, Sucre deplored the policy of intervention which Peru had seen fit to adopt.

After his departure Congress proclaimed as president General Blanco, who was soon imprisoned by political enemies and assassinated.

Congress then invited General Santa Cruz to assume the presidency of the nation. Santa Cruz was a forceful native of Bolivia who had served in both the royalist and the patriot armies during the struggle for independence. While president of the Peruvian council of government, he had formed an ambitious project to unite Peru and Bolivia into a Confederation that would include the major portion of the former Empire of the Incas.

Rise of Santa Cruz

Early in 1829 Santa Cruz accepted the presidency. He soon replaced the Constitution by a provisional statute. At La Paz in August, 1831, a Constituent Assembly adopted a fundamental law which in some particulars was in sharp contrast with the previous Constitution. Bolivia's Constitution of 1831 provided that governmental authority should be exercised by executive, legislative, and judicial departments. The President's term of office was fixed at four years. He was to be aided by three secretaries, and advised by a Council of State selected by Congress. Legislative authority was vested in a Senate and a House of Representatives. In October, 1834, a Congress that had assembled at Sucre promulgated a "reformed Constitution" which in reality was the fundamental law of 1831 with slight modifications.

A chance to realize his cherished project came to Santa Cruz in 1835. He arranged with Provisional President Orbegosa of Peru to send an army into that distracted country to restore order. In June, 1835, the President deputed his executive authority to a council of ministers, and led his soldiers across the frontier. This intervention evoked protests from such Peruvian leaders as Gamarra and Salaverry: Santa Cruz defeated Gamarra, however, at Yanacocha and Salaverry at Socabaya. Meantime Orbegosa had convoked assemblies to meet at Sicuani and Huara to consider the formation of a confederation. The Assembly at Sicuani on March 17, 1836, made known the establishment of the free and independent state of South Peru, composed of the departments of Arequipa, Ayacucho, Cuzco, and Puno, with Santa Cruz as "Supreme Protector." In the following August the Assembly at Huara proclaimed the state of North Peru, with Santa Cruz as protector. A Congress at Tapacarí had already announced that Santa Cruz was the protector of Bolivia.

Confederation of Peru and Bolivia

In a circular letter addressed to the governments of America on August 20, 1836, Santa Cruz explained his motives in creating a Confederation. He declared that the South American states, instead of being disturbed because of "the creation of a body politic in whose structure were to be combined the social guaranties with stability of power and energy of action, should view this organization as a guaranty of order, as a dike erected against the torrent of anarchy, and as a suitable amalgam of interests that had been discordant up to the present time." "Inter-American politics," he continued, "will find only motives of security and fraternity in the policy that the existing government follows with respect to it and in the policy that the government of the Federation will adopt. My system, which, during seven years of a pacific administration, has been recognized by all the republics of the Continent, will furnish them sufficient security concerning the perfect neutrality and the respect with which they are viewed, and concerning the frank and friendly relations that I shall try to maintain with them."

On October 28, 1836, the Protector issued a proclamation which announced the establishment of a Confederation composed of Bolivia, North Peru, and South Peru. He also convoked a General Assembly composed of three deputies from each of the confederated states which was to meet at Tacna on January 24, 1837. Meanwhile he had announced that the civil code of Bolivia should be in force throughout the Confederation. He not only initiated some administrative reforms but also issued regulations which promoted commerce and mining.

But circumstances were against him. In the northern part of the Confederation many Peruvians felt keenly aggrieved at the predominance of Bolivians in the government. That sentiment was not lessened by the Protector's autocratic measures. Chile was aroused at the emergence of a confederated state that included a country in which Freire had organized an expedition against the Chiloé Islands. Dictator Rosas took up arms against the Confederation; and in June, 1838, an Argentine army marched into the Bolivian department of Tarija but was repulsed. With the aid of Peruvian émigrés, Chilean soldiers invaded southern Peru and occupied Arequipa. In November, 1837, however, those invaders were compelled to sign a treaty of peace. Nevertheless, the Chileans soon resumed the struggle, and on January 20, 1839, under General Búlnes they defeated the confederate army at the battle of Yungay. The Peru-Bolivian Confederation then dissolved and Santa Cruz sailed for Guayaquil. If he had realized his dream of uniting Bolivia and Peru under one rule, an Incan federation might conceivably have served to shield their people against foreign aggression.

A Constituent Congress soon assembled at Sucre. Its members declared in the preamble of a new Constitution which was adopted in October, 1839, that, as Bolivia had renounced the Confederation, the Constitution of 1834 was no longer in force. The fundamental law of 1839 made some innovations. It provided for the creation of elective municipal councils in the departmental capitals. In each of these capitals it established a judicial tribunal with special jurisdiction. It declared that citizens should have the right freely to petition the government. Except in specified cases, the death penalty was prohibited.

Constitution
of 1839

Upon the downfall of Santa Cruz, General Velasco was proclaimed president. Shortly afterward he was deposed by revolutionists. In September, 1841, soldiers proclaimed that General José Ballivián, an enterprising native of La Paz, was president of the republic. He soon announced that both the constitutions of 1839 and 1841 were no longer in force and that his policy would be to preserve liberty, property, and the Roman Catholic religion.

Ballivián's
Policies

As President Gamarra of Peru would not desist from an invasion of Bolivia and evidently aimed to annex the department of La Paz, if not to overthrow the government of the republic, Ballivián placed himself at the head of the army. On November 18, 1841, Gamarra was defeated and killed on the plateau of Ingavi, within sight of the snow-capped peaks of Illampu and Illimani. In the following June a treaty was arranged between Bolivia and Peru by which both nations agreed to restore the status quo and to relinquish all claims for indemnities.

In 1843 a National Assembly adopted a new fundamental law for Bolivia. That Constitution much increased the power of the chief magistrate. It provided him with an advisory body which was designated the national council. His term of office was extended to eight years. Among the powers conferred upon him was the authority to dissolve Congress, to remove government officials, and to promote immigration. In consequence of such clauses Bolivia's fourth Constitution has been characterized as a "military ordinance which should be perused in the glow of the sword that conquered at Ingavi."

President Ballivián took a deep interest in public improvements. He promoted the construction of roads, aqueducts, cathedrals, hospitals, and prisons throughout the republic. He dispatched an agent to England who was instructed to interest capitalists and manufacturers in the development of Bolivia. He equipped expeditions that were directed to determine whether or not the river Pilcomayo would furnish Bolivia an exit to the Atlantic Ocean. He formed projects designed to encourage emigration from Europe. Yet his arbitrary régime provoked opposition, especially in the army, and in December, 1847, the President resigned.

It was the news of a rebellion led by a valiant general named Manuel Belzu which caused that resignation. Velasco, who was again proclaimed president, appointed that general as secretary of war. But in October, 1848, Belzu joined insurrectionary soldiers at Oruro. He decisively defeated Velasco's army at Yamparaez on December 6,

1848. The victorious general soon issued a decree declaring that the Constitution of 1839 was in force; but he stated that, if the President should not be able to perform his duties, the Council of State should carry on instead of the president of Congress, as provided by that Constitution. Other decrees evinced his desire to win the support of the lower classes against the aristocratic partisans of Ballivián who were designated the *Rojos*. Belzu thus brought a so-called Democratic party into existence. With the aid of aborigines and the army, he suppressed various rebellions. By good luck he escaped death by an assassin's dagger.

General
Belzu
Becomes
President

In September, 1851, a National Convention brought another Constitution into existence. The fundamental law of 1851 abolished the national council. It fixed the President's term at five years and gave him wide powers. He was given the right, by way of punishment, to suspend government officials from office. The Constitution gave legislative authority to a Congress composed of two coördinate houses. In January, 1853, President Belzu announced that the waters of all navigable streams flowing through Bolivian territory and emptying into the Amazon and the Paraguay rivers should be open to navigation by the vessels of all nations. In the election of 1855 General Jorge Córdova, a disciple of Belzu, was elected president.

President Córdova was much harassed by conspiracies and rebellions. A humane ruler, he did not sanction a single execution. In September, 1857, Linares started a revolt in Oruro. Uprisings soon took place in other cities, and, after Córdova had made a futile attempt to suppress the insurrection, he fled to Peru. José María Linares, who thus realized a long-cherished ambition, was a man of great determination and energy. With the support of aristocratic and intelligent political leaders, he hoped to carry out certain reforms. To the cabinet he added a secretary of public improvement. He reduced the emoluments of many officials, made alterations in the system of central and local administration, and divided the republic into three judicial districts. He established a military college and organized a national guard. By a decree providing for the establishment of ecclesiastical seminaries he displayed his intention to reform the manners and customs of the clergy.

Rise and
Fall of
Linares

When signs of opposition to his measures became apparent, on March 31, 1858, Linares issued a decree frankly announcing that he had assumed the powers of a dictator. The stern policy which he pursued toward seditious conspirators intensified the discontent. Bolivian émigrés commanded by Belzu and Córdova made irruptions into Bolivia from Peru. Upon the eve of the presidential election, two members of his own cabinet conspired against the President; by the aid of military officers in January, 1861, they established a governmental junta. Linares was forced to withdraw from his native land; and Congress elected General José M. de Achá as president.

In August, 1861, a National Constituent Assembly framed the "Political Constitution of the State." This Constitution set the President's term at three years. It established a unicameral legislature and re-established the Council of State. Unusually liberal to foreigners, it declared that all persons within the republic should enjoy civil rights. The massacre of numerous prisoners of state, including ex-President Córdova, by a military commander caused a revulsion of feeling among the populace. Weak and vacillating in character, Achá hesitated to take decisive measures against the chief assassin.

On December 28, 1864, General Mariano Melgarejo took advantage of the growing dissatisfaction and proclaimed himself president.

The Reign of Melgarejo   An intriguing and brutal militarist, Melgarejo showed even less regard for Bolivia's laws and institutions than had his predecessors. Among other measures he speedily proclaimed that the Constitution was abrogated. During the years of his domination the principles of the two political parties, the Rojos and the Colorados, became even less than the mere battle cries of bitter partisans. Upon the point of being deposed by Belzu, who suddenly returned from exile to place himself at the head of a rebellion, Melgarejo slew that rival with his own hand.

Extremely jealous of his authority at home, Melgarejo did not increase the prestige of his nation abroad. In 1867 he authorized a treaty with Brazil by which Bolivia acknowledged the Empire's title to some sixty thousand square leagues of territory upon the Madeira and Paraguay rivers. A dispute that had arisen with Chile about the title to the desert of Atacama, a large portion of which was included in Bolivia by the *uti possidetis* of 1810, was adjusted by a treaty signed on August 10, 1866. This treaty stipulated that Bolivia should cede to Chile the zone between the Salado River and the parallel of 24° south latitude from the Andes to the Pacific. The guano discovered between parallels 23° and 25° and the duties levied upon mineral products exported from that zone were to be divided equally between the parties. Chilean products should be exempt from imposts upon entering the Bolivian port of Mejillones. Within the department of Atacama, as well as in the southern provinces of Peru, energetic Chileans engaged in the exploitation of nitrate deposits. In a misguided moment, to the Nitrate Company of Antofagasta, which was domiciled in Chile, Melgarejo conceded the right to exploit for fifteen years the nitrate deposits in the desert of Atacama.

In November, 1870, revolutionists led by Hilarión Daza repudiated the odious rule of Melgarejo and announced that Colonel Agustín Morales was their leader. Morales, who was proclaimed president after the defeat and flight of Melgarejo, declared that his political motto was "more liberty and less government." After a Constituent Assembly had passed some reform laws, Morales assumed dictatorial authority but was soon killed in a quarrel with some military officers. In May, 1873, Adolfo Ballivián, a son of the victor of Ingavi, was inaugurated as president. An outstanding personality, he attempted to reform the disordered finances of his country. He negotiated a treaty of defensive alliance with Peru, but unfortunately died on February 14, 1874. Ballivián's term was almost completed by Tomás Frías, an old man who had been president of the Council of State. His administration was disturbed by military rebellions.

At this juncture a dispute again arose with Chile about the desert of Atacama. In August, 1874, Bolivia and Chile attempted to adjust the controversy by a treaty which stipulated that their boundary line in the desert should be the parallel of 24°, which ran a short distance south of Antofagasta. As a concession to Chile, Bolivia agreed that for twenty-five years Chileans who might engage in the mining industry in the desert should not be subjected to any additional imposts.

On the eve of the Bolivian presidential election, one of the leading candidates, General Hilarión Daza, who was secretary of war, seized the President. The subservient populace of the capital city proclaimed Daza president on May 4, 1876. This coup d'état marked the accession of a dictator whose rule became notorious in South America for corruption, arbitrary imprisonments, and bacchanalian feasts. In February, 1878, he sanctioned a law which had been indiscreetly passed by Congress to the effect that a tax of ten centavos per hundredweight should be laid upon all nitrate exported from the Bolivian littoral. The Nitrate Company of Antofagasta protested against this law and appealed to the Chilean government. While negotiations were still in progress for the adjustment of the dispute, the Bolivian government decided temporarily to rescind its contract with the nitrate company. On February 14, 1879, which was the date set by Bolivia for the sale of the company's property to ensure the payment of the taxes, Chilean soldiers took possession of Antofagasta. Two weeks later Bolivia announced that in consequence a state of war existed between her and Chile. After the Peruvian government had declined to proclaim its neutrality in the struggle, Chile declared war upon both Bolivia and Peru.

Step by step the controversy between Chile and Bolivia over the exploitation of nitrate deposits in the littoral had moved toward a tragic climax in which Peru was inevitably involved because of her secret treaty with Bolivia. The conflict which ensued was designated by South Americans the "War of the Pacific."

Even before a declaration of war had been made by Chile, her soldiers had taken possession of the Bolivian port of Cobija, and had captured Calama by assault. Delegating executive authority to the Council of State, President Daza hastily led a division of poorly equipped soldiers to Tacna, where he reported to the Peruvian commander, General Mariano Prado. Upon learning of the capture of Pisagua by Chilean soldiers, Daza and Prado decided to make a concerted attack upon the invaders. When, after a toilsome march by way of Arica to the river Camarones, Daza sent a message to Prado declaring that his soldiers refused to advance farther, he was instructed to desist from his march southward. Daza then retreated to Arica. That retrograde movement—*la retirada de Camarones*—was stigmatized as an act of treason by the Bolivians, especially as it was followed by the rout of coöperating Peruvian soldiers.

Soon afterward the Chileans defeated the Peruvian-Bolivian army at Tarapacá. General Daza then formed the resolution to march to La Paz in order to suppress an insurrection. But Bolivian soldiers at Tacna, who were disgusted at his conduct, disavowed his authority and proclaimed that the commander of the Bolivian army in Peru should be Colonel Camacho. As Camacho had no ambition to become the president of Bolivia, he placed himself under the orders of a junta that had been established at La Paz.

When he heard of the deposition of President Daza, General Campero, who had been in command of another division of the Bolivian army, proceeded to Oruro. There, by a decree of January 19, 1880, he assumed the provisional presidency of the distracted republic. He soon convoked a Convention at La Paz, which in June elected him president for four years. At that Convention—far from the thunder of Chilean cannon—a group of leaders framed a centralistic Constitution which was promulgated on October 17, 1880.

The Bolivian Constitution of 1880 provided that Roman Catholicism should be the religion of the State. It prohibited the public exercise of any other faith except in frontier territories. Upon the nomination of the Senate, the President was to appoint bishops and archbishops to vacant sees.

Executive authority was vested in a President and two Vice-Presidents. Those magistrates should be elected by direct vote and were to hold office for four years. The President was given the title of captain general of the army; he might even direct a war in person, and could negotiate treaties. He was to appoint ambassadors and ecclesiastical dignitaries. He was given the authority to exclude papal bulls and rescripts. Members of the cabinet might take part in the debates of Congress, but they must withdraw before a vote was taken.

Congress was to be composed of a House of Deputies and a Senate. Each department of the republic was to have two Senators. In joint session Congress might consider the resignation of the President, approve or reject treaties which he had negotiated, declare war at his instance, set the strength of the permanent military force, and decide conflicts about the jurisdiction of the supreme court. Among specific grants of jurisdiction to that court was the authority to judge disputes arising from contracts and concessions. The administrative system which had been founded in 1826 was, for the most part, preserved.

Though General Campero gave to his country a new Constitution, he could not prevent Chilean soldiers from conquering its seacoast. They took possession of the department of Atacama. At last, after a treaty of peace had been signed between Peru and Chile, at Valparaiso on April 4, 1884, a convention was signed between Chile and Bolivia which was designated an agreement upon an indefinite truce. The Treaty of Valparaiso declared that the state of belligerency between the parties had terminated, and that neither party might renew the war without a year's notification to the other party. It stipulated that during the life of the agreement the victor should retain control of Bolivian territory lying between 23° south latitude and the mouth of the river Loa. Chilean products and manufactures should be allowed to enter Bolivia through her former littoral free of duty, while foreign merchandise destined for that isolated country should pay the imposts laid by the Chilean tariff but should not be liable for other duties. Bolivia should receive 75 per cent of such imposts for use in part on her indemnities that were due to Chile. By the Treaty of Valparaiso the vanquished nation reluctantly waived control of valuable territory that was rich in nitrate deposits and that contained her only seaports. This treaty embodied a thinly veiled cession of the nitrate desert to the victor in the War of the Pacific.

Treaties between Bolivia and Chile

After this treaty was signed, President Campero was succeeded by Gregorio Pacheco. He prepared the way for the accession of Aniceto Arce, who became president in 1888. Both of those presidents aimed to stifle all opposition to their rule. The presidency of Arce was, however, signalized by the opening of a railroad from Antofagasta to Oruro, the first exit by railroad that was afforded to the mediterranean country.

Under Arce's successor, Mariano Baptista, on May 18, 1895, two

significant treaties were signed between Bolivia and Chile which
aimed to settle finally the territorial problems left open by the Treaty
of Valparaiso. One of those treaties provided that Chile should be
definitely assured of the possession of the Bolivian littoral which she
had retained. By the other treaty Chile promised that if she secured
"dominion and permanent sovereignty" over the provinces of Tacna
and Arica by direct negotiations or by a referendum, she would transfer
those provinces to Bolivia. To accomplish this adjustment Chile promised to use her influence separately or in conjunction with Bolivia in
order to obtain for herself a definite proprietary right over Tacna and
Arica. This treaty of peace was supplemented by a protocol dated
December 8, 1895, which stated that the proposed cession of the
Bolivian littoral was to be without effect, if within two years Chile did
not give to Bolivia a port upon the Pacific. In no case were Chile's
obligations to be fulfilled without the transfer of a zone and a port to
serve as an outlet for Bolivia. Although ratifications of these treaties
of May, 1895, were exchanged, yet they were never executed. It would
seem that in framing these treaties Chile, who was menaced by a war
with Argentina, aimed to assure herself of friendly relations with
Bolivia by promising to cede to her a corridor to the Pacific through
Peru's lost provinces—a pledge to which Peru made strenuous objections.

In 1896 Severo Alonso, who had been a secretary of Baptista, became president of Bolivia. In December, 1898, because of an attempt
of the Conservatives to enact a law that would have made
Sucre the permanent capital of the republic—a dignity
which, in reality, it had shared at times with other cities
—the citizens of La Paz took up arms under Colonel José
Pando against the government. On January 17, 1899, a battle was
fought near La Paz between government soldiers and insurgent forces
which resulted in a victory for the revolutionists. In the following
April, after another victory Colonel Pando entered Oruro in triumph.
President Alonso fled to Chile, while the victor organized a provisional
government. In this manner, after a struggle that had lasted more
than a score of years, the ruling oligarchy was shorn of authority
and the so-called Liberal party came into power.

The Revolution of 1899

Elected president without any opposition, Pando was inaugurated
on October 26, 1899. During his administration a long-standing dispute
concerning the boundary with Brazil reached a climax. A treaty between the two countries in 1867 had sketched a frontier line between
them through a tropical region. Subsequently many Brazilians settled
in Bolivian territory near the borders in order to gather rubber. In
July, 1899, they rebelled against its magistrates and announced the

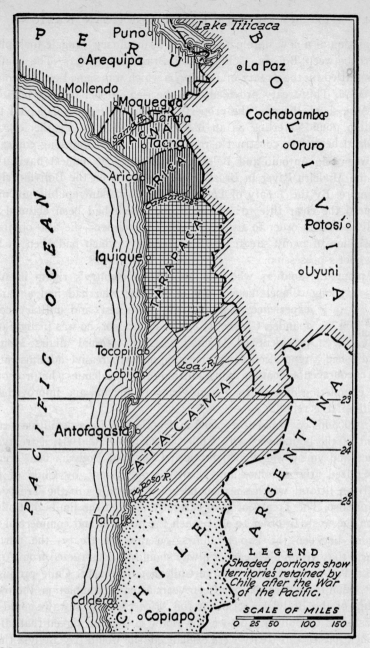

MAP TO ILLUSTRATE TERRITORIAL ADJUSTMENTS RESULTING FROM
"THE WAR OF THE PACIFIC"

formation of a new state named Acre. A sanguinary struggle took place there between Bolivian soldiers and Brazilian pioneers. The conflict was settled by the Treaty of Petropolis which was signed on November 17, 1903. This treaty provided that the rich, rubber-bearing territory of Acre should become the property of Brazil after she had paid two million pounds sterling as an indemnity to Bolivia. Further, Brazil pledged herself to construct a railroad around the imposing cataracts between São Antonio and Bella Vista in order to connect navigation on the Madeira River in Brazil with navigation on the Bolivian river Mamoré. By the Treaty of Petropolis the Brazilian republic not only secured the clear title to a large region which had been claimed by Bolivia but, in order to straighten out her frontiers, she also obtained possession of many square miles of territory which had been in her neighbor's possession.

Among the soldiers who had upheld his country's rights in Acre was a young colonel named Ismael Montes, who had had a varied experience as a journalist, publicist, and military commander. Chosen as Pando's successor, he was inaugurated president in August, 1904. In internal affairs Montes established a reputation as an energetic and progressive administrator. He encouraged education by establishing new academies; he promoted the completion of a railroad from Oruro to Viacha, and improved the credit of the republic.

President Montes

In 1903 his government engaged in negotiations for a definitive settlement of the boundaries with Chile. On October 20, 1904, a treaty of peace and amity was signed between Chile and Bolivia. That treaty recognized "the absolute and perpetual possession" by Chile of the Bolivian littoral which she had occupied according to the Treaty of Valparaiso. The Treaty of 1904 carefully marked the limits of Bolivia upon the west. In order to strengthen the political and commercial relations between the two republics—so ran the treaty—the parties agreed that within one year a railway should be constructed from Arica to La Paz at the expense of the Chilean government. Chile promised that, upon the expiration of fifteen years after its completion, the ownership of the Bolivian section of the Arica-La Paz railway should be transferred to Bolivia. Further, the victor in the war agreed that, after ratifications of this treaty were exchanged, she would pay Bolivia three hundred thousand pounds sterling. Chile also undertook to meet certain outstanding obligations of the vanquished nation. She acknowledged the perpetual right of Bolivia to a commercial transit through her territories and ports to the Pacific Ocean. On November 15, 1904, those nations signed a supplementary protocol by which the sovereignty of Chile over that part of the Atacama Desert lying between the parallels of 23° and 24° and extending from the Argentine boundary to the Pacific Ocean was recognized by Bolivia.

In August, 1906, a law was enacted providing that the public exercise of other religions than Roman Catholicism should be permitted. Three years later Montes, whose term had been extended by Congress for one year upon the sudden death of the president-elect, was succeeded by Elidoro Villazón. A conciliatory statesman with a varied experience in public life, Villazón aimed to continue the policies that had been promoted by Montes. Important railroads were projected; new telegraph lines were built. The foreign commerce of Bolivia increased, while her revenues steadily augmented. On January 7, 1911, Villazón signed a bill which provided for the establishment of the Bank of the Bolivian Nation. Difficulties about the boundary line provoked armed conflicts between Bolivians and Peruvians near the Manuripi River. On December 28, 1912, a protocol was signed by which Bolivia released Brazil from her pledge in the Treaty of Petropolis to build a spur of the Madeira-Mamoré railroad from Villa Murtinho to Villa Bella.

Montes was inaugurated for the second time on August 6, 1913. He took various steps to promote the construction of new railroads or the extension of existing lines. Of economic developments perhaps the most significant was the increased attention which was paid to mining. So pleased were some of the Bolivians with his energetic administration that they styled him "the Great President."

Partly because of her mediterranean position, Bolivia has been vexed by many boundary disputes. As has been indicated, the victory of Chile in the War of the Pacific eventually determined the boundary between Bolivia and Chile. A dispute with Argentina about Bolivia's southern boundary was apparently adjusted by a treaty negotiated in 1889; but, as **Conditions about 1914: Boundary Disputes** modified three years later, it sketched a line of demarcation which was difficult to survey because of the geographical errors or misconceptions that were incorporated in it. The task of surveying this boundary was resumed in 1913 and iron posts were set up along parts of the line. Disputes concerning the Bolivian-Peruvian frontier—largely due to a difference about the boundaries of the audiencia of Charcas—will be considered in connection with Peru.

An isolated state, Bolivia attracted few immigrants. According to a rough enumeration made in 1900, with some allowance for omissions, her population was about 1,700,000. Persons of pure European descent constituted a very small fraction of the population. Possibly the creoles, who resided mainly in the towns and cities, constituted one-tenth of the inhabitants. A very large part of the population was made up of pure-blooded Indians, who even in towns near the capital city of La Paz still preserved their clan organization and customs. In frontier districts the aborigines were in a barbarous state. A considerable part of the population in large towns or cities was composed of mestizos. The whites and the mixed classes spoke Spanish, while the Indians ordinarily used their own dialects. Unnumbered thousands of her people still spoke either the Aymaran or the Quechuan language. In 1914 the size of her regular army was set at 4,600 men. Bolivia had no navy whatever. The chief occupations of her people were farming, grazing, and mining. Her great mineral wealth was being exploited by foreign corporations.

In 1915 the products of her mines constituted over five-sixths of the total value of the exports of Bolivia. Her chief mineral exports in that year were the following: tin, antimony, rubber, copper, bismuth, silver, wolfram, lead, and gold. Bolivia was linked to the outside world by two railways which found their exit to the Pacific at Arica and Antofagasta through territory held by Chile; and by a third railway that passed through Peruvian territory from Lake Titicaca to Mollendo.

Social, Economic, and Intellectual Conditions

Education in Bolivia was very backward. A Bolivian writer estimated that in 1910 only about one-eighth of his fellow countrymen could read. In 1914 there existed in the republic, according to the report of the secretary of public instruction, over six hundred primary schools. Each department of the republic had a so-called university located at its capital. In some of those institutions the instruction was mainly secondary, as there were few advanced students in attendance. National colleges of commerce and of medicine were located at La Paz, while a national college of law was at Sucre.

Because of the large aboriginal element in the population and the backward condition of Bolivia, her literature was comparatively scant. Some books and pamphlets have been written about important events in Bolivian politics, such as the struggles of political parties, the lives of salient personalities, and the need of an outlet to the sea. Manuel Ordóñez López and Luis S. Crespo composed a history of Bolivia which carried the story to 1880. Manuel V. Ballivián made valuable contributions to knowledge, as in his monograph about the rubber industry. Among outstanding Bolivian novels may be mentioned *Casa Solariega*, by Armando Chirveches, which is a romance concerning Latin-American society.

An illuminating sociological study of Andean life is the introspective booklet, "Sick People," published in 1910 by a Bolivian scholar named Alcides Arguedas. A passage from his description of the Bolivian Indian runs thus:

His character partakes of the sternness and aridity of the wilderness. He is stubborn, rancorous, egotistic, cruel, vengeful, and suspicious. He lacks either initiative or perseverance and harbors a profound abhorrence for anyone who is different from himself. Hence his hatred for the white man.

His life is incredibly frugal and crude. . . . For him, to be the owner of an embroidered garment with which he can appear at a festival of the village or the parish and in which he can become as drunk as possible and can remain drunk as long as possible is the height of good fortune. The longer a festival lasts, the better it seems to him. To dance or to drink is his only pleasure; he knows no other. With persons of his own kind he is an expansive animal; away from his habitat, he is reserved and sullen. . . . In the Indian's house there is nothing but squalor, and, according to an anonymous note in a statistical report, it is 'a small and miserable hut composed of mud and stones with a roof of straw. Within this murky and unclean habitation lives an entire family; there it reposes for the night either upon the bare earth or upon decaying sheepskins. Throughout the plains, the mountains, the valleys, and the ravines of the entire republic are scattered Indian ranches upon ground that belongs in most part to landed proprietors.'

Soon after the United States broke off diplomatic relations with Germany because of her ruthless submarine campaign, the Bolivian government expressed its approval of the policy pursued by the government at Washington. On April 13, 1917, Bolivia's secretary of foreign relations sent a note to Germany's representative at La Paz declaring that a ship carrying the Bolivian envoy to Berlin had been sunk by a German torpedo while traversing neutral waters. Hence that secretary gave passports to the Kaiser's agent.

A publicist and banker who had served as secretary of finance under Montes, José Gutiérrez Guerra, was elected president by the Liberals in the campaign of 1917. During his administration the agitation about an outlet to the Pacific Ocean became more and more serious. His secretary of foreign relations took the view that the provinces of Tacna and Arica, **An Outlet to the Pacific** which Peru had allowed Chile to retain after the War of the Pacific, did not belong to either country, and that Bolivia should be granted an outlet to the Pacific through a port in those provinces, preferably Arica. Bolivia's claim to this territory was partly based upon economic considerations and geographical proximity, and partly upon the opinion that before the establishment of her independence Tacna and Arica had been under the jurisdiction of the audiencia of Charcas. Suppositions that the government was quietly negotiating with Chile for an understanding about an outlet to the ocean evidently helped to precipitate a bloodless revolution at La Paz, where a provisional junta was established. On July 13, 1920, that junta issued a decree announcing that it would soon convoke a National Convention composed of delegates chosen by popular vote which would elect a new president, reform the Constitution, and adopt laws to promote the reorganization of the country. President Gutiérrez Guerra was escorted out of Bolivia via the coveted port of Arica. After Bautista Saavedra was inaugurated as president, the delegates of Bolivia presented a plea for the modification of her Treaty of 1904 with Chile to the Assembly of the League of Nations. Their hope was that their country might be restored an outlet to the Pacific Ocean. But, in view of stipulations in the Covenant of the League, the Assembly decided that it could not properly entertain this unilateral request for the modification of an international agreement.

When, as will be narrated in the next chapter, Chile and Peru undertook to submit the Tacna-Arica controversy to the arbitration of the United States, Bolivian statesmen took a keen interest in the proceedings. After the United States proposed that Chile and Peru should engage in direct negotiations, Secretary of State Kellogg suggested that at least a part of the disputed region might be given to Bolivia in return for a compensation to be divided between Chile and Peru. But Peru would not agree to that adjustment. Kellogg then proposed that Bolivia should be conceded a corridor leading to the Pacific. Bolivia, however, did not seem inclined to agree to this compromise.

On November 30, 1926, the American secretary of state proposed that Chile and Peru should, in return for an adequate compensation, make a joint cession of all their rights and interests in Tacna-Arica to Bolivia. The mediterranean state at once unconditionally approved this proposal; Chile accepted it in principle; while alleging that such a sacrifice would be inequitable to her, Peru declined to agree to it. Three years later, as will be shown in the next chapter, a definitive treaty between Chile and Peru provided for the division of Tacna-Arica between them. When the terms of a protocol to that treaty stipulating that neither party should, without the consent of the other party, transfer any portion of the territory assigned to her to a third power became known in La Paz, Bolivian statesmen promptly filed a protest with the government at Washington.

Meanwhile American capitalists were playing an important rôle in Bolivian finance. Shortly after Saavedra came into power, the government had to refund certain large loans made from bankers in the United States. The outcome was the Nicolaus Loan of 1922. This loan, arranged with the Equitable Trust Company of New York as trustee, amounted to $33,000,000. As a security for its payment, Bolivia pledged more than one-half her entire national revenue. A fiscal commission, two members of which were to be named by the American bankers, was to take charge of the collection of taxes in the republic during the life of the loan. A presi-

Industrial Conditions

dential decree soon appointed the American chairman of this commission as the inspector-general of banks and monopolies.

Contemporaneously, American entrepreneurs of industry undertook to exploit Bolivia's mineral wealth. On June 16, 1921, in an attempt to conserve the nation's oil, a law was passed which limited to 100,000 hectares the extent of petroleum land that any person or corporation could exploit, which restricted oil concessions to a term of fifty-five years, and which provided that a maximum royalty of 11 per cent of the value of the oil produced should be paid to the government. By virtue of grants made in 1920, however, a subsidiary of the Standard Oil Company of New Jersey had been prospecting for petroleum in an area of 4,000,000 hectares.

Meanwhile President Saavedra had been granting to persons of Indian descent a participation in the government. Large sums of money were used to make the city of La Paz the industrial center of the country at the expense of other places. Borrowed money was diverted from railway construction for the modernization of that city. Charges on the foreign debt became so large that they aggregated more than one-half of the national revenue. The suspension of constitutional guarantees did not allay the growing discontent. General Kundt, a former German officer, undertook as the chief of the military staff not only to Prussianize the Bolivian army but also to establish a system of espionage. Prominent Bolivian statesmen were forced into exile.

At this juncture, Hernando Siles was allowed to assume the presidency with the apparent understanding that he was to continue Saavedra's policies. But President Siles soon drifted into dictatorship; he exiled the Vice-President. A serious fall **The** in the price of tin stimulated discontent. Although, be- **Revolution** cause of opposition by military officers, Siles relinquished **of 1930** his authority to the cabinet on May 28, 1930, suspicions were rife that he wished changes in the law and custom of the Constitution. Daniel Salamanca, an influential and constructive leader of the Republican party, protested against this unconstitutional régime. University students took up the cry. The garrisons at Oruro and Cochabamba revolted against the government. Cadets in the military academy at La Paz joined the revolutionists, and on June 27 an energetic general named Blanco Galindo captured that city. President Siles was forced to leave Bolivia, while political leaders who had been in exile began to return to their homes.

After taking possession of La Paz, a junta of six military officers undertook to formulate reforms. In August, 1930, a committee designated by this junta announced that it had arranged a coalition ticket for the national elections on which Salamanca was named as the leading

candidate. On March 5, 1931, he took office as president. In his inaugural address he praised the patriotic conduct of the junta and mentioned the social and economic problems that confronted the nation.
Nevertheless he was discredited by the disastrous defeats inflicted on
Bolivian soldiers in the Chaco. During a visit to the front in 1934,
Salamanca was rudely seized and Vice-President Tejada Sorzano
became the chief magistrate. In May he was deposed by a clique of
military officers and Colonel Toro took over the presidency.

For some years politics were dominated by heroes of the Chaco
War. In March, 1937, President Toro achieved notoriety by the expropriation of the Standard Oil Company, whose properties
were valued at $17,000,000. His allegation was that this
corporation had evaded the payment of rentals of petroleum lands. A Bolivian company was directed to take
charge of the confiscated oil properties. Maintaining that it had not
been guilty of fraud, the American company protested against this
seizure. Upon his return from a vacation, on July 15, 1937, Toro was
seized and sent into exile.

Colonel Germán Busch, the son of a German physician, succeeded
to power. In May, 1938, a Constitutional Convention elected him president. In October following he promulgated a new Constitution which
did not much alter the existing frame of government. Article CVI
declared, however, that unoccupied lands with their natural resources,
water rights, and mineral deposits were the property of the State.
A certain clause declared that laborers had the right to strike. The law
was to determine how workmen might participate in the profits of
their respective occupations. Provision was made for the regulation and
protection of Indian communal organizations.

In turn, on April 24, 1939, Busch prorogued Congress and assumed
dictatorial power. In the following August he died in a mysterious
fashion. After a brief interregnum, when the commander of the
army served as the chief executive, General Peñaranda was elected
president. He was inaugurated on April 15, 1940, for a term of four
years. In November of that year the United States government agreed
to purchase set amounts of tin from Bolivian mines during a five-
year period. A similar arrangement was later made concerning pur-
chases of lead, tungsten, and zinc. In 1941 the discovery of an alleged
Nazi conspiracy to subvert the government led to the proclamation of
a state of siege, the incarceration of several suspects, and the expulsion
of the German minister. In January, 1942, Bolivia broke off relations
with the Axis powers.[1] After an animated debate in Congress, the

*Politico-
Military
Fluctuations*

---

[1] On April 7, 1943, Peñaranda issued a decree putting Bolivia in the war against
the Axis.

Peñaranda government finally removed a cause of friction with the United States by agreeing to pay the Standard Oil Company $1,750,000 for the petroleum properties which had been confiscated. The seriously embarrassed finances of Bolivia were somewhat relieved in November, 1942, by an agreement with the United States providing for economic and financial aid.

Among South American nations the republic of Bolivia possesses traits that are unique. The main habitat of the nation is upon a plateau so elevated that the average white man cannot continuously carry on physical labor there. Her industry is to a large extent dependent upon the Aymaran and the Quechuan Indians or upon the large, mixed classes. The party in control of the spoils of office has at times based its power largely upon the quasi-democratized Aymarans, whose rise to political influence has been resented by the Quechuans. The significant part played by the Indians and the cholos who are not only the laborers but also the fighters of the nation, has been vividly illustrated by the military uprisings that have so often rudely disturbed Bolivia's political equilibrium. Those insurrections have occasionally made her institutions appear like the mere shuttlecocks of contending partisans. A leading historian of Bolivia has stated that during the past century one hundred and ninety revolts have disturbed her life. Aboriginal blood which ran in the veins of some of her outstanding leaders seems occasionally to have found expression in statesmanship that was bizarre.

This, as well as the clever and well-informed diplomacy of her antagonists, has had an unfortunate effect upon Bolivia's territorial ambitions and integrity. Her history has been checkered by successive losses of outlying regions to which she had a claim. Even before the Chaco War, on a map of his native land a Bolivian cartographer had indicated those grievous losses by areas which he colored black—in several places his nation's domain thus appeared to have wide borders of mourning. After that war had been liquidated, the territory of Bolivia had been reduced to little more than one half of the domain bequeathed by Marshal Sucre.

SUGGESTIONS FOR FURTHER READING

BALLIVIÁN, A., *Bolivia: Her Resources and Future*, 1920.

BANDELIER, A. F. A., *The Islands of Titicaca and Koati*, 1910.

CARRASCO, J., *Bolivia's Case for the League of Nations*, 1920.

BROWNING, W. E., and Others, *The West Coast Republics of South America*, 1930.

CHAPMAN, C. E., "Melgarejo of Bolivia," *Pacific Historical Review*, Vol. VIII, pp. 37-45.

CLEVEN, N. A. N., *The Political Organization of Bolivia*, 1940.

GALARZA, E., "Debts, Dictatorship, and Revolution in Bolivia and Peru," *Foreign Policy Reports*, Vol. VII, No. 5, 1931.

MCBRIDE, G. M., *The Agrarian Indian Communities of Highland Bolivia*, 1921.

MARKHAM, C. R., *The War Between Chile and Peru*, 1882.

MARSH, M. A., *The Bankers in Bolivia*, 1928.

PARKER, W. B. (ed.), *Bolivians of Today*, 1922.

SANGER, J. W., *Advertising Methods in Chile, Peru, and Bolivia*, 1919.

SCHURZ, W. L., *Bolivia: a Commercial and Industrial Handbook*, 1921.

WALLE, P., *Bolivia: Its People and Its Resources*, 1914.

CHAPTER XVIII

PERU

Modern Peru arose from the viceroyalty of that name. Shortly after the departure of San Martín from Lima, a Constituent Congress which he had convoked became the source of political authority. It soon vested executive authority in a junta composed of three persons. On December 17, 1822, Congress adopted the "Bases of the Political Constitution of Peru." Among its principles was a declaration that the Peruvian provinces combined into one organization composed the nation. Her religion should be Roman Catholicism: the exercise of any other faith was prohibited. Executive authority was not to be held for life, nor should it become hereditary. Legislative authority was to be vested in a unicameral Congress.

Early Constitutional Doctrines

In February, 1823, Congress declared that José de la Riva Agüero should be president. In the following June he was induced to retire from the presidency and two months later José Torre Tagle was made president. On November 12, 1823, he promulgated an organic law which Congress had just adopted. That Constitution abolished certain hereditary privileges and prohibited the slave trade. Executive authority was vested in a President who should serve for four years. He was to be aided by three secretaries or ministers of state. Legislative authority was given to a unicameral Congress. Judicial power was vested in a supreme court, departmental courts, and provincial tribunals. The republic was to be divided into departments, provinces, districts, and parishes.

Congress had already declared that Simón Bolívar was the supreme military and political authority of the republic. On November 14, 1823, it enacted a law declaring that any articles of the Constitution which were incompatible with his authority should be suspended. On February 10, 1824, Bolívar was declared to be Supreme Political Chief of the Peruvian nation. A year later Congress extended Bolívar's dictatorship until such a time as Peru's administration should have been definitely organized. In April, 1825, the dictator temporarily transferred his authority to a council of government. Upon his return from a trip to Bolivia, in September, 1826, he relinquished the dictatorship and departed for Colombia. On November 30 of this year the fundamental law that he had framed for Bolivia, which had been approved by Peruvian electoral colleges, was declared to be the Constitution of Peru. In June, 1827, however, the Liberator's cherished Constitution was discarded; the Peruvian Congress declared that, with some modifications, the Constitution of 1823 would be provisionally in force.

In March, 1828, a Constituent Congress that had been convoked by Santa Cruz, who was president of the council of government, adopted the "Political Constitution of the Peruvian Republic." Executive power was given to a President who was to be chosen by an electoral college. Legislative authority was vested in a Congress composed of a Senate and a Chamber of Deputies. A Council of State was created that was to sit during the recess of Congress. The Judiciary was declared to be completely independent. Prefects of departments were made dependent upon the President, while subprefects of provinces were made dependent upon the prefects.

The Framing of Constitutions

Military rule soon usurped the place of constitutional government. General José de la Mar, who had fought under Sucre in the patriot army at Ayacucho, was first elected president. Not only did La Mar dispatch an expedition against Bolivia, but he also became involved in a war with Colombia. As the Peruvian army was defeated by General Sucre at the battle of Tarqui, the President's hope of annexing southern Colombia was thwarted. A military uprising against La Mar resulted in his deposition and General Gamarra, a native of Cuzco, was elected president. Gamarra was soon succeeded by an aristocrat named Luis Orbegosa. It was a troublous age in Peru's history when the National Convention met in September, 1833, to revise the fundamental law. The discussion of proposed changes lasted several months; on June 10, 1834, another Constitution was promulgated. The Constitution of 1834 differed from the Constitution of 1828 chiefly in phraseology and minor details. Each department was to be represented by five instead of three Senators. The president of the Council of State should act as chief executive in case of the death, absence, or disability of the President. A certain article provided that any person who might become President by sedition or by force was to lose his political rights and that all his acts should be null and void.

Scarcely had the new Constitution been promulgated, when Felipe Salaverry, a talented and ambitious Peruvian, took the leadership in a revolt that broke out in Lima. On February 25, 1835, he proclaimed himself the supreme chief of Peru. In the ensuing civil war the Bolivian President took occasion to intervene on the side of President Orbegosa in order to establish the Peru-Bolivian Confederation, as described in the preceding chapter. After the defeat of Santa Cruz at Yungay, Provisional President Gamarra issued a decree convoking a Congress of delegates to reorganize the political system.

On August 15, 1839, the delegates assembled at Huancayo. A few days later they enacted a law announcing that the Constitution of 1834 was discarded. They declared that the acts of Santa Cruz and the measures taken by the assemblies of North and South Peru were null and void. On November 10, 1839, they adopted a new Constitution which in many particulars resembled the constitutions of 1828 and 1834. The term of office of the President, however, was extended to six years; he might not be reëlected until a presidential term had intervened. The Council of State was to be composed of fifteen members selected by Congress. Judges of the highest courts were to be selected by the chief executive from a list of nominees presented by that council. Gamarra, who had become a leader of the Peruvian nationalistic movement, was elected president. As elsewhere indicated, shortly afterward he led an army into Bolivia, but was defeated and killed at the battle of Ingavi.

In the civil strife that ensued among claimants for the presidency, who followed each other in rapid succession, the rising figure was Ramón Castilla, who had served under Sucre and fought at Ingavi. After defeating General Vivanco, who had **The Age of Castilla** proclaimed himself supreme director, Castilla was inaugurated president in April, 1845. An energetic and resolute ruler, he gave his native land tranquillity; for fifteen years he was virtually dictator. During his first presidential term, from 1845 to 1851, he promoted Peruvian progress in many ways. Though some political agitation took place in the southern provinces, no concerted uprising occurred against his government. He refrained from persecuting the partisans of Vivanco and even appointed some of them to office. He not only reorganized the army but also began the task of creating a navy composed of steamships. He took steps to systematize the administration of the nation's finances. Two years after he was inaugurated, a telegraph line was constructed between Callao and Lima; a few years later a railway was built between those cities.

Early in 1849 the government signed an important contract for the exploitation of the guano that had been discovered in the Chincha Islands. Soon four hundred thousand tons were being exported annually. The exploitation of vast beds of saltpeter in ravines of the province of Tarapacá became a thriving industry which brought a regular income to the Peruvians. About one million tons of nitrate were exported annually from southern Peru. Castilla was able to pay the interest on the debt which had been floated in London. He reorganized the internal debt. With those measures there occasionally went improvidence: some government offices were well-paid sinecures; various taxes were abolished; and the accounts of some branches of the fiscal administration were poorly kept. A speculative spirit became manifest.

In December, 1851, José Echenique, who had become president, announced that the civil code of Peru was to go into force in July, 1852. As corruption and extravagance in the government provoked discontent, Castilla came forward to lead a revolution. Early in July, 1854, he issued a decree abolishing the tribute that had been levied upon the Indians. In October he decreed the immediate emancipation of Negro slaves. After he had routed the soldiers of Echenique and had been elected president, those reforms were sanctioned by Congress.

The legislature also undertook to act as a Constituent Convention. In October, 1856, it adopted a new Constitution which, besides some exotic features, contained a clause abolishing ecclesiastical fueros. After a revolt at Arequipa had been suppressed by the indomitable Castilla, at his instance Congress made further alterations in the fundamental law. The constitutional charter which he promulgated on November 13, 1860, was thus a revised version of the Constitution of 1856.

The Peruvian Constitution of 1860 stipulated that Roman Catholicism should be professed and protected by the State, and that the public exercise of any other religion should not be per-

Constitution of 1860

mitted. Executive authority should be vested in a President elected by the people for four years. He was given the right to veto acts of a bicameral Congress. He was granted control of civil and ecclesiastical patronage and made commander in chief of the army and navy. He might negotiate treaties and admit papal rescripts. But the President might neither leave Peruvian territory nor assume personal command of the armed forces of the nation without the consent of the legislature. His ministers should be responsible to Congress: they were granted the right to attend its debates; they were to answer the interpellations of its members, but should withdraw before a vote was taken. Bills might be introduced into the legislature by the chief executive or by the supreme court, as well as by congressmen. Among the powers of Congress was the right to accept or to reject the resignation of the President and the right to declare war at his instance. A permanent commission composed of congressmen was to exercise certain powers when the legislature was not in session. Judicial authority was vested in a supreme court, superior courts, and justices of the peace.

This centralistic Constitution provided that the republic should be divided into departments and littoral provinces. The departments were subdivided into provinces; and the provinces were carved into districts. Prefects, selected by the President, should govern the departments and the littoral provinces.

By a bull of March 3, 1874, the Papacy recognized the practice which had been followed with regard to ecclesiastical appointments. Explaining his concession by the clause in the Constitution of Peru concerning religion, as well as by the jealous protection of Roman Catholicism by that state, the Pope granted to the President the right of making ecclesiastical appointments under the same conditions as those which had been enjoyed by the Spanish monarchs. This bull stipulated, however, that the property already assigned to the clergy and to the service of the Catholic faith should be conserved with fidelity, and that the Peruvian government should continue to favor and to protect the Roman Catholic religion.

In 1862 General San Román became president. He was soon succeeded by Vice-President Juan A. Pezet who had acted as secretary of war for Castilla. During Pezet's presidency serious difficulties arose with Spain, which had not yet acknowl- **The War with Spain** edged the independence of Peru. This delicate situation was aggravated by the fact that some Spanish citizens still had claims against her government because of alleged injuries during the war for independence. An occasion for a serious controversy was furnished in 1863 by a quarrel that occurred between Peruvians and Spaniards on the hacienda of Talambo. Shortly afterward a squadron under Admiral Pinzón, which had been sent from Spain ostensibly on a scientific expedition, anchored in the harbor of Callao. After a special agent of the Spanish government named Salazar y Mazaredo had failed to reach a satisfactory adjustment with the government of Pezet, he reëmbarked, and, by the aid of Admiral Pinzón seized the Chincha Islands. The acrimonious controversy seemed to be adjusted by a preliminary treaty of peace and friendship that was signed on January 27, 1865. According to this treaty Spain virtually acknowledged Peruvian independence and agreed to return the Chincha Islands. On her part, Peru promised to pay the Spanish claim for indemnity as well as the expenses of Pinzón's expedition.

This treaty was repudiated, however, by Peruvian public opinion, and Colonel Mariano Prado led an uprising in Arequipa against the government. After that revolution triumphed, Dictator Prado ruptured relations with Spain, and made alliances with Chile, Bolivia, and Ecuador against the motherland. During the ensuing war a naval battle took place near the Chiloé Islands between Spanish frigates and war vessels of the allies. Spanish forces attacked Valparaiso, blockaded certain ports of the allies, and in May, 1866, bombarded Callao. By the mediation of the United States an armistice was finally signed by the belligerent nations at Washington in 1871. At intervals during the years from 1871 to 1885 each of the allied nations signed a separate treaty of peace with Spain.

When the difficulties with Spain were in a fair way to be settled, Vice-President Canseco, who had returned from a visit to Europe, and Colonel José Balta reëstablished constitutional rule.

Guano, Loans, and Railroads
In 1868 Balta became president. A vigorous and resourceful leader, he found Peru burdened with a considerable debt. Furthermore, he lacked funds with which to promote internal improvements. In 1869 he accordingly made an important contract with Dreyfus and Company of Paris. Peru granted the firm a monopoly of the export of guano to the amount of 2,000,000 tons. Dreyfus not only agreed to pay that government 350,000 soles for the liquidation of a debt which it had incurred in 1865 but also a bonus of 650,000 soles per month during the delivery of the guano. In 1870 a new loan of 12,000,000 soles was negotiated in Europe; and two years later another loan was floated which funded the outstanding indebtedness,—thus Peru's foreign debt was augmented to more than 35,000,000 soles. With these funds the Peruvian government proceeded to improve harbors at Eten, Pisca, and Callao; it also subsidized foreign contractors to construct railroads.

In December, 1869, it signed a contract with an able and enterprising citizen of the United States named Henry Meiggs for the construction of a railroad up the steep grade from Callao to Oroya. As early as May, 1868, it had made a contract with Meiggs to subsidize the construction of a railroad from Arequipa to the Pacific Ocean which was opened in December, 1870. By other contracts Meiggs agreed to build railways in the Peruvian highlands from Arequipa to Puno and from Juliaca to Cuzco. Steps were thus taken to link the ancient home of the Incas to the Pacific Ocean.

Before those railroads were completed, President Balta had been deposed and murdered. In August, 1872, Manuel Pardo was inaugurated as president. Because of recent, enormous expenditures, Pardo found that the finances were demoralized. Still he arranged for the construction of two new ironclads. To promote economy, however, he reduced the size of the army. Pardo was succeeded by General Mariano Prado in 1876. During that year a contract was made for the disposal of guano which was not so favorable to Peru as the Dreyfus contract. In April, 1877, the government was constrained to issue 20,000,000 soles of inconvertible paper money.

Meanwhile, at Lima on February 6, 1873, Peru signed a secret treaty of defensive alliance with Bolivia. The Treaty of Lima provided that the contracting parties were mutually to guarantee their independence, sovereignty, and territorial integrity against all foreign aggression. In case of acts that tended to deprive one of the parties to this treaty of a portion of her territory, to induce a party to accept a protectorate, to lessen the sovereignty of a party, or to alter the existing government of a party, the alliance was to become effective. Each party expressly retained the right to judge for herself whether or not an offense that might be committed against her ally should be considered as a *casus fœderis*. Once the alliance had been declared effective, the parties agreed that all diplomatic and commercial relations should be broken off with the offending nation. Both allies promised to employ every possible conciliatory measure to prevent a rupture of relations or to end a war. Each party agreed not to sign any boundary treaty or other territorial adjustment without having notified the other party.

Alliance with Bolivia

When the controversy about the activities of Chileans in the desert of Atacama culminated in hostilities between Chile and Bolivia, this alliance led Peru to essay the rôle of a mediator. But the efforts of her diplomats were fruitless. On April 5, 1879, after Peru had declined to proclaim her neutrality in the conflict, the Chilean government which claimed to have been just informed of the secret treaty, declared war upon the allies.

Although the war nominally lasted from February, 1879, until April, 1884, the actual conflict by land and sea was brief. By the destruction of the Peruvian warship "Huascar" in October, 1879, Chile made herself mistress of the Pacific. As indicated in the preceding chapter, her soldiers soon overran the Peruvian provinces of Tarapacá, Tacna, and Arica, which were defended by soldiers of the allies. President Prado was replaced by Nicolás de Piérola, who had been secretary of the treasury. Attempts by the United States to mediate between the belligerent nations failed. On January 13, 1881, the Chilean army defeated Peruvian soldiers at Chorillos, near Callao. Two days later the invaders broke the second line of Peruvian defenses at Miraflores. Nicolás de Piérola, who had become dictator, fled from Lima, which was soon occupied by the exultant victors.

Chile Defeats the Allies

Chile terminated the war by the negotiation of separate conventions with the vanquished nations. At Ancón, on October 20, 1883, a treaty of peace and friendship was signed between Chile and Peru. By Article III of the Treaty of Ancón the vanquished party ceded to the victor the province of Tarapacá. That article continued as follows:

The Treaty of Ancón

The territory of the provinces of Tacna and Arica . . . shall continue in the possession of Chile, subject to Chilean legislation and authority for a period of ten years from the date of the ratification of the present treaty of peace. At the expiration of that term, a plebiscite will decide, by popular vote, whether the territory of the aforesaid provinces shall remain definitely under the dominion and sovereignty of Chile or is to continue a part of Peru. That country to which the provinces of Tacna and Arica remain annexed shall pay to the other country ten million pesos of Chilean silver or Peruvian soles of equal weight and fineness. A special protocol, which shall be considered an integral part of the present treaty, will determine the form in which the plebiscite is to be carried out and the terms and the time for the payment of the ten millions by the nation which remains the owner of the provinces of Tacna and Arica.

This article raised an issue concerning the sovereignty over those provinces. Unfortunately it contained no specifications in respect to the electorate that should participate in the referendum. Another article in the Treaty of Ancón provided that the Lobos Islands were to remain in the possession of Chile until one million tons of guano had been furnished; they were then to be returned to Peru. The net proceeds derived from the exploitation of the guano deposits during the Chilean occupation were to be divided between the contracting parties.

The War of the Pacific was a most significant event in South American history. Chile not only gained the extensive nitrate desert but also retained control of two adjacent provinces of southern Peru. Bolivia was deprived of valuable territory which contained her only seaports. Peru apparently lost one province irretrievably, and, for the time being at least, she waived the control of two other provinces. Indeed the War of the Pacific seemed to spell national collapse for Peru. On the other hand, Chile gained an outlet for her enterprise and capital by the acquisition of a domain that was rich in resources, a domain that she thought essential to her future security and the best pledge of a lasting peace. Certain Peruvians likened Tacna and Arica to Alsace-Lorraine.

Peruvian history after the Treaty of Ancón was in large part the story of recuperation and readjustment. The itinerant government of Miguel Iglesias, which negotiated that treaty, was overturned in December, 1885, by General Cáceres, who served as president from 1886 to 1890. During his presidency the foreign debt was funded and assumed by a group of European bondholders called the Peruvian Corporation. That corporation relieved Peru of all responsibility for her loans of 1869, 1870, and 1872: in return she ceded to it her railroads and guano deposits for sixty-six years. In 1889 a confidential agent was dispatched from Santiago to Lima to present a plan concerning the future of Tacna and Arica. He proposed that his government should pay Peru an indemnity of about one million pounds, while she was to cede the provinces to Chile at once. The Peruvian government declined to consider this proposition.

Cáceres was succeeded by Colonel Morales Bermúdez. He was the candidate of the Civil party which favored order and stability against militarism. During his administration other attempts were made to settle the fate of Tacna and Arica. In 1892 the government at Lima sent a special agent to Santiago with a proposal that his government would make cer- tain commercial concessions to Chile in return for the sovereignty over the lost provinces. Two years later Peru proposed the following bases for a protocol: the referendum should be taken under conditions acceptable to both governments; the nation securing the provinces was to pay the stipulated sum in bonds bearing interest at 4½ per cent; and the Chilean-Peruvian frontiers were to be rectified. When the ten-year period elapsed on March 28, 1894, however, no decision had been reached about the referendum.

The "Question of the Pacific"

It is worth while to notice the chief points of agreement and dis-agreement at that juncture. Chile and Peru had agreed that a refer-endum should be taken to determine the future nationality of the people of Tacna and Arica. Yet they could not agree as to who should administer the two provinces when the ten years had lapsed. The Peruvian government argued that Peru ought to be given control of them, while the Chilean government maintained that Chile should retain them: thus the disputants differed as to the nation that should direct the referendum. Peru wished the vote to be public; Chile wished it to be secret. Neither could they agree as to who should be permitted to participate in the proposed elections. Peru insisted that only native-born inhabitants of Tacna and Arica should vote. On the other side, Chile wished to allow all residents of those provinces to take part.

In 1898 by an exchange of telegrams the two nations nearly ap-proached a settlement of the moot points in the Billinghurst-La Torre Protocol. This virtually provided that the disputed points concerning the referendum should be submitted to the arbitration of the Queen of Spain. Ten million Chilean pesos or their equivalent should be paid to the loser within ten years by the nation securing the territory in dispute. This protocol was approved by Peru; it was sanctioned by the Senate of Chile; but her Chamber of Deputies rejected it, and suggested that the controversy should be adjusted by direct negotia-tions instead of by arbitration.

Meanwhile a transformation had taken place in Peruvian politics. The Democratic party, a radical group whose members sometimes entertained revolutionary doctrines, had changed its political princi-

ples. So far had it altered its views that in March, 1895, it secured the
support of members of the Civil party in a revolution led by Nicolás

Domestic
and Inter-
national
Issues

de Piérola which deposed the President. In September of
that year Piérola was elected to that office. An efficient
administrator, he promoted various fiscal and religious
reforms. During his presidency a series of steps was taken
that looked toward the adoption of the gold standard. Eventually a
law of December, 1897, authorized the mintage of a gold coin called
the *libra* which was to be of the same weight and value as the English
pound. In the same month a law was enacted providing that marriages
might be legally solemnized before civil magistrates; in 1899 it was
supplemented by a decree providing for the legalization of marriages
that had already been performed in Peru by evangelical ministers.
The Peruvian military academy was reorganized under the direction
of French officers. At Lima the construction of several important
public buildings was undertaken.

At this time political parties in Peru were the creatures of personal
politics. A publicist named Francisco García Calderon wrote concerning them in words that are more or less applicable to other Latin-
American states:

Peruvian political parties are unstable groups, formed at the suggestion of a
strong, directing personality. Theoretically they promise reforms in all phases
of national activity; they possess programs and aims, whether ambitious or
feeble; but, in reality, they are divided by personal hatreds, by different traditions, and by the partitions of habit. In the age of military leaders and of political chieftainship the prestige of personality was the only element of unity. Men
then created ephemeral and personal groups whose sole end was the rapid conquest of power. . . . With us political transformations depend upon the ambitions of the leaders; national problems are relegated to a secondary position as
compared with the immediate purposes of the parties' action.

Piérola was succeeded by Eduardo de Romaña in 1899. During his
term of office the Democratic party drew away from the Civil party.
The Democrats became outspoken opponents of the administration.
Capitalists in the United States took steps to mine the enormous
deposits of copper ore at Cerro de Pasco. With respect to Tacna and
Arica, Romaña declared that Peru could not agree to her "own dismemberment." Complications developed with Ecuador about the disputed boundary in the Mainas region. Under Miguel Candamo, who
was elected in 1903 by a combination of the followers of General
Cáceres, who were denominated Constitutionalists, and the Civil party,
a controversy arose with Brazil because of another unsettled boundary.

After José Pardo had become president following the death of
Candamo in 1904, fresh difficulties arose about Peru's boundaries.

Certain clauses of the treaty by which Bolivia definitively ceded the department of Atacama to Chile provoked a protest from the Peruvian government which declared that the provisions of that treaty could not diminish its rights to Tacna and Arica. Nevertheless the Chileans undertook to assimilate those provinces in various ways. They established schools, periodicals, courts, and military law in the province of Tacna, as they designated the territory in dispute. Their purpose was evidently to strengthen their interests in that region.

Peru naturally objected to this policy of Chileanization: she maintained that, in reality, Chile's possession of the territory was only temporary. As time passed Chile altered her contentions respecting Tacna. In November, 1908, soon after Augusto B. Leguía had succeeded Pardo, Chile's authorized spokesman declared that the referendum clause of the Treaty of Ancón was really a disguised cession; that, as she held dominion over the disputed territory, Chile had the right to direct the referendum; that, as Tacna was of vital importance to her northern frontier, she could not submit the disputed points to arbitration; and that she would be justified in abrogating the clause in the Treaty of Ancón providing for a referendum because an agreement concerning its execution was impossible.

Under Guillermo Billinghurst, a former mayor of Lima who became president in 1912, the condition of the aborigines in the extensive frontier region drained by the Putumayo River became the object of public solicitude. In that territory a Peruvian company that was financed mainly by English capital had been gathering rubber by the use of Huitoto Indians. Complaints about their treatment led to the appointment by President Leguía of a commissioner to investigate, and also to the dispatch by the English government of Roger Casement as consul to Peru. Congress protested against the English mission because it seemed to menace intervention. Yet, after that consul's report upon the Putumayo atrocities became known, the government took steps to improve the condition of the oppressed Indians.

Political discontent, which had been occasionally manifested under other presidents, reached a climax under Billinghurst whose arbitrary rule stimulated the disaffection. Rumors concerning his project for the settlement of the long-standing dispute **Revolution-ary Disturbances** with Chile about Tacna and Arica provoked suspicions that he was unduly favorable to that country. After the President had suspended the publication of a newspaper which served as the organ of the opposition and had arrested some prominent politicians, early on the morning of February 4, 1914, Colonel Benavides and other military leaders boldly seized Billinghurst, forced him to resign, and deported him to Chile. Despite the opposition of the Vice-

President, the provisional government which the revolutionists organized was promptly acknowledged by Peruvian authorities as legal. The leading nations of America soon extended diplomatic recognition to the Benavides régime.

As Peru was the heir of the viceroyalty of that name, she had many boundary difficulties. With Bolivia a grievous dispute developed because of conflicting claims to territory occupied by the Chuncha and Moxo Indians. In 1902 Peru and Bolivia agreed to a treaty which provided that this controversy should be submitted to the arbitration of Argentina upon the express condition that she should confirm Bolivia's title to any territory over which the audiencia of Charcas had exercised jurisdiction. When the Argentine President divided the disputed territory between the two neighbors, Bolivia strenuously protested, declared that the award was not according to the terms of the treaty of arbitration, and refused to accept the limits which had been sketched. In 1909 a treaty between the contending parties readjusted this boundary more to Bolivia's satisfaction, and provided for its exact delimitation. Posts were later set up along this boundary line.

Conditions about 1914: Boundary Disputes

Peru's long-standing controversy with Brazil was settled by a treaty signed on September 8, 1909. By that treaty Peru acknowledged the jurisdiction of Brazil over certain portions of the territory of Acre. Further, Peru recognized Brazilian sovereignty over other territory which she had also claimed. Between the two parties this treaty drew a jagged boundary line that stretched in a northwesterly direction from the river Acre to the Yavarí River. Peru's disputes concerning boundaries with Ecuador and Colombia will be considered in connection with the history of those countries.

Immigration from other countries than Spain has played a small part in Peruvian development. Though some Germans and Italians settled in Peru, the main European element in her population remained the Spanish. Negroes and persons of Negro descent were found in her coastal valleys. About the middle of the nineteenth century Oriental immigration to Peru began. It has been estimated that between 1861 and 1872 some 58,000 Chinese landed on Peruvian soil. They ordinarily came under contracts to serve as laborers for a term of years. As certain publicists saw a danger in Chinese immigration, in 1873 the Peruvian Congress passed a law which stipulated that such contracts should be registered in Peru and enforced. In 1893 a law was enacted providing that free transportation, agricultural tools, and grants of land should be offered to European immigrants to Peru. As the immigration of laborers from China eventually became a serious problem, in May,

Social and Economic Conditions

1909, the government issued a decree prohibiting the entrance of Chinese who had less than five hundred libras in cash.

A careful Peruvian scholar named Alejandro Garland calculated that in 1906 Peru's population was about 3,500,000 souls. According to his calculations the most densely populated region was the Andean plateau, while the most thinly settled area was the tropical, trans-Andean forest. Garland estimated that in 1906 the population was composed of the following elements: aborigines, 50 per cent; whites, chiefly of Spanish descent, 15 per cent; Negroes, 2½ per cent; Chinese and Japanese, 1 per cent; and "various ethnic crossbreeds," 31½ per cent. In 1914 the population was probably over 4,000,000. Though Spanish was the language of the educated classes in Peru, Indian dialects were used by the majority of her people. Many Peruvians spoke the language that had been imposed by the conquering Incas.

By a law of December 27, 1896, with certain exceptions, Peruvian male citizens from nineteen to fifty years of age were made liable for military service. Ten years later the actual size of the regular army was about four thousand men. In 1914 the Peruvian navy included about a dozen warships.

The chief occupation in Peru was agriculture. Scattered through the coastal region were numerous plantations of cotton and sugar cane. Cereals and potatoes were raised on the Andean plateau. Cacao, coffee, and crude rubber were the chief products of the wooded eastern slopes of the Andes. Very few minerals were not found in Peru. Peruvian miners were the Indians of the mountains; the capital and the managerial talent for the development of the mines were generally furnished by foreigners. A few factories of cotton and woolen goods had been established at Arequipa and Lima; other manufactures were beverages, cigars, cigarettes, chocolate, and "Panama hats."

Official statistics show that in 1914 Peru exported animal products which amounted to 750,518 libras. The three most important items in that category were the wool of sheep, alpaca wool, and various kinds of hides. In 1914 Peru exported vegetable products which amounted to 4,894,699 libras, the most valuable items being sugar, cotton, rubber, rice, cacao, and straw hats. In that year Peru exported mineral products, largely copper and silver, which amounted to 3,073,865 libras.

Certain parts of the country were in communication with the Atlantic by steam vessels which plied the upper affluents of the Amazon. A Peruvian steamship company furnished regular service between Callao and Panama. Unfortunately Peru had no longitudinal railroad. She had two great trans-Andean lines: one that ran from Mollendo to Lake Titicaca, and thence to Cuzco; and the other that ran from Callao to Oroya, and thence to Cerro de Pasco. The ownership of those railways was in large part. vested in the Peruvian government. Because of the lofty cordilleras the cost of transporting freight by land between certain sections of Peru was enormous. In the Andean region the llama was still the common beast of burden. On the elevated plateau that was once the seat of Inca culture llamas and Indians were still the agents of transportation.

Primary education in Peru, originally in the hands of local authorities, had been taken over by the national government. Secondary
Education   education was placed under the direct control of the secretary of public instruction, justice, and religion. A law of 1901 authorized two different types of secondary schools, the academy and the lyceum. The academy was intended to be preparatory to higher education, while the lyceum was designed to prepare pupils for the practical arts, as agriculture, mining, commerce, and mechanical industry.

Higher education was carried on in four universities and in other national institutions. Among the latter were an engineering school, an agricultural college, and a school of industrial arts. By the law of 1901 Peruvian universities were divided into two classes, namely major and minor. Minor universities, which were to be composed of at least two colleges, were located at Arequipa, Cuzco, and Trujillo. The only major university was the renowned University of San Marcos at Lima which had six colleges: theology, jurisprudence, medicine, philosophy and letters, mathematics and natural sciences, and political and administrative sciences.

Peru has a literature that is rich and varied. Mariano Melgar introduced the melancholy note of the Indian into her poetry. In three
Literature   comedies Felipe Pardo depicted society in the ancient
and Art   capital of the Peruvian viceroyalty; and in a satirical newspaper called *Espejo de mi tierra* he ridiculed Castilla's attempts at democratic reform. A dozen comedies that dealt mainly with the life and manners of Peru were written by Manuel A. Segura. *Al Misti* by Manuel Castillo of Arequipa was a poetic tribute to the wonderful mountain that towers above his native city. Pedro Paz Soldán y Unanue, a versatile poet who subscribed himself "Juan de Arona," seemed equally at home describing Peruvian birds and flowers in *Ruinas,* mocking the achievements of Admiral Pinzón in *La Pinzonada,* and depicting the Peruvian environment in *Cuadros y episodios peruanos. La epopeya del Morro,* in which José Santos Chocano chanted about the heroism of his compatriots during the siege of Arica by Chilean soldiers, made him a favorite poet of the Peruvian nation. From verse Ricardo Palma passed into prose in 1863 with the publication of the first volumes of his *Tradiciones Peruanos.* The best

work of fiction was perhaps Florinda Matto de Turner's *Aves sin nido*, a novel describing the servile life of Peruvian Indians.

Among the writers of Peru since 1821 two historians deserve the highest rank: Manuel de Mendiburu and Mariano Paz Soldán. In his voluminous *Historical and Biographical Dictionary of Peru* Mendiburu produced an encyclopedic work of profound learning. A documented work of a serious type was Paz Soldán's *History of Independent Peru* and also his *War of Chile against Peru and Bolivia*. Two illuminating volumes about Peruvian literature were composed by José de la Riva Agüero: one describes in narrative fashion the *Character of the Literature of Independent Peru;* the other entitled *History in Peru,* is an instructive account of Peruvian historiography which contains original interpretations.

Modern Peruvians have combined some features of Inca architecture and Spanish colonial architecture into a style that has been designated neo-Peruvian. Among Peru's prominent artists should be named Teofilo Castillo, who painted some fine pictures of an historical character. Perhaps his finest existing canvas is that which depicts "A Saint's Day Procession in the Olden Times." Prominent among the musicians of Peru was Valle Riestra, who composed several operas. The most widely known of these works was probably "Ollanta," which was based upon the music of the Andean aborigines.

Benavides was still provisional president when the first World War began. Early in August, 1914, the government declared a moratorium for thirty days. Shortly after José Pardo became president, international complications threatened to involve Peru in the struggle. The announcement of an unrestricted submarine policy by Germany reached Lima at a critical juncture. A Peruvian bark named the "Lorton" had just been torpedoed by a German submarine near the Spanish coast. On February 10, 1917, Peru's secretary of foreign relations accordingly protested against Germany's submarine policy and declared that it was contrary to international law. In October, 1917, he proposed to Congress that diplomatic relations with Germany should be severed. After an animated debate, the proposal was approved on October 5 by a vote of 105 to 6. On the following day the German minister was given his passports.

After his reëlection in August, 1919, Augusto B. Leguía became a dominant personality in Peruvian politics. A versatile business man who had fought bravely against the Chilean invaders at Miraflores, his political life began in 1903 when he was appointed minister of finance. In May, 1908, he had been dragged from the governmental palace and menaced with death unless he would resign the presidencey. Shortly

after his term expired he was driven into exile in England. Upon returning to his native land in February, 1919, he was received with
enthusiasm, re-elected president, and swept into office by
a revolutionary coup. He soon became a leader of those
reformers who felt that the Constitution of 1860 no longer
embodied national aspirations.

Leguía Becomes Dictator

On July 22, 1919, he submitted for popular approval a project for
constitutional reform. As the proposal was approved at elections, a
National Assembly met on September 24 to amend the fundamental
law. The Constitution of 1860 served as a basis for the work of the
convention: more than two-thirds of the new Constitution was taken
verbatim from it.

This Constitution declared that only the State had the right to
establish monopolies, that disputes between capital and labor must be
arbitrated, and that indemnities must be paid to workmen for accidents incurred while engaged in their respective occupations. It provided for a graduated income tax.
It prohibited the issue of irredeemable paper money except when the
nation was involved in a foreign war. With regard to the ownership
of property, aliens were declared to have the same rights and privileges
as Peruvians. The state was to protect the aborigines and to promote
their development.

Constitution of 1920

Though the Peruvian Constitution of 1920 allowed the administrative subdivisions that had been sanctioned in 1860 to persist, it altered
the system of government. A cabinet member might participate in
congressional debates. He could not remain in office, however, after
either house of the legislature had expressed a lack of confidence in
him. Congress was granted the right to sanction annually a budget for
the ensuing year. The initiative in laws concerning the judiciary was
accorded to the supreme court which was given supervision over all
the judicial tribunals of the nation. A peculiar innovation was the
provision that there should be local legislatures in the north, the center,
and the south of Peru. Those legislatures, which were to be composed
of deputies elected by the respective sections, might frame regulations
concerning local affairs. Such measures must, however, be transmitted
to the President; if he considered them contrary to national laws or
inimical to the public welfare, he was to submit them to Congress
for adoption or rejection. This concession to sectionalism seemed to
concede to regional legislatures the right to initiate laws for the nation.
The Constitution of 1920 declared that "the nation professes the
Roman Catholic Apostolic faith and the state protects it." It also
provided that the President should exercise "ecclesiastical patronage in
accordance with the laws and present practices." By and with the

consent of Congress, the President could refuse to allow the promulgation of papal bulls, rescripts, and letters.

A law promulgated on February 5, 1921, placed all branches of education under the department of public instruction. In April, 1922, after having been closed by the government for about a year, the University of San Marcos was recognized under the new education law as a private institution. Soon afterward the President created a commission for the protection and uplifting of the aborigines. In 1922 because of a loan made to the republic the Guaranty Trust Company of New York was conceded a first option on future loans. In the same year Congress amended the Constitution so as to permit Leguía to become a candidate for reëlection in 1924.

Meanwhile the President of the United States had suggested that Peru and Chile should try to settle the Tacna-Arica Controversy by direct negotiations. In 1922 the ministers of these two nations at Washington agreed to submit the differences arising from the nonfulfillment of Article III of the Treaty of Ancón to the United States President for arbitration. The pleas of the two parties were submitted to the arbiter on November 13, 1923. The Chilean brief argued for a referendum to decide whether Tacna and Arica should belong to Chile or to Peru. The Peruvian brief pleaded that changed conditions had made a plebiscite "impractical and unfair," that for practical purposes the plebiscite might be regarded as having been decided against Chile, and that Peru, having been wrongfully deprived of her territory for thirty years, should be conceded an indemnity.

Arbitration in the Tacna-Arica Controversy

In March, 1925, President Coolidge announced his decision. With regard to the boundaries of the disputed territory, he upheld the contention of Peru in respect to the northern boundary, but referred the question of the southern boundary to a special commission for a report concerning the old Peruvian interprovincial boundary lines. The most important clause in the award stipulated that the plebiscite should be held under the supervision of a commission consisting of one Peruvian, one Chilean, and a citizen of the United States appointed by Coolidge. Natives of Tacna-Arica, nationals of the contending countries of at least two years' continuous residence there, and resident foreigners eligible for naturalization were all to be allowed to vote. The citizens of Santiago de Chile were much pleased with the decision, for they considered it a vindication of their country's conduct during the controversy. Peruvians were profoundly dissatisfied; popular demonstrations against the verdict were made in front of the American legation at Lima.

President Coolidge soon appointed General Pershing as the presiding

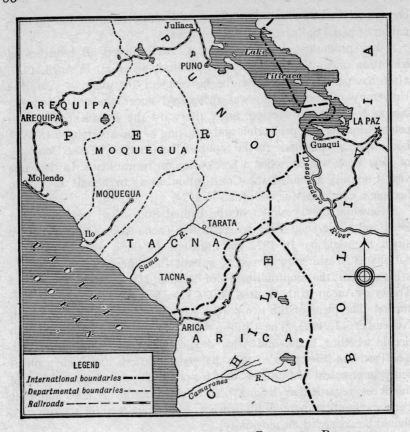

MAP SHOWING THE BOUNDARY BETWEEN CHILE AND PERU DRAWN
BY THE TREATY OF 1929

(Adapted from the special Tacna-Arica number of the *West Coast Leader*)

member of the plebiscitary commission. Early in August, 1925, it met
at Arica to work out the practical details of the plebiscite. The progress
of the commission was often hindered by the objections of one or
another party to rules promulgated by the majority of the commission.
Events proved that it had no power to control the conditions attendant upon the existence of a Chilean government in Tacna-Arica.
Convinced that a fair referendum could not be arranged, General
Pershing relinquished his task. In June, 1926, General Lassiter, who
succeeded Pershing, stated that Peruvians in Tacna-Arica were being
terrorized, that the commission was powerless to secure a just plebiscitary expression of the will of the people, and that in consequence it
had decided that a referendum should not be held. The Chilean government protested against the grounds upon which Lassiter based his

views, but expressed its willingness to coöperate for an amicable adjustment.

Even before the attempt to arbitrate the Tacna-Arica Controversy had failed, United States Secretary of State Kellogg had suggested that Chile and Peru should try to reach an adjustment by direct negotiations. In the autumn of 1928, the parties resumed diplomatic relations, which had been severed for seventeen years. On May 14, 1929, President Hoover submitted through the American ministers at Lima and Santiago a proposal suggesting a settlement founded upon tentative agreements which had been reached between the two parties. On May 15 and 16 the governments of Chile and Peru respectively accepted the proposal.

On June 3, 1929, in the presence of the American Minister at Lima, a treaty was signed between Chile and Peru that ended the controversy over the lost provinces. This treaty provided that Tacna-Arica was to be divided into two portions: Tacna was to become the property of Peru, while Arica should remain in the possession of Chile. The boundary between the two neighbors was to be drawn by a mixed commission. Further, Chile was to construct at her own cost in the Bay of Arica a steamship pier, a customs building, and a terminal railway station for the service of Peru whose commerce should enjoy there all the independence pertaining to a free port. Upon the exchange of the ratifications of this treaty, Chile was to relinquish all the real estate or buildings of state ownership in Tacna. In addition, she was to pay Peru $6,000,000. The acrimonious dispute arising out of Article III of the Treaty of Ancón was thus settled by mutual concessions concerning provinces that were not worth a war.

Division of the Disputed Territory

But this compromise displeased some Peruvians who stigmatized it as the mutilation of their country. Though Leguía had been responsible for the revision of the Constitution, the creation of a new Lima, and the modernization of the country in various ways, he was bitterly criticized. He was attacked because of the increase in the national debt and was accused of favoring foreign financiers. The dictator rudely suppressed the opposition by journalists and statesmen. Many prominent leaders fled into exile or were confined on an island near Callao. On August 22, 1930, the garrison at Arequipa revolted under a brave and energetic colonel named Luis Sánchez Cerro. The insurrection spread into other parts of southern Peru. Leguía's cabinet then resigned. On August 24, 1930, a military junta at Lima compelled the President to relinquish his authority. When Colonel Sánchez Cerro arrived in the capital by airplane on August 27, he was recognized by the junta as provisional president.

Revolution of 1930

The former dictator was confined on board a warship; a Peruvian historian thus described his downfall:

This powerful man, the most powerful and influential of all the presidents of Peru, he who was adulated the most: he who accomplished the greatest works; he who raised up a large number of protégés—this man, who was genuinely strong, was left alone, almost deserted, in the bitter hour of his downfall. Abandoned by sycophants, ill beyond hope of recovery, Leguía fell. With incorruptible guards at the gates of his prison, he was like a wild beast in a corral!

Though an era of Peruvian history was thus dramatically brought to a close, economic and political unrest did not cease. In October, 1931, elections arranged by a provisional junta resulted in the choice of Sánchez Cerro as president. On March 29, 1933, a Constituent Congress promulgated a new fundamental law which retained the administrative divisions outlined in 1860, but prohibited the immediate reëlection of the President. With regard to religion and the patronage, it repeated the clauses in the Constitution of 1920. It made no mention of the regional legislatures created at that time. The councils in the departments, however, were accorded administrative functions. Besides, provision was made for municipal councils in the provincial capitals. This Constitution also provided that communities of aborigines should be given legal recognition.

Soon after this fundamental law was promulgated, a fanatical youth mortally wounded the President. As his successor, on April 30, 1933, Congress selected General Benavides, who was supported by the army. Opposition to his rule mainly centered in a mysterious revolutionary party known as *Apra* (*Alianza Popular Revolucionaria Americana*) which for many years had been a peculiar factor in Peruvian politics. Among other pleas in its program, it advocated restrictions on the use of foreign capital, the nationalization of land and industry, an improvement in the lot of the oppressed aborigines, and joint action by Latin-American nations in matters of common interest. An underground party in Peru, it had partisans in foreign lands.

The Apristas: Inter-American Diplomacy

Among measures of the dictator which partly offset the Aprista program were the following: the maintenance of public order, the reduction of certain imposts, the construction of model homes for laborers, and the building of roads and other important public works. In addition, arrangements were made for a new census, aërial armament was improved, a new civil code was promulgated, a fundamental statute was formulated for the University of San Marcos, and a boundary dispute with Colombia was adjusted.

In April, 1939, Benavides issued a "decree-law" arranging for general elections. Apparently the Apristas did not take part in this campaign. On October 22 Manuel Prado Ugarteche, a banker and professor who belonged to an aristocratic family, was elected president. On December 9, 1939, he was inaugurated for a term of five years. As he was considered the successor of Benavides the attitude of his administration toward existing political alignments became an important issue. In March, 1940, both houses of Congress approved a motion which declared that, unless amended or repealed, all decree-laws of the Benavides régime were to remain in force. An influential leader of the Apristas named Manuel Seoane, who was living in exile, published a significant book entitled *Our America and the War* which marked a departure from the conventional tenets of his party. Omitting the usual Aprista denunciation of Yankee imperialism, he expressed the view that the triumph of totalitarianism over democracy in the second World War would be a universal catastrophe. Further, he not only advocated that the Latin-American nations should form a union to promote their economic, political, and military collaboration in this war but also that they should negotiate an alliance with the United States. After the Japanese attack on Pearl Harbor, Peru granted non-belligerent rights to the government at Washington.

In January, 1942, Peru severed relations with the Axis powers. On May 7 following the Peruvian secretary of finance signed a reciprocal trade agreement with Secretary of State Hull. This was the last of a series of important agreements between Peru and the United States. Among other stipulations, these conventions provided that the Peruvian government would promote the gathering of wild rubber in Amazonia, that the United States would furnish a credit of $25,000,000 to the central bank of Peru for the purchase of American equipment for public works, that the Commodity Credit Corporation would buy all the Peruvian surplus cotton for the duration of the war, that Peru would aid the United States to enforce her Black List, that the American government would give expert advice in such matters as the founding of an agricultural experiment station, and that reciprocal tariff concessions would be granted by both parties on many articles. To crown these important agreements President Prado soon made a voyage to the United States—the first visit that a South American president had made to that country while in office. After President Vargas declared the existence of a state of war with Germany and Italy, the Peruvian government granted non-belligerent rights to Brazil.

Peru set out upon her independent career with a social organization that was fundamentally aristocratic. Such a tendency has been displayed in her political and social life from that time until the present day. This tendency has been encouraged by the fact that some of the most important Peruvian industries have been of such a character as to foster undemocratic organization. The existence of large plantations, of extensive guano deposits, and of mines of copper and silver which have been exploited by semi-servile labor has encouraged a hierarchical arrangement of society. Of this politicians have not been slow to take advantage. Peruvian constitutions have abounded in abstract conceptions of liberty and democracy that have been entertained but not always practiced by the framers of those constitutions. In Peru, as in Bolivia, the hewers of wood and the drawers of water have been the aborigines or their descendants. To supplement the Indians there have come to Peru in recent decades immigrants from the Orient who have mainly settled in coastal towns and cities. The clew to recent Peruvian history is to be found in the sustained attempt that has been made to recuperate from the losses due to the disastrous War of the Pacific. A promising sign in Peruvian politics has been the appearance of an assertive proletariat that is profoundly dissatisfied with its political and social heritage. In 1930 Peru was seized with the throes of a change that seemed to promise a much larger participation of her people in the government. Perhaps the most significant development since that time has been a rapprochement with the United States.

SUGGESTIONS FOR FURTHER READING

BINGHAM, H., *Inca Land,* 1922.

BOWMAN, I., *The Andes of Southern Peru,* 1916.

DENNIS, W. J., *Tacna and Arica,* 1931.

DUFFIELD, A. J., *Peru in the Guano Age,* 1877.

DUNN, W. E., *Peru: A Commercial and Industrial Handbook,* 1925.

ENOCK, C. R., *The Andes and the Amazon,* 1907.

———, *Peru,* 1910.

GÁLVEZ, J. I., *Peru Against Colombia, Ecuador, and Chile,* 1920.

GARLAND, A., *Peru in 1906 and After,* 1908.

HARDENBURG, W. E., *The Putumayo, the Devil's Paradise,* 1912.

HUTCHINSON, T. J., *Two Years in Peru, with Explorations of Its Antiquities,* Vol. I, 1873.

MARTIN, P. F., *Peru of the Twentieth Century,* 1911.

MAÚRTUA, V. M., *The Question of the Pacific,* 1901.

NILES, B., *Peruvian Pageant,* 1937.

PARKER, W. B. (ed.), *Peruvians of Today,* 1919.

PLATT, R. S., "Six Farms in the Central Andes," *Geographical Review,* Vol. XXII, pp. 245-259.

"South America II: Peru," *Fortune,* Vol. XVII, No. 1, pp. 49 ff.

SQUIER, E. G., *Peru, Incidents of Travel and Exploration in the Land of the Incas,* 1877.

STUART, G. H., *The Governmental System of Peru,* 1925.

VIVIAN, E. C., *Peru: Physical Features, Natural Resources, Means of Communication, Manufactures. and Industrial Development,* 1914.

CHAPTER XIX

NEW GRANADA OR COLOMBIA

The history of New Granada or Colombia, as that state is now called, springs from "Great Colombia,"—the nation that was formed during the heroic age of South American history by the union of the provinces in New Granada with those in Quito and Venezuela. A Constitution adopted for Great Colombia by the Congress of Cúcuta in 1821 vested executive authority in a President who should hold his office for four years, who might be reëlected only once without an intermission, and who, in a crisis, was to have absolute power. In case the President acted as commander in chief of the army, his civil functions should devolve upon the Vice-President. The Congress of Cúcuta also enacted some reformatory laws: it made Bogotá the capital of the state, abolished the slave trade, and declared that the children born of slaves should be free. Not only was the tribute levied upon aborigines swept away, but they were declared to be upon the same status as other citizens of the republic. On September 7, 1821, Congress elected Bolívar president. He accepted on condition that he should be allowed to remain in command of the army, while the chief civil authority should be exercised by Vice-President Francisco de Paula Santander, an able and aspiring native of the former viceroyalty.

Accordingly, from 1822 to 1826, while Bolívar was liberating the presidency of Quito and the viceroyalty of Peru, Vice-President Santander acted as the Colombian President. In 1823 Congress authorized the negotiation of a loan of thirty thousand pesos in Europe. During the following year it sanctioned treaties of confederation which Joaquín Mosquera had negotiated with Peru and Chile. It divided the territory of the republic into twelve departments, which were subdivided into provinces and cantons. In June, 1824, it enacted a law providing that the boundary line between the department of Cauca and the department of Ecuador should be the Carchi River.

In 1826 a serious accusation was brought before Congress against General Páez, commandant-general of two Venezuelan departments, namely, that he had ordered soldiers forcibly to conscript men. Despite the advice of Santander, who urged that the accused general should be heard in his own defense, Congress arbitrarily suspended him from

335

his command. As a result the discontent which had been provoked in Venezuela by the choice of Bogotá as the capital of the republic was

Internal
Dissensions

intensified. Spurred on by dissatisfied Venezuelans, in May that general openly rebelled against the government. At the instance of the municipal council of Valencia, he assumed the command from which he had been suspended. When he heard of this rebellion, Bolívar left Peru for Colombia; he arrived at Bogotá on November 14, 1826, whence he soon departed for Venezuela. At Puerto Cabello on January 1, 1827, he published a decree of amnesty which announced that Páez was restored to his command. That general responded not only by acknowledging the authority of Bolívar but also by revoking an invitation which he had issued for the convocation of an assembly of Venezuelan delegates at Valencia.

Still, the republic which Bolívar had founded was torn by factions. Certain Colombians evidently thought that a solution for their political ills would be to acclaim the Liberator as Emperor. Though he did not publicly favor that project, which was suggested to him several times, he was not loath to assume dictatorial power. Upon his return to Bogotá, in February, 1828, he issued decrees announcing that he was invested with extraordinary authority in certain portions of the republic, and declaring that he would also retain the exercise of his regular powers. Bolívar thus deprived Santander of the functions which he had for some time exercised. In April, 1828, delegates, who had been convoked by Congress, assembled at Ocaña in order to revise the Constitution. At the Convention of Ocaña the partisans of Bolívar could make no adjustment with their opponents, who were followers of his rival, Santander. Eventually some delegates even walked out of the Convention, which was soon dissolved.

On the night of September 25, 1828, an unsuccessful attempt was made by political enemies to assassinate Bolívar, who was almost alone in the national palace. Suspicion fell upon Santander, who was tried and condemned to death; this penalty was, however, commuted into exile. In November, 1829, an assembly at Caracas resolved that Venezuela should separate from Colombia. In a rare pamphlet attributed to Bolívar, which was published in the city of Quito, this despairing sentiment was expressed: "There is no faith in America; neither among men nor among nations: their treaties are paper; their constitutions are books, their elections are combats: liberty is anarchy; and life is a torment."

A Constituent Congress which he had convoked at Bogotá tried to prevent the disruption of the republic. In April, 1830, it framed a new fundamental law. The Constitution of 1830 stated that Colombia comprised the provinces formerly included in the captaincy general of

Venezuela and the viceroyalty of New Granada. Though retaining, in general, the existing political framework, it contained some innovations. It created a Council of State which was to serve as an advisory body to the President. It declared that Roman Catholicism was the religion of the republic, and that in the exercise of the patronage of the Colombian Church, the government was to protect the Catholic religion and not to tolerate the public worship of any other faith. Apparently as a concession to the spirit of sectionalism, the Constitution granted to each department the privilege of holding an assembly that could enact local and municipal ordinances and could represent the respective department in matters concerning the general interests of the republic. Yet the administration of the departments was left to prefects who were to be appointed by the national government.

Colombia's Constitution of 1830

On March 1, 1830, Bolívar relinquished the presidency. Weary and disillusioned, on December 17, 1830, he died at Santa Marta of pulmonary consumption. Even before he expired, Colombia had broken into three fragments. In January, 1830, General Páez had invited a convention of delegates from the former captaincy general of Venezuela to meet in April at Valencia. In August of the same year a movement for the separation of the former presidency of Quito from Colombia culminated in a convention of delegates from its provinces at Riobamba; thus the state of Ecuador began to emerge. In November, 1831, a convention at Bogotá announced that the central provinces of Colombia constituted a state designated New Granada. Further, it declared that those provinces would assume their proportionate share of the debt incurred by Great Colombia during the protracted wars for independence.

Disruption of Great Colombia

On February 29, 1832, this convention adopted a new fundamental law. The first "Constitution of the State of New Granada" vested executive authority in a President who was to be chosen for four years by electoral assemblies and who might not be reëlected until four years had elapsed. It provided that the President's cabinet should be composed of three members. Judicial authority was vested in a supreme court and in district tribunals. The territory of the republic was carved into provinces, which were to be composed of cantons. Each province was to be administered by a governor who should serve as the agent of the national administration.

After the Constitution had been framed, the convention elected as president General Santander, who returned from exile and assumed authority on October 7, 1832. In a proclamation which he issued to his fellow countrymen the President expressed his intention to govern in accordance with the Constitution and the laws. A conspiracy against the government led by General Sardá was ruthlessly suppressed.

On December 23, 1834, representatives of Venezuela and New Granada signed an agreement for the division of the debt of "Great Colombia." It provided that 50 per cent of the debt **President Santander** should be paid by New Granada, 28½ per cent by Venezuela, and the remainder by Ecuador. The same negotiators signed a treaty of amity, alliance, commerce, and limits which provided that the *uti possidetis* of 1810 should be the determining principle in respect to the boundary between New Granada and Venezuela. As Venezuela refused to approve the treaty, a dispute soon arose between the parties about their limits. Congress adopted a new coat of arms and a national flag. By various measures Santander promoted education, science, and art. He reëstablished the National Academy which aimed to increase and to diffuse knowledge. A scholar named Joaquín Acosta was placed in charge of the astronomical observatory at Bogotá.

During Santander's presidency political factions appeared in New Granada. A party composed of his followers maintained that the country needed a military man as president. On the other hand, a moderate group of the Civil party supported as a candidate for the presidency José de Márquez, an able and conciliatory statesman. Another party was composed of Bolívar's disciples who were sometimes denominated Bolivarians. Aided by them, the Civil party elected Márquez as president; he was inaugurated on April 1, 1837. In 1839 a decree that suppressed certain monasteries provoked an insurrection in the province of Pasto, which proved to be the beginning of a series of desolating and fratricidal civil wars.

The republic was not pacified until after Pedro A. Herrán, who commanded the government forces against the rebels, was elected president in 1842. A significant result of the internecine strife **Constitution of 1843** was a conviction on the part of some statesmen that their Constitution did not confer sufficient authority upon the national government. Prominent among such thinkers was José R. Mosquera, who presented to Congress a project of a new fundamental law. After some discussion, Congress adopted the "Political Constitution of the Republic of New Granada" which was promulgated on April 20, 1843. The Constitution of 1843 increased the power and influence of the President, who was given the right to appoint and remove national officers. The Council of State was virtually replaced by a council of government made up of the Vice-President and the secretaries of state. Those secretaries were not only given the right to introduce bills into Congress but also to participate in its discussions.

In 1845 Tomás Mosquera, an imperious military hero who had served under Bolívar, became president. Of him it has been said that he first came to power because of the support of a party which desired peace and progress. From 1845 to 1849 he promoted material development in many ways. He initiated negotiations with French engineers for the construction of a railroad across the Isthmus of Panama. In 1846 he negotiated with the United States a commercial treaty which contained significant stipulations. By Article XXXV of the Treaty of 1846 New Granada guaranteed to the United States and her citizens the right of transit across the Isthmus. In return the United States guaranteed to New Granada "the perfect neutrality" of the Isthmus of Panama and her "rights of property and sovereignty" over it. The President vigorously strove to improve his country's finances: at his instance Congress passed laws which reformed the monetary system; colonial and foreign moneys that had been in circulation were replaced by national currency. On April 28, 1847, a law was enacted which prohibited the importation of slaves into the republic and which declared that all slaves who had been introduced should be set free. A democratic clique came into existence which styled itself the Liberal party, while Mosquera's supporters were ordinarily called Conservatives.

The presidency of General José H. López, a soldier of the revolution who became chief magistrate in 1849, was a period of radical reform. Incited by the Liberals, on May 21, 1850, the President ordered that the Jesuits should be expelled **The Liberals in Power** from the republic. In the same year López made a contract with the Italian geographer, Agostino Codazzi, for a geographical survey of the country. As a climax to a series of measures that aimed to ameliorate the condition of Negro slaves, on May 21, 1851, a law was enacted which stipulated that all slaves in New Granada should be free after January 1, 1852. A law of April, 1852, announced that her rivers should be open to navigation by merchant vessels of foreign nations. A year later, General Obando, the candidate of a Liberal faction, was installed as president. On May 20, 1853, Congress adopted a Constitution which embodied legal and political doctrines of the dominant political party.

The Constitution of 1853 stated that all persons born on the soil of New Granada were citizens of that country. It declared that, except in times of war, private property should not be taken for public use without compensation. It promised to all citizens the free exercise of any religion they might profess, provided that they did not disturb the public peace, offend morals, or interfere with the religious practices of others. It guaranteed the free expression of thought and absolute liberty of the press. Jury trial was guaranteed in certain criminal cases. Slavery was prohibited. The right to vote was conceded to every citizen.

This Constitution stipulated that municipal authority should be reserved to the provinces. The power of the national government was also reduced by a provision that the provincial governors should be elected by popular vote. Further, each province was granted the power to make arrangements for its own administration. Article XXVII made possible the amendment of the Constitution by the action of two successive congresses.

In June, 1853, Congress enacted laws which embodied the ideal that Church and State should be completely separated. Dissensions between political parties became so bitter, however, that in April, 1854, Congress was dissolved by revolutionists, and the President was imprisoned. That Œdipus of Granadian history was soon accused of treason and deprived of his magistracy. He was succeeded by Vice-President Manuel Mallarino, whose administration opened auspiciously. On January 28, 1855, the first railroad train crossed the Isthmus of Panama.

During the same year Congress adopted a constitutional amendment which purported to introduce the federal system into New Granada. The "Granadian Confederation" This amendment not only provided that the Isthmus of Panama should be a federal state but it also declared that any other province of New Granada might be similarly transformed. In 1856 and 1857 laws were enacted which created other federal states. Under President Mariano Ospina, who was inaugurated on April 1, 1857, Congress reorganized the governmental system by the adoption of a new Constitution for the republic which was now styled the "Granadian Confederation." That Constitution was promulgated on May 22, 1858; it transformed a unitary-federal nation composed of eight states into a Confederation. The states were declared to have all powers which by the Constitution were not delegated to the confederate government. Strange though it may seem, the powers of that government were not defined. Both the national government and the state governments were prohibited from performing certain acts.

Shortly after this Constitution went into operation, a law providing for the scrutiny of election returns by national officials provoked bitter opposition. In 1860 Congress enacted a law which declared that under certain circumstances state officials were responsible to the national judiciary for the disturbance of public tranquillity. Soon afterward General Tomás Mosquera, who had become a Liberal and was now governor of the state of Cauca, declared his opposition to

the law, and issued a decree announcing that his state had assumed
sovereign power. Similar steps were taken in other states. After several conflicts between revolutionary soldiers and the army of the
Confederation, on July 18, 1861, Mosquera captured Bogotá. The
victorious general assumed the title of Provisional President of the
United States of New Granada.

Partly as a measure of retaliation upon his political opponents,
Mosquera immediately instituted radical politico-religious reforms.
He announced that no priest might exercise his functions without the consent of the State under pain of
exile. He declared that the Jesuits, who had again been
recalled to New Granada, were to be expelled and deprived of their
property. He ordered that the archbishop of Bogotá should be imprisoned because of noncompliance with decrees concerning the
clergy. Property held in the dead hands of religious corporations or
communities was to revert to the nation. All convents, monasteries,
and religious houses were to be suppressed.

The Age of Mosquera

When a civil war had terminated, a convention which was composed
of victorious Liberals assembled in the city of Rionegro (Antioquia).
In March, 1863, the Cæsar of Colombia sent a message to that convention in which he bitterly criticized the Roman Catholic Church. He
accused the clergy of having kept the aborigines in a debased and
superstitious condition and of having used their influence to promote
a civil war. He said to the delegates:

> You know well the evils that have been caused in other countries by fanatics;
> history is full of examples showing the pernicious results to nations because of
> the union of the throne and the altar; and if to avoid these evils we have proclaimed the principle of religious toleration, we have never given such latitude
> to a philosophic thought as to feel that it might result in the establishment of a
> theocratic government in Colombia. . . . The epoch has come to consider the
> exercise of religion in this country not only as a principle of morality and to
> support the religious element as an element of order, but also to view the exercise of religious doctrines in a purely economic aspect.

On May 8, 1863, the convention adopted a new Constitution. The
"Political Constitution of the United States of Colombia," as it was
styled, guaranteed freedom of religion. It declared that, with certain
limitations, the states should control their respective local governments. All powers which were not expressly delegated to the general
government should be reserved to the states. The President, who
should hold his office for two years, was to be elected by the states,
one vote being cast by each state. Congress should be composed of a
Senate and a House of Representatives. Judges of the federal supreme
court should be selected by Congress from lists of nominees made by

the state legislatures. The Constitution prohibited the national government from levying war against the states without the express authorization of Congress and without having exhausted all possible means of conciliation. In a commentary upon the Constitution of Rionegro a Colombian lawyer sagely declared that the powers of the national government were so organized in it that they seemed like guests who were scarcely tolerated in the constitutional mansion.

In accordance with a provisional act of the convention, Mosquera was elected president of the republic. The states soon framed their respective constitutions under the new régime. The dictator, who was reëlected in 1866, was soon accused of malfeasance in office, cast into prison, and exiled in 1867. A significant tendency of the following years was the development of violent opposition to the policy of the Liberals. While the Conservatives clung to tradition and became a clerical party, the Liberals constituted a party of reform which was opposed to the influence of the Church in politics. In 1876, shortly after a Liberal named Aquileo Parra, whose candidacy was supported by the administration, had been made president, certain Conservatives took up arms in behalf of their politico-religious tenets. Organized opposition to the national government developed in the state of Cauca, and, encouraged by certain provisions of the national Constitution, similar movements soon took place in other states. To paraphrase a Liberal writer, many melancholy pages were thus added to the sanguinary story of Colombia's party struggles.

In 1880 the Liberals decided to support the candidacy for president of a versatile and influential politician named Rafael Núñez, who was

Problems Confronting President Núñez apparently a Liberal. A journalist, publicist and political philosopher, as president of the Senate in 1878, Núñez had publicly declared that Colombia was confronted by a dilemma: either she would have to undertake a fundamental political reorganization, or she would suffer a catastrophe. Fiscal embarrassments, the legacy of former presidents, were partly responsible for the dissatisfaction of some Liberals with his first administration. Núñez cut down the size of the army and took other measures to reduce expenses. Protracted negotiations between Colombia and Costa Rica for the settlement of a boundary dispute culminated on December 25, 1880, in the negotiation of a treaty which stipulated that the controversy should be submitted to arbitration. On September 14, 1881, diplomats of Colombia and Venezuela signed a convention by which those nations agreed to submit their dispute about boundaries to the arbitration of the Spanish King.

After making way for his successor, in 1882 Núñez published a series of articles in *El Porvenir,* a journal of Cartagena, in which he advocated the creation of a party that would dedicate itself to the task of political reconstruction. He explained his attitude by citing the Scriptural text: "Render therefore unto Cæsar the things which are Cæsar's; and unto God the things that are God's." "Or if you wish," he continued, "a free church in a free state. There should be neither 'persecuted nor persecutors; neither martyrs nor executioners. In justice there is liberty."

Reëlected president of the republic in 1884, he became the leader of a new party which was composed of Independents who had separated from the radical Liberals and joined the Conservatives to form the so-called Nationalists. It soon became clear that Núñez favored making concessions to the Papacy. Armed strife which broke out between the Nationalists and the extreme Liberals he suppressed by defeating the radicals. Taking his cue from the political antecedents of the Constitution of Rionegro, on September 10, 1885, Núñez issued a decree which invited the governors of the states to send delegates to Bogotá to deliberate in a "National Council" about the reform of the Constitution.

This convention, which was composed of Independents and Nationalists, assembled at Bogotá on November 11, 1885. To it the President made a trenchant address about political reform. He declared that the political achievements of the Colombians for the preceding quarter of a century had all been negative. He urged that the proposed constitution should be in sharp contrast with the charter of 1863, that legislation and administration should be nationalistic, and that the main object of the educational system should be the inculcation of Christian doctrine.

On August 4, 1886, the Council adopted a Constitution which was the fruit of many compromises and concessions. It was sanctioned by the chief executive on the following day. The preamble of Colombia's Constitution of 1886 proclaimed that God was the supreme fountain of all authority. Its first article announced that Colom- **Constitution of 1886** bia was a centralistic republic. The states which had composed the union were now designated departments. Roman Catholicism was declared to be the religion of the nation; public magistrates were charged to give it protection, and to cause it to be respected as an essential factor in the social order. Religious buildings were to be exempt from taxation. Public education should be managed in accordance with the Catholic religion. In addition to a declaration that the Church could act as a juridical person, the provision was made that the government should arrange a concordat with the Papacy.

The President, who was to be elected for six years by direct vote, was given the right to issue decrees having the force of laws. The members of his cabinet were to be the organs of communication between him and the legislature: they might introduce bills and take part in its debates. In case of need, a person selected by Congress should serve as the President's substitute. It should be composed of a Senate and a House of Representatives. The Senate was given the right to accept or reject the President's resignation. Judicial authority was vested in a supreme court, district courts, and inferior courts. In each department the chief executive, who was designated governor, should act as the agent of the national government.

The Constitution of 1886 illustrates tendencies that were significant. It symbolized the triumph of the Clerical or Conservative party. It recognized the primacy of the Catholic Church, strengthened the hands of the central government, and reëstablished the unity of the nation. In December, 1885, the National Council had proclaimed Núñez as the first president under the projected constitution.

As President Núñez was at times absent from Bogotá, presumably because of bad health, his post was occasionally filled by a substitute.

The Concordat

In June, 1887, he assumed the presidency for a short period. At that juncture he authorized the negotiation of a concordat with the Papacy, which was signed on December 31, 1887, and sanctioned by Congress in 1888. This agreement stipulated that the Catholic Church in Colombia should be independent of the civil power; that, as a juridical personage, it should have the right to acquire, to possess, and to manage property; and that it should have the privilege to establish in Colombia religious orders of either sex which could be governed by their respective constitutions. Further, it provided that marriages performed canonically by Catholic priests should be recognized by the civil law; that cemeteries should be under the administration of ecclesiastical authorities; and that the state should compensate the Church for properties which had been confiscated. The article of the concordat which defined the position of the Church ran thus:

The Catholic, Apostolic, Roman Religion is the religion of Colombia: the public authorities recognize it as an essential element of the social order; they agree to protect and to respect it as well as its ministers. At the same time they assure to it the full enjoyment of its rights and prerogatives.

An article which was concerned with public instruction was couched in these words:

In the universities and colleges, in the schools and other centers of teaching, education and public instruction shall be organized and directed in conformity with the dogmas and the morality of the Catholic Religion. In such centers religious teaching shall be obligatory, and the pious customs of the Catholic Church shall be observed.

The accepted doctrine concerning ecclesiastical appointments in Colombia was set forth as follows:

The right to make appointments to vacant bishoprics and archbishoprics pertains to the Holy See. Nevertheless, the Holy Father, as a proof of special deference, and in order to preserve harmony between Church and State agrees that in appointments to episcopal and archiepiscopal seats the desires of the President of the republic shall be consulted. Consequently, in every case of a vacancy the President shall recommend directly to the Holy See the ecclesiastics who in his judgment possess the qualities necessary for the episcopal dignity; and on its part the Holy See, before making the appointment shall make known the names of the candidates whom it wishes to appoint, for the purpose of ascertaining whether the President has motives of a civil or political character to regard such candidates as *personas non gratas*.

In this manner an adjustment was reached between the Papacy and Colombia on the age-long problem of investiture. The right of making ecclesiastical appointments was acknowledged as being vested in the See of St. Peter, but in practice it was to be exercised in such a manner as to please the republic.

The Anti-Clericals or Liberals struggled against the readjustment of political and religious forces for several years. Upon the death of Núñez in September, 1894, a littérateur named Caro, who had been chosen Vice-President, became President, and in the following year he suppressed an insurrection of the Liberals. Four years later he was succeeded by Manuel A. Sanclemente, an aged lawyer and publicist who was a member of the so-called National party. During the following year the government suppressed another Liberal revolt. In the night of July 31, 1900, Vice-President José M. Marroquin, who was a Conservative, boldly assumed the President's power, and prominent Conservatives deftly imprisoned Sanclemente in his own house at some distance from Bogotá. Those measures added fuel to a fierce civil war that was already raging. Marroquin nevertheless retained presidential authority, while the war ended in June, 1903, in another defeat for the Liberals.

To a Congress which assembled while the passions that had been stirred by this conflict still raged, the government submitted a treaty with the United States about the Isthmus of Panama. Designated because of its negotiators as the Hay-Herrán Treaty, it conceded to the United States the right to use a narrow strip of land across the Isthmus for a canal in return for a cash payment of ten million dollars and an annuity of a quarter of a million. Though ratified by the United States Senate, it was rejected by the Congress of Colombia. On November 3, 1903, an insurrection broke out in Panama City. Its leaders promptly declared that the Isthmus was independent. Under color of a clause in the Treaty of 1846 with New Granada the President of the United States sent orders to his war vessels to prevent Colombian soldiers from landing upon the Isthmus. A few days later President Theodore Roosevelt acknowledged the independence of the republic of Panama. Basing her claim upon the Treaty of 1846, Colombia made emphatic protests to the United States. That government, however, refused to submit the dispute about its proceedings in the Panama affair to arbitration. It made a treaty with the Panamanian Republic by which it secured, in return for a money payment, the title to a zone of land for the construction of a canal.

Colombia promptly sent General Rafael Reyes to Washington to secure redress for the loss of Panama. His negotiations were in vain. Secretary of State Hay assumed the view that the United States now had obligations to Panama instead of to Colombia. He refused to submit the political questions that had arisen between the United States and Colombia to The Hague for arbitration.

Shortly after his return to Bogotá from Washington, General Reyes was elected president. He was inaugurated on August 7, 1904. A domineering personality, some acquaintance with the rule of Díaz in Mexico had convinced him that his demoralized country could be transformed by a similar régime. He soon took steps to reorganize the finances, to promote industry, and to encourage the construction of railroads. Attempts of political antagonists to use Vice-President González Valencia against Reyes precipitated the former's resignation. The President placed serious restrictions upon the liberty of the press. As he felt Congress to be an incubus upon his efforts, he arbitrarily dissolved that body. On February 1, 1905, he issued a decree convoking a "National Assembly" that was to be composed of delegates selected by departmental juntas under the direction of the respective governors, whom he had appointed.

At his instance this extra-legal Assembly usurped the functions of Congress. By a series of acts, in March and April, 1905, it made significant alterations in the Constitution. Among other amendments it declared that the Assembly itself should continue to exercise legislative functions until February 1, 1908; that the office of Vice-President should be abolished; that the Council of State should be swept away; that the Constitution could be amended by a National Assembly convoked for this purpose; and that the term of office of President Reyes should be extended until December 31, 1914. By a decree of the National Assembly in April, 1907, the further announcement was made that Congress would not meet until February 1, 1910. Accordingly, by a series of acts that scarcely bore the semblance of legality, the President of Colombia was clothed with dictatorial power for a term of years.

In 1909 through an agent named Enrique Cortés, who was dispatched to Washington, Reyes made another attempt to settle the troublesome dispute with the United States about Panama. A convention was negotiated between Cortés and Secretary of State Root. Treaties were also arranged between the United States and Panama, and between Panama and Colombia. In connection with those treaties the Cortés-Root Convention provided that Colombia should recognize the independence of Panama, that the Treaty of 1846 between Colombia and the United States should be abrogated, and that Colombia should declare Panama to be free of all indebtedness incurred upon her behalf before November, 1903. This convention also stipulated that Panama should pay Colombia two hundred and fifty thousand dollars annually from the cash payments, which, according to treaty stipulations, would be paid to her by the United States.

Public opinion in Bogotá, however, disapproved of this adjustment which legalized the loss of Colombia's most precious possession by a monetary recompense that was deemed inadequate. Caviling critics asserted that the convention with the United States veiled a menace to their nation's integrity. In the cloisters of the national university and in legislative halls a vigorous opposition was displayed. Intense dissatisfaction with the proposed adjustment furnished an occasion for bitter denunciations of the policy of Reyes. Hence, in May, 1909, the President reluctantly decided to withdraw the Cortés-Root conventions from consideration by the Assembly: he issued a manifesto announcing that he had postponed their discussion until the regular session of Congress in February, 1910. So threatening did the demonstrations against the autocrat become, however, that at last he resigned the presidency and left his native land.

In August, 1909, the Assembly elected General Ramón González Valencia provisional president. In his message to that Assembly in May, 1910, President González Valencia pointed out the imperative necessity of modifying the fundamental law. Soon afterward a number of important amendments to the Constitution were made by the Assembly. Capital punishment was prohibited. Only those citizens able to read and write who owned real estate or who possessed an income should be permitted to vote in presidential or congressional elections. The President's term was again limited to four years. Congress was annually to elect two personages who in case of need should exercise the execu-

Constitutional Reforms

tive authority in a designated order. Senators were to be chosen by electoral councils that should be elected by the respective departmental assemblies. The Senate was to determine when the President was physically incapacitated to perform his functions. The supreme court was conceded the right to decide whether or not a law should be enforced that the national government or any citizen had stigmatized as unconstitutional.

An important contract concerning higher education was signed on January 19, 1910, between the superior of the Society of Jesus and **Politico-Religious Problems** the Colombian minister of public instruction. This contract provided that the Jesuits should be left in control of the buildings and the incomes of the College of St. Bartholomew for eighteen years. During that period the national government promised not to occupy these buildings, even for purposes of war. The members of the society were to offer the courses of study, which, according to a decree of October, 1886, constituted the College of Philosophy and Letters of Colombia. Such courses were to be considered university courses: the College of St. Bartholomew was accordingly authorized to confer the degree of bachelor in philosophy and letters. Other colleges of the society within the republic that had a similar plan of studies were granted the same authorization. Jesuit fathers were given the power to fix the conditions of entrance to such institutions, to outline the courses of study, and to select the text books. Though the government was to furnish the equipment for this instruction, it was not to interfere in the teaching or the management of those colleges. The preceptors were to enjoy "complete independence." Many Liberals naturally resented this agreement which conceded to the Jesuits the control of higher education.

In July, 1910, Carlos E. Restrepo, a journalist and publicist of Medellín, was elected President. Inaugurated in the following month, he declared that he was neither the chief of any political party nor the pontiff of any sect, and that he had the welfare of the entire nation at heart. By decrees of October 14 and 18, 1910, he created the office of inspector-general of public instruction, and aimed to bring all grades of public education within the republic under the supervision of the national government. By decrees of October 24 following he directed that instruction in the geography and history of the country should everywhere be taught by Colombian teachers; he also ordered that a council which had been charged with arranging the curricula of colleges and universities should be reëstablished. He signed laws that provided for the reorganization of the departmental assemblies, which had fallen into disuse during the dictatorship of

Reyes. In addition, Restrepo took measures to reform Colombia's finances.

In February, 1914, a Conservative named José Concha was elected president. In selecting the members of his cabinet Concha gave representation to the Liberals. During his administration Congress re-established the Council of State. Like Restrepo, Concha had to undertake the reorganization of the nation's finances.

President Concha also made a well-considered attempt to settle the dispute with the United States about Panama. On April 6, 1914, Francisco Urrutia, Colombia's secretary of foreign rela-tions, and Thaddeus Thompson, minister of the United States at Bogotá, signed a treaty of reconciliation. The Thompson-Urrutia Treaty contained expressions of re-gret by the United States government for the differences which had arisen with the Colombian government because of Panama. That treaty gave Colombia exceptional privileges in the use of either the Panama Canal or the Panama railroad as a commercial highway be-tween her Atlantic and Pacific seaboards. Colombia was to acknowl-edge the independence of the new nation and to negotiate with her a treaty of peace and friendship. Not of least importance to Colom-bians, the treaty provided that the United States should pay to their country twenty-five million dollars as an indemnity for injuries caused by Panama's independence. After some discussion, by a law dated June 9, 1914, the Colombian Congress solemnly sanctioned the Thomp-son-Urrutia Treaty. Upon more than one occasion President Wilson urged the United States Senate to ratify this treaty; but that body did not accede to his wishes largely because of the apologetic phrases, which certain Republicans considered as a reflection upon Roosevelt.

The opening of the present century did not see all the boundaries of Colombia determined. Disputes with her sisters, Ecuador and Vene-zuela, will be considered in connection with the history of those nations. With respect to the boundary dispute between Colombia and Costa Rica, on September 11, 1900, after carefully considering the evidence and the arguments that had been submitted to him, President Loubet of France pronounced his arbitral award. The French President sketched a boundary line between those nations which assigned to Costa Rica some territory on the Atlantic and the Pacific oceans that had been claimed by Colombia. An important step was taken toward an adjustment of the limits between Colombia and Brazil, which had been under consid-eration by both governments since 1826, by the negotiation of a treaty between them in April, 1907, that sketched a boundary line between their coterminous territories and provided for the appointment of a mixed commission which was to survey it. By this treaty Colombia relinquished to Brazil territories that she had claimed around the mouth of the river Caquetá and near the headwaters of the Río Negro.

The long-standing boundary dispute between Colombia and Peru harks back to colonial days, when the Spanish government vaguely indicated the bounds between the viceroyalties of New Granada and Peru. After the defeat of the Peruvians at the battle of Tarqui the governments of Colombia and Peru signed a treaty at Guayaquil by which they agreed to recognize as the boundaries of their respective territories the vague line that had separated the former viceroyalties of Peru and New Granada. Upon the southwest that line was marked by the Tumbes River. Provision was made for the choice of a joint commission which was to demarcate the boundary, but partly because of the disruption of Great Colombia the line was never surveyed.

The President was the commander in chief of the army and might even direct it in person. In 1914 the army was composed of some fourteen thousand men. Colombia had a navy of nine vessels. Though congresses passed laws which aimed to encourage immigration, yet few immigrants settled in this region. According to the census of 1912 Colombia had a population of 5,072,604. The two main elements in the population were the aborigines and the Spaniards. Many inhabitants were of mixed descent; in coastal regions traces of Negro blood were found. The language of the official, as well as of the cultured, classes was Spanish. Citizens of Bogotá spoke the language of Cervantes with a musical intonation.

The main occupations were agriculture, mining, manufacturing, and commerce. In 1895, according to the report of the secretary of the treasury, Colombia exported products which amounted to 28,643,322 pesos. The important items in Colombia's export trade were: coffee, gold, hides, bananas, straw hats, tobacco, and rubber. Colombia had only about six hundred miles of railroad lines; these were of different gauges, and did not even furnish the links for a railroad system. Before the outbreak of the first World War, several lines of steamships connected Cartagena and Santa Marta with Europe and the United States. The main artery for interior traffic was the Magdalena River.

The census of 1912 indicated that about 50 per cent of the population of the republic was illiterate. Education had been under the control of the secretary of public instruction. Primary education was in charge of the respective departments and municipalities. In important towns the clergy maintained parochial schools, while in frontier districts they supported missionaries who were employed in converting the Indians. There were schools of arts and trades in Bogotá, academies in the largest towns, and normal schools in the capitals of departments. After much fluctuation, a college of medicine and natural science, a college of mathematics and civil engineering, and a college of law and political science had been established at Bogotá which were directly under the control of the national government. The Colombian College of Philosophy and Letters, however, remained in clerical hands.

Education, Literature, and Art

Colombia produced a literature notable in Latin America. Its history to 1820 may be followed in the book by Vergara y Vergara entitled *History of the Literature of New Granada*. Among historical writers José M. Restrepo holds a prominent place because of his classic *History of the Revolution in Colombia*. General Joaquín Acosta wrote an *Historical Compendium of the Discovery and Colonization of New Granada,* which has been very useful to students of the Spanish conquest. In his *Ecclesiastical and Civil History,* José Manuel Groot told the story of New Granada up to the opening of the struggle for independence. That work was supplemented by the *Memoirs for the History of New Granada* by José Antonio de Plaza. Early in the present century the National Academy of History, under the auspices of the government, began to publish the *Library of National History,* a series of volumes edited or written by well-known authors which form a collection that is indispensable to every serious student of Colombian history.

Among the writings of the publicist Salvador Camacho Roldán should be mentioned his *Notas de viaje,* which conveys his impressions of a visit to the United States. Jorge Isaacs, the son of a Jamaican Jew who settled in the Cauca Valley, was reckoned the prince of Colombian novelists; his masterpiece was *María,* a romantic story of plantation life. Among Colombia's poets José E. Caro was best known through his patriotic poem "La Bandera Colombiana" and his apostrophe to the picturesque falls of Tequendama. A poet as well as a soldier, Julio Arboleda, who was assassinated during the revolution of 1860, left fragments of a national epic entitled *Gonzalo de Oyón* which sang of the Spanish conquest. A versatile native of Bogotá named Rafael Pombo wrote *El Bambuco* and translated poems from English into Spanish. Rufino José Cuervo wrote scholarly grammatical and philological treatises.

An academy of music was founded at Bogotá about 1882. Four years later a school of fine arts was opened in that city. In parks of the capital were handsome statues of revolutionary heroes by Colombian artists. More than one national artist has attempted to portray the quiet beauty of the adjacent plains. Among paintings of religious subjects by Colombians may be mentioned Ricardo Acebedo Bernal's "Mater Dolorosa" and his picture of "St. Mark," which adorns the cupola of the cathedral. A painting of historical interest is J. M. Zamorra's "The Campaign of Liberation of 1819," which depicts Bolívar and his officers fording the river Apure. Gustavo Arcila Uribe, a young sculptor of Bogotá, won a prize offered annually by the Art Institute of Chicago for the best ideal sculptural representation by his bust entitled "The Sermon on the Mount."

Political parties in Colombia remained as aligned in the struggles that culminated in the concordat. As in the days of Mosquera's dictatorship, the struggle was a species of *Kulturkampf*, **Political Tendencies** with the difference that the Conservative or Clerical party generally held the reins of power. A significant constitutional tendency was the use by Colombian presidents of a custom established by President Núñez, namely, the convocation of national assemblies whose members had been appointed by departmental authorities. When he summoned such an assembly in 1905, the President stated that the justification for his act was found not in the Constitution but in the supreme law of necessity. This practice stimulated a tendency toward centralization. The departments declined in constitutional importance while the national government became well-nigh dominant.

During the administration of President Concha the first World War and its issues affected the politics and life of Colombia. On August 13, 1914, Marco Fidel Suárez, her able secretary of foreign relations, addressed instructions to the governors of the littoral departments directing them to observe certain rules concerning vessels of the belligerent nations in order that Colombia's neutrality might be ensured. Three **Attitude toward the First World War** months later that secretary sent a circular to newspaper editors advising them to be strictly neutral. Upon being officially informed of Germany's intention to renew an unrestricted submarine campaign, he notified Germany's envoy at Bogotá that his government reserved the right to protest against the destruction of neutral property and innocent lives and also to demand justice. On June 2, 1917, he issued an announcement that his government intended to remain neutral in the war between the United States and Germany. It was mainly her remoteness from the titanic struggle and the fact that her merchant vessels were not affected by the German submarine campaign, that kept Colombia aloof from the struggle and enabled her to pursue a policy of neutrality.

In October, 1917, Marco Fidel Suárez, whom the Conservatives had nominated for the presidency, resigned from Concha's cabinet. The ex-secretary was elected president in February, 1918, and inaugurated on August 7. On April 20, 1921, omitting the apologetic clauses and with other modifications, the Senate of the United States approved the Thompson-Urrutia Treaty. By it Colombia was still pledged to recognize Panama. The Treaty of 1921 accorded to Colombia fewer commercial privileges in the use of the Panama Canal and the Panama Railroad than did the original treaty. This treaty also provided that of the twenty-five million dollars indemnity, **Subsequent Developments** five million should be paid by the United States to Colombia within six months after the ratifications of that treaty were exchanged, and the remainder should be paid in four equal annual installments. In the Colombian Congress opposition was made to certain alterations in the Thompson-Urrutia Treaty.

As modified, however, it was favored by President Fidel Suárez. Suspecting that attacks were being made upon his administration because of political motives, as he did not wish to jeopardize the fate of this important treaty, he resigned the presidency. He was succeeded by General Jorge Holguín, a publicist of extensive political experience. On December 22, 1921, Congress ratified the Thompson-Urrutia Treaty as modified by the United States. Two days later, it was approved by the Acting President. In recommending this treaty of reconciliation to the Colombian Senate for approval, the committee on foreign relations expressed the hope that its ratification would "restore the cordial amity which had previously marked the relations between the United States and Colombia."

On February 12, 1922, General Pedro Nel Ospina, a journalist and statesman who was the candidate of the Conservative party, was elected president over the Liberal candidate, General Benjamin Herrera. On March 26, 1922, an old dispute was settled by a treaty with Peru which drew a boundary line along the Putumayo River and conceded to Colombia a corridor which led to the river Amazon. Soon after Nel Ospina was inaugurated, in order to fund its floating indebtedness, the Colombian government borrowed $5,000,000 in the United States. The fiscal condition of Colombia was improved on December 7, 1922, when, in accordance with the modified Thompson-Urrutia Treaty, the United States paid her the first installment of $5,000,000 in compensation for the loss of Panama.

Yet the demoralized condition of her finances and currency induced Colombia to seek financial advisers in the United States who might assist in the task of reform. In accordance with a law of October, 1922, and aided by the advice of the Department of State at Washington, the Colombian government secured the services of a commission of experts. In February, 1923, this commission sailed from New York for Colombia. During a sojourn there of six months its members assiduously investigated her fiscal and currency system, and they presented to the government recommendations for fiscal reform. Prominent among these was a bill providing for the establishment of a national bank and for the reform of the currency. The impromptu formation of the Bank of the Republic by the commission averted what threatened to become a disastrous panic.

Meantime, a serious politico-economic issue had arisen. Shortly after the opening of the first World War, petroleum seepages came to play an important part in Colombian economy. For- **The Oil Industry** eign corporations secured concessions of oil properties. Partly because of inconsistent Colombian legislation, problems soon arose concerning the ownership of such holdings. On November 17, 1927, a law was enacted concerning titles to oil lands, which provided that any one drilling oil wells must present to the Minister of Industries within six months documents proving his lease or ownership of these lands. Further, this law doubled the tax levied on the exploitation of oil seepages which were found under land that was privately owned. Oil prospectors objected to this law. They claimed that it was unconstitutional, that the time limit which it set was too short, and that it virtually suspended all action on pending contract proposals. This law was put into operation, however, by a decree dated January 28, 1928, which oil interests denounced as too stringent. On November 15 of that year the government recognized the title of Brazil to a strip of territory ceded to her by Peru in 1851.

In the campaign of 1930 the Conservative party split into a regular faction and an insurgent faction, each of which nominated a candidate for the presidency. A Socialist party also brought forth a nominee. The election of February 9, 1930, resulted in the choice of the Liberal candidate, Enrique Olaya Herrera, who had been serving as minister to the United States. Making campaign trips via airplane, he promised, if elected, to support woman suffrage. He also declared that he would appoint the most competent men to office, that he favored an open door policy for foreign investors in his country, and that he believed in the development of the oil industry. The triumph of Olaya was a political event of the first magnitude. For the first time since 1884 the Liberals had won a presidential election. Nevertheless, Olaya kept some conservatives in office.

During his administration a dispute took place regarding a strip of land furnishing an outlet to the river Amazon, which the Treaty of 1922 with Peru had assigned to Colombia. Early in September, 1932, the little village of Leticia in this corridor was seized by a band of armed Peruvians. Their government disclaimed responsibility for the attack but, yielding to popular clamor, it opposed the forcible reincorporation of Leticia by Colombia. Instead Peru proposed an alteration in the line drawn in 1922 so as to give her the title to the Leticia corridor in return for the relinquishment of other territory to her neighbor. After hostilities had begun, however, both parties accepted the good offices of the League of Nations. In May, 1933, the Council of the League formulated an agreement which checked the war. Finally, on May 24, 1934, the disputants signed a treaty at Rio de Janeiro by which Peru expressed regret for the seizure of Leticia, and the disputed territory was temporarily placed under the control of an international commission. This treaty also contained stipulations concerning the free navigation of the rivers Amazon and Putumayo. Further, it provided that controversies between the parties were to be settled by the Hague Tribunal. The coveted corridor was returned to Colombia in the following year. As her boundary dispute with Venezuela had also been adjusted as will be shown in a later chapter, by 1936 the territorial limits of Colombia were clearly marked.

Boundary Disputes and Politico-Religious Issues

Because of a dispute between the political parties, the Conservatives did not nominate a candidate for the presidency in the campaign of 1934. The uncompromising Liberal candidate, Alfonso López, was elected president. Despite the non-participation of the Conservatives in politics, in August, 1936, amendments were made to the Constitution which embodied reforms desired by the Liberals. This organic law provided that the territorial divisions of the republic were to be departments, intendancies, and *comisarías*. It declared that because of public necessity or social interest private individuals might be expropriated by the government. Article XI provided that the national government might interfere by law in the management of private enterprise in order to ensure the proper distribution of wealth and adequate protection to laborers. The national government was pledged to give aid to poor people who were unable to earn a living. Liberty of conscience and freedom of religious worship were assured to all cults which were not immoral or unchristian. Freedom of teaching was assured but the state was to have the authority to supervise all educational institutions, both public and private. Not of least importance was a clause in Article XIII which reads thus: "Subject to approval by Congress, the government will negotiate with the Holy See agreements to regulate the relations between the State and the Catholic Church upon bases of reciprocal deference and mutual respect."

These significant amendments not only proposed a modification of the Concordat of 1887, but they also emphatically enunciated the principle of religious freedom. They reëstablished government control of all branches of education, furnished a legal basis for governmental regulation of business enterprise, and forecasted measures that might ensure a more equitable return to labor. By endorsing the practice of expropriation they even envisaged a redistribution of landed property.

The death of Olaya in 1937 deprived the Liberal party of its leading candidate for the presidential nomination. In 1938 Eduardo Santos, the editor of *El Tiempo* of Bogotá, was elected president. During the following year as the Conservatives decided to participate again in congressional elections, they secured some seats in Congress. A split took place in the Liberals, who had controlled the national government since 1930, over the candidacy of former president López for the presidential nomination. In September, 1940, anti-López Senators belonging to the right wing of the Liberal party walked out of Congress accompanied by the Conservative minority. Early in 1941 Colombia and Venezuela agreed to negotiate a treaty of commerce and to allow free navigation on rivers common to both countries. In spite of the division in the ranks of his party, López was nominated by the Liberal convention, elected president on May 3, and inaugurated on August 7, 1942.

Before that date the attitude of Colombia toward the second World War had been determined. For her government had led the way in South America by severing relations with Japan, Italy, and Germany soon after the Japanese attack on Pearl Harbor.

A promising feature of recent politics in Colombia has been the decline of party dissensions. Her citizens have become aroused to the damage wrought their country by fierce civil wars and have evidently settled down to an era of regular constitutional government. The economic development of Colombia has been much retarded, partly because of her physiography, partly because of revolutionary disturbances, and partly because of the lack of good communications. The Magdalena River is still the main artery of her commercial life; as yet no railroad connects the Caribbean coast with the plateau; with the exception of Sucre, Bogotá is the most inaccessible capital in Latin America. During a large part of her history Colombia has lacked the capital necessary for industrial development. In a large measure she remains an agricultural, pastoral, and mining country, rich in material resources but undeveloped. Her political life has been dominated by a capable aristocracy, seated for the most part in the capital city, whose culture reposes upon the industrial activities of the Indians and the mixed classes. Educated Colombians are resourceful, courteous, and watchful of their economic interests. By virtue of their habitat they are destined to be brought into closer and closer relations with the United States. The spirit shown in such measures as the recent constitutional amendments entitles Colombia to a high place among the liberal and progressive nations of Latin America.

SUGGESTIONS FOR FURTHER READING

BELL, P. L., *Colombia: A Commercial and Industrial Handbook*, 1921.

BYNUM, M. L., *The Coffee Industry in Colombia*, 1931.

DENNIS, A. L. P., *Adventures in American Diplomacy*, 1928.

EDER, P. J., *Colombia*, 1913.

GARCÍA, A., *An Outline of Colombian Economy, Commercial Pan America*, No. 80, 1939.

HENAO, J. M., and ARRUBLA, G., *History of Colombia*, 1938.

HUDSON, M. O. (ed.), *The Verdict of the League. Colombia and Peru at Leticia*, 1933.

LEVINE, V., *Colombia: Physical Features, Natural Resources, Means of Communication, Manufactures, and Industrial Development*, 1914.

MECHAM, J. L., *Church and State in Latin America*, 1934.

MINER, D. C., *The Fight for the Panama Route*, 1940.

PARKES, E. T., *Colombia and the United States, 1764-1934*, 1935.

PETRE, F. L., *The Republic of Colombia*, 1906.

REYES, R., *The Two Americas*, 1914.

RIPPY, J. F., *The Capitalists and Colombia*, 1931.

———, "The United States and Colombian Oil," *Foreign Policy Reports*, Vol. V, No. 2, 1929.

CHAPTER XX

ECUADOR

Ecuador took the place on the map which had been occupied by the presidency of Quito. This presidency was liberated from Spanish rule by the victory of General Sucre at Pichincha. As the fundamental law of the Congress of Angostura had provided that it was to be a department of Colombia, Bolívar instructed Sucre that it was to be incorporated in her territory. Five days after the battle of Pichincha, an extraordinary cabildo at the capital city announced that the provinces of Quito had been united with Colombia. Shortly afterward many of its inhabitants swore to support her Constitution.

Origin of Ecuador

In Guayaquil some citizens favored annexation to Peru. On July 13, 1822, Bolívar issued an address to the people of that city in which he expressed his ardent desire to place the presidency under Colombia's protection. He soon declared that it was Colombian soil. In August, 1822, he issued a decree which formally announced that the province of Guayaquil would be organized as a Colombian department. General Salom was soon appointed the intendant of that district. As has been indicated, in 1826 at Tarqui soldiers under the command of Sucre repulsed Peruvian invaders of southern Colombia.

On September 22, 1829, a treaty of peace was signed by Peru and Colombia. To carry out certain articles of that treaty, on August 11, 1830, General Tomás de Mosquera, the Colombian minister at Lima, and the Peruvian minister of foreign relations, Carlos Pedemonte, signed a protocol which sketched a boundary line between the two countries. This line proceeded from the mouth of the Yavarí River up the river Máranon and by an uncertain course from the headwaters of the Máranon to the mouth of the river Tumbes. But during the following century, the claims of the Ecuadorian government sometimes included territory south of the Pedemonte-Mosquera line.

Even before the death of Bolívar, a movement had begun in the city of Quito for separation from Colombia. In May, 1830, a junta in that city appointed as provisional executive General Juan Flores, a comrade and compatriot of Bolívar who had distinguished himself in the revolutionary cause. He soon convoked a Constituent Congress of delegates from the three departments of Colombia near the equator.

This Congress, which assembled at Riobamba on August 14, 1830, framed a Constitution that was promulgated by the President on September 23, 1830.

The first Ecuadorian Constitution declared that the departments of Azuay, Guayas, and Quito formed an independent entity named the "State of Ecuador." The religion of the new state was to be Roman Catholicism to the exclusion of any other. Extensive authority was vested in a President elected for four years, who should be aided by a Council of State. With the approval of that council, the President could appoint bishops, judges, and prefects. Legislative authority was granted to a unicameral legislature which was to be composed of ten members elected from each of the departments. Judicial authority was given to a high court, appellate courts, and other tribunals. The administrative divisions of the territory were to be departments, provinces, and cantons.

Congress elected General Flores president. General Urdaneta promptly proclaimed himself in favor of Colombian unity. When news of Bolívar's death reached Urdaneta's soldiers, however, their opposition to independence vanished, and they accepted the Ecuadorian Constitution. Uprisings that took place against the new government in 1832 were remorselessly suppressed. A territorial dispute soon arose between Ecuador and New Granada; for certain inhabitants of the department of Cauca proclaimed their adhesion to Ecuador. In December, 1832, a treaty was signed in the city of Pasto by commissioners of the two nations which provided that Cauca should belong to New Granada. The river Carchi was made the boundary between the sister republics. Meantime José Villamil took possession of the Galápagos Islands for Ecuador.

Rivalry of Flores and Rocafuerte

In 1832 opposition appeared to the rule of Flores, the Conservative leader who believed that the Catholic Church should be allowed to enjoy large and important privileges. In May, 1833, a Liberal society, which was organized in the capital city, began to publish a periodical of propaganda. Vicente Rocafuerte, a progressive leader who had just returned to his native land from a visit to Mexico, England, and the United States, was elected to the Congress of 1833. He protested against the exercise of extraordinary power by Flores, who undertook to exile Liberal leaders. As a result, Rocafuerte was expelled from Congress and banished from Quito. But insurrectionists at Guayaquil soon proclaimed him supreme chief. After conflicts between followers of the rival chieftains, Rocafuerte was captured by the President's soldiers and cast into a dungeon.

In July, 1834, the Liberal leader made a pact with Flores. This adjustment provided that there should be peace and harmony among Ecuadorians: Rocafuerte was made "superior chief" of the department of Guayas. When the President's term ended, Rocafuerte was proclaimed supreme chief of Ecuador, while his rival became commander in chief of the army.

After the uprisings in various sections had been checked, a Convention that Rocafuerte had summoned to meet at Ambato adopted a new Constitution, which was promulgated on August 13, 1835. This Constitution provided for a bicameral legislature composed of a Senate and a House of Representatives. It stipulated that the republic should be organized into seven provinces, besides the Galápagos Archipelago. In charge of each province should be placed a governor who was to be the President's agent. The Convention elected Rocafuerte president for a term of four years.

The presidency of Rocafuerte was signalized by significant reforms. He issued decrees that aimed to protect the aborigines against fiscal exactions by priests and corregidores. He appointed a commission to formulate civil and penal codes. In 1837 he signed a generous decree of amnesty, which was followed by the return of certain émigrés. He promoted elementary and higher education in various ways: he founded a short-lived school for girls at Quito, and established a military institute. He reconstructed the pyramids that had been built by French scientists to determine the equinoctial line. A critic of Roman Catholicism and the clergy, he tried to secularize public education; he even seems to have dreamed of introducing Protestantism into Ecuador. In a message to Congress he expressed his desire for freedom of conscience and the encouragement of immigration.

Early in 1839 Flores succeeded Rocafuerte, who resumed his former post at Guayaquil. Flores issued a decree which opened Ecuador's ports to Spanish commerce. A treaty was negotiated with England providing for the abolition of the slave trade. In 1841 fruitless negotiations were initiated in Quito between the minister of Peru and the Ecuadorian government for a treaty which would fix the limits of their territories. To a convention which met at Quito the President sent a message urging the need of constitutional reform. That Convention adopted a new Constitution which was promulgated on April 1, 1843. It extended the President's term to eight years. It declared that no other religious faith than Roman Catholicism might be practiced publicly. Meanwhile, despite the protests of Rocafuerte, who went into exile, Flores was reëlected president. Liberals now suspected that he aspired to become dictator for life. His third presidency was tempestuous. In March, 1845, a revolution broke out against him: a few months later he was forced to sign agreements with Liberal leaders by which he recognized their provisional government, was granted a pension, and agreed to leave Ecuador. Even while in exile, however, he did not relinquish his ambitious designs.

In December, 1845, a convention at Cuenca formed a Constitution which provided that the President should be elected for four years by a majority of the members of Congress. Vicente Roca was then elected president. The period from 1846 to 1860 was perhaps the most tumultuous age in Ecuadorian history. Because of the failure to refuse an asylum to General Obando, as requested by New Granada, grave differences arose between the two neighbors. Soldiers of New Granada were stationed along the frontier, while her President was authorized to make war on Ecuador. Yet, on May 29, 1846, an agreement was signed by the contending nations which provided for the negotiation of a treaty that would determine their limits. In March, 1851, Diego Noboa, who became president after a struggle with aspiring rivals, signed a law permitting the Jesuits to return to Ecuador. But he was expelled from the republic as the result of a revolution that began in Guayaquil.

Civil War and International Complications

A new Constitution had scarcely been put into force, when in July, 1851, General Urbina became dictator. He established his capital at Guayaquil. With one cannon Ecuadorian soldiers under Illingsworth and Villamil repulsed a squadron which General Flores led against that city from Peru. A convention which met at Guayaquil on July 17, 1852, adopted a new Constitution that was promulgated on September 6. Though in important particulars it followed the Constitution of 1845, it provided that ordinarily the President and Vice-President should be chosen by electoral assemblies. The convention decreed the expulsion of the Jesuits, and provided for the emancipation of Negro slaves. In accordance with a transitory clause of the Constitution, it elected General José Urbina president. Under General Robles, who became president in October, 1856, Congress issued a decree of amnesty to all political offenders except those who had been engaged in the expedition of Flores. In 1857 Congress adopted the Chilean civil code with some modifications.

While the country was being torn by internal dissensions and civil war, Peruvian warships had blockaded Guayaquil. To the disgust of many Ecuadorians, in January, 1860, General Franco, who had been proclaimed dictator by revolutionists in that city, agreed to a treaty with President Castilla which tentatively recognized as the boundary between Peru and Ecuador the limits of the viceroyalties of Peru and New Granada according to the royal order of 1802. The Peruvian fleet then withdrew. Franco and other Ecuadorian generals were soon driven out of Guayaquil, however, by General Flores and García Moreno, who captured that port on September 24, 1860.

The period from 1861 to 1875 may appropriately be designated the Age of García Moreno. In January, 1861, a convention which had been convoked at Quito elected Gabriel García Moreno presi-

The Age of García Moreno

dent of Ecuador. A brave, energetic, and well-educated man, he had studied in Quito, London, and Paris. During Urbina's dictatorship he had founded an opposition journal called *La Nación*. Its chief theme was that the enslaved Ecuadorian nation should shake off her chains and protest against her oppressors. Unwilling to desist from his propaganda, though warned by the dictator, García Moreno was deported shortly after the second number of his journal was published. From 1854 to 1856 he was in Paris where he became obsessed with the idea that the Catholic Church should be above all earthly powers.

On March 10, 1861, the Ecuadorian convention adopted a new Constitution which García Moreno promulgated a month later. It vested extensive powers in a President, who should be chosen by the direct and secret vote of qualified citizens for four years, and who could not be reëlected until one term had intervened. He was to be aided by a cabinet of three members. Each house of the bicameral legislature was granted special functions and also powers that might only be exercised in conjunction with the other house. The religion of the republic should be Roman Catholic to the exclusion of every other.

The convention elected García Moreno president. His internal policy was one of reform and economy. His own salary he donated to charity and to the State. He made a study of Ecuador's finances. He planned good roads that should stretch from the coast into the foothills of the Andes. He established a new port at Pailon; at Quito he erected a mint and a hospital. He issued decrees against immorality, brigandage, and militarism; he disciplined and reorganized the army, and directed that a prominent revolutionary leader who had become a bandit chief should be shot. The President forced a venturesome Ecuadorian who tried to publish an opposition journal in the capital city to flee incontinently to New Granada. He banished congressmen who opposed his rule; he arbitrarily imprisoned or executed unfortunate individuals who were suspected of disaffection.

With respect to the relations between Church and State President García Moreno authorized a significant agreement. On September 26, 1862, a prelate whom he had dispatched as minister plenipotentiary to Rome signed a concordat with the papal secretary of state. Article I of that agreement ran, in part, as follows: "The Roman Catholic Apostolic Religion shall continue to be the sole religion of the Republic

of Ecuador to the exclusion of any other faith or of any society condemned by the Church. This religion shall be preserved there forever
in its integrity, with all its rights and privileges in accordance with
the law of God and canonical provisions." The clause
which granted to the President a limited participation   The
in ecclesiastical appointments, ran as follows: Concordat

The Church concedes to the President of the republic the right of presentation
to bishoprics and benefices. The bishops will submit to the President the names
of three candidates from which he will make his choice within a period of three
months. Should this period elapse without an appointment being made, the
choice will be made by the Holy See.

Further, the concordat provided that an ecclesiastical seminary
should be established in each diocese. The government of Ecuador was
to furnish facilities for the planting of missions. Public and private
education were everywhere to be conducted "entirely according to the
doctrines of the Christian religion." Bishops were to have the right
to supervise primary schools, academies, and universities, as well as
the right to prohibit the use of books which were "opposed to religion
and good morals." Ecuadorian clergy and laymen were to be permitted
freely to communicate with the Pope. Papal bulls or rescripts were
to be admitted into Ecuador without being scrutinized by the civil
authorities. Bishops should be allowed complete liberty in the administration of their dioceses; they might freely convoke provincial and
diocesan synods. The Church was assured the right to possess and
administer property. Ecclesiastical suits were to be brought "before
ecclesiastical tribunals only": no cases involving the clergy should be
heard by civil courts, and appeals from ecclesiastical tribunals to civil
courts were cut off.

The concordat negotiated at the wish of García Moreno was the
earliest formal agreement between the Papacy and an independent
nation of Latin America respecting the relations between Church and
State. By its terms Ecuador relinquished to the Holy See certain rights
and privileges which the State had assumed upon the separation of
the presidency of Quito from Spain. Assured the exercise of extraordinary privileges, the Ecuadorian Church was encouraged to exert its
powerful influence in support of a theocratic State. This concordat
was for many years the butt of fierce attack by the Liberals.

Discontent was increased by foreign complications. Rumors were
circulated in Quito that the President desired to make Ecuador an
appanage of Spain. The truth of the matter is that, disgusted with
the tumultuous politics of his native land, he felt that it needed the
protection of a strong European state. He believed that, because of

political prestige and religious faith, France was the power that could best aid and uplift his country. Accordingly from December, 1859,

Dream of a French Protectorate

to April, 1862, by secret negotiations with the French consul general at Quito and through the Ecuadorian chargé at Paris, proposals were made to the government of Napoleon III that it should establish a protectorate over the distressed equatorial nation. At times García Moreno dreamed of forming, by the aid of French auxiliaries, a confederation that would ultimately include Peru and Bolivia—a confederation which would eventually become a rival of Brazil. At other times he contemplated the outright annexation of his country by the French Empire. The Ecuadorian chargé at Paris even suggested to the Quai d'Orsay that a "United Kingdom of the Andes" should be formed under the aegis of Napoleon III. Further, he proposed that his government should not only cede to France certain unoccupied lands on the banks of the Amazon but also the Galápagos Archipelago. Though attracted by these proposals, apprehensive of European complications, and skeptical of support by Ecuadorians, the French cabinet finally made known that it would not engage in projects "of territorial acquisition in those distant countries."

About the time that this grandiose scheme was shattered, Julio Arboleda, a revolutionist who was driven out of New Granada, crossed the frontier into Ecuador and defeated García Moreno's soldiers. President Mosquera of New Granada invited Ecuadorians to overthrow their President and to reëstablish "Great Colombia." As a retort General Flores arrogantly led an army into New Granada only to be defeated at Cuaspud on December 6, 1863. Still, New Granada negotiated a generous treaty of peace and amity with Ecuador which restored the status quo. Upon the death of the aged Flores, the President of Ecuador relinquished his civil authority to the Vice-President, placed himself at the head of the armed forces, and ruthlessly suppressed Ecuadorian revolutionists who were using Peruvian territory as a base of operations.

In the election of 1865 the administration candidate, Jerónimo Carrión, was chosen president. The ex-President apparently planned

García Moreno Returns to Power

to use him as a pliant tool. It was during Carrión's administration that Ecuador joined other republics on the Pacific in a struggle against Spain because of her war upon Peru. After the President had experienced grave difficulties with García Moreno and with Congress, he relinquished his post and was succeeded by Javier Espinosa, one of García Moreno's followers. As the result of a barrack insurrection in the capital city, García Moreno became president ad interim on January 17, 1869.

During the following month he promulgated a law which defined benefit of clergy. This law aimed to guarantee the right of ecclesiastics to be tried in church courts in all civil cases, except those of a financial or political character. In civil cases, however, ecclesiastical judges were to be guided by the civil law.

In June, 1869, García Moreno was reëlected by a Convention that had just framed a new Constitution which assured extravagant privileges to the Church. This organic law granted large powers to the President, extended his term to six years, and provided that he might at once be reëlected. Roman Catholicism was declared to be the national religion to the exclusion of any other. Non-Catholics were excluded from citizenship. Persons belonging to societies prohibited by the Church were to lose their political rights. Freedom of the press was not to include matters concerning religion, morality, and public order. Because of such provisions Ecuadorian Liberals stigmatized the Constitution of 1869 as a charter of serfdom to the Vatican.

During what has been designated his third administration, García Moreno became more and more imbued with Catholicism. A Peruvian littérateur said that his governmental program real like a bishop's sermon. The Ecuadorian President decreed that any one who belonged to a sect which was condemned by the Church should lose his civil rights. He protested to the Kingdom of Italy against the confiscation of the papal territories. At his instance, Congress made gifts of money to the Pope from Ecuador's treasury. In October, 1873, the President promulgated a law which solemnly consecrated the republic to the Sacred Heart of Jesus.

At the end of his third term García Moreno was again elected president and would have continued in power, but on August 6, 1875, conspirators finally accomplished their purpose. Assassins fell upon him at the entrance to the capitol and cleft his skull with a machete.

His influence upon Ecuador was twofold. His rule promoted a great increase of clerical influence and fanaticism. On the other side, his rule was marked by significant material improvements. It has been said that the road built during his age which replaced an Indian trail between Guayaquil and Quito was enough to immortalize ten presidents of republics. In his last message to Congress the theocrat indeed compared Ecuador to Lazarus arisen from his sepulcher. For good or ill, the impress of García Moreno's politico-religious despotism long remained upon the "Republic of the Sacred Heart."

Upon the death of the dictator the secretary of the interior assumed executive power. In December, 1875, Antonio Borrero, who had been elected president, picked up the reins. His refusal to convoke a convention to reform the clerical Constitution provoked violent opposition. In Guayaquil the Anti-Clericals or Liberals organized a revolution under General Ignacio de Veintemilla, the government forces were defeated, and Borrero was forced into exile. Clericals and priests, who feared that their powers and privileges would be curtailed, stimulated opposition to the new régime. A convention

Struggles
between
Clericals
and Liberals
that met at Ambato in 1878 framed a Constitution which vested executive power in a President whose term should be four years. This convention elected Veintemilla to that office. Well-grounded suspicion that he aspired to retain his power beyond the constitutional term soon promoted a spirit of discontent. Hence, insurrections against his authority took place. Driven out of Ecuador, the dictator was compelled to take refuge in Peru.

Revolutionary governments that were erected in various sections of Ecuador issued pronunciamientos advocating constitutional reform. Hence the "National Assembly of Ecuador" met at Quito in 1883, framed a Constitution, and elected José Caamaño president. He promulgated the fundamental law on February 13, 1884. The religion of Ecuador was again declared to be Catholic, Roman, and Apostolic, to the exclusion of any other faith. Public authorities were to respect it and to protect its rights and liberties. The term of both President and Vice-President was strictly limited to four years. They might not be reëlected until eight years had elapsed.

The rule of President Caamaño was marked by much turmoil and civil strife. Antonio Flores, who became president in 1888, gave Ecuador a rule of comparative tranquillity. A law passed by Congress during his administration that aimed to exempt the government from claims of foreigners for damages caused by riots, revolts, and civil wars, provoked a protest from the United States government. It declared that the act was "subversive of all the principles of international law." The President, who had opposed this law, then resigned, but Congress would not accept his resignation. He strove to accomplish certain reforms, especially the rehabilitation of Ecuador's embarrassed finances. In 1892 a lawyer and poet named Luis Cordero was elected president. Aid which he furnished Chile in a transaction involving the use of the Ecuadorian flag to cover the sale and transfer of the Chilean cruiser "Esmeralda" to Japan during the Sino-Japanese War aroused the indignation of the Ecuadorian people.

That transaction furnished the occasion for a liberal reaction against the existing régime. On June 5, 1895, the people of

The Rise
of Alfaro
Guayaquil published a proclamation which announced that General Eloy Alfaro, a Liberal who had spent several years in exile, was the ruler of Ecuador. Upon returning to his native land, he organized a revolutionary army and defeated the

soldiers of the government. On September 1, 1895, he entered Quito in triumph. Displeased with some results of autocratic rule, Alfaro thus became the "Supreme Chief of the Republic."

Alfaro soon undertook to institute social reforms. Passages selected from his message to Congress dated October 10, 1896, will suggest, in part, the political transformation that he contemplated:

The indigenous race, who were the masters of the territory before the Spanish conquest, continue in large part to be subject to the most odious slavery under the name of peons. . . . By a decree the Indians have already been relieved from certain contributions. . . . In Ecuador ecclesiastics and military men enjoy certain privileges and immunities that it is necessary to abolish. . . . I believe that in our fundamental charter you should stipulate that all citizens of the republic are equal before the law. . . . You well know that the Ecuadorian government has had a tempestuous life, and that we have lived constantly with arms in our hands, ever threatened by an implacable and insensate enemy. Further, the struggle has not always been on the battle field but has also been against a maze of entanglements, intrigues, and favoritisms which were long ago converted into a system of political life, and which prevented an honorable magistrate from fully performing his duties.

Under his leadership the Liberals tried to purge Ecuador of clericalism. A convention that had assembled at Guayaquil framed a liberal Constitution which was promulgated on January 12, 1897. More tolerant than previous fundamental laws, it provided that Roman Catholicism should be the state religion to the exclusion of all other forms of religious worship that were contrary to morality. There were to be no religious qualifications for the exercise of civil or political rights. The entrance of religious orders into the republic was prohibited; only native-born clergy could hold an ecclesiastical position or administer the property of monastic institutions. Compulsory conscription and confiscation of private property were alike prohibited. Slavery was not to exist within Ecuadorian territory. The main administrative divisions were to be the provinces which should be managed by governors appointed by the President.

After the convention had transferred its seat to Quito, it elected General Alfaro president. Scarcely had it terminated its labors when an insurrection began. As that movement was evidently due to the influence of the Conservative party, Alfaro pursued a policy that was designed to decrease the privileges of the clergy. On September 27, 1899, he promulgated a law which abrogated certain provisions of the concordat. This law provided that papal legates could not exercise jurisdiction in the republic without the consent of the Council of State; bulls or rescripts could not be circulated without the sanction of the President. Revenues for the support of the Church were to be raised by

Politico-Religious Reforms

the State alone. The right to appoint bishops could only be exercised by the national government.

In 1901 General Leonidas Plaza Gutiérrez became president. During his administration Ecuador enjoyed a large measure of peace and liberty. His program of reform included various measures designed to decrease the authority and privileges of the Catholic Church. In a message to Congress on August 10, 1902, he urged that the control of education should be given to laymen. He soon signed bills that legalized civil marriage and made divorce possible. On October 13, 1904, he sanctioned a law providing that any faith which was not contrary to morality or to the laws of Ecuador was to be tolerated, that the ministers of religions which were tolerated should be protected, and that the establishment of new convents and monasteries was prohibited. In 1905 a law was enacted which declared that rural property held by the dead hand of the Church belonged to the nation. The income from these extensive estates was set apart for the support of such institutions as asylums, hospitals, and orphanages.

In 1905 Lizardo García, who was the candidate of Plaza Gutiérrez, was elected president. A few months of power were all that he enjoyed; for early in the following year a revolt began that was supported by former President Alfaro. This movement triumphed in Guayaquil; and on January 17 he occupied Quito.

He soon convoked a Constitutional Assembly that met in Quito and framed the twelfth Constitution of Ecuador, which was promulgated on December 23, 1906. This organic law declared that public education was to be under the control of laymen. Freedom of conscience was to be enjoyed whenever it was not contrary to morals or public order. There should be no arbitrary arrests; liberty of suffrage, of speech, and of the press were to be enjoyed. All personal privileges or immunities were abolished. The transfer of landed property was not to be restricted by primogeniture or entail. Confiscation of property, infamous punishments, or torture were prohibited. In general, foreigners were to enjoy the same civil rights as Ecuadorians. Every contract made by a foreigner with the government of Ecuador, however, was to imply his renunciation of any recourse to diplomacy.

The Ecuadorian Constitution of 1906 furnished the basis for a centralistic republic. It stipulated that the President was to select the governors of the provinces. He was to be advised by a cabinet of five members appointed by himself; upon important matters he was to be advised by a Council of State. Members of the cabinet might participate in congressional debates. Congress should meet annually at Quito on August 10, but the President might convoke it in extraordinary session whenever he judged necessary. The supreme court should be composed of five judges elected by Congress in joint session for six years.

The convention of 1906 elected the revolutionary chieftain president. Alfaro was inaugurated on January 1, 1907. The politico-religious reforms that he had initiated were further advanced by a law which freed education from the control of the Church. It provided that no religious doctrines could be taught in the public schools. A contract that had been signed during Alfaro's first administration between the Ecuadorian government and a citizen of the United States for the construction of a railroad between Guayaquil and Quito was carried out. On June 17, 1908, Américo Alfaro, the President's daughter, drove a golden spike in the last tie of the railway that linked the miasmic coast with the Andean plateau.

Meantime, an opposition had developed that was composed of Conservatives who were aided by discontented Liberals. Alfaro was accused of aiming at the establishment of a dictatorship. The opposition became so strong that he relinquished his authority and went into exile. Unfortunately the Acting President soon died; and party passion again flared up over the succession to the presidency. Partisans of Alfaro urged him to return to lead a revolution. The anticlerical leader accepted the invitation. A barbarous struggle ensued between his partisans and the government's forces. The revolutionary soldiers were badly defeated at Huigra, their leaders were captured, and their aged chieftain was incarcerated in the penitentiary of the capital city. In January, 1912, he was dragged out of his dungeon by the enraged populace and barbarously murdered. Such was the tragic end of the great Liberal champion whose life work had largely undone the clerical achievements of García Moreno!

After December, 1911, the chief magistracy of Ecuador was exercised during an interregnum either by the president of the Senate or by the president of the Chamber of Deputies. On August 31, 1912, General Leonidas Plaza Gutiérrez was again inaugurated president. Partisans of Alfaro had taken refuge in the mountainous province of Esmeraldas, where uprisings soon took place against the government, but after the defeat and capture of their chief leader, the rebels gradually dispersed. Not only did President Plaza Gutiérrez strive to exterminate the bandits who were often responsible for revolutionary disturbances, but he also attempted to initiate certain political reforms.

Attempts at Reforms

In a message to the legislature in 1914 he proposed that the Constitution of the republic should be again altered. As conferences with congressmen produced no tangible results, he brought the matter to

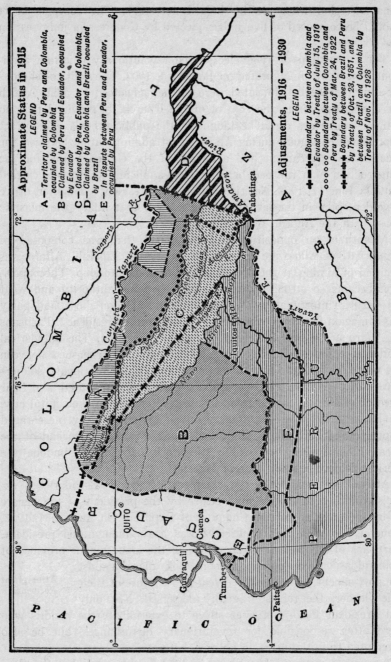

Map illustrating boundary disputes near the headwaters of the Amazon, 1915-1930

the attention of Congress by a special message. Like Batlle of Uruguay, Plaza Gutiérrez deplored the failure of "presidential government." The Ecuadorian President, however, proposed a reorganization through the introduction of a parliamentary system resting upon "complete electoral liberty." Yet Congress could not indorse his projected constitutional amendments which would have made it possible for a Senator or a Deputy to accept a place in the cabinet without relinquishing his seat in Congress, and which would have introduced a system similar to that which had prevailed in Chile under the Constitution of 1833.

In 1914 a treaty was signed in Rio de Janeiro by which Ecuador relinquished to Brazil her claim to territory lying between the river Caquetá and the Amazon River, east of a line drawn from the mouth of San Antonio River to the mouth of the river Apaporis. In 1856 a treaty had been negotiated which provided that the northern boundary of Ecuador should be the line drawn in 1824 by the Congress of Colombia between the departments of Ecuador and Cauca. Subsequently, however, troublesome questions arose about the survey of this line. At Bogotá on July 15, 1916, a treaty was accordingly signed which sketched a boundary line between Ecuador and Colombia, and which provided that a mixed commission should be selected with power to set posts along this boundary and to adjust such reciprocal compensations as might be necessary to determine the line clearly. A year later the commission began this survey, which it completed by July 9, 1919.

Conditions about 1914: Boundary Disputes

The boundary dispute of Ecuador with Peru, however, proved more difficult to adjust. In 1894 a Tripartite Treaty was arranged between Ecuador, Colombia, and Peru which stipulated that Colombia and Ecuador should submit their boundary disputes with Peru to arbitration. This compact was ratified by the congresses of Peru and Colombia but was rejected by the Ecuadorian Congress. On February 19, 1904, a protocol was signed by diplomats of Peru and Ecuador by which their governments agreed to submit their acrimonious controversy to the arbitration of the Spanish King. A commissioner of that monarch visited Lima and Quito but, apparently dreading that the announcement of the decision which he had drafted might provoke a war between Peru and Ecuador, the arbiter withheld his award. A portion of the territory in dispute was subsequently occupied by Peruvians.

In 1914 the total population of Ecuador perhaps amounted to one and one-half million souls. Possibly three-fourths of these were Indians; about one-fifth were half-breeds; while only a small fraction were whites. Few immigrants had entered Ecuador, even from other

Spanish-American countries. The upper classes spoke Spanish, while the lower classes ordinarily used an Indian dialect. On the eve of the first World War the Ecuadorian army numbered about seven thousand men, while the navy was composed of a few small war vessels.

The chief industry was agriculture. More cacao was produced in Ecuador than in any other American country. In various sections coffee was a profitable crop. On the lowlands near the

Social and Economic Conditions coast there were numerous sugar and tobacco plantations. Ivory nuts and crude rubber were gathered in the forests. The ordinary cereals were raised for home consumption, as well as cattle and sheep. Some mining was done; a small amount of gold was exported. Among Ecuador's manufactures were the following: crude chocolate, ponchos, stuffed humming birds, and "Panama hats."

Transportation in Ecuador was extremely backward. Her eastern territory, which Peru claimed, was served by small steamers that plied the branches of the Amazon. Her seaports had rather indifferent steamship service; Guayaquil was generally under a quarantine. Ecuador's smaller ports were reached by coasting vessels. Internal arteries of commerce in Ecuador were the Guayas River, the upper tributaries of the Amazon, and the Guayaquil and Quito Railway. In 1914 the debt of Ecuador, which was largely composed of obligations inherited from Colombia and of loans incurred to promote her chief railway, perhaps aggregated in United States currency some twenty million dollars.

Education was very backward. Though primary education was free and obligatory, the attendance at elementary schools was small. Secondary education was mainly carried on in academies that were often managed by religious orders. Higher education was pursued in the universities of Cuenca, Guayaquil, and Quito. The University of

Intellectual Life Quito offered courses in philosophy, letters, law, medicine, physical and natural science, mathematics, and agriculture. In spite of the liberal reforms, the Church still exercised a politico-religious influence upon many Ecuadorians.

The literature of Ecuador began with the poet Olmedo, who sang about the triumph of Bolívar's arms at Junín. Her most distinguished journalist was García Moreno who wrote a lengthy defense of the Jesuits, besides numerous state papers. Juan Montalvo included in *Siete Tratados* literary essays upon diverse topics. His best-known production was the *Capítulos que se olvidaron á Cervantes*—a volume which was published posthumously. Among poets Numa Pompilio Llona holds a high rank, his best-known poem being "La Odisea del Alma." The most versatile writer of Ecuador was Juan León Mera, the author of novels, verses, and a history of Ecuadorian poetry. His poem "La Virgen del Sol" was based upon a legend of the Spanish conquest. A diplomat named Carlos R. Tobar was not only the author of sketches of society in Quito, but also the formulator of a doctrine allied to the Monroe Doctrine.

Partly because of the impetus given during the colonial era, Ecuador maintained a name as an artistic center that was much superior to her reputation for material progress. Chief among her distinguished painters was Antonio Salas, who was made the official painter of the heroes of the wars for independence. Perhaps the most noteworthy of his portraits and religious paintings is "The Prophets," which was hung in the residence of the archbishop of Quito. Ramón, the son of Antonio Salas, created a new genre of Ecuadorian art by depicting the manners and customs of the people of Quito, which he portrayed in water colors. Rafael Salas, a brother of Ramón, was taught to draw and to paint by his father, studied in Europe, and taught at an academy of fine arts founded by García Moreno. He was instrumental in introducing the art of landscape painting into his native land. When a school of fine arts was reopened at Quito in 1904, he became a member of its faculty where he taught until his death in 1906. In the same year there also died another teacher in that school, Joaquín Pinto, whose best canvas, "Dies Irae," was hung in the national museum. After the death of these two Ecuadorian artists, the faculty of the art school was strengthened by the addition of a number of teachers of painting and sculpture from Europe.

The first World War affected Ecuador in various ways. At once the volume of her imports declined and, in consequence, her revenues decreased. On August 17, 1914, the government announced that it would observe a strict neutrality during the war. In November, 1914, in response to complaints of England and France that Ecuador had permitted violations of neutrality within her jurisdiction, Secretary Elizalde addressed a circular to American governments justifying the neutral policy of his government. Subsequently Ecuador addressed communications to American republics advocating an organization for the defense of their rights and the protection of their interests. This policy was continued under the Liberal, Alfredo Baquerizo Moreno, who became president on August 31, 1916. It does not appear that the Ecuadorian government was ever officially notified by the German government about its ruthless submarine policy. Still, in October, 1917, when the ex-minister of Germany to Lima expressed his intention to proceed to Quito—having been accredited to Ecuador as well as to Peru—he was informed by the Ecuadorian minister at Lima that his reception at Quito would be incompatible with the principles of American solidarity. This step, which was virtually a decision to suspend diplomatic relations with Germany, was promptly made known by the Ecuadorian government to other nations.

Not until after the close of the war did efforts for the sanitation of Guayaquil, which had long been an endemic center for the bubonic plague and yellow fever, terminate in a satisfactory manner. In 1916 a commission of the Rockefeller Foundation made an investigation of the conditions prevailing in that city. A scientific fight against yellow fever was undertaken under the direction of the American sanitary expert, Colonel Gorgas. By May, 1920, that scourge had been eradicated from Guayaquil and also from adjacent districts. The chief seaport of Ecuador was thus relieved from the commercial excommunication which had for many years obstructed her relations with other countries.

Later Trends

In the campaign of 1920 José Tamayo was elected president. In his inaugural address he outlined a legislative program that was designed to suppress brigandage and to promote the social and economic welfare of the people. During his administration steps were taken to provide for the study of agriculture in all national schools, to promote such public improvements as railroads, and to take a census of the Chinese in the republic. In 1922 the activities of petroleum prospectors induced Congress to pass a law concerning the exploitation of oil lands. The President then issued a decree fixing the government's quota from operating wells at 6 per cent of the gross product.

An assembly of leaders of the Liberal party that gathered in Quito in September, 1923, framed a program of reform. Among its proposals were the following planks: agrarian reform, the representation of minorities, the reform of education, the enactment of laws to protect the laborer, the improvement of the position of women, and the maintenance of the principles embodied in the Constitution of 1906. Some time afterward the Conservative party formulated its principles. These included declarations in favor of Catholic teaching in all training schools, obligatory military service, liberty and respect for the Catholic Church, and friendly relations with the Vatican.

By a large majority, Gonzalo Córdoba, a legislator and diplomat of wide experience, was elected president for the term 1924-1928. During his administration an economic crisis, which was severely felt in Guayaquil, reached a climax. On the morning of July 9, 1925, the leaders of the army deposed the President; and a junta composed of civilians was placed in charge of the government. But neither this junta nor another that followed it succeeded in finding a remedy for the economic evils. As a result of the revolution of 1925, a Socialist party came into existence. In April, 1926, the army proclaimed Isidro Ayora, who had been directing the ministry of labor, as provisional president. Dictator Ayora initiated certain reforms. He compelled offending bankers to withdraw their illicit paper money from circulation. As a temporary solution for the currency problem, he founded a bank of redemption. To secure a thorough economic and financial reform Ayora secured the services of a group of foreign financial experts headed by Professor Kemmerer. This commission recommended that a series of reform laws should be enacted concerning such matters as the banks, the budget, the currency, and the customs service.

After these reforms were initiated, elections were held for the choice of delegates to a Constitutional Assembly. In 1929 this Assembly adopted a Constitution which slightly modified the Constitution of 1906. In March, 1929, it elected Ayora president. On September 28, 1930, mainly because of opposition to budgetary reforms, Ayora resigned the presidency, but Congress refused to accept his resignation, and two days later he resumed office for a short time.

The history of Ecuador from 1930 to 1940 was very tumultuous. During that decade no less than thirteen persons undertook to exercise the functions of president or acted as dictator. More than one Congress was dissolved as the result of a coup d'état. During three months of 1939 seven different cabinets were formed. One cabinet member dared to state to Congress that none of the labor partisans or of the intellectual leaders engaged in the political orgies of his country had acted with any other motive than to overthrow the government so that they might themselves secure power. A sharp decline in the price of cacao due to plant diseases promoted economic instability. There were frequent signs of bitter discontent among the oppressed Indians who were still kept in a servile condition on the haciendas of the landholding aristocracy.

In the election which took place in January, 1940, Carlos del Río, the leader of a faction of the Liberal party, was elected president. During his administration the old boundary dispute again brought Ecuador to the brink of war with her **End of** southern neighbor. Though commissioners had been ap- **Boundary Controversies** pointed by both parties to designate the *de facto* boundaries, disquieting reports reached Quito about the penetration of Peruvian soldiers into the hinterland. In May, 1941, Argentina, Brazil, and the United States proposed to mediate in the bitter controversy but Peru would not accept their offer. A little later Ecuadorians complained that the Peruvians had even invaded the coastal province of Oro. On August 3, 1941, popular discontent because of defeats to the soldiers of Ecuador in the undeclared war induced Congress to grant to the President authority which transcended the extraordinary power

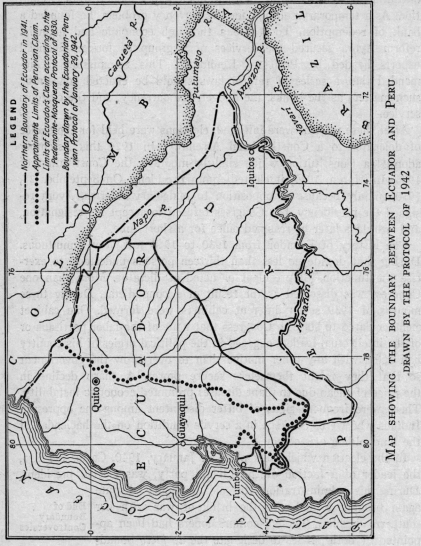

LEGEND

Northern Boundary of Ecuador in 1941.

Approximate Limits of Peruvian Claim.

Limits of Ecuador's Claim according to the Pedemonte-Mosquera Protocol of 1830.

Boundary drawn by the Ecuadorian-Peruvian Protocol of January 29, 1942.

MAP SHOWING THE BOUNDARY BETWEEN ECUADOR AND PERU DRAWN BY THE PROTOCOL OF 1942

(Adapted from a map in the *Inter-American Monthly*, June, 1942.)

which had not infrequently been granted to the chief magistrate in times of peace.

Fortunately, however, immediately after the third meeting of the ministers of foreign affairs at Rio de Janeiro, on January 29, 1942, and in accordance with its resolution condemning inter-American conflicts, the two parties signed a protocol which ended the long controversy. This protocol provided that a compromise line was to be drawn by a mixed commission through places designated in that agreement. By this adjustment Peru was conceded sovereignty over the upper Amazon River and the lower courses of its tributaries, while Ecuador retained control of the major portion of the Andean foothills with the right of navigation on the tributaries of the Amazon which traversed those slopes.

Shortly after agreeing to this demarcation of the boundary, the government at Quito announced that it had severed relations with the Axis. Some months later, it granted the United States the right to establish an air base in the Galápagos Islands.

Ecuador has been very slow in development. Because of her inaccessibility, due in some measure to the pestiferous conditions that long prevailed at her chief port, that republic has in many essentials lagged behind her northern neighbor. Politicians of Guayaquil struggling against the domination of politicians of Quito and vice versà, an aggressive Clerical party anxious to retain as many as possible of the privileges gained during the age of García Moreno, barrack uprisings of aboriginal soldiers that have been occasionally marked by acts of savage cruelty—these have been some of the outstanding traits of Ecuadorian revolutions and counter-revolutions. Ecuadorian constitutional changes do not appear to have often signalized the triumph of any political principles. The phrase which Bolívar used in despair while speaking of the constitutions of Spanish America seems to be particularly applicable to Ecuador: her constitutions are paper. This has been so largely because of the intractable aboriginal element in her population, an element that at times suddenly breaks through the dikes which have been raised by the cultured leaders. At many points the Liberals have made gains against the Clericals in recent decades; the Republic of the Sacred Heart has been much changed by the spirit of liberalism. Her economic development has been stunted because of the unprogressive character of large classes in her population, because of the lack of good communications, and because of the relatively slight contact with the outer world. The sanitation of Guayaquil made possible a great improvement in the relations of Ecuador with foreign nations. More recently her international relations have been further improved by the peaceful adjustment of the boundary with her southern neighbor which had been in dispute for more than a century.

SUGGESTIONS FOR FURTHER READING

BEEBE, C. W., *Galápagos, World's End,* 1924.
BEMELMANS, L., *The Donkey Inside,* 1941.
ENOCK, C. R., *Ecuador,* 1914.
ESTRADA, V. E., *Money and Banking in Ecuador,* 1925.
HASSAUREK, F., *Four Years among Spanish Americans,* 1868.
NILES, B., *Casual Wanderings in Ecuador,* 1923.
ORTON, J., *The Andes and the Amazon,* 1870.
ROBERTSON, W. S., "García Moreno's Dream of a European Protectorate,"
   Contribuciones para el estudio de la historia de América (1941), pp. 125-143.
ROSS, E. A., *South of Panama,* 1915.
SIMSON, A., *Travels in the Wilds of Ecuador,* 1886.
TOMLINSON, E., *New Roads to Riches in the Other Americas,* 1940.
VON HAGEN, V. W., *Ecuador, the Unknown,* 1940.

CHAPTER XXI

VENEZUELA

A convention which, at the instance of General Páez, assembled at Valencia in May, 1830, re-created the state of Venezuela. In September, 1830, it published a Constitution which provided that the republic was to include the territory designated the captaincy general of Venezuela before the Revolution of 1810. This fundamental law was a compromise between the federalistic and the centralistic types of government. Executive authority was to be vested in a President chosen by electoral colleges. The unit of local government was to be the autonomous province. Each province was to have a legislature made up of members chosen by an electoral college. The governor of each province should be selected by the President from a list of nominees presented by the respective legislature. The convention also undertook to modify certain laws of Great Colombia so as to make them suit the new nation.

As their chief magistrate the Venezuelans chose that dashing, inconsistent, and refractory lieutenant of Bolívar who had been the chief leader of the separatist movement. Early in 1831 General Páez was installed as president. In May Congress passed a law which provided that the capital of Venezuela should be at Caracas. After leading the army triumphantly against opponents of the new régime, Páez issued a decree of amnesty. By a law of March 31, 1833, Congress declared that the Colombian law of 1824, which vested the right of patronage in the national government, was in force in Venezuela. This law also declared that the government had the right to inspect and to protect the Venezuelan Church. A law of April, 1833, abolished the tithes and provided that the expenses of the Church in Venezuela should be paid from the national exchequer. Early in 1834 the President signed a law which stipulated that there should be no prohibition upon religious liberty.

As no candidate secured the required majority of electoral votes in the next presidential election, early in 1835 Congress proceeded to choose a president. To the chagrin of military men the choice fell upon José Vargas, the learned rector of the University of Caracas. He took up the duties of chief magistrate with reluctance, and, when the legislature passed a bill over his veto, he resigned. Yet Congress

379

declined to accept his resignation. In July, 1835, an insurrection led by General Mariño, who was designated the chief of the revolution of reform, deposed Vargas and sent him into exile. Tradition records that when a revolutionist peremptorily asked Vargas to renounce the presidency, exclaiming that the world was for the valiant man, Vargas responded that the world was for just and honorable men. Upon the eve of his departure, he appointed General Páez as commander of the government forces. That general took the field against the so-called reformers, occupied Valencia and Caracas; and on March 1, 1836, captured Puerto Cabello. Soon afterward, President Vargas, who had returned from exile, again resigned his office.

Congress accepted his resignation, and Vice-President Narvarte, who succeeded Vargas, soon gave way to Carlos Soublette, a conciliatory hero of the war for independence. In January, 1836, a treaty of friendship and commerce was negotiated between the United States and Venezuela. By a law of February, 1837, the announcement was made that laws of Great Colombia, which had suppressed certain monasteries, should be in force. In March, 1837, President Soublette sanctioned a law providing that Spanish merchant vessels would be admitted into Venezuela's ports. On April 19, 1838, on behalf of Congress, Soublette presented a sword to General Páez in testimony of his services in defense of the Constitution and laws of Venezuela against revolutionary reformers.

In 1838 Páez was reëlected president. The years from 1839 to 1843 were marked by social and economic progress. The President persuaded Congress to adopt the policy of building roads

President Páez

between seaports and important cities of the republic. In April, 1839, it enacted a law which granted more freedom to the press and provided for the punishment of such persons as might abuse that liberty. Another important law was passed that aimed to encourage immigration to Venezuela. A group of German immigrants was granted lands in the beautiful valley of Aragua. Páez issued a decree that made provision for the funding of the national debt. In May, 1841, he signed a law which provided for the establishment of a national bank with a capital of two and one-half million pesos. In accordance with a law directing the President to take measures to civilize the aborigines, he issued an ordinance for the regulation of missions that were to be established by friars in the province of Guiana. A treaty of commerce and navigation was negotiated between Venezuela and the Kingdom of Sweden and Norway. With Great Britain a convention was arranged which contained provisions that aimed to abolish the slave trade. During the decade from 1831 to 1841, Venezuela's imports and exports more than trebled in value.

In 1843 General Soublette became president again. He continued the policies of Páez. In June, 1843, an elaborate law was enacted containing regulations about Venezuelan universities. Another law made provisions concerning naval schools that had been established at Maracaibo and on the island of Margarita. An appropriation was made to promote the construction of a highway between La Guaira and Caracas. A commercial code was promulgated. An index of the prosperity of Venezuela is shown by the fact that from 1830 to 1845 her public debt had been reduced from some nine million pesos to two million.

The oligarchy which had ruled Venezuela under an electoral system restricting suffrage to owners of property became known as the Conservative or *Godo* party. Members of that party believed in the conservation of property and order, if necessary by military force. To oppose the Conservatives a party designated the Liberals had appeared. In 1840 that anti-oligarchical party founded a journal called *El Venezolano*. In its first number the editor, Antonio Guzmán, characterized his followers as the "new men." His attacks upon the political domination of Páez and Soublette stimulated the opposition of the lower classes to the ruling oligarchy. Guzmán was an unsuccessful candidate for the presidency in 1846 in opposition to General José Tadeo Monagas, who was supported by Páez.

One of the first acts of President Monagas was magnanimously to commute the punishment of Guzmán, who had been condemned to death because of the propaganda which he had directed in his journal against the existing régime. That penalty the President commuted into exile. In truth Monagas was himself somewhat affected by liberal principles; his presidency was a period of transition in politics. In May, 1847, in accordance with an early law of Colombia, which had declared that that republic had the right of patronage, he signed a law providing for the establishment of two new bishoprics. Bitter strife, however, soon took place between the President and Congress; for Monagas replaced a cabinet of conservatives by a liberal cabinet, and his policies were attacked by the conservative press. The oligarchy was contemplating the impeachment of the President, when on January 24, 1848, he arbitrarily dissolved Congress. Against that coup d'état Páez protested, but the conservative oligarchy refused longer to support him, the insurrectionary soldiers whom he led were defeated, and in 1850 he was forced into exile. Meantime Guzmán, the apostle of reform, who was elected vice-president in 1848, had returned to his native land.

José Tadeo Monagas, the founder of the so-called Monagas dynasty, was succeeded in 1851 by his brother, General José Gregorio. Another liberal oligarch, he was viewed askance by the followers of Guzmán and Páez alike. Two revolts against the younger Monagas were sternly repressed.

During his administration anti-slavery propaganda steadily increased. An animated discussion about Negro slavery took place. On March 10, 1854, the President sent a message to Congress in which he cited Bolívar's statement that slaveholding was contrary to all laws and an infringement upon human dignity. He argued that Venezuela should no longer appear to the eyes of the world bearing the horrible stain of slavery. In the name of Venezuela and of her Constitution, he asked the congressmen, "with all the enthusiasm of his republican heart," to abolish that institution. Congress approved his plea. On March 24, 1854, Monagas signed a law which provided that slavery should be forever abolished in Venezuela. This law declared that the liberated slaves should not only be exempt from any obligation for service, but also that they should enjoy the same liberty as born freemen. It provided that the owners of emancipated slaves should be paid indemnities out of the proceeds of certain taxes. It prohibited the importation of slaves into the republic; any bondsmen who might be introduced should immediately gain their liberty.

The Dynasty of the Monagas

In 1855 José Tadeo Monagas became president for the second time. In April, 1856, Congress enacted a law which provided that there were to be twenty provinces in the republic. That law gave to the President the right to appoint provisional governors for all the provinces. It provided that the provincial electoral colleges should at once proceed to elect senators and representatives. To the new legislature the President sent a message in January, 1857, which urged that the Constitution should be amended. This Congress framed an ephemeral, fundamental law that was promulgated on April 10, 1857. That Constitution did not prohibit the immediate reëlection of the President whose term was made six years. It conceded to him the exclusive power to appoint the governors of provinces, and it granted certain autonomous rights to the cities. When a reactionary movement against the Constitution of 1857 broke out, Monagas renounced the presidency, and a convention was promptly convoked to frame another fundamental law.

The convention assembled at Valencia, invited Páez to return from exile, and, after some discussion, adopted a new Constitution. The charter of 1858 provided that the governors of provinces were to be elected by the voters but that they should act as agents of the national government. The President of the republic was to be elected by universal suffrage. The adoption of this Constitution was followed by a protracted civil war between the Conservatives, who generally supported it, and the Liberals, who wished a federal type of government. In March, 1861, General Páez returned to Venezuela. He gathered all the power into his own hands, abrogated the new Constitution in September, 1861, and crowned his picturesque career by becoming dictator. In 1862 he promulgated a civil code for Venezuela. As a consequence of some bloody conflicts, federalist leaders gained the ascendancy, and on May 22, 1863, agents of the contending factions signed a truce.

Constitutional Readjustments

This agreement provided that a National Assembly was to be convoked composed of members selected in equal numbers by "the supreme chief of the republic," General Páez, and by General Juan Falcón, who was styled "the provisional president of the Federation." Páez faithfully promised to transfer his power to the Assembly which was to establish a new government, pending the political reorganization of the state. Both Páez and Falcón promised to promote the establishment of a régime that would enable the republic to heal the wounds caused by internecine war. The "Founder of Venezuela," as Páez has been called by admiring fellow countrymen, again went into exile and spent his last years in the United States. Although a concordat which he had negotiated with the Papacy conceded the right of patronage to the republic, yet it was rejected by Congress because it was not in harmony with Venezuela's law and custom concerning freedom of religion and the press.

The National Assembly soon elected General Falcón president. His magnanimous spirit was displayed in a decree dated August 18, 1863, which guaranteed civil and political rights to all Venezuelan citizens in the most ample fashion. On March 28, 1864, the Assembly adopted a Constitution for "the United States of Venezuela." This fundamental law, which marked the introduction of the federal system, declared the Venezuelan provinces to be autonomous states that retained all sovereign power which was not expressly delegated to the national government. Falcón was soon elected president of the Confederation for four years.

In May, 1867, the President promulgated a new civil code for his country which was to go into force in the following October. He was much harassed by uprisings against his rule in various sections; hence, upon more than one occasion, he temporarily transferred executive authority to a substitute and led his soldiers against rebels. In Congress unrelenting opposition to his administration reached a climax a few months before his term expired. To intimate friends Falcón ultimately made known his high resolve not to use military force against Congress.

In the belief that the opposition was directed against him personally, on May 2, 1868, he published an address to his fellow citizens announcing that he had transferred executive authority to his ministers. He denounced the insurrection against his government as anti-patriotic, decried the fact that a cordial and sincere union of parties had not been effected, and ascribed his country's bitter misfortunes to a rebellious spirit. General José T. Monagas, who had become the leader of the party of opposition designated the *Azules*, soon led his victorious soldiers into the capital city. An exile from his native land, there expired in the island of Martinique the "Great Citizen,"—as Congress had styled Falcón in the days of his glory.

A leader soon emerged who seized the mantle that had fallen from the shoulders of Páez. In November, 1868, under General Antonio Guzmán Blanco, a son of the radical journalist, the Liberals rose in arms against Monagas. On April 27, 1870, the *Jaunes,* as they were designated, entered Caracas in triumph. Guzmán Blanco was soon made provisional president. Armed opposition to the new régime was not thoroughly suppressed, however, until May, 1872, when Matías Salazar, a renegade associate of the new leader, was defeated and executed. Magnetic, eloquent, and energetic, Guzmán Blanco was an extraordinary personage. With extensive experience both as a civil and a military administrator, that resourceful leader dominated Venezuelan politics for almost two decades.

During that period he promoted certain reforms which had been initiated under previous presidents. On June 27, 1870, he issued a decree which provided that public education should be gratuitous and obligatory. Soon afterward he took steps to reorganize the national debt and to restore the public credit. In May, 1871, he issued a decree that regulated the coinage. He promoted the building of a railroad between Caracas and La Guaira. He provided for the construction of roads, bridges, customhouses, parks, and boulevards. His commissions prepared codes of civil and commercial law and of military and penal procedure. On January 1, 1873, he issued a decree which made civil marriage legal.

The Reign of Guzmán Blanco

Convents and monasteries were suppressed throughout Venezuela. Their properties were sequestrated by the State. A famous church in the capital city was transformed into a national pantheon. In 1873 the Venezuelan secretary of foreign affairs informed the papal secretary of state that his government would not allow the exercise within its territory of any ecclesiastical authority except that of those bishops or archbishops who had been chosen by Congress and presented to His Holiness and of vicars who had been appointed to vacant seats by the respective cabildos with the approval of the executive authority.

Not only did Venezuela thus claim the exclusive right of patronage, but she also made known her policy to exclude any papal delegate or nuncio whose functions were not purely diplomatic. A grand master of the Masonic order, Guzmán Blanco even dreamed of establishing a national Church that would be independent of the Papacy.

Some of his fellow countrymen displayed a tendency to adulate him. Statues were erected in his honor. A boulevard which encircled a hill overlooking the capital city was given his name. Congress proclaimed him president for four years and bestowed upon him the title of "Illustrious American, Regenerator, Pacificator."

While descanting upon the magical influence by which Guzmán Blanco had transformed Venezuela, his father, the veteran Liberal, indulged in the following homily on Venezuelan politics, which may serve as an apology for Spanish-American dictatorship:

Sixty-three years of vicissitude, martyrdom, and terrorism that seemed endless rendered it impossible for us to form the rare virtue of civic valor, which is the sentiment of personal independence. We cannot inherit that virtue. Under absolute monarchs, under the ferocious Inquisition, and under the viceroys and captains general, free will remained dormant. What resulted from this condition? Yesterday saving fortune from peril, to-day rescuing the hearth and the family, to-morrow preserving life itself; passing from the camp to the gibbet or perhaps from the bed to the gloom of the barracks or the dungeon; amidst apprehensions about the guerrilla or in the shock of his attack, how could the Venezuelans be of good heart, or acquire sensible ideas, or mold and strengthen their convictions, so as to form finally the inexorable consciences of true republicans?

Disgusted Liberals and former Conservatives who rose against the dictator were forced to lay down their arms. It was due to his influence that in 1874 an Assembly framed another Constitution which provided for voting by ballot, which limited the President's term to two years, and prohibited his reëlection. Three years later the President quietly gave up his power and left ostensibly on a mission to seven European courts. Upon the death of his successor, President Alcántara, Guzmán Blanco returned from Europe, and was proclaimed supreme director by a revolutionary party. As chief magistrate of Venezuela, on March 31, 1879, he issued a decree which provided that a coin designated the bolívar should be the monetary unit. Soon afterward he left the executive authority in the hands of Diego Urbaneja and made another visit to Paris.

In 1880 Guzmán Blanco was elected "constitutional president" for two years. At his suggestion in 1881 a new Constitution was adopted which stipulated that there should be nine states in the Venezuelan republic. It provided that the President and his substitute should be elected for two years by a federal council composed of Senators and

Deputies. It established a tribunal of representatives of the states which was designated the court of cassation. In 1882 the federal council elected Guzmán Blanco president. The following year, which was the centenary of Bolívar's birth, was made memorable in various ways. An academy, which was a correspondent of the Royal Spanish Academy, was inaugurated in the Venezuelan capital. The railroad between Caracas and La Guaira was opened to traffic. At public expense there were published the memoirs of General O'Leary, an aide-de-camp who had preserved the Liberator's papers. Meanwhile one young Venezuelan journalist after another took up the pen against a dictator who was not always benevolent.

In 1884, after substitutes had exercised authority in place of Guzmán Blanco, who had again proceeded to Europe as an envoy extraordinary, Joaquín Crespo was elected president. He was a lieutenant of the dictator who had worthily occupied important civil and military offices. This President promoted internal improvements and public instruction. He strove to preserve the autonomy of the states as well as to protect the aborigines from exploitation. His nation's credit he upheld despite the economic stress due to a plague of locusts. After suppressing revolts in the eastern part of the republic, he treated their leaders with rare magnanimity. Upon being accused of forsaking the political views of Guzmán Blanco, he published a defense of his absent chief. When he relinquished his authority to make way for that personage who was again elected president in April, 1886, Congress appropriately bestowed upon him the title of the "Hero of Duty."

President Crespo

In a short time Guzmán Blanco bestowed his authority as President upon a member of his council; and in July, 1887, he again proceeded to Europe on a diplomatic mission. In February, 1888, Dr. Juan Rojas Paul, whose candidacy had been supported by Guzmán Blanco, was elected president. Eight months later a violent reaction took place against the absent dictator: the people of the capital city cast his statues to the earth. A Venezuelan historian states that a group of young men offered the head from a statue of this discredited leader to Crespo but that he refused to accept it, saying that that glory belonged not to him but to President Rojas. After this incident the absent dictator relinquished any hope he may have entertained of longer dominating Venezuelan politics. Proposals to reform the Constitution so as to extend the chief magistrate's term of office encouraged the next President, Raimundo Andueza Palacio, to lay plans to retain his power beyond the fixed term. A group of congressmen vigorously opposed that projected change in the legal order.

Those publicists invited General Crespo to lead a small band which opposed the threatened usurpation. He became the chief of a revolution that may be said to have favored legitimism. After sanguinary conflicts with the well-equipped soldiers of the government, and after thwarting the attempts of aspiring leaders to acquire supreme power, on October 6, 1892, that revolutionary leader entered Caracas. On the next day he issued a decree announcing that he had assumed the executive power. He published a broadside which declared that the Venezuelans had recovered their sovereignty, that he would guarantee their civil and political rights, and that all the decrees and laws of the republic which were not antagonistic to the legitimist revolution would remain in force.

The Legitimist Revolution

He convoked a National Convention which adopted a new Constitution for the United States of Venezuela that was promulgated on July 5, 1893. This Constitution provided that foreigners in the republic were to enjoy all the civil rights which citizens enjoyed; and that in case of need, they might have recourse to the same legal proceedings as Venezuelans. The right of property was expressly guaranteed to citizens; their possessions might be taken from them only by legislative act or judicial decree. Without due process of law no citizen could be deprived of his liberty because of political reasons. Every public contract was to contain a clause to the effect that controversies arising under it were to be decided by tribunals of Venezuela and according to her laws.

The National Assembly formally approved all the acts which Crespo had performed either as revolutionary leader or as chief executive. After being duly elected president, he was inaugurated on March 14, 1894. During his second presidency a dispute about the boundary of British Guiana assumed a menacing aspect. Expanding from the colony definitely acquired by England from the Dutch in 1814, her pioneers had entered a region which the republic claimed by virtue of decrees of the Spanish King. In 1844 Secretary Fortique of Venezuela argued that the Essequibo River marked the western limits of British Guiana, while Lord Aberdeen proposed a new boundary which to a large extent followed a line that had been surveyed in 1841 by an explorer named Schomburgk. In 1881 vain proposals for the adjustment of the controversy were made by both parties.

Boundary Dispute with England

Meanwhile English frontiersmen pushed farther and farther into the debatable land. As England refused to submit the dispute to arbitration, Venezuela eventually broke off diplomatic relations with her, and appealed to the United States for redress. In 1895 Secretary Olney sent a trenchant dispatch to the United States minister in London which gave a most liberal interpretation to the Monroe Doctrine and which declared that the Anglo-Venezuelan boundary dispute came within the purview of that doctrine. President Cleveland championed the same view in a vigorous message to Congress. Partly because of his belligerent attitude, England agreed to submit the dispute to arbitration, but upon the express condition that the possession of land during fifty years should be judged to constitute a good title. In view of that principle the arbitral tribunal awarded the major portion of the territory in dispute to England, but Venezuela was conceded a clear title to valuable territory at the Orinoco's mouth.

Before the Anglo-Venezuelan boundary controversy was adjusted, Crespo had been succeeded by General Ignacio Andrade, who had served as Venezuela's minister at Washington. A revolt against Andrade was suppressed by forces under the command of General Crespo, who unfortunately was killed in battle. During the night of May 23, 1899, from the banks of the river Tachirá, General Cipriano Castro, a brave and illiterate cowboy, with a few supporters launched an insurrection. On the following day that general issued a manifesto which denounced the policy of Congress and asserted that the President had infringed the Constitution. The tree of liberty, exclaimed Castro, had to be fertilized by more Venezuelan blood!

Andrade soon fled from the capital city, and Castro entered it in October, 1899. At the request of a subservient Congress, he formally assumed the duties of Provisional President in February, 1901. In July, 1902, shortly after being chosen "Constitutional President," he temporarily transferred his civil authority to Vice-President Juan Gómez and left the capital in order to quell revolts.

General Castro Becomes President

Foreign complications soon arose to trouble the President. Largely through revolts and civil wars, foreigners residing in the republic had suffered injuries for which they demanded indemnities. Because of such disturbances Venezuela had been unable to pay the interest upon foreign indebtedness incurred for the construction of railways. Citizens of England, Germany, and Italy consequently appealed to their governments for indemnities through diplomatic channels.

As those governments failed to secure such redress, they decided to blockade certain Venezuelan ports. Accordingly in 1902 English, German, and Italian warships undertook a pacific blockade of La Guaira and Puerto Cabello. When this developed into a warlike blockade, Castro published an indignant protest. An agreement was finally reached between Venezuela and the creditor nations by which their claims were submitted to mixed commissions for arbitration. These commissions adjudged that Venezuela should pay sums which

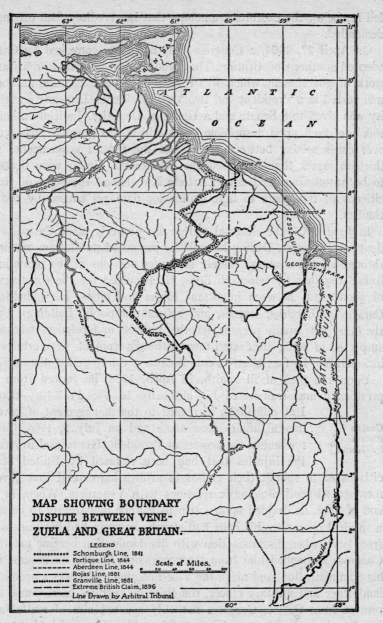

MAP SHOWING BOUNDARY DISPUTE BETWEEN VENE-
ZUELA AND GREAT BRITAIN.

LEGEND
•••••••••• Schomburgk Line, 1841
——————— Fortique Line, 1844
— — — — Aberdeen Line, 1844
— · — · — Rojas Line, 1881
••••••••• Granville Line, 1881
— — — — Extreme British Claim, 1896
————— Line Drawn by Arbitral Tribunal

Scale of Miles.
20   40   60   80   100

MAP SHOWING BOUNDARY DISPUTE BETWEEN VENEZUELA AND
GREAT BRITAIN

(From Robertson's *Hispanic-American Relations with the United States*)

fell far below the exorbitant amounts that her creditors had originally demanded.

On April 27, 1904, a Congress that had been convoked by Castro adopted another Constitution. That fundamental law provided a framework of government which was federal in type. Executive authority was vested in a President and two Vice-Presidents. Legislative authority was given to a Senate and a House of Deputies. Judicial authority was conferred upon a supreme court which was granted jurisdiction over cases arising between states and the federal government. The thirteen states that composed the Venezuelan Union were declared to be autonomous and equal. Article XV denied the right of either citizens or foreigners to urge claims for damages caused by revolutionists.

In June, 1905, the electoral college unanimously made Castro president for six years. During his rule he promoted public improvements throughout the country. Widely separated sections of the republic he linked together by telegraph lines. He provided for the construction of good roads between important towns and cities. He embellished Caracas with parks, statues, and substantial public buildings. Upon the other side, many persons, whether citizens or foreigners, who were suspected of being disaffected toward the government, were arbitrarily incarcerated. In fact Castro's rule became a thinly veiled dictatorship.

Upon the plea of ill health, in April, 1906, he retired from the presidency and transferred his authority to Vice-President Gómez.

Castro Succeeded by Gómez But difficulties in regard to the management of governmental affairs soon arose and on July 5, 1906, Castro reassumed the powers of President. His refusal to redress the injuries that had been suffered by United States citizens or to submit their claims to arbitration caused that government to suspend diplomatic relations with Venezuela. When, in the end of 1908, he decided upon a trip to Europe, apparently to undergo a surgical operation, his hour had struck. Scarcely had his ship sailed from port, when dissatisfaction with his domination became manifest. Congress suspended him from the presidency, started an inquest into his administration, and made the Vice-President, who was a prominent landowner and military officer, the chief magistrate. In response to a protest from Castro, Congress not only accused him of malfeasance in office but also expressed its confidence in Gómez. In May, 1909, that general issued a decree which announced that he was exercising the powers of the President. He effectively suppressed opposition to his rule that had been manifested in certain sections.

On December 19, 1909, Gómez was loudly acclaimed provisional president. He expressed a desire to preserve liberty and order, to respect the sovereignty of the states, and to seek a decorous solution for disputes with other nations. When he made known to the United States his desire to settle satisfactorily the pending dispute about claims of her citizens, that government took steps to resume diplomatic relations with his country. Success attended the measures which he took to adjust the claims of French citizens because of injuries suffered during Castro's régime.

In August, 1909, a new Constitution was promulgated which vested executive authority in a President who should hold office for four years but should not be eligible for reëlection for the ensuing term. He was to be aided by a cabinet and a council of government. A bicameral legislature, a court of cassation, and other courts were to function. Twenty political entities which had been established by law in 1856 were acknowledged as states.

On August 27, 1910, Gómez was elected president. He called to his council table some of the most inveterate revolutionaries and able publicists of his country. Profiting doubtless by their advice, the President initiated reforms in public administration. The tariff laws were revised; and deliberate attempts were made to encourage foreign commerce. So much did the financial condition of the country improve that a number of foreign claims were paid. By a decree of July, 1911, the revolutionary debt of Venezuela and other national obligations were converted into the national internal debt. The diplomatic and consular service was improved: consuls were appointed to posts where there had not been any since the age of Guzmán Blanco, and provision was made for six foreign legations of the first class. By a decree of May 18, 1912, the decimal system was adopted for use by state and national governments. A special feature of this administration was the attention paid to the construction and improvement of important roads.

As former President Castro tried to regain his power, early in August, 1913, Gómez entrusted his civil authority to a littérateur named José Gil Fortoul, who was president of the council of government, and left the capital to wage a campaign for the restoration of order and tranquillity. The partisans of Castro were suppressed, and early in January, 1914, General Gómez entered Caracas at the head of his victorious soldiers. At once he reassumed the President's functions.

Shortly afterward, a Congress of Deputies was convoked, and in June, 1914, a new fundamental law was adopted for the United States of Venezuela. The Constitution of 1914 vested executive authority in a President who should be chosen for seven years by Congress in secret election. His substitute should be a cabinet minister to be selected by the President himself. Among the extensive powers which were conferred upon the chief magistrate was the right to arrest, to expel, or to exclude pernicious foreigners.

The states were declared to have all the authority that was not delegated by the Constitution to the national government. Religious liberty was assured to Venezuelans under laws that entrusted the supervision of all forms of worship to the national executive.

Two articles of the new Constitution proved to be of prime significance. Article CXXXVII stipulated that the Provisional President

Constitution of 1914
should hold office until the new constitutional magistrates were inaugurated. The following article stipulated that the commander in chief of the national army should exercise his functions until the inauguration of the republic's constitutional president.

Meanwhile Gómez had relinquished the presidency. On April 19, 1914, the Congress of Deputies had elected Victoriano Márquez Bustillos, who had been secretary of war and the navy, provisional president. Congress also elected ex-President Gómez commander in chief of the national army. On May 3, 1915, the first Congress chosen under the new Constitution unanimously elected General Gómez president for the term ending April 19, 1922. Yet he did not assume the President's duties: in accordance with special provisions of the new Constitution, the Provisional President continued to exercise the functions of chief magistrate, while Gómez, evidently believing that military authority would enable him to retain his power as well as to promote peace, remained at the head of the army. The refusal of the president-elect to assume the functions of President—while remaining the military chieftain during the term for which he had been chosen chief executive—was without a parallel in the strange chronicles of Latin America.

Since the disruption of Great Colombia, Venezuela has had two boundary disputes with her neighbors. Negotiations with Brazil for

Conditions about 1914: Boundary Disputes
the demarcation of the frontiers began as early as 1843. Sixteen years later the governments of Brazil and Venezuela signed a treaty which sketched a boundary line between their territories. That boundary was surveyed by 1880; but a part of the line was in a sense obliterated by the decision of the Spanish King concerning the limits between Venezuela and Colombia. By a protocol signed in Caracas in 1905 between diplomats of Brazil and Venezuela, that part of the Brazilian-Venezuelan boundary line which had been surveyed was mutually acknowledged as the true boundary. In 1914-1915 a mixed commission proceeded to place marks along another part of the boundary line. On July 24, 1928,

an agreement was signed by representatives of the two parties which was to take the place of the protocol of 1905. The new agreement stipulated that the boundary marks set up by the commission of 1914-1915 were to be considered as permanent, and that a new commission should proceed to complete the survey of the line sketched in the Treaty of 1859. This commission set up boundary marks along the limits between the two countries from the island of São José in the Río Negro to Mount Roraima, where the bounds of Brazil, Venezuela, and British Guiana converged.

With respect to the limits between Venezuela and Colombia, in 1881 both powers agreed to submit the dispute to the arbitration of the Spanish King, who was to determine the line which in 1810 separated the captaincy general of Venezuela from the viceroyalty of New Granada. In the award made by that monarch on March 16, 1891, he drew a boundary line between the two states which had sprung from Great Colombia. Acrimonious correspondence, however, took place between the governments of Venezuela and Colombia about that line, mixed commissions determined a part of it, and Colombia occupied districts which belonged to her. After the first World War began, they decided to submit the dispute to the arbitration of the federal council of Switzerland which was to entrust to engineers the exact demarcation of the boundary. Swiss experts accordingly undertook to determine the ownership of portions of the disputed territory. By an exchange of notes, on December 17, 1928, the governments of Colombia and Venezuela made known that the demarcation line between the two countries had been successfully drawn.

In the second decade of the nineteenth century Venezuela seemed to be revolution-weary. It has been estimated that within three-quarters of a century she had suffered from fifty revolts. Frequent revolutionary disturbances undoubtedly checked immigration. Various attempts by law to encourage foreigners to settle there met with slight success. In 1912 the net increase by immigration was 1,634.

The upper class in large cities was mainly of Spanish descent; the lower classes were mixed. There was a Negro element on the coast, and in the interior were many Indians. Upon the distant frontiers were about a dozen tribes of aborigines who had been little affected by civilization. According to official statistics, on January 1, 1913, the population of Venezuela was 2,755,638. Religious orders were excluded from Venezuela by law. The Constitution of 1914 declared that Venezuelans were guaranteed religious liberty in accordance with the laws and subject to the supervision of the federal executive.

Agriculture, cattle raising, and manufacturing were the main industries. In fertile valleys of Venezuela many large plantations were devoted to the culture of coffee, cacao, sugar, and cotton. Large numbers of cattle, goats, horses, and sheep roved over her hills and grassy plains. As in other Latin-American countries, the factories of Venezuela were engaged for the most part in the transformation of native products. The chief manufactures were lumber, leather, cotton goods, cocoanut oil, cigarettes, and chocolate. The twelve most important exports in 1912-1913 were coffee, cacao, balata, hides, gold, tonka beans, rubber, asphalt, heron feathers, cattle, raw sugar, and pearls.

Largely because of her topography and location Venezuela had a better transportation system than Colombia. Upon the eve of the first World War, steamships from Europe and the United States touched at La Guaira, Puerto Cabello, and Cumaná. Spanish merchantmen regularly made voyages between Barcelona, Habana, Panama, and Venezuelan ports. Vessels from the United States made trips between such ports and New York City. Ships plied with regularity on the Orinoco River. Venezuela had only some five hundred miles of railroad, which were mostly lines from Caracas to other important cities. Her railroad system, however, was supplemented by roads that had been built by her dictators.

For a considerable period educational facilities in Venezuela were extremely poor. In part elementary education was supported by the nation, in part by the states, and in part by municipalities. Secondary education was mainly carried on in academies that were attended by boys and girls. Separate schools of arts and crafts had been established for boys and girls at Caracas. A school of engineering was also located there. In addition Venezuela had seminaries of philosophy and divinity, besides normal schools. Higher education was furnished by the universities of Caracas, Los Andes, and Mérida. In those universities considerable attention was paid to the study of law, medicine, and theology.

No nation of Latin America has produced a literature more characteristic of her life than Venezuela. Here, as in Chile, the earliest literary figure was Andrés Bello, who was a poet even before he left Venezuelan soil. Rafael M. Baralt, who resided in Madrid, wrote a standard history of his native land. Upon his plantation on the river Choroní, José A. Maitín composed verses that contain suggestive descriptions of Venezuelan life. José A. Calcaño, a member of a literary family, wrote lyric poems in which he used his native land as a background. A national note was struck by Juan Vicente González, the author of *Mesenianas*, which is a series of flowery eulogies upon certain national leaders. Cecilio Acosta was not only the author of poems and essays, but also of studies of politics. A poet named Juan Antonio Pérez Bonalde added a philosophic note to Venezuelan poetry; his *Vuelta á la patria* and *Poema del Niagara* are widely known.

Venezuelan novelists have a flavor of their own. Julio Calcaño composed a novel about the Italian renaissance which he entitled *Blanca de Torestella,* and also compiled a book concerning the peculiarities of the Castilian language as it was used in Venezuela. *Peonía,* a novel by Manuel Romero García, which dealt with life on a Venezuelan plantation, marked the beginning of the so-called creole influence in Venezuelan fiction. Another author who has published novels of the same type as well as poems was Rufino Blanco-Fombona. His famous story of *El Hombre de hierro* described Venezuelan revolutions. Poet, novelist, philosopher, and publicist, José Gil Fortoul established his reputation as a historian by writing a constitutional history of Venezuela. Picón-Febres made an excellent survey of his country's literature in a book entitled *Literatura venezolana en el siglo XIX.*

Felipe Larrazábal founded a conservatory of music in Caracas about 1868. Subsequently Venezuelan composers produced many pieces of music. The annals of painting in Venezuela go back to the days of Pedro Lovera who founded a school for artists in the capital city. Later a local society established there an academy of painting that was ably directed by Antonio J. Carranza. One of his disciples named Manuel Cruz produced a painting which depicted the soldiers of Bolívar fording the river Apure. Tovar y Tovar produced a noteworthy series of paintings, mainly of a historical character: among those were a canvas depicting the battle of Ayacucho and a famous picture of the members of the Venezuelan Congress signing the Declaration of Independence. Arturo Michelena produced some genre and religious paintings. Among Venezuelan sculptors two names, at least, should be mentioned: Eloy Palacios, who made statues of heroes of the revolutionary epoch, besides one of José Vargas; and Rafael de la Cova who modeled statues of Bolívar that were cast in bronze.

In his message to Congress on April 28, 1916, the Provisional President expressed his gratitude to General Gómez for advice furnished in regard to problems of state. In a message to Congress on the same day that general stated that he would assume the presidency of the republic whenever he might consider such a step convenient and opportune. Thus it would appear that ordinarily the Provisional President had pursued policies which were sponsored either by the president-elect or by that dignitary's advisers.

Near the end of 1916 Márquez Bustillos issued decrees providing for the construction of two great highways that were to run from the capital city through the eastern and western portions of Venezuela. He also issued decrees which radically modified the system of higher education: a school of political science, a school of dentistry, and a school of pharmacy were founded at Caracas. A school of wireless telegraphy was created for the training of military and naval officers. With certain exceptions, a law of June, 1919, made military service compulsory for adult male citizens. In time of peace every man was obliged to serve for two years either in the army or the navy, while in war time he could be constrained to serve during the pleasure of the President.

Even before General Gómez became president-elect, Venezuela had experienced ill effects from the first World War. The cost of necessities of life increased. A sharp decrease in the amount of dutiable imports soon caused her customs revenues to decline. As early as August, 1914, the government issued a decree which not only abolished certain offices but also decreased official salaries 25 per cent. This retrenchment was followed by other economies; thus the national credit was maintained intact. During the same month the government informed national and state officials that it would maintain a strict neutrality during the war. After being informed of the policy which the United States was pursuing toward Germany, on February 14, 1917, the secretary of foreign relations declared that the policy of his government would accord with the principles of international law and with the relations of peace and friendship which it had with all the belligerents. Soon afterward the United States minister at Caracas was informed that, while fulfilling her duties as a neutral, Venezuela would not relinquish any of her rights. Certain of her statesmen deeply sympathized with the United States in the war, yet as their nation was not directly affected by the German submarine campaign, she adhered to her policy of neutrality throughout the struggle.

Venezuela and the First World War

In May, 1922, Gómez was unanimously reëlected president of Venezuela. On June 19 a new Constitution was promulgated which made slight changes in the fundamental law. Articles CXXXVII and CXXXVIII of the Constitution of 1914, which allowed the president-elect to remain commander in chief of the army, were omitted. Further, the Constitution of 1922 provided that in case of the permanent disability of the President he should be succeeded by the ranking Vice-President. The president-elect now decided to emerge from retirement on his estate at Maracay. On June 24, 1922, he assumed the powers of President for the term ending in 1929. General Juan C. Gómez, the brother

Gómez Takes Direct Control

of the dictator, became First Vice-President, while one of the President's sons became Second Vice-President. This seemed to presage the founding of a Gómez dynasty. A group of Venezuelan Liberals who were living in exile addressed to the Congress of the United States a memorial protesting against this domination. The world was startled on July 1, 1923, by the news of the murder of General Juan C. Gómez in the presidential palace.

Meanwhile significant industrial progress had been taking place under the protection of the dictator. Not only were public works being constructed and the foreign debt being extinguished, but valuable oil fields were being exploited. After the close **Oil and** of the first World War, American, British, and Dutch **Constitutional Alterations** companies secured from the government concessions of oil lands, especially in the basin of Lake Maracaibo. From 1919 to 1927 the production of oil virtually doubled each year: in 1927 the output of Venezuelan oil amounted to sixty-four million barrels. This marvelous development not only furnished remunerative employment for laborers who often forsook the farms for the oil fields, but also had an influence upon the political régime. In 1925, at the behest of Gómez, the Constitution was again revised. Though the old frame of government was in the main retained, the authority given to Congress in 1922 to pass upon concessions of land to foreign oil and mining companies was transferred to the President.

As the time for the election of 1929 drew near, speculation was rife in regard to the presidential succession. The great question was: "Who will succeed Gómez?" When Congress met on April 19 it unanimously reëlected the septuagenarian President for a seven-year term. Avowing that he wished to retire to his estates, he declined the post, but Congress persisted. The dictator then suggested that a new president should be chosen. Hence, on May 30, Congress elected as president the chief justice of the supreme court, Juan Bautista Pérez; but it selected Dictator Gómez to serve as commander in chief of the army.

Besides, a modification of the Constitution was promptly adopted. Article CXXVIII made the position of commander-in-chief a constitutional position that was to be filled by Congress at the same time as the presidency and for the same term. Most significant was the unique clause which stipulated that the President and the commander in chief should exercise certain authority jointly. Among their joint powers were to be such functions as the selection of the cabinet, the suspension of civil rights, and the declaration of war. The commander of the army was nevertheless to remain in complete control of the nation's forces by land or sea. This amendment accordingly much

decreased the power and prestige of the President and corresponding-
ly increased the authority of the chief military commander.

But this scheme did not work to the satisfaction of the dictator.
Pérez relinquished the presidency, and Gómez again took direct
charge of the government. To celebrate the centenary of the death
of Bolívar in 1930 the government paid off the remainder of its
foreign debt. After twenty-seven years of autocratic rule, the dictator
died on December 17, 1935. Free to express his views, a Venezuelan
historian denounced the Gómez régime in passages from which the
following excerpt is taken:

The entire country was transformed into an immense personal estate of the
dictator and his favorites who monopolized commerce, industry, and the development of the country. They destroyed free competition and throttled the
free development of private initiative. There did not exist any distinction between the public treasury and the dictator's private purse. . . . Without any
ideals of government, avaricious and cruel, he subordinated everything to his
personal ambition, without a thought of anything else than to increase his personal possessions and to perpetuate himself in command.

Eleázar López Contreras, a tall general, who had served as secretary of war and the navy, filled out the unexpired term. After the
dreaded dictator's death, his régime was liquidated. The populace of
Caracas demanded a free press, the restoration of civil rights, and the
dismissal of his officials. The houses of Gómez, of his kinsmen, and
of his protégés were looted. Congress declared that his property
worth some five hundred million bolívares was confiscated to the
State. Many of his adherents fled.

The passing of the dictator marked a great divide in Venezuelan
history. In April, 1936, Congress elected López Contreras president.

The Régime
of Reform
He not only unlocked the dungeons in which political
prisoners were incarcerated but also opened the ports to
expatriated Venezuelans. He signed laws which aimed to
improve the lot of the laboring classes; trade unions were accorded
legal recognition. Article XXXII of a Constitution which he promulgated on July 20, 1936, announced that the national government had
the power to expropriate from private individuals unexploited lands
for the public benefit. Another article of this fundamental law declared that neither anarchists nor communists should enjoy civil rights
and that to profess their doctrines was treason. Clauses in the Constitution of 1909 which accorded a dual rôle to the commander of the
armed forces were omitted. In 1939 a commission which had been
organized in the United States, acting in conjunction with official
representatives of the government, drew up a tentative program of
action with regard to serious social problems of the country. This

program contained recommendations for reform in such matters as sanitation, charity, taxation, education, immigration, agricultural development, and "social ideals in government." Because of many improvements in education, hospitals, roads, and bridges, during the last year of this transitional administration, the national expenditures were twice as large as those of the Gómez régime.

On April 28, 1941, General Isaías Medina Angarita was elected president. Like his three immediate predecessors he was a native of the Andean state of Tachirá. Inaugurated on May 5, Medina spoke favorably of the reforms under López Contreras and of the friendly policy of the United States. Emphatically did he declare that his country was able to protect herself "against any possible encroachment by totalitarian powers." Shortly after the Japanese attack on Pearl Harbor, the government of Venezuela severed relations with the Axis.

Venezuela has not been so backward in her economic development as Colombia. This has been so, partly because of a more advantageous geographical position, partly because the problem of intercommunication in Venezuela is less serious, and partly because her government has recently much improved transportation facilities by the construction of good roads. Then, too, her capital city is located where quick communication may be had with both the West Indies and the United States. From the viewpoint of territorial possessions, Venezuela has retrograded since 1831; she has been constrained to relinquish territory to Brazil and also to England. In the elements of her population Venezuela so far resembles Colombia in that a capable and progressive aristocracy of wealth and culture reposes upon the labor of ignorant, mixed classes.

Venezuelan political history has been marked by odd contrasts: with influential leaders like Simón Bolívar and Antonio Guzmán, whose addresses and writings contain passages imbued with a lofty patriotism that is sometimes democratic, it has nevertheless been checkered by lamentable lapses into arbitrary government. Venezuela is redeeming herself from the reputation which she acquired under Castro and Gómez of being one of those countries of South America where infringements of personal liberty and arbitrary imprisonments were most frequent. From a fiscal viewpoint the nation should be happy; her finances were so carefully husbanded by her last dictator that they are now upon a much better basis than those of either Ecuador or Colombia. Like those countries, Venezuela should share in increasing measure in the advantages that flow from the completion of the Panama Canal. The phenomenal development of her oil fields has not only ensured employment and prosperity to a considerable number of her citizens but has also been responsible for a large influx of foreign capital. The recent change of rulers seems to promise a renaissance of that liberal political spirit which on former occasions distinguished Venezuelan politics.

SUGGESTIONS FOR FURTHER READING

ARCAYA, P. M., *The Gómez Régime in Venezuela*, 1936.

BINGHAM, H., *The Journal of an Expedition across Venezuela and Colombia*, 1909.

BONSAL, S., "Castro: A Latin-American Type," *North American Review*, Vol. CLXXVI, pp. 747-757.

DALTON, L. V., *Venezuela*, 1912.

DROUGHT, J. M., *Social Economy, Venezuela*, 1939.

FERGUSSEN, E., *Venezuela*, 1939.

HILL, H. C., *Roosevelt and the Caribbean*, 1927.

ROBERTSON, W. S., "Hispanic American Appreciations of the Monroe Doctrine," *Hispanic American Historical Review*, Vol. III, pp. 1-16.

ROURKE, T., *Gómez, Tyrant of the Andes*, 1936.

SCRUGGS, W. L., *The Colombian and Venezuelan Republics*, 1905.

"South America V: Venezuela," *Fortune*, Vol. XIX, No. 3, pp. 74 ff.

SPENCE, J. M., *The Land of Bolívar*, 2 vols., 1878.

VERRILL, A. H., *Colombian and Venezuelan Republics*, 1910.

WATTERS, M., *A History of the Church in Venezuela*, 1933.

WHEELER, W. R., and BROWNING, W. E., *Modern Missions on the Spanish Main*, 1925.

WILGUS, A. C. (ed.), *The Caribbean Area*, 1934.

CHAPTER XXII

THE INSULAR REPUBLICS

CUBA

During the second decade of the nineteenth century revolutionary breezes from the mainland reached the Spanish colonies in the West Indies. Though conspiracies were formed, and revolts broke out in Cuba, its inhabitants did not gain their coveted autonomy. A guerrilla warfare that began in 1868 ended in the capitulation of the insurgents ten years later. By a decree of March 1, 1876, Spain granted the Cubans representation in the Cortes. At a later time the Spanish Constitution, the Spanish code of civil procedure, and the Spanish civil code were extended to Cuba. Still, at the opening of the last decade of the nineteenth century, the evils of maladministration were no less keenly felt in that island than they had been in the adjacent continent.

Cuba, 1823-1898

In 1895 Máximo Gómez led a bloody revolt in Cuba against Spanish domination. During the ensuing struggle Spain resorted to the policy of concentrating defenseless Cubans in camps encircled by barbed wire. Property belonging to citizens, as well as foreigners, was destroyed. In his message to Congress on December 7, 1896, President Cleveland said that the obligations of the United States to the sovereignty of Spain might be superseded by higher obligations.

The explosion of the United States battleship "Maine" in the harbor of Habana on February 15, 1898, which killed about two hundred and fifty American citizens, brought public opinion in that country to the fighting point. Her ambassador at Madrid was instructed to present an ultimatum to Spain asking for immediate peace in Cuba through the good offices of his government. Though at last Spain reluctantly granted the demands of the United States, her concessions were considered by that government as mere attempts to gain time.

Explosion of the "Maine"

On April 11, 1898, President McKinley sent a message to Congress which argued that forcible intervention was the only remedy for Cuba's ills. After some debate, on April 19 Congress adopted a joint resolution which contained the following declarations: (1) that the Cubans were independent; (2) that the United States demanded that Spain should

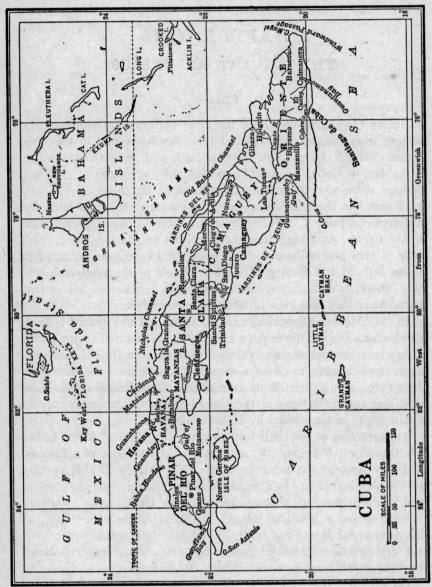

relinquish her authority over Cuba at once; (3) that the President was authorized to use the land and naval forces to carry out these resolutions; and (4) that the government of the United States disclaimed any intention to exercise control over Cuba except for her pacification and asserted its intention to leave the government and the management of the island to her own people.

This was equivalent to a declaration of war against Spain. After the President signed the resolution on April 20, the Spanish minister at Washington asked for his passports, the American minister left Madrid, and the navy of the United States **American Intervention in Cuba** was ordered to blockade Cuba. The war which ensued was short and decisive. In a little more than a month after American soldiers sailed for the island, Santiago de Cuba capitulated. Article I of the treaty of peace between Spain and the United States which was signed at Paris on December 10, 1898, provided that Spain should relinquish her sovereignty over Cuba. The United States undertook to protect life and property in that island as long as her occupation lasted.

Until May, 1902, Cuba was occupied by United States soldiers. On January 1, 1899, General John R. Brooke, military governor of Cuba, issued a proclamation announcing the intentions of his government. He declared that the United States intended to give protection to the island, announced that the civil and criminal codes which formerly prevailed there would remain in force, and urged that the Cubans should coöperate in the work of rehabilitation. During the first year of occupation significant changes were made in Cuban administration: some taxes were abolished; civil marriage was made legally valid; and steps were taken to prepare a census. Under Governor Leonard Wood measures were taken to standardize Cuban schools. United States army surgeons not only improved sanitary conditions upon the island but also demonstrated that yellow fever was transmitted by the female *stegomyia* mosquito. During the second year of occupation attempts were made to alter Spanish practices which prevailed in Cuban courts and legal processes.

Steps were also taken for the reorganization of civil government in the island. In accordance with an order of the military governor, municipal elections were held on June 16, 1900. On July 25 an order was issued directing that elections should be held for the choice of delegates to a convention to adopt a constitution which should contain provisions about the relations between the government of Cuba and the government of the United States. This convention was also to make arrangements for the election of Cuban magistrates to whom governmental authority should be transferred. After some interesting debates, on February 21, 1901, the delegates adopted the Constitution of the Cuban republic.

That fundamental law vested executive power in a President, a Vice-President, and a cabinet. The President was to be chosen by an electoral college. Legislative power was granted to a Congress composed of a Senate and a House of Representatives. Judicial authority was vested in a supreme court and such other courts as might be provided by law. The unit of local organization was the province. Each of the six provinces should be administered by a governor and a provincial council elected by the people. As originally adopted, the Constitution contained no provision about future relations between Cuba and the United States.

Constitution of Cuba

On March 2, 1901, certain clauses concerning Cuba and the United States which had been inserted in the army appropriation bill of the United States at the instance of Senator Platt became law. This law, ordinarily known as the Platt Amendment, provided that the Cuban republic would never enter into any compact with a foreign power which might impair her independence, that she would contract no excessive debt, that the acts of the United States in Cuba during the Spanish War were validated, that the Cuban government would carry out certain plans for the sanitation of the island, that the new republic would lease to the United States the lands necessary for coaling stations, and that the United States government might exercise the right to intervene in Cuba to preserve her independence and to maintain a government capable of protecting life, property, and individual liberty. After a vain attempt to modify the Platt Amendment, on June 12, 1901, the Constitutional Convention reluctantly made it a part of the Cuban Constitution.

The Constitutional Convention also adopted a law which provided that a general election should be held on December 31, 1901. On February 24, 1902, the presidential electors met and chose Tomás Estrada Palma as president. Estrada Palma was inaugurated on May 20, 1902. In the following year a reciprocity treaty was negotiated with the United States.

President Estrada Palma

A Liberal party developed that opposed the policies of the President, who became the leader of the Conservatives. Political dissensions soon culminated in uprisings against the government. Hence in September, 1906, the Cuban government appealed to the United States. President Roosevelt sent Secretaries Taft and Bacon to Habana to reconcile the discordant factions. After conferences with various leaders these commissioners proposed that certain magistrates should resign, that the insurgents should lay down their arms, and that new elections should be held. But this compromise was inacceptable to the Cubans.

On September 28 the President and his cabinet resigned. After Congress received his resignation, it adjourned without electing a successor.

Taft accordingly proclaimed a provisional government which was to conform, so far as possible, to the Cuban Constitution. He declared that besides restoring order, peace, and confidence, his object was to reestablish a permanent government. The Cuban insurgents and the militia were then disarmed. Soon after Charles E. Magoon assumed the duties of provisional governor, officers of the United States army were stationed in Cuba. During the second military occupation by the United States tranquillity was maintained in the island, public improvements were introduced into towns and cities, and the criminal and electoral laws were revised.

In November, 1908, a general election was held. Congressmen and electors of president and vice-president were chosen. The Cuban Congress assembled on January 23, 1909, and, after scrutinizing the election returns, it announced that General José Gómez, a Liberal leader who had fought against **Political Problems** Spain in the revolt of 1895, had been elected president. He was inaugurated on January 28, 1909. Magoon left the island, and the army of occupation was soon withdrawn. Congress passed a law granting amnesty to many political offenders but adjourned without acting definitely upon the budget. In November, 1910, the first congressional elections under the new régime took place.

At that juncture the Liberal party divided into two factions: a moderate group which advocated the abrogation of the Platt Amendment; and a radical faction which demanded the enactment of anticlerical legislation. In certain sections of the island Negro politicians took steps toward the organization of a political party which was to include in its ranks all colored voters. In 1911 many complaints of extravagance and corruption were made against the Gómez administration. Dissensions, riots, and armed uprisings induced the government of the United States to take measures preparatory to intervention. In the presidential campaign of April, 1912, the Conservative candidate, General Mario García Menocal, was elected president.

The inauguration of Menocal took place on May 20, 1913. In response to a congratulatory message from President Wilson, the new chief magistrate expressed his intention to improve the friendly relations that bound Cuba to the United States. In a message to Congress Menocal advocated fiscal reform. He soon **Conditions about 1914** took steps to abrogate certain concessions that had been made during the Gómez régime. He had difficulties with Congress about the budget, but that body eventually sanctioned a loan of fifteen million pesos to pay outstanding debts and to finance internal improvements. The United States did not altogether release the Cubans from leading-strings; for in 1914 she made known her opposition to a proposed amnesty law, because it did not seem designed to promote the preservation of law and order.

Her insular position and the existence of over 2,000 miles of railroads, besides good highways, gave Cuba one of the best transportation systems in Latin America. Steamship lines connected her ports with the United States and with the leading countries of Europe. Her population in 1914 was estimated at somewhat less than 2,500,000. The upper classes prided themselves on their Spanish descent, while in the veins of the lower classes ran some Negro blood.

Cuba was in a flourishing condition. The chief occupations of her inhabitants were agriculture and mining. Sugar was the most important crop. In the fiscal year 1913-1914 the main exports were sugar, unmanufactured tobacco, manufactured tobacco, iron, gold, and copper ores, hides and skins, molasses, and fruits. After the negotiation of a reciprocity treaty with the United States in 1903, which allowed Cuban sugar to enter the United States at 20 per cent of the existing rates, an increasing amount of Cuba's commerce was with that country.

In the campaign of 1916 Menocal was opposed by Alfredo Zayas, a Liberal who was supported by ex-President Gómez. So close was the election that both parties claimed the victory. Without waiting for a definite decision upon the returns, the Liberals led by Gómez rose in rebellion. Urging the Cubans to refrain from civil war, Secretary of State Lansing declared that his government would not recognize a régime established by violence. American marines were landed at Santiago de Cuba to aid in the preservation of order. After Gómez had been defeated and captured, the President expressed his appreciation of the policy pursued by the United States. In May, 1917, he entered upon his second term.

Shortly after the first World War began, it became clear that Cuba sympathized with the Allies. When the imperial German government declared the existence of a submarine zone around the British Isles, the Cuban government issued a protest. After the United States had declared the existence of a state of war with Germany, Menocal sent a message to Congress which denounced the German submarine campaign. He declared emphatically that Cuba could not remain indifferent "in the face of such stupendous violations of international law." On April 7, 1917, Congress unanimously adopted a resolution declaring that a state of war existed between Cuba and Germany. It authorized the President to float a large loan and to use the land and naval forces to promote the war. It levied heavy taxes to raise funds for extraordinary expenditures. In August, 1917, Cuba delivered to the United States four German steamers that had been interned in her ports. During the following year a law was enacted that required obligatory military service from all adult male citizens who were not expressly exempted.

When the war terminated the Cubans became absorbed in local problems. Dissensions again arose. As many publicists were convinced of the need of reform in elections, a new electoral law was enacted which had been framed by the aid of Major-General Crowder of the United States army. That law aimed to check fraud by requiring each voter to bring with him to the polls an identification card and by stipulating that the ballots should be counted publicly upon election day. In the campaign of 1920 General Gómez, who had only been punished by a few months' imprisonment for leading a rebellion, was the presidential candidate of the Liberals. In opposition to Gómez was his former Vice-President, Alfredo Zayas, a well-educated leader who had been nominated by the "National League," a third party which was a coalition composed of Conservatives and members of the so-called "Popular" party. Throughout the campaign emphasis was placed upon personalities rather than upon political issues: the partisans of Gómez were dubbed Miguelistas, while the adherents of Zayas were designated Zayistas.

The election took place in November amid intense excitement. Its results were never officially announced, because returns were not received from many districts, and because charges of fraud and intimidation were made by both parties. At this juncture the collapse of the sugar market, which had induced the government to declare a moratorium in January, 1920, precipitated a financial stringency. Early in 1921 the United States accordingly sent General Crowder to Habana on board the cruiser "Minnesota." After supplementary elections took place in some provinces, Zayas was declared to be elected president. He was inaugurated on May 20, 1921.

President Zayas soon began to frame remedial legislation. He established by decree an extralegal advisory commission composed of congressmen, cabinet ministers, and General Crowder. This commission cut down government expenditures, sent a commercial mission to Washington, and authorized domestic and foreign loans. On October 7, 1921, Dwight W. Morrow agreed to a contract with Zayas, on behalf of J. P. Morgan and Company, for a loan of $5,000,000 to Cuba. The proceeds were used largely to pay interest and amortization upon the foreign debt. In revising the tariff, the Congress of the United States made Cuba's preferential rate on sugar 1.84 cents. Early in 1922 the American

The Mission of General Crowder

government asked Cuba to recognize her right under the Platt Amendment to investigate certain departments of her government. Though Zayas protested, Crowder proceeded to do so, aided by American experts. That general sent memoranda to Zayas which maintained that certain grave problems of Cuban administration should be solved. The establishment of a financial protectorate by the United States over Cuba seemed to be imminent.

Many objections were made in Cuba to Crowder's activities. Congress nevertheless reduced the republic's budget to $55,000,000. It authorized an external loan and provided for a tax on gross sales. Scarcely had the effects of these reform measures become apparent when an economic revival took place. General Crowder soon sailed for home; in 1923 he returned as the first ambassador from the United States to Cuba. When he relinquished his post in 1927, as certain politico-economic evils of Cuba had been remedied, the fear of intervention by the United States had vanished.

Meanwhile "nationalism" had become the slogan of Cuban politicians. It became the cry of General Gerardo Machado, a business man and Liberal politician who advocated social and administrative reform and also the revision of the Platt Amendment. In November, 1924, the Liberals triumphed in the presidential election; and on May 20, 1925, Machado was inaugurated. In a very real sense he was a Cuban President. Legislation was enacted largely by executive decrees. Political pressure was brought to bear upon objectionable partisans. Work was at last begun on a great central highway. The tariff law was soon judiciously revised with a view to promote home industry in Cuba as well as to develop her foreign markets. In September, 1927, a national sugar defense commission was created whose function should be to regulate the production and marketing of sugar which had suffered from foreign competition. The Machado government also framed a constitutional reform that was styled the Prorogue Law, which not only provided for an independent judiciary but also for a six-year term for the President, who was not to be eligible for reëlection. But these changes did not still the discontent.

During 1930 conditions in Cuba grew steadily worse. The price of sugar fell to an unprecedented figure. "Poverty and unemployment," said an American Senator who visited Cuba, "are feeding the flames of political unrest." He urged that the United States should exercise her influence in order to prevent trouble. After student riots had occurred in the streets of Habana, on October 4, Congress granted Machado the power to suspend constitutional guarantees. On December 11 following, he issued a decree suspending for sixty days such

From
Machado to
Batista

guarantees as freedom of speech, inviolability of correspondence, and protection against arbitrary arrests.

On February 5, 1931, Congress granted the President the unlimited right to suspend constitutional guarantees indefinitely. Two days later he signed a decree which suspended those guarantees "over all national territory, and as long as conditions of unrest" continued. On August 10 Machado proclaimed a state of martial law throughout the republic. Despite social unrest and revolutionary uprisings, it was 1933 before the rising tide of opposition swamped him. On August 12 he transferred his authority to Secretary of State Céspedes and went into exile. As large stores of sugar could not be marketed because of the economic crisis and falling prices, in September, 1933, a politico-military revolt replaced Céspedes by Grau San Martín whose rule lasted scarcely four months. On January 18, 1934, a young engineer named Hevia was elevated to the chief magistracy which he held for a scant twenty-four hours. Then Colonel Carlos Mendieta, a leader of the National party, became provisional president. During his brief administration the Platt Amendment was abrogated on May 29, 1934, by an agreement with the government at Washington.

By another revolutionary change on December 11, 1935, Mendieta was succeeded by José Barnet. Elections held on January 10, 1936, resulted in the choice of Miguel Gómez, a son of the second Cuban President, as the chief executive. His administration only lasted from May, 1936, until December of that year when he was succeeded by Vice-President Federico Laredo Bru, who filled out the unexpired term. During these troublous years the power behind the kaleidoscopic changes was an aspiring and capable young military officer named Fulgencio Batista.

In November, 1939, elections were held for delegates to a constitutional convention. After considerable debate, this convention adopted a prolix Constitution which changed somewhat the régime established in 1901. The new fundamental law contained several articles instituting social reforms, such as insurance for laborers. The President elected for a term of four years by popular vote was to be ineligible for immediate reëlection. He was to be aided by a council of ministers who were to be responsible to Congress in either house of which they might hold seats. Each province was to have nine senators, who should be elected by popular vote. Meanwhile, on July 14, 1940, the electoral college which still functioned, elected Colonel Batista president. He was inaugurated on October 10, 1940, the same day as that on which the new Constitution went into operation.

Early in his administration attempts were made to check the subversive activities of Falangists in the island. Compulsory military service was introduced. Within a week after the Japanese assault on Pearl Harbor, the Cuban government declared war on the Axis. Congress conferred war powers on the President. After Batista made a speech denouncing the Germans as "vicious animals," the Berlin radio warned him that he lived only a short distance from the sea. Soon afterward, because of the intimate relations existing between Berlin and Madrid, the Habana government prohibited the exportation of foodstuffs to Spain.

The Dominican Republic

The island of Española or Santo Domingo, as it came to be known, has a checkered history. In 1697 by the Treaty of Ryswick, France secured from Spain the western half of that island which Origins became known as Haiti; and in 1795 by the Treaty of Bâsle she secured the eastern half from Spain. As many inhabitants of eastern Santo Domingo preferred to be under Spanish rule, in 1808 a rebellion began against the French. With the aid of an English squadron, on July 9, 1809, revolutionists captured the city of Santo Domingo. Spain's title to the eastern half of the island was reasserted in 1814 by the Treaty of Paris. Incited by the example of their brethren in South America, in 1821 the Dominicans, as the inhabitants of eastern Santo Domingo were eventually designated, deported the Spanish governor, proclaimed their independence of Spain, and expressed their desire to become incorporated in Colombia. As Bolívar could not extend them any aid, President Boyer of Haiti soon invaded the eastern half of the island, and early in 1822, he captured Santo Domingo City. For twenty-two years Haitians dominated the entire island. They tried to transform it into a unified black republic.

In 1838 Juan Pablo Duarte, an aspiring young Dominican who had been educated in Europe, founded a secret society which aimed to promote his country's independence. On February 27, 1844, a group of dissatisfied Dominicans captured the chief gate of Santo Domingo City, and shortly afterward the Haitian commander surrendered to the revolutionists. Soon a provisional council was formed to administer Dominican affairs. A convention drafted a Constitution which was promulgated on November 6, 1844. Scarcely had it been adopted when revolts broke out. In addition, for several years the republic was forced to defend herself against the attempts of Haiti to destroy her autonomy. In February, and in December, 1854, and also in February, 1858, short-lived Dominican constitutions were promulgated.

Frequent insurrections against the government, and a conviction that the country needed the protection of a foreign power, incited President

Santana in 1861 to make a treaty which transferred his nation to Spain. This treaty provided that the Dominican Republic should be considered as a Spanish province. On March 18, 1861, the incorporation of the republic with Spain was proclaimed in the Dominican capital. Santana was appointed the provincial governor and captain general. But in various quarters opposition to that metamorphosis soon became manifest. On August 16, 1863, a planter named Cabrera started a revolution which became known in history as "the War of the Restoration." After a destructive struggle the small Spanish army was forced to take refuge in the capital city. On May 1, 1865, the Spanish Queen sanctioned a law of the Cortes which provided that the colony in Santo Domingo should be abandoned.

The history of the Dominican Republic from 1865 to the end of the nineteenth century was extremely turbulent. A convention which assembled in 1865 proclaimed that the Constitution of 1858 should be the fundamental law. Scarcely had General Antonio Pimentel been elected president when an insurrection against his government began. As a result General Buenaventura Báez was proclaimed president. The Constitution of 1854, which had given the President large powers, was declared to be in force again. In 1868, after he became president for the second time, Báez negotiated a treaty with the United States which provided for the annexation of the Dominican Republic to that country. His compatriots approved the treaty by a referendum in February, 1870; but the United States Senate declined to ratify it. After a series of changes in the presidency, in 1882 General Ulises Heureux, a Negro politician, became chief magistrate. To prolong his rule he had the existing Constitution amended more than once. A new fundamental law which was promulgated in 1896 accorded to him very extensive powers. Dictator in everything but name, Heureux was cruel and relentless to his political enemies. At last he was assassinated by Ramón Cáceres, who had entered into a conspiracy against him. Around two leaders of the opposition to Heureux's domination, Juan Jiménez and Horacio Vásquez, cliques or party groups had formed. Jiménez, who became president in November, 1899, gave peace to his country for a few years. He was overthrown by a revolution led by Vice-President Vásquez in 1902. A civil war then broke out which developed into a three-cornered fight. Finally Carlos Morales was elected president and Ramón Cáceres vice-president. Morales was inaugurated on June 19, 1904.

He found the republic in a condition of apparently hopeless bankruptcy. In September, 1904, her debt was estimated at over $32,000,000. About one-half of that debt was held by subjects of Belgium, England, France, and Germany, while a small part of it was held by United

States citizens. At that date the annual revenue of the insular republic was estimated at $1,850,000. The annual expenditures, including payments on the indebtedness, amounted to $3,900,000. In the latter part of 1904 rumors were rife that certain European nations would intervene to collect debts which were due their citizens. It seemed that intervention by armed force might lead to the occupation of Dominican territory for an indefinite period. The demoralized condition of the republic furnished President Theodore Roosevelt a chance to apply his corollary of the Monroe Doctrine, a corollary which will be discussed in the last chapter of this book.

John Hay, secretary of state for the United States, accordingly instructed Minister Dawson to sound the Dominican government with respect to aid from Washington. In February, 1905, a protocol was signed which provided that the United States should adjust the debts of the Dominican Republic and administer her customhouses for the service of the debt, a fixed amount of the revenue being set apart to pay the current expenses of the insular government. A clause in the convention provided that the United States should furnish such further assistance as might be necessary to restore the credit, maintain the order, and promote the welfare of the country. Largely because of that clause, which was interpreted to signify the establishment of a protectorate over the embarrassed republic, the Senate of the United States declined to ratify the treaty.

Yet President Roosevelt made an executive arrangement with the Dominican government which embodied the essential features of the rejected treaty. On April 1, 1905, he put that *modus vivendi* into force in the bankrupt republic. An agent from the United States was placed in charge of her fiscal administration. The marked improvement which then took place in her economic, social, and political condition, altogether aside from the fact that her debt was readjusted and her credit restored, strengthened the sentiment in the United States in favor of a treaty arrangement.

Fiscal Intervention by the United States

On February 8, 1907, a treaty was accordingly signed which arranged for assistance by the United States in the collection and use of the customs duties of the insolvent republic. The Treaty of 1907 provided that the government at Washington should for fifty years administer the customs of the Dominican Republic for the service of her debt. Besides the reduction of the Dominican debt, many beneficial results followed the execution of this treaty: customs receipts greatly increased; import and export trade expanded, and many internal improvements were carried out. On the other hand, the administration of Dominican finances by the United States led to interference with the government of that Latin-American republic—interference which infringed upon her sovereign authority.

Meantime a convention that sat in Santiago de los Caballeros promulgated a new Constitution for the republic. The Dominican Constitution of 1908 vested executive authority in a President who should be elected by indirect vote for six years. Among the powers specifically granted him was that of commander in chief of the army. He was to be aided by a cabinet of seven secretaries. **Constitution of 1908** Legislative authority was granted to a bicameral Congress. Judicial authority was granted to a supreme court that should hold its sessions at the capital city. The republic was divided into twelve provinces which were to be administered by governors appointed by the chief magistrate.

Ramón Cáceres, the first President under this Constitution, was inaugurated on July 1, 1908. At a juncture when a new era seemed to be dawning for his people, unfortunately he was assassinated by a political enemy. At the instance of a military commander, a weak man was elected president, and the country was soon torn by dissensions and civil war. A special commission sent by the United States government induced Congress to accept the President's resignation and to elect Archbishop Noel as provisional president for two years. Monsignor Noel, however, became tired of his difficult post, and in March, 1913, he resigned the presidency. Congress then selected a compromise candidate as provisional president for one year. At the end of his term revolts began in various sections. In consequence a commission was again sent from the United States to pacify the republic. In October, 1914, an election was held which resulted in the choice of Juan Jiménez as president for the second time.

The population of the Dominican Republic in 1914 was probably about 700,000. Many inhabitants were of Spanish descent. In some sections there was a large Negro element. The chief occupation in the republic was agriculture and related **Social and Economic Conditions** industries. Her rich soil produced large crops; extensive areas were covered with valuable timber; and certain portions were well suited for cattle raising. A few factories of cigars, cigarettes, and chocolate had been established. In 1914 her chief exports were raw sugar, cacao, leaf tobacco, coffee, hides, wax, and fine woods. Early in 1915 through the efficient administration of her customs service by the United States government, the debt of the republic had been reduced to $21,500,000.

To suppress disturbances, however, Dominican officials soon incurred fresh debts without the approval of the United States. That government then demanded that a convention supplementary to the Treaty of

1907 should be arranged which would provide for the appointment of a financial adviser to the republic and for the control of her constabulary by the United States. To this the Dominicans refused to consent. In April, 1916, a young military officer named Arias issued a proclamation in which he declared that Jiménez was deposed and that he had assumed the President's powers. As this was followed by disorder, the United States landed a detachment of marines upon Dominican soil who, after a short campaign, suppressed the revolutionists. Congress then elected Francisco Henríquez y Carvajal provisional president. As the government again refused to sign a convention supplementary to the Treaty of 1907, the United States refused to recognize it. On November 29, 1916, Captain Knapp of the United States navy issued a proclamation which announced that the Dominican Republic was under the military administration of the United States. He declared that his government did not intend to destroy the sovereignty of the republic but that it wished to enable her to restore internal order so that she might observe her international obligations. The administration of Dominican affairs was assigned by the United States to Admiral Snowden with the title of military governor.

In April, 1917, the military governor canceled the exequaturs of German consular representatives in the Dominican Republic. Diplomatic relations between that republic and the German **Armed Intervention** Empire were thus technically severed. During the military occupation by the United States tranquillity was restored, regulations providing for compulsory education were enforced, sanitary conditions were much improved, and finances were again restored to a sound basis. In 1919 the military government modified the tariff so as to favor American goods. It provided for an extensive free list that included agricultural and industrial machinery, building materials, and many petroleum products.

Yet the Dominicans were naturally dissatisfied with foreign military rule. In 1919 commissioners headed by Henríquez y Carvajal went to Europe to lay a plea for the restoration of liberty in the insular republic before the League of Nations. The commission then proceeded to Washington. In December, 1920, Admiral Snowden informed the Dominican people that his government wished to withdraw from the responsibilities which it had assumed in the affairs of their republic.

At Washington on June 30, 1922, four representatives of different Dominican parties signed a "Memorandum of the Agreement of Evacuation" with the American Department of State. Although the Dominicans did not secure any of the desired modifications of the tariff law imposed on them in 1919, yet they were assured that the marines would be withdrawn. The negotiators and Archbishop Noel chose a provisional president and a cabinet. After this government was inaugurated in the autumn of 1922, the marines were concentrated at certain places. Juan Vicini Burgos took an oath of office as provisional president. By the aid of American advisers, the new rulers of the insular republic proceeded to formulate the "necessary amendments" to the Constitution and laws as specified in the evacuation memorandum. The President announced that all the existing American administrative provisions would remain in force until a legislature was established. A special commissioner was soon dispatched from Washington to Santo Domingo City.

The spring elections of 1924 resulted in the choice of General Horacio Vásquez as president. A Constituent Assembly framed a fundamental law in harmony with the evacuation agreement. This Constitution provided for direct elections of President and congressmen, reëstablished the position of Vice-President, and extended the term of both President and Vice-President to six years. Further, it prohibited capital punishment, the levying of export duties, and the issue of paper money. It provided that no foreigner could belong to the Dominican constabulary. It contained detailed provisions that aimed to ensure peaceful succession to the presidency. The armed forces were declared to be in strict subordination to the government. {.marginnote Constitutional and Political Changes}

On July 12, 1924, General Vásquez was inaugurated as president. Soon afterward the United States flag was lowered and the withdrawal of the marines was begun. The new government soon showed a desire to Dominicanize the republic. It declined to float a $25,000,000 loan that had been proposed by Americans. By a series of laws enacted in 1925, it radically modified the American tariff of 1919. A law signed by President Vásquez on November 24, 1925, levied heavy import duties on certain American manufactures. In other particulars Vásquez continued the reforms that had been started by the American military government. Roads were built, harbors improved, and agriculture stimulated.

Early in 1929 a new Constitution for the Dominican Republic was adopted. This Constitution provided that the President, the Vice-President, and the members of Congress were to be elected for four-year terms. The Senate was to be composed of one Senator from each of the twelve provinces, while the Chamber of Deputies was to be made up of members elected from specified districts at the ratio of one member for every 30,000 inhabitants. The outgoing President was prohibited from becoming a candidate for either President or Vice-President for the term immediately succeeding his own.

After a brief interregnum, General Rafael Trujillo was elected president in May, 1930; he was reëlected in 1934. By vigorous measures and by the aid of a well-trained army, he gave his country a good peace. Though injured by the world economic crisis, the republic rapidly recovered. The government undertook to distribute land among the peasants, to build roads and bridges, and to promote education. Many new elementary schools were opened. A college of philosophy and letters was added to the Central University. An academy of history was founded that proceeded to publish a journal called *Clio*. On June 9, 1934, a constitutional convention proclaimed a Constitution which did not much alter the existing frame of government. It did, however, declare that the western boundary of the Dominican Republic was the line which in 1793 separated the Spanish colony on the island from the French colony of Saint-Domingue. In 1935 the two neighbors signed a treaty which made an adjustment of that long-disputed boundary. Early in the next year Congress honored the dictator by changing the name of the capital to Ciudad Trujillo.

In 1938 Trujillo declined to become president for a third term. Jacinto Bienvenido Peynado was elected to that position. When he died in 1940, another figurehead, Vice-President Troncoso, took his place. The power behind the chief magistrate, however, was still General Trujillo, who was given credit for the negotiation of a treaty with the United States, which when ratified by the Senate in February, 1941, brought to an end the customs receivership that had been initiated sixteen years before. Within a week after the attack on Pearl Harbor, the Dominican Republic declared war on the Axis. After Trujillo was again elected president in May, 1942, Troncoso resigned and his predecessor was sworn in as president three months before the regular date for the inauguration.

HAITI

In 1697 Spain ceded the western half of the island of Santo Domingo to France. This colony became known as Haiti, which was the
aboriginal name of the island. French emigrants went
A French there in considerable numbers. Meanwhile the Indians
Colony had been exterminated. To furnish the servile labor for their farms, French landowners brought Negroes from Africa. The foundations were thus laid for an economic system in which French proprietors tilled their plantations by slave labor.

Missionaries were soon sent to the colony to convert the heathen to Christianity. In 1685 Louis XIV provided that Haiti should be administered by a royal council composed of a governor, an intendant, and other personages. The colony was carved into three administrative districts, the North, the South, and the West. Each of these districts was furnished with a deputy-governor and a court of justice. By the middle of the eighteenth century society in Haiti had become stratified. There were four distinct classes: Frenchmen, creoles, free colored people, and Negro slaves. It has been estimated that in 1789 there were in Haiti 30,000 Frenchmen and creoles, 27,000 free colored persons, and 465,000 Negro slaves.

News of the French Revolution altered the face of society. Local assemblies gathered at various points, declared that they were entitled to representation in the *tiers état,* and dispatched deputies to Paris. When a republic was proclaimed in France, colored agents were sent there to defend Haitian rights. Dissensions broke out in Haiti between the dominant whites and the aspiring blacks.

On March 8, 1790, the National Assembly of France decreed that assemblies should be formed in those colonies where they did not already exist. The news of this decree reached Haiti at the very juncture when there was an Assembly composed of whites in session at St. Marc. On May 18, 1790, this Assembly proclaimed itself the sole legal representative of the colony. It further declared that in extreme cases the importation into Haiti of articles required for the subsistence of its inhabitants was not to be considered as a breach of the monopolistic French colonial system. These and other stipulations of May 18, 1790, were declared to form a part of the colony's constitution. Thus there became manifest in Haiti aspirations for local autonomy. During the war between France and England General Whitelocke invaded the island. To enlist aid against the invaders on August 29, 1793, the French government announced the liberation of all slaves.

As a reward for leading the resistance against the English, the French government appointed a remarkable Negro called Toussaint L'Ouverture as military governor of Haiti. He soon extended his rule over the eastern part of the island   Toussaint L'Ouverture which had meanwhile been ceded to France by Spain. In July, 1801, he promulgated a Constitution for Santo Domingo which had been framed by a convention composed of delegates from both the French and the Spanish parts of the island. This Constitution declared that "Saint-Domingue" was a part of the French Empire but subject to special laws. It prohibited slavery. The only religion that could be publicly professed was Roman Catholicism. Toussaint, who was made governor of the island for life, was to transmit this fundamental law to France for approval. When his envoy submitted the Constitution to Napoleon for ratification, the Emperor took the view that it contained provisions "contrary to the dignity and sovereignty of the French people." In response the "First of the Blacks" proudly asked why the Dominicans should not aim at independence.

Discarding the mask of allegiance to France, the black leader then undertook to champion the independence of his country. Hence in 1802 a French army under General Leclerc disembarked at various points in the island and began the subjugation of the blacks. With other Negro leaders, L'Ouverture was induced to capitulate to Leclerc under the terms of an agreement that was not kept. Betrayed by his own followers, in June, 1802, he was delivered to the French, and ended his life miserably in a prison cell.

When it became known that the French commander planned to re-establish slavery in Haiti, an insurrection against French rule began that soon spread over the entire island. On January 1, 1804, a Declaration of Independence was framed at Gonaives, where the decision was also reached to designate the new state Haiti. A patriot leader named Dessalines was proclaimed by his comrades governor-general for life, a title which was soon changed to that of Emperor. In May of the following year a Constitution was framed for "the Empire of Haiti," which gave Dessalines the right to choose his successor, provided for freedom of religious worship, and stipulated that slavery should be forever abolished.

After the assassination of the Emperor in 1806, a Constituent Assembly framed a Constitution for the Republic of Haiti. An aspiring general named Henri Christophe soon became the president. In 1811 he erected a petty kingdom in northern Haiti, while another leader named Alexandre Pétion ruled in the south. About 1820 Jean Boyer became president over all of Haiti; he also extended his control over the eastern part of the island.

During the rule of Boyer, negotiations that had been going on for the acknowledgment of Haitian independence by France bore fruit. On April 17, 1825, citing Articles XIV and LXXIII of the French Charter, King Charles X promulgated an ordinance that defined the status of the former French colony. The ordinance provided that the complete independence of French Santo Domingo was granted on two conditions: (1) That the ports of Haiti should be open to the commerce of all nations on the following terms: import duties and port dues were to be equal for the ships of all nations, except those of France that were to pay only one-half of the regular charges. (2) That the Haitians should pay an indemnity of 150,000,000 francs to former French colonists of the island in order to recompense them for their loss of property.

Haitian Independence Acknowledged by France

Thus did the French King conditionally concede to the Haitians the independence that they actually enjoyed. Accompanied by a show of force and dignity, these terms were submitted to President Boyer, who soon accepted. But the royal ordinance which recognized the political existence of Haiti imposed a heavy financial burden.

In 1826 Boyer promulgated a rural code that relegated the peasants of Haiti to a condition of serfdom. This code stipulated that Negroes and mulattoes should live outside the limits of towns and cities. It consequently divided the Haitians into two antagonistic camps, the peasants and the townspeople. It was largely responsible for the ensuing rapine, revolts, and civil wars. In the course of these struggles, the eastern portion of the island again established its independence of the black republic.

After several fresh essays, another Constitution for Haiti was adopted in 1889. This Constitution provided for a President who was to be assisted by a cabinet that should be responsible to the lower house of the legislature. The country was divided into departments, arrondissements, communes, and rural districts. French legal codes were to be in force. Though parliamentary in form, in practice this system often became dictatorial.

The population of Haiti in 1914 was about 2,000,000. Its capital, Port au Prince, had a population of 90,000. The chief occupation of the Haitians was agriculture; coffee was the most important crop. Other important exports were cacao, cotton, and logwood. There was in circulation a large quantity of irredeemable paper money that fluctuated in value.

Conditions in 1914

Partly because of the heavy indemnity promised France in 1825, the government had been forced to float a series of loans in Paris. By 1915 Haiti had a foreign and domestic debt that amounted to some $35,000,000. Her import and export duties were pledged to guarantee its payment. She was paying the interest as required, but was in arrears with respect to the sinking fund. Further, in 1914 the Haitian government had a controversy with an American syndicate that had secured control of a railway concession. It also became involved in difficulties over the reorganization of the national bank, which had been controlled by Parisian financiers. In December, 1914, in response to an appeal from the vice-president of that bank, the State Department of the United States transferred $500,000 in gold from its vaults to New York City. Haiti was now compelled to issue paper money. She tried to secure control of the customs duties that had generally been turned over to the bank.

These entanglements prepared the way for intervention by the United States. This step was partly due to the desire of the government at Washington to guard the Panama Canal. In the autumn of 1915

Haiti signed a convention by which the United States agreed to aid her in the development of her resources and the rehabilitation of her finances. It provided that, upon the nomination of the President of the United States, the Haitian President was to appoint a receiver-general of the customs and also a financial adviser. The revenues collected were to be used to meet the expenses of the financial administration, to pay the public debt, to support a constabulary, and to meet current expenditures. The Haitian government agreed to im-

prove the sanitary condition of the island under the direction of American engineers. The United States promised to aid in the preservation of Haitian independence and the maintenance of a government that would keep order. This treaty was approved by the Haitian Congress under pressure from an American naval commander.

Intervention by the United States

After the system of fiscal supervision by the United States went into operation, American officials in Haiti apprehended that certain provisions of her Constitution might make their position untenable. On June 19, 1917, Admiral Caperton arbitrarily dissolved the Haitian Assembly and established a military government. A new organic law was now framed, ostensibly by Haitian officials.

The Haitian Constitution of 1918 preserved the existing frame of government. It declared that the measures taken by the United States in Haiti were approved. It provided that foreigners should be accorded in Haiti the same rights as her citizens. Provision was made for the election of a new legislature, but pending its convocation legislative power was to be exercised by a Council of State.

Meanwhile the control of the United States over Haiti steadily increased. The republic was managed through a military governor, who was generally the commander of the American marine brigade, and by the American minister at Port au Prince. The Treaty of 1915 was interpreted so as to allow the exercise of more and more authority by American officials over the republic's expenditures and legislation. In 1928 a series of amendments was made to the Constitution which gave the government power to restrict the freedom of the press. Though the fiscal administration of the republic was reformed, the debt reduced, and the social condition of the country improved, some Haitians bitterly criticized the United States because it was interfering with the sovereign rights of their nation.

Hence, in 1921 the Senate of the United States sent a committee to the island to investigate the intervention. This committee decided that the personnel of American officials in Haiti should be improved, that the United States had failed to centralize responsibility, and that she had not developed a constructive policy. It recommended that a high commissioner should be appointed by the United States to coördinate the activities of treaty officials. In 1922 the State Department appointed General Russell to that office. However, complaints about the nature and methods of American intervention did not cease.

In 1929 President Hoover accordingly appointed a new commission headed by W. Cameron Forbes to study Haitian conditions. The report of that commission was made public on March 29, 1930. It urged that American occupation and control should be reduced. On the other hand, it recommended that the amount of Haitian control should be increased. The office of high commissioner should be abolished. American marines should be withdrawn. In fine, it recommended the Haitianization of the republic under American direction.

Haitianization

On May 15, 1930, Eugene Roy, who was the choice of the Forbes Commission, was inaugurated as provisional president of Haiti. President Roy selected a cabinet that was to serve until the constitutional system should be restored through elections. The withdrawal of President Borno, who had served under American auspices for eight years, and the accession of Roy, were greeted with enthusiasm by the Haitians who viewed it as an important step toward self-rule.

In the end of 1930 Sténio Vincent, a patriotic lawyer, was elected president. He soon took steps to bring the American occupation of the country to an end. In August, 1933, an agreement was reached with the United States for the transfer of the constabulary to the Haitians and for the withdrawal of the marines. Though the collection of the customs was to be placed in Haitian hands, for a time the American fiscal representative remained in charge. On August 15, 1934, the American marines were completely withdrawn. Under home management, however, the debt of the republic increased. In March, 1935, Haiti entered into a reciprocal trade agreement with the United States which placed coffee and bananas on the free list.

On June 2, 1935, a new Constitution, which extended Vincent's term of office to May 15, 1941, was approved by a plebiscite. The massacre in 1937 of thousands of Haitians, who had crossed the border from their own over-crowded country to secure work on Dominican plantations, brought the jealous neighbors to the verge of war. By the good offices of the United States, however, hostilities were avoided and the Dominican government agreed to pay Haiti an indemnity. On August 9, 1939, a slightly revised form of the Constitution of 1935 was promulgated. This fundamental law set the President's term at five years and further provided that he might be reëlected. Members of the cabinet might appear in either house of Congress to support governmental measures. The President, who might prorogue the legislature, was given authority to appoint almost one-half of the members of the Senate. By virtue of a concordat, the Roman Catholic Church was to have a privileged position.

In March, 1941, the Chamber of Deputies extended Vincent's term another five years, but he declined to serve. On April 15, 1941, Elie Lescot, the minister to Washington, was chosen his successor. In his inaugural address he declared that his country's destiny was closely linked to that of the United States. Shortly after the infamous Japanese attack on Pearl Harbor, Haiti declared war on Japan, Italy, and Germany.

In the Spanish West Indies many poets flourished. During the age when Cuba was striving for independence, Diego Vicente Tejera wrote *Al ideal de la independencia de Cuba,* Enrique Varona edited the *Revista Cubana,* and in exile from his native land a gifted Cuban patriot named José Martí served as correspondent for *La Nación* of Buenos Aires. Of poets and romancers who were natives of the Dominican Republic may be mentioned Manuel de Jesús Galván, author of *Enriquillo,* a novel of the Spanish conquest, and Pedro Henríquez Ureña, who wrote *Antología Dominicana* and *Romances en América.* Among the Haitians who wrote impassioned verse in the patois of the common people, perhaps the most notable is Oswald Durand, the author of a poem of love entitled "Choucoune."

Literature of these Caribbean States

The states considered in this chapter stand in a peculiar relation to their great Anglo-American neighbor. Because of the manner in which she attained her independence, and because of the Platt Amendment that defined her status with regard to the United States, Cuba was long under the tutelage of that government. Because of chronic fiscal difficulties which seemed to menace interference in her domestic concerns by creditor nations of Europe, the Dominican Republic was induced to agree to an arrangement by which the United States government undertook to administer her finances, and, as the sequel showed, her affairs, for a term of years. Though that arrangement undoubtedly resulted in many advantages to the debtor republic, it led to virtual domination by the United States in Dominican affairs, a domination which many Dominicans hotly resented. In accordance with an evacuation agreement framed by representative Dominicans and the State Department of the United States, in 1924 the Dominicans framed a new Constitution. American marines were withdrawn from the republic and a native government was again installed. Conditions existing in Haiti similar to those in her sister republic led the United States to intervene there also. Native resentment against that proceeding was largely responsible for the decision of the United

States to modify her policy. The Haitianization of that republic under American direction has been brought to an end.

SUGGESTIONS FOR FURTHER READING

COMMISSION ON CUBAN AFFAIRS, *Problems of the New Cuba*, 1935.
BELLEGARDE, D., *Haiti and Her Problems*, 1936.
BUELL, R. L., *The American Occupation of Haiti*, 1929.
CHAPMAN, C. E., *A History of the Cuban Republic*, 1927.
DAVIS, H. P., *Black Democracy, the Story of Haiti*, 1936.
FITZGIBBON, R. H., *Cuba and the United States*, 1935.
JENKS, L. H., *Our Cuban Colony*, 1928.
KNIGHT, M. M., *The Americans in Santo Domingo*, 1928.
LEYBURN, J. G., *The Haitian People*, 1942.
MILLSPAUGH, A. C., *Haiti under American Control*, 1931.
MONTAGU, L. L., *Haiti and the United States*, 1940.
MUNRO, D. G., *The United States and the Caribbean Area*, 1934.
NILES, B., *Black Haiti*, 1926.
PARKER, W. B. (ed.), *Cubans of Today*, 1919.
SCHOENRICH, O., *Santo Domingo*, 1918.
TANSILL, C. C., *The United States and Santo Domingo*, 1938.
VANDERCOOK, J. W., *Black Majesty*, 1928.
WAXMAN, P., *The Black Napoleon*, 1931.
WELLES, S., *Naboth's Vineyard*, Vol. II, 1928.
WILGUS, A. C. (ed.), *The Caribbean Area*, 1934.

CHAPTER XXIII

THE CENTRAL AMERICAN REPUBLICS

The captaincy general of Guatemala acquired independence from Spain through its adherence to the Plan of Iguala. When General Filisola, who commanded a military expedition that the Mexican Emperor had sent to Central America, heard of the downfall of Agustín I, he decided to summon delegates to an assembly which might establish its independence. Elections were accordingly held, and on June 24, 1823, delegates from provinces of Central America gathered at Guatemala City. As the province of Chiapas had been incorporated in Mexico, it was not represented.

On July 1, 1823, this National Assembly announced that the provinces of the former captaincy general were free and independent states which formed a nation entitled the United Provinces of Central America. It established a provisional government with three departments, declared in favor of the freedom of the press, and stipulated that Roman Catholicism should be the religion of the State. Early in August, 1823, General Filisola left Guatemala City. On August 20, at the instance of a Central American agent, the Mexican Congress acknowledged the independence of the united provinces. In October following the Assembly passed a decree instructing the deputies from Central America to withdraw from that Congress. In April, 1824, it decreed that slavery should be abolished.

On November 22, 1824, the Assembly promulgated a brief Constitution which had evidently been patterned after the United States Constitution. By the Constitution of 1824 the provinces of Costa Rica, Guatemala, Honduras, Nicaragua, and Salvador associated themselves in a Federation. That fundamental law conceded some executive authority to a bicameral legislature. It conferred the highest judicial authority upon a supreme court. Meanwhile the provinces had organized their governments.

Early in 1825, the Federation of Central America began its troubled career. On April 21 Congress chose a Liberal named Manuel José Arce as president. Several nations of America and Europe recognized the new nation. In March, 1825, diplomats of Central America had negotiated a treaty of union, league, and perpetual confederation with

424

Colombia. A commercial treaty was signed between Central America and the United States. Diplomatic relations were also initiated with England.

Parties soon appeared which differed with regard to the political organization of the State. The Moderate party was composed of persons who desired a centralized form of government. They took a favorable attitude toward the Church and were sometimes called by their opponents the "Serviles." The Radicals, who ordinarily favored the existing régime, were called Liberals: sometimes their opponents designated them "Anarchists." President Arce soon found himself hedged about with difficulties. As he tried not to displease the Servile party, he lost the support of his own partisans. Some Central Americans were dissatisfied because the seat of the Federation was located at Guatemala City which was the capital of the province of Guatemala. Other provinces became jealous of that province because it was allotted the largest number of members in Congress. Dissensions also arose because of the establishment of a new bishopric in the province of Salvador without the sanction of the Pope. *Political Problems*

In October, 1826, Arce convoked an extraordinary Congress, which some persons considered an unconstitutional step. The President arrested Barrundia, the Liberal leader of Guatemala, upon the charge that he was planning a revolt. The murder by infuriated Indians of a Guatemalan official named Flores, who had taken refuge in a church, was followed by a desolating civil war. In that war the President espoused the cause of the Serviles, who wished to abolish the bishopric of Salvador; meanwhile Francisco Morazán became the efficient leader of the Liberals. On April 12, 1829, Guatemala City fell into the hands of his soldiers.

Dictator Morazán was the most distinguished publicist of the Central American Federation. After capturing the capital city, he took measures against his real or supposed enemies. His puppet, President Barrundia, fearing a Spanish invasion, sanctioned a law which provided that the property of Spaniards should be confiscated. Barrundia proscribed or exiled Servile leaders; he dictated the appointment of dignitaries of the Church. Because of a suspicion that certain ecclesiastics were plotting against the government, he ordered the arrest and expulsion of the archbishop of Guatemala and also of many members of the Dominican, Franciscan, and Recollet orders. Soon afterward Congress announced that members of religious orders would neither be received nor recognized in the Federation. Their buildings were sequestrated by the government. After Morazán was elected president, in May, *Politico-Religious Innovations*

1832, Congress announced that religious liberty should prevail through-out the country. Some years later it declared that marriage was merely a civil contract.

The scene was thus set for a politico-religious war. An occasion for that conflict was afforded by an epidemic of cholera. As priests intimated that this scourge was caused by the poisoning of wells by Liberals, in June, 1837, fanatical Indians in the district of Mita rose against the government.

At the head of a frenzied band there soon appeared a youth of mixed blood named Rafael Carrera. An illiterate but dashing leader, with much influence among the Indians and the mestizos, he secured the support of embittered ecclesiastics. Attempts of Morazán to ar-range a peace by negotiations failed, and at the head of a nondescript horde of soldiers Carrera entered Guatemala City on February 1, 1838. About five months later the last Congress of the Federation adjourned. Morazán continued to campaign against Carrera; but on March 19, 1839, he was defeated at Guatemala City, and shortly after-ward sailed for Peru. The Federation of Central America dissolved into the preëxisting provinces.

Carrera soon became dictator of Guatemala. In 1842 delegates from Honduras, Nicaragua, and Salvador framed articles at Chinandega which instituted a league designated the Central Amer-
Fresh At-tempts at Central American Union
ican Confederation. Those articles stated that other nations of Central America might join the league. A certain article declared that the contracting states ac-knowledged the principle of nonintervention with regard to their internal affairs. Provision was made for an executive, an advisory council, and a supreme court. In March, 1844, this Confedera-tion was organized at San Vicente, but the states that had signed the articles did not observe them. Its chief executive was soon reduced to impotence.

Certain leaders, however, were loath to relinquish the idea of a union. In November, 1849, commissioners from Honduras, Nicaragua, and Salvador met at León: they agreed that those three states should coöperate in the management of their foreign relations; and that they would arrange a federal plan. They decided that Guatemala and Costa Rica might join this confederation, if they so desired. Though those states declined to join, the three contracting parties sent delegates to a Constituent Congress, which elected a supreme chief of the Federa-tion and framed a fundamental law. The assemblies of Nicaragua and Salvador alleged, however, that this Congress had acted beyond its authority. A war which broke out in 1863 between Guatemala and Salvador precipitated the disruption of the new Federation. Still, the idea of a federal union did not vanish from the minds of Central Americans.

COSTA RICA

Costa Rica was somewhat isolated from the rest of Central America. In November, 1838, her Congress announced that she had left the Federation. At that juncture Braulio Carrillo, an aspiring native of Cartago, was serving as chief of the state. Early in 1840 he selected Costa Rica's flag and coat of arms; about a year later he issued a decree containing regulations which provided that he should hold office for life. Opponents of his dictatorial rule, however, invited Morazán to return from Peru. He landed in Costa Rica in April, 1842, and issued a manifesto announcing that he intended to establish a government distinguished by order and progress. As many Costa Ricans joined his standard, he entered the capital city without opposition, and convoked a Constituent Assembly at San José, which on July 15, 1842, elected him provisional chief. But reactionaries who were encouraged by Serviles in Guatemala attacked the Liberals, Morazán was besieged at San José, defeated, captured, and shot on September 15, 1842.

In 1843 a convention framed a Constitution for the "State of Costa Rica," which was promulgated on April 11, 1844. The Constitution provided that executive authority should be exercised by one man, while legislative authority should be vested in a bicameral Congress. While José M. Castro was acting as executive, a Constituent Assembly formed an organic law which was promulgated in March, 1847. This Constitution vested executive power in a President and a Vice-President, while legislative power was given to a unicameral Congress. It declared that Roman Catholicism was the state religion. On August 30, 1848, Congress declared that Costa Rica was a sovereign and independent nation with the title of the "Republic of Costa Rica."

Under Juan Mora, who became president in November, 1849, and who was again elected to that post in 1859, Costa Rica enjoyed peace and relative prosperity. His second administration was strongly opposed by the conservative classes, however, and on the night of August 14, 1859, he was driven from the national palace. A convention was soon convoked which adopted a Constitution stipulating that the only religion to be tolerated was Roman Catholicism. After President Castro had been deposed, an assembly framed another fundamental law providing that Roman Catholicism should be the state religion, but that other religions should be tolerated. The next President was deposed by a coup d'état in April, 1870; and in August, 1871, Dictator Guardia convoked another constitutional convention.

On December 7, 1871, that convention adopted a new Constitution for Costa Rica. This Constitution provided that the Roman Catholic Apostolic religion should be supported by the State, but that other religions which were not contrary to morality or good customs should be tolerated. Foreigners, who should not be subject to extraordinary taxes, were to enjoy all the civil rights of citizens. Executive authority was vested in a President and a cabinet. The President, who should be chosen by an electoral college for four years, was declared to be ineligible for immediate reëlection. At the head of each executive department should be a secretary who might attend the meetings of Congress, and might introduce bills, but could not vote. Legislative authority was vested in one house which was styled the Constitutional Congress. Judicial authority was vested in a supreme court and other courts. The local subdivisions of the republic were provinces, cantons, and districts. In charge of each province should be placed a governor appointed by the President, who was to act as the agent of the national government.

Constitution of 1871

Because of the habitat of the Costa Ricans upon a small, central plateau, and because of the absence of a large aboriginal population, their political and economic life was different from that of the other nations of Central America. The public lands of Costa Rica largely passed into the hands of many small proprietors. There the tendency was strong toward the formation of a democratic and law-abiding citizenry.

Traits of Costa Rica

Costa Rica was primarily an agricultural and mining country. In 1914 her chief exports were bananas, coffee, gold, silver, lumber, hides, cacao, and rubber.

With the exception of a revolution in 1917 led by Secretary of War Tinoco, her recent domestic life has been relatively tranquil. On September 21 of that year Costa Rica severed relations with the imperial German government; on May 21 following she declared war on Germany. Immediately after the Japanese attack on Pearl Harbor, which took place on December 7, 1941, this republic set the example for the Spanish-American nations by declaring war on Japan. Later she also declared war on Italy and Germany.

SALVADOR

On January 30, 1841, the Salvadoran legislature passed a law providing that the new nation should be designated the Republic of Salvador. Shortly afterward a Constitution was promulgated which vested governmental authority in a President and a bicameral legislature. In a few years Provisional President Juan J. Guzmán was succeeded by a Conservative named Francisco Malespin, who was soon deposed and driven into Honduras. Doroteo Vasconcelos, a Liberal who became president in 1848, cherished the dream of organizing a republic that would include all the states of Central America. But an armed band of Salvadorans, Hondurans, and Nicaraguans whom he led into Guatemala against Carrera was defeated, and he was deposed by Congress.

Francisco Dueñas, who became president in 1852, adjusted disputes with Guatemala and Honduras. As the result of a war waged against him by Carrera, President Barrios, who became chief executive in 1860, was deposed and Dueñas again became president in 1864. Soon afterward the Salvadorans adopted a conservative Constitution which recognized only the Roman Catholic religion. A very conservative ruler, Dueñas was favored by the Clerical party, and was reëlected in December, 1868. When a quarrel broke out with Honduras because of alleged protection granted her political refugees, Salvadoran Liberals sought to profit by that circumstance to secure the triumph of democratic principles. Dueñas was defeated by General Santiago González on April 10, 1872, and soon afterward Congress announced that he was deposed. Under a Constitution adopted in 1871, González was elected president. Five years later, while he was acting as vice-president, Salvador was accused of affording an asylum to political refugees. Hence, Guatemalan soldiers compelled the Salvadorans to sign a treaty by which they agreed to change the personnel of their government. Under the next President, Rafael Zaldívar, some economic progress was made, and a liberal Constitution was adopted. After President Barrios of Guatemala vainly attempted to reëstablish the Federation of Central America by force of arms, the time appeared ripe for the framing of a new fundamental law. Francisco Menéndez, who became provisional president of Salvador in May, 1885, accordingly invited his fellow citizens to choose delegates to a constitutional convention.

An article in her Constitution of 1886 declared that Salvador's ability to join other states of Central America to form a union was unimpaired. In a list of rights and guarantees of citizens was a prohibition upon slavery. All civil and ecclesiastical corpora- **Constitution of 1886** tions were prohibited from acquiring real estate, except for the actual service of the respective corporation. Both President and Vice-President should be elected for four years by popular vote. The cabinet should be composed of four secretaries of state, who might attend meetings of the legislature but were to withdraw before a vote was taken Legislative authority was vested in a unicameral Congress. The judiciary was to be composed of a supreme court and inferior courts. The territory of the republic was to be divided into departments, districts, and municipalities or cantons. At the head of each department should be placed a governor appointed by the President.

In 1914 the main industries of Salvador were agriculture and mining. Coffee raised on the slopes of the mountains was the chief crop. In the coastal sections of the country were many sugar plantations and cattle ranches. Some articles were manufactured from native products. In 1914 the chief exports of Salvador were coffee, gold, silver, hides, sugar, and Peruvian balsam.

Social and Economic Conditions

Salvador had a unique position. She was the smallest of the Central American republics and the only nation of Middle America that did not have a coast line on both oceans. Though Indian blood flowed through the veins of a majority of her people, Spanish was the language generally used. Many of the lower classes were mestizos. With some 1,700,000 inhabitants Salvador was the most densely populated Central American country.

A new Constitution was promulgated on January 26, 1939, which slightly changed the political framework of 1886. The President was to hold office for six years, while the vice-presidency was abolished. Significant social provisions were concerned with education, labor and the family.

GUATEMALA

For three decades after the defeat of Morazán, the history of Guatemala hinged around Carrera. Reactionary decrees took the place of liberal laws upon the statute books, while special privileges were restored to the clergy. In November, 1843, a new coat of arms was adopted for the republic. An abortive revolt against Carrera in 1849 was followed by a policy of proscription.

In October, 1851, an assembly in Guatemala City adopted a fundamental law that was designated the Constituent Act of the Republic of Guatemala. This Constitution provided that the President, who was clothed with absolute authority, should be elected for four years by an assembly. If the President was temporarily absent from the capital, the chief executive authority should be vested in a council of government. Churches and other corporations were by a decree granted representation in Congress. Under that Constitution the first President was Carrera, who, on October 21, 1854, was proclaimed chief magistrate for life. Invested with almost monarchical power, Carrera ruled despotically over Guatemala until his death in 1865.

His disappearance from the political stage was followed by an increase in the power and influence of the Liberals. Led by Justo R.

Barrios, an energetic and idealistic Guatemalan, they defeated the Conservatives in battle and triumphantly entered the capital city in June, 1871. President Barrios adopted an anti-clerical policy which resembled that of Morazán. Tithes were abolished, monasteries were suppressed, ecclesiastical privileges were swept away, and freedom of religious worship was decreed. In December, 1879, a convention adopted a liberal Constitution for the republic.

Under this Constitution Barrios was chosen president. One of his cherished designs was a union of the Central American states. His secretary cited the following expressions of Barrios as indicative of his views: "I have no desire to follow the footsteps of Carrera and become a life-president, but if I could leave a worthy and united country to the inhabitants of Central America, I would consider myself happy." "I have nothing to live for but the Union." "We shall never be a great country until we are a united country, with sufficient financial resources, with a navy on both seas and an army capable of meeting our most powerful neighbor."

On February 28, 1885, Barrios accordingly issued a decree which proclaimed the reëstablishment of the Central American Union. He arrogantly declared that he had assumed the rôle of supreme military chief with absolute authority, that a general assembly of representatives from each republic should meet at Guatemala City in May following to frame a constitution for the union, and that any one who dared to oppose the execution of this decree would be considered as a traitor to Central America. He issued a manifesto to the Central American people asserting that he was not animated by personal ambition; for he had tasted the bitterness of office-holding. But this Guatemalan champion of union was opposed by Costa Rica, Nicaragua, and Salvador who appealed to Mexico and the United States to interfere on their behalf. On March 22, 1885, those republics entered into an offensive and defensive alliance against Guatemala. In consequence Barrios soon invaded Salvador, and on April 2, 1885, he was killed in battle.

Barrios and Central American Union

In 1887 the Guatemalan Constitution was modified. Freedom of religious worship was guaranteed. Entail was prohibited and also the retention of property in dead hands, except by charitable institutions. The President should be elected by direct popular vote for a term of six years; he might not be re-elected until six years had elapsed. In case of death or disability his place should be taken by substitutes in the order designated by Congress. Members of the cabinet might attend sessions of the legislature and take part in its deliberations. A Council of State, which was to be

Constitution of 1887

made up of persons selected by the President and the legislature, was to act as his advisory body. Legislative authority should be vested in a unicameral legislature called the National Assembly, which was to be composed of members elected by direct popular vote for four years. Judicial authority was vested in a supreme court which should be composed of five members chosen by direct popular vote. The basis of local administration should be departments that were to be managed by political chiefs appointed by the President.

In 1903, while Manuel Estrada Cabrera was chief magistrate, the Constitution was altered so as to allow the immediate reëlection of the President. Under the amended Constitution, Cabrera acted as the dictator of Guatemala for many years. In 1920 a rebellion broke out. After the revolutionists had proclaimed a prominent sugar planter named Carlos Herrera president of the republic, they captured Guatemala City. There they were besieged and shelled by government forces for several days. When it became clear that he was doomed to defeat, Cabrera capitulated and resigned his post. At once Provisional President Herrera undertook economic and fiscal reforms. He issued a proclamation which announced that he would not be a candidate for the presidency himself. Eventually the fundamental law was altered so as to prevent the reëlection of the President until twelve years had elapsed after he had left office.

The chief industry about 1914 was agriculture. Many coffee plantations were located on the slopes of volcanoes near the Pacific coast. Coffee, which was the main crop, had gained an enviable reputation in the world's market. On the southern coastal plain were sugar cane plantations and cattle ranches. Upon the plateau above the coffee plantations sheep were raised. In recent decades many banana plantations have been started near the Gulf of Honduras. A few factories have been established where native cotton is made into cloth. In 1914 the chief exports of Guatemala were coffee, bananas, sugar, hides, lumber, and chicle.

Social, Economic, and Political Conditions

Social conditions were in some respects unlike those in Costa Rica. In Guatemala there were thousands of aborigines. Many were held on the plantations by a system of compulsory labor, while others owned or controlled portions of the common land of their respective villages. The plantation system of the country was based upon aboriginal laborers who were in economic dependence upon the dominant class. Pure-blooded aborigines far outnumbered the whites and the mixed classes. In 1930 the population of Guatemala probably amounted to 3,000,000.

In 1931 General Jorge Ubico was elected president. By personal supervision he much improved the efficiency of public officials. On

July 11, 1935, Article LXVI of the Constitution was suspended and Ubico's term was extended until March 15, 1943. His administration was marked by material progress: swamps were drained, learned societies were founded, and the chief cities were connected by good roads. In April, 1936, a reciprocal trade agreement was made with the United States by which among other articles bananas and coffee were admitted into that country free of duty. A boundary treaty with Salvador was signed, and an arrangement was made for the adjustment of the boundary dispute with Honduras. Steps were taken to restrict the political activities of aliens and of foreign political organizations throughout the republic.

HONDURAS

The history of Honduras was perhaps more complicated than that of Guatemala. On October 26, 1838, a Constituent Assembly at Comayagua proclaimed that the State of Honduras was free, sovereign, and independent. A Constitution adopted in 1848 provided for freedom of conscience and religion. Shortly afterward President Lindo became involved in a controversy with England about the boundary of the colony of Belize which was eventually terminated by a treaty that conceded the English claims. General Santos Guardiola, a *zambo* who was under the influence of Carrera, served as president from 1856 to 1862, when he was assassinated. A Constitution adopted by Honduras in 1865 provided that Roman Catholicism should be the state religion to the exclusion of all other faiths. Under José Medina, who became president in the same year, a war broke out with Salvador which resulted in the occupation of Comayagua by Salvadoran soldiers. A little later the presidents of Guatemala and Salvador intervened in the politics of Honduras in order to replace President Arias by a chief executive selected by themselves. In 1885 Honduras promised her coöperation in the project of Barrios to establish a Central American union, but after his death she made peace with the dissentient states.

Central American Politics

At Amalpa, on June 20, 1895, Honduras, Nicaragua, and Salvador agreed to establish a common political system for the control of their external relations. This organization was to be known as the Greater Republic of Central America. In December, 1896, the President of the United States recognized this Federation by the reception of its minister. At Managua, on August 27, 1898, the three nations signed a Constitution for the United States of Central America, which provided for the admission of Costa Rica and Guatemala into the Federation. In pursuance of its stipulations, a provisional executive council for the union was installed at Amalpa on November 1, 1898, but a movement directed against the Federation occurred in Salvador, and in a short time the confederates resumed their independent sovereignty.

In 1904, at the instance of President Bonilla, a Constituent Assembly was convoked in Honduras. On September 2, 1904, that Assembly promulgated a new Constitution for the state. Executive authority was granted to a President, who was to be elected by direct popular vote for six years, but who should be ineligible for the succeeding term. Members of the cabinet might attend Congress and take part in its debates but they should have no vote. Legislative authority was vested in a unicameral Congress composed of deputies elected by direct popular vote for four years. Judicial authority was granted to a supreme court of five judges selected by Congress. Honduran territory was to be divided into departments. In a Constitution that was adopted in September, 1924, the above-mentioned provisions were repeated, except with respect to the President's term of office, which was reduced to four years.

In the main the people of Honduras were of mixed descent. Indian or Negro blood coursed in the veins of many of her citizens and a pure Caucasian was not frequently encountered. In 1914 the population of Honduras was estimated to be 562,000. Aboriginal dialects had become practically extinct; Spanish was the official language of Honduras, and also the language of her people.

The chief occupations of the people were agriculture, cattle raising, and mining. The most important agricultural products were bananas, cocoanuts, and coffee. Cattle and hogs were raised in **Social and Economic Conditions** large numbers, especially near the northern coast. Among Honduran mines the most important was a gold and silver mine in the San Juancito district near Tegucigalpa. In 1913 the main exports of Honduras were bananas, precious metals, live cattle, cocoanuts, and hides.

The history of Honduras after 1914 was checkered by military and political fluctuations. After she declared war on Germany in 1918, a state of siege was proclaimed throughout the republic. By a Constitution adopted in September, 1924, the fundamental law of 1904 was reordained except with respect to the President's term of office which was reduced to four years. In January, 1936, a commercial agreement was made with the United States which reduced the duties on certain imports from that country. On March 28 following a new fundamental law was promulgated which separated Church and State. By this Constitution the President's term of office was again set at six years as provided in 1924. In accordance with this provision, another article in that fundamental law extended the term of the energetic General

Carias Andino, who had become president in February, 1933, to January 1, 1943.

NICARAGUA

On April 30, 1838, a Constitutional convention at Managua declared that Nicaragua was independent. Her boundary problems proved very troublesome. They involved her in a dispute with England who, as the protector of the Mosquitoan Indians, **Early Problems** urged a claim to territory within the region that was designated Nicaragua. In 1850 the Clayton-Bulwer Treaty between England and the United States stipulated that neither party could occupy, fortify, colonize, or exercise dominion over any portion of Central American territory. By a later treaty England ceded to Nicaragua her protectorate over the Mosquitoan Indians. In April, 1854, a Constituent Assembly adopted a Constitution for Nicaragua which vested governmental authority in a President and a unicameral Congress. Fruto Chamorro was made provisional president.

Among the Liberals who opposed the government of Chamorro was Francisco Castellon who, through a mutual acquaintance, invited a daring adventurer named William Walker to bring colonists from the United States to Nicaragua. In May, 1855, Walker sailed from San Francisco for Central America. His original plan was evidently to aid Nicaraguan Liberals in their struggle against the Serviles. After being defeated by the Serviles, he captured Granada by a night attack. He declined the presidency of Nicaragua which was offered him but accepted the post of commander in chief of her army. Soon afterward, however, the filibuster had a bitter quarrel with influential financiers in the United States upon whom he depended for aid. Further, his enemies aroused the other states of Central America against him: soldiers from Costa Rica, Guatemala, Honduras, and Salvador joined the Serviles of Nicaragua. Walker was ultimately forced to desist from the ambitious design which he had formed of establishing a state that should include Central America, Mexico, and possibly Cuba. Instead of founding a tropical empire where Negro slavery would have been a recognized institution, he was captured by the Hondurans, court-martialed, and executed.

Politics in Nicaragua ran a tortuous course. Progressives, who moved slowly to avoid antagonizing other parties, were occasionally called the Liberals, while at other times they were designated Liberal-Conservatives. About 1870 certain persons who **Party Struggles** styled themselves Democrats had become attached to the clergy and were known as Moderates. A number of young politicians, who were anxious to introduce reforms, were styled Radicals. In 1881 difficulties arose because certain clerics were suspected of having instigated the Indians to revolt. The Jesuits became incensed because of a liberal speech made by a Spanish professor at the opening of a national educational institute at León; they incited an uprising against the government that encouraged such doctrines, and finally had to be expelled from the republic. When Barrios of Guatemala tried to reweld the Central American states into a union, Nicaragua joined Salvador and Costa Rica to shatter his plans.

General José Santos Zelaya, a member of the Liberal party, emerged as the leader of a successful insurrection in 1893. Soon afterward he was elected president for four years under a new Constitution. In 1895, because he arrested and expelled certain English citizens who were suspected of conspiring against his government, he became involved in a dispute with England. Despite this controversy which led to the dispatch of an English warship to Central America but was settled by the payment of an indemnity, and despite uprisings against his government, Zelaya maintained his power and was reëlected president in 1902 and again in 1906. A man of initiative and energy, he secured the completion of a railroad from the Atlantic Ocean to Lake Nicaragua; he also promoted the construction of wharves and electric lighting plants. He took steps to improve his country's monetary system; but his concessions to monopolistic companies provoked much dissatisfaction. He did not succeed in satisfactorily adjusting Nicaragua's debts. Arbitrary in his methods of rule, but a clever politician, he was viewed by his partisans as a great leader who might ensure tranquillity to the discordant and belligerent republics of Central America.

In 1905 the Nicaraguans adopted a Constitution which provided for a President, a unicameral legislature, and federal courts. That Constitution made the department the local unit of organization.

War with Honduras

Among the wars which were subsequently waged by Nicaragua, none was more significant than the conflict that broke out in 1907 with Honduras. This war was terminated largely because of good offices exerted by the United States and Mexico. Upon its close the belligerents signed a convention stipulating that until a general arbitration treaty was adopted by the nations of Central America, any differences which might arise between contracting parties should be settled by the arbitration of the presidents of Mexico and the United States.

Soon afterward, as war seemed imminent between Nicaragua and Salvador, Presidents Díaz and Roosevelt proposed that a peace conference should be held by the nations of Central America. In September, 1907, a preliminary conference of the ministers of the Central

American states and representatives of Mexico and the United States was held at Washington. At that meeting the five republics of Central America agreed to send delegates to a conference to discuss the measures necessary to adjust any differences which might arise among those republics and to frame a treaty that should define their general relations.

Accordingly Presidents Díaz and Roosevelt soon invited the republics of Central America to send representatives to a conference. In November and December, 1907, delegates from those republics and also diplomats of Mexico and the United States gathered at Washington. The Central American Conference agreed to certain conventions concerning peace and amity, extradition, and future conferences. Other conventions established a Central American court of justice, a pedagogical institute, and a Central American bureau. The last-mentioned convention provided that the republics concerned should found and support a bureau which was to promote the interests of Central America, to maintain an organ of publicity, and to serve as a medium of intelligence.

The Central American Conference of 1907

The Treaty of Peace and Amity declared that a first duty of the contracting parties was to preserve peace. They pledged themselves to adjust in a Central American court of justice any differences that might arise among themselves. A citizen of one nation residing in another country of Central America was to have the same civil rights as citizens of that country. Legal documents of one state should be valid in the other states. The territory of Honduras should be absolutely neutral. Revolutionary leaders should not be allowed to reside in districts adjacent to a country where they might disturb the peace. The convention concerning a Central American court of justice provided for the establishment of a permanent tribunal at Cartago in Costa Rica, composed of one judge from each state, which was to take cognizance of certain controversies. The five nations agreed to enforce the decisions of that court. Certain members of the Conference even suggested that the republics should again form one political organization, but most of the delegates held that, at this juncture, a Central American union was impracticable.

The Peace Conference of 1907 seemed to prescribe efficacious remedies for chronic Central American maladies. On May 25, 1908, the court of justice was installed at Cartago. Its decisions were not without influence in checking the interference of one or more states in the affairs of a neighbor. Still, revolutions in Central America did not cease.

The storm center of Central American politics was Nicaragua. Suspicions were rife that President Zelaya designed to impose his authority upon neighboring states. In February, 1909, Zelaya evidently encouraged a filibustering expedition against Salvador. To promote the execution of the Washington conventions the United States sent warships to Central American waters. At Bluefields in October, 1909, General Estrada started an insurrection against the government of Nicaragua. Early in December, 1909, United States Secretary of State Knox gave the Nicaraguan minister at Washington his passports. Knox declared that, in violation of the treaties of 1907, President Zelaya had kept Central America in turmoil and that his administration was "a blot on the history" of Nicaragua. In the face of civil war and international complications, Zelaya decided to relinquish his authority. Upon accepting his resignation the National Assembly protested against the American policy of intervention.

Yet after Zelaya went into exile, Nicaragua asked the United States for advice about her political and fiscal reorganization. On November 6, 1910, an agreement was reached between those two nations which provided for a convention that should elect Provisional President Estrada as president. This agreement also stipulated that a loan should be secured for Nicaragua upon the basis of her customs duties. Any claims which might be pending against that state should be
Intervention by the United States adjusted according to a plan formed by the United States and Nicaragua. Early in the next year Secretary Knox signed a treaty with Nicaragua which provided for the refunding of her national debt and for a loan that should be guaranteed by her customs receipts. This treaty further provided that the collector-general of Nicaragua's customs should be approved by the President of the United States. Although it was not ratified by the United States Senate, yet according to an executive agreement, President Taft selected a collector who was given charge of the Nicaraguan customs service.

In March, 1912, a new Nicaraguan Constitution was put into operation. That Constitution vested executive authority in a President who should be elected by direct popular vote for four years. He was declared to be ineligible to succeed himself, and was to be aided and advised by secretaries of state. Members of both the Senate and the House of Deputies were to be chosen by direct popular vote. One deputy was to be elected from every district into which a department might be divided. Each department of the republic should elect one senator for every two deputies. The national judiciary was to be composed of a supreme court and three inferior courts.

The largest in territory of the Central American republics, in many particulars Nicaragua resembles Salvador and Honduras. To a considerable extent the aborigines have become amalgamated with the Spanish element of the population. The most numerous class is probably the mestizo. In 1914 the population of Nicaragua was estimated at 703,540 souls. There the language and religion of the Spaniards have been imposed upon a stock which has often preserved aboriginal agricultural customs. The chief cities of Nicaragua are located on the plains near lakes Nicaragua and Managua.

Social and Economic Conditions about 1914

The main Nicaraguan industries were agriculture and cattle raising. Coffee, bananas, sugar, and cacao were the important crops. A large number of cattle roamed over the grassy plains. In 1914 the chief exports of Nicaragua were as follows: coffee, gold, bananas, lumber, hides and skins, and rubber.

Nicaragua has also had difficulties and embarrassments in regard to her loans. So serious did her fiscal problems become that United States bankers undertook to aid in the reorganization of her banking and monetary systems. In October, 1910, an agreement was reached between the United States and Nicaragua which provided that this republic should take steps to reorganize her finances by negotiating a loan secured by her customs duties. Subsequently Nicaragua entered into an agreement by which the United States government should choose a collector who was to supervise her fiscal administration.

In 1916 an important treaty that had been negotiated between Secretary Chamorro of Nicaragua and Secretary of State Bryan was ratified. By that treaty the United States government agreed to pay Nicaragua $3,000,000. In return the United States was granted the exclusive right to construct and maintain an interoceanic canal across Nicaragua, and she was given a lease of Great and Little Corn Islands near the eastern terminus of the proposed canal. As Costa Rica and Salvador made objections to the Bryan-Chamorro Treaty, when it was ratified by the United States Senate that body declared that none of its provisions were intended to affect any existing right of any other nation of Central America.

The nations of Central America showed a remarkable unanimity in their attitude toward the first World War. In 1917 certain of those nations announced that their diplomatic relations with Germany were severed. By August, 1918, Costa Rica, Honduras, Guatemala, and Nicaragua had declared the existence of a state of war with the imperial German government. Although Salvador remained neutral, yet she evidently declared that she was friendly to the government at Washington.

Meanwhile the finances of Nicaragua had become badly demoralized. Her government was harassed by "floating debts and miscellaneous

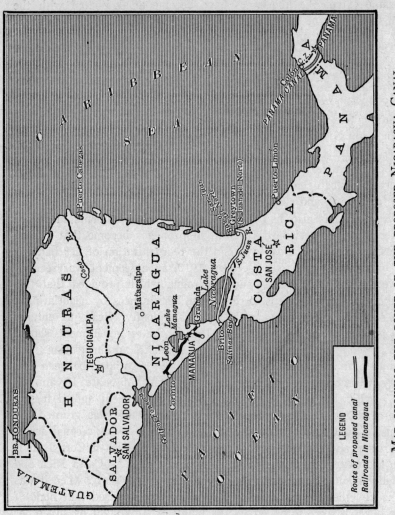

Map showing the route of the proposed Nicaragua Canal

(Adapted from Foreign Policy Association, Information Service Bulletin, IV, 6)

claims." Exacting demands made by the holders of such obligations often prevented the government from paying the salaries of its employees. By the aid of the United States a plan for the rehabilitation of Nicaragua's finances was formed. This plan provided for the introduction of a budgetary system, for an adjustment of the floating debt, and for the financing of the deferred interest and sinking fund obligation of the bonded indebtedness. A high commission was to be established composed of representatives of Nicaragua and the United States. This commission was to serve as an agency to ensure the payment of bonds that were guaranteed by import duties. Aided by payments from the canal fund paid by the United States, the execution of this plan resulted in a substantial reduction of Nicaragua's debt.

Fiscal Rehabilitation of Nicaragua

At this juncture prominent publicists entertained high hopes that the Central American nations might attain their political salvation in a Federation. Arrangements were accordingly made for a conference of delegates from the five states. At San José, Costa Rica, on January 19, 1921, delegates of Guatemala, Salvador, Honduras, and Costa Rica signed a "Treaty of Union." This compact provided that, after its ratification by three states, they would unite in "a perpetual and indissoluble union" to constitute a nation designated the "Federation of Central America." It formulated a Provisional Constitution for the Federation. According to that Constitution each state was to preserve her control of internal affairs and was to exercise such powers as were not granted to the federal government. The constitutions of the states of Central America were to remain in force so far as they were not contrary to the federal pact. After the Swiss example, executive authority was to be vested in a federal council. To that council each state was to elect by popular vote a councilor and an alternate for a term of five years. From their own number the councilors were to select a President and a Vice, President who should serve for one year. Legislative authority was to be exercised by a Senate and a Chamber of Deputies. Judicial authority was to be vested in a supreme court and inferior courts established by law.

Central American Federation of 1921

After three states had ratified the "Treaty of Union," a provisional federal council was to be elected composed of one delegate from each state. That council was to convoke a National Constituent Assembly composed of fifteen delegates from each state which should frame a permanent constitution for the Federation according to the bases laid down in the Treaty of Union.

Fearing that to accept the compact might jeopardize its rights under the Bryan-Chamorro Treaty, the Nicaraguan government declined to

sign the Treaty of San José. The Congress of Costa Rica finally rejected the Treaty of Union by a close vote. It was ratified, however,
by the congresses of Honduras, Guatemala, and Salvador. Members of
the provisional federal council were then elected, and the National
Constituent Assembly was convoked at Tegucigalpa, Honduras, to
pass laws and to frame a constitution. But a coup d'état in Guatemala
City in December, 1921, which resulted in the deposition of President
Herrera by General Orellana, ensured the failure of this political
experiment.

The collapse of the union, the disintegration of the court of justice
because of a dispute concerning the Bryan-Chamorro Treaty, and a
belief that steps should be taken to avoid heavy military
expenditures stimulated the sentiment in Central America
in favor of common action. The five republics invited the
United States to send delegates to a new conference at Washington.
This assembly, which deliberated from December 4, 1922, to February
7, 1923, framed and adopted twelve treaties and three protocols. A
Treaty of Peace and Amity contained provisions concerning relations
among the republics which closely resembled those adopted by the
Conference of 1907. This treaty also provided that disputes arising
among the republics should be investigated by commissions of inquiry.
Another treaty stipulated that these commissions were to examine the
circumstances attending a dispute between nations of Central America
and to elucidate them in a report. The Treaty for a Central American
court of justice provided that controversies which were neither adjusted by diplomatic means nor submitted to other modes of settlement
should be decided irrevocably and without appeal by three judges
who were to be selected by the disputants from a panel of thirty
jurists nominated by the five republics. The Convention for the Limitation of Armaments provided that for five years after it came into
force none of the republics should maintain an armed force in excess
of a stipulated number.

A few years later a troublesome situation had again developed in
Nicaragua. In November, 1926, immediately after a Conservative
named Adolfo Díaz had entered upon his duties as president, he appealed to the United States for aid to oppose
a Liberal revolt led by General José Moncada and also
to prevent hostilities with Mexico. President Coolidge
took the view that Mexico was attempting to set up in Nicaragua a
government hostile to the United States. Hence, large numbers of
American marines were landed in that country who erected neutral
zones around certain cities. Díaz even proposed a treaty of alliance
with the United States that would concede to her the right to intervene

in Nicaragua whenever necessary to make certain guarantees of that convention effective.

In March, 1927, Henry L. Stimson was sent by Coolidge to Nicaragua to investigate conditions. He concluded that a deadlock between the contending parties had been reached, but that the Nicaraguans wished the United States to supervise their approaching national elections. At his instance, an agreement was reached between the factions to the effect that the Liberal soldiers would lay down their arms, provided that the United States would arrange to give Nicaragua a fair election in 1928. A lieutenant of Moncada named Sandino, however, refused to abide by this agreement, and, in consequence, American marines engaged in a strenuous campaign against him. Sandino demanded the evacuation of his country by the marines, the appointment of an impartial civilian president for Nicaragua, and the supervision of her elections by Latin America. The intransigent Nicaraguan Liberal was driven into exile. Meanwhile, in accordance with the Stimson agreement, on November 4, 1928, the Nicaraguan presidential election took place under the supervision of General Frank McCoy. The result was the election of General Moncado by a large majority.

Early in 1931 Stimson, who had meanwhile become the American secretary of state, announced that the number of marines in Nicaragua would soon be greatly decreased and that after the presidential election of 1932 they would be completely withdrawn. By the beginning of 1933 all the American forces had left that country. In 1936 General Anastasio Somosa rose to power and during the next year he became president of Nicaragua. On March 22, 1939, a constitutional convention adopted a new fundamental law which did not much alter the existing political framework. It did, however, extend the President's term of office to six years and provided that ex-Presidents who had been elected to that office should be entitled to seats in the Senate. Among a long list of social guarantees, the Catholic Church was assured that it would be allowed to remain in possession of such structures as were actually used for religious purposes. By a special dispensation of the Constitution it was stipulated that Somosa was to continue as chief magistrate until May 1, 1947.

PANAMA

Though the Isthmus of Panama formed a part of the terrritory of Colombia until the revolution in the city of Panama on November 3, 1903, the independent state which was at once erected on that Isthmus is now often grouped with the Central American republics. On November 4 the council of that city framed a declaration that the people under its jurisdiction had severed the political bonds which had connected them with Colombia. It further declared that in union with other towns in the state of Panama it had formed an independent government.

A constitutional convention was soon convoked to organize the new nation. On February 13, 1904, it adopted a Constitution for the republic of Panama. The territory of the republic was declared to be that which had been included within the state of Panama by a Colombian law, subject to the arbitral award of the French President in the pending boundary dispute of Colombia with Costa Rica. Article XXVI of the Constitution recognized Roman Catholicism as the religion of the majority of the republic's inhabitants but stipulated that religious worship should be free. Executive authority was vested in a President who should serve for four years. Members of his cabinet were to act as an advisory council. Legislative authority was vested in a unicameral legislature called the National Assembly which should be composed of members elected from districts for four years. Judicial power was given to a supreme court and other courts that were to be established by law.

The territory of the republic was divided into seven provinces. In each province the chief executive should be a governor who was to be appointed and removed by the President. Article CXXXVI provided that if the United States government should by treaty assume the obligation of guaranteeing the independence and sovereignty of Panama, it should have the power to intervene in any part of the republic "to reëstablish public peace and constitutional order."

Meanwhile, on November 18, 1903, a treaty had been signed by Secretary Hay and Philippe Bunau-Varilla, Panama's agent. By the Hay–Bunau-Varilla Treaty the United States guaranteed the independence of the isthmian republic. Panama granted to the United States not only a strip of land ten miles wide across the Isthmus for the construction of the canal but also the nominal right of sovereignty over that zone and its adjacent waters. In return for the privileges and rights thus granted, the United States agreed to pay that nation $10,000,000 and during the life of the treaty an annual sum of $250,000 to begin nine years after its ratifications were exchanged. Other nations soon followed the example of the United States and recognized the new republic. Profoundly dissatisfied with the Panama affair, however, Colombia refrained from acknowledging her independence.

Though the Panamanian Constitution contained a clause providing that the President should be a natural-born citizen of the republic, yet in recognition of his services to the cause of independence the conven-

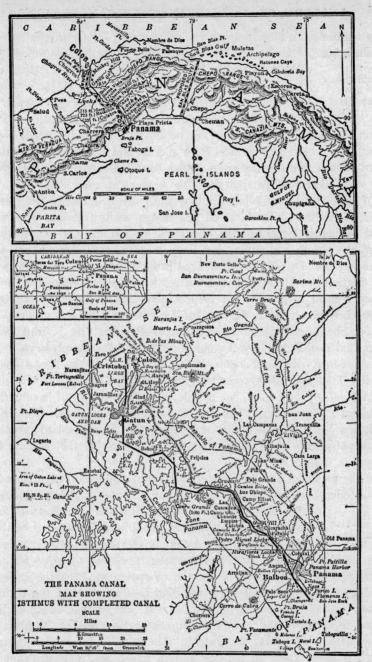

MAP OF THE PANAMA REPUBLIC, SHOWING THE CANAL ZONE

tion unanimously elected to that office a native of Cartagena named
Manuel Amador Guerrero. The convention was then transformed into
a legislative body. It enacted a law stipulating that the
legal codes of Colombia should remain in force whenever they were not repugnant to the laws of Panama. It
established the gold standard and adopted a national flag.
Upon the coat of arms that it sanctioned for the republic there were
depicted a sword and a musket, a pickax and a shovel, a horn of
plenty and a rosette with wings, which were surmounted by the scroll
pro mundi beneficio, pendant from the beak of an eagle.

**Establish-
ment of an
Independent
Government**

Of the ten million dollars paid by the United States for the Canal
Zone, six millions were invested in Panama, while the remainder was
used to finance certain public utilities in that country. A controversy
soon arose with Colombia, for there was no agreement about the
boundary line. Dissensions that raged in 1908 because of the approaching election in which two Conservatives were candidates for the presidency seemed to presage a rebellion. The United States accordingly
dispatched warships to the city of Panama and landed marines at
Colón. She informed the government of Panama that if fraud was
permitted in the elections, it would become her duty to preserve order
in accordance with the Panamanian Constitution and the Hay–Bunau-
Varilla Treaty. After a commission composed of citizens of Panama
and officials of the Canal Zone had declared that charges of irregularity
had been grossly exaggerated, one of the candidates for the presidency
withdrew his name, with the explanation that he wished to promote
party unity as well as to prevent the occupation of the republic by
American soldiers.

In the presidential election of July, 1908, Domingo de Obaldia, who
had acted as chief executive, was chosen president. Obaldia was inaugurated on October 1, 1908; he died in March, 1910, and
was succeeded by Carlos Mendoza. In September of that
year the National Assembly elected as the first substitute for the President, Pedro Arosemena, who was to serve for the
remainder of Obaldia's term. In the campaign of 1912 the Liberal
candidate, Dr. Belisario Porras, who had been minister to the United
States, was elected president. During 1913 a law was enacted that
aimed to conserve the natural resources of the country. Difficulties
arose with Chinese residing within the republic because of a law
which required them to register and to pay a fee. The government
withdrew the exequatur of the Chinese consul-general at Panama City,
who was reported to have advised his fellow countrymen to refuse
obedience to the obnoxious registration law. Partly as a result of the
protests of Chinese residents, the National Assembly ultimately en-

**Panamanian
Conditions**

acted a law that authorized the President to expel objectionable foreigners from the republic.

In 1912 the population of the republic of Panama was estimated to be about 341,000. Negroes composed a not inconsiderable element. In certain parts of the country were remnants of aboriginal stocks that had scarcely been affected by civilization. There were many mulattoes and mestizos, especially in the capital city. Some attention was paid to mining, but agriculture and cattle raising were the chief industries. In the cities of Colón and Panama many persons were employed in mercantile pursuits. Besides bananas, the important exports of the republic were rubber, cocoanuts, manganese, ivory nuts, hides, cabinet woods, and pearls.

While the new republic had been learning the art of government, the United States had been digging the great ditch to connect the Atlantic Ocean with the Pacific. In August, 1914, the canal across the Isthmus of Panama was opened to traffic. The completion of the Panama Canal and the imperative need of protecting it, especially in war times, caused the United States government to take measures that augmented its influence in the isthmian nation. In September, 1914, that nation ratified a treaty with the United States which defined the boundaries between Panama and the Canal Zone. This treaty conceded to the United States control over the waters of Ancón and Colón at the Atlantic terminus of the canal; it transferred to that nation two small islands in Ancón harbor, and gave her the site for a coastal battery upon that water front. *Panama during the First World War*

On April 7, 1917, the National Assembly declared war upon Germany. Upon the same day Ramón Valdez, who had become President on October 1, 1916, issued a proclamation in which he declared that the very existence of his republic was linked to that of the United States. He appealed to his people to coöperate in the protection of the Panama Canal and of their own territory. In 1917 soldiers from the United States were landed in Colón and Panama City to quell election disturbances. During the next year the United States felt compelled to assume police power in the isthmian republic.

That republic inherited a troublesome boundary dispute. As already indicated, Colombia's limits with Costa Rica under the Loubet award had not been completely demarcated when Panama declared her independence. Although Costa Rica and Panama reached a satisfactory solution about their boundary under that award upon the Pacific side, yet they could not agree about their limits upon the Atlantic side. An acrimonious dispute seemed to end when, through the good offices of the United States, *Boundary Disputes* in March, 1910, the two nations agreed to a treaty stipulating that the chief justice of the United States should decide which was the boundary line between Panama and Costa Rica "most in accordance" with the Loubet award.

By the award of Chief Justice White, which was announced in 1914, a line drawn from the mouth of the Sixaola River upon the Atlantic side to a point near 9° north latitude beyond Cerro Pando was declared to be the boundary most in accordance with the intent of President Loubet. The isthmian republic, however, objected to White's award and charged that he had exceeded his authority. In 1920 she even proceeded to occupy a part of the territory in dispute. Armed conflicts occurred between Panama and Costa Rica which threatened to involve certain of their neighbors. When he became secretary of state under President Harding, Hughes took a firm stand. He declared that Panama's allegations were groundless and insisted that she accept the limits that had been drawn in the arbitral award of Justice White. At that very juncture, the boundary between Panama and Colombia was sketched by Article III of the modified Thompson-Urrutia Treaty.

Because of the control of the Canal Zone by the United States, the recent history of Panama is closely related to the policy of that country. On July 28, 1926, diplomats of the two nations signed a treaty that aimed clearly to define their mutual relations. This treaty provided that in case the United States should become involved in a war the Panamanian republic should also consider herself in a state of war. Panama was then to turn over to the United States her aircraft, wireless stations, and other warlike equipment. Further, she was to yield to the United States the control of military operations in any part of the republic. Besides, the United States was to be given the right "to expropriate privately owned lands" and also "the use, occupation, and control in perpetuity" of Manzanillo Island and Colón harbor.

Relations with the United States

The Panamanians, however, raised various objections to this agreement. In part their opposition was based on the contention that the Hay–Bunau-Varilla Treaty did not concede complete sovereign rights over the Canal Zone to the United States. The League of Nations took the view that the Treaty of 1926 was not in keeping with Panama's obligations to that society. In January, 1927, the National Assembly adopted a resolution postponing the further consideration of that treaty.

On January 2, 1931, a revolution promoted by a patriotic society designated the *Acción Comunal* overthrew the government of President Arsomena and installed a temporary régime. At the same time the supreme court made known its decision that the presidential election of October, 1930, was illegal. The succession to the presidency thus devolved upon Ricardo J. Alfaro, the minister to the United States, who soon assumed the duties of that office. The government of the United States treated the new régime as the legal government of Panama. President Alfaro soon announced his intention of reopening negotiations for a modification of the pending treaty with the United States in order to fulfill as fully as possible the hopes of his people for the enjoyment of a larger measure of the benefits flowing from the opening of the Panama Canal.

On October 1, 1932, Harmodio Arias was inaugurated as president. During his administration the protracted negotiations for a readjustment of Panama's relations with the United States bore fruit in a new treaty signed on March 2, 1936. By that treaty the two parties agreed that, in case of any menace or of an international war, they would be jointly responsible for the security of the republic and of the canal. Further, the United States agreed to pay Panama $250,000 annually. This treaty was not ratified by the Senate of the United States until July 29, 1939.

Juan D. Arsomena, who had meanwhile become president, died in December, 1939. After a brief interlude, Arnulfo Arias became the chief magistrate. At once he took steps to frame a new Constitution which would be both "democratic and unitarian." The National Assembly promptly adopted this fundamental law which extended the term of the President and the assemblymen to six years. Certain articles authorized the intervention of the government in business and in the formation of public monopolies. The article formally providing for the protectorate of the United States was stricken out. Buildings used by the Catholic Church for religious purposes were to be exempt from taxation. Early in 1941 the new Constitution was put into operation.

After the President flew secretly to Cuba ostensibly for medical attention, without the required consent of the legislature, the cabinet declared that his position was vacant and Ricardo de la Guardia was then made the chief executive. In contrast with his predecessor, Guardia soon showed that he would not be sympathetic toward the Axis powers.

In pursuance of the precedent set in the Dominican republic, and because of similar conditions, the United States undertook to aid in the financial rehabilitation of Nicaragua. In Central America, as in the West Indies, this process of fiscal reconstruction led to measures by the United States which constituted an infringement upon the sovereign rights of a Latin-American nation. American marines sometimes followed the bankers to support what has been designated financial imperialism. Largely because of the attitude of a good neighbor taken by the United States, however, she has recently renounced the policy of forcible intervention. Meanwhile the acquisition by the United States of the Panama Canal Zone and the completion of the canal had led to an increasing interest in the administration of the isthmian republic, especially in war times. In almost all of the Central American republics there has recently been displayed a peculiar tendency, namely the policy of the chief executive to evade constitutional limitations in order to continue in office. A remarkable unanimity was shown by these republics toward the second World War, for shortly after the Japanese attack on Pearl Harbor, every one of them declared war on the Axis powers.

SUGGESTIONS FOR FURTHER READING

BELT, T., *The Naturalist in Nicaragua*, 1928.

BUNAU-VARILLA, P., *Panama, the Creation, Destruction, and Resurrection*, 1914.

BURGESS, P., *Justo Rufino Barrios*, 1926.

COX, J. I., *Nicaragua and the United States*, 1927.

CUMBERLAND, W. W., *Nicaragua: An Economic and Financial Survey*, 1928.

DOMVILLE-FIFE, C. W., *Guatemala and the States of Central America*, 1913.

FRANK, H. A., *Tramping through Mexico, Guatemala, and Honduras*, 1916.

HILL, R. R., *Fiscal Intervention in Nicaragua*, 1933.

JONES, C. L., *The Caribbean since 1900*, 1936.

———, *Costa Rica and Civilization in the Caribbean*, 1935.

———, *Guatemala, Past and Present*, 1940.

KEPNER, C. D., and SOOTHILL, J. H., *The Banana Empire*, 1935.

MARTIN, P. F., *Salvador of the Twentieth Century*, 1911.

MOE, A. K., *Honduras*, 1904.

MUNRO, D. G., *The Five Republics of Central America*, 1918.

———, *The Latin American Republics*, 1942.

NOGALES, R. DE, *The Looting of Nicaragua*, 1928.

SCRUGGS, W. O., *Filibusters and Financiers*, 1916.

STEPHENS, J. L., *Incidents of Travel in Central America, Chiapas, and Yucatan*, 1841.

STIMSON, H. L., *American Policy in Nicaragua*, 1927.

VERRILL, A. H., *Panama of Today*, 1927.

WALKER, W., *The War in Nicaragua*, 1860.

CHAPTER XXIV

IMPERIAL AND REPUBLICAN RULE
IN MEXICO

Emperor Agustín I established a court in the City of Mexico. To reward his followers he founded a fraternity designated the Imperial Order of Guadelupe. Yet his Empire did not endure long. Heavy expenses caused by the Revolution, by the forma- tion of a new government, and by a lavish distribution of offices and pensions embarrassed the finances of a monarch who had no organized system of finance. Royalists opposed his rule because he had not placed a Spanish prince upon the Mexican throne as provided by the Plan of Iguala. Republicans objected to a native monarch, protested against the paraphernalia of royalty, and clamored for a republic. As bitter opposition to his rule developed among congressmen, by a decree dated October 30, 1822, the Emperor arbitrarily dissolved Congress, after having imprisoned some of its leading members.

Collapse of the First Empire

Agustín I then appointed certain congressmen to a junta which served as a council of government. With its advice he tried, by the issue of paper money and by making forced loans, to prevent the Empire from becoming bankrupt. Near the end of 1822, a discontented military commander named Antonio de Santa Anna started an insurrection. On February 1, 1823, with other military leaders, he signed at Casa Mata a proclamation which denounced imperial rule and declared that sovereignty resided in the people.

The Plan of Casa Mata asserted that the cause for the uprising was the lack of a national Congress. As this plan found supporters in many parts of Mexico, and as the Emperor soon realized that it was impossible to compromise with the revolutionists, on March 19 he sent a letter of resignation to Congress. Asserting that he did not wish his name to be made a pretext for civil war, and that his presence might be made an excuse for civil disturbances, he declared that he was willing to expatriate himself. On April 7, 1823, Congress decreed that the coronation of Iturbide was illegal and that the acts of the imperial government were null. It granted the deposed ruler a pension upon the condition that he should reside abroad. Further, it declared that, in so far as the Plan of Iguala and the Treaty of Córdoba had created a governmental system, they were null and void. Shortly afterward the former Emperor sailed for Italy.

On March 31, 1823, Congress had decreed that the executive authority should be vested in generals Bravo, Victoria, and Negrete. This triumvirate selected a cabinet and also took steps to reorganize the government. In May, 1823, Congress issued a decree which provided that delegates should be elected to a Constituent Congress. In that Congress, which assembled in November, the Republicans were divided into two factions: the Federalists and the Centralists. Some of Iturbide's followers joined the Federalist party, while the Royalists generally allied themselves with the Centralists.

Political Reorganization

On October 4, 1824, the Constituent Congress promulgated a constitution for the United Mexican States. Article IV of this Constitution declared that Roman Catholicism should be perpetually the religion of the Mexican nation. It provided that members of the clergy should retain their privileges. Executive authority was vested in a President who should be elected for four years by the state legislatures and who, in a crisis, might be granted "extraordinary powers." Legislative authority was given to a Congress made up of a Senate and a House of Deputies. Judicial authority was granted to inferior courts and to a supreme court which was to be made up of judges chosen by the state legislatures. Shortly after the adoption of this fundamental law, the Constituent Congress passed an act which provided for the organization of a federal district that was to include Mexico City.

The first President of Mexico under a republican régime was a Federalist with little political ability, General Guadalupe Victoria. He was inaugurated on October 10, 1824; and on January 1, 1825, the first constitutional Congress of Mexico opened its sessions. Several months later the Spanish garrison in the castle of San Juan de Ulúa capitulated. President Victoria soon established commercial relations with England by treaty and received Joel Poinsett as minister from the United States. Partly as a result of Poinsett's influence, Masonic lodges began to play an important rôle in Mexican politics. In 1827 a conspiracy was discovered which apparently aimed to reëstablish Spanish rule in Mexico. The legislatures of certain states therefore decreed that Spaniards should be expelled; on December 20, 1827, Congress enacted a law to the same effect. In the election of 1828 Victoria's secretary of war, Manuel Gómez Pedraza, defeated General Vicente Guerrero, a revolutionary hero. When the result became known, Guerrero's followers appealed to arms under the leadership of Santa Anna and Lorenzo Zavala. After a bloody struggle in the streets of the capital

Early Politico-Military Problems

city, the revolutionists were victorious, Gómez Pedraza fled, and Congress named Guerrero president. By the insurrection of Acordada, as it was called, the party defeated at the polls had triumphed by the use of the sword.

One of Guerrero's first steps was to execute the law providing for the expulsion of Spaniards. Possibly that measure stimulated King Ferdinand VII to send General Barradas from Cuba with an expedition against Mexico. After capturing Tampico, Barradas was forced to capitulate. At Jalapa, on December 4, 1829, Vice-President Anastasio Bustamante, who was in command of a division of the republic's soldiers, declared in favor of the restoration of the Constitution and the laws. President Guerrero marched against Bustamante but was soon deserted by his soldiers, and the rebels captured Mexico City. Shortly after the Vice-President assumed the presidency, Guerrero was treacherously captured and executed. In 1832 Santa Anna issued a pronunciamiento against Bustamante who, after some bloody conflicts, was forced to sign an agreement by which he relinquished the presidency to Gómez Pedraza.

In 1833, Santa Anna, the candidate of the so-called Liberal party, was elected president. Wily, passionate, and inordinately ambitious, he apparently had no fixed political principles, except to dominate Mexican politics. A Mexican contemporary likened him to a chameleon. By a strange whim Santa Anna allowed Vice-President Gómez Farias to assume the powers of President upon inauguration day; these two men served alternately as President during 1833 and 1834. At this time, under the leadership of Gómez Farias, the Liberal party essayed certain politico-religious reforms. The government assumed the right to make ecclesiastical appointments, withdrew the support which it had given in the collection of tithes, and prohibited the clergy from engaging in public instruction. Those measures caused much discontent among the Conservatives, who were largely composed of monarchists and supporters of clerical privilege.

Pronunciamientos were issued in favor of the Roman Catholic religion and ecclesiastical privileges. Though Santa Anna had evidently approved some of the objectionable measures, he became the leader of the Conservatives, annulled the reform laws, and forced Gómez Farias into exile. A Congress which Santa Anna convoked approved his actions and appointed General Miguel Barragán provisional president. At the instance of Congress, in October, 1835, Barragán promulgated a decree which established a centralistic system of government.

Under his successor, José Justo Corro, Congress acting as a Constituent Assembly framed a species of Constitution that was embodied in seven laws—designated by some Mexicans as the "Seven Plagues" —which were promulgated on December 30, 1836. Those measures provided that the chief executive authority was to be vested in a President who should serve for eight years. He should be aided by a council of government. Besides providing for legislative and judicial departments, those fundamental laws created a commission of congressmen denominated "the supreme conservative power," which was entrusted with the task of keeping the executive, legislative, and judicial magistrates in their proper spheres. Further, the Constituent Assembly not only suppressed the state legislatures but also designated the states as departments. A *de facto* revolution thus became a revolution *de jure*.

Meanwhile events of international significance were taking place. Grave difficulties had arisen in Texas which, with Coahuila, had formed a state in the Mexican republic. In imitation of the first empresario, Stephen F. Austin, who, according to a contract with the Mexican government, had established a settlement of United States citizens on the Brazos River, other enterprising Americans led colonists

Independence of Texas

to Texas. Many of those settlers were from regions in the United States where slavery legally existed. By one device or another they retained that institution in Texas, even though Negro slavery was prohibited by Mexican law. Among those settlers the centralistic measures of the government provoked great dissatisfaction. On March 2, 1836, the Texans accordingly held a convention which adopted a Declaration of Independence from Mexico. David G. Burnet was elected president of the Republic of Texas, and Samuel Houston, an adventurous leader who had just arrived from the United States, was made commander in chief of the patriot soldiers. After some spectacular conflicts, on April 21, 1836, the Texans defeated the Mexican army under Santa Anna at San Jacinto. While that commander was a prisoner, they induced him to sign a species of treaty which stated that the limits of Texas were not to extend beyond the Rio Grande. By a law of the Texan Congress, this river was declared to be the western boundary of the republic.

In March, 1839, when President Bustamante left the capital at the head of an army to fight his opponents, the supreme conservative

Santa Anna as Dictator

power appointed Santa Anna provisional president. He soon retired from the presidential stage again, and after other fluctuations in the government had taken place, on September 28, 1841, he proclaimed the Plan of Tacubaya. This plan proposed that the executive and legislative authorities established by the laws of 1836 should be swept away, that the commander in chief should choose two representatives for each department who were to elect a provisional president, and that the new executive should reorganize the government.

In October, 1841, Santa Anna returned to the capital city. At once he appointed the members of a junta, who selected him as provisional president. From October 10, 1841, to December 6, 1844, he ruled as a dictator, either directly or through chosen substitutes. As the Congress convoked in accord with the Plan of Tacubaya attempted to frame a constitution which did not suit him, he arbitrarily dissolved it, and appointed a junta of notables which on June 12, 1843, promulgated a new Constitution for Mexico that was entitled the "Organic Basis" of the republic. This fundamental law provided for a centralistic government which has been styled a constitutional despotism. Soon afterward, Santa Anna, the will-o'-the-wisp of Mexican politics, was again made president: he governed directly or through a substitute until December, 1844. At that time he was deposed by revolutionists led by General Paredes who had issued a pronunciamiento denouncing the existing government as a régime which ensured the domination of the privileged classes.

After a brief interregnum, a junta of representatives of the departments elected Paredes president. Relations between Mexico and the United States, which had been disturbed for some time because of the claims of American citizens for damages **Dispute with the United States** or injuries suffered south of the Río Grande, became acute because of the annexation of Texas by the United States in accordance with a joint resolution of March 1, 1845. An attempt by the American government to adjust the differences concerning the disputed boundary between Texas and Mexico failed. Hence, those Mexicans who maintained that the incorporation of Texas into the United States was a just cause for war acquired predominance in the national councils. After President Polk ordered soldiers under General Taylor to occupy territory on the left bank of the Río Grande, which Mexico claimed did not of right belong to Texas, conflicts took place between those soldiers and Mexican forces. On May 11, 1846, Polk sent a message to Congress stating that American blood had been shed upon American soil and that war existed by the act of Mexico.

On May 13, 1846, the Congress of the United States declared the existence of a "state of war" with Mexico. In June, 1846, General Kearney was directed to lead an expedition into Upper California via Santa Fé. In August he occupied that city, and in September he started for California. Meanwhile, United States naval forces under Commodores Sloat and Stockton had taken possession of Monterey, San Francisco, and Los Angeles. American soldiers under General Wood and Colonel Doniphan invaded Chihuahua. The army of General

Taylor drove the Mexicans across the Rio Grande, defeated them at Monterey, and occupied the capitals of Coahuila and Tamaulipas. After Santa Anna had been decisively defeated by Taylor at Buena Vista, General Scott captured Vera Cruz. On April 8, 1847, his soldiers began their march from Vera Cruz to the city of Mexico. After they had won the battle of Cerro Gordo, they stormed the castle of Chapultepec, and on September 14, 1847, they occupied the capital city.

The war was ended by a treaty which was signed at Guadelupe Hidalgo on February 2, 1848. By this treaty the vanquished nation ceded to the United States the regions known as Upper California and New Mexico as well as the northern portions of the states of Sonora, Coahuila, and Tamaulipas. In return the United States not only undertook to satisfy certain claims of her citizens against Mexico but also agreed to pay that nation fifteen million dollars in gold. The United States thus gained a vast domain but aroused the apprehensions of Latin-American nations.

The victories of the invaders had precipitated changes in the Mexican government. After the Treaty of Guadelupe Hidalgo became known, President Herrera suppressed a revolt led by Paredes **Results of the War** and promoted some much needed reforms. A law was enacted which limited the size of the army. Steps were taken to build a navy. Despite the funds paid by the United States, Mexico was financially embarrassed. Attempts were consequently made to readjust her foreign debt and to consolidate her domestic debt. The government formed a project for the establishment of military colonies that should serve as a buffer along the northern frontier.

President Mariano Arista, who was inaugurated in 1851, did not have decided views upon political questions. In the main, he followed the policy of Herrera. Arista tried to rehabilitate Mexico's finances by reducing the salaries of officials. The discontent produced by his attempt at economy was increased by the fact that he pursued a vacillating course in politics. On the one hand, he provoked the opposition of the Conservatives who hoped that his downfall would be followed by the accession of Santa Anna; while, on the other hand, he aroused the apprehensions of Liberals who feared that he might become a dictator. In certain quarters revolts broke out, while various pronunciamientos were issued by aspiring reformers. A colonel of the national guard proclaimed himself in favor of the deposition of the President. On January 5, 1853, Arista relinquished the presidency.

After a brief interregnum, when the functions of chief magistrate were exercised by provisional presidents, in 1853 Santa Anna was elected president again. Upon returning from exile, he was greeted with enthusiasm. He selected a cabinet composed of prominent Conservatives, among whom was the historian, Lucas Alamán. Two new cabinet members were selected: a secretary of the interior and a secretary of public improvements. Santa Anna now arbitrarily suppressed the legislatures of the departments. He made appointments and removals largely with a view to strengthen his own authority and prestige. A strict law was enacted which was directed against conspiracies; secret police were established and espionage prevailed to an extraordinary extent. The press was deprived of all liberty. There were published in the capital city only those journals which acted as organs of the administration. In a vain attempt at retrenchment, the national government took control of all property that had belonged to the departments. When the secretary of finance proposed, however, that unused church property should be hypothecated to secure a government loan, the clergy raised such a vigorous protest that he relinquished his post. Yet new and onerous taxes were imposed upon laymen.

Santa Anna as a Conservative

Santa Anna considerably increased the army. He not only reëstablished the Imperial Order of Guadelupe but also conferred upon himself the title of Most Serene Highness. On December 16, 1853, he issued a decree which announced that he would continue to exercise dictatorial powers so long as he might deem necessary. Rumors were even circulated that the aged dictator intended to promote the establishment of a European monarchy in Mexico.

On March 1, 1854, Colonel Villareal proclaimed a daring plan at Ayutla. The Plan of Ayutla was a program for reform which embodied the views of those persons who objected to domination by privileged classes. It was composed of articles designed to furnish the basis for a provisional government. After he vainly attempted by force of arms to defeat the revolutionists, realizing that they were steadily gaining in strength, Santa Anna reluctantly decided to expatriate himself. In August, 1855, he sailed ingloriously from Vera Cruz on a vessel bound for Habana. After the reform plan was proclaimed in Mexico City, a junta of Liberals selected General Juan Alvarez as provisional president. As signs of dissension appeared in the ranks of the victorious Liberals, in accordance with a clause in the Plan of Ayutla Alvarez renounced his authority in favor of his secretary, General Ignacio Comonfort.

During Comonfort's presidency a number of significant measures were adopted. In November, 1855, a law was promulgated, which was called the Juárez Law after the secretary of justice, that abolished the privileges of the clerical and the military classes. In June, 1856, the President approved a bill which has ordinarily been designated the Lerdo Law after the secre-

Religious Reforms

tary of finance who framed it. Its object was to abolish the rights to properties held by the dead hand that were not actually used by the Church or by religious corporations. It defined corporations so as to include religious communities of both sexes. Its first article stipulated that all properties leased by tenants from religious corporations might be purchased by those tenants from the Church at a price which was to be determined by the rent. In reality this law was a reform designed to abolish ecclesiastical privileges.

The clergy denounced this law, especially at Puebla where a pronunciamiento was actually issued against the government. Upon being informed of a clerical conspiracy in the capital city, President Comonfort ordered that the monastery of Franciscans in that city should be suppressed, and that their property should be sequestrated, with the exception of their principal church. Those measures served greatly to embitter the opposition party. Priests fervently exhorted the people to take up arms against the Liberals who wished to wrest time-honored privileges from the Church.

Meanwhile a Constituent Congress had been framing another Constitution. On February 5, 1857, a new organic law was signed by the members of Congress. President Comonfort promptly swore to recognize and support it.

An entire section of the Mexican Constitution of 1857 dealt with the rights of man. A certain article stipulated that within the Mexican republic no person should be judged by special laws or by extraordinary tribunals, and that no individual or corporation should have special privileges or enjoy emoluments which were not in compensation for public services as stipulated by law. Another article declared that the Church and the State were independent of each other. Congress was not to enact laws "establishing or forbidding any religion." Marriage was declared to be a civil contract. No religious corporation or institution was to be allowed to acquire real estate beyond that destined for its services.

Constitution of 1857

The Constitution of 1857 vested the executive authority in a President, who should be chosen for four years by indirect election. Ecclesiastics were made ineligible to that office. The President was granted very extensive authority; he could select his own cabinet and make other important appointments. Legislative authority was vested in a Senate and a House of Deputies. Under certain conditions, Congress might form new states within the limits of existing states. Bills might be introduced into the national legislature by the President, by congressmen, or by state legislatures. Provision was made for a permanent deputation that should exercise special powers during the recess of Congress. Judicial power was vested in supreme, district, and circuit courts. The states were restored to the status which they had been granted in 1824. Those powers which were not expressly granted to the national government were reserved to the states. Each state was to adopt a republican and representative form of government for its internal régime. The federal government should protect the states against invasion or internal violence.

Many Liberals acclaimed this Constitution. On the other hand, clerical leaders denounced it: for it contained a generous bill of rights; it deprived them of cherished privileges, and also ex- **The Conserva-** cluded them from political office. No sooner was it pro- **tive Reaction** mulgated than Catholic bishops issued edicts which declared that any one who swore to obey it would be excommunicated. Though General Comonfort, who was elected president, was a brave man on the field of battle, he was timid and vacillating in politics. A conspiracy was soon formed to abrogate the Constitution; and at Tacubaya on December 17, 1857, General Félix Zuloaga published a plan directed against the new régime.

The Plan of Tacubaya proposed that the Constitution of 1857 should be annulled and that supreme authority should be vested in Comonfort, who should be empowered to convoke an extraordinary Congress which was to frame another constitution. Though Congress protested, after some hesitation, the President officially announced his acceptance of the plan. He then dissolved Congress and cast into prison some Liberal leaders. Among them was Benito Juárez, a judge of the supreme court, who had been a model governor of the state of Oajaca. Certain Mexican states protested against the arbitrary measures of Comonfort, while some adherents of the Plan of Tacubaya deserted him. After struggling against his enemies in the capital city for some time, and after liberating Juárez, in January, 1858, accompanied by a few faithful followers, Comonfort sailed from Vera Cruz for the United States. In his place the Conservatives had proclaimed Zuloaga president.

On January 11, 1858, the Liberals proclaimed as provisional president Benito Juárez, who established his government at Vera Cruz. The man who thus became a salient figure in a stirring drama was a full-blooded Zapotec Indian. The choice of **Rôle of** Juárez and Zuloaga as presidents by opposing parties was **Benito** followed by three years of internecine conflict. This **Juárez** struggle was between the Liberals, who supported the politico-religious laws which had been placed upon the statute books, and the Conservatives, who opposed those measures. During this strife diplomatic relations between Mexico and certain foreign nations were for a time severed. The Conservative leaders secured aid from the clergy. Upon the other side, the supporters of Juárez were inspirited by the news

that their government had been recognized by the United States. The
Liberals established their center of operations at Vera Cruz, while
the Conservatives held the capital city. The flames of civil war soon
spread over all of Mexico.

As a war measure, at Vera Cruz in July, 1859, Juárez promulgated
certain laws which aimed to carry the anti-clerical struggle of the Liberals to its logical climax. Those reform laws provided
that Church and State should be completely separated:
all ecclesiastical property, except churches and their con-
tents, should be confiscated to the nation; and all monastic orders and religious communities should be suppressed. Roman
Catholicism was to be protected just like any other religion. Thenceforth a civil ceremony was to be the only legal mode of matrimony
within the republic; civil authorities should register births, marriages,
and deaths. The control of cemeteries was transferred from the Church
to the State. These laws served as a program for the Liberals in the
so-called "War of the Reform."

The "War of the Reform"

On December 22, 1860, the army of the Conservatives was decisively
defeated at Calpulalpan. General Miramon and other Conservative
leaders hastily fled from the capital, and three days later a Liberal
general named González Ortega occupied that city. Three years of
bloody and fratricidal war had terminated in the defeat of the clerical
party.

In January, 1861, President Juárez began the difficult task of reconstruction. He soon ordered that the diplomatic representatives of
Spain, Guatemala, Ecuador, and the Holy See should be
expelled from Mexico because of aid which they had
furnished the Conservatives. He replaced the ministers
who represented Mexico at foreign courts by other diplomats, and
even directed that certain bishops of the Mexican Church should be
exiled. Despite armed opposition, he executed the reform laws throughout Mexico. In June, 1861, Congress announced that Juárez had been
elected president.

Reconstruc-
tion

As a result of the costly civil war, Mexico's finances were much embarrassed. On July 17, 1861, Congress therefore enacted a law providing that the government should suspend all payments of interest
for two years, even upon foreign claims which were guaranteed by
customs duties. That law caused the governments of England, France,
and Spain to enter into a treaty at London on October 31, 1861. The
Treaty of London provided that those nations might occupy portions
of the Mexican coast in order to enforce the payment of claims of their
citizens: it stipulated, however, that the autonomy and integrity of
Mexico should be respected. By January, 1862, Spanish, French, and

English soldiers had disembarked at Vera Cruz. Soon afterward President Juárez issued a proclamation announcing the intention of his government to pay all just claims and exhorting all Mexicans to unite in order to save the honor and independence of the republic. After the English and the Spanish detachments had left Mexican soil, the purpose of Napoleon III, who was aping his great namesake, was disclosed as a project to subvert the republic of Mexico. In the pursuit of his design he was encouraged by certain Mexicans in Europe who fondly hoped that a monarchy might be established upon the ruins of the republic.

In May, 1863, French soldiers occupied Puebla. On June 7 they entered the capital city. There, under the auspices of the French commander, General Forey, a junta was assembled which on July 10 made the following declarations: that the Mexican nation adopted as her form of government a hereditary monarchy with a Catholic prince as a ruler, that her sovereign should have the title of Emperor of Mexico, and that the Mexican imperial crown should be offered to Archduke Maximilian of Austria. When a commission of Mexicans offered this phantom crown to that prince in his beautiful home on the shores of the Adriatic, he foolishly accepted it. Meanwhile in certain parts of distracted Mexico, patriots were fighting French soldiers and their adherents. By successive steps the seat of the patriot government was transferred from San Luis Potosí to Chihuahua. At last it was located at El Paso del Norte—later known as Juárez. On July 12, 1864, Emperor Maximilian entered the City of Mexico.

French Intervention

The United States, which was being torn by the Civil War, declined to recognize Emperor Maximilian; for she viewed President Juárez as the true head of the Mexican government. Secretary of State Seward informed the French government of his dissatisfaction with the establishment in Mexico of an exotic monarchy. After the close of the Civil War, Seward made strong and insistent protests to Napoleon III against the operations of French troops in Mexico. Partly because of those protests, Napoleon III at last decided completely to withdraw his soldiers. Early in 1867 the last detachments of the French invaders sailed from Vera Cruz. But, relying upon assurances of aid given him by Napoleon III, the misguided Prince remained in Mexico. Captured by soldiers of the republic, he was court-martialed and shot at Querétaro on June 19, 1867. Empress Charlotte lost her reason. A tragedy ended what some Mexican historians have called their second war for independence.

President Juárez entered the capital city on July 15, 1867, amid the plaudits of his people. At once he took measures to reëstablish a national government. On August 14 he issued regulations which provided for the election of state and federal magistrates. When Congress assembled in December, 1867, it announced that Juárez had been elected president of the republic. On January 8, 1868, it issued a manifesto announcing that the government would not oppose the reëstablishment of diplomatic intercourse with nations which had recognized Emperor Maximilian, provided that their governments would base the new relations upon justice and reciprocal interest. On October 13, 1870, an amnesty law was passed that included all persons who had been guilty of conspiracy, sedition, or treason against the government. In December, 1870, President Juárez promulgated a civil code for the federal district and for the territory of Lower California which was to go into effect on March 1, 1871. In the campaign of that year Juárez, Lerdo de Tejada, and Porfirio Díaz were candidates for the presidency. As no candidate secured the required majority, Congress declared in October that Juárez was the constitutional president. On July 18, 1872, he suddenly fell ill and died. His body was interred in the cemetery of San Fernando in the capital city where the Mexicans often gather to do homage to their greatest national hero.

Lerdo de Tejada, who was chief justice of the supreme court, quietly assumed the position of provisional president. He was elected president shortly afterward. On December 1, 1872—retaining the cabinet of President Juárez—he began his constitutional term of four years. His administration was marked, on January 1, 1873, by the opening of the railroad between Vera Cruz and Mexico City. As there was still opposition to the politico-religious reforms of Juárez, on September 25, 1873, the legislature adopted constitutional amendments which were intended to reënforce those measures. Church and State were declared to be independent of each other: Congress was inhibited from passing laws that would establish or prohibit any religion. Marriage was declared to be a civil contract. Religious institutions were prohibited from acquiring real estate, except on certain conditions. The religious oath which had been required of witnesses was abolished. A declaration was made that the Mexican government might neither recognize monastic orders nor permit their establishment for whatever purpose.

Meanwhile opposition to the administration of President Lerdo de Tejada came to a head. The leader of that movement was Porfirio Díaz, who advocated electoral liberty and maintained that the President should not be eligible for reëlection. In December, 1875, he left Mexico and established a base of operations at Brownsville, Texas. About a month later in the state of Oaxaca one of his partisans pro-

Juárez as President

Religious Reforms

claimed the Plan of Tuxtepec which renounced the national magistrates. That plan was hailed with joy in other sections. The election of 1876 thus took place in the midst of civil dissensions. After Congress announced that Lerdo de Tejada had been reëlected, many Mexicans repudiated the election and joined Díaz who led an uprising in the state of Puebla. On November 16, 1876, the revolutionists encountered government forces at Tecoac and defeated them. Shortly afterward the capital city surrendered to the revolutionary army; and Diaz assumed the position of provisional president. On May 2, 1877, Congress announced that he had been elected president. It soon amended the Constitution to stipulate that four years should elapse before a President might be reëlected.

Porfirio Díaz had been baptized in the city of Oaxaca on September 15, 1830. From the maternal side, Indian blood ran in his veins. Upon his father's side he was descended from an Andalusian who had emigrated to Mexico in the sixteenth century. The narrative of Porfirio's early life reads like a romance—he became a man of daring, resource, and iron will. A lover of Mexican independence with a fondness for autocratic rule, he was a chieftain whose descent inspired confidence in the Indians, while his genuine ability won the respect and support of the upper classes.

On May 5, 1877, Díaz became president of Mexico for the first time. As advisers he at first selected his own partisans. Eventually, he also appointed followers of Juárez and Lerdo to office: thus he won the confidence of some of his political opponents. **First Presidency of Díaz** The President soon gave to Mexico what Ramón Castilla had given to Peru—a good peace. Clever bandits he induced to enroll as rural police who were employed to check the depredations of their former companions. He not only gave a stimulus to public education but also promoted the establishment of astronomical and meteorological observatories. He reduced the size of the army, abolished many sinecures, and thus improved the nation's finances. His secretary of the treasury undertook negotiations with foreign capitalists for the construction of railroads.

In September, 1880, in accordance with the action of Congress, President Díaz signed a contract with the Sonora Railroad Company, which was organized under the laws of Massachusetts, for the construction of a railroad from Guaymas in the state of Sonora to the northern frontier of Mexico to connect with a railway in the United States. As an aid to the construction of this railway, the Mexican government granted to the company the right of way through the republic and also promised to pay it three thousand five hundred pesos for each mile of railroad that it constructed. During the same month

Díaz made a similar contract for the building of a railway through central Mexico that should stretch from the capital city to El Paso del Norte. This contract had scarcely been signed when workmen began to lay the ties of the Mexican Central Railroad.

Significant steps were taken in international relations. Diplomatic intercourse with Spain, Germany, Italy, Switzerland, Portugal, Belgium, and even France was resumed. Relations were reëstablished with a majority of the Latin-American states. With the United States, which for a time did not recognize the Díaz government, there were difficulties caused by the raids of Mexican Indians who attacked towns north of the border. Yet the awards made to American citizens by a claims convention which was signed in 1876, were regularly paid by the Mexican government. Díaz protested against instructions given by the United States to a military commander to pursue marauding Indians across the borders into Mexico; but in July, 1882, a convention was signed by both countries for the reciprocal crossing of the frontier by soldiers in pursuit of savages.

Meanwhile his term had elapsed, and though some states proposed that he should again be a candidate for the presidency, he declined to run. But his candidate, General Manuel González, was elected president. President González appointed Díaz secretary of public works. The period from 1880 to 1884 was accordingly in some particulars a continuation of the previous administration. Early in 1883 the Sonora railroad was opened to traffic. By April, 1884, the main line of the Mexican Central Railroad was in operation from El Paso del Norte to the City of Mexico. The construction of bridges, wharves, custom-houses, and telegraphs was promoted. A national bank was founded in the capital city. Attempts which were made to reorganize the debt that Mexico owed to English bankers were not entirely successful, while the coinage of a large quantity of subsidiary nickel coins of low intrinsic value provoked much discontent. A commercial code and a civil code were promulgated. With respect to subsoil resources, the doctrine of the Ordinances of Aranjuez was discarded in the Mexican Mining Code of 1884 which provided that petroleum belonged to the owner of the surface soil.

In the same year Díaz was reëlected; he was inaugurated President for the second time on December 1, 1884. He was reëlected in 1888, 1892, 1896, 1900, 1904, and 1910. This was made possible

Reëlections of Díaz

by three successive changes in the Constitution. If we may trust the statements of Mexican Liberals, during this period there was no open political opposition to Díaz,—presidential elections were a farce.

During more than twenty-five years he engrossed the power of the

State. More truthfully, perhaps, than Dictator Rosas of Argentina might he have said *l'état c'est moi*. This remarkable man was a dictator who, at times, in spite of his errors and faults, might have been characterized as benevolent. It is to be presumed, however, that the intelligent Mexican would have said—had he felt free to speak frankly— that Díaz ruled by the clever use of an iron hand. To him the national Congress was like clay.

Under Díaz the Mexican government began to play a part in international politics. When President Barrios of Guatemala tried to reestablish the Central American Union, Díaz expressed his disapproval of that policy. The death of Barrios, which occurred soon afterward, extricated Mexico from **Character of His Rule** a delicate international situation. As indicated in the preceding chapter, when hostilities broke out in 1907 between Honduras and Nicaragua, Mexico coöperated with the United States in good offices to terminate that struggle. When war between Nicaragua and Salvador appeared imminent, Díaz joined hands with Roosevelt to propose that a peace conference of the nations of Central America should be held at Washington.

A difficult problem was the reduction and reorganization of Mexico's increasing debt. In June, 1885, laws were enacted that aimed to improve the fiscal situation. One law authorized the issue of bonds amounting to twenty-five million pesos which bore interest at 6 per cent. Another law provided for the funding of the national debt which should include not only the floating debt incurred since 1882 but also various foreign claims that had been urged against the republic. In accordance with a law of December 13, 1887, a loan of £10,500,000 sterling was contracted in the following year with a German banking firm. This loan seems to have been partly used to satisfy the holders of the English debt against Mexico. Subsequently additional loans were made by the Díaz government for other purposes: to pay subsidies to railway contractors, to liquidate the finances of the national bank, and to raise money for the construction of a railroad across the Isthmus of Tehuantepec. In 1899, under Secretary of the Treasury José Limantour, who was one of the most capable Mexican statesmen of the Díaz era, the debt was again funded. Critics of Díaz, however, claimed that those readjustments caused millions of pesos to flow into the pockets of the ruling autocracy and its supporters.

Various public improvements went on apace. A harbor was built at Tampico. Existing railroads were extended, and new lines were built. By contracts with English financiers President Díaz secured the construction of a railroad across the Isthmus of Tehuantepec from Coatzacoalcos to Salina Cruz. In 1904 he purchased for the government the railway which was being built between Córdoba and the Tehuantepec railway. Five years later he secured control of the most important railway lines in the country at the cost of about two hundred million dollars. Díaz thus greatly increased the national debt. Yet in 1936 there was a surplus in the treasury.

An important work of his régime was the construction of a canal to prevent the inundation of the valley in which the capital city was located. In viceregal days the Spaniards had compelled Indians to dig a canal called Nochistengo to drain the valley, but that ditch did not prevent floods. Díaz soon took steps to complete and perfect the drainage canal: in 1886 definite plans were adopted; and on May 17, 1900, the big ditch was formally inaugurated. This work, which cost some twenty-five million pesos, was composed of a canal about twenty-two miles long emptying into a tunnel of five miles in length that conveyed the water to the valley of Tequixquiac. The valley of Mexico was thus drained of surplus water and the sanitary condition of the capital city was much improved.

A vital problem which Díaz did not solve successfully concerned the ownership of land. When he came to power countless acres in

System of Land Holding

Mexico were held by descendants of prominent families that had succeeded the conquistadors. Those proprietors cultivated their large estates by a servile peasantry composed of aborigines. Lands held by Indian pueblos or tribes in common ownership were called *egidos*. Here and there strips of land were held in private ownership by Indians or by mestizos. Frequently the Indian who lived upon a small strip of land had not taken the legal steps necessary to secure the title, although he was the rightful owner. Thus when a new land law was enacted in 1886 that gave to any person the right to preëmpt a strip of land as unoccupied and to acquire possession of it upon making a payment to the State, many small landowners lost their holdings. Further, some of the tribal lands were carved up and distributed. Many portions of land ultimately passed into the possession of large landowners, while other strips became the property of foreigners.

With the decrease in number of the small landed proprietors and with the disappearance of the communal lands belonging to the lower classes, the condition of the Mexican peon became almost intolerable. He was often induced or compelled to borrow money; he was bound to service for the payment of his debts; frequently, except in name, he became a serf. Indians were captured by force in the state of Sonora, transported to the plantations of Yucatan, and, with the connivance of federal officials, sold into bondage. Obviously the plight of the lower classes held the bitter seeds of a class revolution.

Another feature of the Díaz régime which much disturbed some of his fellow citizens was a steady increase in the interest of the Americans in their country. Not only were United States citizens largely instrumental in the construction of important railroads, but they became financially interested in Mexican lands, mines, and factories. Partly because of their enterprise, in various sections of Mexico steel plows took the place of crooked sticks, modern methods were used in the extraction and reduction of ores, and cotton mills and machine shops were erected. Arid lands were irrigated. Electricity was introduced into important cities. Farmers from the United States purchased lands south of the Río Grande; and at times the rights of native Mexicans to the soil were none too scrupulously regarded. Under the legislation of **Interest of United States Citizens in Mexico** 1884, American capitalists purchased titles to valuable lands with subsoils containing minerals and petroleum. A careful observer estimated in 1904 that the United States capital invested in the lands and mines of Mexico aggregated more than four hundred million dollars. As early as the beginning of the present century, there were students of Mexican politics who inquired: "What would be the policy of the United States if a revolution should break out in Mexico?"

At that time political parties, as understood in the United States, scarcely existed south of the Río Grande. The political fortunes of Mexico were in the hands of Porfirio Díaz and his cabinet. As the dictator grew older, he lost his grip on public affairs. In consequence the destinies of his country passed more and more into the hands of a group of his political advisers who were known as the Científicos. Those politicians looked upon Vice-President Corral as their leader. A group of Mexicans who considered General Reyes—at one time governor of Nueva León—as a rising publicist were designated Reyistas. There is reason to belive that occasionally the uncrowned King of Mexico seriously thought of choosing a successor, but evidently finding that task extremely difficult, he clung to his post until the storm burst.

His dictatorial rule was brought to an end through a propaganda promoted by Francisco I. Madero, a scion of an influential family in northern Mexico who had received part of his education in the United States. In December, 1908, Madero published a booklet entitled "The Presidential Succession in 1910" which was dedicated to the heroes of Mexico, to the **The Apostle of a New Freedom** Mexican press, and to all good Mexicans. In that volume he made an analysis of conditions in his country: he described the good and the evil of the Díaz régime; he criticized its muzzled press, its autocratic tendencies, and its policy of truckling to the United States.

In particular he criticized the restrictions and limitations upon elections. He insisted that in the approaching presidential election the people of Mexico should be allowed freely to express their desire whether or not General Díaz should be reëlected. Bitterly did he criticize the nomination of the Vice-President as a candidate for reelection; he intimated that Corral had the qualifications which Díaz required his successor to possess. Two clauses from this glowing polemic became a slogan for the opponents of Díaz: liberty of suffrage, and no reëlection of the president. "We do not say," reasoned this apostle of social and political reform, "that General Díaz should not continue for another term, if such is the will of the people, but we do insist that the people should be allowed to express their will without any coercion."

The anti-reëlection party nominated Madero for the presidency. A few days before the presidential election, however, he was arrested and taken to San Luís Potosí. Eluding the vigilance of federal officials, he escaped to San Antonio, Texas, where he issued a manifesto stating that the elections of June, 1910, were illegal. He also published a plan which was dated at San Luís Potosí, October 5, 1910. In this plan he declared that the lands which had been unlawfully seized should be restored to their rightful owners; that the principle that important magistrates should not be reëlected was a part of the republic's supreme law, pending the amendment of the Constitution; and that he assumed the position of provisional president of Mexico with the power to make war upon the illegal government of Díaz. He named November 20, 1910, as the date for a general uprising against the usurper. During the anti-Díaz agitation certain agrarian and social reforms were championed by Madero's followers, especially an increase of wages for the laborers and the division of landed estates among the proletariat.

At the beginning of the revolt, Madero's supporters were most numerous in northern Mexico, especially in the states of Durango and Chihuahua. During the early months of 1911, the revolu-

Triumph of Madero tionists gained strength with surprising rapidity. The much-vaunted army of Díaz seemed to vanish into skeleton regiments. In April, 1911, the octogenarian dictator so far yielded to the storm as to read a message to Congress in which he proposed that the President of Mexico should not be reëlected, that the administration of the government should be reformed, and that large landed estates should be divided. He even made changes in his cabinet. Still, the reformer insisted that there could be no peace in Mexico until the dictator retired. On May 21, 1911, an agreement was signed at Juárez by an agent of Díaz and representatives of the revolution, which provided that both Díaz and Corral should retire. For the time being, Francisco de la Barra, secretary of foreign relations, was recognized as the chief executive who should make the arrangements necessary for general elections.

During the interregnum a group of reformers organized the Constitutional Progressive party which nominated Madero for the presidency. That party won the special presidential election in October, 1911. Madero was inaugurated as president of Mexico in the following month, while Pino Suárez became vice-president. Meantime Congress amended the Constitution to prohibit the reëlection of either President or Vice-President.

Yet, the zealous idealist who had spread the gospel of reform throughout Mexico did not succeed as chief magistrate. As he gave certain disciples of Díaz seats in his cabinet, Madero was suspected of being an apostate. When he tried in other ways to conciliate partisans of the fallen dictator, he lost the support of extreme reformers. He was denounced because he did not properly carry out cherished plans for a distribution of land at nominal prices among the poor, landless class. His enemies accused him of not having brought evil-doers of the former régime to justice. In an open letter to the secretary of the interior, a prominent Mexican educator penned the following indignant criticism:

You have shown that you lack the holy wrath of the Redeemed. You have demonstrated that you cannot dispense the bolt-like justice which strikes terror to the evil-doer, nor yet the consuming fire of Jehovah which cuts down and purifies. . . . Mr. Minister, the oppressed and the expropriated, who thought they had come into their own again, do not care to listen to all this talk of legal formalities, because they know that it was behind the shield of those very laws that Don Porfirio committed his various atrocities.

After Díaz came the deluge. General Reyes tried to start an insurrection in the state of Nueva León but was captured and imprisoned in Mexico City. Victorious rebels under the leadership of General Orozco captured Chihuahua, only to be defeated by federal soldiers. A nephew of the exiled dictator, Félix Díaz by name, taking as his battlecry the motto, "Peace and Justice," then assumed the revolutionary leadership and seized Vera Cruz. After being captured by a federal general, because of the supposed insecurity of the fortress of San Juan de Ulúa, Díaz was incarcerated in a penitentiary in the capital city. The crisis came early on the morning of February 9, 1913, when Anti-Maderistas freed General Reyes and the younger Díaz whom they had selected as their leaders. Ten bloody days followed: the capital city was bombarded by revolutionists; thousands of innocent people were slaughtered in the streets; and Reyes, whom some Mexicans viewed as a possible savior, was killed.

Toward this bombardment the federal commander, a general of Aztec descent named Victoriano Huerta, took a dubious attitude. On February 18, after the imprisonment and enforced resignation of both President and Vice-President, Huerta assumed the authority of chief magistrate. The chief of the republic's soldiers now stood forth as a reactionary. On the night of February 23, while Madero and Pino Suárez were being transferred from the "national palace" to the penitentiary, their escort was attacked, during the ensuing scuffle shots were exchanged, and, when the smoke cleared away, the two prisoners of state were found dead.

An act of treachery thus ushered into the presidency a strong, cunning personality who flattered himself that he was "a man of iron." A political disciple and a former military commander of the great dictator, it was not strange that in many particulars Huerta followed his master's example. American newspapers printed a cablegram from the new dictator to the exiled Díaz which declared that "the revolution against you has been avenged."

The "Man of Iron"

The means by which Huerta had acceded to power at once provoked opposition in northern Mexico. On March 26, 1913, at the hacienda of Guadalupe certain Mexicans framed a project which declared that Huerta had committed treason to secure the presidency. The Plan of Guadalupe repudiated his government, declared that Venustiano Carranza, governor of Coahuila, was "First Chief" of the "Constitutional" army, and that he would become the provisional president of the republic when his army took possession of the capital city. A stubborn country gentleman was thus proclaimed the leader of a movement that aimed to overthrow Huerta. A more picturesque figure in that revolution was Pancho Villa, a cattle rustler, outlaw, bandit, and revolutionist who became a rival of Carranza.

Opponents of Huerta were encouraged by the policy adopted by the United States. President Wilson refused to recognize him, because he was suspected of having connived at Madero's murder. The dictator disdainfully refused to enter into an arrangement proposed by John Lind, a special agent of the United States, which included a pledge to the effect that he would not become a candidate in the approaching presidential election. During the series of sanguinary struggles that occurred between Huerta's soldiers and the Constitutionalists, the properties and the lives of many foreigners were ruthlessly sacrificed.

At this delicate juncture an affront by Mexicans to United States soldiers at Tampico caused Admiral Mayo to demand an apology from the dictator in the form of a salute to the Stars and Stripes. As Huerta refused to accede to this demand, **A B C Mediation** marines from the United States took possession of Vera Cruz, and the American Congress adopted a joint resolution which disclaimed any intention to make war upon the Mexican republic. The occupation of that port provoked intense excitement in certain capitals of South America; while the A B C powers, Argentina, Brazil, and Chile, undertook to mediate between the United States and Mexico. Accordingly, in May, 1914, there assembled in Canada representatives of Huerta, agents of the United States, and the ministers of the mediatory powers to Washington. The Constitutionalists were asked to send delegates to the conference; but, as Carranza would not agree to an armistice and to a discussion of internal conditions in Mexico, the mediators withdrew the invitation. In June, 1914, a protocol was signed which arranged for the establishment of a provisional government in Mexico that was to be recognized by the mediating nations and by the United States.

Shortly afterward Huerta resigned. He was succeeded by Provisional President Carvajal. Negotiations for a settlement of the difficulties between Carvajal and Carranza were futile, and on the night of August 12, 1914, the Provisional President and his followers evacuated Mexico City. On August 15, soldiers of the constitutionalist army entered the capital. Five days later General Carranza assumed the executive power. Dissensions between him and Villa soon broke out which resulted in a civil war between the two factions. Carranza, Villa, and Zapata occupied the capital city in rapid succession. In September, 1915, the United States and the A B C Powers, with Bolivia, Guatemala, and Uruguay, agreed to recognize that Mexican faction which should display the most success in the maintenance of order. The result was the recognition of Carranza as *de facto* president of Mexico on October 19, 1915, by nine American nations.

After a gang of Mexican bandits under Villa had crossed the border and attacked a town in New Mexico, in 1916 the United States government dispatched a detachment of soldiers under General Pershing to pursue the marauders. When a second punitive expedition from the United States had crossed the frontiers in pursuit of outlaws, Carranza's government strenuously objected. As Villa, by the aid of sympathizers, succeeded in eluding Pershing's soldiers, the attempts of the United States to preserve tranquillity upon her southern border merely served to stimulate in Mexico the spirit of opposition to foreigners.

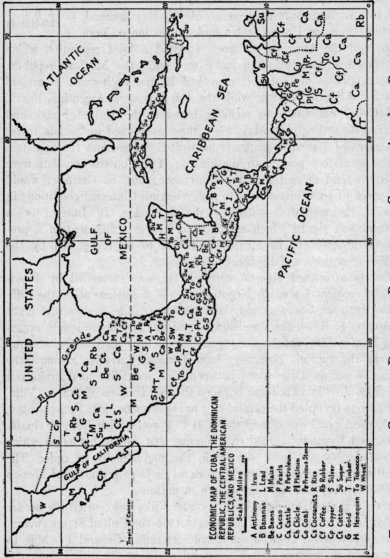

ECONOMIC MAP OF CUBA, THE DOMINICAN
REPUBLIC, THE CENTRAL AMERICAN
REPUBLICS, AND MEXICO

Scale of Miles

A Antimony	I Iron
B Bananas	L Lead
Be Beans	M Maize
C Cacao	P Pearls
Ca Cattle	Pe Petroleum
Ch Chicle	Pl Platinum
Co Coal	Pr Precious Stones
Cs Coccanuts	R Rice
Cf Coffee	Rb Rubber
Cp Copper	S Silver
Ct Cotton	Su Sugar
G Gold	To Tobacco
H Henequen	T Timber
	W Wheat

Economic Map of Cuba, the Dominican Republic, the Central American Republics,
and Mexico

Revolutionary outbreaks had seriously disturbed Mexico's educational system. A law of 1896 had provided for free, elementary instruction for children between six and twelve years of age. National schools had been supplemented by academies established by Protestant missionaries. Imposing educational structures had been erected at public expense. Various institutions of higher education were supported by missionaries or by the national government. The very name of university, however, was absent from the annals of public instruction from 1865, when Maximilian definitely closed the venerable University of Mexico, until 1910. Despite attempts to improve educational facilities, it is clear that the instruction of the lower classes was neglected. During the civil wars, from 1910 to 1917, private and public schools in some sections of the republic were closed. **Conditions about 1914**

In time of peace the chief occupations in Mexico were agriculture, cattle raising, and mining. Among the main crops were corn, sugar, cacao, tobacco, coffee, henequen, and cotton. Valuable woods were obtained from Mexican forests, such as cedar and mahogany. In certain parts of Mexico large numbers of cattle and sheep grazed upon the fertile lowlands or roamed over the grassy uplands. Mexico had valuable deposits of silver, gold, copper, and lead; but many of her mines were at times closed because of civil wars. The production of coal in Mexico had not been enough to supply home consumption. Mexican manufacturing establishments were mainly cotton and woolen factories, ore reduction plants, paper mills, saw mills, breweries, and sugar mills. During revolutionary disturbances, incited by the desire to secure booty, many peons took part in guerrilla warfare. **Economic Conditions**

During the administrations of Huerta and Carranza conditions in Mexico were very unstable. Statistics of industry and commerce during this epoch are often incomplete. An inkling of the industrial activities of the country may, however, be obtained from the figures of Mexico's exports for 1918. In 1918 the exports were as follows in United States currency: vegetable products, $64,468,662; mineral products, $106,-966,171; and petroleum, $70,250,000. Among the vegetable products exported in that year henequen from Yucatan amounted to $12,000,000.

By a law of 1905 the gold peso was made the monetary unit of Mexico. Ordinarily that coin was worth, in United States currency, about fifty cents. In 1910 the total foreign debt of Mexico amounted to $295,000,000. In May, 1913, a 6 per cent loan aggregating $80,-000,000 was authorized by President Huerta. Even before the first World War began, the interest payments upon almost all of the foreign debt of Mexico were in default.

Poetry and prose in Mexico ran the entire gamut of her history. José J. Pesado in *Las Aztecas* presented in Spanish dress the poems of an Aztec chieftain. Perhaps the most learned of Mexican historians who have written about the Spanish régime was Joaquín García Icazbalceta. José de Jesús Díaz dealt with such dramatic episodes in the separation of Mexico from Spain as *The Shooting of Morelos*. That revolution also furnished the background for Juan Díaz Covarrubia's historical novel concerning the insurgent, Gil Gómez. In his *Historical Survey of the Revolution* Carlos Bustamante made himself a useful chronicler of that epoch. Roa Bárcena described his country's war with the United States in his *Recollections of the American Invasion*. Besides contributing a volume to a notable coöperative history of Mexico, Vicente Riva Palacio wrote a novel that was concerned with French intervention. A versatile professor named Alfredo Chavero produced learned treatises concerning aboriginal antiquities and also stirring dramas about the Aztecs. Gutiérrez Nájera composed musical verses after the French model; he also founded a literary journal named the *Blue Review*. The statesman Lucas Alamán wrote a notable history of Mexico in five volumes, parts of which are, however, colored by bias. A younger publicist was Federico Gamboa, a "dissector of souls" who not only penned realistic novels but also caustic rejoinders to Wilson's demands for Huerta's resignation.

In the days of Juárez an academy of painting and sculpture was replaced by a National School of Fine Arts. Before the downfall of Díaz there were in that school some religious paintings by Mexican artists, as well as a few paintings by European masters. In the hall of the ambassadors of the national palace were portraits of distinguished Mexican leaders from Hidalgo to Díaz. In the boulevards and plazas of the capital city there were statues to such national heroes as Guerrero and Morelos. Towering among those monuments was a bronze statue of Cuauhtemoc, the last of the Aztec monarchs, by Miguel Noreña. Upon the sides of its base were bronze representations of dramatic scenes from that chieftain's life by Gabriel Guerra, such as, the arrival of the Spanish conquistadors in Mexico, and the torture of Cuauhtemoc by Cortés. Carved by the Islas brothers, in the cemetery of San Fernando was a beautiful monument in white marble at the tomb of Benito Juárez.

In the wake of the Madero Revolution there came to Mexico a renaissance of aboriginal art. Back to the themes, the motifs, and the color of pre-Columbian art became the cry of the Mexican artist. A leader in this movement was Adolfo Best Maugard, who discovered the fundamental motifs in Aztec art, and who, as director of drawing for the Mexican government, developed this knowledge into a technique of art instruction which was being used to train the children of Mexico. Among modern Mexican artists who drew their inspiration largely from Aztec arts and crafts was Saturnino Herrán, who colorfully depicted "Our Gods" and "A Mexican Dance." The leading exponent of this unique school was Diego Rivera, a talented painter of mixed blood. A most prolific artist, in decorating the walls of the Ministry of Public Education with frescoes, Rivera painted a panorama of the renaissant Mexico that has been arising from the ruins of the Díaz régime: peasants, weavers, miners, markets, festivals, folk dances, urban aristocrats, martyrs of the revolution, and the distribution of land.

Much of the unrest in Mexico was due to social conditions. Immigration from European countries other than Spain affected Mexico little before the first World War. Spanish immigrants remained a notable element in the population. They **Social Conditions** often engaged in mercantile pursuits in towns or cities. Of some 15,000,000 inhabitants, persons of European ancestry constituted perhaps 10 per cent. In the hot, humid regions along the coast were some persons with Negro blood in their veins—numerically perhaps an almost negligible factor. The aboriginal element was composed of scattered tribes using different dialects or languages. Those Indians, in large part still barbarous, constituted probably from 15 to 25 per cent of the population. While from 65 to 75 per cent of the people belonged to the mestizo class.

Unfortunately those widely dissimilar elements had not been amalgamated into a homogeneous nation. In an interpretative spirit a Mexican journalist aptly pointed out that the crucial political problem of his country was to establish a form of government that would suit the different ethnic types: the pure-blooded aborigines who possessed a fifteenth-century civilization; the mixed classes who had, for the most part, an eighteenth-century culture; the educated, mixed class who were fitted for a nineteenth-century government; and the aristocratic Mexicans of Caucasian race, who with the immigrants desired twentieth-century political institutions.

On January 31, 1917, a convention at Querétaro adopted a new Constitution. In respect to the framework of government many of the provisions in the organic law of 1917 were essentially the same as in 1857. Some significant changes were made **The Constitution of 1917** with regard to the President. His term of office was set at five years; it was stipulated that he could not be reëlected. It was provided that he must be the son of native-born Mexicans; that he could not be a minister of any religion; that, if he were a military man, he must have retired from active service at least ninety days before the election; and that he must not have taken part, directly or indirectly, in any military uprising or coup d'état. Among the personal guaranties was an article which stipulated that no Mexican should be compelled to render personal service without due compensation and without his full consent, with the exception of labor imposed as a punishment by a judicial sentence.

A politico-religious clause declared that every one should be free to worship as he chose. Another clause stipulated that the titles to all real property held by religious institutions should be vested in the nation. Only a Mexican by birth might be "a minister of any religious faith in Mexico." Instruction in primary schools or in public institutions should be secular. No cleric or religious corporation could establish or direct elementary schools.

This Constitution contained certain articles which had their origin partly in a spirit of reaction against exploitation by foreigners. Article CXXIII declared that workmen engaged in an industrial or commercial enterprise should have the right to share in the profits of the respective business through commissions appointed by local authorities. Strikes might be considered as lawless only when a majority of the workmen engaged in them should resort to acts of violence. Article XXXIII conferred upon the President the right to expel from Mexico, without "judicial process," any foreigner whose presence he might deem inexpedient.

Article XXVII provided that churches should not have the right to acquire, hold, or administer real property within the republic. It stated that the ownership of the land and the waters within the republic was originally vested in the Mexican people. It not only declared that the nation might impose limitations upon private property but also that the necessary measures should be taken to divide large landed estates and to protect small holdings. Further, it stipulated that only Mexicans or Mexican companies had the right to acquire concessions to develop mineral fuels in the republic. A foreigner might secure that right only if he renounced the privilege of recourse to his government for redress through diplomatic channels. Reënunciating a doctrine that was held in Mexico prior to 1884, it affirmed that the title to minerals and other subsoil deposits was vested in the people of Mexico.

The provisions about the ownership of subsoil deposits provoked a discussion concerning the rights of foreign capitalists who had secured control of oil lands. Carranza's contention appeared to be that the laws and decrees dating from the Díaz régime which permitted foreigners purchasing lands in Mexico to acquire titles to underlying petroleum and minerals were unconstitutional. Foreign corporations, which had gained control of valuable oil lands, viewed Article XXVII as the herald of a policy of confiscation.

On February 10, 1918, by virtue of power vested in the treasury department by the Mexican Congress—so ran the announcement—Carranza, who had been elected president, issued a decree imposing a graduated tax upon contracts for the exploitation of lands which had been made before May 1, 1917. Sixty per cent of the revenues accruing from this tax should belong to the federal government, while the remainder should be divided between the state governments and the municipalities. Any persons or corporations acquiring petroleum contracts by transfer or otherwise, as well as owners of oil lands wishing to exploit them upon their own account, were required to report to the government any sale, lease, or concession. All oil concessions that had not been certified by the department of the treasury within three months should be declared vacant. This comprehensive decree evidently aimed to bring the productive oil industry of Mexico under the control of the federal government.

The implication of national ownership of oil deposits which that law conveyed, as well as the heavy taxes imposed, provoked the oil producers. Citizens of England and the United States appealed to their respective governments for protection. **Controversy over Oil** The United States informed Mexico that she would not tolerate measures aiming at the confiscation of property rights which her citizens had acquired south of the Río Grande. Carranza's decision not to allow foreign corporations to drill fresh oil wells without the payment of a license fee aggravated the difficulty. Further, a tax of some twenty pesos per barrel was levied upon all oil exported from Mexico. Eventually a temporary solution was reached by the President, who decided to permit foreign corporations to develop their petroleum concessions without prejudice to Mexico's contention about the title to the subsoil, provided that they paid the taxes and duties imposed by his government.

Other complications arose. Though customs receipts increased, the government failed to administer the finances properly. Foreigners claimed enormous indemnities for damages suffered during the bitter and protracted civil wars. International relations were further complicated by the failure of President Carranza to pay interest on the foreign debt.

A most serious complication was caused by the peculiar policy which the President pursued in regard to the first World War. Although Mexican officials stated that they were neutral in the struggle, yet their government actually proposed to other American republics a policy which was not in harmony with the attitude of a neutral, namely, that

American states should prohibit the export of munitions to the belligerent nations of Europe. Just before the United States entered

Mexico's Policy toward the First World War　the war, German agents intrigued with Carranza against that government. They even proposed that Mexico should form an alliance with Japan and undertake to attack those portions of the United States which she had formerly possessed. Certain Mexicans plainly desired that the Central Empires should triumph in the war. A hope was apparently entertained that Germany might thus be enabled to play a rôle in the Three Americas which would check the increasing power of the United States.

Fatal in its consequences, however, was Carranza's attempt to control the succession to the presidency. Anxious to perpetuate his régime, he promoted the candidacy of Ignacio Bonillas, who had served as ambassador to the United States. Other candidates for the presidency were the popular soldier, General González, and Alvaro Obregón, a dashing, one-armed military leader. The President's attitude toward Bonillas furnished the occasion for a revolt which began in the state of Sonora.

The program of the Anti-Carranzistas was formulated at Agua Prieta on April 23, 1920. In the Plan of Agua Prieta the policies of President Carranza were denounced and his administration was repudiated. The plan provided that until the states joining the revolt should indicate their desires, the governor of Sonora, Adolfo de la Huerta, was to act as the civil and military chief of the insurrection. It also contained a provision which stipulated that freedom of suffrage should be observed and which declared that the President of Mexico should not be reëlected. With regard to foreign interests in Mexico, the plan announced that the leaders of the new cause would protect the legal rights of all foreigners.

The disaffection spread with surprising rapidity in western Mexico. González went over to the insurrectionary camp. Obregón escaped from

Downfall of Carranza　the capital city and placed himself at the head of the revolution. On May 5 Carranza issued a manifesto to declare that he would fight to the end. He expressed the opinion that no citizen of Mexico ought to become president by the use of the army, by insubordination, or by treason. Scarcely had this manifesto been published when, accompanied by his cabinet, other officials, soldiers, and treasure, the President left Mexico City with the intention of transferring the government to Vera Cruz. His convoy was fiercely attacked by insurgents, however, and he was forced to abandon his railway coach. While the fugitive magistrate was sleeping in a rude hut in the mountains, he was assassinated by one of his former followers. Obregón's partisans promptly denounced and disavowed the treacherous deed.

Meanwhile the soldiers of Obregón had entered Mexico City. On May 25, 1920, Adolfo de la Huerta became acting president. A light vote was cast in the election which resulted in the choice of General Obregón, the candidate of the Liberal Constitutional party, as president.

Obregón selected for his cabinet able and ambitious men from different cliques of the Constitutionalists. His task was Augean. His administration's interest in popular education was soon manifested by the reëstablishment of a national department **The Policies of Obregón** of public instruction, which was placed under the inspiriting direction of José Vasconcelos, a well-known educator who had been rector of the University of Mexico. Despite the reluctance of the United States to recognize the *de facto* government, in June, 1922, Secretary of the Treasury Adolfo de la Huerta reached an agreement with a group of international bankers for an adjustment of Mexico's enormous foreign debt and for the payment of part of the current interest. According to the terms of a presidential decree of August, 1923, a large number of poor, landless Mexicans secured plots of land from the national government which were to be used for farming or stock raising.

On May 27, 1921, the chargé d'affaires of the United States in the Mexican capital presented to the government a communication from Secretary Hughes. This note invited Mexico to sign a convention of amity and commerce with the United States. Besides an agreement for the settlement of a boundary dispute, the proposed treaty contained provisions for the creation of a commission for the adjudication of claims of United States citizens for injuries to person and property in Mexico. Most important were the stipulations by which the Mexican government bound itself not to interpret retroactively Article XXVII of the Constitution. The signing of this treaty by the United States would have constituted the formal recognition of the Obregón régime in Mexico.

Yet Obregón declined to favor the proposal. He explained that Article XV of the Constitution provided that no treaty should be negotiated by the government which would abridge the constitutional rights of individuals. His idea evidently was that as an autonomous state Mexico should not be required to meet certain conditions before being recognized as a member of the family of nations.

By declining to recognize President Obregón, because of a desire to protect the rights of United States citizens which had so often been flagrantly violated south of the Río Grande, Secretary Hughes brought about an *impasse*. In April, 1923, a solution of the vexatious problem of recognition was made possible through an agreement between

Mexico and the United States that two commissioners

Impasse with the United States Broken

from each government should meet in the Mexican capital to discuss the steps necessary to promote a mutual understanding. As a result of meetings held by these commissioners an adjustment of the controversy was reached. They agreed that Article XXVII of the Mexican Constitution should not be made to apply to titles to petroleum lands acquired prior to the adoption of that fundamental law. They recommended that their governments should agree to the negotiation of two claim conventions: the first convention was to adjust the claims of citizens of the United States for damages suffered during the revolutionary disturbances in Mexico, and the second was to adjust other claims of United States citizens against Mexico and any claims of Mexicans against the United States. On August 31 both governments announced that, in view of these recommendations, they had decided to renew diplomatic relations. At noon on September 3, 1923, the United States government received an agent of Mexico as chargé d'affaires, and simultaneously the Obregón government received the letters of credence of the American chargé in the City of Mexico.

On September 9, 1923, General Plutarco Calles resigned his post as secretary of the treasury in order that he might become a candidate for the presidential nomination by Obregón's followers who were now often styled the Coöperative party. In November a convention, which was mainly composed of delegates of labor groups, nominated Adolfo de la Huerta as its presidential candidate. Another faction had meanwhile nominated General Calles, who was favored by the President. Opposition to Obregón came to a head at Vera Cruz on December 5, 1923, where a group of military officers framed a politico-military program. After hostilities had broken out in several states between rebel forces and national soldiers, the chief of the rebellion proclaimed that President Obregón and his supporters should be disavowed. Early in 1924 the United States government sold much-needed arms and ammunition to the Obregón government. Further, it announced that a ban would be placed on all exports of war supplies to the insurgent faction. General Calles was elected president and inaugurated in December, 1924.

Both Calles and Obregón represented in Mexican politics the chastened spirit of the reform movement. They became what may not inappropriately be designated nationalist dictators. Among other measures President Calles carried on for some time Obregón's policy of dividing the large landed estates into small holdings. Occasionally these plots for landless Mexicans were carved out of haciendas held by Americans. It has been estimated that during the rule of Obregón and Calles perhaps 20,000,000 acres of land were thus distributed among the peons.

In December, 1925, Congress passed a new land law. This law stipulated that no alien could own lands within a certain distance of the Mexican borders or seacoast. It provided that the government was to take over the ownership of all subsoil properties in other parts of the country and to lease them to operators. Persons who had concessions granted before May 1, 1917, were to have their holdings confirmed by the government, if they contained oil. In response to protests by the United States, in March, 1926, Secretary Sáenz of Mexico assured that government that this land law would not be applied retroactively. Under its provisions, Americans holding oil lands in Mexico took steps to have their titles confirmed. In March, 1928, after Dwight W. Morrow became United States Ambassador to Mexico, a confirmatory regulation concerning oil was signed by President Calles to the effect that the titles to oil lands which had been secured by Americans before the date when the new Mexican Constitution went into effect were to "stand in perpetuity."

Calles Carries on Obregón's Policies

An issue that was even more delicate was provoked by the decision of Calles to carry out the politico-religious clauses of the Constitution. On February 11, 1926, the Mexican government announced not only that all church property not already in the possession of the nation had been nationalized but also that orders had been issued for the arrest and deportation of all foreign priests. On the following day an order was issued that all schools, seminaries, and religious houses where religious instruction was given should be closed. The result was that a large number of foreign-born priests were deported from Mexico. Ecclesiastical institutions that had been giving religious instruction were allowed to reopen only on condition that such instruction should be omitted. In an interpretative decree issued by President Calles on July 3, 1926, he added that no political meetings should be held in any church, that priests inciting the people against the law should be punished, and that members of the clergy were forbidden to express political views or to criticize governmental measures. To complete the dismay of the clerical faction, he further announced that religious orders in Mexico were to be dissolved.

The Politico-Religious Conflict

The stage was thus set for a Kulturkampf more bitter perhaps than any that had taken place in South America. A report of an interview with President Calles in January, 1927, thus set forth his contention:

The clergy of the Roman Catholic Church in all Latin-American countries has constituted itself as a power superior to that of the State and has always aimed at temporal power. It has not limited itself to its mission, it has invaded the sphere of politics, it has organized and conducted internal wars. . . . What the government has tried to do is to define the two camps, to limit the clergy to its proper sphere of religion, and to leave the State free to exercise its functions.

The Catholic Church strenuously opposed the politico-religious policy of Calles. Pope Pius XI accused the Mexican government of persecuting Roman Catholics. He protested against the expulsion of an apostolic delegate. He prohibited communicants in Mexico from joining any political party under the name of Catholic. In March,, 1927, it became necessary for the Archbishop of Mexico to announce that, in the absence of priests, Catholic laymen were authorized to perform the sacraments of marriage and extreme unction. After the assassination of President-Elect Obregón, Portes Gil, who was unanimously elected provisional president by Congress to serve until February 5, 1930, announced that his task would be "to continue the policies developed by President Calles in all branches of public administration, and also to procure the fulfillment of the social programs outlined by the late General Obregón."

During the administration of Portes Gil a new civil code was promulgated which embodied concepts springing from the recent Revolution. It provided that "in view of the notorious intellectual backwardness" of some persons, judges might exempt culprits from penalties incurred by the violation of laws of which they were ignorant. The right of private property was declared to be subject to restrictions imposed in the interest of society. A certain article enumerated circumstances under which private property might be taken for public use with compensation. Among those circumstances were expropriation for homestead purposes and for works of collective benefit. Another article reiterated the view that subsoil resources did not belong to the owner of the surface soil. People living in the territories or in the federal district were obligated to use their property so as not to injure social interests. Men and women were declared to be on an equality before the law. Civil marriage was made obligatory, while divorce was permitted. Concubines, as well as illegitimate children, were accorded rights in cases of intestate succession. Tenant farmers whose crops were seriously injured by an act of Providence were to be entitled to a reduction in the rent.

In the election of November, 1929, the two candidates for the presidency were José Vasconcelos, who had been minister of education under Obregón, and Pascual Ortiz Rubio, who had served his country as a diplomat and statesman. The election was won by Ortiz Rubio, who was inaugurated on February 5, 1930. He declared his intention to follow the policy of Calles. In June following the latter decided to check the agrarian reform by setting narrow limits to the distribution of land. Meanwhile, in the state of Tabasco anticlerical "Redshirts" persecuted Catholic priests. But in June, 1930, an agreement was reached between the government and the Catholic Church to the effect that its temples were the property of the Mexican nation and subject to governmental supervision. During the next year Mexico was seriously affected by the prevailing economic crisis. Because of a decline in the value of silver and a large deficit in the budget, the government was compelled to undertake fiscal reforms. It reduced the pay of soldiers as well as of civil officials. By legislation that became effective in July, 1931, Mexico relinquished the gold standard; the silver peso became the unit of her monetary system. Soon after Ortiz Rubio undertook to remove from office certain politicians who were protégés of Calles, that president-maker announced that the President had resigned. In September, 1932, a prosperous banker named Rodríguez was chosen to serve as chief magistrate.

A new political organization designated the National Revolutionary party (P.N.R.) was formed and given official sanction. In May, 1933, Calles suggested in vague terms a plan which involved a radical change in the scheme for agrarian reform. At the convention of the National Revolutionary party in December, 1933, a six-year plan was drawn up which reenunciated certain political ideals. **The Six-Year Plan** This program declared that the only limitation upon the distribution of land should be the complete satisfaction of the agricultural needs of the centers of rural population. Free competition should be restricted by understandings among competitors. It was declared to be the duty of the State to ensure that trade unions should perform their functions as efficiently as possible without going beyond their proper sphere. Collective bargaining for wage earners was to be encouraged so as to make it the prevailing form of "employee-employer relationship." With regard to Articles XXVII and CXXIII of the fundamental law, the announcement was made that they would be enforced until they constituted "an integral reality" in the social life of the country.

In reality this plan framed a social and economic program for the next administration. As its presidential candidate the P.N.R. selected Lázaro Cárdenas, an astute and masterful general of Tarascan descent who was the choice of Calles. In his campaign Cárdenas visited every one of the Mexican states and explained the six-year plan. Soon after his inauguration he declined to follow the behest of Calles and forced that aged politician into exile.

At first the President was inclined to follow the policy of Calles toward the Church. Early in 1936 the Mexican bishops issued a pastoral letter that denounced the government's "socialist" program which prohibited religious teachings in the public schools. In March of that year Cárdenas stated that his administration did not consider the religious issue as paramount in the reform program. Early in 1937 he declared that Catholics were at liberty to attend their religious services, that his administration was not hostile to the Church, and that Mexican priests had recognized that it was useless to meddle in politics. His educational policy remained nonreligious; it was distinguished by the construction of many new school buildings.

Cárdenas made a deliberate attempt to transfer economic control to the peasants and the laborers. During the first four years of his rule he gave ejidos to some 800,000 peasants. In 1936 in the Laguna district in the states of Coahuila and Durango, where cotton was the main crop, farms were organized on the coöperative principle. Similar innovations were introduced in Sonora and Yucatan. A bank of ejido credit was established to advance loans to needy farmers. In a few years collectivist agriculture was producing the major part of the cotton, henequen, rice, and wheat of Mexico.

Significant progress was made by organized labor. When a strike took place, the Cárdenas government ordered that the financial management of the company be investigated so that it could Expropriation determine whether adequate wages were being paid. In accordance with a Mexican legal dictum, the President maintained that the law favored the weaker party. He reasoned that, if the employers became weary of the struggle, they should "turn over their factories to the government or to the workers." Applying this doctrine to industry, the government took possession of the sugar haciendas, while peasants and laborers formed collective societies which undertook to produce sugar. The light and power company of the capital city, which was controlled by the British, was induced to pay higher wages to its employees. In 1937 the national railways were expropriated and later turned over to the union of railway workers.

Meanwhile a score of petroleum workers' organizations had been coalesced into one industrial union. In 1936 this union submitted to the foreign oil companies a comprehensive general contract that involved increases in wages and social security amounting to over 100,-000,000 pesos. This the companies refused to grant. After conferences of the contending parties failed to reach an agreement, on May 28, 1937, the union ordered a general strike. Upon investigation a committee of experts appointed by the government decided that the oil companies ought to increase their payrolls by some 26,000,000 pesos annually. Though the workers were willing to accept this solution, the companies refused even after the findings of the experts were upheld by a conciliation tribunal and also by the Supreme Court. Furthermore, the operators announced that they would not observe Article CXXIII of the Constitution. On March 18, 1938, Cárdenas retorted that the oil industry of his country had been nationalized and that the companies affected were to be compensated for their holdings. The petroleum industry thus became national property which was to be exploited by Mexicans.

Downing Street not only maintained that the properties of the British oil companies should be returned to them but also severed diplomatic relations with Mexico. Secretary Hull admitted that she had the right to expropriate the companies but reasoned that compensation should be made to the dispossessed Americans.

In 1938 the P.N.R. was transformed into a party composed of laborers, peasants, and soldiers which was called the party of the Mexican Revolution (P.M.R.). The official candidate for the presidency in 1940 was General Manuel A. Camacho, while the opponents of the Cárdenas régime nominated General Juan A. Almazán. Both sides claimed to have won at the polls; Congress decided that Camacho was the victor. Meanwhile the P.M.R. had framed a program known as the second six-year plan for the period of transition from 1941 to 1946. This program praised the achievements of Cárdenas in the nationalization of Mexican industry. It declared that the State should undertake to transform the economic system into a régime of collective ownership. Education in public schools should continue to be "socialistic."

Soon after Camacho took office a solution was reached in the expropriation controversy with the United States. On April 18, 1942, a joint commission announced that the value of oil properties belonging to American companies expropriated in Mexico amounted to $23,-995,991,—only about one-eighth of the amount claimed by the companies. The English government had meanwhile resumed diplomatic relations with Mexico.

Issues provoked by the second World War overshadowed all others. In the spring of 1941 Mexico and the United States agreed to coördinate their preparations for defense. A little later each party undertook to allow the free passage through its territory of troops of the other party. After the dastardly attack of the Japanese on Pearl Harbor, the Mexican government severed diplomatic relations with Germany, Italy, and

Camacho and the Second World War

Japan. Axis ships in Mexican ports were seized. Nevertheless, as in-dicated by the views of the able internationalist, Isidro Fabela, many Mexicans still wished that their country could remain aloof from the titanic conflict. On May 13, 1942, however, the *Potrero del Llano,* a Mexican tanker, was blown up by an Axis submarine. Not only did a protest against this outrage go unheeded, but on May 20 another Mexican vessel, the *Faja de Oro,* was torpedoed. A wave of indignation swept over the capital city. On May 30 Congress passed a law which gave the President power to declare the existence of a state of war. On June 1 Camacho accordingly issued a decree declaring that diplomatic measures to secure redress had failed and that he consequently proclaimed "the existence of a state of war imposed upon Mexico by the hostility of the totalitarian governments." In October, 1942, General Cárdenas was made a member of a reorganized defense ministry which was placed in supreme command of the army, navy, and air forces.

The history of independent Mexico furnishes a strange pageant. To many Mexicans the successive announcements of new plans for politi-cal and constitutional reorganization meant little or nothing. Though the firm rule of Díaz kept the country tranquil and promoted much-needed internal improvements, he did not promote the welfare of the lower classes. Against domination by a favored clique Madero directed his revolution, but he proved unable to control the weird elements which he had conjured up. Huerta failed as a ruler largely because the United States withheld the recognition of his government on moral grounds. At the very juncture when relations with her northern neigh-bor were being adjusted, the vexatious problem of the succession to the presidency again occasioned an insurrection. More fortunate than his immediate predecessors, Obregón suppressed those revolutionists who wished to make the choice of a chief magistrate depend upon the outcome of an armed conflict.

Events arising from the apostleship of Madero and the adoption of the Constitution of 1917—events appropriately styled by Mexicans as "The Revolution"—constitute the most significant development in the national history of Mexico. Her debt was considerably increased because of obligations incurred by the distribution of lands among the peons and by the expropriation of oil companies. Under Cárdenas, however, the long conflict between Church and State was at least temporarily stilled. Workmen were more adequately paid for their labor. Such measures as the nationalization of petroleum properties and the system of coöperative farming indicated that Mexico was moving toward a régime of collective socialism. In sharp contrast with her policy toward World War I, because of the ruthless submarine policy of the Axis, Mexico was forced into the second World War on the side of the United States.

SUGGESTIONS FOR FURTHER READING

BEALS, C., *Porfirio Díaz*, 1932.

BETETA, R., *The Mexican Revolution, a Defense*, 1937.

BLAKESLEE, G. H. (ed.), *Mexico and the Caribbean*, 1920.

BRADERMAN, E. M., *A Study of Political Parties and Politics in Mexico since 1890*, 1938.

BURKE, U. R., *A Life of Benito Juárez*, 1894.

CALDERÓN DE LA BARCA, *Life in Mexico during a Residence of Two Years in That Country*, 1931.

CALLCOTT, W. H., *Church and State in Mexico*, 1926.

———, *Santa Anna*, 1936.

CORTI, E. C., *Maximilian and Charlotte of Mexico*, Vol. II, 1928.

DILLON, E. J., *President Obregón*, 1922.

GRUENING, E., *Mexico and Its Heritage*, 1928.

HACKETT, C. W., *The Mexican Revolution and the United States*, 1926.

International Conciliation Bulletin, No. 345 (Mexican Expropriation), 1938.

KELLEY, F. C., *Blood-Drenched Altars*, 1935.

KING, R. E., *Tempest over Mexico*, 1935.

KLUCKHOHN, F. L., *The Mexican Challenge*, 1939.

McBRIDE, G. M., *The Land Systems of Mexico*, 1923.

MACMAHON, A. W., and DITTMAR, W. R., "The Mexican Oil Industry since Expropriation," *Political Science Quarterly*, Vol. LVII, pp. 28 ff.

"The Mexican Constitution of 1917 Compared with the Constitution of 1857," Supplement to the *Annals of the American Academy of Political and Social Science*, Vol. LXXI.

"Mexico in Revolution," *Fortune*, Vol. XVIII, No. 4, pp. 75 ff.

PARKES, H. B., *A History of Mexico*, 1938.

PORTES GIL, E., *The Conflict between the Civil Power and the Clergy*, 1934.

REDFIELD, R., *Tepoztlan: A Mexican Village*, 1930.

ROBERTSON, W. S., "The Tripartite Treaty of London," *Hispanic American Historical Review*, Vol. XX, pp. 167-189.

SCHMECKEBIER, L. E., *Modern Mexican Art*, 1939.

SIMPSON, E. N., *The Ejido: Mexico's Way Out*, 1937.

TANNENBAUM, F., *The Mexican Agrarian Revolution*, 1929.

TERRY, T. P., *Terry's Guide to Mexico*, 1938.

TURNER, J. K., *Barbarous Mexico*, 1912.

WEYL, N. and S., *The Re-Conquest of Mexico, the Years of Lázaro Cárdenas*, 1939.

WHELESS, J., *Compendium of the Laws of Mexico*, 1938.

WOLFE, B. D., *Diego Rivera: His Life and Times*, 1939.

CHAPTER XXV

SOCIAL PROBLEMS AND POLITICAL IDEALS OF THE LATIN-AMERICAN NATIONS

The nations that developed within the bounds of the former colonial empires of Spain and Portugal have been confronted with some problems which are more or less common. Among them are those connected with the theory and practice of their constitutions. In Latin America relations between Church and State are of perennial importance. The conception of a legal code which is cherished under the Southern Cross deserves an explanation. Race problems worthy of careful consideration have persisted in Latin America to the present day. Economic and fiscal problems, such as tariff systems and foreign loans, are still pressing Latin-American publicists for adequate solutions. Certain international problems have at times loomed ominously on the horizon. The rôle which certain Latin-American publicists have from time to time desired that their nations should assume in the New World is also a theme of present interest.

The proper viewpoint for a consideration of the political ideals of the Latin-American nations is that they were launched upon their independent careers with very little political training or experience. Unlike the people of the English colonies in America, the Latin Americans had had little or no training in deliberative assemblies. Hence, their earliest attempts at political organization were often imitative. Some of the first constitutions adopted in Spanish America were patterned to an extent after the United States Constitution. This was true of the Mexican Constitution of 1824, of the Venezuelan Constitution of 1811, and of the Argentine Constitution of 1853. In some Spanish-American constitutions traces can be found of French influence. Certain declarations which they contained about the rights and privileges of citizens, although influenced by constitutions of North America, were also affected by French declarations regarding the rights of man.

In certain details of those constitutions there may be detected the impress of colonial customs and Spanish precedents. Occasionally, as in the Bolivian Constitution of 1826, there may be found the vestiges of ancient political ideals. Some English influence may also be discerned, as in constitutional provisions permitting cabinet members to participate in congressional debates. In contrast with Spanish America, the sources of the first Constitution of Brazil were mostly European, and largely Portuguese. In the Brazilian Constitution of 1824 scarcely a trace can be found of influence emanating from the North American Republic.

To a citizen of the United States perhaps the most striking feature of the early constitutions of Spanish America was the manner in which they organized the local divisions. According to those constitutions, provinces or intendancies of the colonial régime were frequently dignified with the name or invested with the attributes of a state in a federal system. A dominant characteristic of many early Spanish-American constitutions was artificiality. The newly created states could not function as organic parts of the respective systems to which they belonged. The people were given institutions for which they were not ripe. Indeed, while arguing against a greater federalization of the Argentine government in 1860, Alberdi emphatically said: "In order to dissolve the unity of the Argentine Republic, it would be sufficient to apply strictly the United States Constitution and to treat as sovereign states those units which hitherto were provinces within a state."

In some nations of Spanish America the trend in the making of constitutions has been away from the North American exemplar. French influence has frequently prevailed rather than the influence of the United States. The Centralistic party has triumphed in many Latin-American countries. If we accept as a criterion the relation between the central government and the main administrative divisions, as shown, for example, in the mode of appointment of the chief magistrate—ordinarily designated the governor—of those divisions, we are forced to the conclusion that only a few of the existing Spanish-American governments are, in any sense of the word, federalistic. In some cases the main administrative division of the state is designated a department or a province; and the chief executive of that area is appointed by the president. Further, in certain states, as in Colombia, the central government has frequently interfered in the management of the affairs of the provinces or departments. Even in cases where special institutions and processes borrowed from the United States or from other countries have been incorporated in the constitutional charter, those supposed adaptations have occasionally proved to be mere fictions. To Spanish-American publicists the United States Constitution has often been little more than an inspiring ideal.

Centralistic and Federalistic Tendencies

To a greater extent perhaps than anywhere else in the world do constitutional provisions in Latin America sometimes exist only on paper. Whatever the character of the constitution of a Spanish-American nation, there has frequently been displayed an irresistible tendency for the chief executive to engross the authority of the State. Spanish-American dictators have not always been benevolent. In certain nations of Latin America the struggle for true democratic government has not yet terminated. Latin-American constitutional history has indeed frequently been marked by two tendencies: by attempts to embody progressive principles in liberal constitutions, and by flagrant violations of individual rights on the part of despotic dictators. This tendency on the part of Latin-American dictators has occasionally been due to the fact that paper guarantees of individual rights were being used to justify license rather than liberty.

The Latin-American trend toward dictatorial rule was dramatically broken in 1930 and 1931 by successful revolts against the existing governments in Argentina, Bolivia, Peru, Ecuador, Chile, and Brazil: the most significant series of revolts that has swept over South America since the epochal year 1810 when the protracted struggles for independence began. To a considerable extent these recent military coups were due to the difficulty of marketing such raw materials as coffee, rubber, meat, grain, tin, and nitrate, except at low prices. The economic depression greatly increased dissatisfaction with the existing régimes, while at the same time it not only reduced government revenues but also threatened to dislodge the holders of lucrative positions. Under such circumstances, patriots as well as politicians turned against the party in power and rode into office on a wave of popular discontent. Occasionally there has in reality been an alternation between liberal fundamental laws and illiberal constitutions. Not infrequently the deposition of a chief magistrate has been followed by the formulation of a new fundamental law: new dictator—new constitution! Indeed the tendency toward the framing of new constitutions has been so marked that under circumstances when Anglo-Saxons would be content with amending the fundamental law, Spanish Americans have been satisfied with nothing less than a brand-new constitution, a constitution which nevertheless contained many clauses taken bodily from the old charter.

Several Latin-American nations have constitutions which in certain particulars were modeled after the United States Constitution. Among recent constitutions of that class are those of Cuba and Panama. The nations in which existing constitutions sanction what may be designated federal unions are Argentina, Brazil, Mexico, and Venezuela. In these nations the local units are either designated states or they are assigned positions comparable to those of states in the United States federal system. In Argentina, as already indicated, the trend has been to treat

Federal Governments

MAP SHOWING COUNTRIES IN SOUTH AMERICA WHERE THE POLITICAL
RÉGIMES WERE ALTERED BY REVOLUTIONS IN 1930 AND 1931

the subdivisions, which were designated provinces, rather as administrative divisions than as states. In Venezuela there has been a decided tendency to centralize authority in the national government at the expense of the states; coupled with this have been influences emanating from France and Switzerland.

The nation in which constitutional customs most resembled those in the United States was probably Brazil under the Constitution of 1891. As indicated in a preceding chapter, by the revolution of 1889-1890 the Brazilians adopted a Constitution which was closely modeled upon the Constitution of the United States. Though the semi-autonomous provinces of Brazil furnished some basis for state organizations, they were far from the stage of development that had been reached by the Thirteen States of North America in 1787. With the Brazilians, customs, precedents, and ideals derived from the motherland also affected constitutional development.

Articles guaranteeing the rights of citizens, which resemble bills of rights in state constitutions of the United States, have appeared in increasing numbers in recent constitutions of Latin America. Noteworthy also are provisions concerning the relations between capital and labor, the amelioration of the lot of the oppressed aborigines, and the expropriation of individuals or corporations. Here and there a tendency has been displayed toward the centralization of political authority. In countries so widely different as Paraguay and Brazil, this trend has recently been so marked that their existing political systems have been termed totalitarian. Perhaps it should be added that, as the 1937 Constitution of Brazil has not been ratified by a referendum as required, a recent American writer on Vargas has called it "a ghost constitution."

Certain features of existing Latin-American constitutions are admirable. Among these are the frequent attempts to define citizenship: the mode of acquiring it; its privileges and responsibilities, and the manner in which its prerogatives might be lost. The status of foreigners residing within a country of Latin America is often defined in the constitution. Recent constitutions of Mexico and northern South America have contained clauses that would debar foreigners from applying for judicial redress for injuries to any other tribunals than those of the respective republic. Some of the clauses in Latin-American constitutions about the disability or the resignation of the president are not unworthy of study in the United States. Not the least suggestive perhaps has been the attempt in some countries to make the cabinet a link that fastens the executive to the legislative department of government. Of this trend, Chile under the Constitution of 1833 was the best illustration. Other nations have recently shown a similar tendency.

Progress in political life has been largely dependent upon economic development. In countries where the natural resources have been developed the interest in good government has ordinarily been strengthened. The organization of parties in Latin America has often been more or less in contrast with party organization in the United States. In backward **Party Organization and Practice** countries, like Ecuador, it has not always been customary for opposing parties even to unite upon their respective presidential candidates. At the other extreme, in a nation like Argentina or Chile, party organization is comparatively complex: there may now be found local committees, political conventions, and the formal nomination of candidates, at least for important national offices. Very infrequently, however, have Latin-American political parties clearly formulated their programs. As in the case of Hipólito Irigoyen in 1916, a presidential candidate may sedulously refrain from making any declaration whatever about his political intentions, or, much more rarely perhaps, as in the case of Ruy Barbosa or Arturo Alessandri, he may boldly indicate what political principles or reforms he intends to champion.

Electoral qualifications differ somewhat, both in theory and in practice, in Latin-American states. Where adult manhood suffrage is not assured, there is ordinarily a tendency in that direction; and in certain countries the right to vote has been granted to women. But the ballots are not infrequently influenced by moral suasion, by coercion, or by bribery. Especially in remote or backward regions elections have occasionally been nothing more than fierce conflicts between the "ins" and the "outs." Party struggles have thus often in essence been concerned mainly with personalities or with the spoils of office. A most remarkable political development has recently taken place in Mexico where the National Revolutionary party has not only held national conventions to nominate candidates for the presidency but has also framed plans designed to serve as programs for action.

Relations between Church and State in Latin America present a marked contrast with the United States. Throughout Latin America early constitutions and laws provided that Roman Catholicism should be the religion of the State. Sometimes the public exercise of any other faith was absolutely prohibited. Especially in rural districts, friars and priests exerted a great influence upon life and manners. In some **The Relations between Church and State** Latin-American states, however, a species of kulturkampf has taken place in which the Liberal party has been more or less victorious. Occasionally that struggle was initiated and waged largely by citizens of the respective state; as for example, by Mosquera's followers in New Granada, while in other states some influence has also been

exerted through the activities of Protestant sects. Although missionaries from England and the United States have occasionally provoked
antagonism by their proselyting propaganda, on the other hand, at
times they have helped to liberalize religious thoughts and ideals. This
was true even in Bolivia, Ecuador, and Peru, the countries where
Protestants suffered the longest under religious and social disabilities.

In some Latin-American countries Church and State are still closely
connected. Of them, as of England, one may say that there is an established Church. Though ordinarily tithes are no longer levied by ecclesiastical authorities, the State regularly provides in her budget for
the support of the religious establishment. On the other hand, in certain countries there has become evident a tendency toward the separation of Church and State. The best illustration of this tendency is
the arrangement made under the Chilean Constitution of 1925. Even
in Colombia, where the Constitution and a concordat conceded for
decades a dominant part in religion and education to the Roman Catholic Church, an anti-clerical spirit has again been displayed and the
Church has been shorn of some of its most cherished privileges.

Legal codes of Latin America amaze some citizens of the United
States. Like their European ancestors, Latin-American publicists have
displayed a keen desire to codify their legislation. The
**Legal
Codes** chief nations of Latin America have often drawn the
inspiration for the codification of their laws from French,
Spanish, or Portuguese sources. In certain particulars the civil code
of a Latin-American country may be considered as a supplement to
the existing constitution.

In nineteenth-century civil codes of Latin America the family was
envisaged as the social unit. Marriage was a sacrament. Annulment of
marriage or the legal separation of husband and wife was permitted
but not absolute divorce. The father of a family was a trustee who
managed the property. But those codes deliberately ignored the interests of the lower classes. Sanction was generally given to the time-
honored custom of keeping landed estates intact and of handing them
down from one generation to another. Liberal ideas did not ordinarily
affect the civil codes of Latin America until the dawn of the twentieth
century. The influence of such ideas can be detected in the civil code
of Brazil which was put into force in 1917. An extreme example of
such influence is found in that civil code of Mexico which was adopted
after "The Revolution" had leavened the thought of progressive Mexicans. After 1938 clauses concerning social interests found their way
in increasing numbers into the legal codes of Latin-American countries.
Nevertheless, in the judgment of Phanor J. Eder, a careful student of
their law and custom, the people are not litigious: "No adage is more

frequently heard or carried out than that a poor settlement is better than a good lawsuit."

Latin-American jurists have also drawn up codes of mercantile and criminal law. In Brazil the law merchant in vogue was based largely upon European codes. For decades after certain countries achieved their independence from Spain, the Ordinances of Bilbao served as their mercantile law. The codes concerning grievous offenses against the State which were adopted in various Spanish-American countries during the nineteenth century were mainly based on French and Spanish law.

The most distinctive contribution made by Latin-Americans to legal literature has been in the field of international law. Not only have they published numerous treatises on that subject, but they early favored a proposal that a uniform code of international law should be formulated. In 1928 a draft of a code of private international law was approved at the Sixth Pan American Conference. As Dr. Antonio Bustamante of Cuba played a leading part in the framing of this code, it was appropriately named the Bustamante Code. It is concerned with civil, mercantile, admiralty, and air law and with procedure.

A leavening influence has been exerted upon certain nations of Latin America by immigration. Argentina is that Latin-American nation where immigration from Europe has been most marked, and where, in consequence, the need of labor for the **Immigration** development of farms, ranches, and factories has not in recent years been very keenly felt. There public attention was earliest and most emphatically directed to the imperative necessity of encouraging immigration. This was done upon various occasions by Juan Bautista Alberdi. He maintained that in Latin America the natural increase of the population was an imperfect and slow method of upbuilding a state. Let us bring, said he, from abroad the finished products required for the creation of a nation—without a large and civilized population no great development can take place! After Argentina, Brazil is probably the country which has most striven to bring foreigners to her shores. Until recently immigration from all nations has been uniformly encouraged or permitted, except in some countries where restrictions were placed upon immigrants from China and Japan. Because of a large Japanese influx in recent years, the Brazilian Constitution of 1934 restricted immigration from any country to an annual quota of two per cent of the number of immigrants coming from the respective country in the last fifty years.

Immigration has tended to differentiate the nations of Latin America. A detailed study of Latin-American conditions would presumably show that many significant contrasts exist in the structure of society in different countries. Still, certain general tendencies prevail in some regions. Ordinarily the capital cities, like Bogotá, Rio de Janeiro, and

The Structure of Society

Buenos Aires, are the chief social centers of their respective nations. The hegemony of those capitals cannot be successfully disputed by cities like Medellín or São Paulo or Córdoba. The customs of the Spaniards or of the Portuguese have had a pervasive influence upon Latin-American society. In many regions caste distinctions still exist. Leadership in important cities is ordinarily in the hands of descendants of Portuguese or of Spaniards who constitute an intellectual aristocracy. The social aristocrats of Latin-American capitals are often members of the official bureaucracy, who have occasionally become a more or less permanent class, or wealthy landowners who have retired from their haciendas to live in urban centers.

Here and there can be detected the influence of another nation than Spain or Portugal upon social customs. English influence can be traced in customs like afternoon teas and horse racing in Montevideo and Buenos Aires. The German language and German customs prevail in large portions of southern Brazil and southern Chile. Important provincial cities sometimes imitate the manners and customs of metropolitan capitals. In certain countries, as in Bolivia and Chile, the vice of alcoholism calls for wise reform.

The aboriginal element in the population is less important numerically in Argentina than in other states. There it is being steadily assimilated by the Caucasian element. In many sections, and especially in remote countries, as Bolivia, the Indians or the mixed classes exert a much greater influence than in urban communities. Throughout the vast and more or less unexplored regions of the remote interior are scattered tribes almost as savage as the head-hunters of the equatorial Andes. Even in regions adjacent to interior towns and cities, aboriginal languages, customs, and superstitions frequently prevail.

A vital issue in Latin America is the problem of races and labor. In most Latin-American countries the population is still very sparse.

Races, Labor, and Capital

An extreme example of this is Bolivia, which, with an area of about seven hundred thousand square miles, has only a population of some three million. The demand for laborers is a crying need in some Latin-American countries. That demand has been accentuated because of the inherited disposition that still prevails among the white inhabitants in certain regions to view manual labor with contempt. The abolition by law of Negro slavery in Latin-American states has not ordinarily improved the condition of the aboriginal race.

In remote sections of Latin America the entrepreneur of industry, whether native or foreign, has been induced or compelled to employ persons of aboriginal descent to develop estates, to exploit mines, and to gather the products of the forests. If we may trust the accounts of observant travelers, the condition of many Indians or persons of Indian descent, especially in Bolivia, Ecuador, and Peru, is still virtually that of peonage, a status resembling serfdom. It is the servile labor of the aborigines that raises the sugar, cotton, tobacco, coffee, cacao, and other products of the landed estates which, under various names, have been handed down as a heritage from colonial days.

Coupled with the scarcity of labor in many countries of Latin America, there is a great lack of capital to develop industry. Strange though it may seem, citizens of Latin-American nations who possess available capital have occasionally been loath to invest it in the industries of their respective countries. Sometimes they have preferred to deposit their money in banks and to draw a high rate of interest rather than to promote the economic development of their own country by investing in national enterprises. This is one reason why foreign financiers have found an attractive field for investment in certain Latin-American countries.

The tariff systems of the countries of Latin America possess many similarities. In contrast with the historic policy of the United States, the import duties which are levied by Latin-American nations are primarily for revenue. In so far as the products of Latin-American nations are subjected to imposts, they are most frequently taxed upon being exported from the respective countries. Incidentally some attention has been paid to the levy of duties for the protection of domestic industries. Such a tendency has probably been most marked in Chile, although similar tendencies have also been shown in Brazil, Argentina, and Peru. Between a few South American countries treaty arrangements have at one time or another been made for mutual concessions of certain duties laid upon the interchange of goods. In 1913 every South American nation, except Brazil and Venezuela, secured a part of her revenue by a tax upon exports. During that fiscal year the relative amount of customs revenue accruing from duties imposed upon imports and exports varied from the minimum duty of one-tenth of one per cent in Argentina to more than 58 per cent in Chile, the relatively high per cent in the latter country being due to the tax laid upon the exportation of nitrate.

Tariffs, Income, and Expenditure

Official statistics of Chile show that of her total revenue amounting in 1913 to 220,173,450 gold pesos, 159,259,254 pesos accrued from customs duties of one sort or another. Of that sum 90,128,621 pesos were derived from the nitrate duty. In Venezuela official statistics for the fiscal year 1913-1914 told a similar story: of 65,438,328 bolívares which represented the total national revenue, 49,888,479 were derived from customs duties. Largely because of the lack of highly developed manufacturing industries, and because of the opposition to direct taxes as an important source of revenue, Latin-American states have ordinarily been dependent upon import and export duties for a large portion of the income that supports the government and that pays the interest on their indebtedness.

The comparatively small national revenues of Latin-American governments have been partly responsible for the burdensome foreign debts which they have often accumulated. In a state like Argentina, where population and wealth are rapidly increasing, such debts may even be considered as in a sense an asset rather than a liability. Yet, as indicated in a preceding chapter, the finances of Brazil have at times been seriously embarrassed because of her heavy and almost unmanageable foreign debt. Further, as will be demonstrated in the following chapter, the payment of foreign claims by Latin-American states have upon several occasions involved certain governments in acrimonious controversies with European nations which threatened forcible intervention.

One of the most serious economic problems that confronts Latin-American people is transportation. Despite the improved steamship service of recent years, and despite the increase in railway mileage, in some countries of Latin America the means of intercommunication are still woefully inadequate. There is a deplorable lack of railroads running from east to west in portions of South America. In certain regions where railroads have been built, a broken and mountainous terrain renders the cost of transportation very high. In northern South America there are no railroads of great length. Though the Venezuelan government has partly remedied this condition by promoting the construction of good roads, those do not fully meet the needs. Colombia still lacks a railroad from Santa Marta to Bogotá; and, unfortunately capitalists have been reluctant to undertake so costly a project. The vast interior of South America is in large part still inaccessible by railroads. By linking together existing railroads by new lines a Pan-American railroad has been planned. Pan-American congresses have approved the idea, but in part this railroad exists only on paper. Many years ago a Pan-American highway was planned to extend from Alaska to Argentina, but some sections in the Latin-American portion of that road, as in Ecuador and Central America, have not yet been built.

Many topics of interest to students of Latin America have been connected with boundary disputes. For the most part those disputes originated because of the vague character of the grants or delimitations of territory which were made by Spain and Portugal during the colonial period. As in the case of early English land grants in North America, not only were natural boundaries inaccurately understood but limitary points were sometimes mentioned which later could not be located. Again, some laws and decrees concerning boundaries were never executed. There were cases in which the grants presumably overlapped. With the exception of endeavors to locate the Spanish-Portuguese boundary line, scarcely any attempts were made to survey the inter-American boundaries before the Spanish and Portuguese colonies separated from their respective motherlands. Indeed, so far as the Spanish Indies were concerned, there was little need of such delimitation; for the entire dominions of Spain in America were viewed as one vast estate which should be exploited for the benefit of the motherland. Again, the actual settlement of the wilderness was so slow that the problem of bounds seldom arose as a practical question. Thus it was that when, upon the attainment of independence, Spanish-American publicists stipulated in their treaties, laws, and constitutions that the limits of a new state should coincide with the limits of the corresponding colonial administrative area, whether it had been a viceroyalty, or a captaincy general, or a presidency, they were unwittingly sowing the seeds of future discord.

Boundary Disputes

Although the view that the boundaries of the emancipated nations of Spanish America should ordinarily coincide with the boundaries of the corresponding colonial administrative divisions or subdivisions was not embodied in any general treaty among the new nations, yet its general acceptance as a guiding principle by Latin-American publicists caused it to be designated as the *uti possidetis* of 1810. Advocated by some statesmen partly as a defense against possible claims to territory in America by European powers upon the ground that some of it was *res nullius,* this principle became the theoretical basis for the territorial delimitation of the Spanish-American states. However, as this doctrine rested not upon actual surveys of the metes and bounds of those colonial areas, but upon the laws and orders of a government seated in Lisbon or Madrid, it led to a large number of troublesome boundary disputes.

The Uti Possidetis of 1810

As elsewhere indicated, a most striking feature of those disputes has been the success with which Brazil has urged her claims against her Spanish-American neighbors. This has come about partly because Spain made concessions to Portugal in the eighteenth century, partly because of the skill of Brazilian diplomats, and partly because the Brazilians have often reënforced their paper claims by the actual occupation of disputed territory. By 1943 all the major boundary disputes in Latin America had been settled. Perhaps the most pleasing feature of those contentions about territory, which frequently neither of the contending parties vitally needed, was the development of the practice of submitting international disputes to arbitration.

It is scarcely too much to say that in the use of arbitral procedure the Latin-American nations have set an example to the world. Colombia had championed the use of arbitration for the adjustment of international disputes even before the battle of Ayacucho. In instructions to Joaquín Mosquera, who was sent as an envoy by Colombia to Peru and Chile in 1822, he was directed to bring to the attention of the governments to which he was accredited the fact that though the states arising in South America had distinct sovereignties, they ought to live together as sister nations. On July 6, 1822, that Colombian signed with Bernardo Monteagudo, the agent of Peru, a treaty of perpetual union, league, and confederation. This treaty provided that the exact demarcation of the boundary between Peru and Colombia should be determined by peaceful and conciliatory means. In a supplementary treaty those diplomats suggested that an assembly of American states should be convoked which might serve as an arbiter in their disputes. Identical provisions were found in treaties that were negotiated contemporaneously by Colombia with Chile and Mexico.

Arbitration in Latin America

The belief in peaceful methods of adjusting controversies has been with publicists of Latin America more than an ideal. After 1823 Latin-American states entered into numerous treaties which embodied the arbitral principle in one form or another. Occasionally those treaties provided for the arbitration of boundary disputes. Sometimes they arranged that international claims should be decided by arbitration. Many times they contained clauses providing for the arbitration of general disputes that might arise between the contracting parties. At other times they stipulated that this method should be used to adjust controversies about the interpretation of treaties. The rôle of arbiter in some of those disputes, was by the consent of both parties, assigned to the United States.

Upon various occasions the United States has also attempted, with more or less success, to mediate in controversies or wars of Latin-American nations. During the war between Spain and certain nations upon the Pacific coast of South America, the United States offered her services as mediator. Through her insistence that dispute was at last amicably adjusted by treaties which were signed long after the hostilities had ended. Yet the United States failed in her policy of mediating in important disputes which involved the government of Argentina.

Similarly she did not succeed in her policy of mediation in the War of the Pacific. It later became clear, however, that the main contention of the United States in that fruitless negotiation was not altogether wrong, namely, that Chile ought not to demand from the conquered nations as a *sine qua non* such extensive territorial cessions as would leave them badly crippled.

Latin-American leaders have frequently cherished thoughts of forming a union. Even before the wars for independence began, Francisco de Miranda had formed a project for a confederation that was to include all the Spanish colonies in America. In 1811 a Chilean revolutionary leader named Juan Egaña drafted a declaration of rights of the Chilean people which proposed the convocation of an international congress composed of delegates of the independent American states. The most suggestive proposals about a union of the revolted colonies of Spanish America were made by that prolific thinker, Simón Bolívar. In a letter addressed on September 6, 1815, to a gentleman of Jamaica who had displayed a keen interest in the Spanish-American Revolution, the Liberator expressed views which have been styled prophetic. Bolívar ventured the prediction that the Spanish Empire in America would ultimately be disrupted and that several independent states would be formed. He believed that differences of conditions in those states would make the establishment of one unified republic impossible but suggested that an international congress should be convoked to meet on the Isthmus of Panama.

Other Latin-American thinkers have favored the idea of an international organization. When the first envoy of Brazil to the United States was received at Washington, he suggested to President Monroe the wisdom of a union of all the independent American nations. Spanish Americans have sometimes been content to suggest plans for a confederation that would not necessarily include Brazil and that would ordinarily exclude the United States. The founding of Great Colombia and Bolívar's veiled attempt to include other portions of South America within his system, was probably the closest approach to the realization of this ideal.

Proposals of a Latin-American union have occasionally been made because of apprehensions concerning the attitude of the United States or of her citizens toward Latin America. As illustrations of such provocation may serve: Walker's filibustering expeditions to Nicaragua; the war between the United States and Spain; and the separation of Panama from Colombia. More often, however, such proposals have been evoked by fear of European intrusion in America. Because of French intervention in Mexico certain Chilean leaders organized a society which was styled the "American Union" whose objects were to sustain the independence of the American states and to promote their union. After Germany, Italy, and England had established a blockade of the ports of Venezuela in 1902, a Venezuelan publicist proposed that a conference of delegates from Spanish-American nations should be assembled at Panama to formulate the basis of an association of those nations which would serve as a protection against European aggression.

The most notable indication of the desire of Latin Americans to form an association of nations has been found in their international

International Congresses

congresses. Here again we must turn back to Bolívar, who on December 7, 1824, sent from Lima an invitation to Brazil, La Plata, Chile, Colombia, Central America, and Mexico to send delegates to a Congress on the Isthmus of Panama. The Liberator proposed that this Congress should serve the Spanish-American nations as a council in great danger, as an interpreter of treaties, and as an umpire and conciliator in case of controversies. The meetings of the Panama Congress, which were attended only by delegates from four Spanish-American nations, occurred in June and July, 1826. Those delegates framed some conventions about the projected Spanish-American confederation, but the states which were represented at Panama did not ratify them. Still, this congress was significant because it was the first of a series of international American conferences that served to formulate the ideas of Spanish-American publicists about inter-American relations.

On December 11, 1847, a Congress of delegates from Bolivia, Chile, Ecuador, New Granada, and Peru met at Lima. That Congress also adopted a number of treaties concerning the relations of American states. Among those was a treaty of confederation which provided that the contracting states would mutally sustain by force their independence, integrity, and sovereignty. Only one of the treaties, however, was ever ratified by any of the contracting republics. On January 23, 1865, a Congress of delegates from Bolivia, Chile, Colombia, Ecuador, Peru, Salvador, and Venezuela, who had gathered at Lima, signed a treaty of "union and alliance" by which they mutually guaranteed their independence, sovereignty, and territorial integrity against aggression.

At the so-called "Bolivian Congress," which was composed of representatives of nations liberated largely through the efforts of Bolívar, that met at Caracas in 1911, the delegates of Peru, Ecuador, Colombia, Bolivia, and Venezuela discussed various matters of common interest. Among other measures they adopted a resolution which pledged their respective states mutually to concede in return for reciprocal concessions any commercial advantage that they might grant separately to any one of the five nations. The delegates also agreed that their respective nations would promote the adoption of uniform customs regulations. Though the treaties which proposed a union, alliance, or confederation of Spanish-American nations had no practical results, they kept alive the ideal of Bolívar and encouraged Latin-American peoples to think in continental terms.

At a later period this spirit was expressed not only in what was styled Pan-Americanism—as will be shown in the following chapter—but also in various congresses which were held by Latin Americans. In the domain of science the Argentine government led the way by the invitation which it issued to scientists from Latin-American countries to assemble in Buenos Aires in order to celebrate the anniversary of the founding of the Argentine Scientific Society. In response to that invitation, in April, 1898, scholars from various Latin-American countries assembled in the First Latin-American Scientific Congress at Buenos Aires to discuss scientific and economic questions. A second Congress of this type gathered in Montevideo in March, 1901; and a third Congress met at Rio de Janeiro in August, 1905. Not only was the discussion of topics in mathematics, physical science, and the social sciences profitable to Latin Americans but the movement for such congresses redounded to the advantage of all America. At the meeting in Rio de Janeiro the decision was reached to transform the Latin-American scientific congresses into gatherings which might be attended by scientists from all the nations of the New World.

The closest approximation toward the ideal of a Latin-American union or confederation has been the rapprochement of Argentina, Brazil, and Chile. The association of those three powers, the strongest economically and politically in South America, was no chance grouping. With the adjustment of the **The A B C Powers** dispute about their Andean boundary, Chile and Argentina felt the strengthening of bonds that had existed since 1817. At the other extremity of Latin America from that over which the United States has been extending hegemony, the publicists of Argentina, in particular, have believed that the nations of southern South America ought to form an association which might serve to counterbalance the influence of the Anglo-Saxon Republic. Into this group Argentina and Chile were naturally inclined to admit Brazil because she possessed the most extensive territory of any Latin-American nation. In September, 1910, the Argentine secretary of foreign relations referred to the fraternity existing between Chile, Argentina, and Brazil, and proposed that, as the three strongest states of South America, they should direct the other nations of that continent along the path of progress. Other countries, he declared, would see in the friendship between those powers a strong guaranty for peace.

An inspiration to the formation of a tripartite treaty was apparently the negotiation by Secretary of State Bryan of a series of peace treaties with the nations of America. At Buenos Aires, on May 25, 1915, the secretaries of foreign relations of Argentina, Brazil, and Chile signed a treaty which gave a definite basis to the tripartite understanding. The A B C treaty stipulated that any controversy which might arise among the contracting parties and which could neither be settled by diplomatic means nor adjusted by arbitration should be submitted to investigation by a permanent commission. That commission should be composed of one person representing each of the contracting parties, while they bound themselves not to commit any hostile acts until the commission had made its report or until one year had elapsed. The dominant idea was that the lapse of time would render an armed conflict between disputants unlikely. The tripartite treaty was thus evidently intended to prevent wars among Latin-American states and to shield them against foreign attacks. This treaty remained an aspiration, however, for it was not ratified by all of the parties.

Foreign perils have been to Latin America a great bugaboo. During the wars for independence many Spanish-American publicists feared—
without reason, as it now appears—that the association of
Foreign Perils European powers known as the Holy-Alliance might intervene to restore the dominion of Spain over her revolted colonies in America. Fears of the intervention of European powers, which would destroy the autonomy of Spanish-American nations, were entertained in Argentina during the reign of Dictator Rosas, in Peru at the time of the dispute with Spain that was precipitated by the Talambo affair, and in Mexico and Venezuela when European nations threatened permanently to occupy their territory. More recently, European aggression was apprehended in certain sections of Latin America because of the colonizing and commercial enterprise of Germany. That part of southern Brazil which was settled by Germans was considered by some patriotic Brazilians as a menace to the independence and autonomy of their nation. In a speech which he made before the College of Law and Social Sciences of the University of Buenos Aires in August, 1916, Ruy Barbosa eloquently voiced the conviction that if Germany should be victorious in the first World War, she would defy the United States and boldly seize a portion of South America. Years ago a brilliant Peruvian writer expressed the opinion that, because of the aggressiveness of the Japanese, the Empire of the Rising Sun was a menace to the autonomy of Latin-American nations.

With the outbreak of the second World War, the foreign menace to

Latin America took on a dangerous form. In certain Latin-American countries there were large minorities composed of natives of Germany, Italy, and Japan and of the descendants of those nationals. A careful study of Axis minorities in 1942 revealed the following startling figures. There were 12,000 Italians and 80,000 Germans in Chile. In Uruguay there were 16,000 Germans and 600,000 Italians. There were 1,450,000 Germans, 2,280,000 Italians, and 235,000 Japanese in Brazil. While in Argentina there were 50,000 Germans, 60,000 Japanese, and 4,800,000 Italians. Members of disloyal, pro-Axis minorities in those countries and elsewhere not only engaged in subversive activities but also harbored agents of the *Gestapo*. Such persons often disregarded the frontier of the countries where they lived. The region of Misiones in Argentina, where there were many Germans, became a corridor for communication with Fifth Columnists in Brazil and Paraguay. Though by February, 1943, Axis powers had been forced to give up their embassies and consulates in nineteen Latin-American countries, in certain regions their sympathizers had retired behind a false front. A strong bulwark of defense against their nefarious activity, however, was the spirit of ideological nationalism in those countries.

SUGGESTIONS FOR FURTHER READING

BORCHARD, E. M., *Guide to the Law and Legal Literature of Argentina, Brazil, and Chile*, 1917.

BOWMAN, I., *The New World*, 1922.

BRYCE, J., *South America*, 1914.

CAMPBELL, J. C., "Political Defense of the Americas," *Inter-American Monthly*, Vol. I, pp. 7-11.

COOPER, C. S., *Understanding South America*, 1918.

EDER, P. J., "Law and Justice in Latin America," *Law, A Century of Progress*, pp. 39-82, 1937.

ESQUIVEL OBREGÓN, T., and BORCHARD, E. M., *Latin-American Commercial Law*, 1921.

FILSINGER, E. B., *Commercial Travellers' Guide to Latin America*, 1922.

HARING, C. H., *South America Looks at the United States*, 1928.

International American Conference, Vol. IV, 1899.

IRELAND, G., *Boundaries, Possessions, and Conflicts in South America*, 1938.

———, *South American Current Practices*, 1933.

JANE, C., *Liberty and Despotism in Spanish America*, 1929.

KIRKPATRICK, F. A., *Latin America*, 1938.

QUESADA, G. DE, *Arbitration in Latin America*, 1907.

RODRÍGUEZ, J. I., *American Constitutions*, Vol. I, 1905.

Royal Institute of International Affairs, *The Republics of South America*, 1937.

SCHURZ, W. L., *Latin America*, 1941.

SPEER, R. E., *South American Problems*, 1912.

WILGUS, A. C., *The Development of Hispanic America*, 1941.

CHAPTER XXVI

RELATIONS OF LATIN-AMERICAN NATIONS WITH OTHER STATES

There remains to consider those relations that have been formed between the family of Latin-American nations and other states. Though the United States has in some respects lagged behind certain European countries in the cultivation of intercourse with Latin America, during recent decades her people have displayed an increasing interest in the history, the politics, and the destinies of those nations that occupy the southern portion of the New World. After a consideration of the interest displayed by certain European powers in Latin America, the major portion of this chapter will accordingly be devoted to a discussion of various phases of inter-American relationships. By these are meant the Monroe Doctrine, the commercial intercourse between the United States and Latin-American nations, and the educational influence as well as the scientific investigations of United States citizens in those countries. A description of the inception and development of the Pan-American sentiment may not be omitted, nor a consideration of the influence exerted by the first World War upon American comity. Notice will also be taken of the attitude of Latin-American nations toward the Axis powers in the second World War.

On the whole it may safely be said that Portugal has kept in closer touch with Brazil than Spain has with Spanish America. A current of emigration from the motherland to Brazil has flowed **Relations with the Motherlands** more or less constantly from 1808 to the present day. Many merchants in important Brazilian towns and cities are either Portuguese or of Portuguese descent. The commercial relations maintained between Brazil and Portugal are not inconsiderable. In 1905 Brazil imported from Portugal merchandise that amounted to some 34,000,000 milreis; eight years later Portuguese imports into Brazil amounted to some 44,000,000 milreis.

The protracted struggles for independence and the long delay of the motherland in recognizing the independent status of her former colonies hindered the development of commercial relations between Spain and the nations of Spanish America. Although Spanish emigrants have proceeded in considerable numbers to certain Spanish-American countries, as Argentina, Chile, and Uruguay, yet Spanish civilization is not

so pervasive or so dominant as one might suppose. Prominent merchants in cities of Spanish America are often Spaniards, frequently
Basques or Catalonians, and leaders of the intellectual coteries boast
of their Spanish ancestors, but the presence of a large aboriginal element and the currents of immigration from other countries than Spain
tended to lessen Castilian influence. In recent decades, however,
Spanish publicists and scholars have made attempts, and with some
degree of success, to cultivate the sympathy and good will of Spanish-
American nations. Those attempts have aimed to cultivate in Spain
an intellectual interest in Spanish America and to promote the development of commercial relations between Spain and the American nations
that speak the language of Cervantes.

Other Romance nations than Spain and Portugal have exercised an
influence on the Latin nations of the New World. A stream of Italian
immigration that went chiefly to eastern and southern
South America has in recent decades had an appre- France
ciable influence upon Latin-American society. It is and Latin
America
probably still safe to assert, however, that the foreigners
who have been, in general, most admired in the intellectual circles of
Latin America are the French. This was not because the French displayed an intense desire to emigrate to Latin-American countries. It
was not because they invested millions of francs in the industries of
Brazil, Uruguay, and Argentina. Nor was it because certain French
manufactures were by some Latin Americans most highly esteemed.
It was not only because of the homage which the thinkers of certain
Latin-American nations render the French genius but also because a
feeling was commonly entertained that France and her people had
more intellectual sympathy for Latin America and for Latin Americans
than almost any other people. This tendency was stimulated by the
formation in France of organizations for the encouragement of close
relations with Latin America. Gallic interest in the Latin nations of
the New World was stimulated by the residence in Paris of distinguished Latin-American diplomats. In 1910 a chair for the study of
Brazilian history and culture was founded at the University of Paris.

Another proof of the deep interest of France in Latin America is
found in the scientific expeditions which Frenchmen have made to
South America. Those notable expeditions were initiated by the trip
of Jean B. Boussingault, a chemist and meteorologist, who from 1825
to 1831 explored portions of Bolivia and northern Peru. Important
contributions to geographical knowledge were made by a naturalist
named Alcide d'Orbigny who, after visiting the basin of La Plata
River, studied the geography of the central Pacific coast of South
American and also of Bolivia. In 1845, by order of the government

of France, Count Castelnau led a scientific expedition into the central portion of South America, explored certain plateaus and cordilleras of Bolivia and Peru, and then boldly descended the Amazon River to the ocean. In 1876 and the following years an enterprising lieutenant of the French navy named Jules Crevaux made geological researches near the Oyapoc River on the northeastern boundary of Brazil, surmounted the Tumuc Humac Mountains, and reached the Amazon River. After 1879 he devoted his energies to the exploration of two northern tributaries of the Amazon. Next he ascended the Magdalena River, climbed the Colombian cordilleras, and proceeded down the Guaviare River into the Orinoco.

The interest of England in Latin America dates from the beginnings of her commercial relations with the Spanish Main and the estuary of La Plata River. After designs entertained by some of her **England and Latin America** officials for colonial expansion in the last-mentioned region had been rendered futile largely by governmental ineptitude, a number of daring Englishmen enlisted under the patriot standards in Spanish America. Those who served under Bolívar in northern South America won an enviable reputation for the "British Legion." It was during this epoch that London bankers began to advance money to the governments of the new states.

After the independence of the Latin-American nations was recognized by Canning, the English undertook to induce certain Latin-American countries to buy goods manufactured at Manchester, Sheffield, or Birmingham. As the years passed, adaptable commercial agents from London began to skirt the coasts of South America and to sail up its great rivers. English banks were eventually planted in Spanish-American capitals. By the opening of the present century millions of pounds sterling had been invested by Englishmen in Mexico and South America. Though in recent decades some Britons have settled upon sheep ranches in Patagonia, nowhere did men of British birth plant "colonies" like those of Germany in southern Brazil. In certain countries of South America, Englishmen married into prominent families: Brazilian and Chilean family names still attest the mingling of English and Latin-American blood. English bankers, merchants, and commercial practices became influential factors in many sections of Latin America. Until the outbreak of the first World War, international exchange in South America generally was reckoned in English pounds.

After the struggles for the independence of Spanish America had terminated, the English people began to develop an interest in the conversion of the aborigines. The earliest deliberate attempt of Anglican missionaries to spread Protestant beliefs in South America was made among the rude Indians of Patagonia. About 1844 the Patagonian

Missionary Society was founded in England, an organization that was later known as the South American Missionary Society. In time the interest of English Protestants in the evangelization of South America widened: Anglican missionaries were sent to convert the Araucanian Indians and also the barbarous aborigines of the Chaco. Episcopalian chapels were built in many towns and cities throughout Chile, Argentina, Uruguay, and Brazil. Recently the labors of English missionaries in South America have been reënforced and supplemented by the activities of certain missionary societies of Canada. The Canadian Baptist Mission Board developed a special interest in Bolivia.

In a sense English scientific interest in Latin America may be said to have originated with Lord Kingsborough. His curious notion that the Aztecs were descendants of the lost tribes of Israel impelled him to make a collection of material upon that theme in his *Antiquities of Mexico,* which has served as a mine of information for students of pre-Columbian Mexico. Among a distinguished list of naturalists who have explored the wildernesses of South America the name of Charles Darwin is preëminent. He left England in the ship "Beagle" on December 27, 1831, and visited the southern and western portions of South America. His studies of man and nature in such widely separated regions as Tierra del Fuego and the Galápagos Islands unquestionably had an influence upon the formulation of his scientific theories.

Another noteworthy trip was that made by Henry Bates and A. R. Wallace, who in April, 1848, left England upon a joint expedition to investigate the natural history of the Amazon basin. After spending some four years traversing in a canoe the tributaries of the Amazon River, Wallace unfortunately lost his collection of specimens of South American fauna by the shipwreck of the vessel in which he was returning home. His companion lived in the Amazonian wilderness seven years longer. Then Bates brought safely to England a magnificent collection of specimens of South American fishes, birds, insects, and butterflies. Darwin estimated that this collection contained representatives of some eight thousand species "that were previously unknown to science." An English botanist named Richard Spruce spent fifteen years wandering over the mountains and through the forests of northern South America. Fortunately, he left his manuscript notes to be edited by the sympathetic hand of Wallace. Among Englishmen who have scaled mountain peaks and made travels in South America the most distinguished is Viscount Bryce, whose interpretative *Observations and Impressions* have spread a knowledge of Latin America among English-speaking peoples.

Germany's interest in Latin-American countries may be traced back as far as the age of Emperor Charles V, when Germans settled in present Venezuela. In the nineteenth century streams of immigrants proceeded from Germany to Brazil and Chile. Some Germans were, in course of time, scattered through other Latin-American countries, but nowhere else did they plant such settlements as in Chile and Brazil. There

Germany and Latin America

they preserved the German language and culture; indeed the ties connecting the settlers with the Fatherland were so sedulously preserved that the towns were called "German colonies." Yet, such settlements might in any strict sense of the term be designated colonies only in so far as certain Germans presumably took advantage of a law which provided that they could retain their German citizenship even though they swore allegiance to the land of their adoption. As the years passed, however, some Germans tended to become assimilated in the mass of the population.

The most striking exception to this was southern Brazil. There the persistence of German customs and a sympathy with German ideals caused grave apprehension to the Brazilian government after the outbreak of the first World War. In other sections of South America than Brazil and Chile, the Germans have been mainly interested in the promotion of trade between the new nations and the Fatherland. They established German banks, acted as commercial agents, and furnished Latin-American merchants with long terms of credit. During the first World War in several Latin-American nations Germans published newspapers that were used as vehicles of propaganda for the Central Powers.

The beginnings of the scientific interest of Germans in Latin America date from the famous trip of Alexander von Humboldt who visited Cuba, Mexico, and northern South America near the end of the colonial régime. In 1840 Prince Adelbert of Prussia explored the Xingu River in Brazil for some distance from its mouth. More than forty years elapsed before Karl von den Steinen with other Germans descended that river from its headwaters and disembarked at Pará. In 1850 Hermann Burmeister forsook his professorship of zoölogy at the University of Halle and travelled for two years mainly in Brazil. Some years afterward he crossed the Argentine pampas, scaled the Andes, and returned from Chile to Argentina where he became professor of natural history at the University of Córdoba. During the last decade of the nineteenth century Hans Steffen and other Germans made a series of remarkable exploring trips in the lake region of the southern Argentine-Chilean cordillera. Wilhelm Reis and Alphons Stübel prosecuted geological investigations in the Colombian cordilleras. From Colombia they crossed the frontier into Ecuador where they made similar studies. In 1875 they not only carried on important researches in the aboriginal acropolis of Ancón but also explored northern Peru.

In 1892 Theodor Wolf published a most instructive volume about Ecuadorian geology which was based upon his own patient research. An outstanding figure among German explorers of Central America was Karl Sappers who traversed that region from Guatemala to Costa Rica.

Of special significance in the relations of the Latin-American states with other nations has been the doctrine which was formulated by James Monroe. That doctrine was promulgated at a juncture when the United States was apprehensive of **The Monroe Doctrine** Russian encroachments on the western coast of North America, and when, in common with states of Latin America, she viewed the association of European powers called the Holy Alliance as a menace against the independence and integrity of American nations. In accordance with an agreement reached at the Congress of Verona, France had just overthrown the constitutional government of Spain and restored Ferdinand VII to absolute power. Prominent publicists in both North and South America feared that the Holy Alliance, which had authorized French soldiers to intervene in Spain, might send an expedition to subjugate the rising nations of Latin America.

In his message of December 2, 1823, after mentioning the threat of Russian encroachment, the President declared that America should no longer be open to colonization by European powers. After mentioning the menace of the Holy Alliance, Monroe announced that his government could only view the intervention of a European power in America as the proof of an unfriendly disposition toward the United States. Incidentally he said that it was the policy of his government not to meddle in European politics.

The declarations thus aimed against European colonization or interposition in America were hailed by South American publicists with delight. One or the other of the two essential principles of the Monroe Doctrine was acceptable to such statesmen as Bolívar, Santander, and Rivadavia. Some journalists of South America warmly praised the policy of the United States that had made herself the sponsor of new nations. Although the President apparently did not have Brazil in mind when he composed his famous message, yet Carvalho e Mello, the Brazilian minister of foreign relations, was the first Latin-American statesman to give his official approval to the Monroe Doctrine.

A favorable attitude was also taken by Latin-American publicists upon later occasions when the ægis of the United States was felt to be necessary against the menace of European interference or when such menace had actually been translated into action. The protests of Secretary Seward against the establishment of an exotic monarchy in Mexico, which probably influenced the French government to with-

draw its soldiers from that country, induced President Díaz to declare
that he was a partisan of the Monroe Doctrine. When a crisis was
reached in the Anglo-Venezuelan boundary controversy
invoking the Doctrine of Monroe, Venezuelan statesmen
and journalists appealed to the United States to prevent
England from extending her dominions in South America
at the expense of their country. The aggressive policy which was
adopted by President Cleveland evoked favorable appreciations of
the Monroe Doctrine in Colombia, Brazil, Ecuador, Central America,
and Mexico.

*Apprecia-
tions of that
Doctrine*

When Germany, Italy, and England in 1902 tried forcibly to coerce
Venezuela to pay certain exorbitant claims and threatened to establish
a warlike blockade of her coasts, certain Venezuelan publicists viewed
that policy as an attempt of the Kaiser to test the efficacy of the
famous Doctrine. After this acrimonious dispute was adjusted, President Castro expressed his warm appreciation of the success of the
United States in compelling the creditor nations to agree to a peaceful
mode of adjusting the financial dispute. The Argentine publicist Roque
Sáenz Peña declared that the Monroe Doctrine had become an india-
rubber doctrine.

Attempts of European powers to collect debts from Venezuela, and
also Theodore Roosevelt's statement that the coercion of a Latin-
American state was not contrary to the Monroe Doctrine
provided that such punishment did not result in the acquisition of territory by a non-American power, evoked
a significant response from Argentina's secretary of foreign affairs, Luis M. Drago. As the view which he then expressed was
largely a restatement of the Calvo Doctrine, that doctrine should first
be described. Many years earlier Carlos Calvo, a noted Argentine
publicist, had in his work on international law declared that the recovery of debts and the collection of private claims did not justify
armed intervention by governments. He also denied the responsibility
of a state for injuries that had been suffered by aliens during internal
dissensions or revolts. Calvo accordingly protested against the use of
force by European nations to collect either private claims or debts
in Latin America.

*The Calvo
and the
Drago Doc-
trines*

On December 29, 1902, in a note to Martín García Mérou, the
Argentine minister in Washington, Secretary Drago enunciated his doctrine. In forcible words he reasoned that proceedings for the collection
of debts by European nations in America could not rightly be undertaken against a sovereign state. He insisted that the public debt of a
Latin-American state could justify neither "armed intervention" nor
even the actual occupation "of the territory of American nations by a

European power." Drago's note was thus a protest of the Argentine government against forcible intervention by European powers to collect debts which had been incurred by a Latin-American nation.

That note was not without some influence upon the theory and practice of the United States with regard to the collection of debts by European nations in America. On December 5, 1905, in a message to Congress, President Roosevelt took the view that attempts of foreign nations forcibly to collect debts from Latin-American republics might embarrass the United States; for such attempts might result in the permanent acquisition of territory in America by foreign nations. In his message to Congress a year earlier, Roosevelt had declared that "chronic wrong-doing" or a "loosening of the ties of civilized society" might force the United States to exercise "an international police power" in the New World. This interpretation of the historic rôle of the United States, which became known as the "Roosevelt Corollary of the Monroe Doctrine," beckoned American statesmen into endless vistas.

It is noteworthy that the United States and certain nations of Latin America exerted a significant influence upon the proceedings of the Second Peace Conference at The Hague. In 1907 delegates appeared there from all the important nations of America. General Porter of the United States presented to the Second Peace Conference a proposal that when contractual debts were owing from a certain nation to citizens of another state, the nations represented at The Hague Conference would agree not to use "armed force for the collection of such contractual debts." This stipulation should not be operative, however, when the debtor nation refused to arbitrate, or neglected to fulfill an arbitral decision, or rendered a compromise impossible. The principle of a prohibition upon the use of armed force which was embodied in the Porter proposition was favored by a large number of delegates and finally approved by the conference. By the action of the United States and some Spanish-American nations the Second Hague Conference thus formally disapproved the use of armed force to collect certain contractual debts.

Applications of the Roosevelt Corollary

The application of the Roosevelt Corollary to controversies arising between Latin-American states and creditor European nations because of debts led to significant results. As indicated in preceding chapters, that corollary was first applied to the bankrupt Dominican Republic, and then, in a modified form, to Nicaragua. Although the administrative and fiscal results of such intervention by the United States in the affairs of her Caribbean neighbors have been, in the main, good, yet a policy which in the West Indies culminated in naval and military occupation of disturbed republics provoked much criticism of the United States.

It will be appropriate, therefore, to devote some attention to animadversions upon the Monroe Doctrine by Latin Americans. A classic criticism of the Doctrine, though little known in the United States, was an attack upon her policy which was made in 1893 by an erudite resident of São Paulo named Eduardo Prado. In a work entitled *A Illusão Americana* that author published so bitter an attack upon the policy of the United States toward her Latin-American neighbors that his book was suppressed by the Brazilian government. A second edition of *The American Illusion* was printed at Paris in 1895; and in 1902 a third edition was published at São Paulo. Prado argued that Monroe's words about European intervention in America were platonic. This he proved to his own satisfaction by a consideration of proceedings of the United States that were indicative of her policy toward Latin America but which frequently had little or no relation to the Monroe Doctrine. Among the acts which he surveyed was the recognition by the United States of King Miguel of Portugal in 1830, the acknowledgment of Texan independence by the United States, and her war with Mexico. He expressed the conviction that the United States was neither sympathetically nor helpfully inclined toward Latin America; hence he argued that Brazil should follow a policy of her own. Animated by anti-Republican principles, Prado struck the keynote of many later criticisms of the Monroe Doctrine both in the United States and in Latin America: he confused that doctrine with a policy which the United States had at one time or another pursued toward Latin America!

Latin-American Criticism

After the United States had begun the war with Spain, Alberto del Solar, a Chilean writer who resided in Argentina, taking his inspiration partly from that event and partly from Prado's diatribe, delivered an address in which he attacked the Monroe Doctrine. Solar's remarks were illustrated by incidents that were almost as inappropriate as those selected by Prado. By an examination of the policy of the United States toward Latin-American republics he essayed to show that her protestations of friendship and sympathy were hollow. These two illustrations may serve to point the moral, namely, that Latin Americans have sometimes directed attacks against measures of the United States which could be scarcely considered as applications of the Monroe Doctrine.

It is undoubtedly true that Latin Americans have made adverse criticisms of the policy of the United States which would be accepted as just by some students of international relations. Forgetting that

England had never clearly relinquished her claim, Argentine writers have insistently asserted that the seizure of the Falkland Islands by England was a violation of the Monroe Doctrine for which the United States was responsible. From time to time bitter criticisms have been made of the Great Republic of the North because of the fact that by successive annexations she added to her dominions much territory which was at one time controlled either by Spain or Mexico.

The measures by which the United States acquired the right to dig the canal across the Isthmus of Panama had a bad influence upon the peoples of Latin America. Roosevelt's phrase, "I took the Isthmus," was echoed and reëchoed throughout the Latin-American world. Conditions in Mexico, which at times have invited intervention to secure the establishment of a régime of peace and progress, have aroused the apprehensions of certain Latin Americans who believe that the interposition of the United States in that country would almost inevitably lead to annexation. In general, criticisms of the United States have often been made because fear was entertained of the increasing power of the Anglo-American Republic.

Unfavorable criticisms of Latin-American journalists and publicists have most often been directed to those applications of the Monroe Doctrine that have been made in accordance with the Roosevelt Corollary. When he heard that Woodrow Wilson was soon to be inaugurated president of the United States, an Argentine littérateur named Manuel Ugarte addressed a public letter to the president-elect and implored him to reverse the foreign policy of his government that was transforming portions of Latin America into new Moroccos and new Egypts. In an article about the Monroe Doctrine, Manoel de Oliveira Lima, a Brazilian ex-diplomat who warmly admired the United States, rightly declared that Latin-American peoples might be excused for tremors of apprehension about the foreign policy of a giant nation that had extended her influence over the West Indies and Central America.

Trade between the United States and Latin America had its origins in the intercourse of the Thirteen Colonies with the Spanish Indies. Soon after the Constitution of the United States was adopted, Yankee sloops were taking fish and flour to the **Commercial Relations** Spanish West Indies to exchange for spirits and molasses. During the first decade of the nineteenth century vessels from the United States undertook to trade with ports in South America. After the Spanish Americans had won their independence, treaties of commerce were negotiated between the United States and certain Latin-American nations.

A few statistics will indicate the drift of inter-American commercial relations during the nineteenth century. In the year ending June 30, 1850, imports into the United States from Latin-American countries amounted to $16,676,669, while exports from the United States to Latin-American countries aggregated $9,117,796. Partly because of the Civil War in the United States, and partly because of keener competition from European nations, during the period from 1850 to 1875 the exports of the United States to Latin-American countries relatively declined, while the imports from those countries to the United States continued to increase. In the year ending September 30, 1875, the total imports into the United States from Latin-American nations amounted to $79,291,858, while United States exports to those nations aggregated $28,627,909. The succeeding quarter of a century was marked by a considerable increase in the exports of the United States to Latin-American countries.

The basis of commercial intercourse between the United States and Latin America has been chiefly the fact that the products of those sections to a large extent supplement each other. Coffee, cocoa, bananas, rubber, lumber, hides, wool, and various minerals are sent from Latin-American countries to the United States; while that nation exports to Latin America agricultural implements, machinery, boots and shoes, cotton and woolen goods, flour, and furniture.

The great differences between the chief exports of the United States and those of Latin-American countries led some publicists to believe at one time or another that reciprocity might promote their commercial intercourse. Through the influence of Secretary of State James G. Blaine the McKinley Tariff Act of October 1, 1890, contained a section which aimed to encourage reciprocity between the United States and countries that produce sugar, molasses, coffee, tea, and hides. This section provided that on and after January 1, 1892, the President might suspend the provisions of the act concerning the free introduction of such articles into the United States whenever he judged that the duties imposed upon products of the United States by nations exporting the enumerated articles were "reciprocally unjust or unequal." It virtually empowered the President to make commercial arrangements with certain countries.

Secretary Blaine accordingly negotiated reciprocity agreements with Salvador, Nicaragua, Honduras, and Guatemala. On the other hand, the President suspended the free introduction into the United States of the enumerated articles from Colombia and Venezuela because those nations levied duties upon imports from the United States that were reciprocally unequal. All of the reciprocity agreements that were negotiated under the McKinley Tariff Act were terminated by the Wilson Tariff of 1894. The reciprocity arrangement framed between the

United States and Cuba in 1903 much encouraged trade between those countries.

Though manufacturers and exporters in the United States have not always shown much adaptability in their methods, nothing could stop the growth of commerce between the United States and Latin America. In the year ending June 30, 1913, the exports of the United States to Latin-American countries amounted to $314,278,949, while the imports from those countries into the United States aggregated $440,531,463.

Citizens of the United States have influenced the industrial development of Latin-American countries in manifold ways. Here a few illustrations must suffice. The Central and South American Telegraph Company, which was founded by James A. Scrymser of New York City, laid submarine cables from the United States, via Vera Cruz and Panama, to Callao and Valparaiso. Aside from the exploitation of petroleum wells by corporations of the United States, through the influence of her citizens such public utilities as sewers and street cars were introduced into certain cities of Mexico. A corporation of the United States exploited a huge asphalt lake in Venezuela. Oil prospectors from the United States operated oil wells in northern Venezuela and Colombia. Machinery made in the United States was set up in Peruvian and Brazilian sugar mills. In the basin of La Plata River corporations of the United States erected huge meat packing establishments. At Chuquicamata members of the Guggenheim family secured extensive properties containing low-grade copper deposits and established there a unique plant for the extraction of copper from the ore by an electrolytic process. They built there a mining town for their Chilean workmen as well as a clubhouse for their engineers. In 1917 that plant produced some forty-four thousand tons of copper. The prince of railway contractors in South America was a United States citizen named Henry Meiggs. To crown his difficult enterprises in Chile and Peru, he planned and partly constructed a railway from Callao to Cerro de Pasco—a veritable railway among the clouds.

Industrial Activities of the United States in Latin America

In various ways the United States has exercised an influence upon public instruction in Latin-American countries. Through his study and residence in the United States, Sarmiento became imbued with her educational ideals. In consequence he initiated a reform of the educational systems of Chile and Argentina, especially by the establishment of normal schools. Other South American publicists followed in his footsteps. During the present century the Peruvian government has undertaken to reform and to reorganize its system of public instruction by the employment of educators from the United States. In connection with the missions and

Educational Influence of the United States

churches which Protestant sects from the United States have planted throughout Latin-American countries, they have frequently established day schools and night schools and occasionally technical institutes. At various places they have also founded academies, seminaries and colleges.

Since 1824 an increasing stream of students has proceeded from Latin America to the North. Instead of sending their sons to European schools to be educated, Latin-American fathers have sometimes sent them to schools and colleges in the United States, especially to study agriculture, engineering, and the mechanic arts. More than one Latin-American government has at one time or another paid regular stipends to young men who were studying agriculture, engineering, medicine, veterinary science, and educational methods in United States colleges or universities. Various universities in the United States have offered scholarships or fellowships to students from Latin America. During recent years the Guggenheim Foundation has awarded fellowships to graduate students in the United States who wished to study in Latin America and also to Latin-American students who desired to study in the United States. As part of a comprehensive program for the improvement of inter-American cultural relations, the Department of State has recently promoted the exchange of students and teachers between the United States and Latin-American countries.

Among the trips made to South America by scientists of the United States, that of Louis Agassiz is outstanding. In April, 1865, with several companions, Agassiz left New York City for Rio de Janeiro. After reaching that capital he was aided by the Brazilian government to make an expedition up the Amazon River in search of fish. The specimens which he collected, as well as the delightful journal written by his wife, are memorials of his investigations. In 1867-1868 Professor James Orton with a few companions climbed the trail from Guayaquil to Quito, thence went down the rivers Napo and Coca to the Amazon River, and then proceeded to Pará,—they were the first white men to make that trip since the days of Orellana. On his second trip in 1873, Orton proceeded from Pará up the Amazon and went overland to Lake Titicaca, where he made ethnographical collections. In 1880 Dr. Edwin R. Heath, a companion of Orton upon his last trip, proceeded down the river Beni to the mouth of the Madre de Dios River. A tributary of the Madre de Dios was named after this daring explorer the Heath River. Professor Hiram Bingham of Yale University led an exploring expedition to South America in 1912, which unearthed the ruins of a remarkable Inca city at Machu Picchu.

Activities of North American Scientists

The most interesting geographical reconnaissance which has been made by a citizen of the United States in Latin America was perhaps that of ex-President Theodore Roosevelt. Accompanied by some adventurous scientists, in 1913 Roosevelt left the United States under the auspices of the American Museum of Natural History. After this party arrived in Brazil, it was accorded generous coöperation by the government of that country. Under the direction of the famous Brazilian explorer, Colonel Rondon, the expedition made a trip through the Brazilian wilderness to the Rio da Duvida. The Roosevelt-Rondon expedition discovered the course of a large, unknown river that flowed through five degrees of latitude—a river which the Brazilian government christened the Rio Roosevelt. Lastly, notice must be taken of the sanitary activities of the Rockefeller Foundation directed against insidious diseases in the tropics from Central America to Peru. The discovery by the eminent Japanese, Dr. Noguchi, of the bacteria which transmit yellow fever, and the perfection of a system of inoculation against that disease, heralded the day when that scourge would be completely extirpated from the New World.

During the century of independent life which the Latin-American states have enjoyed, Pan-Americanism, meaning by that a tendency shown by independent nations of America to associate themselves together, has made significant progress. In Latin America, as indicated in the preceding chapter, that **Pan-Americanism** spirit originated during the struggles for independence. An early apostle of Pan-Americanism in the United States was Henry Clay. His most significant remarks were made in Congress on May 10, 1820, when he expressed the opinion that the United States might create a system of which she would be the center and in which South America would act with her. The United States, he declared, could "become the center of a system" that would serve as a counterpoise to "the despotism of the Old World."

The great advocate of Pan-Americanism in the United States during the nineteenth century, however, was James G. Blaine. On November 29, 1881, Blaine, who was secretary of state under President Garfield, issued an invitation to the independent states of North and South America to send delegates to a congress to be held in Washington for the purpose of considering "the methods of preventing war" between American nations. Several Latin-American states accepted that invitation, but the assassination of President Garfield was followed by the withdrawal of the invitation by Secretary Frelinghuysen.

Still the project of a Pan-American conference was not discarded. In accordance with a law enacted in May, 1888, Secretary Bayard issued invitations to all the independent nations of Latin America to send delegates to a conference that should assemble at Washington. Among the subjects which were mentioned by Bayard as topics for consideration by the conference were arbitration, reciprocity, transportation, and a common system of coinage. The Latin-American states sent to that conference men who had attained prominence as scholars, lawyers, and statesmen. By a fortunate chance Blaine had become secretary of state under President Harrison, when on October 2, 1889, delegates of the independent nations of America gathered at Washington.

Secretary Blaine presided over the First Pan-American Conference, which used Bayard's invitation as its program. In respect to the improvement of commercial intercourse among American nations, a committee which considered the proposal for an American Zollverein reported in favor of the negotiation of a series of reciprocity treaties. Members of the conference approved a project for the completion of the Pan-American railway. They framed treaties concerning copyrights, patents, and trademarks. The delegates eventually approved a convention which declared that the nations represented should adopt arbitration "as a principle of American international law" for the adjustment of their disputes. This convention, like other conventions approved by the delegates, was merely in the nature of a recommendation to the respective nations represented at the conference. A recommendation that there should be established at Washington a bureau of information for all the American republics was sanctioned by them. Those republics appropriated money for the support of that organization, which became known as the International Bureau of the American Republics.

The Second International American Conference was held at Mexico City in 1901-1902. Again the delegates agreed to a series of conventions, which partook of the nature of recommendations to the states participating in the conference. Almost all of the delegates signed a protocol of adherence to The Hague Convention of 1899 for the amicable adjustment of international disputes. Many delegates signed a treaty which provided for the arbitration of certain financial claims that could not be settled by diplomatic negotiations. The Third International American Conference met in 1906 at Rio de Janeiro. It unanimously adopted a resolution which recommended that the nations represented should instruct their delegates to the next Hague Conference to favor the adoption of a universal treaty of arbitration. Other conventions were adopted which concerned the codification of international law, the arbitration of financial claims, and the status of naturalized citizens who returned to their native land.

The Fourth International American Conference assembled at Buenos Aires in 1910. It adopted an important resolution to the effect that the International Bureau of American Republics, which was henceforth to be called the Pan American Union, should be managed by a board composed of the diplomatic envoys of the American republics to the United States and her secretary of state. The functions of the Union were enlarged. The Fifth International American Conference met at Santiago, Chile, in 1923. It stipulated that the chairman of the Pan American Union should be elected by the board. It adopted conventions and resolutions which aimed to improve inter-American commercial relations. It approved a treaty extending to all the American republics a system of conciliation which provided for a commission of inquiry to adjust such disputes as could not be settled by diplomatic means. Nevertheless it was not able to reach a definite conclusion about the reduction and limitation of armaments by the American republics.

At the Sixth International American Conference, which met at Habana early in 1928, an attempt was made to get the American nations to declare themselves opposed to intervention by one state in the affairs of another state. An unsuccessful attempt led by Argentina was also made to transform the Pan American Union into an American Zollverein. An important decision, however, was reached to de-diplomatize that Union and incidentally to reduce the influence of the United States in it. The Conference decided that the governing body of the Union should be composed of members appointed by the member-states, and that its chairman should continue to be elective.

A resolution adopted by the Habana Conference provided that a Pan-American Conference should be held at Washington to consider arbitration and conciliation in America. The only American republic that did not send a delegation to this conference was Argentina. The Pan-American Conference on Conciliation and Arbitration drew up two treaties, a general treaty of international American arbitration, and a convention of international American conciliation. By the treaty of conciliation, the contracting parties agreed to submit to the consideration of commissions of inquiry established by the Santiago Conference certain controversies which had not been settled by diplomatic means. The treaty of arbitration provided that the contracting parties should submit to arbitral processes certain international differences of a juridical character that could not be adjusted by diplomacy.

Intellectual leaders of America have also stimulated the Pan-American spirit. As a result of the Latin-American Scientific Congresses a movement began for the assemblage of a scientific congress in which all the American nations might participate. Invitations to the First Pan-American Scientific Congress were issued in 1907 by the president of the University of Chile. Members of that Congress met in Santiago de Chile

Pan-American Scientific Congresses

in December, 1908, where interesting papers were read concerning topics of common interest to the Three Americas. In December, 1915, the Second Pan-American Scientific Congress met at Washington, where delegates from the independent nations of America read articles upon topics of mutual interest. That Congress was of special Pan-American significance because the President of the United States in a noteworthy address took occasion to develop certain ideas about the relations of the American countries.

In his message to Congress on December 7, 1915, President Wilson said that the neutral policy which American nations had adopted toward the belligerent powers of Europe had made them more conscious of a community of interest. He declared that the United States cherished the spirit of President Monroe: that she still meant to champion the "common cause of national independence and of political liberty in America"; but that all the independent American governments stood upon a footing of equality and independence.

Wilson's Pan-American Monroe Doctrine

The moral is that the states of America are not hostile rivals but coöperating friends, and that their growing sense of community interest, alike in matters political and in matters economic, is likely to give them a new significance as factors in international affairs and in the political history of the world. It presents them as in a very true and deep sense a unit in world affairs, spiritual partners, standing together, quick with common sympathies and common ideals. Separated, they are subject to all the cross currents of the confused politics of a world of hostile rivalries; united in spirit and purpose, they cannot be disappointed of their peaceful destiny.

The ideals thus praised by President Wilson in reality constituted a Pan-American Monroe Doctrine. He was the first President of the United States to express the view that the famous Doctrine should be internationalized. The Wilson Doctrine, as it may be called, was elucidated by the President on January 7, 1916, in an address to the Second Pan-American Scientific Congress. Though some adverse comment was made, his ideal of a Pan-American Monroe Doctrine was hailed with delight by the editors of prominent newspapers in Rio de Janeiro, Lima, Santiago de Chile, and Buenos Aires.

As elsewhere suggested, the first World War brought the United States into closer relations with certain countries of Latin America. More than one of the Latin-American nations that severed relations with Germany did so because of the identical issue which had forced the United States to declare the existence of a state of war, that is, Germany's ruthless submarine campaign. In the discussions concerning the policy of their respective governments several Latin-American publicists laid such emphasis upon "continental solidarity" as to indi-

Effects of the First World War on Inter-American Relations

cate that the crucial issue of that great war had stimulated the Pan-American spirit.

After that war began, an increase took place in the import trade of the United States with Latin-American countries. This was accompanied, however, by a temporary decline in the total exports from the United States to Latin America. Still, certain Latin-American nations took a larger percentage of goods from the United States in 1915 and 1916 than they had taken in 1913. In 1916 the United States was supplying about 33 per cent of the total imports of South America, as compared with about 15 per cent in the year before the war. This phenomenal increase was partly due to the great advance in prices. During the year ending June 30, 1917, the aggregate trade of the United States with Latin-American countries swelled prodigiously. An increase of some sort was noticeable in the import and export trade of the United States with almost every country of Latin America. In 1917 the United States exported to Latin-American countries domestic and foreign goods which totaled $577,367,238, while she imported from those countries products amounting to $956,001,028. Because of the handicap imposed by war conditions, the United States had far outstripped England, her keenest competitor for that trade. This unprecedented increase continued through the fiscal year ending June 30, 1920. During that year the United States exported to the Latin-American nations domestic and foreign goods aggregating $1,134,630,268, while she imported from those nations products amounting to $1,760,721,618.

Soon after the outbreak of the war, certain statesmen felt the necessity of promoting closer commercial and fiscal relations among the nations of America. In accordance with a law of March 4, 1915, Secretary of State Bryan invited each of the independent nations of America, except Mexico, to send delegates to a conference which should assemble in the United States to consider problems of banking, transportation, and commerce among the countries represented.

Pan-American Financial Conferences

On May 24, 1915, the First Pan-American Financial Conference met at Washington. That Conference, which was composed of from one to three delegates from seventeen Latin-American nations, besides representatives of Haiti and the United States, conducted its business through a series of committee meetings. A special committee was appointed to consider each Latin-American state. Two general committees were selected to consider the improvement of commercial relations between the United States and Latin-American countries. One general committee made reports concerning inter-American policy, which aimed to improve transportation facilities between the United

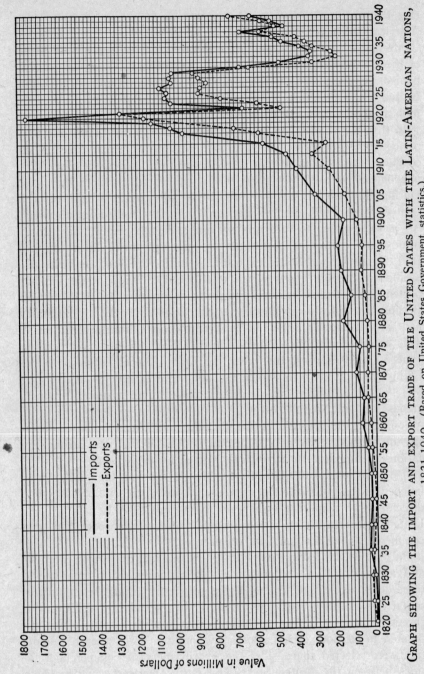

GRAPH SHOWING THE IMPORT AND EXPORT TRADE OF THE UNITED STATES WITH THE LATIN-AMERICAN NATIONS, 1821-1940. (Based on United States Government statistics.)

States and the states of South and Central America. The other general committee recommended the establishment of an Inter-American High Commission to promote the uniformity of commercial laws among American nations. A commission of that type, which was composed of jurists and financiers representing each American nation, was later organized. A report of the activities of that commission was laid before the Second Pan-American Financial Conference which subsequently met at Washington. On January 23, 1920, this Conference, which was made up of delegates from nineteen American republics including Mexico, adopted a series of resolutions that aimed to improve commercial and fiscal relations among the American republics.

Upon the close of the first World War, some problems which earlier confronted merchants and manufacturers in the United States concerning European competition for Latin-American trade arose again. As aids in the strife for markets, under the Federal Reserve Act branches of national banks were planted in Latin America, and through the instrumentality of the Department of Commerce the technic of the trade was improved. The Inter-American High Commission undertook to serve as an advisory body concerning commercial and financial matters to independent American governments. Disturbance of the economic equilibrium resulting from the war provoked some tantalizing fluctuations of international exchange which for a time affected the commerce of the United States with Latin-American countries unfavorably. The low rate of exchange between those countries and Europe encouraged commercial intercourse with England, France, and Germany, while a high rate of exchange between most Latin-American countries and the United States hampered trade. A phenomenal decline, which seems to have been partly due to the reaction from a period of heavy buying and selling, was followed in 1923 by a revival of the commerce between the United States and Latin America.

Problems of Reconstruction

That revival was most marked in respect to northern and western South America. In 1913 Colombia and Venezuela bought from the United States goods amounting to ten million dollars. In 1927 the amount purchased by those two countries had increased ninefold. What made this increase particularly significant was the fact that it was composed of distinctive American products such as automobiles, movie films, office appliances, and agricultural implements.

The opening to traffic of the Panama Canal on August 15, 1914, gave a great stimulus to trade between the United States and the countries on the west coast of South America. In 1901 the United States took 8 per cent of the total exports from those countries. In 1927 she took 35 per cent of those exports. The lowest percentage of exports taken by the United States from South America was from the Platean countries. In reality, because of the similarity of their products to those of the United States, Argentina and Uruguay constitute a special case. The chief products of Argentina are similar to our own; hence, our exports to her have been relatively low. For some years the tariff laid heavy duties on Argentine wheat and meat brought to the United States.

Recent
Commercial
Tendencies

The share of the United States in the total Latin-American trade fell from over 50 per cent of the total in 1920 to about 38 per cent in 1929. Still, that quota was a greater amount than the aggregate imports furnished to Latin America by France, Germany, and Great Britain. The commercial intercourse of the United States with her southern neighbors was influenced by the tendency for trade to follow the dollar. After the close of the first World War, American corporations invested large sums in such enterprises as banks, mining plants, and electric light and power companies in Latin America. In 1930 the total amount of United States money invested in Latin-American republics came to more than five billion dollars.

From 1930 to 1940 the export trade of the United States with Latin-American countries fluctuated considerably. It reached the lowest point in 1932 and the highest in 1940. Still, in 1932 exports of the United States to those countries aggregated about 12 per cent of her total exports. In 1940 those exports amounted to $726,776,000, which was 18 per cent of her total exports. In fact, her gain in export trade with her southern neighbors in that year was almost equivalent to the loss suffered by Germany in her commerce with the Latin-American countries. Mainly on account of the shift to United States markets because of the second World War, her exports to those countries in 1940 increased $232,000,000. Especially noticeable was the increase of her export trade with the countries in southern South America which had depended largely upon Germany for certain manufactures. In particular the United States replaced Europe in furnishing chemicals and products of iron and steel.

Though the general imports of the United States from Latin-American countries showed only a slight increase in 1940 over 1939, yet the nature of those imports was significant. They were largely such strategic commodities as wool, hides, tin, manganese, copper, lead, antimony, and rubber. In addition the United States furnished a market for a large quantity of gold and silver. According to their official statistics, in 1940 the commerce of every nation of Latin America showed an excess of exports over imports.

Meanwhile the earth was rapidly shrinking. Marvelous advances have recently been made in international telephone service. The first system of that kind available to a Latin-American country was opened in 1921 by the Cuban-American Telephone Company. This service was carried on by a submarine cable that stretched from Key West to Habana. Important business interests in Cuba and the United States promptly made use of that line. Through the American Bell System this service was later extended to Mexico.

The first international telephone service between the countries of South America was informally opened by the International Telephone and Telegraph Company between Montevideo and Buenos Aires. Soon afterward Argentina, Chile, and Uruguay were included in a telephone circuit. International telephone service has helped business men to get into touch with prospective clients and has aided diplomats to secure prompt communication with their home governments. It has enabled the presidents of countries thus linked to converse with each other. During the Chaco boundary controversy, on behalf of the League of Nations, the French statesman Briand carried on a telephone conversation from Geneva with the French ambassador in Buenos Aires. During the Argentine revolution of 1930 American Ambassador Bliss made reports to Washington by telephone concerning its developments. The inter-American radiotelephone has not only become an instrument in diplomacy, but also in business. By means of a prearranged code that ensures secrecy, investors and bankers could carry on important financial negotiations by long-distance radio messages. By 1930 radio telephone circuits were in operation between New York City and the following countries: Cuba, Costa Rica, Panama, Colombia, Venezuela, Brazil, Argentina, and Chile.

> The Shrinking Earth

The phenomenal development in aviation has promoted closer relations between widely separated sections of America as well as more intimate intercourse between Latin-American states and European countries. By 1930 Mexico had attained the leadership in commercial air transportation in Latin America. The Aeronautic Transportation Company of Mexico had established air-mail, passenger, and express routes from Brownsville, Texas, to Mazatlán, and from El Paso to Mexico City. As early as 1920 an air service for mail, parcel post, and express routes was in operation in Colombia. In November, 1927, the first flight took place in that country between an Atlantic and a Pacific port. Since April, 1928, daily flights have taken place between Barranquilla and Girardot, the terminal port for Bogotá. In July of that year the Colombian air line was extended southward as far as Guayaquil. In February, 1929, the Chilean government opened its first air route that led from Arica to Santiago. By August, 1930, that government had completed its longitudinal air service by opening a line that connected Magellanes, the southernmost city in the world, with Santiago.

In that capital there met airplanes of an American line from Panama and the planes of a French line. By November, 1930, the Pan-American Airways System had established air routes between the United States and thirty colonies or nations of America which included Cuba, the Dominican Republic, Nicaragua, and South American countries. By 1941 United States air lines had not only been further extended but had also been enlarged by the addition of affiliated lines. By that time Dutch airways had connected Paramaribo, Curaçao, and Maracaibo. Italian lines had linked Bahia to Rio de Janeiro. Meanwhile, German airplanes had not only skirted the coast of Brazil from Belem to Porto Alegre but at some points had also flown beyond her coastal plain. In addition German affiliated air routes had not only linked Buenos Aires to Tierra del Fuego but had also connected various cities on the Bolivian plateau.

Diplomatic concomitants of the first World War raised a question about the future relations of Latin-American peoples with the United States and also about their relations with the leading
American Nations at the Versailles Conference
powers of Europe. For the first time in history certain Latin-American nations, as well as the United States, were represented in a conference which was held at the conclusion of a war. When the Peace Conference assembled at Paris on January 18, 1919, provision was made for the attendance of diplomatic representatives of several nations of Latin America. As members of the group known as the Allied and Associated Powers, representatives of Bolivia, Brazil, Cuba, Ecuador, Guatemala, Haiti, Honduras, Nicaragua, Panama, Peru, Uruguay, and the United States signed the Treaty of Versailles. The Latin-American states were represented upon the commission of Associated Nations that formulated the Covenant of the League of Nations. Latin-American nations that through their representatives signed the treaty of peace between the Allied and Associated Powers and Germany also subscribed the Covenant of the League of Nations, which was an integral part of that treaty. An annex to the Covenant provided that other states were invited to join the League. Among those states were Argentina, Chile, Colombia, Paraguay, Salvador, and Venezuela. The accession of such a state was to become effective by the filing with the secretariat of the League within two months after the Covenant went into force a declaration that it had been accepted without reservations.

The Treaty of Peace with Germany was signed at Versailles on June 28, 1919. The date originally set for the Treaty of Versailles to become effective was the anniversary of the signing of the Armistice between Germany and the Allied and Associated Powers. Because of a delay in the ratification of that treaty by the United States, which was caused by the debate over ratification with reservations in the Senate, the date set for it to become operative was postponed. Finally, on January 10, 1920, a *procès verbal* was signed at Paris by the representatives of certain nations that had been parties to the Treaty of Versailles. Of the American nations which had subscribed that treaty only Bolivia, Brazil, Guatemala, Panama, Peru, and Uruguay signed the *procès verbal*. As soon as this was signed, the president of the interallied Peace Conference sent a note to the nations designated in the annex to the original covenant to inform them that the Treaty of Versailles had gone into force. Although that treaty failed of ratification in the United States Senate, yet every nation of Latin America which signed it, except Ecuador, subsequently signified her accession to the Covenant of the League of Nations. Each of the Latin-American nations which was invited to join the League filed its acceptance within the specified time. In the autumn of 1931 Mexico accepted a tardy invitation to join the Society of Nations. Besides the United States, the only other American state that ultimately failed to join this Society was Ecuador, whose Congress voted to postpone the ratification of the peace treaty.

The refusal of the United States Senate to ratify the Covenant of the League of Nations with or without reservations raised some significant and tantalizing problems. Article XXI of the Covenant stipulated that nothing therein should be considered as having affected the validity of regional understandings to secure the maintenance of peace, such as the Monroe Doctrine. In the resolution of ratification which was proposed in the United States Senate on November 19, 1919, and again in the resolution proposed on March 19, 1920, a clause was included stipulating that the United States would not submit any questions to the consideration of the League of Nations which in her judgment involved the Monroe Doctrine. Though the Treaty of Versailles was not ratified by the Senate even with reservations, this clause indicated the attitude of many citizens of the United States toward the declarations of the Covenant of the League of Nations about her traditional American policy. Nevertheless by 1930 fifteen Latin-American nations had declared their intentions to support the World Court which had been founded by the League of Nations.

Even before the Senate of the United States rejected the Covenant of the League largely in order to protect a cardinal principle of American diplomacy, a Latin-American diplomat had protested against

Article XXI because it did not undertake to define the Monroe Doctrine. The President of Honduras reasoned that because of this article the nations which ratified the Covenant would be considered as having impliedly sanctioned any policy that the United States might deign to designate with the name of. Monroe. This sentiment became more pronounced when South American statesmen began to play a significant

The League and the Monroe Doctrine

part in the activities of the Assembly and the Council at Geneva. Delegates of Spanish-American states served on important committees. Latin-American statesmen were elected to preside over the Assembly of the League; they also served as presidents of its Council. With ominous apprehensions concerning the expanding power of the United States constantly in their minds, and in view of the fact that that nation had not adhered to the League, what wonder that the publicists of various Latin-American countries occasionally displayed a tendency to submit their controversies rather to the tribunal at Geneva than to statesmen at Washington.

At the Ninth Assembly of the League, after Costa Rica, which had announced her intention to withdraw, had been asked by the Council to resume membership, that tiny republic presented a statement declaring that as "under Article XXI the international legal scope of the Monroe Doctrine was extended," she wished to be informed of the "interpretation placed by the League of Nations on the Monroe Doctrine and the scope given to that Doctrine when included in Article XXI of the Covenant."

By way of response, the Council cited Article XX by which the members of the League agreed to abrogate all understandings between themselves that were incompatible with the terms of the Covenant. With regard to the reference to the Monroe Doctrine in Article XXI, the Council unanimously assured the members of the League that this mention "neither weakens nor limits any of the safeguards provided in the Covenant," and that it cannot have the effect of giving them a "sanction or validity" not previously possessed. The Council cautiously refrained from defining international engagements in the belief that such a definition would be "liable to have the effect of restricting or enlarging their sphere of application."

The actual participation of the leading South American states in the League of Nations, however, soon began to wane. When the delegates to the Eighth Assembly of the League met at Geneva, there were present no representatives from Argentina, Brazil, Bolivia, Honduras, and Peru. Among eleven Latin-American states represented there, only one, Chile, could be reckoned as a first-rate American power. The two other A B C nations had both practically withdrawn from the League.

One by one other nations withdrew. After the opening of the second World War the august tribunal at Geneva ceased to function.

Nevertheless, there were signs of a revival of interest in an American League of Nations. A leading advocate of this association in its recent form was Balthasar Brum, who had served both as secretary of foreign relations and as president of Uruguay. In a lecture to the students of the University of Montevideo on April 21, 1920, Brum reasoned that the Monroe Doctrine should be transformed from a unilateral policy of the United States into a Pan-American Monroe Doctrine. He argued that all the na-   *An American Society of Nations* tions of the New World should make a declaration of adherence to Pan-American principles. He proposed that the authority to decide on common action by America, if a non-American state acted against the rights of an American state, should be vested in "the American League." This organization could be no other than an "American Society based on the absolute equality of all the associate countries." This new league would have a double purpose: to adjust disputes that might arise among its own members; and to deal with controversies between American states and non-American nations.

Among the agenda drawn up for the Pan-American Conference which met at Santiago de Chile in March, 1923, was a proposal for an American league of nations. But the unfavorable attitude of the delegates sent by the United States government, who announced that they considered the Monroe Doctrine as a unilateral policy, inhibited Latin-American publicists from bringing Brum's plan into the focus of attention. Largely due to similar conditions, the Pan-American Conference at Habana also failed to approve proposals recognizing that phase of Pan-Americanism.

Intriguing problems were also involved in the policy adopted by the United States with respect to the Kellogg-Briand Peace Pact, which abjured war as an instrument of national policy. When this pact was submitted to the Senate for ratification on December 4, 1928, certain members of that body assumed the attitude that this multilateral treaty should not be   *Recent Interpretations of the Monroe Doctrine* ratified by the Senate without an accompanying interpretation.

Early in 1929 some twenty-five Senators signed a plea demanding that an interpretative statement about the Monroe Doctrine should be submitted with the resolution of ratification. A senatorial agreement, however, was reached that this accompanying report should not be a formal part of the ratification. With the recommendation that the Multilateral Peace Pact should be ratified by the Senate, the Committee on Foreign Relations accordingly submitted an interpretative report. It recommended the ratification of the treaty "with the understanding that the right of self-defense is in no way curtailed or impaired by the terms or conditions of the treaty." Regardless of the pact, each nation was to remain the sole judge of the necessity of self-defense and of the extent of the same. The Monroe Doctrine was thus interpreted: "The United States regards the Monroe Doctrine as a part of its national security and defense. Under the right of self-defense allowed by the treaty must necessarily be included the right to maintain the Monroe Doctrine, which is a part of our system of national defense."

The action of the committee and the tacit agreement of the Senate to a conservative interpretation of the President's Message of December 2, 1823, constituted a distinct improvement in the attitude of the United States toward the "cardinal principle" of American diplomacy. For the first time in history the legislative tribunal that is constitutionally authorized to pass upon the foreign policy of the United States undertook to interpret the cardinal feature of her diplomacy—and the interpretation was conservative!

In agreement with the Senate's views was the opinion expressed by Under Secretary of State Clark. In a memorandum dated December 17, 1928, Clark did not justify under the Monroe Doctrine such intervention as that which had taken place in Haiti, Nicaragua, and the Dominican Republic. He held that this Doctrine stated the case of the United States *versus* Europe and not the case of the United States *versus* Latin America.

After Franklin D. Roosevelt became president, proposals of Latin-American publicists that the policy of intervention should be curbed received careful attention. In his first inaugural address on March 4, 1933, the President suggestively linked the Monroe Doctrine and Pan-Americanism "The essential qualities of a true Pan-Americanism," he said, "must be the same as those which constitute a good neighbor, namely mutual understanding, and through such understanding, a sympathetic appreciation of the other's point of view." He declared that the Monroe Doctrine was directed at the maintenance of independence by the peoples of the New World. It was aimed against the acquisition in any way of "additional territory in this hemisphere by any non-American power." In December, 1933, the Seventh Pan-American Conference at Montevideo adopted a resolution to the effect that "no state has the right to intervene in the internal or external affairs of another." At that conference Secretary Hull added that no government need fear any intervention by the United States during the existing administration. By these announcements the United States renounced the corollary which Theodore Roosevelt had added to the Monroe Doctrine.

The Good Neighbor Policy

A few years later rumors of a European war incited the United States to propose an American conference on peace. On January 30, 1936, President Franklin D. Roosevelt invited other American republics to send delegates to a conference at Buenos Aires to discuss how peace might be maintained in the New World. By the Collective Security Pact signed at that conference the independent American governments resolved that they were to consult with each other whenever it was necessary to find a peaceful mode of coöperation. Further, they agreed that their foreign offices would furnish the mechanism to determine when such consultation should take place. The Protocol Relative to Non-Intervention stipulated that interference in the affairs of an American nation should be deemed a sufficient menace to set the newly constructed protective mechanism into operation. The modified Monroe Doctrine was thus Pan-Americanized for the purpose of shielding the American republics against any menace of aggression from overseas.

The Eighth Pan American Conference which met in Lima in 1938 undertook to implement the agreements reached at Buenos Aires. The provocation was the implied threat to America because of the policy adopted by Hitler toward Germans living beyond the boundaries of the Reich. His doctrine concerning racial minorities startled Latin-American nations where there were thousands of people who had been born in Germany or were of German descent. Accordingly, among important statements of Pan-American policy formulated at this conference was the Declaration of Lima. In that declaration the republics of the New World reaffirmed their "continental solidarity" and announced their intention to defend their common interests against any foreign intervention. They proclaimed that a threat to the peace, security, or territorial integrity of any American nation would become a matter of their common concern. To facilitate joint action the twenty-one republics agreed that at the invitation of any one of them, their secretaries of state should assemble to deliberate about the proper steps to be taken. This declaration made known the determination of the signatory nations to present a common front against any attempt by a European dictator to undermine their institutions, to disturb their tranquillity, or to seize their territory.

The Declarations of Lima and Panama

After the outbreak of the second World War, the President of Panama invited the American secretaries of state to a meeting to discuss the effects of that war upon the nations of the Western Hemisphere. On behalf of those nations the Panama Conference undertook to set up standards of neutral conduct. It established an economic war board to sit in Washington for the purpose of determining how the evil effects of the war upon the economic structure of American nations might be decreased. Most important of all, it drew up a resolution styled the Declaration of Panama by which those nations agreed to notify the belligerents that a neutrality zone had been delimited in American waters. This safety zone was to extend from the northeastern

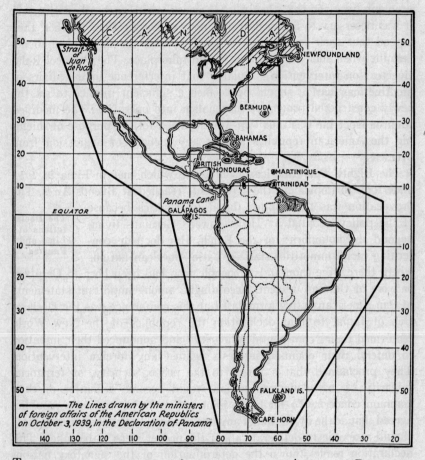

THE NEUTRAL MARITIME ZONE CREATED BY THE AMERICAN REPUBLICS

boundary of the United States to Cape Horn and from Porto Rico to the Galápagos Islands. Within this two-ocean zone, which stretched far beyond American territorial waters, the respective nations might establish naval patrols. The creation of a neutral zone within which the European belligerents were prohibited from engaging in maritime activity was in reality an attempt by all the American nations to extend a principle of the Monroe Doctrine to the high seas.

The Japanese attack on Pearl Harbor, as noticed in earlier chapters, brought declarations of war against the Axis from nine nations of Middle America. Three other Spanish-American states severed relations with Axis powers, while a number of others announced that they would accord to the United States a status of non-belligerency. At the third conference of the foreign ministers at Rio de Janeiro in January, 1942, a discussion took place concerning the assistance which other American nations were to lend the United States. These ministers resolved that steps should be taken to mobilize the economic resources of the American continents. They advised that the American states take effective measures to terminate all commercial or financial intercourse between themselves and the Axis countries. Further, they reënunciated the resolution of their nations to prevent "espionage, sabotage, and subversive propaganda" by member states of the Tripartite Pact. They emphatically condemned the Japanese attack on Pearl Harbor. They recommended that all the American republics ought to sever their diplomatic relations with Japan, Germany, and Italy, but that each country might act in conformity with its own procedure and special circumstances. This phraseology enabled the ministers of Argentina and Chile to sign this resolution, while still leaving the actual decision to their respective governments. As a result of this meeting, with the exception of those two states, every American nation that had not already done so at once broke off relations with the Axis powers. By March, 1943, every Latin-American nation except Argentina had severed diplomatic relations with the Axis, while eleven of those nations had either declared war on Italy and Germany or had announced that a state of war existed between them and those European Powers.

The Americas and the Second World War

When German legions had subjugated the Netherlands and France, fears arose that the status of their Caribbean colonies might be altered. Accordingly in June, 1940, Secretary Hull notified Germany and Italy that his government would not recognize a transfer of "any geographic region of the Western Hemisphere from one non-American power to another non-American power." At the same time he proposed to the American nations that the second meeting of their foreign ministers scheduled for Habana should take place at once. Among the resolutions adopted by that conference in July, 1940, was one which condemned hostilities within the maritime zone created by the Declaration of Panama as prejudicial to the republics of America. Another resolution provided that whenever any lands or islands in the possession of non-American nations were in danger of becoming the objects of barter "or change of sovereignty," they might be placed temporarily under the administration of the American republics. Still another resolution announced that "any attempt on the part of a non-American State against the integrity or inviolability of the territory, the sovereignty, or the political independence of an American State shall be considered as an act of aggression" against the signatory powers. This resolution further provided for the negotiation of other agreements to arrange for the defense and assistance which those states were to lend each other in case of aggression.

In the cause of hemispherical defense the government of the United States has recently aided the Latin nations of the New World in various ways. Among other measures, it has sent military, naval, and aerial missions to several of their capitals. There met at Washington in March, 1942, a joint Mexican–United States commission which was organized to study problems concerning the mutual defense of those countries. The Inter-American Defense Board created by the third conference of American foreign ministers assembled at the same capital on March 30 to study problems of continental defense. By March, 1943, lend-lease agreements had been signed between the United States and sixteen Latin-American nations. Perhaps the most important of these agreements was that signed with Brazil. By this agreement the United States granted a credit of $100,000,000 to that nation to enable her to build up her armaments and thus to fortify the defense of the Americas. On May 18, 1942, the republic of Panama agreed to allow the United States to develop areas in the Isthmus for military, naval, and aërial bases. The Isthmian Republic thus demonstrated her willingness to co-operate in the guardianship of the Panama Canal so as to contribute to the defense of the hemisphere. On their part, other Latin-American republics furnished the use of strategic bases and also supplied the United States with essential war materials. A mere mention of reciprocal action thus taken clearly indicates that not only has the development of Pan-Americanism promoted the defense of the Western Hemisphere against European and Oriental aggressors, but it has also stimulated in an unprecedented manner the spirit of neighborliness among the American nations.

SUGGESTIONS FOR FURTHER READING

ALVAREZ, A., *The Monroe Doctrine*, 1924.
BEALS, C., *The Coming Struggle for Latin America*, 1940.
BIDWELL, P. W., *Economic Defense of Latin America*, 1941.
BOLTON, H. E., "The Epic of Greater America," *American Historical Review*, Vol. XXXVIII, pp. 448-474.
CLARK, J. R., *Memorandum on the Monroe Doctrine,* 1930.
FERNÁNDEZ ARTUCIO, H., *The Nazi Underground in South America*, 1942.

GOETZ, D., and FRY, V., *The Good Neighbors*, 1939.

GREEN, P. L., *Pan American Progress*, 1942.

HALL, M., and PECK, W., "Wings for the Trojan Horse," *Foreign Affairs*, Vol. XIX, pp. 347-369.

HARING, C. H., *Argentina and the United States*, 1941.

HERSHEY, A. S., "The Calvo and Drago Doctrines," *American Journal of International Law*, Vol. I, pp. 26-45.

INMAN, S. G., *Problems in Pan Americanism*, 1921.

International Conciliation Bulletin, No. 300 (Montevideo Conference); No. 328 (Buenos Aires Conference); No. 349 (Lima Conference); No. 356 (Panama Meeting); No. 362 (Havana Meeting); No. 378 (Rio de Janeiro Meeting), 1934-1942.

International Reference Service, U. S. Department of Commerce, Vols. I and II, 1941-1942.

KELCHNER, W. H., *Latin American Relations with the League of Nations*, 1930.

McCULLOCH, J. I. B., *Challenge of the Americas*, 1940.

MANGER, W., *The Americas and the War*, 1942 [mimeographed].

——, *Evolution of the Pan American Movement*, 1942 [mimeographed].

MANNING, W. R., *Diplomatic Correspondence of the United States, Inter-American Affairs, 1831-1860*, Vol. I, 1932.

MARTIN, P. A., *Latin America and the War*, 1925.

NERVAL, G., *Autopsy of the Monroe Doctrine*, 1934.

PERKINS D., *Hands Off: A History of the Monroe Doctrine*, 1941.

RAUSHENBUSH, J., *Look at Latin America*, 1940.

RÍOS, F. DE LOS, "South American Perplexities," *Foreign Affairs*, Vol. XX, pp. 650-663.

RIPPY, J. F., *Historical Evolution of Hispanic America*, 1940.

——, *Latin America in World Politics*, 1940.

ROBERTSON, W. S., *Hispanic American Relations with the United States*, 1923.

——, "The Monroe Doctrine in Our Own Times," *The American Scholar*, Vol. IX, pp. 284-295.

STUART, G. H., *Latin America and the United States*, 1938.

INDEX

(16)

Date Due

MAY 1 '57			
APR 18 '58			
APR 25 '58			
MAR 28 '60			
APR 8 '60			
APR 21 '60			
MAY 4 '60			
APR 17 '62			
APR 17 '62			
DEC 11 '63			
JAN 3 '64			
MAY 13 '64			
JAN 12 '68			
	PRINTED	IN U. S. A.	